T0202781

Lecture Notes in Computer Science 14259

The series Lecture Notes in Computer Science (LNCS), including its subseries Lecture Notes in Artificial Intelligence (LNAI) and Lecture Notes in Bioinformatics (LNBI), has established itself as a medium for the publication of new developments in computer science and information technology research, teaching, and education.

LNCS enjoys close cooperation with the computer science R & D community, the series counts many renowned academics among its volume editors and paper authors, and collaborates with prestigious societies. Its mission is to serve this international community by providing an invaluable service, mainly focused on the publication of conference and workshop proceedings and postproceedings. LNCS commenced publication in 1973.

Lazaros Iliadis · Antonios Papaleonidas ·
Plamen Angelov · Chrisina Jayne
Editors

Artificial Neural Networks and Machine Learning – ICANN 2023

32nd International Conference on Artificial Neural Networks
Heraklion, Crete, Greece, September 26–29, 2023
Proceedings, Part VI

Editors
Lazaros Iliadis
Democritus University of Thrace
Xanthi, Greece

Antonios Papaleonidas
Democritus University of Thrace
Xanthi, Greece

Plamen Angelov
Lancaster University
Lancaster, UK

Chrisina Jayne
Teesside University
Middlesbrough, UK

ISSN 0302-9743 ISSN 1611-3349 (electronic)
Lecture Notes in Computer Science
ISBN 978-3-031-44222-3 ISBN 978-3-031-44223-0 (eBook)
https://doi.org/10.1007/978-3-031-44223-0

This Springer imprint is published by the registered company Springer Nature Switzerland AG
The registered company address is: Gewerbestrasse 11, 6330 Cham, Switzerland

Paper in this product is recyclable.

Preface

The European Neural Network Society (ENNS) is an association of scientists, engineers and students, conducting research on the modelling of behavioral and brain processes, and on the development of neural algorithms. The core of these efforts is the application of neural modelling to several diverse domains. According to its mission statement ENNS is the European non-profit federation of professionals that aims at achieving a worldwide professional and socially responsible development and application of artificial neural technologies.

The flagship event of ENNS is ICANN (the International Conference on Artificial Neural Networks) at which contributed research papers are presented after passing through a rigorous review process. ICANN is a dual-track conference, featuring tracks in brain-inspired computing on the one hand, and machine learning on the other, with strong crossdisciplinary interactions and applications.

The response of the international scientific community to the ICANN 2023 call for papers was more than satisfactory. In total, 947 research papers on the aforementioned research areas were submitted and 426 (45%) of them were finally accepted as full papers after a peer review process. Additionally, 19 extended abstracts were submitted and 9 of them were selected to be included in the front matter of ICANN 2023 proceedings. Due to their high academic and scientific importance, 22 short papers were also accepted.

All papers were peer reviewed by at least two independent academic referees. Where needed, a third or a fourth referee was consulted to resolve any potential conflicts. Three workshops focusing on specific research areas, namely Advances in Spiking Neural Networks (ASNN), Neurorobotics (NRR), and the challenge of Errors, Stability, Robustness, and Accuracy in Deep Neural Networks (ESRA in DNN), were organized.

The 10-volume set of LNCS 14254, 14255, 14256, 14257, 14258, 14259, 14260, 14261, 14262 and 14263 constitutes the proceedings of the 32nd International Conference on Artificial Neural Networks, ICANN 2023, held in Heraklion city, Crete, Greece, on September 26–29, 2023.

The accepted papers are related to the following topics:

Machine Learning: Deep Learning; Neural Network Theory; Neural Network Models; Graphical Models; Bayesian Networks; Kernel Methods; Generative Models; Information Theoretic Learning; Reinforcement Learning; Relational Learning; Dynamical Models; Recurrent Networks; and Ethics of AI.

Brain-Inspired Computing: Cognitive Models; Computational Neuroscience; Self-Organization; Neural Control and Planning; Hybrid Neural-Symbolic Architectures; Neural Dynamics; Cognitive Neuroscience; Brain Informatics; Perception and Action; and Spiking Neural Networks.

Neural applications in Bioinformatics; Biomedicine; Intelligent Robotics; Neurorobotics; Language Processing; Speech Processing; Image Processing; Sensor Fusion; Pattern Recognition; Data Mining; Neural Agents; Brain-Computer Interaction; Neuromorphic Computing and Edge AI; and Evolutionary Neural Networks.

September 2023

Lazaros Iliadis
Antonios Papaleonidas
Plamen Angelov
Chrisina Jayne

Organization

General Chairs

Iliadis Lazaros	Democritus University of Thrace, Greece
Plamen Angelov	Lancaster University, UK

Program Chairs

Antonios Papaleonidas	Democritus University of Thrace, Greece
Elias Pimenidis	UWE Bristol, UK
Chrisina Jayne	Teesside University, UK

Honorary Chairs

Stefan Wermter	University of Hamburg, Germany
Vera Kurkova	Czech Academy of Sciences, Czech Republic
Nikola Kasabov	Auckland University of Technology, New Zealand

Organizing Chairs

Antonios Papaleonidas	Democritus University of Thrace, Greece
Anastasios Panagiotis Psathas	Democritus University of Thrace, Greece
George Magoulas	University of London, Birkbeck College, UK
Haralambos Mouratidis	University of Essex, UK

Award Chairs

Stefan Wermter	University of Hamburg, Germany
Chukiong Loo	University of Malaysia, Malaysia

Communication Chairs

Sebastian Otte	University of Tübingen, Germany
Anastasios Panagiotis Psathas	Democritus University of Thrace, Greece

Steering Committee

Stefan Wermter	University of Hamburg, Germany
Angelo Cangelosi	University of Manchester, UK
Igor Farkaš	Comenius University in Bratislava, Slovakia
Chrisina Jayne	Teesside University, UK
Matthias Kerzel	University of Hamburg, Germany
Alessandra Lintas	University of Lausanne, Switzerland
Kristína Malinovská (Rebrová)	Comenius University in Bratislava, Slovakia
Alessio Micheli	University of Pisa, Italy
Jaakko Peltonen	Tampere University, Finland
Brigitte Quenet	ESPCI Paris, France
Ausra Saudargiene	Lithuanian University of Health Sciences, Lithuania
Roseli Wedemann	Rio de Janeiro State University, Brazil

Local Organizing/Hybrid Facilitation Committee

Aggeliki Tsouka	Democritus University of Thrace, Greece
Anastasios Panagiotis Psathas	Democritus University of Thrace, Greece
Anna Karagianni	Democritus University of Thrace, Greece
Christina Gkizioti	Democritus University of Thrace, Greece
Ioanna-Maria Erentzi	Democritus University of Thrace, Greece
Ioannis Skopelitis	Democritus University of Thrace, Greece
Lambros Kazelis	Democritus University of Thrace, Greece
Leandros Tsatsaronis	Democritus University of Thrace, Greece
Nikiforos Mpotzoris	Democritus University of Thrace, Greece
Nikos Zervis	Democritus University of Thrace, Greece
Panagiotis Restos	Democritus University of Thrace, Greece
Tassos Giannakopoulos	Democritus University of Thrace, Greece

Program Committee

Abraham Yosipof	CLB, Israel
Adane Tarekegn	NTNU, Norway
Aditya Gilra	Centrum Wiskunde & Informatica, Netherlands
Adrien Durand-Petiteville	Federal University of Pernambuco, Brazil
Adrien Fois	LORIA, France
Alaa Marouf	Hosei University, Japan
Alessandra Sciutti	Istituto Italiano di Tecnologia, Italy
Alessandro Sperduti	University of Padua, Italy
Alessio Micheli	University of Pisa, Italy
Alex Shenfield	Sheffield Hallam University, UK
Alexander Kovalenko	Czech Technical University in Prague, Czech Republic
Alexander Krawczyk	Fulda University of Applied Sciences, Germany
Ali Minai	University of Cincinnati, USA
Aluizio Araujo	Universidade Federal de Pernambuco, Brazil
Amarda Shehu	George Mason University, USA
Amit Kumar Kundu	University of Maryland, USA
Anand Rangarajan	University of Florida, USA
Anastasios Panagiotis Psathas	Democritus University of Thrace, Greece
Andre de Carvalho	Universidade de São Paulo, Brazil
Andrej Lucny	Comenius University, Slovakia
Angel Villar-Corrales	University of Bonn, Germany
Angelo Cangelosi	University of Manchester, UK
Anna Jenul	Norwegian University of Life Sciences, Norway
Antonios Papaleonidas	Democritus University of Thrace, Greece
Arnaud Lewandowski	LISIC, ULCO, France
Arul Selvam Periyasamy	Universität Bonn, Germany
Asma Mekki	University of Sfax, Tunisia
Banafsheh Rekabdar	Portland State University, USA
Barbara Hammer	Universität Bielefeld, Germany
Baris Serhan	University of Manchester, UK
Benedikt Bagus	University of Applied Sciences Fulda, Germany
Benjamin Paaßen	Bielefeld University, Germany
Bernhard Pfahringer	University of Waikato, New Zealand
Bharath Sudharsan	NUI Galway, Ireland
Binyi Wu	Dresden University of Technology, Germany
Binyu Zhao	Harbin Institute of Technology, China
Björn Plüster	University of Hamburg, Germany
Bo Mei	Texas Christian University, USA

Brian Moser	Deutsches Forschungszentrum für künstliche Intelligenz, Germany
Carlo Mazzola	Istituto Italiano di Tecnologia, Italy
Carlos Moreno-Garcia	Robert Gordon University, UK
Chandresh Pravin	Reading University, UK
Chao Ma	Wuhan University, China
Chathura Wanigasekara	German Aerospace Centre, Germany
Cheng Shang	Shanghai Jiaotong University, China
Chengqiang Huang	Huawei Technologies, China
Chenhan Zhang	University of Technology, Sydney, Australia
Chenyang Lyu	Dublin City University, Ireland
Chihuang Liu	Meta, USA
Chrisina Jayne	Teesside University, UK
Christian Balkenius	Lund University, Sweden
Chrysoula Kosma	Ecole Polytechnique, Greece
Claudio Bellei	Elliptic, UK
Claudio Gallicchio	University of Pisa, Italy
Claudio Giorgio Giancaterino	Intesa SanPaolo Vita, Italy
Constantine Dovrolis	Cyprus Institute, USA
Coşku Horuz	University of Tübingen, Germany
Cunjian Chen	Monash, Australia
Cunyi Yin	Fuzhou University, Singapore
Damien Lolive	Université Rennes, CNRS, IRISA, France
Daniel Stamate	Goldsmiths, University of London, UK
Daniel Vašata	Czech Technical University in Prague, Czech Republic
Dario Pasquali	Istituto Italiano di Tecnologia, Italy
David Dembinsky	German Research Center for Artificial Intelligence, Germany
David Rotermund	University of Bremen, Germany
Davide Liberato Manna	University of Strathclyde, UK
Dehao Yuan	University of Maryland, USA
Denise Gorse	University College London, UK
Dennis Wong	Macao Polytechnic University, China
Des Higham	University of Edinburgh, UK
Devesh Jawla	TU Dublin, Ireland
Dimitrios Michail	Harokopio University of Athens, Greece
Dino Ienco	INRAE, France
Diptangshu Pandit	Teesside University, UK
Diyuan Lu	Helmholtz Center Munich, Germany
Domenico Tortorella	University of Pisa, Italy
Dominik Geissler	American Family Insurance, USA

DongNyeong Heo	Handong Global University, South Korea
Dongyang Zhang	University of Electronic Science and Technology of China, China
Doreen Jirak	Istituto Italiano di Tecnologia, Italy
Douglas McLelland	BrainChip, France
Douglas Nyabuga	Mount Kenya University, Rwanda
Dulani Meedeniya	University of Moratuwa, Sri Lanka
Dumitru-Clementin Cercel	University Politehnica of Bucharest, Romania
Dylan Muir	SynSense, Switzerland
Efe Bozkir	Uni Tübingen, Germany
Eleftherios Kouloumpris	Aristotle University of Thessaloniki, Greece
Elias Pimenidis	University of the West of England, UK
Eliska Kloberdanz	Iowa State University, USA
Emre Neftci	Foschungszentrum Juelich, Germany
Enzo Tartaglione	Telecom Paris, France
Erwin Lopez	University of Manchester, UK
Evgeny Mirkes	University of Leicester, UK
F. Boray Tek	Istanbul Technical University, Turkey
Federico Corradi	Eindhoven University of Technology, Netherlands
Federico Errica	NEC Labs Europe, Germany
Federico Manzi	Università Cattolica del Sacro Cuore, Italy
Federico Vozzi	CNR, Italy
Fedor Scholz	University of Tuebingen, Germany
Feifei Dai	Chinese Academy of Sciences, China
Feifei Xu	Shanghai University of Electric Power, China
Feixiang Zhou	University of Leicester, UK
Felipe Moreno	FGV, Peru
Feng Wei	York University, Canada
Fengying Li	Guilin University of Electronic Technology, China
Flora Ferreira	University of Minho, Portugal
Florian Mirus	Intel Labs, Germany
Francesco Semeraro	University of Manchester, UK
Franco Scarselli	University of Siena, Italy
François Blayo	IPSEITE, Switzerland
Frank Röder	Hamburg University of Technology, Germany
Frederic Alexandre	Inria, France
Fuchang Han	Central South University, China
Fuli Wang	University of Essex, UK
Gabriela Sejnova	Czech Technical University in Prague, Czech Republic
Gaetano Di Caterina	University of Strathclyde, UK
George Bebis	University of Nevada, USA

Gerrit Ecke	Mercedes-Benz, Germany
Giannis Nikolentzos	Ecole Polytechnique, France
Gilles Marcou	University of Strasbourg, France
Giorgio Gnecco	IMT School for Advanced Studies, Italy
Glauco Amigo	Baylor University, USA
Greg Lee	Acadia University, Canada
Grégory Bourguin	LISIC/ULCO, France
Guillermo Martín-Sánchez	Champalimaud Foundation, Portugal
Gulustan Dogan	UNCW, USA
Habib Khan	Islamia College University Peshawar, Pakistan
Haizhou Du	Shanghai University of Electric Power, China
Hanli Wang	Tongji University, China
Hanno Gottschalk	TU Berlin, Germany
Hao Tong	University of Birmingham, UK
Haobo Jiang	NJUST, China
Haopeng Chen	Shanghai Jiao Tong University, China
Hazrat Ali	Hamad Bin Khalifa University, Qatar
Hina Afridi	NTNU, Gjøvik, Norway
Hiroaki Aizawa	Hiroshima University, Japan
Hiromichi Suetani	Oita University, Japan
Hiroshi Kawaguchi	Kobe University, Japan
Hiroyasu Ando	Tohoku University, Japan
Hiroyoshi Ito	University of Tsukuba, Japan
Honggang Zhang	University of Massachusetts, Boston, USA
Hongqing Yu	Open University, UK
Hongye Cao	Northwestern Polytechnical University, China
Hugo Carneiro	University of Hamburg, Germany
Hugo Eduardo Camacho Cruz	Universidad Autónoma de Tamaulipas, Mexico
Huifang Ma	Northwest Normal University, China
Hyeyoung Park	Kyungpook National University, South Korea
Ian Nabney	University of Bristol, UK
Igor Farkas	Comenius University Bratislava, Slovakia
Ikuko Nishikawa	Ritsumeikan University, Japan
Ioannis Pierros	Aristotle University of Thessaloniki, Greece
Iraklis Varlamis	Harokopio University of Athens, Greece
Ivan Tyukin	King's College London, UK
Iveta Bečková	Comenius University in Bratislava, Slovakia
Jae Hee Lee	University of Hamburg, Germany
James Yu	Southern University of Science and Technology, China
Jan Faigl	Czech Technical University in Prague, Czech Republic

Jan Feber	Czech Technical University in Prague, Czech Republic
Jan-Gerrit Habekost	University of Hamburg, Germany
Jannik Thuemmel	University of Tübingen, Germany
Jeremie Cabessa	University Paris 2, France
Jérémie Sublime	ISEP, France
Jia Cai	Guangdong University of Finance & Economics, China
Jiaan Wang	Soochow University, China
Jialiang Tang	Nanjing University of Science and Technology, China
Jian Hu	YiduCloud, Cyprus
Jianhua Xu	Nanjing Normal University, China
Jianyong Chen	Shenzhen University, China
Jichao Bi	Zhejiang Institute of Industry and Information Technology, China
Jie Shao	University of Electronic Science and Technology of China, China
Jim Smith	University of the West of England, UK
Jing Yang	Hefei University of Technology, China
Jingyi Yuan	Arizona State University, USA
Jingyun Jia	Baidu, USA
Jinling Wang	Ulster University, UK
Jiri Sima	Czech Academy of Sciences, Czech Republic
Jitesh Dundas	Independent Researcher, USA
Joost Vennekens	KU Leuven, Belgium
Jordi Cosp	Universitat Politècnica de Catalunya, Spain
Josua Spisak	University of Hamburg, Germany
Jozef Kubík	Comenius University, Slovakia
Junpei Zhong	Hong Kong Polytechnic University, China
Jurgita Kapočiūtė-Dzikienė	Vytautas Magnus University, Lithuania
K. L. Eddie Law	Macao Polytechnic University, China
Kai Tang	Independent Researcher, China
Kamil Dedecius	Czech Academy of Sciences, Czech Republic
Kang Zhang	Kyushu University, Japan
Kantaro Fujiwara	University of Tokyo, Japan
Karlis Freivalds	Institute of Electronics and Computer Science, Latvia
Khoa Phung	University of the West of England, UK
Kiran Lekkala	University of Southern California, USA
Kleanthis Malialis	University of Cyprus, Cyprus
Kohulan Rajan	Friedrich Schiller University, Germany

Koichiro Yamauchi	Chubu University, Japan
Koloud Alkhamaiseh	Western Michigan University, USA
Konstantinos Demertzis	Democritus University of Thrace, Greece
Kostadin Cvejoski	Fraunhofer IAIS, Germany
Kristína Malinovská	Comenius University in Bratislava, Slovakia
Kun Zhang	Inria and École Polytechnique, France
Laurent Mertens	KU Leuven, Belgium
Laurent Perrinet	AMU CNRS, France
Lazaros Iliadis	Democritus University of Thrace, Greece
Leandro dos Santos Coelho	Pontifical Catholic University of Parana, Brazil
Leiping Jie	Hong Kong Baptist University, China
Lenka Tětková	Technical University of Denmark, Denmark
Lia Morra	Politecnico di Torino, Italy
Liang Ge	Chongqing University, China
Liang Zhao	Dalian University of Technology, China
Limengzi Yuan	Shihezi University, China
Ling Guo	Northwest University, China
Linlin Shen	Shenzhen University, China
Lixin Zou	Wuhan University, China
Lorenzo Vorabbi	University of Bologna, Italy
Lu Wang	Macao Polytechnic University, China
Luca Pasa	University of Padova, Italy
Ľudovít Malinovský	Independent Researcher, Slovakia
Luis Alexandre	Universidade da Beira Interior, Portugal
Luis Lago	Universidad Autonoma de Madrid, Spain
Lukáš Gajdošech Gajdošech	Comenius University Bratislava, Slovakia
Lyra Puspa	Vanaya NeuroLab, Indonesia
Madalina Erascu	West University of Timisoara, Romania
Magda Friedjungová	Czech Technical University in Prague, Czech Republic
Manuel Traub	University of Tübingen, Germany
Marcello Trovati	Edge Hill University, UK
Marcin Pietron	AGH-UST, Poland
Marco Bertolini	Pfizer, Germany
Marco Podda	University of Pisa, Italy
Markus Bayer	Technical University of Darmstadt, Germany
Markus Eisenbach	Ilmenau University of Technology, Germany
Martin Ferianc	University College London, Slovakia
Martin Holena	Czech Technical University, Czech Republic
Masanari Kimura	ZOZO Research, Japan
Masato Uchida	Waseda University, Japan
Masoud Daneshtalab	Mälardalen University, Sweden

Mats Leon Richter	University of Montreal, Germany
Matthew Evanusa	University of Maryland, USA
Matthias Karlbauer	University of Tübingen, Germany
Matthias Kerzel	University of Hamburg, Germany
Matthias Möller	Örebro University, Sweden
Matthias Müller-Brockhausen	Leiden University, Netherlands
Matus Tomko	Comenius University in Bratislava, Slovakia
Mayukh Maitra	Walmart, India
Md. Delwar Hossain	Nara Institute of Science and Technology, Japan
Mehmet Aydin	University of the West of England, UK
Michail Chatzianastasis	École Polytechnique, Greece
Michail-Antisthenis Tsompanas	University of the West of England, UK
Michel Salomon	Université de Franche-Comté, France
Miguel Matey-Sanz	Universitat Jaume I, Spain
Mikołaj Morzy	Poznan University of Technology, Poland
Minal Suresh Patil	Umea universitet, Sweden
Minh Tri Lê	Inria, France
Mircea Nicolescu	University of Nevada, Reno, USA
Mohamed Elleuch	ENSI, Tunisia
Mohammed Elmahdi Khennour	Kasdi Merbah University Ouargla, Algeria
Mohib Ullah	NTNU, Norway
Monika Schak	Fulda University of Applied Sciences, Germany
Moritz Wolter	University of Bonn, Germany
Mostafa Kotb	Hamburg University, Germany
Muhammad Burhan Hafez	University of Hamburg, Germany
Nabeel Khalid	German Research Centre for Artificial Intelligence, Germany
Nabil El Malki	IRIT, France
Narendhar Gugulothu	TCS Research, India
Naresh Balaji Ravichandran	KTH Stockholm, Sweden
Natalie Kiesler	DIPF Leibniz Institute for Research and Information in Education, Germany
Nathan Duran	UWE, UK
Nermeen Abou Baker	Ruhr West University of Applied Sciences, Germany
Nick Jhones	Dundee University, UK
Nicolangelo Iannella	University of Oslo, Norway
Nicolas Couellan	ENAC, France
Nicolas Rougier	University of Bordeaux, France
Nikolaos Ioannis Bountos	National Observatory of Athens, Greece
Nikolaos Polatidis	University of Brighton, UK
Norimichi Ukita	TTI-J, Japan

Oleg Bakhteev	EPFL, Switzerland
Olga Grebenkova	Moscow Institute of Physics and Technology, Russia
Oliver Sutton	King's College London, UK
Olivier Teste	Université de Toulouse, France
Or Elroy	CLB, Israel
Oscar Fontenla-Romero	University of A Coruña, Spain
Ozan Özdenizci	Graz University of Technology, Austria
Pablo Lanillos	Spanish National Research Council, Spain
Pascal Rost	Universität Hamburg, Germany
Paul Kainen	Georgetown, USA
Paulo Cortez	University of Minho, Portugal
Pavel Petrovic	Comenius University, Slovakia
Peipei Liu	School of Cyber Security, University of Chinese Academy of Sciences, China
Peng Qiao	NUDT, China
Peter Andras	Edinburgh Napier University, UK
Peter Steiner	Technische Universität Dresden, Germany
Peter Sutor	University of Maryland, USA
Petia Georgieva	University of Aveiro/IEETA, Portugal
Petia Koprinkova-Hristova	Bulgarian Academy of Sciences, Bulgaria
Petra Vidnerová	Czech Academy of Sciences, Czech Republic
Philipp Allgeuer	University of Hamburg, Germany
Pragathi Priyadharsini Balasubramani	Indian Institute of Technology Kanpur, India
Qian Wang	Durham University, UK
Qinghua Zhou	King's College London, UK
Qingquan Zhang	Southern University of Science and Technology, China
Quentin Jodelet	Tokyo Institute of Technology, Japan
Radoslav Škoviera	Czech Technical University in Prague, Czech Republic
Raoul Heese	Fraunhofer ITWM, Germany
Ricardo Marcacini	University of São Paulo, Brazil
Riccardo Renzulli	University of Turin, Italy
Richard Duro	Universidade da Coruña, Spain
Robert Legenstein	Graz University of Technology, Austria
Rodrigo Clemente Thom de Souza	Federal University of Parana, Brazil
Rohit Dwivedula	Independent Researcher, India
Romain Ferrand	IGI TU Graz, Austria
Roman Moucek	University of West Bohemia, Czech Republic
Roseli Wedemann	Universidade do Estado do Rio de Janeiro, Brazil

Rufin VanRullen	CNRS, France
Ruijun Feng	China Telecom Beijing Research Institute, China
Ruxandra Stoean	University of Craiova, Romania
Sanchit Hira	JHU, USA
Sander Bohte	CWI, Netherlands
Sandrine Mouysset	University of Toulouse/IRIT, France
Sanka Rasnayaka	National University of Singapore, Singapore
Sašo Karakatič	University of Maribor, Slovenia
Sebastian Nowak	University Bonn, Germany
Seiya Satoh	Tokyo Denki University, Japan
Senwei Liang	LBNL, USA
Shaolin Zhu	Tianjin University, China
Shayan Gharib	University of Helsinki, Finland
Sherif Eissa	Eindhoven University of Technology, Afghanistan
Shiyong Lan	Independent Researcher, China
Shoumeng Qiu	Fudan, China
Shu Eguchi	Aomori University, Japan
Shubai Chen	Southwest University, China
Shweta Singh	International Institute of Information Technology, Hyderabad, India
Simon Hakenes	Ruhr University Bochum, Germany
Simona Doboli	Hofstra University, USA
Song Guo	Xi'an University of Architecture and Technology, China
Stanislav Frolov	Deutsches Forschungszentrum für künstliche Intelligenz (DFKI), Germany
Štefan Pócoš	Comenius University in Bratislava, Slovakia
Steven (Zvi) Lapp	Bar Ilan University, Israel
Sujala Shetty	BITS Pilani Dubai Campus, United Arab Emirates
Sumio Watanabe	Tokyo Institute of Technology, Japan
Surabhi Sinha	Adobe, USA
Takafumi Amaba	Fukuoka University, Japan
Takaharu Yaguchi	Kobe University, Japan
Takeshi Abe	Yamaguchi University, Japan
Takuya Kitamura	National Institute of Technology, Toyama College, Japan
Tatiana Tyukina	University of Leicester, UK
Teng-Sheng Moh	San Jose State University, USA
Tetsuya Hoya	Independent Researcher, Japan
Thierry Viéville	Domicile, France
Thomas Nowotny	University of Sussex, UK
Tianlin Zhang	University of Manchester, UK

Tianyi Wang	University of Hong Kong, China
Tieke He	Nanjing University, China
Tiyu Fang	Shandong University, China
Tobias Uelwer	Technical University Dortmund, Germany
Tomasz Kapuscinski	Rzeszow University of Technology, Poland
Tomasz Szandala	Wroclaw University of Technology, Poland
Toshiharu Sugawara	Waseda University, Japan
Trond Arild Tjostheim	Lund University, Sweden
Umer Mushtaq	Université Paris-Panthéon-Assas, France
Uwe Handmann	Ruhr West University, Germany
V. Ramasubramanian	International Institute of Information Technology, Bangalore, India
Valeri Mladenov	Technical University of Sofia, Bulgaria
Valerie Vaquet	Bielefeld University, Germany
Vandana Ladwani	International Institute of Information Technology, Bangalore, India
Vangelis Metsis	Texas State University, USA
Vera Kurkova	Czech Academy of Sciences, Czech Republic
Verner Ferreira	Universidade do Estado da Bahia, Brazil
Viktor Kocur	Comenius University, Slovakia
Ville Tanskanen	University of Helsinki, Finland
Viviana Cocco Mariani	PUCPR, Brazil
Vladimír Boža	Comenius University, Slovakia
Vojtech Mrazek	Brno University of Technology, Czech Republic
Weifeng Liu	China University of Petroleum (East China), China
Wenxin Yu	Southwest University of Science and Technology, China
Wenxuan Liu	Wuhan University of Technology, China
Wu Ancheng	Pingan, China
Wuliang Huang	ICT, China
Xi Cheng	NUPT, Hong Kong, China
Xia Feng	Civil Aviation University of China, China
Xian Zhong	Wuhan University of Technology, China
Xiang Zhang	National University of Defense Technology, China
Xiaochen Yuan	Macao Polytechnic University, China
Xiaodong Gu	Fudan University, China
Xiaoqing Liu	Kyushu University, Japan
Xiaowei Zhou	Macquarie University, Australia
Xiaozhuang Song	Chinese University of Hong Kong, Shenzhen, China

Xingpeng Zhang	Southwest Petroleum University, China
Xuemei Jia	Wuhan University, China
Xuewen Wang	China University of Geosciences, China
Yahong Lian	Nankai University, China
Yan Zheng	China University of Political Science and Law, China
Yang Liu	Fudan University, China
Yang Shao	Hitachi, Japan
Yangguang Cui	East China Normal University, China
Yansong Chua	China Nanhu Academy of Electronics and Information Technology, Singapore
Yapeng Gao	Taiyuan University of Technology, China
Yasufumi Sakai	Fujitsu, Japan
Ye Wang	National University of Defense Technology, China
Yeh-Ching Chung	Chinese University of Hong Kong, Shenzhen, China
Yihao Luo	Yichang Testing Technique R&D Institute, China
Yikemaiti Sataer	Southeast University, China
Yipeng Yu	Tencent, China
Yongchao Ye	Southern University of Science and Technology, China
Yoshihiko Horio	Tohoku University, Japan
Youcef Djenouri	NORCE, Norway
Yuan Li	Military Academy of Sciences, China
Yuan Panli	Shihezi University, China
Yuan Yao	Tsinghua University, China
Yuanlun Xie	University of Electronic Science and Technology of China, China
Yuanshao Zhu	Southern University of Science and Technology, China
Yucan Zhou	Institute of Information Engineering, Chinese Academy of Sciences, China
Yuchen Zheng	Shihezi University, China
Yuchun Fang	Shanghai University, China
Yue Zhao	Minzu University of China, China
Yuesong Nan	National University of Singapore, Singapore
Zaneta Swiderska-Chadaj	Warsaw University of Technology, Poland
Zdenek Straka	Czech Technical University in Prague, Czech Republic
Zhao Yang	Leiden University, Netherlands
Zhaoyun Ding	NUDT, China
Zhengwei Yang	Wuhan University, China

Zhenjie Yao	Chinese Academy of Sciences, Singapore
Zhichao Lian	Nanjing University of Science and Technology, China
Zhiqiang Zhang	Hosei University, Japan
Zhixin Li	Guangxi Normal University, China
Zhongnan Zhang	Xiamen University, China
Zhongzhan Huang	Sun Yat-sen University, China
Zi Long	Shenzhen Technology University, China
Zilong Lin	Indiana University Bloomington, USA
Zuobin Xiong	Georgia State University, USA
Zuzana Cernekova	FMFI Comenius University, Slovakia

Invited Talks

Developmental Robotics for Language Learning, Trust and Theory of Mind

Angelo Cangelosi

University of Manchester and Alan Turing Institute, UK

Growing theoretical and experimental research on action and language processing and on number learning and gestures clearly demonstrates the role of embodiment in cognition and language processing. In psychology and neuroscience, this evidence constitutes the basis of embodied cognition, also known as grounded cognition (Pezzulo et al. 2012). In robotics and AI, these studies have important implications for the design of linguistic capabilities in cognitive agents and robots for human-robot collaboration, and have led to the new interdisciplinary approach of Developmental Robotics, as part of the wider Cognitive Robotics field (Cangelosi and Schlesinger 2015; Cangelosi and Asada 2022). During the talk we presented examples of developmental robotics models and experimental results from iCub experiments on the embodiment biases in early word acquisition and grammar learning (Morse et al. 2015; Morse and Cangelosi 2017) and experiments on pointing gestures and finger counting for number learning (De La Cruz et al. 2014). We then presented a novel developmental robotics model, and experiments, on Theory of Mind and its use for autonomous trust behavior in robots (Vinanzi et al. 2019, 2021). The implications for the use of such embodied approaches for embodied cognition in AI and cognitive sciences, and for robot companion applications, was also discussed.

Challenges of Incremental Learning

Barbara Hammer

CITEC Centre of Excellence, Bielefeld University, Germany

Smart products and AI components are increasingly available in industrial applications and everyday life. This offers great opportunities for cognitive automation and intelligent human-machine cooperation; yet it also poses significant challenges since a fundamental assumption of classical machine learning, an underlying stationary data distribution, might be easily violated. Unexpected events or outliers, sensor drift, or individual user behavior might cause changes of an underlying data distribution, typically referred to as concept drift or covariate shift. Concept drift requires a continuous adaptation of the underlying model and efficient incremental learning strategies. Within the presentation, I looked at recent developments in the context of incremental learning schemes for streaming data, putting a particular focus on the challenge of learning with drift and detecting and disentangling drift in possibly unsupervised setups and for unknown type and strength of drift. More precisely, I dealt with the following aspects: learning schemes for incremental model adaptation from streaming data in the presence of concept drift; various mathematical formalizations of concept drift and detection/quantification of drift based thereon; and decomposition and explanation of drift. I presented a couple of experimental results using benchmarks from the literature, and I offered a glimpse into mathematical guarantees which can be provided for some of the algorithms.

Reliable AI: From Mathematical Foundations to Quantum Computing

Gitta Kutyniok[1,2]

[1]Bavarian AI Chair for Mathematical Foundations of Artificial Intelligence, LMU Munich, Germany
[2]Adjunct Professor for Machine Learning, University of Tromsø, Norway

Artificial intelligence is currently leading to one breakthrough after the other, both in public life with, for instance, autonomous driving and speech recognition, and in the sciences in areas such as medical diagnostics or molecular dynamics. However, one current major drawback is the lack of reliability of such methodologies.

In this lecture we took a mathematical viewpoint towards this problem, showing the power of such approaches to reliability. We first provided an introduction into this vibrant research area, focussing specifically on deep neural networks. We then surveyed recent advances, in particular concerning generalization guarantees and explainability methods. Finally, we discussed fundamental limitations of deep neural networks and related approaches in terms of computability, which seriously affects their reliability, and we revealed a connection with quantum computing.

Intelligent Pervasive Applications for Holistic Health Management

Ilias Maglogiannis

University of Piraeus, Greece

The advancements in telemonitoring platforms, biosensors, and medical devices have paved the way for pervasive health management, allowing patients to be monitored remotely in real-time. The visual domain has become increasingly important for patient monitoring, with activity recognition and fall detection being key components. Computer vision techniques, such as deep learning, have been used to develop robust activity recognition and fall detection algorithms. These algorithms can analyze video streams from cameras, detecting and classifying various activities, and detecting falls in real time. Furthermore, wearable devices, such as smartwatches and fitness trackers, can also monitor a patient's daily activities, providing insights into their overall health and wellness, allowing for a comprehensive analysis of a patient's health. In this talk we discussed the state of the art in pervasive health management and biomedical data analytics and we presented the work done in the Computational Biomedicine Laboratory of the University of Piraeus in this domain. The talk also included Future Trends and Challenges.

Contents – Part VI

A Further Exploration of Deep Multi-Agent Reinforcement Learning with Hybrid Action Space

Hongzhi Hua, Ruiwei Zhao, Guixuan Wen, and Kaigui Wu(✉)

College of Computer Science, Chongqing University, Shazheng Street, Chongqing 400044, China
{hongzhihua,guixuanwen,kaiguiwu}@cqu.edu.cn, ruiweizhao@stu.cqu.edu.cn

Abstract. The research of extending deep reinforcement learning (DRL) to multi-agent field have solved many complicated problems and made great achievements. However, almost all of these studies only focus on discrete or continuous action space and there are few works having ever applied multi-agent deep reinforcement learning (MADRL) to discrete-continuous hybrid action space which is common in practice problems. In this paper, two novel approaches are proposed to address multi-agent problems in discrete-continuous hybrid action space with centralized training but decentralized execution framework. The first approach, multi-agent hybrid deep deterministic policy gradients (MAHDDPG), extends the hybrid deep deterministic policy gradients (HDDPG) to multi-agent settings. However, like most other DRL algorithms, MAHDDPG still faces the problem that it may converge to the local optimal solution. To alleviate this problem, the second approach, multi-agent hybrid soft actor-critic (MAHSAC) is proposed. It extends hybrid soft actor-critic (HSAC) to multi-agent settings which introduces the idea of maximum entropy to strengthen the exploration of action space. Our experiments are running on a multi-agent particle world and a challenging task, whose results show that these methods are effective and significantly outperform independent HDDPG and HSAC methods.

Keywords: multi-agent system · deep reinforcement learning · hybrid action spaces

1 Introduction

In recent years, DRL [1,2] has been applied in multi-agent fields to handle practical tasks, such as multiplayer games and autonomous driving whose research have made great progress. However, there are also many problems and challenges about MADRL [3,4]. In previous research on MADRL, researchers have

H. Hua and R. Zhao—These authors made equal contributions to this work and should be considered cofirst authors.

L. Iliadis et al. (Eds.): ICANN 2023, LNCS 14259, pp. 1–12, 2023.
https://doi.org/10.1007/978-3-031-44223-0_1

made many explorations to improve the performance of algorithms. [5] considers a decentralized multi-agent policy gradient algorithm. Multi-agent deep deterministic policy gradients (MADDPG) [6] adopts multi-agent setting with a centralized Q-function to deep deterministic policy gradients (DDPG) [7].

The combination of hybrid action space and multi-agent system is common in reality, especially in video games, such as the release of skills in multiplayer games. First, a specific skill is selected which is a discrete action, and then the release position of this skill is selected which are continuous parameters. The development of video games has promoted the growth of the demand for built-in AI in video games. However, there was little research on this field in the past which could train good policy for it.

Those popular MADRL algorithms almost require the action space to be discrete or continuous which is not consistent with many practice environments which the action space is discrete-continuous hybrid, such as real time strategic (RTS) games [8] and robot movements [9]. In those settings, each agent usually needs to select a discrete operation and its related continuous parameters at each time step. In order to solve this problem, one approach is to simply approximate hybrid action space by a discrete set or relax it into a continuous set [10,11]. However, such methods suffer from a number of limitations. For the continuous part of hybrid action, establishing a good approximation usually requires a huge number of discrete actions. For the discrete part of hybrid action, relaxing them into a continuous set might significantly increase the complexity of the action space. A better solution is to learn directly over hybrid action space [12]. HSAC [13] is a successful algorithm to solve hybrid action space problem following this mind. Besides, [10] improves DDPG algorithm to get good policy in hybrid action space. However, the attempt to apply those methods directly to multi-agent settings is not ideal because of instability. Therefore, explicit coordination mechanism among agents' hybrid action space needs to be introduced.

In this paper, two novel approaches are proposed to address multi-agent problems in discrete-continuous hybrid action space. The first approach, MAHDDPG, extends the HDDPG to multi-agent settings. However, like most other DRL algorithms, MAHDDPG still faces the problem that it may converge to the local optimal solution. To alleviate this problem, we propose the second approach, MAHSAC. It extends HSAC to multi-agent settings which introduces the idea of maximum entropy to strengthen the exploration of action space. Empirical results on multi-agent particle environment and standard benchmark game Half Field Offense (HFO) show the superior performance of our approaches compared to independent hybrid DDPG and HSAC.

2 Background and Related Work

2.1 Deep Multi-agent Reinforcement Learning

DRL has abilities of feature extraction and sequence decision making which can solve many complex decision problems. It often uses Markov decision models to decompose problems and collects the state s_t, action a_t, reward r_t, next state

s_{t+1} as a tuple $(s_t\ , a_t, r_t, s_{t+1})$ at each time step to form a set (S, A, R, S'). The optimization objective is the strategy $\pi : s \rightarrow a$, and the cumulative reward which is obtained at the time t by (1) can be maximized by optimizing this objective.

$$R = \sum_{t'=t}^{T} \gamma^{t'-t} r_t \tag{1}$$

where, γ represents the discount factor. Then, the Q function can be defined as $Q^{\pi} = E\left[R_t \mid s_t, a_t\right]$, and the optimal strategy π^* is selected as the optimization goal to maximize the expectation of (1), which means (2) is accurate.

$$Q^{\pi^*}(s, a) \geq Q^{\pi}(s, a)\, \forall s, a \in S, A \tag{2}$$

When DRL is applied to multi-agent system, the environment becomes more complex, each agent needs to process more information, and the stability of the whole system will face bigger challenges. Centralized training but decentralized execution (CTDE) is the most popular multi-agent training architecture. The landmark methods such as MADDPG [6], QMIX [14] are built based on this architecture. CTDE focuses on learning a centralized critic $Q^{\mu}(x, a_1, ..., a_N)$ to take as input actions of all agents $(a_1, ..., a_N)$ in addition to global state information $x = (o_1, ..., o_N)$, and output the centralized action-value for each agent i.

2.2 Hybrid Deep Deterministic Policy Gradients

DDPG [7] is a classical algorithm which is usually used to deal with continuous action values. DDPG can be regarded as an extended version of DQN [17]. The difference is that DQN finally outputs an action vector, while DDPG finally outputs only one action deterministically. Moreover, DDPG allows DQN to be extended to a continuous action space.

[10] extends the DDPG algorithm into hybrid action space. Assuming that there are K discrete actions and each action corresponds to an m-dimensional continuous parameter x_k, the hybrid action space can be expressed as

$$A = \{(k, x_k) \mid x_k \in X_k \subset R^m\ for\ all\ k \in [K]\} \tag{3}$$

At each time step, the actor network μ takes as input the state which has two output layers: one for the discrete action and another for the continuous parameters. The discrete action is selected by the maximum value from the actions output, which is paired with related continuous parameters from the parameters output. The critic network Q takes as input the action a and state s while outputs a single scalar Q-value.

Compared with the standard temporal difference update originally used on Q-Learning [18], the update of critic network in HDDPG is basically unchanged. However, the actor needs to provide the next-state action $a' : \mu(s', \theta^{\mu})$ for the update target. Therefore, this process is greatly influenced by the actor's policy.

At the same time, the critic's knowledge of action values is then harnessed to learn a better policy for the actor.

One can think about those updates as simply interlinking the actor and critic networks: On the forward pass, the actor's output is passed forward into the critic and evaluated. Next, the estimated Q-Value is backpropagated through the critic, producing gradients $\nabla_a Q$ that indicate how the action should change in order to increase the Q-Value. On the backwards pass, these gradients flow from the critic through the actor. An update is then performed only over the actor's parameters.

By employing the target network and replay memory D to ensure convergence and stability, the critic loss and actor update can be expressed by the following:

$$\begin{aligned} L_Q(\theta^Q) = E_{s_t,a_t,r_t,s_{t+1}\sim D}[(Q(s_t,a_t) \\ - (r_t + \gamma Q'(s_{t+1},\mu'(s_{t+1}))))^2] \end{aligned} \tag{4}$$

$$\nabla_{\theta^\mu}\mu = E_{s_t\sim D}[\nabla_a Q(s_t,a \mid \theta^Q)\nabla_{\theta^\mu}\mu(s_t)\mid_{a=\mu(s_t)}] \tag{5}$$

2.3 Hybrid Soft Actor-Critic

Soft actor-critic (SAC) [15] is a popular off-policy algorithm that is originally proposed for continuous action space. Traditional reinforcement learning methods often maximize the return of agent which make the results of training easy to fall into local optimal solution due to their small scope of exploration in complex environments. SAC aims to maximize both return and entropy of action from the agent which can prevent the agent's strategy from converging prematurely to the local optimal solution [16], that is maximizing

$$E_\pi\left[\sum\nolimits_t \gamma^t\left(r_t + \alpha\mathcal{H}\left(\pi\left(\cdot \mid s_t\right)\right)\right)\right] \tag{6}$$

where, policy π is used to calculate distributions of the trajectory (s_t, a_t) for the entropy $\mathcal{H}(\cdot)$ of the strategy. α is used to pay more attention to entropy or reward, and a higher α will especially be conducive to explore possibility by encouraging agents to take actions which are more random.

HSAC [13], an extension of SAC, can directly handle hybrid action space without any approximation or relaxation. The definition of hybrid action space in HSAC is the same as Sect. 2.2.

By injecting standard normal noise ξ and applying tanh nonlinearity to keep the action within a bounded range, actor can output the mean μ^c and standard deviation vectors σ^c which are used to sample continuous parameter a^c. Besides, the shared hidden state representation h produces additionally a discrete distribution π^d to sample the discrete action a^d. Then, the critic can estimate the corresponding Q-value for all discrete actions by taking both state s and continuous parameter a^c as input.

SAC algorithm is based on the idea that the entropy increment proportional to the entropy of $\pi(a \mid s)$ is given. As long as the action has a discrete part, the joint entropy definition with the weighted sum of discrete action and continuous parameters in HSAC becomes:

$$\begin{aligned}\mathcal{H}(\pi(a^d, a^c \mid s)) = &\alpha^d \mathcal{H}(\pi(a^d \mid s)) \\ &+ \alpha^c \sum_{a^d} \pi(a^d \mid s)\mathcal{H}(\pi(a^c \mid a^d, s))\end{aligned} \tag{7}$$

Among them, the hyperparameters α^d and α^c encourage the exploration of discrete action and continuous parameters respectively.

3 Methods

3.1 Multi-Agent Hybrid Deep Deterministic Policy Gradients

In this part, HDDPG is extended to multi-agent settings based on CTDE paradigm. The structure of this algorithm is shown in Fig. 1. For each agent i, the same settings in single-agent HDDPG shown in Sect. 2.2 is applied. The actor μ_i takes as input the local observation o_i and outputs the action a_i, including the discrete action and continuous parameters. μ_i is updated by minimizing the following:

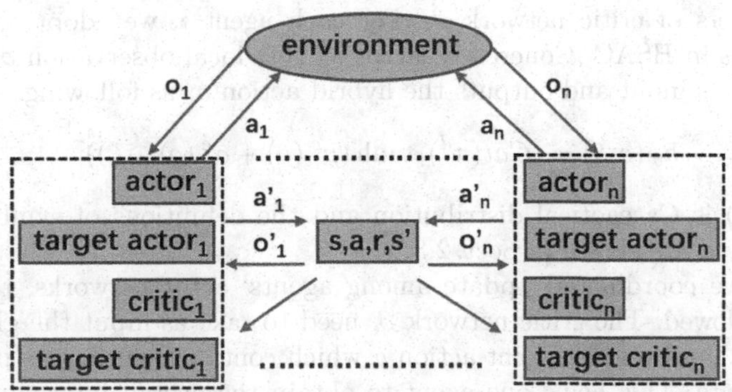

Fig. 1. Architecture of MAHDDPG and deep MAHSAC

$$L_\mu(\theta^{\mu_i}) = E_{s_t, a_t \sim D}[-Q_i(s_t, a_t \mid \theta^{Q_i})] \tag{8}$$

where, the global state s and joint action a are also stored in the experience replay buffer D for updating. Each agent i has its own independent global critic network which takes as input the combination set of state s and action a. Here, the action a taken by policy is a set of discrete action and continue parameters from all agents in addition to the state $s = \{o_i, ..., o_i\}$. Besides, each agent's critic network can be updated by the loss:

$$\begin{aligned}L_Q(\theta^{Q_i}) = E_{s_t, a_t, r_t, s_{t+1} \sim D}[&(Q_i(s_t, a_t) \\ &- (r_t + \gamma Q_i'(s_{t+1}, a_{t+1})))^2]\end{aligned} \tag{9}$$

It is very important to explore the action space, which helps agents to maximize long-term rewards. In this method, ϵ-greedy exploration is employed to hybrid action space where the discrete action is selected randomly and the associated continuous parameters are sampled from a uniform random distribution with the probability ϵ. And ϵ will change from 1.0 to 0.1 over the first 10,000 updates.

Compared with the well-known MADDPG algorithm, our algorithm modifies the structure of actor, so that it can output the discrete action and the corresponding continuous parameters, while changing the structure of critic according to this modification. Finally, the HDDPG algorithm is successfully extended to the setting of multi-agent and has stronger practical value. However, MAHDDPG still faces the problem that it may converge to the local optimal solution which will affect the performance of this algorithm.

3.2 Deep Multi-Agent Hybrid Soft Actor-Critic

To address the problem mentioned in previous section, the second method is an extension of single-agent HSAC based on CTDE paradigm, and the architecture is roughly the same as MAHDDPG in Fig. 1.

N agents are set up in the system to suit various situations, and the actor networks of these agents are a set: $\pi_\theta = \{\pi_1, \pi_2, ..., \pi_n\}$, while the Q_i^β represents the parameters of critic network β_i. For each agent i, we adopt roughly the same settings in HSAC. Concretely, actor π_i gets local observation o_i from the environment as input and outputs the hybrid action a_i as following:

$$\tilde{a}_\theta(o, \xi) = (Cat(\pi^d), \tanh(\mu^c(o) + \sigma^c(o) \odot \xi)) \tag{10}$$

where, $Cat()$ is Categotical distribution and the definitions of symbols in the above equation are shown in Sect. 2.3.

To achieve coordinated update among agents' actor networks, the idea of CTDE is followed. The critic network β_i need to take as input the global state $s = \{o_1, o_2, ..., o_n\}$ and the joint action a which contains continuous parameters from all agents. This helps one agent to obtain the overall information of the system better and realize the influence of other agents' actions on itself.

Depending on the soft policy iteration approach, MAHSAC updates the actor network by minimizing Kullback-Leibler (KL) divergence [15], and needs to minimize the following goals:

$$J_{\pi_i}(\theta) = E_{s\sim D, a\sim\pi_\theta}[\log(\pi(a_i \mid o_i)) - Q_\beta(s_i, a_i)] \tag{11}$$

The idea of maximum entropy helps MAHSAC explore the action space as much as possible to find the global optimal solution. The expectations of $J_{\pi_i}(\theta_i)$ can be approximated by taking samples out of experience replay buffer D. The gradient of resulting optimization objectives can be written as:

$$\begin{aligned}\nabla_\theta J_{\pi_i}(\theta) = {} & \nabla_\theta \log(\pi(a_i \mid o_i)) \\ & + (\nabla_{a_i} \log(\pi(a_i \mid o_i)) - \nabla_{a_i} Q_\beta(s_i, a_i)) \nabla_\theta \tilde{a}_\theta(o, \xi)\end{aligned} \tag{12}$$

According to the maximum entropy principle, the critic network $J_Q(\beta)$ can be updated by minimizing the Bellman error:

$$J_Q(\beta_i) = E_{s,a,r,s'}[\frac{1}{2}(Q^{\beta_i}(s,a) - y)^2] \tag{13}$$

y is represented as:

$$y = r_i + \gamma E_{a' \sim \pi_{\overline{\theta}_i}}[Q^{\overline{\beta}_i}(s',a') - \log(\pi(a'_i \mid o'_i))] \tag{14}$$

where, (s', a', a'_i, o'_i) represents the trajectory of one agent at next time step.

4 Experiment

In this section, the proposed algorithms are evaluated in 1) a multi-agent particle world, 2) the standard benchmark game HFO. Those algorithms, MAHDDPG and MAHSAC are compared with independent HDDPG and HSAC in all our experiments.

4.1 The Multi-Agent Particle World

This experiment adopts a simple multi-agent particle environment which consists of N agents and L landmarks inhabiting a two-dimensional world. This environment is modified so that it can meet the demand of discrete-continuous hybrid action space. Agents may take physical actions and continuous parameters that get broadcasted to other agents in the environment. Each agent has accelerations on the X axis and Y axis respectively. The discrete actions is a set (x^+, x^-, y^+, y^-) which means directions of acceleration to be applied. The continuous parameters are values of acceleration which $\in$ [0,1] corresponding to discrete actions. There are two different scenarios with different topics in the environment: cooperative and competitive.

There are three agents and three target points for the cooperative navigation scenario. Agents observe the relative positions of other agents and target points. After moving, they will be collectively rewarded based on the proximity of any agent to each target. In addition, the agents occupy significant physical space and will be punished when they collide with each other. They need to learn to infer which targets they must cover and move there while avoiding other agents.

Besides, there are 3 predators, 1 prey, and 2 obstacles for the Predator-Prey scenario. The goal of predators is to cooperate with each other to capture the prey, while the prey is aimed at avoiding the predators. Therefore, there is competition between the predators and the prey, and there is cooperation between the predators.

In the cooperative navigation scenario, agents will be rewarded according to the distance from the target and be punished when they collide with each other. The reward of all agents r_c in this scenario is defined as:

$$r_c = -dist_c - col_c \tag{15}$$

where, $dist_c$ is the mean value of distances from each target to the nearest agent and col_c is the total number of collisions between agents per episode. Therefore, in this scenario, multi-agent and decentralization training models are compared in terms of the reward value, number of collisions and distance from the target.

After 20000 episodes of training, the reward value curves of the agents are shown in Fig. 2. The sum of all 3 agents' reward is recorded per episode and the average value every hundred episodes is saved.

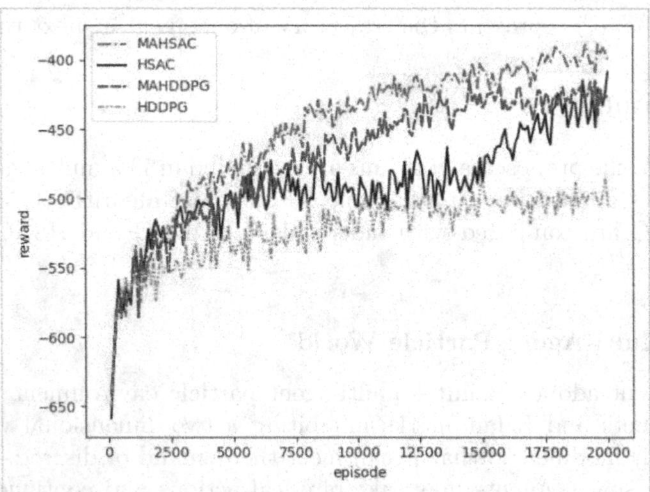

Fig. 2. Agent reward on cooperative communication after 20000 episodes

Table 1 shows the number of collision between agents and distance from the target after algorithm convergence which corresponds to the performance of agents.

Table 1. The average number of collision and proxy distance per episode in the cooperative navigation scenario

Agent	Collisions	Dist
MAHSAC	1.76	0.24
HSAC	1.81	0.32
MAHDDPG	1.84	0.27
HDDPG	2.09	0.38

Besides, in the Predator-Prey scenario, the reward r_p is as following:

$$r_p = (-1)^a 10col_p \tag{16}$$

Here, $a = 0$ for predator while 1 for prey. Col_p means the number of times prey is touched by all predators per episode. Due to the competition between predators and prey, the reward value curve of agents is unstable and cannot reflect the real performance of algorithms. Therefore, the average number of times prey is touched by predators per episode is recorded. Here, in order to concretely show the difference between different algorithms, four situations are set where multi-agent setting and independent methods are respectively applied to predators and prey.

The test results are shown in Table 2, a higher number of collisions indicates that predators can catch their prey more easily.

Table 2. Average number of times prey is touched by predators per episode in the predator-prey scenario

Agent	adversary	touches
MAHSAC	MAHSAC	2.90
MAHSAC	HSAC	20.59
HSAC	MAHSAC	2.22
HSAC	HSAC	1.87
MAHDDPG	MAHDDPG	0.73
MAHDDPG	HDDPG	2.34
HDDPG	MAHDDPG	1.30
HDDPG	HDDPG	1.45

The above data shows that our methods can train policy that will achieve the goal faster and better in both cooperative and competitive environment than independent algorithms. Especially, independent agent has a bad performance when directly pitted against multi-agent setting policy in the competitive scenario. This proves the advantages of the joint hybrid strategy between explicit coordination agents. Besides, MAHSAC outperforms MAHDDPG after convergence. It is believed that this is due to SAC's maximum entropy mechanism which can effectively prevent the agent's strategy from converging to the local optimal solution prematurely. A note is that MAHSAC agents learn policies a little slower than MAHDDPG in terms of the number of time steps required. The underlying reason is that MAHSAC needs to train additional models to adjust the weights in the definition of joint entropy.

4.2 Half Field Offense

HFO is a RoboCup 2D game which features in a hybrid action space. In this section, we apply our proposed algorithms on the challenging multi-agent problems of HFO including defense and offense. The opponent played against are all built-in hand-coded agents.

The observation of each agent is a vector consisting of its position and orientation; distance and angle to the ball and goal; an indicator if the agent can kick etc. The action space of this experiment is a set: **KickTo**($target_x, target_y, speed$); **MoveTo**($target_x, target_y$); **DribbleTo**($target_x, target_y$); **Intercept**(). Valid values for $target_{x,y} \in [-1, 1]$ and $speed \in [0, 3]$. In this environment, it's almost impossible for the random action of the agent to achieve the goal of shooting or defending to gain traction on a reward that only consists of scoring goals. Therefore, the reward settings of previous work [19] is applied in our paper to alleviate the sparse reward problem.

In the defense scenario, there are two agents with the shared objective of defending the goal against one opponent. Note that for defensive agents, only two actions **MoveTo** and **Intercept** are applicable. The reward is calculated as a weighted sum of the following three types of statistics at each time step: a reward proportional to the change in distance between the agent and the ball; a punishment if there's no defensive agent in the goal area; extra positive points if defensive agents successfully defend the goal and vice versa.

In the offense scenario, there are two agents with the shared objective of scoring the goal against one goalie. This mode has larger action space and the coordinating tasks is more challenging. The offensive agent has a extra discrete action **shoot**() which has totally five types of actions. The reward is also a weighted sum of the following types of statistics at each time step: a reward proportional to the change in distance between the agent and the ball; A reward proportional to change in distance between the ball and the center of the goal; a punishment if the ball is too far away from both agents when it is still outside the goal area; extra points if offensive agents successfully score a goal.

The defense rates in the defense scenario and goal rates in the offense scenario of our algorithms and independent methods are successfully recorded. Within 10000 episodes after algorithms converges, the above data are recorded and the average value is calculated. As Table 3 shows, MAHDDPG and MAHSAC outperform independent methods in both two modes which demonstrates that our methods can train good policies in a challenging task. Especially, we observe that the independent agents rarely pass and shoot in the offense scenario. The main reason may be the lack of information from teammates. Besides, MAHSAC still outperforms MAHDDPG which further validates that the introduction of maximum entropy mechanism can help agents find better actions. It indicates that MAHSAC framework provides a better way to handle problems with hybrid action space.

Table 3. Defense rates and goal rates for MAHDDPG, MAHSAC and independent methods

Agent	Defense rate	Goal rate
MAHSAC	0.63	0.56
HSAC	0.49	0.11
MAHDDPG	0.56	0.51
HDDPG	0.44	0.04

5 Conclusion

This paper extends HDDPG and HSAC to multi-agent settings while providing two novel ways to apply deep reinforcement learning in multi-agent environments to handle practical problems with discrete-continuous hybrid action space. This further fills the vacancy in this area. Under the paradigm of centralized training but decentralized execution, MAHDDPG and MAHSAC algorithms are proposed and the experimental results show their superiority to independent hybrid methods under a multi-agent particle world and a RoboCup 2D game. For future work, we want to apply more advanced and effective neural network structures to the research of multi-agent hybrid action space setting or test the potential of other DRL approaches in this area. This will make our algorithms to adapt to more diversified and complicated environments while showing more excellent performance. We also hope to combine our approaches with the most advanced and challenging operating environments in the future to contribute to the development of artificial intelligence and machine learning.

References

1. Arulkumaran, K., Deisenroth, M.P., Brundage, M., Bharath, A.A.: Deep reinforcement learning: a brief survey. IEEE Signal Process. Mag. **34**(6), 26–38 (2017)
2. Mousavi, S.S., Schukat, M., Howley, E.: Deep reinforcement learning: an overview. IntelliSys (2), 426–440 (2016)
3. Nguyen, T.T., Nguyen, N.D., Nahavandi, S.: Deep reinforcement learning for multi-agent systems: a review of challenges, solutions and applications, CoRR abs/1812.11794 (2018)
4. Tampuu, A., et al.: Multiagent cooperation and competition with deep reinforcement learning, CoRR abs/1511.08779 (2015)
5. Foerster, J.N., Assael, Y.M., de Freitas, N., Whiteson, S.: Learning to communicate with deep multi-agent reinforcement learning. In: NIPS 2016, pp. 2137–2145 (2016)
6. Lowe, R., Yi, W., Tamar, A., Harb, J., Abbeel, P., Mordatch, I.: Multi-agent actor-critic for mixed cooperative-competitive environments. In: NIPS, pp. 6379–6390 (2017)
7. Lillicrap, T.P., et al.: Continuous control with deep reinforcement learning. In: ICLR (Poster) (2016)
8. Xiong, J., et al.: Parametrized deep Q-networks learning: reinforcement learning with discrete-continuous hybrid action space, CoRR abs/1810.06394 (2018)
9. Kalyanakrishnan, S., Liu, Y., Stone, P.: Half field offense in RoboCup Soccer: a multiagent reinforcement learning case stud. In: RoboCup 2006, pp. 72–85 (2006)
10. Hausknecht, M.J., Stone, P.: Deep reinforcement learning in parameterized action space. In: ICLR (Poster) (2016)
11. van Hasselt, H., Wiering, M.A.: Using continuous action spaces to solve discrete problems. In: IJCNN, pp. 1149–1156 (2009)
12. Bester, C.J., James, S.D., Konidaris, G.D.: Multi-pass Q-networks for deep reinforcement learning with parameterised action spaces, CoRR abs/1905.04388 (2019)
13. Delalleau, O., Peter, M., Alonso, E., Logut, A.: Discrete and continuous action representation for practical RL in video games, CoRR abs/1912.11077 (2019)

14. Rashid, T., Samvelyan, M., de Witt, C.S., Farquhar, G., Foerster, J.N., Whiteson, S.: QMIX: monotonic value function factorisation for deep multi-agent reinforcement learning. In: ICML 2018, pp. 4292–4301 (2018)
15. Haarnoja, T., Zhou, A., Abbeel, P., Levine, S.: Soft actor-critic: off-policy maximum entropy deep reinforcement learning with a stochastic actor. In: ICML 2018, pp. 1856–1865 (2018)
16. Haarnoja, T., et al.: Soft actor-critic algorithms and applications, CoRR abs/1812.05905 (2018)
17. Mnih, V., et al.: Playing Atari with deep reinforcement learning, CoRR abs/1312.5602 (2013)
18. Watkins, C.J.C.H., Dayan, P.: Technical note Q-learning. Mach. Learn. **8**, 279–292 (1992)
19. Fu, H., Tang, H., Hao, J., Lei, Z., Chen, Y., Fan, C.: Deep multi-agent reinforcement learning with discrete-continuous hybrid action spaces. In: IJCAI, pp. 2329–2335 (2019)

Air-to-Ground Active Object Tracking via Reinforcement Learning

Xin Liu, Weiya Ren, Jie Tan, Xiaochuan Zhang, Xiaoguang Ren(✉), and Huadong Dai

Academy of Military Science, Beijing, China
rxg_nudt@126.com

Abstract. Over the years, active object tracking has emerged as a prominent topic in object tracking. However, most of these methods are unsuitable for tracking ground objects in high-altitude environments. Therefore, the paper proposes an air-to-ground active object tracking method based on reinforcement learning for high-altitude environments, which consists of a state recognition model and a reinforcement learning module. The state recognition model leverages the correlation between observed states and image quality (as measured by object recognition probability) as prior knowledge to guide the training of reinforcement learning. Then, the reinforcement learning module can actively control the PTZ camera to achieve stable tracking and successfully recover tracking after object loss. Additionally, the study introduces a UE-free simulator that increases the efficiency of the training process by over nine times. High-altitude experimental results with the proposed method show significantly enhanced stability and robustness compared to the PID method. Furthermore, the results also indicate that the proposed method can significantly improve the image quality of the observation.

Keywords: Active object tracking · Reinforcement learning

1 Introduction

Object tracking is a subject of interest for decades, with a focus on robotics and unmanned aerial vehicles (UAV) applications [15]. The purpose of object tracking is to locate the position of a moving target in a sequence of image frames and keep it in the image field of view. Object tracking can be categorized into active object tracking and passive object tracking. The passive method [10] assumes that the camera is stationary and the object is within the camera's field of view. In contrast, the active method requires adjusting the posture of pan-tilt-zoom (PTZ) cameras to maintain continuous visibility within the image, which is more practical and challenging.

Active object tracking has been extensively researched across various fields [4]. However, most studies have focused on ground or low-altitude scenarios, while the research on active object tracking in high-altitude environments is

L. Iliadis et al. (Eds.): ICANN 2023, LNCS 14259, pp. 13–24, 2023.
https://doi.org/10.1007/978-3-031-44223-0_2

limited. In addition, previous methods have taken less account of the interference caused by the external environment on the controller and the resulting problem of object disappearance and recovery. However, in high-altitude environments, atmospheric disturbance and complex ground environments can interfere with the tracking process and easily lead to object loss.

To address the problem of active object tracking in a complex high-altitude environment, we propose an air-to-ground (i.e., high-altitude UAV tracks a vehicle on the ground) active object tracking method based on reinforcement learning. Specifically, we build a state recognition model and introduce it to the reinforcement learning training process as prior knowledge, which considers the correlation between the observation states and the quality of the observed images. Then, we design a reinforcement learning module to achieve stable tracking by actively controlling and guiding the PTZ camera, and successfully recovering tracking after object loss.

The results have shown that our proposed active object tracking method is significantly more stable than the PID control method in all proposed scenarios. In particular, in the case of object rectilinear motion, the tracking stability of our model is better than that of the S-curve and random motions. One possible reason is that our method could predict the object's motion based on its historical information and control the camera accordingly in time, especially for rectilinear motion. Regarding the disturbance, PTZ camera vibration has a certain effect on tracking stability, while the object-specific disturbance (i.e., the object's speed and direction) has less impact. Such a result indicates that it is important to maintain the stability of the PTZ camera during tracking and that our method has good adaptability regardless of the object's movement.

Moreover, our method can significantly improve the accuracy of object recognition by automatically adjusting the magnification, i.e., the image quality of the observation is improved. Furthermore, we find that the object has a lower chance of reappearing in the field of view after being lost, even for a short period of time, while our method can quickly retrieve the object and resume tracking. In contrast, the conventional PID control method can only recover tracking in the few cases where the object is still in the field of view after being lost. Therefore, our method is significantly better than the PID control method in terms of robustness during tracking.

In summary, our main contributions include the following:

- An air-to-ground active object tracking reinforcement learning method is proposed to achieve tracking in high-altitude environments, and its tracking stability and robustness outperform the traditional PID method in all the proposed scenarios, i.e., different object motions and disturbance modes.
- A novel reward function involving the state recognition model is proposed and the object recognition probability is utilized as a part of the reward function to effectively guide reinforcement learning to adjust the PTZ camera focus and improve the input image quality.
- A memory-enabled actor-critic neural network is designed specifically for active object tracking, and the training efficiency is significantly improved,

i.e., over nine times compared to the UE simulator, by introducing a UE-free simulator and optimizing the training strategy.

2 Related Work

The goal of active object tracking is to lock the object by autonomously adjusting the position and attitude of the camera given a visual observation as input [12]. The method has been applied to a range of platforms, including PTZ cameras [13], vehicles [3], and UAVs [12]. For instance, Kyrkou [5] proposed a real-time and lightweight C^3Net for roadside monitoring. Zhang et al. [16] implemented an end-to-end tracking method for UAVs by introducing GRU into the reinforcement learning network. However, these methods are not suitable for tracking tasks in high-altitude environments due to the relatively close distance between the tracker and the object.

Researchers have studied disturbance factors, including similar objects [12], occlusion [2], and obstacles [6] to increase the robustness of tracking methods. Such as Zhong et al. [18] and Yao et al. [14] improved the robustness of models by introducing occlusion during training. However, they do not consider the disturbance of vibration-induced tracker or target loss during active object tracking.

Combining prior knowledge with reinforcement learning can improve tracking performance, for example, a common approach involves combining PID as a knowledge module [7,17]. However, the application of the PID is restricted due to problems such as vibration, object loss, and low image quality in high-altitude object tracking scenarios. Thus, we propose an active object tracking method that is well-suited to high-altitude environments and solves such problems.

3 Approach

3.1 Overview

Active object tracking aims to control the motion of a PTZ camera based on the object's position in the image. In this paper, we propose an air-to-ground active object tracking reinforcement learning method, as shown in Fig. 1. The method includes two main components: the state recognition model and the reinforcement learning module with the improved Proximal Policy Optimization (PPO) [11] algorithm. A brief description of each of these modules is given below.

In some scenarios, it is necessary to maintain the highest possible image quality during the tracking process to obtain additional information from the observed images, which can further improve tracking performance. For this purpose, we introduce a state recognition model as prior knowledge into reward shaping, which is proposed to establish a relationship between image quality (as measured by object recognition probability) and the observed camera states through supervised learning. The model can guide the motion of PTZ cameras to further improve the quality of observed images and enhance the object tracking performance. Meanwhile, it can also avoid the vast computational burden caused by direct image processing with the reinforcement learning method.

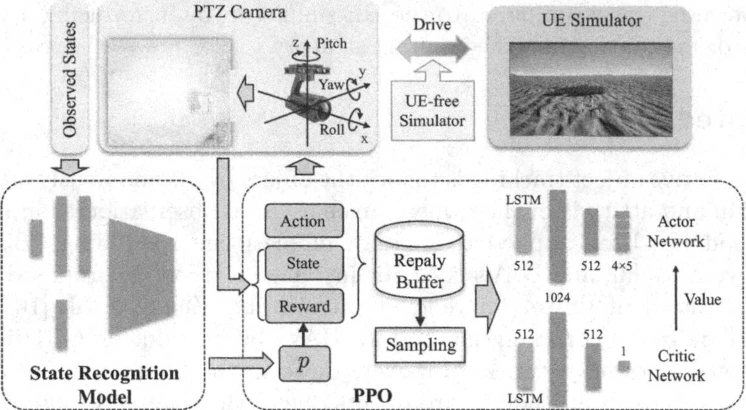

Fig. 1. The overall framework

A PPO-based reinforcement learning module is conducted to control the PTZ camera and, thus, address the high-altitude active object tracking task. To improve the efficiency of reinforcement learning training, we introduce a UE-free simulator. The trained model exhibits excellent tracking performance in the simulator, which is based on the UE engine to create a realistic desert environment with mild undulating terrain, forests, vehicle and UAVs. The movements of UAVs and vehicle follows the laws of physics.

3.2 State Recognition Model

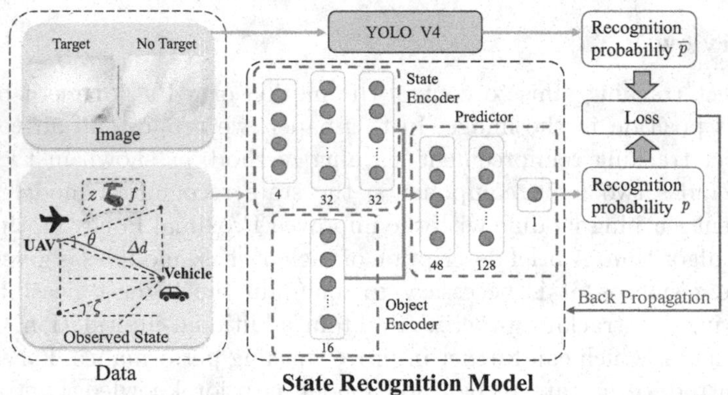

Fig. 2. State recognition model. (together with the observed states)

Figure 2 illustrates the structure of the state recognition model. The model takes the observed states as the input and the object recognition probability measuring the image quality as the output, and establishes the relationship between the input and output through supervised learning. The observed states consist of five parameters: $[\Delta d_t, \zeta_t, \theta_t, z_t, f_t]$, where Δd_t represents the distance between the UAV and the vehicle, ζ_t illustrates the azimuth angle of the vehicle relative to the UAV, θ_t represents the pitch angle of the PTZ camera, z_t indicates the camera magnification (the camera is autofocus). In addition, f_t functions as a status flag to distinguish whether the object is present in the image, assigning a value of 1 if the object exists and 0 otherwise.

As shown in Fig. 2, the network structure of the state recognition model is comprised of three parts: a state encoder, an object encoder and a predictor. The state encoder processes the observed states through three fully connected layers and returns a 32-dimensional vector. The object encoder processes the object status flag in a fully connected layer and outputs a 16-dimensional vector. The predictor joins the two vectors outputted by the state and object encoders, respectively, and feeds them into three fully connected layers to generate the object recognition probability. Moreover, both encoders employ the ReLU activation function, while the predictor applies the softmax activation function. Furthermore, the number of neurons in each network layer is present in Fig. 2.

Training Process. We collect 24,000 images with the corresponding observed states from the UE simulator, and train the state recognition model using supervised learning based on pre-trained YOLOv4. Specifically, we take the images as the input and use the object recognition probability $\bar{p}$ generated by YOLOv4 as the supervision signal, combined with the object recognition probability p generated by the state recognition model, to form the loss function[1].

To improve the stability and convergence speed of the learning process, a gradient clipping approach with a threshold of 0.5 was conducted to dynamically adjust the learning rate[2]. The neural network parameters of the state recognition model were optimized using the Adam optimizer during the training process, and the state recognition model showed convergence after 30 iterations.

3.3 Reinforcement Learning Module

Active object tracking keeps the object within the field of view by continuously controlling the motion of the PTZ cameras. Such a process can be formulated as a classic reinforcement learning problem, and an improved proximal policy optimization (PPO) reinforcement learning algorithm is employed as an agent. The parameterization of the Markov Decision Process (i.e., state space, action space, and reward shaping) and the network architecture are described below.

The state space s_t at the moment t can be defined as given below:

$$s_t = \left[\frac{x_t}{w}, \frac{y_t}{h}, \frac{z_t}{z_{\max}}, \frac{px_t}{(w \cdot h)}, f_t\right]^T$$

[1] $Loss = \frac{\sum_{i=1}^{N}|p-\bar{p}|}{N}$, where N represents the batch size of training.

[2] The rule for updating the learning rate: $lr_{epoch} = \frac{1}{1+0.02\times epoch}$, where *epoch* represents the number of iterations.

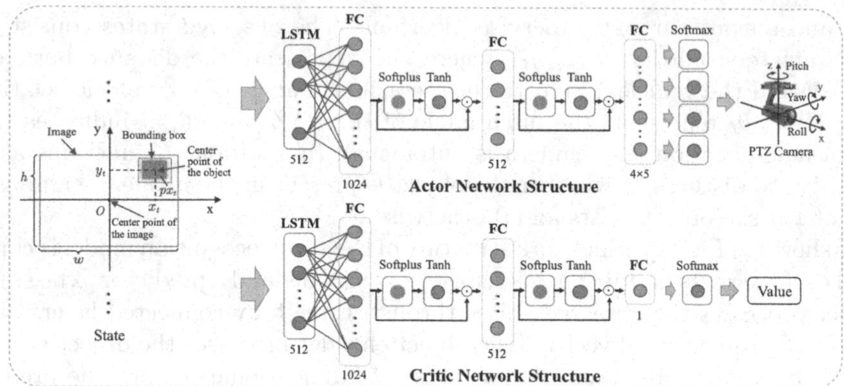

Fig. 3. Reinforcement learning module

where x_t and y_t donate the coordinates of the object concerning the center of the field of view, w and h represent the width and the height of the image, respectively (as shown in Fig. 3). In addition, px_t represents the pixel area of the object, z_t and z_{max} represent magnification and maximum magnification. In particular, when the object is lost at the time t, s_t is set to $\left[0, 0, \frac{z_t}{z_{\max}}, 0, 0\right]^T$. In this paper, the values of w, h, z_{max} are 1024, 768 and 400x, respectively.

At the time t, we define the $action_t$ as $[pitch_t, yaw_t, roll_t, zoom_t]$, where $pitch_t, yaw_t, roll_t$, and $zoom_t$ are integers with values ranging from -2 to 2, and represent the actions of the PTZ camera's pitch angle θ, yaw angle ψ, roll angle ϕ, and camera magnification z, respectively. When executing the $action_t$, the camera state at the time $t-1$, i.e., $[\theta_{t-1}, \psi_{t-1}, \phi_{t-1}, z_{t-1}]$, is added with increments $\alpha \cdot [pitch_t/z_{t-1}, yaw_t/z_{t-1}, roll_t/z_{t-1}, zoom_t \cdot \beta]$ to obtain the required camera state at the time t, and adjust the PTZ camera. The α and β are coefficients.

In the proposed active object tracking process, the shaping of the reward function involves: 1) the agent should improve the object recognition probability p by actively performing actions, and 2) the center of the object should be as close to the center of the image as possible to achieve continuous and stable object tracking. In particular, the agent gets a time penalty when the object is out of the image. Therefore, the reward function is obtained by:

$$r_t = \begin{cases} mp_t - n\sqrt{\left(\frac{x_t}{w}\right)^2 + \left(\frac{y_t}{h}\right)^2}, & f_t = 1 \\ -n, & f_t = 0, \end{cases}$$

where m, n are the coefficients used to limit the total accumulated reward value.

The actor and critic in PPO are represented as neural networks, with the structures shown in Fig. 3. In particular, the output layer of the actor network has four parallel fully-connected networks with five neurons each, corresponding to the four actions passed through a softmax activation function. The critic network has a similar structure to the actor network, except that it has only one neuron in the output layer that directly outputs the Q value. A Block composed of softplus and tanh activation functions is used after the second and third layers, which makes the networks easier to optimize.

Training Process. Reinforcement learning requires iterative optimization through continuous interaction with mass data in the environment. However, the simulation environment built with UE engines usually runs slowly, hindering fast model training. Thus, we propose and construct a UE-free simulator based on environment abstraction, which can provide crucial parameters involved in the simulation environment and significantly improve training efficiency.

We propose an improved training procedure for the PPO algorithm (pseudocode below) to address the challenge of recovering the tracking process when the object has been lost for a long time. The core idea is to accumulate the rewards r_t for different moments satisfying certain criteria into a variable r_{sum} after each interaction between the agent and the environment, i.e., UE-free simulator. Then, the current episode is terminated when the value of r_{sum} falls below a predefined threshold, and a new round of training is started.

Algorithm 1. Improved PPO Algorithm.

Require: Initialize parameters θ of actor network and ϕ of critic network, respectively.

```
for episode = 1,2,... do
  Initialize set to store trajectory D ← ∅;
  Initialize flag to determine whether to end the episode r_sum ← 0;
  Randomly initialize state s_0;
  for step = 1,2,... do
    Get the state s_t from the UE-free simulator;
    Run old policy π_θ' to select action action_t;
    Execute action action_t, receive r_t and obtained status s_{t+1};
    if r_t > 0 then
      r_sum ← min ([0.02, r_t]) + r_sum;
    else
      r_sum ← max ([−0.01, r_t]) + r_sum;
    end if
    if r_sum < −2.0 then
      break;
    end if
    Collect trajectory D ← D ∪ (s_t, action_t, r_t);
    if the data in D reaches mini-batch and step % 50 == 0 then
      for Iteration = 1,2 do
        Sample a random mini-batch trajectory from buffer D;
        Compute advantage estimates Â_t with GAE;
        Update θ and φ with clipped surrogate objective and value functions loss;
      end for
    end if
  end for
end for
```

In the training process, we initialize the actor and critic parameters, interact with the UE-free simulator to obtain the training data and store it in a replay buffer. Then, we sample a mini-batch of 256 from the replay buffer as our dataset and use Adam (the learning rate of actor and critic is $1e-4$ and $2e-4$) to optimize the network. The generalized advantage estimation (GAE) parameter λ and clipping ϵ are set at 0.95 and 0.2. The maximum global episodes and maximum steps N are 8K and 400. For the reward function, the values of the γ, m and n are 0.99, 0.1 and 0.1, and the action coefficient α, β are 50 and 5, respectively. We use TensorFlow as a deep learning framework to train the actor and critic networks with a PC containing an AMD Ryzen 7-5800H (3.20 GHz $\times 16$) processor, 16 GB of RAM, and an NVIDIA RTX 3050 with 4 GB of VRAM.

4 Experimental Setup and Results Analysis

4.1 Baseline and Evaluation Criteria

As a baseline, we choose the commonly used and effective PID controller to control the pitch and yaw actions of the PTZ camera. The PID formula under discrete control is:

$$u_k = K_p \cdot e_k + K_i \sum_{j=0}^{k} e_j + K_d \left(e_k - e_{k-1} \right),$$

where at time k, u_k represents the increment of pitch and yaw actions, and e_k represents the Euclidean distance from the image center to the object centroid. Moreover, K_p, K_i and K_d are the tuning hyperparameters, which can be set to -0.005, 0.003 and 0.003, respectively, after multiple experiments. Furthermore, the magnification in the PID controller is set to 50 times.

The performance evaluation includes the following three criteria:

- **Stability.** The stability of the tracking process is measured in terms of center location error, which represents the Euclidean distance (in pixels) between the object centroid and the image center in a step. Continues smaller values of center location errors indicate better stability.
- **Robustness.** Ro is used to evaluating the robustness of the active tracker, which is the percentage of frames in which the tracker loses the object during the tracking process. Smaller Ro means better robustness.
- **Image quality.** Object recognition probability is adopted to measure image quality. Higher probability indicates better image quality is obtained during the object tracking process.

4.2 Experiments and Results

To conduct the experiments, we randomly initialized the starting position and orientation of the vehicle and the UAV, with the vehicle moving at 12 m/s and the UAV flying at 300 m altitude. Initially, the camera was set at a magnification of 50x and precisely aimed at the vehicle.

Stability. We compared the object tracking stability for three different vehicle motions, i.e., rectilinear, S-curve and random. In addition, we introduced three disturbance modes, i.e., the vehicle speed and direction, and the PTZ camera vibration, to further verify the tracking stability. Regarding the vehicle, the speed changes randomly in the range of 0 to 20 m/s and the direction turns arbitrarily. For the PTZ camera, we applied a slight vibration by setting random changes in the pitch and roll angles, which caused the object to vibrate within the camera viewfinder frame. Moreover, we also compared the results obtained in each scenario with the tracking performance of the PID control method.

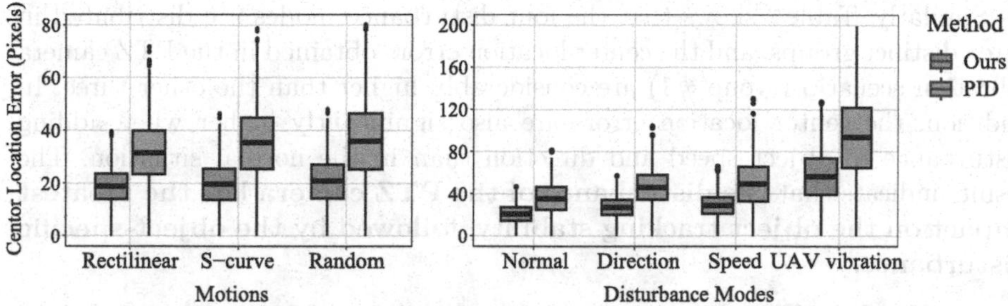

Fig. 4. Comparison of the tracking stability obtained in different scenarios

Figure 4 shows a series of box plots depicting the distribution of center location errors of our proposed and PID control methods in 30 episodes (i.e., 12000 steps) for each of the above-mentioned scenarios. According to Fig. 4, the center location errors of our method are almost two times smaller than those of the PID control method in all scenarios. To further evaluate the significance of the difference for each scenario, we calculated the Wilcoxon Signed Rank test [9] and Cliffs Delta Effect Size [1] on the center location errors of our method and PID control method. The results of the statistical tests reveal that the difference between the center location errors of our method and the PID control method in each scenario is significant (i.e., p-value < 0.05), and with a large effect size[3]. Thus, **the proposed method is significantly more stable than the PID control method in object tracking for all proposed scenarios.**

To evaluate the significance of different scenarios on the stability of our proposed tracking method, we performed a Scott-Knott effect size difference (ESD) test to group the different scenarios into statistically distinct ranks based on their center location errors. Tables 1 and 2 illustrate the ranks of tracking stability for three object motions and four disturbance modes, respectively. From Table 1, we found that the three object motions are distributed in two distinct groups, and in particular, the center location errors of S-curve and random motions (group #1) are relatively higher than rectilinear motion. Thus, **in the case of object**

[3] The magnitude is assessed using the thresholds provided by Romano et al. [8], $|delta|$ >0.474 is large.

Table 1. Ranks of object motions according to the Scott-Knott ESD tests

Group	Object Motions
1	S-curve, random
2	rectilinear

Table 2. Ranks of disturbance modes according to the Scott-Knott ESD tests

Group	Disturbance Modes
1	PTZ camera vibration
2	object speed and direction
3	normal

rectilinear motion, the tracking stability of our model is better than that of the S-curve and random motions.

Similarly, Table 2 shows that the four disturbance modes are distributed in three distinct groups, and the center location errors obtained in the PTZ camera vibration scenario (group #1) are considerably higher than the other three. In addition, the center location errors are also significantly higher when adding disturbance to object speed and direction than in the normal situation. The results indicate that **the disturbance of the PTZ camera has the greatest impact on the object tracking stability, followed by the object-specific disturbance.**

Image Quality. The object recognition probabilities of 210 episodes obtained from the above seven scenarios using our method and the PID control method at the initial PTZ camera magnification (50x), respectively, all have an average of about 0.123. In other words, both methods have an accuracy of only about 0.123 for object recognition at the initial moment. During the tracking process, our proposed method improves the object recognition probability close to 1 in a short time (about 40 steps) and continues until the end of the tracking task by controlling the PTZ camera magnification (zoom in to approximately 400x). However, the PID control method has almost no improvement in the object recognition probability during the tracking process and ends with an average accuracy of 0.124. Therefore, **our method can significantly improve the accuracy of object recognition by automatically adjusting the magnification, i.e., the image quality of the observation is improved.**

Robustness. We evaluate the robustness of the proposed method by comparing the tracking performance after losing the object due to various reasons (e.g., interference or occlusion) during the UAV flight with the PID control method. We set the object vehicle to move randomly within an episode (400 steps) and to be lost (i.e., no longer receiving the tracking signals) at step 100. After the loss, the movements of the object vehicle and the UAV remain constant, and an attempt is made to re-observe and re-track the object at step 120. Since the object vehicle and the UAV continue to remain in motion, there are two situations when the object is re-observed at step 120 through the PTZ camera, 1) the object is still in the field of view ($inFoV$) and 2) the object is no longer observed, i.e., out of the field of view ($outFoV$).

Table 3 shows the number of occurrences (numbers in parentheses) for $inFoV$ and $outFoV$ after 50 experiments using our method and the PID control method,

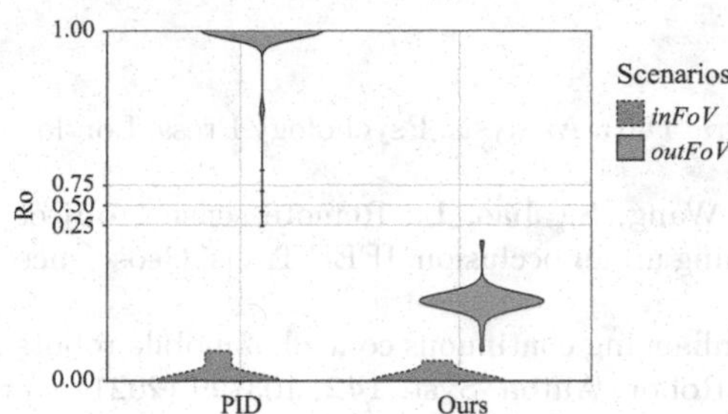

Fig. 5. Distribution of Ro

Table 3. Ro values in different scenarios

Scenarios	PID	Ours
inFoV	0.20% (9)	0.12% (6)
outFoV	95.69% (41)	2.84% (44)
Total	**78.50%**	**2.51%**

respectively, and the corresponding average value of Ro, i.e., the percentage of frames in which the tracker lost the object after step 120. In addition, the "Total" row represents the average Ro values in a total of 50 experiments. From Table 3, *outFoV* has a much higher probability of occurrence than *inFoV*, which means **the object has a lower chance of reappearing in the field of view after being lost for a short period of time** (e.g., only 20 steps).

Moreover, Table 3 also reveals the lower Ro values for our method, especially in the *outFoV* situation. This can be further visualized in Fig. 5, where the violin plots comparing the change in Ro values for *inFoV* and *outFoV* situations can be visualized for each method. The more elongated the shape of the violin, the larger the variance in the corresponding group; and the wider the violin plot, the higher the density. By observing Fig. 5, we note that the Ro values of our method in the *inFoV* situation are slightly lower than those of the PID control method. In stark contrast, the Ro values of our method in the *outFoV* situation are surprisingly smaller than those of the PID control method. These results highlight that **our method is significantly better than the PID control method in terms of robustness during tracking, especially when re-tracking after object loss.**

5 Conclusion

This paper proposes an air-to-ground active object tracking method based on reinforcement learning for a high-altitude tracking environment. The method consists of two parts: a state recognition model and an improved PPO algorithm. By incorporating the state recognition model's output into the reward function, the proposed reinforcement learning algorithm adjusts the PTZ camera to improve image quality during tracking. Moreover, a UE-free simulator is introduced to accelerate the training process. The experimental results indicate that our proposed method offers a higher level of robustness and stability in the tracking process as compared to PID control method.

However, due to the limitations of experimental conditions, future work will focus on deploying our method in physical environments and solving more disturbance factors in high-altitude environments to further enhance its applicability.

References

1. Cliff, N.: Ordinal Methods for Behavioral Data Analysis. Psychology Press, London (2014)
2. Cui, Y., Hou, B., Wu, Q., Ren, B., Wang, S., Jiao, L.: Remote sensing object tracking with deep reinforcement learning under occlusion. IEEE Trans. Geoscience Remote Sens. **60**, 1–13 (2021)
3. Devo, A., Dionigi, A., Costante, G.: Enhancing continuous control of mobile robots for end-to-end visual active tracking. Robot. Auton. Syst. **142**, 103799 (2021)
4. Jeong, H., Hassani, H., Morari, M., Lee, D.D., Pappas, G.J.: Deep reinforcement learning for active target tracking. In: 2021 IEEE International Conference on Robotics and Automation (ICRA), pp. 1825–1831. IEEE (2021)
5. Kyrkou, C.: C^3Net: end-to-end deep learning for efficient real-time visual active camera control. J. Real-Time Image Proc. **18**, 1421–1433 (2021)
6. Luo, Y., et al.: Calibration-free monocular vision-based robot manipulations with occlusion awareness. IEEE Access **9**, 85265–85276 (2021)
7. Ma, X., Wang, Y., Yang, S., Niu, W., Ma, W.: Trajectory tracking of an underwater glider in current based on deep reinforcement learning. In: OCEANS 2021, San Diego-Porto, pp. 1–7. IEEE (2021)
8. Romano, J., Kromrey, J.D., Coraggio, J., Skowronek, J.: Appropriate statistics for ordinal level data: should we really be using t-test and Cohen's d for evaluating group differences on the NSSE and other surveys. In: Annual Meeting of the Florida Association of Institutional Research, vol. 177, p. 34 (2006)
9. Rosner, B., Glynn, R.J., Lee, M.L.T.: The Wilcoxon signed rank test for paired comparisons of clustered data. Biometrics **62**(1), 185–192 (2006)
10. Ross, D.L., Lim, J.L., et al.: Incremental learning for robust visual tracking. Int. J. Comput. Vis. 77(1r3), 125r141 (2008)
11. Schulman, J., Wolski, F., Dhariwal, P., Radford, A., Klimov, O.: Proximal policy optimization algorithms. arXiv preprint arXiv:1707.06347 (2017)
12. Xi, M., Zhou, Y., Chen, Z., Zhou, W., Li, H.: Anti-distractor active object tracking in 3D environments. IEEE Trans. Circuits Syst. Video Technol. **32**(6), 3697–3707 (2021)
13. Yang, J., Tang, Z., Pei, Z., Song, X.: A novel motion-intelligence-based control algorithm for object tracking by controlling pan-tilt automatically. Math. Probl. Eng. 2019 (2019)
14. Yao, B.: GARAT: generative adversarial learning for robust and accurate tracking. Neural Netw. **148**, 206–218 (2022)
15. Yun, S., Choi, J., Yoo, Y., Yun, K., Choi, J.Y.: Action-driven visual object tracking with deep reinforcement learning. IEEE Trans. Neural Netw. Learn. Syst. **29**(6), 2239–2252 (2018)
16. Zhang, H., He, P., Zhang, M., Chen, D., Neretin, E., Li, B.: UAV target tracking method based on deep reinforcement learning. In: 2022 International Conference on Cyber-Physical Social Intelligence (ICCSI), pp. 274–277. IEEE (2022)
17. Zhao, W., Meng, Z., Wang, K., Zhang, J., Lu, S.: Hierarchical active tracking control for UAVs via deep reinforcement learning. Appl. Sci. **11**(22), 10595 (2021)
18. Zhong, F., Sun, P., Luo, W., Yan, T., Wang, Y.: Towards distraction-robust active visual tracking. In: International Conference on Machine Learning, pp. 12782–12792. PMLR (2021)

Enhancing P300 Detection in Brain-Computer Interfaces with Interpretable Post-processing of Recurrent Neural Networks

Christian Oliva[1(✉)], Vinicio Changoluisa[2], Francisco B. Rodríguez[1], and Luis F. Lago-Fernández[1]

[1] Grupo de Neurocomputación Biológica, Departamento de Ingeniería Informática, Escuela Politécnica Superior, Universidad Autónoma de Madrid, Madrid, Spain
{christian.oliva,f.rodriguez,luis.lago}@uam.es

[2] Grupo de Investigación en Electrónica y Telemática, Universidad Politécnica Salesiana, Quito, Ecuador
fchangoluisa@ups.edu.ec

Abstract. Brain-computer interfaces (BCIs) are innovative systems that allow individuals to communicate with external devices without physical movements. These systems commonly use Event-Related Potentials (ERPs), particularly P300, as the signal control. However, despite their wide acceptance, there are still issues to be resolved, such as inter- and intra-subject variability. To address this challenge, we propose a novel approach based on post-processing the output of a Recurrent Neural Network using a Post-Recurrent Module (PRM). The PRM processes the temporal information extracted from the recurrent layer to make the final decision. This work shows that simple approaches, such as a reduce-max operation or a logistic regression layer, can improve the balanced accuracy by more than 9% compared to state-of-the-art results. Our findings also contribute to the interpretability of RNNs since we have deepened the internal mechanisms of the model through an extensive analysis of the PRM layer. Overall, this study enhances the performance of ERP-based BCIs.

Keywords: Elman RNN · LSTM · Deep Learning · Bayesian Linear Discriminant Analysis · Interpretability · Brain-Machine Interface · Inter- and Intra-subject Variability · ERP Detection

1 Introduction

Brain-computer interfaces (BCIs) are advanced systems enabling individuals to establish direct communication with external devices or applications by processing and decoding their brain signals, bypassing the requirement for physical movement. These interfaces can potentially revolutionize the field of human-computer interaction by offering an alternative means of control, for instance, for

L. Iliadis et al. (Eds.): ICANN 2023, LNCS 14259, pp. 25–36, 2023.
https://doi.org/10.1007/978-3-031-44223-0_3

those with physical disabilities or limitations. Event-related potentials (ERPs) are the stereotyped electrophysiological brain responses to certain external stimuli, being the most commonly used signals in BCIs to explore the human brain. These ERPs can be detected non-invasively by recording electrical activity in the brain with electroencephalography (EEG) technology. One of the most widely used ERPs is the P300 [1], which is associated with various cognitive processes such as memory, learning, and attention [3].

The P300-ERP is a positive deflection evocated with the presentation of frequent and infrequent stimuli [14]. Although this positive deflection usually appears around 300 ms after the presentation of the infrequent (or target) stimulus, there is abundant literature showing that it is variable in time and that it can appear between 250 and 900 ms [18]. Moreover, it does not always manifest as a single positive deflection but usually includes other positive and negative deflections that appear with the target stimulus. In other words, the P300 wave is not a mere and simple deflection at 300 ms, but rather a signal with a complex temporal structure that presents a clear inter- and intra-subject variability [1,5–8]. This complex temporal structure and its variability in signal characteristics make it difficult to identify the brain activity related to the target stimulus. Although several methodologies have recently been proposed to deal with these variability problems [7], they are still a pending challenge in ERP-based BCIs.

Advances in Artificial Intelligence (AI) algorithms have improved the detection of such activity and therefore the performance of ERP-based BCIs [15]. One of the branches of AI that have been most successful in improving BCI performance is deep learning [2,20]. Several architectures have been used in this context, including Recurrent Neural Networks (RNNs), Convolutional Neural Networks (CNNs), and Deep AutoEncoders (DAEs). Although CNNs have been more widely used for EEG signals [2], in recent years the use of RNNs has also been explored, due to their good performance for time series analysis. This type of network allows extracting temporal characteristics of EEG [20]. Thus, in this work, we present a post-processing methodology for RNNs that identifies the temporal structure of P300 ERPs. It consists of incorporating a Post-Recurrent Module (PRM) that processes the temporal outputs of the recurrent network to make its decision. Specifically, we show that even a simple PRM, such as a reduce-max operation or a logistic regression layer, outperforms the state-of-the-art models. Additionally, we deepen into the interpretability of the model and we demonstrate that it is effectively detecting the occurrence of the P300 event after approximately 250 ms. Furthermore, our results suggest that the models have learned to discard redundant or noisy information from the input data.

The remaining of the article is organized as follows. First, in Sect. 2, we introduce the materials and methods used in our research: we describe the dataset used in our experiments, the preprocessing we apply to the data, and the models that we use. Then, in Sect. 3 we perform an analysis of the interpretability of the proposed PRM and present our results. Finally, in Sect. 4 we present the conclusions and further lines of research.

2 Materials and Methods

2.1 Data Description and Preprocessing

The dataset used in this work was created by Hoffman et al. [12] and is based on a six-choice P300 paradigm. It comprises EEG recordings from eight participants who viewed randomized sequences of six images with an Inter-Stimulus Interval (ISI) of 400 ms. Each image was presented for 100 ms, followed by a 300 ms blank screen. The EEG signals were captured using the standard 32 electrodes of the 10–20 international system [13] and sampled at 2048 Hz. A sixth-order forward-backward Butterworth bandpass filter was applied with cut-off frequencies set to 1 Hz and 12 Hz, and the signals were downsampled to 32 Hz.

For preprocessing the data, 1000 ms windows were extracted starting from the stimulus onset and the classification problem consists of predicting the corresponding class (*Target stimulus* for target image and *Non-target stimulus* for non-target image) using these windows. Although this approach is used in most research studies, it poses several challenges. For example, there is an intrinsic overlap in the 1000 ms windows, since the images are presented with an ISI of 400 ms. Hence, each window contains information related to the subject's response to three different images, which adds noise and variability to the problem.

2.2 Models

Bayesian Linear Discriminant Analysis (BLDA). Initially used by Hoffman et al. [12] for the P300-ERP recognition problem, BLDA is an extension of Linear Discriminant Analysis [4] that conducts regression within a Bayesian framework. The method automatically estimates the degree of regularization to prevent overfitting in noisy and high-dimensional environments. For our experiments, we employ the scikit-learn implementation [19].

Recurrent Neural Network (RNN). RNNs are a kind of neural network designed to process sequential or time-series data, thanks to the introduction of recurrent connections. These connections allow learning the temporal dependencies within a sequence of data, making RNNs well-suited for many tasks, such as language modeling, speech recognition, or time series prediction. In this work, we use Elman RNNs [10], the most basic type of neural network in which these recurrent connections are introduced, and Long Short-Term Memory (LSTM) networks [11]. Elman RNNs define their hidden state as follows:

$$\mathbf{h}_t = tanh(\mathbf{W}^{hx}\mathbf{x}_t + \mathbf{W}^{hh}\mathbf{h}_{t-1} + \mathbf{b}^h), \quad (1)$$

where $\mathbf{x}_t$ is the input to the recurrent layer at time t, $\mathbf{h}_t$ is the activation vector of the recurrent layer at time t, $\mathbf{W}^{h*}$ represents the weights associated to vector $*$, and $\mathbf{b}^h$ is the recurrent bias. Here, the recurrent connection is introduced by the inclusion of the term $\mathbf{W}^{hh}\mathbf{h}_{t-1}$. On the other hand, the LSTM hidden state is given by:

$$\mathbf{f}_t = \sigma(\mathbf{W}^{fx}\mathbf{x}_t + \mathbf{W}^{fh}\mathbf{h}_{t-1} + \mathbf{b}^f) \tag{2}$$
$$\mathbf{i}_t = \sigma(\mathbf{W}^{ix}\mathbf{x}_t + \mathbf{W}^{ih}\mathbf{h}_{t-1} + \mathbf{b}^i) \tag{3}$$
$$\mathbf{o}_t = \sigma(\mathbf{W}^{ox}\mathbf{x}_t + \mathbf{W}^{oh}\mathbf{h}_{t-1} + \mathbf{b}^o) \tag{4}$$
$$\mathbf{z}_t = tanh(\mathbf{W}^{zx}\mathbf{x}_t + \mathbf{W}^{zh}\mathbf{h}_{t-1} + \mathbf{b}^z) \tag{5}$$
$$\mathbf{c}_t = \mathbf{f}_t \odot \mathbf{c}_{t-1} + \mathbf{i}_t \odot \mathbf{z}_t \tag{6}$$
$$\mathbf{h}_t = \mathbf{o}_t \odot tanh(\mathbf{c}_t), \tag{7}$$

where, as before, $\mathbf{W}^{**}$ are weight matrices and $\mathbf{b}^*$ are bias vectors. The $\odot$ operator denotes an element-wise product, and σ is the logistic sigmoid function. In both network architectures, the hidden state $\mathbf{h}_t$ (Eqs. 1 or 7) is used for calculating the network output as:

$$y_t = \sigma(\mathbf{W}^{yh}\mathbf{h}_t + b^y), \tag{8}$$

where $\mathbf{W}^{yh}$ is a weight matrix and b^y is the bias. Note that, as we are facing a binary classification problem, only one neuron is used at the output layer.

In previous work [16,17], we introduced a methodology for training these networks in a sample-level way that requires the use of two hyperparameters to define the expected output for each time step. With these, the networks can detect the presence of a P300 event by focusing the attention on an interest interval that is individually defined for each subject. The aim of this work is to avoid the definition of these two hyperparameters while maintaining, if not improving, the model's accuracy and interpretability.

Post-Validation Neural Ensemble (PVNE). On the RNN models previously defined, a post-validation neural ensemble (PVNE) can be constructed by extracting the most informative neurons, using the weights that connect the recurrent and output layers to assess their relevance [16]. The neurons are ranked based on their contribution towards generating the network's output, and a selection is made to combine their individual predictions for the final model's decision. This process eliminates neurons that may be more involved in maintaining the network's hidden state than in generating the network's output, leading to an overall improvement in performance with respect to the base models. The PVNE has been shown to be highly effective in detecting the temporal structure of P300 event-related potentials at the sample level, surpassing standard RNN models. However, PVNE requires a sample-level preprocessing [16]. Thus, it is not an alternative choice as a post-processing methodology.

2.3 Post-Recurrent Module (PRM)

We have shown in previous works [16,17] that using recurrent neural networks for learning the temporal dependencies of the P300 EEG signals in a sample-level way outperforms the state-of-the-art models, probably due to a better adaptation to the to inter- and intra-subject variability. However, as we mentioned above, this method requires an exhaustive search of the two hyperparameters, the *offset*

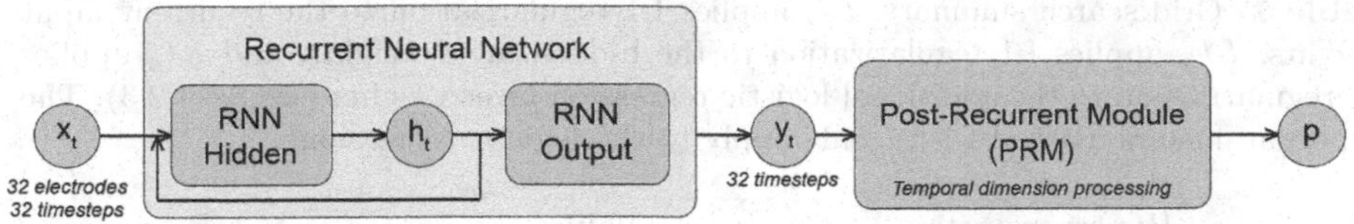

Fig. 1. Explanatory diagram of the PRM. This module jointly processes the RNN's outputs to give the final prediction p.

and the *window size*, that define, for each user, the region where the model must focus its attention on. In order to avoid this search, the present work aims to enable the models to self-learn the relevant temporal information by adding a post-recurrent module (PRM) into the network's architecture. Figure 1 shows an explanatory flowchart of this procedure, in which the outputs of the RNN at each time step are jointly processed by the post-recurrent module. The PRM automatically processes the time dimension to obtain the final prediction. In the following sections, we present two different strategies in order to achieve this objective.

Reduce-Max Strategy (RM). The first strategy that we consider consists of applying a reduce-max operation on the RNN outputs, across the temporal dimension. Departing from the standard recurrent network output at each time step, y_t (Eq. 8), the network outputs a 32-component vector, $\mathbf{y}_{[0::32]}$, for each 1000 ms window (note the 32 Hz downsampling, see Sect. 2.1). With this output vector $\mathbf{y}_{[0::32]}$, the RM strategy follows this simple equation:

$$p = \max(y_t) \text{ for each } y_t \text{ in } \mathbf{y}_{[0::32]}. \tag{9}$$

This idea arises from the fact that the P300 event may occur at any time step due to the big inter- and intra-subject variability. Therefore, by choosing the maximum, we let the model focus the attention on different regions for different users, hence allowing the detection of the P300 time dependencies in an autonomous way.

Logistic-Regression Strategy (LR). The second strategy consists of applying a logistic regression model on the previously defined output vectors $\mathbf{y}_{[0::32]}$:

$$p = \sigma(\mathbf{w}^p \mathbf{y}_{[0::32]} + b^p), \tag{10}$$

where $\mathbf{w}^p$ is a weight vector and b^p is the bias. This approach allows the model to learn how to combine and scale the contributions for each time step, y_t, for giving the final output p.

2.4 Experiments

The complete dataset has 8 users and four different sessions for each user. We perform a K-Fold cross-validation with K = 4, using three of these sessions as

Table 1. Grid search summary. $L1_i$ applies L1 regularization to the recurrent input weights, $L1_h$ applies L1 regularization to the hidden layer weights, and $L1_o$ applies L1 regularization to the additional logistic regression layer weights (see Sect. 2.3). The hyperparameters marked with * only apply to the logistic regression.

	Hyperparameters	Values
	L1 Regularization Input ($L1_i$)	$\{0, 10^{-4}, 10^{-3}, 10^{-2}, 10^{-1}\}$
	L1 Regularization Hidden ($L1_h$)	$\{0, 10^{-4}, 10^{-3}, 10^{-2}, 10^{-1}\}$
*	*L1 Regularization Output* ($L1_o$)	$\{0, 10^{-4}, 10^{-3}, 10^{-2}, 10^{-1}\}$

training and the remaining one as the test session. All the models are trained with some fixed hyperparameters, such as the number of units in the recurrent layer (50), the batch size (16), the learning rate (0.0003), or the optimizer (Nadam [9]). There are also some variable hyperparameters, like the L1 regularization strength, which are optimized using a grid search (see Table 1).

For evaluation, we use the balanced accuracy metric, $BAC = (recall + specificity)/2$, because this problem has an intrinsic imbalance: there are five negative stimuli against only one positive stimulus. In addition, the training has also been weighted to resolve this imbalance.

3 Results

The initial focus of this section is to assess the interpretability of the implemented models, ensuring that they align with this article's goal of self-learning the temporal characteristics of the P300 events. We start by analyzing the temporal dynamics of the models when using the RM and the LR strategies, in Sect. 3.1. Then, in Sect. 3.2, the results of the two strategies regarding the BAC metric are presented.

3.1 Interpretability Analysis

Reduce-Max Analysis. The RM strategy combines the 32 RNN outputs in a single 1000 ms window by computing their maximum (Eq. 9). Hence, we can analyze the temporal behavior of the model by looking at the specific intervals where the maxima occur and comparing the target and non-target activation averages at these intervals. This procedure allows the identification of the interest regions with maximum discrimination in which the recurrent network is focusing for making its prediction. Figure 2 portrays this comparison with an example network trained with user 7, for all the target (red lines) and non-target (blue lines) stimuli. The thick lines represent averages over stimuli.

It is interesting to observe the huge difference between target and non-target averages in the interval [312.5 ms, 437.5 ms], which clearly defines the relevant temporal window that the network is using for giving its final prediction. From this model, we can infer that the P300-ERP occurs at about 375 ms from the

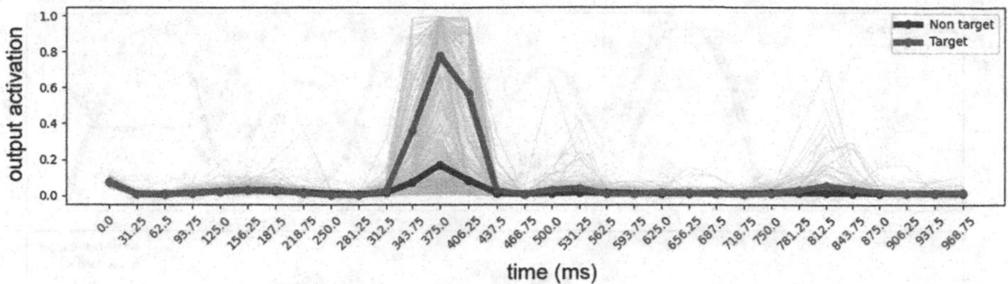

Fig. 2. Target and non-target activations of the recurrent layer at each time step of an Elman RNN with RM strategy trained with user 7. Red and blue curves represent the target and non-target averages when tested on the target and non-target stimuli, respectively. (Color figure online)

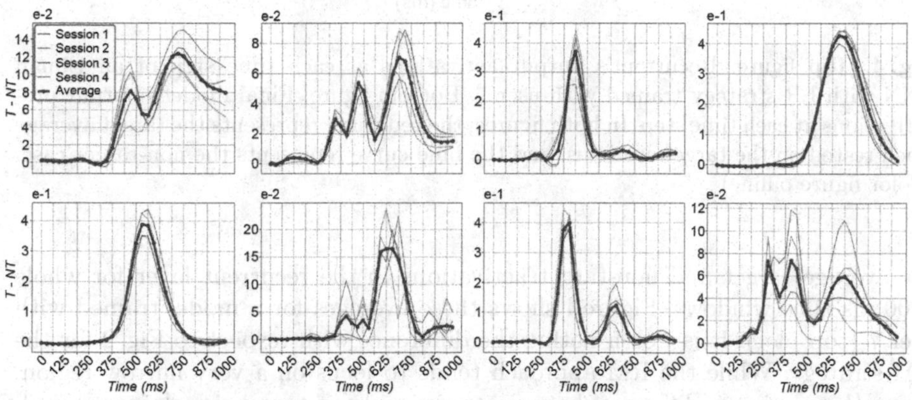

Fig. 3. Average target (T) and non-target (NT) difference of 400 different executions for the available eight users. Thicker lines in blue represent the averages of the four sessions. (Color figure online)

stimulus onset, for user 7. Results for other users are shown in Fig. 3, where each line is an average of the difference between the target and non-target RNN outputs of 400 different models trained for each user and session. Thicker lines in blue represent the averages of the four sessions for each user. These plots illustrate the large inter- and intra-variability between users. Note that, in many cases, the P300 ERPs do not appear as a single peak, so the models must consider different time regions. The pertinent regions consistently emerge after 250 ms, which aligns with the theoretical notion that the P300 event usually takes place approximately 300 ms after the stimulus.

Logistic Regression Analysis. The LR strategy uses a logistic regression model on the RNN outputs (Eq. 10). As before, we can analyze the model's behavior, and its differences with respect to the previous approach, by observing

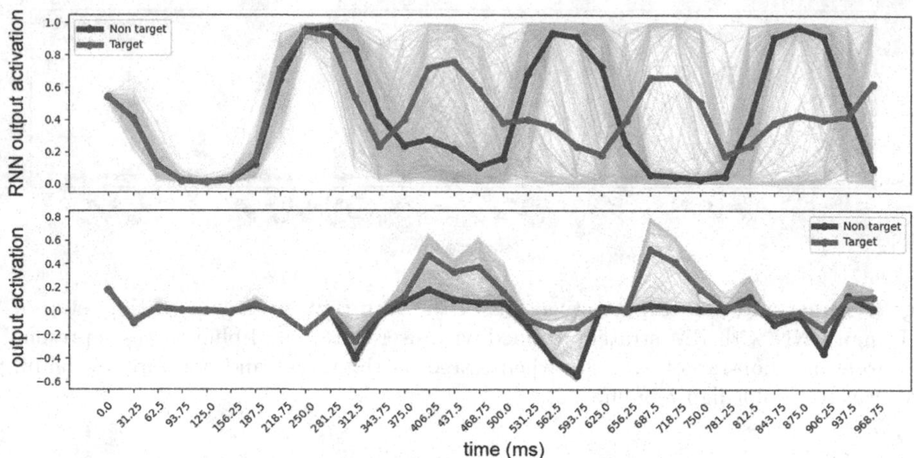

Fig. 4. Top figure: Recurrent's output activations at each time step of an Elman RNN with LR strategy trained with user 7. Bottom figure: Final model's output pre-activations at each time step. In both figures, the red curve represents the target average when tested on the target stimulus, and the blue curve represents the non-target case. (Color figure online)

the average target and non-target activations in the recurrent layer for whole 1000 ms time windows. Figure 4 shows these averages for a model trained with user 7 (top plot). It is worth noting the difference with respect to Fig. 2 for the RM strategy. While the RM approach tends to focus on a very narrow region, where the maximum difference between target and non-target signals is observed, the LR strategy considers a wider interval that spans from approximately 250 ms to the end of the window.

The final output in the LR model is mediated by the weight vector $\mathbf{W}^p$. Hence it is interesting to observe how each weight in $\mathbf{W}^p$ scales its corresponding component in the RNN output vector $\mathbf{y}_{[0::32]}$. The bottom plot in Fig. 4 shows these scaled values, emphasizing the regions [375 ms, 500 ms], [531.25 ms, 625 ms], and [658.25 ms, 781.25 ms], where the most significant differences between target and non-target averages are observed.

The results for the other users, measured as the difference between the target and non-target signals, are displayed in Fig. 5. As before, different lines are averages of 400 models trained with different sessions and users, and thick lines show averages of the four sessions for each user. The plots suggest that the networks are actively learning to differentiate between P300 and non-P300 stimuli since, after approximately 250 ms, there is a noticeable increase in these differences. It is now more evident that the model utilizes all the information from 250 ms onwards to make its prediction.

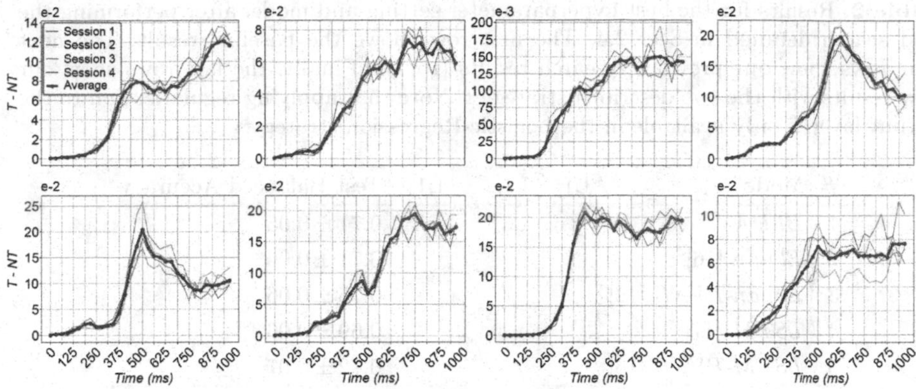

Fig. 5. Average target (T) and non-target (NT) difference of 400 different executions for the available eight users. Thicker lines in blue represent the averages of the four sessions for each user. (Color figure online)

3.2 P300 Detection Accuracy

In this section, we present the results, in terms of accuracy (BAC), of the two former strategies, and make a comparison with other methods in the literature. Table 2 shows the BAC score obtained for each model, after hyperparameters have been tuned using the grid search detailed in Sect. 2.4. The first row shows the baseline result, obtained with the BLDA model by Hoffman et al. [12], which represents the state of the art. The following four rows display the results obtained with our previous sample-level approach [16,17]. Finally, the last four table rows contain the results obtained with the two strategies presented in this work, using both Elman and LSTM RNNs.

We can extract several conclusions from the table. First, the Elman RNN enhanced with the LR module achieves the best test BAC (80%), improving the second best result by 3% points (compare row 7 with rows 6 and 9). Interestingly, the LSTM yields lower results compared to the Elman RNN. Additionally, it is worth mentioning that, for the Elman RNN, the optimal hyperparameter settings always involve applying the maximum value of the L1 regularization to the input layer and zero to the rest. This may indicate that the models are receiving redundant and noisy information that needs to be discarded. Moreover, both strategies consistently achieve equal or better results than those obtained by the homonymous standard model (rows 6 and 7 versus row 2).

Table 2. Results for the best hyperparameter setting and model after performing the grid search detailed in Sect. 2.4. The first row shows the baseline result. The next four rows show our previous research results [16,17]. Finally, the last rows show our new results with the two described strategies. Note that applying regularization to the output layer is only available in the Logistic-Regression strategy.

#	Model	$L1_i$	$L1_h$	$L1_o$	Test Balanced Accuracy
1	*BLDA*				0.71 ± 0.05
2	*Elman* [16]				0.71 ± 0.06
3	*Elman-PVNE* [16]				0.75 ± 0.06
4	*LSTM* [17]				0.69 ± 0.06
5	*LSTM-PVNE* [16]				0.72 ± 0.07
6	*Elman-RM*	0.1	0.0	n/a	0.77 ± 0.05
7	*Elman-LR*	0.1	0.0	0.0	$\mathbf{0.80 \pm 0.05}$
8	*LSTM-RM*	0.01	0.0	n/a	0.72 ± 0.07
9	*LSTM-LR*	0.01	0.0001	0.01	0.77 ± 0.06

4 Conclusion and Discussion

This article introduces a post-processing technique for Recurrent Neural Networks that effectively identifies the temporal structure of P300 event-related potentials. The methodology incorporates a Post-Recurrent Module (PRM) (see Sect. 2.3) that processes the outputs of the recurrent network at each time step, considering the time dependencies extracted by the recurrent layer, to make the final prediction. An advantage of the PRM approach is that it eliminates the need to define the expected output for each time step and the interval of interest [16], enabling more accurate decisions by the combination of the temporal information, and outperforming other state-of-the-art models. Additionally, the PRM improves the training efficiency compared with our previous research since it avoids the computational costs invested in finding the best interest interval. Specifically, even a simple PRM, such as a reduce-max operation or a logistic regression layer, can significantly improve the results, as shown in Table 2, in more than 9% balanced accuracy compared to the state-of-the-art BLDA model, and more than 5% concerning our previous works based on a sample-level approach. Moreover, the PRM classifier can be replaced by any complex-enough model to solve the task at hand, having the possibility of further increasing the model's performance. This should be the subject of future study to find the most appropriate PRM for the P300 ERP detection.

Our work demonstrates that the additional PRM model effectively detects the occurrence of the P300 event, making the network actively learn to distinguish between P300 and non-P300 stimuli since, after approximately 250 ms, there is a noticeable difference in the activations from the two classes. This ability is helpful when identifying event-related potential waves. Our findings contribute to the interpretability of recurrent neural networks since we have gained valuable insights into the internal workings of the model through our analysis of the PRM layer. Further research could focus on the recurrent layer's analysis to ensure confidence in the signal features. Interestingly, our results suggest that the models learn to discard redundant or noisy information from the input data, as the best results settings always introduce L1 regularization into the input layer. This last idea joins with other research [6,7] that demonstrates that not all electrodes have the same relevance to reach maximum accuracy. Those findings contribute to the enhancement of the ERP-based BCI performance, a pending challenge in the field, and the management of inter- and intra-subject variability.

Acknowledgments. This work has been partially funded by Spanish project PID2020-114867RB-I00, (MCIN/AEI and ERDF-"A way of making Europe"), Universidad Politécnica Salesiana 034-02-2022-03-31 and by Predoctoral Research Grants 2015-AR2Q9086 of the Government of Ecuador through SENESCYT.

References

1. Allison, B.Z., Kübler, A., Jin, J.: 30+ years of P300 brain-computer interfaces. Psychophysiology **57**(7), e13569 (2020)
2. Altaheri, H., et al.: Deep learning techniques for classification of electroencephalogram (EEG) motor imagery (MI) signals: a review. Neural Comput. Appl. 1–42 (2021)
3. Amin, H.U., Malik, A.S., Kamel, N., Chooi, W.T., Hussain, M.: P300 correlates with learning & memory abilities and fluid intelligence. J. Neuroeng. Rehabil. **12**(1), 1–14 (2015)
4. Bishop, C.M.: Pattern Recognition and Machine Learning. Springer, New York (2006)
5. Changoluisa, V., Varona, P., Rodríguez, F.B.: An electrode selection approach in P300-based BCIs to address inter-and intra-subject variability. In: 2018 6th International Conference on Brain-Computer Interface (BCI), pp. 1–4. IEEE (2018)
6. Changoluisa, V., Varona, P., Rodriguez, F.B.: A fine dry-electrode selection to characterize event-related potentials in the context of BCI. In: Rojas, I., Joya, G., Català, A. (eds.) IWANN 2021. LNCS, vol. 12861, pp. 230–241. Springer, Cham (2021). https://doi.org/10.1007/978-3-030-85030-2_19
7. Changoluisa, V., Varona, P., Rodríguez, F.B.: A low-cost computational method for characterizing event-related potentials for BCI applications and beyond. IEEE Access **8**, 111089–111101 (2020)
8. van Dinteren, R., Arns, M., Jongsma, M.L., Kessels, R.P.: P300 development across the lifespan: a systematic review and meta-analysis. PLoS ONE **9**(2), e87347 (2014)
9. Dozat, T.: Incorporating nesterov momentum into adam. In: ICLR Workshop (2016)
10. Elman, J.L.: Finding structure in time. Cogn. Sci. **14**(2), 179–211 (1990)
11. Hochreiter, S., Schmidhuber, J.: Long short-term memory. Neural Comput. **9**(8), 1735–1780 (1997)
12. Hoffmann, U., Vesin, J.M., Ebrahimi, T., Diserens, K.: An efficient P300-based brain computer interface for disabled subjects. J. Neurosci. Methods **167**, 115–25 (2008)

13. Hu, L., Zhang, Z.: EEG Signal Processing and Feature. Springer, Singapore (2019). https://doi.org/10.1007/978-981-13-9113-2
14. Luck, S.J.: An Introduction to the Event-Related Potential Technique, 2nd edn. MIT Press, Cambridge (2014)
15. Mansoor, A., Usman, M.W., Jamil, N., Naeem, M.A.: Deep learning algorithm for brain-computer interface. Sci. Program. **2020**, 1–12 (2020)
16. Oliva, C., Changoluisa, V., Rodríguez, F.B., Lago-Fernández, L.F.: Detecting P300-ERPs building a post-validation neural ensemble with informative neurons from a recurrent neural network. In: Maglogiannis, I., Iliadis, L., MacIntyre, J., Dominguez, M. (eds.) AIAI 2023, pp. 90–101. Springer, Cham (2023). https://doi.org/10.1007/978-3-031-34111-3_9
17. Oliva, C., Changoluisa, V., Rodríguez, F.B., Lago-Fernández, L.F.: Precise temporal P300 detection in brain computer interface EEG signals using a long-short term memory. In: Farkaš, I., Masulli, P., Otte, S., Wermter, S. (eds.) ICANN 2021. LNCS, vol. 12894, pp. 457–468. Springer, Cham (2021). https://doi.org/10.1007/978-3-030-86380-7_37
18. Patel, S.H., Azzam, P.N.: Characterization of N200 and P300: selected studies of the event-related potential. Int. J. Med. Sci. **2**(4), 147 (2005)
19. Pedregosa, F., et al.: Scikit-learn: machine learning in Python. J. Mach. Learn. Res. **12**, 2825–2830 (2011)
20. Zhang, X., Yao, L., Wang, X., Monaghan, J., McAlpine, D., Zhang, Y.: A survey on deep learning-based non-invasive brain signals: recent advances and new frontiers. J. Neural Eng. **18**(3), 031002 (2021)

Group-Agent Reinforcement Learning

Kaiyue Wu and Xiao-Jun Zeng(✉)

The University of Manchester, Manchester M13 9PL, UK
{kaiyue.wu,x.zeng}@manchester.ac.uk

Abstract. It can largely benefit the reinforcement learning (RL) process of each agent if multiple geographically distributed agents perform their separate RL tasks cooperatively. Different from multi-agent reinforcement learning (MARL) where multiple agents are in a common environment and should learn to cooperate or compete with each other, in this case each agent has its separate environment and only communicates with others to share knowledge without any cooperative or competitive behaviour as a learning outcome. In fact, this scenario exists widely in real life whose concept can be utilised in many applications, but is not well understood yet and not well formulated. As the first effort, we propose group-agent system for RL as a formulation of this scenario and the third type of RL system with respect to single-agent and multi-agent systems. We then propose a distributed RL framework called DDAL (Decentralised Distributed Asynchronous Learning) designed for group-agent reinforcement learning (GARL). We show through experiments that DDAL achieved desirable performance with very stable training and has good scalability.

Keywords: Group-agent system · Reinforcement learning · Distributed learning

1 Introduction

Currently reinforcement learning (RL) problems are considered in two types of systems, which are single-agent system and multi-agent system. For single-agent RL problems, there is only one intelligent agent involved in the learning process. It learns through interacting with its surroundings in order to achieve the objective of optimal individual behaviour. For multi-agent RL problems, there are multiple agents involved in the learning process. They can learn not only through interacting with their surroundings but also through interacting with each other, with the objective of not only optimal individual behaviour but also optimal team behaviour of cooperation or equilibrium behaviour of competition. These two parts of the learning objective are not separable since cooperative or competitive behaviour is actually an essential part of individual behaviour in multi-agent reinforcement learning (MARL).

However, there are some real-world RL scenarios which cannot be classified into either of the two categories and still lack understanding. In existing literature, there is a lack of understanding for pure cooperative learning and an

L. Iliadis et al. (Eds.): ICANN 2023, LNCS 14259, pp. 37–48, 2023.
https://doi.org/10.1007/978-3-031-44223-0_4

ambiguity between cooperative learning and learning to cooperate. In a typical multi-agent problem, such as robotic soccer playing, all the agents perform learning activities together in a common environment. For each single agent, the other agents are part of its environment which becomes non-stationary due to the continually changing behaviour of those agents [17]. In this case, all agents from one team are learning together to cooperate with each other to achieve a common goal. Obviously learning to cooperate often involves cooperative learning (completely independent learning is also possible) which is the learning process with knowledge shared among agents, since agents would probably need information from others to cooperate with them. But from the other way around, cooperative learning does not involve learning to cooperate very often. Agents can be learning with different goals in their own separate environment which is not affected by others and purely communicating knowledge to benefit each other's learning process without any cooperative or competitive behaviour as a learning outcome. The only cooperation is the communication during learning process, which is native and not learned behaviour. We name this learning system a group-agent system that aims at connecting learning agents that are naturally geographically distributed for the purpose of improving learning behaviour.

This scenario is fundamentally different from MARL since it is doing pure cooperative learning for the purpose of acquiring only optimal individual behaviour (potentially diversified and not containing cooperative or competitive behaviour) faster and better while MARL is learning to cooperate or compete. And it certainly cannot be categorised as single-agent RL since it involves a group of agents with separate tasks. In another word, it identifies a gap which has not been addressed by traditional RL framework. A simple real-life example would be multiple students study by themselves in different countries through environment interactions while also communicate with each other online in a "study group" to share knowledge. These countries are geographically distributed thus not affected by each other, and Internet serves as the communication channel between them. We can see from the example that via this pure cooperative learning each agent is able to learn faster to achieve its goal in its own environment. It can be useful in many applications, such as autonomous driving and networking, which motivates us to formulate it as group-agent reinforcement learning (GARL) to inspire dedicated approaches to solve it. In this paper, we propose a cooperative distributed RL framework called DDAL (Decentralised Distributed Asynchronous Learning) as a proof-of-concept effort to tackle GARL. The empirical evaluation shows DDAL achieved good performance with remarkable training stability.

2 Background

RL is a process of learning by trial and error. In this process, there is one or several intelligent agents interacting with their surroundings from which they could get feedbacks for the actions they take. In this way, the agents are able to obtain knowledge on how to behave better and gradually improve their performance. Single-agent RL is often modeled as a Markov Decision Process (MDP) [2]. All the states satisfy the memoryless state transition property

$P[S_{t+1}|S_t] = P[S_{t+1}|S_1, S_2, ..., S_t]$ where the next state is only relevant to the current state without being affected by any previous states or we can say that the current state grabs all necessary information from past states. An MDP is basically a tuple

$$< \mathcal{S}, \mathcal{A}, \mathcal{P}, \mathcal{R}, \gamma > \quad (1)$$

where $\mathcal{S}$ is a finite set of environment states, $\mathcal{A}$ is a finite set of actions, $\mathcal{P}$ is the state transition probability matrix where $P_{s,s'} = P[S_{t+1} = s'|S_t = s]$ is the probability of transiting from state s to s', $\mathcal{R}$ is reward function, and γ is the discount factor used in the Bellman equation formulation of value functions. For example, the state value function $V(s)$ can be stated as $V(s) = E[R_{t+1} + \gamma V(S_{t+1})|S_t = s]$. Given the action selection policy $\pi(a|s)$ which is a probability distribution over all possible actions under state s, we can further have $P[S_{t+1} = s'|S_t = s] = \sum_a P[S_{t+1} = s'|S_t = s, A_t = a] \cdot \pi(a|s)$.

Multi-agent reinforcement learning is often modeled as a stochastic game which is a generalisation of MDP to the multi-agent case [3]. It is stated by the following tuple

$$< \mathcal{S}, \mathcal{A}_1, \cdots, \mathcal{A}_n, \mathcal{P}, \mathcal{R}_1, \cdots, \mathcal{R}_n, \gamma > \quad (2)$$

where n is the number of agents, $\mathcal{S}$ is a finite set of environment states, $\mathcal{A}_i, i = 1, \cdots, n$ are the finite sets of actions of every agent, $\mathcal{P}$ is the state transition probability matrix, $\mathcal{R}_i, i = 1, \cdots, n$ are the reward functions of every agent, and γ is the discount factor. From this formulation, we can see that all the agents are in a common environment so that we have only one set of environment states, and the state transition is the same from every agent's point of view.

3 Related Work

Methods for single-agent RL can be classified into two broad categories, basic algorithms and distributed variants (parallelisation) of the basic algorithms. For basic algorithms, there are the well-known Q-learning introduced by [22] which maintains and updates a Q-table during training. Replacing the Q tables with deep neural networks, called Q networks, we have DQN (Deep Q-Network) [12] which takes raw RGB images as input and is trained to output the Q values for all possible state-action pairs (s, a_i). Other than the value-based methods, we also have actor-critic track. A2C, short for Advantage Actor-Critic, is a typical kind of actor-critic method for RL. It has two neural networks for approximating policy function π_θ and state-value function $V(s)$. Another popular actor-critic method is PPO [18], short for Proximal Policy Optimisation, which introduces an innovative clipped surrogate loss for the policy function.

For the distributed variants, there are A3C (asynchronous advantage actor-critic) [11] which is an asynchronous version of distributed A2C, Gorila [13] which is distributed DQN, and APPO [8] which is asynchronous PPO. A3C has a central copy of network models asynchronously receiving gradients from multiple parallel A2C workers and periodically synchronises the workers with the central copy. Gorila has multiple learner processes training a central Q-network copy with experiences generated by multiple parallel actor processes interacting with environment. APPO has a PPO learner paired with multiple actor processes who generate experiences. The experiences are stored in a circular buffer and will be discarded after being used in training. These distributed RL algorithms are single-agent parallelisation and cannot be applied to GARL. But each agent in GARL should be able to apply any one of the single-agent algorithms. DDPPO [23], short for decentralised distributed PPO, is another parallel single-agent algorithm, but is a bit different in that it involves multiple "agents", respects the completeness of each "agent" and does not parallelise the internal processes of an agent such as actor or learner processes as the other distributed algorithms do. It is completely decentralised without any central network copy. All the "agents" update their models locally after communicating gradients directly with each other. However, it does global synchronous control among the "agents" – the communication and model updates all happen synchronously with all updates that happen at the same time being identical. This breaks the autonomy of the "agents" and actually makes them worker copies of one single agent. Hence it is still a single-agent learning system, but when GARL agents all work on same tasks we can say that GARL is generalisation of it that additionally respects agent autonomy. We will compare our proposed method DDAL with the synchronous method behind DDPPO in Sect. 6.

Methods for multi-agent reinforcement learning can be classified into three broad categories, cooperative algorithms, competitive algorithms and algorithms for a mix of cooperation and competition. The competition or cooperation here refers to the interactions between agents which is learned behaviour and the nature of the problem, in comparison to cooperative learning where the cooperation is only knowledge communication and not learned behaviour. MARL methods do not apply in GARL due to the inherent difference in problem definition. To justify more, multi-agent problem can be approached through methods with only independent learner which optimises its own policy ignoring the other agents and assuming environment stationarity [5,10]. More approaches would consider environment non-stationarity and study the joint behaviour of the agents instead [9,21,24]. For example, [7] considers a centralised critic that takes the states and actions of all agents and outputs the Q value for each agent, while also maintains approximated policies of other agents at each agent. In GARL, the agents share knowledge with each other (thus not independent) only to benefit each other's learning (thus joint behaviour optimisation is not necessary). Besides, MARL happens in a common environment thus the environment state is identical to every agent at any time point, while in GARL the environment states are varied (the agents can be at different pace even though with same tasks). Considering this variousness is an important task of GARL methods. And the multiple geo-distributed environments in GARL also introduce many issues from the systems side. In real applications geo-distributed agents would need real communication and subsequently be managed by a networking protocol, resulting in a real system rather than just a machine learning algorithm.

We also notice that multi-task learning is trying to learn a single policy that works across a set of related tasks within the same environment [20]. It can be studied in either single-agent system or multi-agent system while the nature of the multi-tasking problem is not affected. An agent learns for a generalised policy that works across a set of related tasks in its own single environment or within the common environment [15]. This diverges from our focus of studying the group learning behaviour where multiple autonomous agents separately learn in their own environment while communicate with each other to benefit each other's learning process that only focuses on its own task, which will result in different policies with possibly different expertise among the agents.

4 Group-Agent Reinforcement Learning (GARL)

In GARL, there are multiple agents doing RL together in a "study group", which is abstracted from a very common real-life behaviour in human intelligence. When we humans study, there are basically two knowledge sources, learning through trial and error in our environment (RL) and learning cooperatively through retrieving available knowledge from other people. Hence we often study together in groups to benefit the latter process. It does not have to happen in a single environment, but can rather work across multiple environments. GARL agents learn through trial and error in their separate environment while communicating with each other to obtain available knowledge. Each of these environments is stationary because no one will interfere with others' environment. From another perspective, what GARL does is connecting distributed autonomous learning agents for them to share knowledge, leveraging the power of the learning community.

We take autonomous driving as an example application to give further explanation. The training of self-driving cars can well take place with RL [16]. We describe it through three training stages, where stage 2 is an example of GARL.

- Stage 1: Given a certain city environment, one single self-driving car is doing RL to obtain driving knowledge in one neighbourhood. Its environment, namely this neighbourhood, is stationary. Learning only happens through trial and error.
- Stage 2: Still in the same city environment, there are now multiple self-driving cars all doing RL simultaneously, each in a different neighbourhood. Each of their environments, namely the neighbourhoods, is still stationary. The goal of every agent is to learn to drive in its own neighbourhood environment. We can see that the goals among the agents are slightly different due to the difference between the neighbourhoods. However since these neighbourhoods belong to the same city environment, they share much similarity. Therefore, it will largely benefit learning if we create communication channels between the agents for them to exchange their knowledge acquired through environment exploration. It is very possible that one car is not able to explore its environment thoroughly and leave out many environment states, but some other peer car explores them well, so that sound knowledge can be obtained through communicating with that peer car. In this case, learning happens in a group-agent setting.

- Stage 3: With the help of GARL, the multiple self-driving cars all learned to drive in its own environment well and fast. Now some of the cars drive out of their neighbourhoods to meet other peer cars. In one neighbourhood, there are several cars on the road. They need to learn to cooperate with each other to safely co-exist on the road, not causing any car crashes. This neighbourhood environment becomes non-stationary since each of these cars becomes a part of the others' environment and their behaviours are continually evolving. This turns to be an MARL scenario.

Note that GARL cannot be viewed as a simplified version of MARL with just the objective of cooperation or competition gotten rid of. In GARL, since each agent is in a separate environment, they can have different state sets and diversified individual learning goals. There is inherently much more freedom for the agents compared to MARL where the agents are very restricted by each other. We present this more clearly with a formal formulation as follows.

Recall from Sect. 2 that single-agent RL can be modeled as an MDP and MARL can be modeled as a stochastic game. Here we propose group MDP to state GARL, in the following tuple

$$\begin{aligned} < \mathcal{S}_1, \cdots, \mathcal{S}_n, \mathcal{A}_1, \cdots, \mathcal{A}_n, \mathcal{P}_1, \cdots, \mathcal{P}_n, \mathcal{R}_1, \cdots, \mathcal{R}_n, \\ \gamma_1, \cdots, \gamma_n, \mathcal{K}_1, \cdots, \mathcal{K}_n, \mathcal{K}_{-1}, \cdots, \mathcal{K}_{-n} > \end{aligned} \tag{3}$$

where n is the number of agents, $\mathcal{S}_i, \mathcal{A}_i, \mathcal{P}_i, \mathcal{R}_i, \gamma_i, \mathcal{K}_i, \mathcal{K}_{-i}, i = 1, \cdots, n$ are the sets of environment states, the sets of actions, the state transition probability matrixes, the reward functions, the discount factors, the sets of knowledge from local environment interactions and the sets of received knowledge of every agent in the group. Note that $\mathcal{K}_{-i} = \{\mathcal{K}_{1,i}, \cdots, \mathcal{K}_{i-1,i}, \mathcal{K}_{i+1,i}, \cdots, \mathcal{K}_{n,i}\}$ where $\mathcal{K}_{i,i'} \subseteq \mathcal{K}_i$ is the knowledge of agent i shared to agent i', and for at least one pair of $i, j \in \{1, \ldots, n\}$, $\mathcal{S}_i \cap \mathcal{S}_j \neq \emptyset$. Each agent can send its knowledge to any other agents arbitrarily and store its received knowledge in local memory for training. From this formulation, we can see that different from MARL where the state set and state transition probability matrix are shared among all agents, each agent in GARL works in its own separate environment so that it has its own set of environment states, and an agent's environment is independent of any other agent's environment so that it has its own state transition probability matrix. Every agent has its own set of actions, reward function, discount factor, set of local knowledge and set of received knowledge. Note that the knowledge shared among agents can be in various forms, such as raw experiences (state, action, reward tuple), policy parameters, state/action values, gradients at each update iteration, etc. With this knowledge sharing, GARL aims to benefit each single agent's learning quality and speed. It can be applied to the training of video game playing and autonomous driving. Besides, we claim that it has great potential in network routing problems due to the independent environment of each network node and the natural communication network between them.

5 Decentralised Distributed Asynchronous Learning (DDAL)

This section introduces DDAL as a proof-of-concept learning framework designed for GARL. The idea is fourfold:

- Decentralised control: The group-agent system naturally comes in a decentralised manner where every agent is autonomous and can learn independently. Artificially having them managed by a central controller can be expensive and sometimes meaningless or unrealistic. Thus we apply decentralised control.
- Asynchronous communication: To give as much freedom as possible to the agents and respect their nature of autonomy, we design to let the communication happen in an asynchronous manner. Synchronous communication among distributed autonomous agents means that the agents should all agree to dedicated communication stages when they are all sending or receiving messages. This can be very difficult in real-world applications since organising these autonomous agents needs lots of efforts from the perspective of distributed systems. Thus we apply asynchronous communication where each agent can send knowledge to other agents or receive knowledge from them at any convenient time, avoiding the need for a communication protocol.
- Independent learning at beginning stage: To explain this from intuition, we are probably not able to acquire very accurate knowledge at the beginning stage of our learning by trial-and-error (due to the inaccurate measurement of error under insufficient prior knowledge) and sharing of beginners' mistakes would have negative effect on others' learning processes, hence it is good practice to start group communication after everyone has reached a relatively stable learning status.
- Weighted gradient average: Here we use gradients as the form of knowledge among agents and require that all gradients ever generated will be shared to every other agent ($\mathcal{K}_{i,i'} = \mathcal{K}_i,\ i, i' = 1, \cdots, n$). Each piece of gradients (for one model update) from any agent is accompanied with two extra pieces of information, the learning experience so far and its relevance to the agent that it's going to. For example, the number of training epochs performed by an agent can represent the learning that the agent has experienced so far, namely the amount of training so far for the piece of gradients just generated by this agent. We quantify these two pieces of information with T_j (training experience) and R_j (relevance) for the $j-th$ piece of gradients represented as g_j in a chunk of received gradient pieces. When agent i is ready to perform a model update involving received gradients, it retrieves m pieces of gradients from $\mathcal{K}_i \cup \mathcal{K}_{-i}$ and calculates a weighted gradient average according to the equation $\overline{g} = \frac{1}{2}(\sum_{j=1}^{m} \frac{T_j}{\sum_{j=1}^{m} T_j} g_j + \sum_{j=1}^{m} \frac{R_j}{\sum_{j=1}^{m} R_j} g_j)$, then perform the update with $\overline{g}$. The average operation allows us to mitigate the influence introduced by poor experiences and introducing weights lowers the influence of immature or irrelevant knowledge.

Algorithm 1. DDAL at the $i - th$ agent

Require: Initialise knowledge set $\mathcal{K}_i$ and $\mathcal{K}_{-i}$

for each *epoch* **do**
  Generate k experiences
  Compute average loss
  Compute gradients
  if *epoch* $<$ *threshold* **then**
    Update model with the gradients
  else
    Append the gradients with weighting information T and R
    Store the gradients in $\mathcal{K}_i$
    Send a copy of the gradients to every other agent j (stored in $\mathcal{K}_{-j}$) ($j = 1, \cdots, i-1, i+1, \cdots, n$)
    if *epoch%minibatch* $==0$ **then**
      Get (and remove) m pieces of gradients from $\mathcal{K}_i \cup \mathcal{K}_{-i}$
      Compute $\overline{g}$ of these gradients
      Update model with $\overline{g}$
    end if
  end if
end for

The algorithm at each agent is shown in Algorithm 1. After being trained for a number of epochs, the agent starts to send its gradients to other agents and perform model updates with received gradients every few epochs. The threshold and minibatch size are hyper parameters. We do not have global organising mechanism for the agent system thus each agent is basically on its own. In our implementation, this decentralised control and asynchronous communication is realised through multiprocessing queues. Every agent has its own queue to hold the knowledge received from other agents, and these queues are shared among all agents so that each agent is free to send its knowledge to any other agent's queue. The agents are implemented with Salina [4]. We claim that DDAL should not be restricted by agent type. The single-agent algorithms as discussed in Sect. 3 should all be able to serve as our agent's brain. Here we discuss a classic A2C agent.

5.1 Decentralised Distributed Asynchronous Advantage Actor-Critic (DDA3C)

For a classic A2C agent, with the relation $Q(s_t, a_t) = A(s_t, a_t) + V(s_t)$ where $A(s_t, a_t)$ is the advantage value, we have the gradients for policy network as $\nabla_\theta log\pi_\theta(a_t|s_t)A(s_t, a_t) = \nabla_\theta log\pi_\theta(a_t|s_t)(Q(s_t, a_t) - V(s_t))$ where $Q(s_t, a_t) = r + \gamma V(s_{t+1})$ (=r, for terminal s_{t+1}). With this A2C agent, we name the complete algorithm as DDA3C.

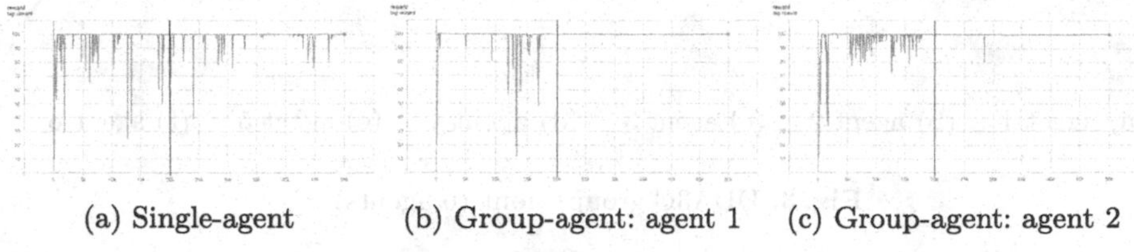

(a) Single-agent (b) Group-agent: agent 1 (c) Group-agent: agent 2

Fig. 1. DDA3C single-agent vs. group-agent (2 agents)

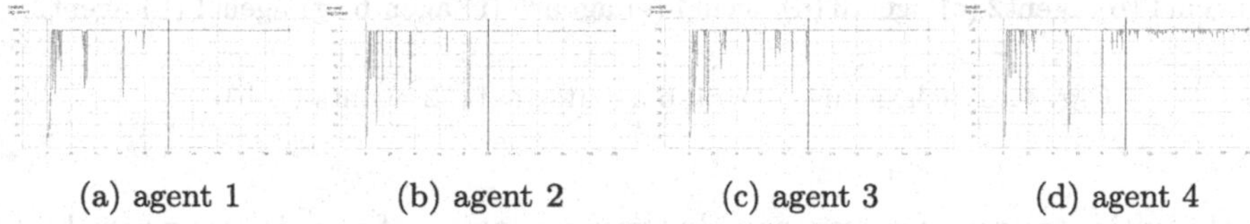

(a) agent 1 (b) agent 2 (c) agent 3 (d) agent 4

Fig. 2. DDA3C group-agent (4 agents)

6 Evaluations

In this section, we evaluate DDA3C on a scenario where there is a group of agents each of whom plays a separate instance of the same computer game while sharing knowledge with each other. Due to the consistency in learning environments and goals, every agent's knowledge is of equal relevance to other agents so that we set the R_j parameters of gradients all equal to each other. And since all agents start at the same time, the T_j parameters are also set identical for every piece of gradients. m is the total number of gradient pieces in $\mathcal{K}_i \cup \mathcal{K}_{-i}$ at the time. Note that the result is from a single run but can represent the average performance. We have run the experiments for quite a number of times and are very confident about the result. The reason why we did not do real average performance is that for each single run the big performance fluctuations happen at different time and doing an average will seriously reduce the significance of the fluctuations.

6.1 DDA3C

We test DDA3C on the task of CartPole-v0 game in OpenAI Gym. In each epoch, we run one episode of CartPole-v0 with a limitation of maximum 100 steps. CartPole-v0 environment will give a reward of +1 for every timestep that the pole remains upright and end when terminal states reached. Hence a total reward of 100 means an optimal policy for a 100-step episode – every move scores. The epoch minibatch size is set to 100. k is set to 120.

In Fig. 1, we do the training for totally 50k epochs (the x-axis is the epoch number) and start the knowledge sharing at 20k-th epoch (threshold) for the two-agent group learning case. Every point of the first model update involving shared knowledge in Fig. 1, 2, 3 is marked by a dark line. Figure 1a is the single-agent baseline, in which we can see that the total reward keeps having big fluctuations

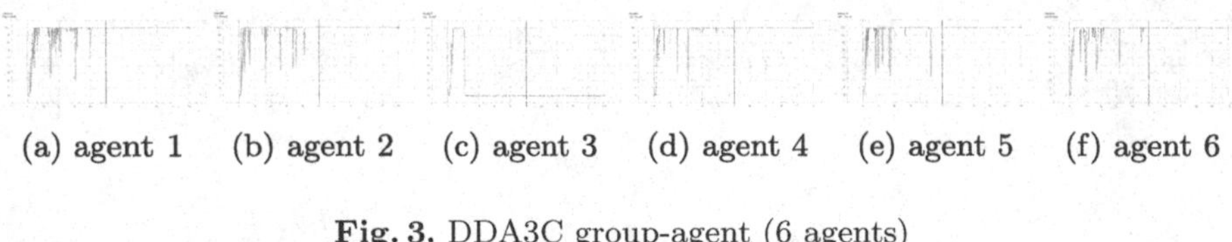

(a) agent 1 (b) agent 2 (c) agent 3 (d) agent 4 (e) agent 5 (f) agent 6

Fig. 3. DDA3C group-agent (6 agents)

(a) agent1 (b) agent2 (c) agent3 (d) agent4 (e) agent5 (f) agent6 (g) agent1 (h) agent2

Fig. 4. Synchronous control: 6 agents (a–f), 2 agents (g–h)

over the entire training process, namely there are quite a few episodes where bad actions were chosen. The training was unstable and never managed to converge to a stable optimal policy that can choose good actions all the time. In contrast, Fig. 1b and Fig. 1c keep very stable at 100 after knowledge sharing starts at 20k-th epoch, showing that two-agent group learning quickly managed to maintain a stable optimal policy.

For the game of CartPole-v0, group learning with two agents already has very good performance. We perform more experiments to test DDA3C's ability to scale to more agents. With more agents, we have more experiences that are diversified and the influence of each single early-stage learning mistake can be smaller so that we made attempts to start knowledge sharing earlier. For 4 agent case in Fig. 2, we train for totally 20k epochs and start sharing at 10k-th epoch, and for 6 agent case in Fig. 3 we train for totally 10k epochs and sharing starts at 5k-th epoch. They show that we still reached good results. Agent 4 in the 4-agent group has some very small fluctuations after 10k-th epoch as shown in Fig. 2d, meaning that the training stability is near-optimal. All other three agents have converged to stable optimal policy with group learning. As shown in Fig. 3c, agent 3 in the 6-agent group was trapped in a bad state before knowledge sharing started and not able to get over it in following studies. It happens sometimes that certain individuals are not doing well, and the probability to see this case can rise when the number of agents in the group goes up. What's interesting is that even in the presence of outliers, others are not affected which shows the robustness of the group learning system. The majority of agents in this 6-agent group works well (5 out of 6) – stable optimal policy learned after knowledge sharing starts at 5k-th epoch.

6.2 Comparison with Synchronous Method

In Fig. 4, we show the reward curve of a 2-"agent" and a 6-"agent" learning system with A2C agent on CartPole-v0 task under synchronous control. This synchronous control is realised through Pytorch DDP (Distributed Data Parallel) library as in DDPPO. We can see that the curves have severe fluctuations during the entire training period (the more "agents", the more fluctuations), much worse than the single-agent baseline in Fig. 1a. As discussed in Sect. 3, these "agents" are actually worker copies of a single agent and do not form a group learning system. Their learning errors are accumulated during training leading to the worse fluctuations, while in our group-agent learning system the agents took knowledge from peers in an asynchronous manner which gives them the autonomy to utilise knowledge in their own way that could possibly benefit themselves the most.

7 Conclusion

GARL describes a very common and important type of real-life learning scenario – human learning behaviour, which is very promising with regard to application. Any geographically distributed reinforcement learning agents who want to benefit from remote peer learners could join a study group which can be managed by a group agent system. Confirmed by social learning theory [1], rather than being isolated, people learn in a social context with behaviours such as observing and imitating others. This successful learning behaviour of real intelligence should inspire us when we try to create artificial intelligence. Joining a group-agent learning system, an agent will be exposed to senior peers and able to learn from them through communication. It provides the agents with the social context that enables them to learn in a more near-human way. There is a body of work adopting social learning [14] or imitation learning [6,19] in their agents under single or multi-agent setting. These promising results further reinforce our confidence in the performance that GARL could possibly reach. For future work, we will investigate more sophisticated approaches that work with different types of agents or environments within the group.

References

1. Bandura, A., Walters, R.H.: Social Learning Theory, vol. 1. Prentice Hall, Englewood Cliffs (1977)
2. Bellman, R.: A Markovian decision process. J. Math. Mech. **6**(5), 679–684 (1957). http://www.jstor.org/stable/24900506
3. Buşoniu, L., Babuška, R., Schutter, B.D.: Multi-agent reinforcement learning: an overview. In: Innovations in Multi-Agent Systems and Applications-1, pp. 183–221 (2010)
4. Denoyer, L., de la Fuente, A., Duong, S., Gaya, J.B., Kamienny, P.A., Thompson, D.H.: Salina: sequential learning of agents (2021). https://github.com/facebookresearch/salina
5. Foerster, J., et al.: Stabilising experience replay for deep multi-agent reinforcement learning. In: International Conference on Machine Learning, pp. 1146–1155. PMLR (2017)
6. Guo, X., Chang, S., Yu, M., Tesauro, G., Campbell, M.: Hybrid reinforcement learning with expert state sequences. In: Proceedings of the AAAI Conference on Artificial Intelligence, vol. 33, pp. 3739–3746 (2019)

7. Lowe, R., Wu, Y.I., Tamar, A., Harb, J., Pieter Abbeel, O., Mordatch, I.: Multi-agent actor-critic for mixed cooperative-competitive environments. In: Advances in Neural Information Processing Systems, vol. 30 (2017)
8. Luo, M., Yao, J., Liaw, R., Liang, E., Stoica, I.: Impact: importance weighted asynchronous architectures with clipped target networks (2020)
9. Ma, X., Yang, Y., Li, C., Lu, Y., Zhao, Q., Jun, Y.: Modeling the interaction between agents in cooperative multi-agent reinforcement learning. arXiv preprint arXiv:2102.06042 (2021)
10. Matignon, L., Laurent, G.J., Le Fort-Piat, N.: Independent reinforcement learners in cooperative Markov games: a survey regarding coordination problems. Knowl. Eng. Rev. **27**(1), 1–31 (2012)
11. Mnih, V., et al.: Asynchronous methods for deep reinforcement learning. In: International Conference on Machine Learning, pp. 1928–1937. PMLR (2016)
12. Mnih, V., et al.: Human-level control through deep reinforcement learning. Nature **518**(7540), 529–533 (2015). https://doi.org/10.1038/nature14236
13. Nair, A., et al.: Massively parallel methods for deep reinforcement learning (2015)
14. Ndousse, K.K., Eck, D., Levine, S., Jaques, N.: Emergent social learning via multi-agent reinforcement learning. In: International Conference on Machine Learning, pp. 7991–8004. PMLR (2021)
15. Omidshafiei, S., Pazis, J., Amato, C., How, J.P., Vian, J.: Deep decentralized multi-task multi-agent reinforcement learning under partial observability. In: International Conference on Machine Learning, pp. 2681–2690. PMLR (2017)
16. Sallab, A.E., Abdou, M., Perot, E., Yogamani, S.: Deep reinforcement learning framework for autonomous driving. Electron. Imaging **2017**(19), 70–76 (2017)
17. Samsami, M.R., Alimadad, H.: Distributed deep reinforcement learning: an overview. CoRR abs/2011.11012 (2020). arxiv.org/abs/2011.11012
18. Schulman, J., Wolski, F., Dhariwal, P., Radford, A., Klimov, O.: Proximal policy optimization algorithms (2017)
19. Stadie, B.C., Abbeel, P., Sutskever, I.: Third-person imitation learning. arXiv preprint arXiv:1703.01703 (2017)
20. Vithayathil Varghese, N., Mahmoud, Q.H.: A survey of multi-task deep reinforcement learning. Electronics **9**(9), 1363 (2020)
21. Wang, J., Ren, Z., Liu, T., Yu, Y., Zhang, C.: QPLEX: duplex dueling multi-agent Q-learning. arXiv preprint arXiv:2008.01062 (2020)
22. Watkins, C.J.C.H.: Learning from delayed rewards (1989)
23. Wijmans, E., et al.: DD-PPO: learning near-perfect PointGoal navigators from 2.5 billion frames (2020)
24. Zhang, K., Yang, Z., Basar, T.: Networked multi-agent reinforcement learning in continuous spaces. In: 2018 IEEE Conference on Decision and Control (CDC), pp. 2771–2776. IEEE (2018)

Improving Generalization of Multi-agent Reinforcement Learning Through Domain-Invariant Feature Extraction

Yifan Xu[1,2], Zhiqiang Pu[1,2(✉)], Qiang Cai[1,2], Feimo Li[1], and Xinghua Chai[3]

[1] Institute of Automation, Chinese Academy of Sciences, Beijing 100190, China
[2] School of Artificial Intelligence, University of Chinese Academy of Sciences, Beijing 100049, China
zhiqiang.pu@ia.ac.cn
[3] The 54th Research Institute of China Electronics Technology Group Corporation, Beijing, China

Abstract. The limited generalization ability of reinforcement learning constrains its potential applications, particularly in complex scenarios such as multi-agent systems. To overcome this limitation and enhance the generalization capability of MARL algorithms, this paper proposes a three-stage method that integrates domain randomization and domain adaptation to extract effective features for policy learning. Specifically, the first stage samples environments provided for training and testing in the following stages using domain randomization. The second stage pretrains a domain-invariant feature extractor (DIFE) which employs cycle consistency to disentangle domain-invariant and domain-specific features. The third stage utilizes DIFE for policy learning. Experimental results in MPE tasks demonstrate that our approach yields better performance and generalization ability. Meanwhile, the features captured by DIFE are more interpretable for subsequent policy learning in visualization analysis.

Keywords: multi-agent reinforcement learning · domain adaptation · domain randomization

1 Introduction

As reinforcement learning (RL) continues to achieve success in games [13,18,24], researchers are currently working on broader applications [14,16,20]. Implementation of RL in complex tasks like applications in real world demands algorithms that can adapt to variations, unlike tasks with static environments, for example, board games [3] and video games [24]. However, traditional RL methods struggle to maintain performance when faced with even slight differences between training and testing environments, particularly in complex and dynamic multi-agent settings. To improve agents' generalization ability, domain randomization (DR) has emerged as a common method [15,17,21]. DR uses a distribution,

L. Iliadis et al. (Eds.): ICANN 2023, LNCS 14259, pp. 49–62, 2023.
https://doi.org/10.1007/978-3-031-44223-0_5

rather than fixed parameters, to model environment dynamics, inducing uncertainty during training processes. Ranging from image-based observations [17] to internal dynamics [14], all accessible parameters are available for randomization. Tobin [21] and Sadeghi [17] first implement DR in robotics by randomizing visual variants in input images under simulation where various training environments improve object detection accuracy when transferring the policy to reality. Peng [15] randomizes dynamic variations of a robotics arm in push tasks and shows that memory-based models achieve high performance than memoryless models through experiments. Chen [2] fills the blank of theoretical analysis in DR by deriving the upper bound of the gap between optimal policies in simulation and reality. In the assumptions of [2], obtaining the optimal policy in DR is formulated as solving a latent Markov decision process (LMDP), where an LDMP contains a series of MDPs. The sample complexity of policy optimization in LMDP grows exponentially with the number of MDPs in LMDP [9]. Therefore, sample-efficient algorithms for training policies in DR are in great demand. OpenAI [14] proposes automatic curriculum training to improve sample efficiency. However, a delicately crafted curriculum evaluation protocol is needed to guarantee that algorithms learn progressively according to task difficulty. Mandlerkar [12] creates an adversary policy to sample environments where current policies fail. However, the adversarial approach leads to learning pessimistic samples and the training process is likely to be unstable. In general, optimizing RL policy in domain randomization remains intractable.

In the context of multi-agent reinforcement learning (MARL), the inherent uncertainty of the environment is exacerbated due to dynamic multi-agent systems. The number of agents and agents' configurations can vary greatly among different environments, leading to variations in agent interactions and making policy transfer even more challenging.

In order to improve generalization performance of RL, it is essential that the optimal policy in the LMDP and the optimal policies in individual MDPs exhibit similarities [6]. To effectively learn policies in domain randomization, we introduce domain adaptation (DA) into our methodology, thereby leveraging this similarity. Initially used for style migration in image classification tasks, DA helps to discover shared feature spaces across different image classes and filter out irrelevant features [10]. Methods in DA contain discrepancy-based approaches [11,22], adversarial-based approaches [4,7], and reconstruction-based approaches [1] [5]. The discrepancy-based approaches focus on reducing the distributional discrepancy between the source and target domains. This discrepancy is often measured using distance metrics such as the maximum mean discrepancy (MMD) [22], second-order moment, or k-oder moment [19]. However, these metrics only accurately capture differences under specific assumptions, which can lead to suboptimal adaptation performance. Besides, labeled target domain data is required to compute the distance, which is costly in some scenarios. The adversarial-based approaches learn domain-invariant representations by training a domain discriminator to distinguish between the source and target domains [4]. The features are extracted in an unsupervised manner, without requiring labeled target domain data [23]. However, training the discriminator to accurately distinguish between the source and target domains requires lots of data and may cause unstable training [26]. The reconstruction-based approaches learn domain-invariant representations by reconstructing the input data from the learned features. These methods leverage the idea that a good domain-invariant representation should preserve the essential information needed to reconstruct the input data while removing the domain-specific information. Bousmalis [1] learns disentangled domain-invariant and domain-specific features through shared and private encoders, respectively. Xing [25] uses cycle consistency to learn feature disentanglement in autonomous driving. In RL simulations, it is convenient to collect a vast amount of unlabeled data, which makes the use of reconstruction models a promising option for feature extraction.

Therefore, our work proposes a method that uses DA to learn a latent representation across a series of randomized environments in multi-agent scenarios. We train a module called domain-invariant feature extractor (DIFE) in domains with randomized parameters and use a cycle-consistent variational autoencoder (cycle-consistent VAE) [8] to disentangle general and specific feature embeddings. This allows agents to utilize domain information in downstream policy learning.

Experiments are conducted in a series of multi-agent coverage tasks with different parameter configurations. Results show that our approach yields better performance and generalization ability. Meanwhile, the features captured by DIFE are more interpretable for subsequent policy learning in visualization analysis.

2 Preliminaries

2.1 Multiagent Reinforcement Learning

Multi-agent reinforcement learning is a sub-field of reinforcement learning that focuses on learning how multiple agents can interact with each other in a dynamic environment to achieve common goals. This process can be described by a Markov game (N, S, A, T, r, γ), where N represents the number of agents, S is the joint state space of agents $S = S_1 \times \cdots \times S_i \times \cdots \times S_N$, where S_i is the state space of agent i, A is the joint action space of agents $A = A_1 \times \cdots \times A_i \cdots \times A_N$, where A_i is the action space of agent i, T is the transition function, $T : S \times a_1 \times \cdots \times a_i \times \cdots \times a_N \times S \rightarrow [0, 1]$, where a_i is the action of agent i. $r_i(s_t, a_1, \ldots a_i, \ldots, a_N, s'_{t+1})$ is the reward function for agent i, where s_t is the state of agent i at time step t and s'_{t+1} is the state of agent i at time step $t + 1$. In MARL, each agent perceives an observation of their surrounding environment o_t at time step t. Based on this information, the agents select joint actions according to policy π. After carrying out the actions, states of the agents and the environment change based on transition function T. Meanwhile, each agent receives a reward signal from the environment, which is used to update the policy.

2.2 Domain Randomization and LMDPs

In this section, we introduce domain randomization (DR) under the framework of latent Markov decision process (LMDP). An LMDP is composed of a set of MDPs $\mathcal{M}$ and a distribution μ over $\mathcal{M}$. An MDP M_l in $\mathcal{M}$ can be sampled from the distribution μ, and can be represented by (S, A, T_l, R_l, ρ_l), where S and A are shared state space and action space in $\mathcal{M}$, T_l is the sampled transition function, R_l is the sampled reward function, ρ_l is the sampled initial states in each episode. The optimal policy in LMDPs is defined as the policy π with the best expectation performance over μ:

$$V_{\mathcal{M}}^* := \max_{\pi \in \Pi} \sum_{l=1}^{|\mathcal{M}|} w_l \mathbb{E}\pi \left[\sum_{t=1}^{H} r_t \right]$$

where $V_{\mathcal{M}}^*$ is the optimal total value function in $\mathcal{M}$ of the optimal policy π^* in a policy set Π, ω_l is the weight coefficient for M_l, H is the episode horizon for each MDP.

In DR, similar MDPs of the same task form the MDP set $\mathcal{M}$ in LMDP. Considering two MDPs M_i and M_j in $\mathcal{M}$, M_i and M_j are represented by $(S_i, A_i, T_i, R_i, \gamma)$ and $(S_j, A_j, T_j, R_j, \gamma)$, respectively. To guarantee the performance of the optimal policy, it is essential that the optimal policy in the LMDP and the optimal policies in individual MDPs exhibit similarities. Therefore, M_i and M_j must have similar state space, action space, transition functions and reward functions, i.e. $S_i \approx S_j, A_i \approx A_j, T_i \approx T_j, R_i \approx R_j$. The values of S_i, A_i, T_i, R_i for MDP M_i are indirectly determined by the parameters of environment in M_i. Therefore, the distribution μ of MDPs in $\mathcal{M}$ can be transformed to a distribution over tunable environmental parameters in $\mathcal{M}$. During training, an MDP M_l in $\mathcal{M}$ is sampled at the start of each episode and remains fixed throughout the whole episode. Agents interact with M_l without knowing the identity.

2.3 Domain Adaptation

In this subsection, we introduce domain adaptation (DA) in the framework of transfer learning. In transfer learning, data is categorized into source domains and target domains. In reinforcement transfer learning, a domain is viewed as an MDP. A source domain is defined as M_s and a target domain is defined as M_t. Transfer learning methods utilize knowledge learned in M_s to facilitate learning in M_t.

For policy optimization in a single static MDP, the underlying trajectory distributions of training and testing are the same, i.e. $M_s = M_t$. However, in MDPs with dynamic environments, traditional RL algorithms fail due to domain shift, i.e. $M_s \neq M_t$. DA addresses this issue by extracting shared latent state representations among the source and target domains, which can be utilized in multi-domain policy optimization. However, DA does not explicitly consider action space, dynamics transitions and reward functions. Therefore, to apply

DA, the targeted MDPs should have the same action space, similar transitions, similar reward functions and distinct state spaces, i.e. $A_s = A_t, T_s \approx T_t, R_s \approx R_t, S_s \neq S_t$. In our method, we use DA to optimize policies in DR.

3 Method

In this section, we adopt the formulations and expressions presented in Sect. 2. To improve the generalization ability of MARL algorithms, we first employ domain randomization to generate an LMDP with various environmental parameter configurations in our method. To optimize policies in this LMDP, we leverage domain adaptation to discover shared feature space among MDPs and design curricula for policy training. Finally, our policy is evaluated on a set of MDPs sampled from distributions in domain randomization. Our method comprises three stages: 1) Environment sampling. 2) Pretraining. 3) Policy learning. Figure 1 shows the framework of our method.

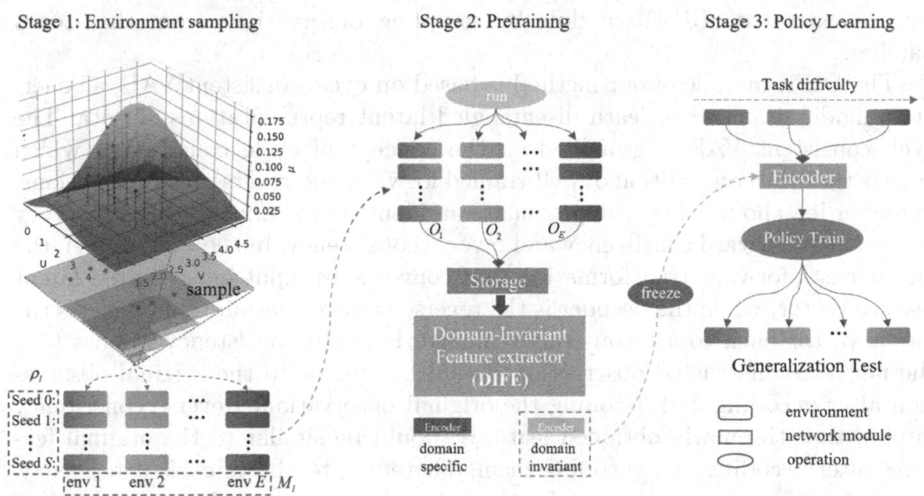

Fig. 1. The framework of our method

3.1 Environment Sampling

For a given task, the complexity of the task is primarily determined by some decisive parameters. To create a smooth task space for generalized policy training, we first reveal the relations of these decisive parameters and build reasonable distributions for them. Then, we sample environments based on the distributions to form an environment set.

Consider an LMDP $\mathcal{M}$ with K environmental variable parameters $v_i, i = 1, 2, \ldots, K$, each parameter has a predefined value range. Firstly, a base policy

π_b is trained in a base environment E_b and evaluated in environment i with variations in v_i compared to E_b. To assess the importance of each parameter, a performance decrease threshold P_{th} is defined. After K groups of evaluation, parameters with performance decrease above P_{th} are identified as decisive parameters. To build a sampling distribution μ over (u, v), regression analysis is performed based on the performance of π_b in different environments with varying values of (u, v). Once we obtain distribution μ through experiments, we use it to randomly generate E environments and sample S seeds for the initial states ρ_l of agents in each environment.

3.2 Pretrain

After collecting $E \times S$ environments, we can exploit the mutual information present within these environments through pretraining, as depicted in Stage 2 of Fig. 1. Specifically, we execute a scripted searching policy in these E environments (with each environment running S seeds), collect and store E batches of observations denoted as $O_1, O_2, \cdots, O_E$. Next, we train our domain-invariant feature extractor (DIFE) module by sampling observations from the stored batches.

The DIFE module of our method is based on cycle-consistent VAE, a generative model designed to learn disentangled latent representations of data. The cycle-consistent VAE is grounded on the concept of cycle consistency, which asserts that the composition of well-trained forward and reverse transformations, in any order, should closely approximate an identity function. Cycle consistency comprises of forward consistency and reverse consistency. In the VAE model, the encoder is a forward transformation that converts an input image into a latent feature vector, while the decoder is the reverse transformation that converts the latent vector back to a reconstructed image. Forward consistency implies that the newly reconstructed observation should be similar to the original observation after encoding and decoding the original observation. Reverse consistency implies that the newly obtained features should be similar to the original features after decoding and encoding them. Therefore, to obtain cycle consistency, we use two reconstruction losses for the forward and backward transformations. To provide a comprehensive overview of the training process of the DIFE module, we discuss a simple scenario involving two domains, where in our work each domain represents an MDP with a distinct set of environmental parameters.

As depicted in Fig. 2, assuming that two domains of data are provided, domain i and domain j. O_i and O_j represent the observation sets in domain i and domain j. o_1^i and o_2^i are two different observations in O_i. o_3^i and o_4^j are random observations in O_i and O_j, respectively. The encoder function $\text{Enc}_\theta(\cdot)$ is parameterized by θ and the decoder function $\text{Dec}_\phi(\cdot)$ is parameterized by ϕ . Processed by the encoder, the observations are mapped into latent feature embeddings $o_1^i \to z_1^i = \langle \bar{z}_1^i, \hat{z}_1^i \rangle, o_2^i \to z_2^i = \langle \bar{z}_2^i, \hat{z}_2^i \rangle, o_3^i \to z_3^i = \langle \bar{z}_3^i, \hat{z}_3^i \rangle, o_4^j \to z_4^j = \left\langle \bar{z}_4^j, \hat{z}_4^j \right\rangle$, where $z_1^i, z_2^i, z_3^i, z_4^j$ are latent features of $o_1^i, o_2^i, o_3^i, o_4^j$, $\bar{z}_1^i, \bar{z}_2^i, \bar{z}_3^i, \bar{z}_4^j$ are domain-invariant features in $z_1^i, z_2^i, z_3^i, z_4^j$ and $\hat{z}_1^i, \hat{z}_2^i, \hat{z}_3^i, \hat{z}_4^j$ are domain-specific features in $z_1^i, z_2^i, z_3^i, z_4^j$. The loss function of DIFE contains two parts.

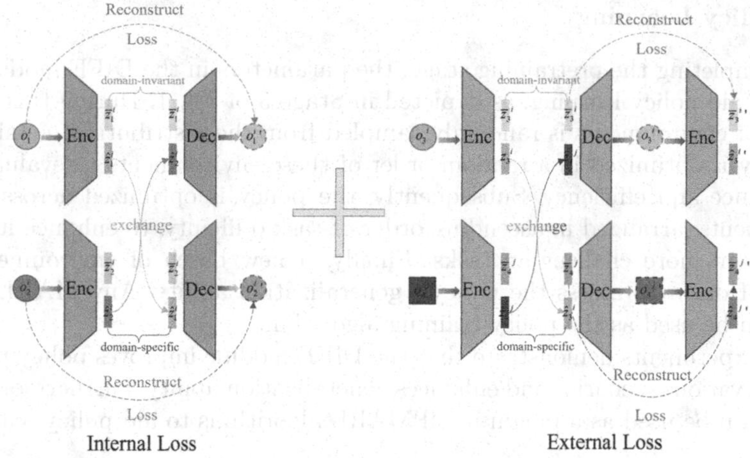

Fig. 2. Cycle-consistent VAE

Internal Loss. This loss corresponds to forward transformation in cycle consistency and contains both the self-reconstruction loss for VAE and the reconstruction loss for domain-specific feature extraction. Domain-specific features exhibit variation across domains but remain constant within a given domain. Therefore, if two features within the same domain have their domain-specific components swapped, the reconstructed observations should restore the original observations, which is $o_1^i \neq o_2^i, \bar{z}_1^i \neq \bar{z}_2^i, \hat{z}_1^i = \hat{z}_2^i$. The internal loss contains both VAE reconstruction loss and domain-specific feature extraction loss.

$$\mathcal{L}_{\text{internal}} = \mathcal{L}_{\text{VAE}} + k_1 \mathcal{L}_{\text{specific}}$$

$$\mathcal{L}_{\text{VAE}} = \mathbb{E}_{\text{Enc}_\theta\left(\bar{z}_1^i, \hat{z}_1^i \mid o_1^i\right)} \left[\log \text{Dec}_\phi \left(o_1^i \mid \bar{z}_1^i, \hat{z}_1^i\right)\right]$$

$$\mathcal{L}_{\text{specific}} = \mathbb{E}_{\text{Enc}_\theta\left(\bar{z}_1^i, \hat{z}_1^i \mid o_1^i\right) \cdot \text{Enc}_\theta\left(\bar{z}_2^i, \hat{z}_2^i \mid o_2^i\right)} \left[\log \text{Dec}_\phi \left(o_1^i \mid \bar{z}_1^i, \hat{z}_2^i\right)\right]$$

where $\mathcal{L}_{\text{internal}}$ represents the internal loss of DIFE, $\mathcal{L}_{\text{VAE}}$ represents the VAE loss, $\mathcal{L}_{\text{specific}}$ represents the loss for domain-specific feature extraction, and k_1 is the weight coefficient for $\mathcal{L}_{\text{VAE}}$ and $\mathcal{L}_{\text{specific}}$.

External Loss. This loss corresponds to reverse transformation in cycle consistency. Domain-invariant features contain little domain-specific information but can be reconstructed across all domains. Therefore, if the domain-specific feature $\hat{z}_3^i$ of the observation o_3^i is replaced by $\hat{z}_4^j$, the embedding of the reconstructed observation $o_3^{i'} = \text{Dec}_\phi\left(\bar{z}_3^i, \hat{z}_4^j\right)$ can still restore the domain invariant feature $\bar{z}_3^i$.

$$\mathcal{L}_{\text{external}} = \mathbb{E}_{\bar{z}^i}\left[\left\|\text{Enc}_\theta\left(\text{Dec}_\phi\left(\bar{z}_3^i, \hat{z}_4^j\right)\right) - \bar{z}_3^i\right\|_1\right]$$

$$\mathcal{L}_{\text{total}} = \mathcal{L}_{\text{internal}} + k_2 \mathcal{L}_{\text{external}}$$

where $\mathcal{L}_{\text{external}}$ represents the external loss of DIFE, $\mathcal{L}_{\text{total}}$ represents the overall loss of DIFE, and k_2 is the weight coefficient for $\mathcal{L}_{\text{internal}}$ and $\mathcal{L}_{\text{external}}$.

3.3 Policy Learning

Upon completing the pretraining stage, the parameters in the DIFE module are frozen to aid policy learning, as depicted in Stage 3 of Fig. 1. During this stage, a batch of environments is randomly sampled from the distribution μ. Initially, the policy is optimized in a random order of these environments to evaluate its performance and efficiency. Subsequently, the policy is optimized across these environments, arranged in ascending order of task difficulty, to enhance its performance in more challenging tasks. Finally, a new batch of environments is sampled from μ to assess the policy's generalization ability. Any MARL algorithm can be used as the policy training algorithm.

Our experiments demonstrate that the DIFE module improves policy performance in various scenarios and enhances generalization ability. Furthermore, this module can be used as a plugin in all MARL algorithms to aid policy learning.

4 Experiment

We selected the multi-agent particle environment (MPE) as our test platform due to its diverse configurations of multi-agent environments. In our previous work [27], we addressed the challenging problem of cooperative coverage and connectivity maintenance in MPE by utilizing graph attention networks. This task encompasses a broader range of environmental configurations compared to other MPE tasks. The primary experiments are conducted in this task, and more details can be found in [27]. Agents in this task need to cooperate in a 2D space to cover targets within their coverage range while maintaining communication links with other agents within their communication range. The goal of this task is to cover as many targets as possible while ensuring a connected communication topology among the agents. The evaluation metrics for this task include training reward, coverage rate, disconnection rate, and success rate. The coverage rate is the percentage of covered targets, the disconnection rate is the percentage of stpng where agents are disconnected, and the success rate is the percentage of episodes where agents cover 90% of the targets while maintaining connectivity.

To identify the most influential parameters of this task, we first conduct experiments on a range of parameters. We use MAPPO as our base algorithm. Our testing results indicate that the size of the arena h and the number of agents N are the primary factors. Intuitively, if we represent the joint state space as $S = S_1 \times \cdots \times S_i \times \cdots \times S_N$, where S_i is the state space of an individual agent i and N is the number of agents, the arena size h determines the range of individual state spaces, while the range of joint state space increases exponentially with N.

During the pretraining process, we employ a scripted searching policy to gather observations from sampled environments. By analyzing the testing performance of our base policy, we establish correlations between h and N, and determine a sampling distribution of the two parameters. We then randomly sample 100 environments in this distribution to gather observations.

After pretraining, we freeze the encoder layers to generate domain-invariant features in downstream policy training. We select three representative configurations with different N and h to illustrate the performance of our method in Fig 3.

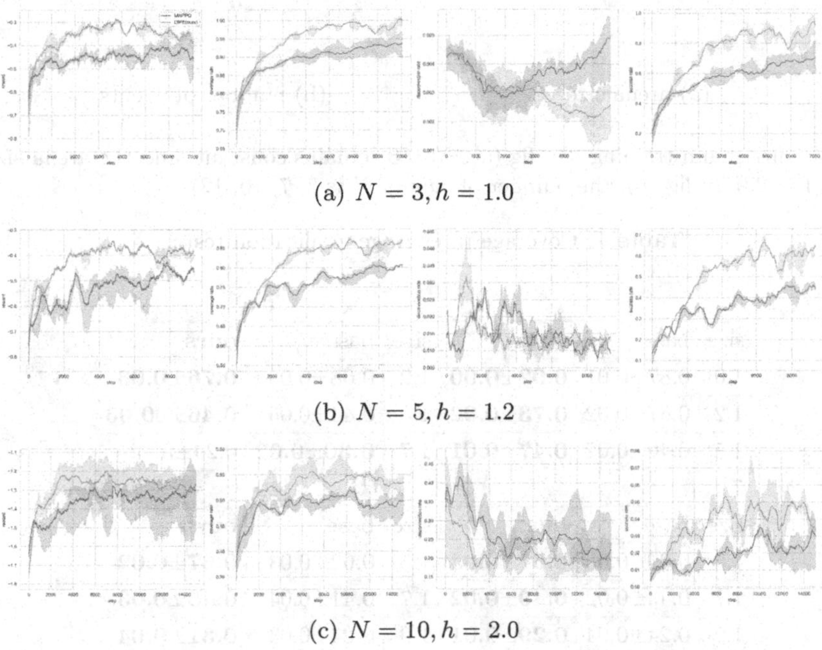

(a) $N = 3, h = 1.0$

(b) $N = 5, h = 1.2$

(c) $N = 10, h = 2.0$

Fig. 3. Training curves of MAPPO and DIFE (ours) in 3 representative scenarios. (Three rows represent three scenarios, respectively. Four columns, from left to right, represent training reward, coverage rate, disconnection rate, and success rate)

The results of our experiments illustrate that, with similar disconnection rates, our method consistently outperforms MAPPO in terms of success and coverage rates, as well as reward. This indicates that our DIFE module is a highly effective means of improving policy performance.

To improve the policy performance in more complex scenarios, we arrange the sampled environments in the sequence of increasing values for h and N. The results indicate that our feature extractor can effectively enhance learning performance as h increases while showing less improvement as N increases. This is due to the fact that in MARL, the optimization complexity increases exponentially with the number of agents. Learning unified latent feature embeddings have limited impacts on optimizing policies in such complex scenarios.

We also performed generalization tests by randomly sampling environments using domain randomization. The policies trained in the base environments were then evaluated in these sampled environments. We selected 12 representative environments to demonstrate the generalization ability of our method (Fig. 4).

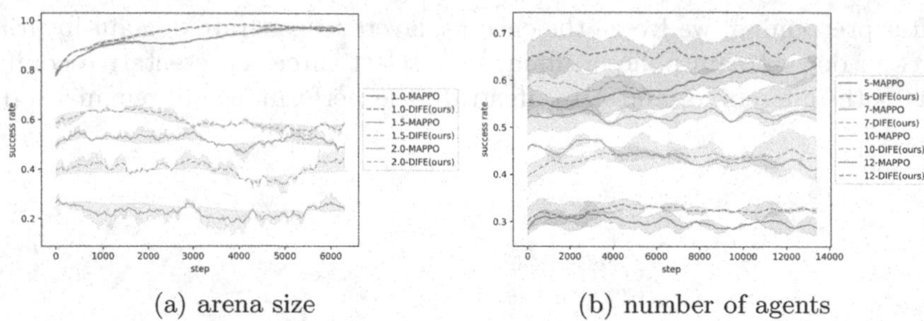

(a) arena size (b) number of agents

Fig. 4. Curriculum training. (In fig (a), $N = 3$ remains constant, and the arena size h is 1.0, 1.5, 2.0. In fig (b), the number of agents N is 5, 7, 10, 12)

Table 1. Coverage rates in generalization tests

3			5		
size	base	**ours**	size	base	**ours**
1.0	0.87±0.01	**0.92±0.00**	1.2	0.68±0.05	**0.76±0.03**
1.2	0.67±0.02	**0.73±0.02**	1.5	0.44±0.05	**0.46±00.06**
1.5	0.40±0.02	**0.47±0.01**	1.7	**0.30±0.02**	0.29±0.02
7			10		
size	base	**ours**	size	base	**ours**
1.5	0.60±0.05	**0.67±0.03**	1.5	0.62±0.03	**0.67±0.02**
1.7	0.43±0.02	**0.49±0.02**	1.7	0.41±0.04	**0.45±0.03**
1.9	0.24±0.04	**0.29±0.01**	1.9	0.24±0.03	**0.31±0.04**

Table 2. Disconnection rates in generalization tests

3			5		
size	base	**ours**	size	base	**ours**
1.0	0.67±0.05	**0.33±0.05**	1.2	2.33±0.12	**0.00±0.00**
1.2	4.00±0.08	**0.33±0.05**	1.5	4.00±0.08	**0.00±0.00**
1.5	5.00±0.08	**0.33±0.05**	1.7	3.33±0.09	**0.00±0.00**
7			10		
size	base	**ours**	size	base	**ours**
1.5	1.67±0.12	**1.00±0.00**	1.5	**0.67±0.05**	1.0±0.08
1.7	0.67±0.05	**0.67±0.05**	1.7	0.67±0.09	**0.33±0.05**
1.9	0.00±0.00	**0.00±0.00**	1.9	0.33±0.05	**0.33±0.05**

As illustrated in Tables 1 and Table 2, policy performance tends to deteriorate as the arena size or the number of agents increases. Nonetheless, our method exhibits better adaptability with higher coverage rates and lower disconnection rates than the base policy.

To assess the effectiveness of our approach, we visualize the output of both the attention module in our method and the base policy in Fig. 5. In the first row, it is evident that the attention map computed by the base policy focuses heavily on agents 0 and 3, likely due to a preference for maintaining connectivity, resulting in a conservative and overfitting policy. In contrast, the attention computed by our method corresponds more closely with the distance map, offering a more flexible and interpretable approach to deploying agents.

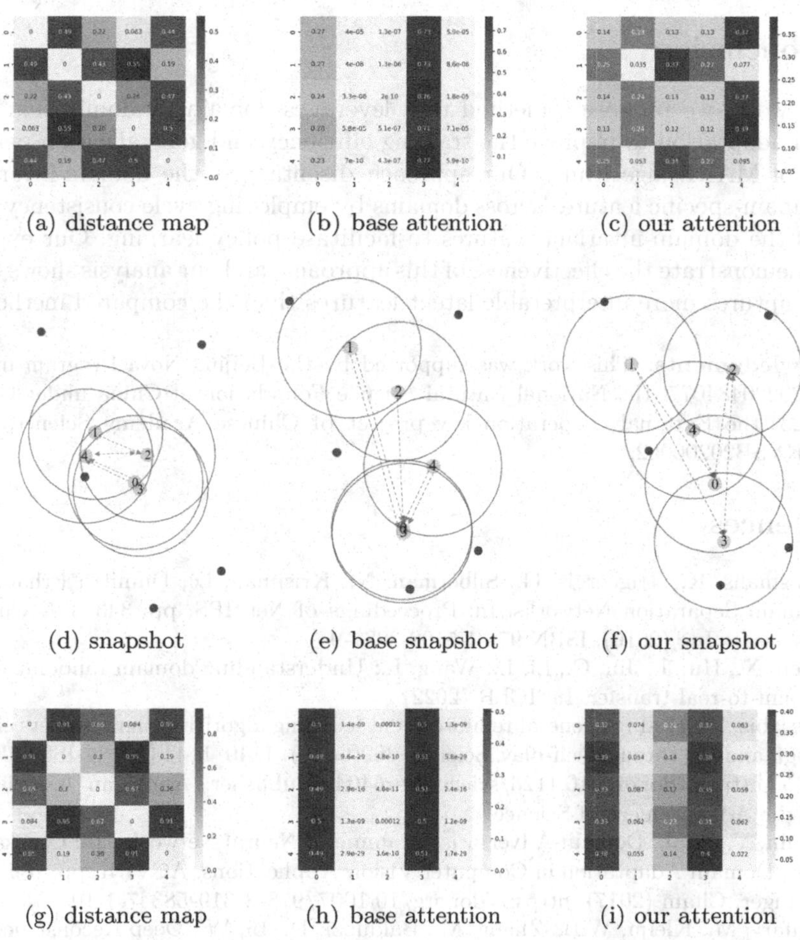

Fig. 5. Attention Visualization for $N = 5, h = 1.2$ in the same episode. (The first row shows visualization maps at the beginning of the episode. The second row shows the rendering snapshots. In the snapshots, the red dotted lines with arrows are the highest attention for each agent. fig (d) shows the snapshot at the beginning of the episode, fig (e) shows the snapshot of MAPPO at the end of the episode, fig (f) shows the snapshot of our method at the end of the episode. The third row shows visualization maps at the end of the episode) (Color figure online)

In the second and third rows, the base policy concentrates its attention almost exclusively on agents 0 and 3, resulting in overlap between the two agents. Our method, on the other hand, attends not only to these two agents but also to agent 2, which is responsible for covering the upper right target and is at risk of disconnecting from the system. Moreover, it is observed that our method distributes attention more uniformly across all agents at the end of the episode, in contrast to the base policy. These results suggest that the observations collected across domains assist in learning a more effective and explainable feature extractor that captures latent domain-invariant features.

5 Conclusion

In this work, we propose a method that leverages domain randomization and domain adaptation to improve the training efficiency and generalization performance of MARL algorithms. Our approach disentangles the domain-invariant and domain-specific features across domains by employing cycle consistency and utilizes the domain-invariant features to facilitate policy learning. Our experiments demonstrate the effectiveness of this approach, and our analysis shows that DIFE captures more interpretable latent features than the compared method.

Acknowledgments. This work was supported by the Beijing Nova Program under Grant 20220484077, the National Natural Science Foundation of China under Grant 62073323, the External cooperation key project of Chinese Academy Sciences No. 173211KYSB20200002.

References

1. Bousmalis, K., Trigeorgis, G., Silberman, N., Krishnan, D., Dumitru Erhan, D.: Domain Separation Networks. In: Proceedings of NeurIPS, pp. 343–351. Curran Associates Inc (2016). ISBN 978-1-5108-3881-9
2. Chen, X., Hu, J., Jin, C., Li, L., Wang, L.: Understanding domain randomization for sim-to-real transfer. In: ICLR (2022)
3. Hassabis, D., et al.: A general reinforcement learning algorithm that masters chess, shogi, and Go through self-play. Science, 362(6419), 1140–1144 (2018). ISSN 0036-8075. https://doi.org/10.1126/science.aar6404. Publisher: American Association for the Advancement of Science
4. Ganin, Y., et al.: Domain-Adversarial Training of Neural Networks. In: Csurka, G. (ed.) Domain Adaptation in Computer Vision Applications. ACVPR, pp. 189–209. Springer, Cham (2017). https://doi.org/10.1007/978-3-319-58347-1_10
5. Ghifary, M., Kleijn, W.B., Zhang, M., Balduzzi, D., Li, W.: Deep Reconstruction-Classification Networks for Unsupervised Domain Adaptation. In: Leibe, B., Matas, J., Sebe, N., Welling, M. (eds.) ECCV 2016. LNCS, vol. 9908, pp. 597–613. Springer, Cham (2016). https://doi.org/10.1007/978-3-319-46493-0_36
6. Ghosh, D., Rahme, J., Kumar, A., Zhang, A., Adams, R.P., Levine, S.: Why Generalization in RL is Difficult: Epistemic POMDPs and Implicit Partial Observability. In: M. Ranzato, A. Beygelzimer, Y. Dauphin, P. S. Liang, and J. Wortman Vaughan, editors, Advances in NeurIPS, vol. 34, pp. 25502–25515. Curran Associates Inc (2021)

7. Hoffman, J., Tzeng, E., Darrell, T., Saenko, K.: Simultaneous Deep Transfer Across Domains and Tasks. In: Csurka, G. (ed.) Domain Adaptation in Computer Vision Applications. ACVPR, Springer, Cham (2017). https://doi.org/10.1007/978-3-319-58347-1_9
8. Jha, A.H., Anand, S., Singh, M., Veeravasarapu, V.S.R.: Disentangling Factors of Variation with Cycle-Consistent Variational Auto-encoders. In: Ferrari, V., Hebert, M., Sminchisescu, C., Weiss, Y. (eds.) ECCV 2018. LNCS, vol. 11207, pp. 829–845. Springer, Cham (2018). https://doi.org/10.1007/978-3-030-01219-9_49
9. Kwon, J., Efroni, Y., Caramanis, C., Mannor, S.: RL for Latent MDPs: Regret Guarantees and a Lower Bound. In: M. Ranzato, A. Beygelzimer, Y. Dauphin, P. S. Liang, and J. Wortman Vaughan, eds, Advances in NeurIPS, vol. 34, pp. 24523–24534. Curran Associates Inc (2021)
10. Liu, A.H., et al.: A unified feature disentangler for multi-domain image translation and manipulation. In: Proceedings of NeurIPS, pp. 2595–2604 (2018). https://papers.nips.cc/paper/7525-a-unified-feature-disentangler-for-multi-domain-image-translation-and-manipulation
11. Long, M., Cao, Y., Wang, J., Jordan, M.I.: Learning transferable features with deep adaptation networks. In: Proceedings of ICML, ICML'15, pp. 97–105. JMLR.org (2015)
12. Mandlekar, A., Zhu, Y., Garg, A., Fei-Fei, L., Savarese, S.: Adversarially robust policy learning: active construction of physically-plausible perturbations. In: Proceedings of IROS, pp. 3932–3939 (2017). https://doi.org/10.1109/IROS.2017.8206245. ISSN: 2153-0866
13. OpenAI, Christopher Berner, C., et al.: Dota 2 with large scale deep reinforcement learning. arXiv:1912.06680 (2019)
14. OpenAI, Akkaya, I., et al.: Solving Rubik's Cube with a Robot Hand. arXiv:1910.07113 (2019)
15. Peng, X.B., Andrychowicz, M., Zaremba, W., Abbeel, P.: Sim-to-real transfer of robotic control with dynamics randomization. In: Proceedings of ICRA, pp. 3803–3810 (2018). https://doi.org/10.1109/ICRA.2018.8460528. arXiv:1710.06537
16. Reed, S., et al.: A Generalist Agent. arXiv:2205.06175 (2022)
17. Sadeghi F., Levine, S.: CAD2RL: real single-image flight without a single real image. arxiv.org/abs/1611.04201arXiv:1611.04201 (2017)
18. Silver, D., et al.: Mastering the game of Go with deep neural networks and tree search. Nature 529(7587), 484–489 (2016). ISSN 1476-4687. https://doi.org/10.1038/nature16961. Number: 7587 Publisher: Nature Publishing Group
19. Sun, B., Saenko, K.: Deep CORAL: Correlation Alignment for Deep Domain Adaptation. In: Hua, G., Jégou, H. (eds.) ECCV 2016. LNCS, vol. 9915, pp. 443–450. Springer, Cham (2016). https://doi.org/10.1007/978-3-319-49409-8_35
20. Adaptive Agent Team, et al.: Human-timescale adaptation in an open-ended task space. arXiv:2301.07608 (2023)
21. Tobin, J., et al.: Domain randomization for transferring deep neural networks from simulation to the real world, arXiv:1703.06907 (2017)
22. Tzeng, E., J., H., Zhang, N., Saenko, K., Trevor Darrell, T.: Deep domain confusion: maximizing for domain invariance. arXiv:1412.3474 (2014)
23. Tzeng, E., Hoffman, J., Saenko, K., Darrell, T.: Adversarial discriminative domain adaptation. In: Proceedings of CVPR, pp. 2962–2971 (2017). https://doi.org/10.1109/CVPR.2017.316. ISSN: 1063–6919

24. Vinyals, O, et al.: Grandmaster level in StarCraft II using multi-agent reinforcement learning. Nature, 575(7782), 350–354 (2019). ISSN 1476–4687. https://doi.org/10.1038/s41586-019-1724-z. Number: 7782 Publisher: Nature Publishing Group
25. Xing, J., Nagata, T., Chen, K., Zou, X., Neftci, E., Krichmar, J.L.: Domain adaptation in reinforcement learning via latent unified state representation. In: Proceedings of AAAI, vol. 35, pp. 10452–10459 (2021). https://doi.org/10.1609/aaai.v35i12.17251
26. Xing, Y., Song, O., Cheng, G.: On the algorithmic stability of adversarial training. In: M. Ranzato, A. Beygelzimer, Y. Dauphin, P. S. Liang, and J. Wortman Vaughan, editors, Advances in NeurIPS, vol. 34, pp. 26523–26535. Curran Associates Inc (2021)
27. Yifan Xu, Y., et al.: A double-observation policy learning framework for multi-target coverage with connectivity maintenance. In: Ren, Z., Wang, M., Hua, Y., eds, Proceedings of CCSICC, pp. 1279–1290. Springer Nature Singapore (2023). https://doi.org/10.1007/978-981-19-3998-3_120

Latent-Conditioned Policy Gradient for Multi-Objective Deep Reinforcement Learning

Takuya Kanazawa[1(✉)] and Chetan Gupta[2]

[1] Research and Development Group, Hitachi, Ltd., Kokubunji, Tokyo185-8601, Japan
takuya.kanazawa.cz@hitachi.com

[2] Industrial AI Lab, Hitachi America, Ltd. R&D, Santa Clara, CA 95054, USA
chetan.gupta@hal.hitachi.com

Abstract. Sequential decision making in the real world often requires finding a good balance of conflicting objectives. In general, there exist a plethora of Pareto-optimal policies that embody different patterns of compromises between objectives, and it is technically challenging to obtain them exhaustively using deep neural networks. In this work, we propose a novel multi-objective reinforcement learning (MORL) algorithm that trains a single neural network via policy gradient to approximately obtain the entire Pareto set in a single run of training, without relying on linear scalarization of objectives. The proposed method works in both continuous and discrete action spaces with no design change of the policy network. Numerical experiments demonstrate the practicality and efficacy of our approach in comparison to standard MORL baselines.

Keywords: Deep reinforcement learning · multi-objective optimization · Pareto frontier · policy gradient theorem · implicit generative network

1 Introduction

In recent years Reinforcement Learning (RL) has grown into a major part of the machine learning research. RL offers a powerful and principled framework to solve sequential decision making problems under uncertainty [28]. The goal of RL is to find an optimal policy that maximizes cumulative rewards over multiple time steps. Rapid progress in the field of deep neural networks (NN) has enabled deep RL to solve a number of complex nonlinear control tasks at a level comparable to or even beyond human experts [16]. RL can be extended to incorporate vector-valued rewards, which is known as Multi-Objective Reinforcement Learning (MORL) [11,15,26]. Such an extension is motivated by the fact that many real-world control problems require balancing multiple conflicting objectives. The trade-off between objectives naturally leads to an *ensemble* of best solutions (known as *Pareto-optimal policies*), and the goal of MORL is to obtain a set of policies that approximates such an ensemble as closely as possible.

L. Iliadis et al. (Eds.): ICANN 2023, LNCS 14259, pp. 63–76, 2023.
https://doi.org/10.1007/978-3-031-44223-0_6

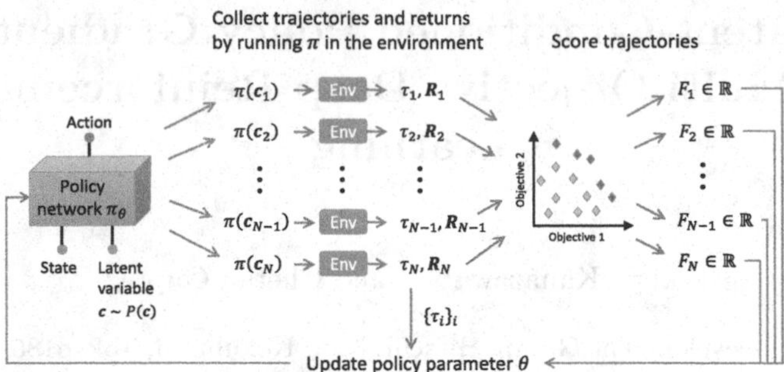

Fig. 1. Illustration of the proposed algorithm (LC-MOPG) for a bi-objective problem. There is an alternative version that uses value networks in addition to the policy network (LC-MOPG-V)

In MORL problems, the set of true Pareto-optimal policies often consists of many (or even *infinite*) diverse and disparate solutions, which hampers a naïve application of conventional RL techniques. One of the popular approaches to tackling this difficulty is to convert the original MORL problem into a series of single-objective RL problems and solve them by training an ensemble of agents [18]. This method is simple but suffers from a high computational cost. Another popular method is to train a single agent that receives preference (linear weight vector) over objectives as additional input to the value function [5,6]. This approach is computationally efficient but linear scalarization hampers finding the concave part of the Pareto frontier (PF) [9,30].

In this work, we propose a novel model-free on-policy MORL algorithm that obtains infinitely many inequivalent policies by training just a single policy network. In this approach, as illustrated in Fig. 1, a stochastic policy receives a random latent variable sampled from a fixed external probability distribution as additional input. We train this latent-conditioned NN via policy gradient. We introduce a novel exploration bonus that helps to substantially enhance diversity of the policy ensemble. The proposed method, coined as Latent-Conditioned Multi-Objective Policy Gradient (LC-MOPG), is applicable to both continuous and discrete action spaces, and can in principle discover the whole PF without any convexity assumptions, as LC-MOPG does not rely on linear scalarization of objectives. We confirm the effectiveness of LC-MOPG numerically. Our source codes are available at GitHub [12]. An extended version of this paper with a full list of hyperparameters, a more in-depth survey of related work, and additional numerical results, is available at [14].

2 Related Work

There are a number of MORL methods that employ some parametric scalarization function to combine multiple objectives into a single objective. Van Moffaert et al. [31] proposed the use of the Chebyshev scalarization function. Linear scalarization (i.e., taking a weighted sum of objectives as the target of optimization) is an alternative approach: Castelletti et al. [5,6] developed multi-objective fitted Q iteration; Mossalam et al. [18] introduced a NN architecture with vector output; Abels et al. [1] investigated a setup with a dynamically changing linear weight; Yang et al. [35] introduced *envelope Q-learning*; Basaklar et al. [2] introduced a Q-learning scheme that contains a cosine similarity term between projected weight vectors and Q values.

While the methods outlined above are value-based, there are also policy-based approaches for MORL that combine policy gradient with linear scalarization. Chen et al. [7] proposed a meta-learning approach to MORL; Xu et al. [33] proposed an evolutionary algorithm in which a population of policies are trained in parallel using various weighted sums of objectives. These methods require training an ensemble of policy networks to cover the PF. We believe our work is the first policy-based approach for MORL that efficiently learns an ensemble of policies by training a single NN.

Miscellaneous MORL approaches that do *not* rest on scalarization techniques have also been developed: Van Moffaert and Nowé [17] developed *Pareto Q-learning*; Reymond et al. [24] extended the framework of reward-conditioned policies [27] to MORL; Parisi et al. [21] developed two policy gradient methods, called *Radial Algorithm* (RA) and *Pareto-Following Algorithm* (PFA); Pirotta et al. [20,22] proposed a manifold-based policy search algorithm in which a policy is sampled from a continuous manifold in the policy parameter space; Parisi et al. [19] proposed a generalization of natural evolution strategies to MORL called MO-NES. Our algorithm, LC-MOPG, is similar to [19,20,22] in that a continuous PF (i.e., infinitely many policies) can be learnt in a single run of training. However, unlike [19,20,22], LC-MOPG is a nonparametric approach, meaning that we need not manually design the parametric form of the distribution over policies. Moreover, LC-MOPG can train deep policies with thousands of parameters efficiently over a high-dimensional continuous state space.

NN that receive a latent variable as additional input are generally called *latent-conditioned NN* or *implicit generative networks* (IGN). Unlike plain NN of the form $\mathbf{y} = f_\theta(\mathbf{x})$ with $\mathbf{x}$ the input features and $\mathbf{y}$ the label, IGN is of the form $\mathbf{y} = f_\theta(\mathbf{x}, \mathbf{c})$ where the latent variable $\mathbf{c}$ is sampled from a fixed (discrete or continuous) probability distribution such as $\mathcal{N}(\mathbf{0}, \mathbb{1})$. IGN has been employed for uncertainty quantification of deep learning models [4,13]. In RL, IGN is used to model a return distribution [8]. IGN is also effective for unsupervised skill discovery, as demonstrated in [10].

3 Problem Formulation

In conventional single-objective RL, we consider sequential decision making problems that are formally described as a Markov Decision Process (MDP): $\langle S, A, P, r, \gamma\rangle$ where S and A are the state and action spaces, $P : S \times A \times S \to [0, \infty)$ is the transition probability (density), $r : S \times A \times S \to \mathbb{R}$ is the reward function, and $\gamma \in [0, 1]$ is the discount factor. A policy π specifies which action is taken in a given state. A deterministic policy $\pi : S \to A$ yields action, while a stochastic policy $\pi : S \times A \to [0, \infty)$ gives a probabilistic distribution over A. The (discounted) cumulative sum of rewards $G_t = \sum_{k=0}^{\infty} \gamma^k r_{t+k}$ is called *return*. The goal in RL is to (approximately) find the optimal policy π_* that maximizes the expected return for all $s \in S$.

Policy-based methods iteratively update the parameters θ of a policy π_θ to improve the expected return. REINFORCE algorithm [32] for episodic environments runs a stochastic policy, samples trajectories $\{(s_t, a_t)\}_t$, and optimizes π_θ as $\theta \leftarrow \theta + \eta \sum_t G_t \nabla_\theta \log \pi_\theta(a_t|s_t)$, where $\eta > 0$ is the learning rate. Intuitively this update rule implies that actions that lead to higher returns are reinforced more strongly than those that lead to lower returns. This method, based on the Monte Carlo estimate of return, is prone to high variance. To remedy this, we may utilize an *advantage function* $A_\phi : S \times A \to \mathbb{R}$, which is trained concurrently with the policy via recursive Bellman updates. The policy is then optimized iteratively as $\theta \leftarrow \theta + \eta \sum_t A_\phi(s_t, a_t) \nabla_\theta \log \pi_\theta(a_t|s_t)$.

MDP may be generalized to multi-objective MDP (MOMDP), in which the reward function $\mathbf{r} : S \times A \times S \to \mathbb{R}^m$ becomes vector-valued, with $m \geq 2$ the number of objectives. In MOMDP, a policy π induces a vector of expected returns $\mathbf{G}^\pi \equiv (G_1^\pi, G_2^\pi, \cdots, G_m^\pi) = \mathbb{E}\left[\sum_{t=0}^{\infty} \gamma^t \mathbf{r}(s_t, a_t, s_{t+1}) \middle| a_t \sim \pi(s_t)\right] \in \mathbb{R}^m$. A policy π is said to *dominate* another policy π' if $G_i^\pi \geq G_i^{\pi'}$ for all i and $G_i^\pi > G_i^{\pi'}$ for at least one i. (With a slight abuse of terminology, we also say that $\mathbf{G}^\pi$ dominates $\mathbf{G}^{\pi'}$.) If there exists no policy that dominates π, then π is said to be *Pareto-optimal*. The set of all such policies is called the *Pareto set*, and the set of expected returns of all Pareto-optimal policies is called the *Pareto frontier* (PF), which is a submanifold of $\mathbb{R}^m$. The goal in MORL is to find a set of policies that best approximates the true Pareto set.

There are several metrics to assess the quality of an approximate PF. Some metrics require knowing the true PF, which is often difficult in practice. A widely used metric that does not require knowing the true PF is the *hypervolume* indicator (HV) [29,36], which is the volume of regions in $\mathbb{R}^m$ that are dominated by a given (approximate) PF. HV is the only unary indicator that is known to be Pareto compliant [37].

4 Methodology

In this section, we introduce a novel policy-gradient approach to MORL coined as LC-MOPG. The pseudocode is presented in Algorithm 1. The main idea is quite simple: train a latent-conditioned NN as a parameter-efficient representation of a diverse collection of policies in the Pareto set of given MOMDP. The training is done on-policy. Over the course of training the policy's stochasticity decreases, signaling convergence.

Note that the latent variable $\mathbf{c}$ that is fed to the policy network carries no such intuitive meaning as "preference over objectives." In the proposed algorithm, $\mathbf{c}$ is simply a mathematical steering wheel to switch policies. We will use a uniform distribution over $[0,1]^{d_{\text{lat}}}$ as a latent space distribution $P(\mathbf{c})$. The dimension $d_{\text{lat}} \in \mathbb{N}$ is an important hyperparameter of the algorithm.

The policy NN used in this work has the structure shown in Fig. 2. It provides a mapping from a state+latent space to action distribution. The outputs of policy are parameters of any parametric probability distribution, e.g., the mean and variance if a Gaussian distribution is chosen. For a continuous bounded action space, we use the Beta distribution $B(\alpha, \beta)$ with $\alpha, \beta > 0$ for each action dimension. For a discrete

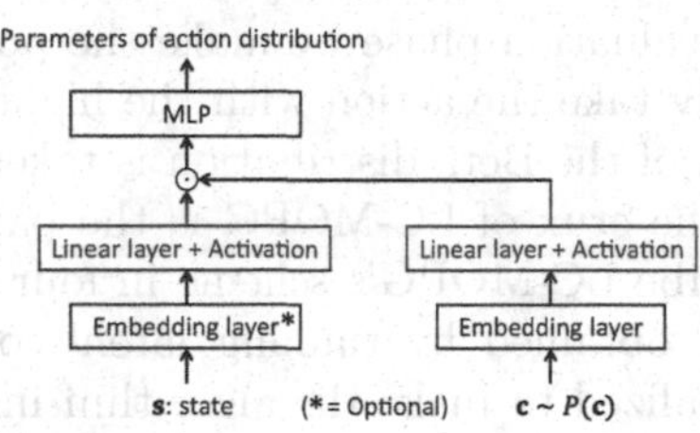

Fig. 2. Architecture of the policy network.

Algorithm 1 Latent-Conditioned Multi-Objective Policy Gradient (LC-MOPG)

Require: π_θ: policy network, $\gamma \in (0,1]$: discount rate, $d_{\text{lat}} \in \mathbb{N}$: dimension of latent variables, $\beta \geq 0$: bonus coefficient, $N_{\text{lat}} \in \mathbb{N}$: number of latent variables sampled per iteration

Initialize π_θ
while π_θ has not converged **do**
  for i in $\{1, 2, \cdots, N_{\text{lat}}\}$ **do**
    Sample $\mathbf{c}_i \sim \text{Uniform}\left([0,1]^{d_{\text{lat}}}\right)$
    Obtain trajectory $\tau_i = \{(\mathbf{s}_t, \mathbf{a}_t)\}_t$ and return $\mathbf{G}_i$ by running policy $\pi_\theta(\mathbf{c}_i)$ in the environment
  end for
  Compute normalized returns $\{\widehat{\mathbf{G}}_i\}_{i=1}^{N_{\text{lat}}}$ from $\{\mathbf{G}_i\}_{i=1}^{N_{\text{lat}}}$
  Compute scores $\{f_i\}_{i=1}^{N_{\text{lat}}}$ from $\{\widehat{\mathbf{G}}_i\}_{i=1}^{N_{\text{lat}}}$ ▷ Algorithm 2
  Compute bonuses $\{b_i\}_{i=1}^{N_{\text{lat}}}$ from $\{\widehat{\mathbf{G}}_i\}_{i=1}^{N_{\text{lat}}}$ ▷ Algorithm 3
  for i in $\{1, 2, \cdots, N_{\text{lat}}\}$ **do**
    $F_i \leftarrow \max(f_i + \beta b_i, 0)$
  end for
  Update θ via gradient descent of loss

$$\mathcal{L}_\pi(\theta) = -\sum_{i=1}^{N_{\text{lat}}} \left\{ F_i \sum_{(\mathbf{s},\mathbf{a}) \in \tau_i} \log \pi_\theta(\mathbf{a}|\mathbf{s}, \mathbf{c}_i) \right\}$$

end while
return π_θ

Algorithm 2 Score computation

Require: Normalized returns $\{\widehat{\mathbf{G}}_i \in \mathbb{R}^m\}_{i=1}^{N_{\text{lat}}}$

Obtain the set of undominated points $\mathfrak{pf} = \text{PF}\left(\{\widehat{\mathbf{G}}_i\}_i\right)$
for $i \in \{1, 2, \cdots, N_{\text{lat}}\}$ **do**
  $\mathfrak{D} \leftarrow \left\{ \min_{z \in \mathfrak{pf}} \|z - \widehat{\mathbf{G}}_i\|_2 \right\}$
  for $j \in \{1, 2, \cdots, m\}$ **do**
    $\mathfrak{D} \leftarrow \mathfrak{D} \cup \left\{ \max_{z \in \mathfrak{pf}} z_j - \left(\widehat{\mathbf{G}}_i\right)_j \right\}$
  end for
  $f_i \leftarrow -\min \mathfrak{D}$
end for
for $i \in \{1, 2, \cdots, N_{\text{lat}}\}$ **do**
  $f_i \leftarrow f_i - \text{avg}(\{f_i\}_i)$ ▷ avg $\in$ {mean, median}
end for
return Scores $\{f_i\}_{i=1}^{N_{\text{lat}}}$

Algorithm 3 Bonus computation

Require: Normalized returns $\{\widehat{\mathbf{G}}_i\}_{i=1}^{N_{\text{lat}}}$, scores $\{f_i\}_{i=1}^{N_{\text{lat}}}$, and parameter $k \in \mathbb{N}$

for $i = \{1, 2, \cdots, N_{\text{lat}}\}$ **do**
  $\text{mask}_i \leftarrow 1$ if $f_i > 0$ else 0
  $d_i \leftarrow$ distance from $\widehat{\mathbf{G}}_i$ to its kth nearest neighbor in $\{\widehat{\mathbf{G}}_i\}_{i=1}^{N_{\text{lat}}}$
  $b_i \leftarrow \text{mask}_i * d_i$
end for
return $\{b_i\}_{i=1}^{N_{\text{lat}}}$

---

action space, the outputs of policy are logits of action probabilities. The feature embedding layer for latent input is the same as in [8]. Finally, the outputs of state layers and latent layers are mixed through a dot product. We note that in the evaluation phase we make the policy deterministic: for discrete actions, we simply take the action with the highest probability; for continuous actions, the mean of the Beta distribution is taken.

The crux of LC-MOPG is the parameter update scheme of policy. We now describe LC-MOPG's scheme in four steps. In the first step, raw returns $\{\mathbf{G}_i \in \mathbb{R}^m\}_i$ obtained by running latent-conditioned policies $\pi_\theta(\mathbf{c}_i)$, $\mathbf{c}_i \sim P(\mathbf{c})$ are normalized to make the algorithm insensitive to the scale of rewards. We shall adopt one of the three normalization conventions: standard normalization, robust normalization, and max-min normalization. We refer to [14] for more details. The second step is the computation of score f_i for each normalized return $\widehat{\mathbf{G}}_i$, as summarized in Algorithm 2. The main idea is to first determine the current PF (= the set of undominated points) $\mathfrak{pf} = \mathrm{PF}(\{\widehat{\mathbf{G}}_i\}_i)$; Next, compute the distance between $\mathfrak{pf}$ and each $\widehat{\mathbf{G}}_i$; Finally, use the negative of this distance as a score (higher is better). The third step is the computation of bonus, denoted b_i, which is added to the score f_i for the sake of better exploration and higher diversity of policies. The procedure of bonus computation is outlined in Algorithm 3. The essential feature is that a high bonus is given to a trajectory i whose return $\widehat{\mathbf{G}}_i$ is dissimilar to other returns. The dissimilarity is quantified by the local density of returns $\left\{\widehat{\mathbf{G}}_i\right\}_{i=1}^{N_{\mathrm{lat}}}$ in $\mathbb{R}^m$. The fourth step is to clip the sum of score and bonus at zero (line 11 of Algorithm 1). This step yields the final score of the ith trajectory as $F_i = \max(f_i + \beta b_i, 0)$, which is used in the subsequent policy gradient update. This clipping means that, unlike standard policy gradient methods, we do not penalize (or weaken) actions in inferior trajectories. We found this expedient to stabilize the entire learning process well. This completes the description of the overall design of the proposed algorithm LC-MOPG. More details on the motivation behind each step can be found in [14] and are omitted here due to the limitation of space.

In single-objective RL it is well known that on-policy trajectory-based methods (REINFORCE) are generally outperformed by methods with *advantage* functions such as A2C and PPO. The advantage function $A(\mathbf{s}_t, \mathbf{a}_t)$ enables to estimate a proper update weight for each transition (state-action pair), which therefore provides a more fine-grained policy update than a trajectory-based update. We can consider a similar generalization of LC-MOPG, named LC-MOPG-V. In this method we train two additional NN, $\{Q_\phi, V_\psi\}$. The role of these NN is to estimate the contribution of individual states and actions within each trajectory to the full score $\{F_i\}_i$. Full pseudocode of LC-MOPG-V is somewhat lengthy and is given in [14]. Both LC-MOPG and LC-MOPG-V require collecting N_{lat} trajectories at every iteration, which benefits from parallelization over multiple CPU cores.

5 Environments

In this section, we describe the benchmark environments used in Sec. 6.

Deep Sea Treasure (DST) is a simple grid world proposed by Vamplew et al. [29]. Many prior works employed DST to evaluate MORL methods. As shown in Fig. 3, a submarine controlled by the agent starts from the top left cell and moves over the 11×11 grid by taking one of the four actions {up, down, left, right}. There are two objectives in DST: time cost and treasure reward. At each time step, the agent incurs a time cost of -1. The treasure reward is 0 if the agent is in blue cells and is equal to the treasure value $\in \{\mathsf{T1}, \mathsf{T2}, \cdots, \mathsf{T10}\}$ if it reaches one of the treasures (orange cells). The episode ends if either the agent reaches a treasure or moves into a cliff (gray cells). The exact PF of DST is given by trajectories of minimum Manhattan distance from the start cell to each treasure. There are some variations in the literature. We shall consider:

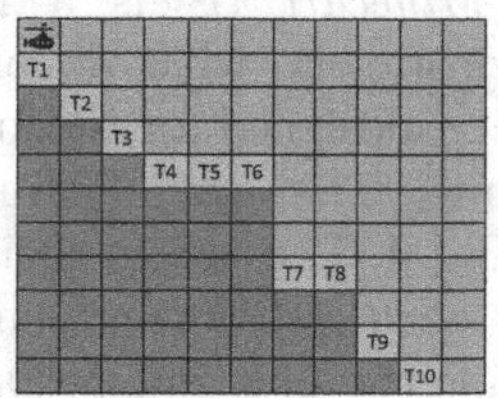

Fig. 3. The DST environment. Orange cells are treasures and blue cells are the ocean. (Color figure online)

- Original version [17,21,24,25,29]: $\{\mathsf{T}n\}_{n=1}^{10} = (1, 2, 3, 5, 8, 16, 24, 50, 74, 124)$.
- Convex version [2,35]: $\{\mathsf{T}n\}_{n=1}^{10} = (0.7, 8.2, 11.5, 14.0, 15.1, 16.1, 19.6, 20.3, 22.4, 23.7)$.

The convex version is easier to solve because all solutions on the PF can in principle be discovered with linear scalarization methods. Note that upper treasures such as T1 and T2 are easy to find while farther treasures such as T10 are substantially more difficult to find. Thus, despite its deceptive simplicity, DST poses a hard challenge of solving the exploration vs. exploitation dilemma in RL.

Fruit Tree Navigation (FTN) [35] is a binary tree of depth d. The state space is discrete and two-dimensional: $\mathbf{s} = (i, j) \in \mathbb{N}^2$ with $0 \le i \le d$ and $0 \le j \le 2^i - 1$. At every non-terminal node, the agent selects between left and right. At a terminal node the agent receives a reward $\mathbf{r} \in \mathbb{R}^6$ and finishes the episode. Thus the length of every episode is equal to d. The challenge for MORL methods is to discover all the 2^d Pareto-optimal policies, which gets harder for higher d. In this paper we consider $d \in \{5, 6, 7\}$ following [2,35]. We use the code available at GitHub [34].

Linear Quadratic Gaussian Control (LQG) is a well-known classic problem in control theory with continuous state and action spaces. LQG has been considered as a test problem in a number of RL and MORL studies. Specifically, we consider the multi-objective version presented in [19–21]. Let m denote the dimension of state and action spaces. The state transition dynamics is defined by $\mathbf{s}_{t+1} = \mathbf{s}_t + \mathbf{a}_t + \sigma\boldsymbol{\varepsilon}$, where $\mathbf{s} \in \mathbb{R}^m$ and $\mathbf{a} \in \mathbb{R}^m$ are state and action, $\boldsymbol{\varepsilon}$ is a Gaussian noise, and $\sigma \ge 0$ is the noise strength parameter. The reward $\mathbf{r} \in \mathbb{R}^m$ is defined as in [19–21]. As for the noise we consider both $\sigma = 0$ and 1. Part of the motivation to consider LQG stems from the fact that the optimal policy for LQG can be obtained by numerically solving the Riccati difference equation (see [14] for more details).

Minecart [1] is a multi-objective environment with a continuous state space, designed for testing MORL algorithms. The map of Minecart is shown in Fig. 4. The cart is initially at the top-left corner $(0, 0)$ and can go anywhere inside the unit square $[0, 1]^2$. There are five mines with distinct ore profiles, to which the cart must travel to perform mining. Inside a mine (blue disk) the cart can mine and get two kinds of ores. Once the cart returns to the home port (red circle), it sells all the ores, acquires rewards, and terminates the episode. The return in Minecart is three-dimensional: the first two components are the amount of mined ores, and the last component is the total fuel cost. The cart can take six discrete actions, [*Mine*, *Turn Left*, *Turn Right*, *Accelerate*, *Brake*, *Do Nothing*]. The underlying state space is $\mathbb{R}^6$, consisting of the cart's position, speed, angle, the mined amounts of ore1 and ore2. We use the source code of Minecart available at [23].

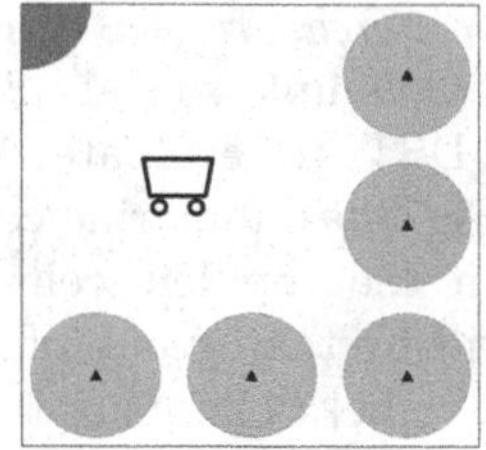

Fig. 4. Minecart environment. The cart departs from the top-left corner, goes for mining at the 5 mines (blue circles), and returns home (red quarter circle) to sell ores. (Color figure online)

6 Numerical Experiments

In this section we report the results of numerical experiments. All implementational details can be found in [14]. The computation of HV is done with an external multi-objective optimization library pymoo [3]. All performance scores in this section show the mean ± one standard deviation over 5 independent runs.

Results for DST. The performance for the two versions of the DST environment is summarized in Table 1. We found that LC-MOPG found the true PF in all runs. The bonus factor β plays an essential role in obtaining this result. Namely, for $\beta = 0$ the policy gets trapped in local optima (i.e., the treasures T1 and T2 located near the initial position) and never discovers the true PF; see [14] for additional figures.

Results for FTN. Next, we report numerical results in the FTN environment with the depth parameter $d = 5, 6, 7$ in Table 2. For $d = 5$ and 6, our method was able to discover the true PF in all runs. For $d = 7$ our method discovered the true PF in 4 out of 5 runs. The mean score is hence very close to the highest possible HV for $d = 7$, which is 12302.34. We conclude that LC-MOPG solved all cases almost exactly. For $d = 7$ our score is 7.6% higher than the best baseline score (PD-MORL). However, we found that very careful tuning of the bonus parameter β, the latent dimension d_{lat}, and the hidden layer width of policy NN was necessary to attain this result.

Table 1. Comparison of methods in the DST environment (**Left:** convex version, **Right:** original version). Results for baselines are taken from [2,24,35]. Besides HV, the CRF1 score [35] (higher is better, the maximum is 1) is also shown for reference. Best values are marked with an asterisk

	CRF1 (↑)	**HV** (↑)
Envelope [35]	0.994	227.89
CN+DER [1]	0.989	—
PD-MORL [2]	1.0*	241.73*
LC-MOPG (Ours)	1.0*	241.73 ±0*

	HV (↑)
RA [21]	22437.40 ± 49.20
MO-NES [19]	17384.83 ± 6521.10
PCN [24]	22845.40 ± 19.20
LC-MOPG (Ours)	22855.0 ± 0*

Table 2. Comparison of methods in the FTN environment. Results for baselines are taken from [2]. Best values are marked with an asterisk

	HV (↑)		
	$d = 5$	$d = 6$	$d = 7$
Envelope [35]	6920.58*	8427.51	6395.27
PD-MORL [2]	6920.58*	9299.15	11419.58
LC-MOPG (Ours)	6920.58 ± 0*	9302.38 ± 0*	12290.93 ± 22.82*

Results for LQG. We conducted experiments in three cases: two-dimensional deterministic ($\sigma = 0$) LQG, two-dimensional stochastic ($\sigma = 1$) LQG, and three-dimensional deterministic ($\sigma = 0$) LQG. Due to the limitation of space, we relegate the results of the latter two cases to [14]. Our main results for the first case are summarized in Table 3. The optimal HV value is obtained by solving the Riccati equation. It is observed that LC-MOPG with $d_{\text{lat}} = 2$ attained the best score equal to 98.0% of the optimal HV. We have also tested LC-MOPG-V that uses the generalized value functions Q and V, and obtained the final score equal to 94.7% of the true HV. It is concluded that LC-MOPG was able to solve the problem accurately and that LC-MOPG outperformed LC-MOPG-V on this

Table 3. Comparison of methods in the two-dimensional deterministic LQG environment

	HV (↑)
Optimal value	1.1646
LC-MOPG ($d_{\text{lat}} = 1$)	1.1408 ± 0.0061
LC-MOPG ($d_{\text{lat}} = 2$)	1.1457 ± 0.0040
LC-MOPG ($d_{\text{lat}} = 3$)	1.1408 ± 0.0076
LC-MOPG-V ($d_{\text{lat}} = 2$)	1.1031 ± 0.0090

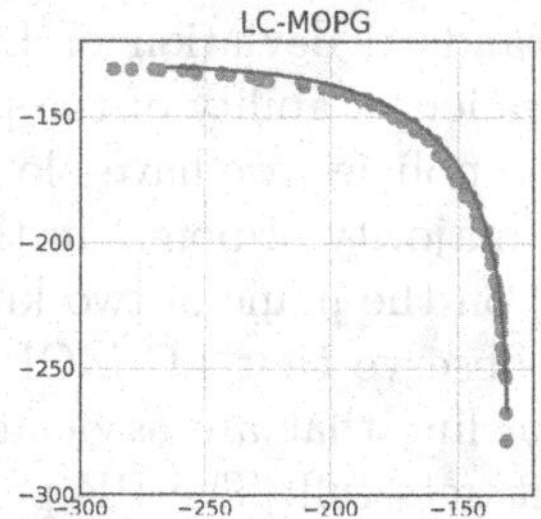

Fig. 5. The PF obtained with LC-MOPG in the two-dimensional LQG environment, overlayed with the optimal PF (red solid line)

problem. To visually inspect the approximate PF, we have randomly sampled 1000 latent variables, fed them into the trained policy network of LC-MOPG, obtained 1000 returns, and identified the PF. The result is shown in Fig. 5. The PF obtained by LC-MOPG is observed to lie in the close vicinity of the true PF. The convergence of the return set $\{\mathbf{G}_i\}_i$ towards the optimal PF during training is displayed in Fig. 6. The return set at iteration 25 is of low quality, but as the training progresses, the returns gradually move to the top-right area of the return space. At iteration 500 most returns cluster near the true PF.

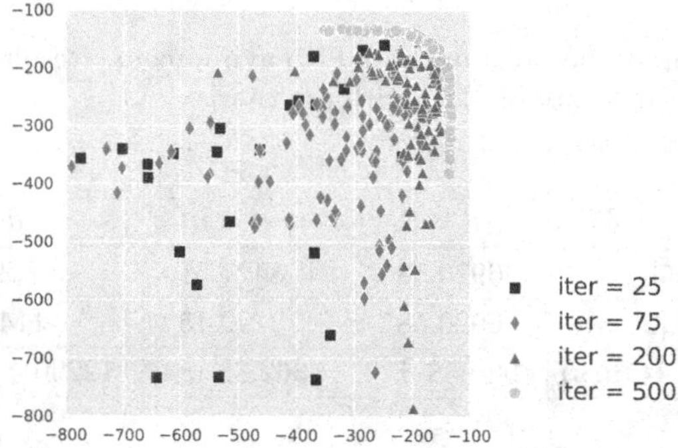

Fig. 6. Progression of the return set of LC-MOPG during training in the two-dimensional LQG environment. Some low-lying returns are out of the scope of this figure

Results for Minecart. Finally, we discuss numerical results in the Minecart environment. We have trained the agent of LC-MOPG using the hyperparameter values in [14]. The training with 5 random seeds took approximately 29 h. After training, we fed 2000 random latent variables to the policy network and evaluated the HV. The result is summarized in Table 4.

We observe that LC-MOPG outperformed all baselines in terms of HV. The attained score of LC-MOPG is close to that of PCN [24], but it is noteworthy that the standard deviation of LC-MOPG is less than half of that of PCN, indicating salient stability of the proposed approach. To gain more insight into the obtained policies, we have plotted the PF of LC-MOPG in Fig. 7. As shown in [24], the majority of points in the PF lie on the straight line between $(0, 1.5)$ and $(1.5, 0)$ on the plane of two kinds of mined ores because the cart's capacity is 1.5. We observe that LC-MOPG was able to discover all the 17 points on the diagonal line that are associated with trajectories in which the cart mines ores until it gets full. The PF point at the origin $(0, 0)$ is associated with an exceptionally short trajectory in which the cart departs home and then returns immediately, without ever reaching mines. The three isolated points below the diagonal represent trajectories in which the cart returns home before it gets full. Although ore1 and ore2 are symmetric in this environment, these three PF

Table 4. Comparison of methods in the Minecart environment. Results for baselines are taken from [24]. Best value is marked with an asterisk

	HV (↑)
RA [21]	123.92 ± 0.25
MO-NES [19]	123.81 ± 23.03
PCN [24]	197.56 ± 0.70
LC-MOPG (Ours)	$198.17 \pm 0.32^*$

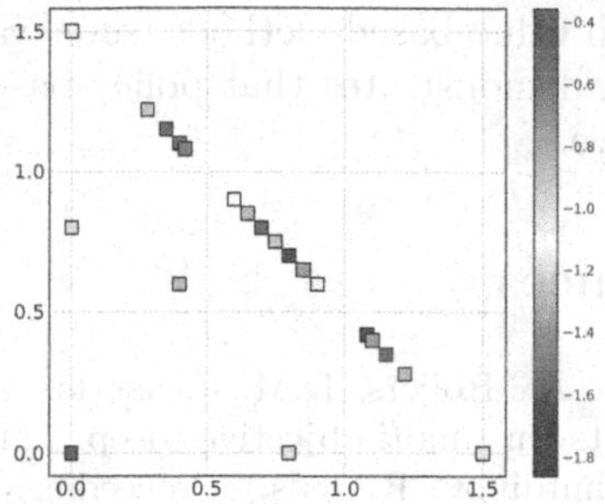

Fig. 7. The PF obtained by LC-MOPG projected onto the first two dimensions. The color of each point indicates the third component of the return

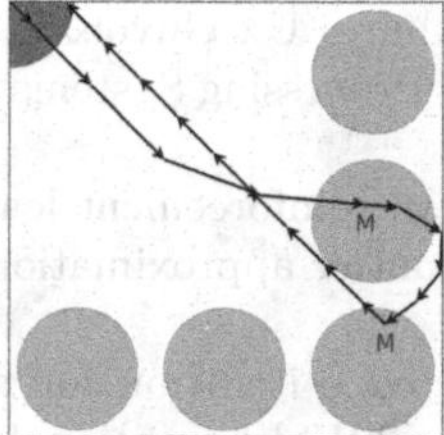

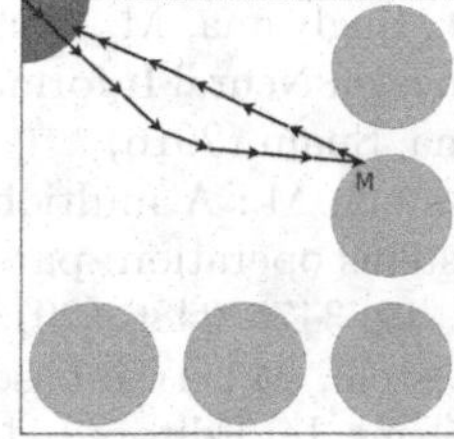

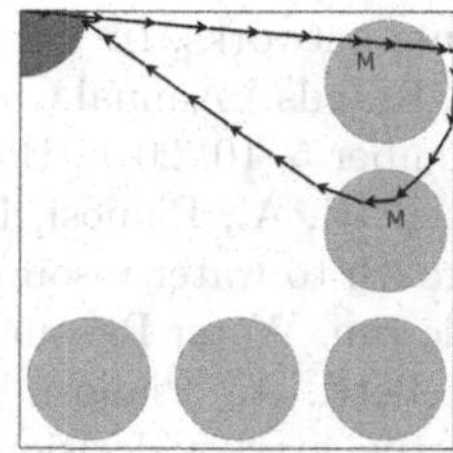

Fig. 8. Example trajectories in the Pareto set. All these trajectories were generated by the same policy network conditioned on different latent values. The symbol 'M' indicates that the agent mined ores at that point

points are not symmetric, which implies that a hidden fourth point at (0.6, 0.4) has been missed by our agent.

In Fig. 8 we present three example trajectories generated by the trained policy network. It is satisfactory to see that a single policy network can actually produce markedly different behaviors when it is conditioned on different values of the latent input.

7 Conclusions and Outlook

Optimal control problems in real life often involve multiple objectives that are hard to maximize simultaneously, such as the speed and safety in car driving. Single-objective RL is inadequate to solve such problems. In this work, we introduced LC-MOPG, an MORL algorithm that obtains infinitely many policies in a single run of training. It uses a latent-conditioned NN to learn diverse behaviors in a parameter-efficient way. It does not rely on linear scalarization and hence is capable of finding the concave part of the PF. In numerical experiments we confirmed that LC-MOPG performed on per with or even better than standard baselines from the MORL literature. While recent work on MORL predominantly focuses on value-based methods (some variants of Q learning) [1,2,5,6,18,25,35], our work demonstrates that policy-based methods still stand as a competitive alternative.

References

1. Abels, A., Roijers, D.M., Lenaerts, T., Nowé, A., Steckelmacher, D.: Dynamic weights in multi-objective deep reinforcement learning. In: Chaudhuri, K., Salakhutdinov, R. (eds.) Proceedings of the 36th International Conference on Machine Learning, ICML 2019, pp. 9–15 June 2019, California, USA (2019)
2. Basaklar, T., Gumussoy, S., Ogras, Ü.Y.: PD-MORL: preference-driven multi-objective reinforcement learning algorithm. CoRR abs/2208.07914 (2022)
3. Blank, J., Deb, K.: Pymoo: multi-objective optimization in python. IEEE Access **8**, 89497–89509 (2020)
4. Bouchacourt, D., Mudigonda, P.K., Nowozin, S.: DISCO Nets : dissimilarity coefficients networks. In: Lee, D.D., Sugiyama, M., von Luxburg, U., Guyon, I., Garnett, R. (eds.) Annual Conference on Neural Information Processing Systems 2016, December 5–10, 2016, Barcelona, Spain (2016)
5. Castelletti, A., Pianosi, F., Restelli, M.: A multiobjective reinforcement learning approach to water resourcessystems operation: pareto frontier approximation in a single run. Water Resour. Res. **49**, 3476–3486 (2013)
6. Castelletti, A., Pianosi, F., Restelli, M.: Tree-based fitted q-iteration for multi-objective markov decision problems. In: Editors (ed.) The 2012 International Joint Conference on Neural Networks (IJCNN), Brisbane, Australia, June 10–15, 2012. pp. 1–8. IEEE (2012)
7. Chen, X., Ghadirzadeh, A., Björkman, M., Jensfelt, P.: Meta-learning for multi-objective reinforcement learning. In: Editors (ed.) 2019 IEEE/RSJ International Conference on Intelligent Robots and Systems (IROS). pp. 977–983 (2019)
8. Dabney, W., Ostrovski, G., Silver, D., Munos, R.: Implicit quantile networks for distributional reinforcement learning. In: Dy, J.G., Krause, A. (eds.) Proceedings of the 35th International Conference on Machine Learning, ICML 2018, Stockholm, Sweden, July 10–15, 2018 (2018)
9. Das, I., Dennis, J.E.: A closer look at drawbacks of minimizing weighted sums of objectives for Pareto set generation in multicriteria optimization problems. Struct. Optim. **14**, 63–69 (1997)
10. Eysenbach, B., Gupta, A., Ibarz, J., Levine, S.: diversity is all you need: learning skills without a reward function. In: Editors (ed.) 7th International Conference on Learning Representations, ICLR 2019, New Orleans, LA, USA, May 6–9, 2019. OpenReview.net (2019)
11. Hayes, C.F., et al.: A practical guide to multi-objective reinforcement learning and planning. Auton. Agents Multi Agent Syst. **36**(1), 26 (2022)
12. Kanazawa, T.: (2023), www.github.com/TaTKSM/LCMOPG
13. Kanazawa, T., Gupta, C.: Sample-based uncertainty quantification with a single deterministic neural network. In: Bäck, T., van Stein, B., Wagner, C., Garibaldi, J.M., Lam, H.K., Cottrell, M., Doctor, F., Filipe, J., Warwick, K., Kacprzyk, J. (eds.) Proceedings of the 14th International Joint Conference on Computational Intelligence, IJCCI 2022, Valletta, Malta, October 24–26, 2022. pp. 292–304. SCITEPRESS (2022)

14. Kanazawa, T., Gupta, C.: Latent-conditioned policy gradient for multi-objective deep reinforcement learning. CoRR abs/2303.08909 (2023)
15. Liu, C., Xu, X., Hu, D.: Multiobjective reinforcement learning: a comprehensive overview. IEEE Trans. Syst. Man Cybern. Syst. **45**(3), 385–398 (2015)
16. Mnih, V., et al.: Human-level control through deep reinforcement learning. Nature **518**(7540), 529–533 (2015)
17. Moffaert, K.V., Nowé, A.: Multi-objective reinforcement learning using sets of pareto dominating policies. J. Mach. Learn. Res. **15**(1), 3483–3512 (2014)
18. Mossalam, H., Assael, Y.M., Roijers, D.M., Whiteson, S.: Multi-objective deep reinforcement learning. In: NIPS 2016 Workshop on Deep Reinforcement Learning, CoRR abs/1610.02707 (2016)
19. Parisi, S., Pirotta, M., Peters, J.: Manifold-based multi-objective policy search with sample reuse. Neurocomputing **263**, 3–14 (2017)
20. Parisi, S., Pirotta, M., Restelli, M.: Multi-objective Reinforcement Learning through continuous pareto manifold approximation. J. Artif. Intell. Res. **57**, 187–227 (2016)
21. Parisi, S., Pirotta, M., Smacchia, N., Bascetta, L., Restelli, M.: Policy gradient approaches for multi-objective sequential decision making. In: Editors (ed.) 2014 International Joint Conference on Neural Networks, IJCNN 2014, Beijing, China, July 6–11, 2014. pp. 2323–2330. IEEE (2014)
22. Pirotta, M., Parisi, S., Restelli, M.: Multi-Objective Reinforcement Learning with Continuous Pareto Frontier Approximation. In: Bonet, B., Koenig, S. (eds.) Proceedings of the Twenty-Ninth AAAI Conference on Artificial Intelligence, January 25–30, 2015, Austin, Texas, USA. pp. 2928–2934. AAAI Press (2015)
23. Reymond, M.: (2022), www.github.com/mathieu-reymond/pareto-conditioned-networks/tree/main/envs/minecart
24. Reymond, M., Bargiacchi, E., Nowé, A.: Pareto Conditioned Networks. In: Faliszewski, P., Mascardi, V., Pelachaud, C., Taylor, M.E. (eds.) 21st International Conference on Autonomous Agents and Multiagent Systems, AAMAS 2022, Auckland, New Zealand, May 9–13, 2022. pp. 1110–1118 (2022)
25. Reymond, M., Nowe, A.: Pareto-DQN: approximating the Pareto front in complex multi-objective decision problems. In: Editors (ed.) Proceedings of the Adaptive and Learning Agents Workshop 2019 (ALA-19) at AAMAS (2019)
26. Roijers, D.M., Vamplew, P., Whiteson, S., Dazeley, R.: A survey of multi-objective sequential decision-making. J. Artif. Intell. Res. **48**, 67–113 (2013)
27. Schmidhuber, J.: Reinforcement learning upside down: don't predict rewards - just map them to actions. CoRR abs/1912.02875 (2019)
28. Sutton, R.S., Barto, A.G.: Reinforcement learning: an introduction. MIT Press, second edn. (2018)
29. Vamplew, P., Dazeley, R., Berry, A., Issabekov, R., Dekker, E.: Empirical evaluation methods for multiobjective reinforcement learning algorithms. Mach. Learn. **84**(1–2), 51–80 (2011)
30. Vamplew, P., Yearwood, J., Dazeley, R., Berry, A.: On the Limitations of Scalarisation for Multi-objective Reinforcement Learning of Pareto Fronts. In: Wobcke, W., Zhang, M. (eds.) AI 2008: Advances in Artificial Intelligence, pp. 372–378. Springer, Berlin Heidelberg, Berlin, Heidelberg (2008)
31. Van Moffaert, K., Drugan, M.M., Nowé, A.: Scalarized multi-objective reinforcement learning: Novel design techniques. In: Editors (ed.) 2013 IEEE Symposium on Adaptive Dynamic Programming and Reinforcement Learning (ADPRL). pp. 191–199 (2013)

32. Williams, R.J.: Simple statistical gradient-following algorithms for connectionist reinforcement learning. Mach. Learn. **8**, 229–256 (1992)
33. Xu, J., Tian, Y., Ma, P., Rus, D., Sueda, S., Matusik, W.: Prediction-guided multi-objective reinforcement learning for continuous robot control. In: Proceedings of the 37th International Conference on Machine Learning, ICML 2020, pp. 13–18 July 2020 (2020)
34. Yang, R.: (2019), www.github.com/RunzheYang/MORL/blob/master/synthetic/envs/fruit_tree.py
35. Yang, R., Sun, X., Narasimhan, K.: A Generalized algorithm for multi-objective reinforcement learning and policy adaptation. In: Wallach, H.M., Larochelle, H., Beygelzimer, A., d'Alché-Buc, F., Fox, E.B., Garnett, R. (eds.) Annual Conference on Neural Information Processing Systems 2019, NeurIPS 2019, December 8–14, 2019, Vancouver, BC, Canada (2019)
36. Zitzler, E., Thiele, L.: Multiobjective evolutionary algorithms: a comparative case study and the strength Pareto approach. IEEE Trans. Evol. Comput. **3**(4), 257–271 (1999)
37. Zitzler, E., Thiele, L., Laumanns, M., Fonseca, C.M., da Fonseca, V.G.: Performance assessment of multiobjective optimizers: an analysis and review. IEEE Trans. Evol. Comput. **7**(2), 117–132 (2003)

LIIVSR: A Unidirectional Recurrent Video Super-Resolution Framework with Gaussian Detail Enhancement and Local Information Interaction Modules

Kaishan Lin and Jianping Luo(✉)

Guangdong Key Laboratory of Intelligent Information Processing, Shenzhen Key Laboratory of Media Security and Guangdong Laboratory of Artificial Intelligence and Digital Economy (SZ), Shenzhen University, Shenzhen, China
linkaishan2021@email.szu.edu.cn, ljp@szu.edu.cn

Abstract. The most popular methods for video super-resolution either rely on a time-sliding window approach to handle low-resolution frames, or utilize a recurrent structure that leverages previously estimated hidden features to recover the current frame. The existing methods do not make better use of initialization and local information. In this paper, we propose a video super-resolution (LIIVSR) framework with Gaussian detail enhancement and local information interaction modules. The proposed Gaussian detail enhancement module enhances the detail part of the hidden features to retain more motion details. To effectively utilize inter-frame local information, we propose a local information interaction module as a propagation framework. The information initialization module effectively extracts relevant information for video frames as the starting information for subsequent long-distance propagation. The multi-residual module obtains local forward and backward information from the coarse extraction of features. The local refinement module further interacts with features to extract fine local forward and backward information. Finally, this local information is used to derive the final super-resolution (SR) output. Our proposed LIIVSR framework achieves state-of-the-art performance on several benchmark datasets, outperforming existing methods in both speed and performance.

Keywords: Video super-resolution · Gaussian detail enhancement · Local information interaction · Information initialization

1 Introduction

The purpose of super-resolution is to generate high-resolution (HR) images from corresponding low-resolution (LR) images. Single image super-resolution [4,12,18] based on deep learning mainly relies on learning a large number of datasets

L. Iliadis et al. (Eds.): ICANN 2023, LNCS 14259, pp. 77–88, 2023.
https://doi.org/10.1007/978-3-031-44223-0_7

to obtain correlations within the image and similarity information between pixel blocks to generate high-resolution images.

In video super-resolution, there exists valuable spatio-temporal information between successive frames of the input. Several methods [17,20,22] attempt to extract temporal information by adopting explicit motion compensation. However, this approach can lead to significant image distortion, performance degradation, and increased model complexity. Moreover, this method is not applicable to many real-world scenarios. On the other hand, some methods [10,25] leverage motion information by implicit motion compensation. However, the implicit motion compensation module necessitates caching numerous video frames in advance, which is computationally intensive and results in more inter-frame redundant computations.

In recent years, in the pursuit of practicality and efficiency, many video super-resolution methods [2,3,6,7,9,17,24] have adopted a recurrent framework. This approach utilizes the output and hidden states of the previous frame as input information for the next frame to incorporate past temporal and spatial information. As a result, the framework can achieve video super-resolution with reduced processing time. Although the bidirectional recurrent framework can achieve better performance metrics, it is unsuitable for real-time or online tasks as it requires caching all video frames and consumes significant server resources. In contrast, the unidirectional recurrent framework is more efficient in solving real-time or online tasks with fewer resource requirements.

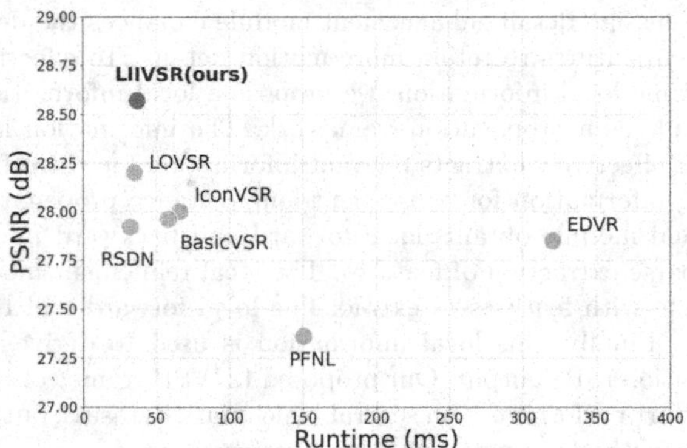

Fig. 1. Comparing the VSR performance of Vid4 in terms of PSNR and runtime, our proposed LIIVSR method achieves a highly competitive performance, surpassing other state-of-the-art models while maintaining efficiency

In this paper, we propose a unidirectional recurrent video super-resolution framework with Gaussian detail enhancement and local information interaction modules. The Gaussian detail enhancement module is introduced to enhance the detail edges of warp frames and retain more motion details. We employ a second-order network to continuously explore the potential spatio-temporal information between frames and design a local information interaction module as a propagation framework. The information initialization module extracts the feature information of video sequences as the starting information. The coarse local information is extracted in the first stage, and the fine local information is extracted in the second stage. The main contributions of this study can be summarized as follows:

(1) We propose a Gaussian detail enhancement module (GDEM) to enhance hidden features after motion compensation and learn more distinguishable image details, which is also important for long-range propagation.
(2) We propose an information initialization module (IIM) to obtain relevant feature information by first feature extraction of video frame sequences, which can be used as the starting information for subsequent long-distance recurrent propagation and can better guide the recovery of video pre-frames.
(3) We propose a video super-resolution (LIIVSR) framework with Gaussian detail enhancement and local information interaction modules. Experimental results show that LIIVSR significantly surpasses existing state-of-the-art, including BasicVSR, IconVSR and LOVSR, while maintaining high efficiency, as shown in Fig. 1.

2 Related Work

The rapid development of deep learning has triggered extensive research in super-resolution, with single image super-resolution techniques benefiting greatly from this progress. SRCNN [4] was the first to propose the reconstruction of HR images from LR images using convolutional neural networks. Since then, many frameworks have emerged, including ESPCN [18], which proposed sub-pixel convolutional modules as an efficient reconstruction method, and VDSR [12], which proposed super-resolution networks with residual structures. More image super-resolution algorithms can be obtained from [23].

The key to video super-resolution is to recover the current frame by leveraging the information from previous and adjacent frames. Moreover, video super-resolution can be classified into two categories according to their network frames: sliding frames and recurrent frames. Among them, VSRnet [11] can improve the reconstruction quality by jointly processing multiple input frames. VESPCN [1] is the first end-to-end video super-resolution algorithm for training optical flow estimation and motion compensation. DUF [10] proposed a 3D convolutional layer with dynamic upsampling filters as the core part of the network as implicit motion compensation. EDVR [21] proposed pyramidal, cascaded, and deformable (PCD) alignment module and temporal attention fusion module (TSA). PFNL [25] proposed a progressive fusion network with non-local correlation extraction. TGA [8] proposed group based on inter-frame distances and performed inter-group fusion using 2D and 3D convolution modules. However, all these methods have the drawback of extremely slow running time. For recurrent methods, FRVSR [17] proposed a recurrent framework that can propagate information across a large number of frames without increasing the computational effort. RLSP [5] presented a method to recover frames by utilizing two consecutive frames and hidden information. Although it has a simple model and fast speed, its performance is suboptimal. RRN [9] used residual blocks for information transmission. RSDN [6] proposed a dual-branch recurrent framework that utilizes details and structure to enhance the robustness of the model. All those methods suffered from the inability to fully leverage the information contained in subsequent frames, leading to limited performance. BasicVSR, IconVSR and BasicVSR++ [2,3] proposed a bidirectional recurrent propagation framework that iteratively refined the features to improve their expressiveness. However, bidirectional recurrent does not apply to the real-time online situation. It required caching all frames to complete the bidirectional situation, which consumed many resources, although the performance was good. LOVSR [24] combined the non-local progressive fusion module initiated by PFNL [25] and proposed a universal framework. However, it is worth mentioning that the model was trained on a dataset that is not commonly used in the field. ETDM [7] was used to model the temporal differences between adjacent time steps to pass the intermediate SR information from the past and future to the current time frame. A back-and-forth refinement module was proposed in ETDM [7], and inspired by this, we use a local refinement module to improve the model's performance.

3 Method

3.1 Overview

In this section, we first introduce the overall framework of LIIVSR, as shown in Fig. 2. Given a sequence of low-resolution frames $I_{t:t+n}^{LR} \in \mathbb{R}^{H\times W\times C}$, at each time step, three consecutive frames and hidden features are received, and the network adopts a unidirectional recurrent structure with the output I^{HR}.

Specifically, the preliminary $I_j^{LR}(j = 0, 1, \cdots, k; k \leq n)$ is first used as the input of the information initialization module (IIM) to extract the initially hidden features and initial recovery frames required for subsequent long-range recurrent propagation. A Gaussian Detail Enhancement Module (GDEM) is added to the motion compensation section to sharpen and enhance the warp frames, trying to recover the lost details and enhance the edge detail information. Then, the Local Information Interaction Module (LIIM) takes the output of the IIM as the initial information. The initial information, hidden features, and three consecutive frames are input to LIIM. The Multiple Residuals Module (MRBM) performs coarse extraction to get the coarse local information. After sending the coarse local information to the Local Refinement Module (LRM), the fine local information is generated. The fine local information and the previously estimated SR results are reconstructed using sub-pixel upsampling to derive the final SR output. We also introduce the specific details of each module in the subsequent subsections.

3.2 Gaussian Detail Enhancement Module

In video super-resolution tasks, motion compensation modules are often used to process adjacent frames and align them with the target frame. However, due to the recurrent nature of the structure, the details in the hidden features are

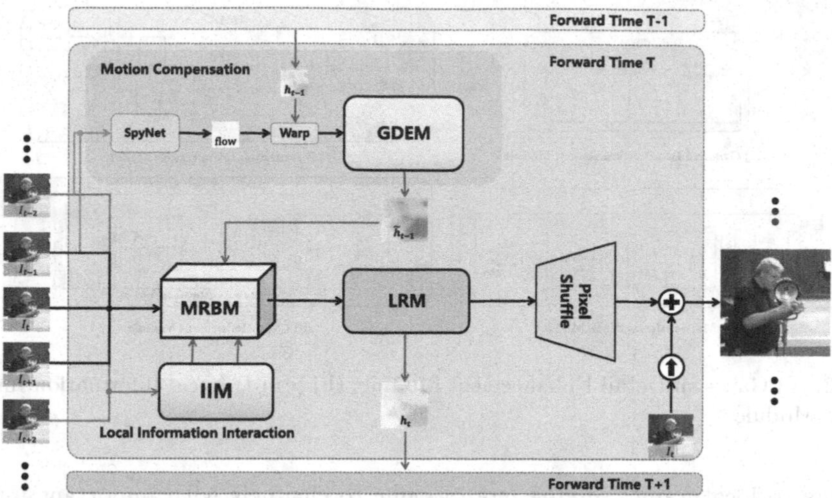

Fig. 2. The overall framework of the proposed LIIVSR method. The framework performs VSR in a unidirectional manner. Green, black, and blue arrows indicate motion compensation, local information interaction, and information initialization, respectively (Color figure online)

prone to loss or blur during the continuous expansion of the time step. These details play a crucial role in recovering the current frame. Therefore, we design a Gaussian Detail Enhancement Module (GDEM) that follows the motion compensation module, as shown in Fig. 3(a). This module helps the model capture more detailed information, thus learning more sophisticated texture information.

A suitable Gaussian kernel is constructed by adjusting the standard deviation σ of the Gaussian distribution and the convolution kernel ks. The Gaussian kernel GF_{2d} is convolved with the output being hidden feature image $\tilde{h}_t$ after motion compensation. The output result is subtracted from the input image $\tilde{h}_t$ to obtain the image enhancement result $\tilde{h}_{GDEM}$. Finally, the desired detail-enhanced hidden feature $\tilde{h}_t$ is obtained using the residual enhancement method.

$$f_{GS} = \tilde{h}_t - GF_{2d}(\sigma, ks) * \tilde{h}_t \tag{1}$$

$$\tilde{h}_{GDEM} = \alpha * f_{GS}(\tilde{h}_t, \sigma, ks) \tag{2}$$

where f_{GS} is the Gaussian smoothing, the GF_{2d} is the Gaussian kernel, σ is the standard deviation, which is usually set to 1.5, ks is the convolution kernel size, which is usually set to 3, and α is the enhancement factor.

3.3 Local Information Interaction Module

Information Initialization Module. To achieve the information initialization phase of the local information interaction module, we introduce an Information Initialization Module (IIM), shown in Fig. 3(b). When processing video frames within a local time step I_j^{LR}, we utilize an SE attention module to assign

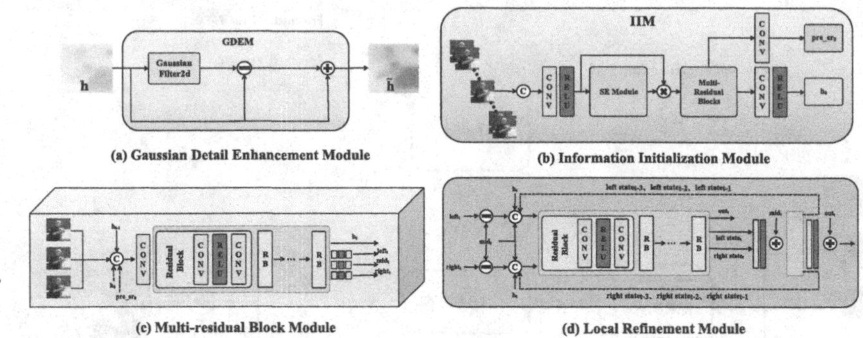

Fig. 3. (a) Gaussian Detail Enhancement Module. (b) (c) (d) Local Information Interaction Module

weights to local frames, giving more weight to channels with important information and reducing redundant information between features. Features filtered by the SE attention module are convolved multiple times using a multi-residual block, enabling the model to learn deeper features. Subsequently, the required initialization information for the recurrent frame is output through a convolution layer and ReLU activation function as h_0 and pre_sr_0 respectively, serving as initialization auxiliary information.

$$\tilde{h_0} = ReLU \left\{ \text{Conv} \left[Concat \left(I_j^{LR} \right) \right] \right\} \tag{3}$$

$$h_0, \text{pre\_sr}_0 = MRB \left[\tilde{h_0} * \text{SE} \left(\tilde{h_0} \right) \right] \tag{4}$$

where the SE attention module first squeezes the input feature map and then applies adaptive recalibration to enhance the network's focus on important features. Specifically, the module applies adaptive average pooling to the input feature map, reducing its dimensions from $C \times H \times W$ to $C \times 1 \times 1$. This compressed feature map represents the weights of global information. Next, two convolutional layers expand the feature map dimensions back to $C \times H \times W$ and activate the feature channels. Finally, the weight matrix is multiplied by the feature map. The MRB extracts deep features from the weight-enhanced feature map using 16 residual blocks and outputs the initialization information.

Multi-residual Block Module. Figure 3(c) shows the main function of the coarse feature extraction module in the local information interaction module. It takes three consecutive frames I_{t-1}, I_t, I_{t+1} as input, concatenated with the hidden feature h_{t-1} from the previous step. Multiple residual blocks perform coarse extraction of concatenate features, and four paths are utilized as output paths. The output paths are hidden feature h_t, local forward information $left_t$, local backward information $right_t$, and keyframe information mid_t, respectively. The same output can generate feature channels with different features by different paths, which can distinguish the difference between local information and keyframe more effectively. The whole procedure is formulated as:

$$h_t, left_t, mid_t, right_t = MRBM\left(h_{t-1}, I_{t-1}^{LR}, I_t^{LR}, I_{t+1}^{LR}\right) \tag{5}$$

where $MRBM$ consists of three main parts: feature adjustment, multi-level feature extraction, and feature output, and its model parameters are initialized before each recurrent. Specifically, all features are concatenated and the dimension of features is adjusted by 2 residual blocks. Then, 16 residual blocks are employed for multi-level feature extraction to output hidden features. Finally, feature output generates feature channels $(S \times S \times 3) \times H \times W$ with different characteristics by utilizing four different convolutional layers and non-linear activation paths. Here, S represents the upscaling factor. If it is the initialization phase, the hidden feature is the output of the information initialization module.

Local Refinement Module. In this paper, we adopt the local refinement module as the feature refinement extraction module of the local information interaction module, as shown in Fig. 3(d). This module has the ability to cache the state information of local video frames. The LRM module updates the local information generated by each time step and uses a cache state buffer to store the local information. The buffer follows a first-in-first-out principle for updates. Currently, our model stores three states at a time, and the oldest state is removed by updating the remaining states. Multiple residual blocks are utilized to continuously refine the output by caching multiple time steps of local information states. The final video super-resolution image is generated by adding the sub-pixel convolutional layer and bicubic interpolation. The whole procedure is formulated as:

$$left\_state_t, out_t = f_{LRM}\left\{\text{Concat}\left[(mid_t - left_t), mid_t, h_t, left\_buffer\right]\right\} \tag{6}$$

$$left\_buffer = append\left(left\_state_t\right) \tag{7}$$

where f_{LRM} consists of 8 residual blocks, several convolutional layers, and activation functions, which refine the output out_t. Taking the local forward channel as an example, $mid_t - left_t$ mainly captures the temporal difference information of the current time step. $left\_buffer$ accumulates the local forward states of the previous three-time steps, $left\_state_{t-3}$, $left\_state_{t-2}$, $left\_state_{t-1}$. Similarly, we can obtain the status update and caching of the local backward information.

3.4 Loss Function

During training, we calculate the coarse extraction loss $\mathcal{L}_t^{mid}$ and the fine extraction loss $\mathcal{L}_t^{SR}$, which are then subtracted from the ground-truth $\mathcal{L}_t^{GT}$ to obtain the reconstruction loss. The results are used as the reconstruction loss. Furthermore, the model is indirectly supervised using the local forward information loss $\mathcal{L}_t^{left}$ and the local backward information loss $\mathcal{L}_t^{right}$.

$$\mathcal{L}_t^{left} = \sqrt{\|left\_state_t^{GT} - left\_state_t\|^2 + \varepsilon^2} \tag{8}$$

$$\mathcal{L}_t^{\text{mid}} = \sqrt{\|\text{I}_t^{GT} - \text{mid}_t\|^2 + \varepsilon^2} \tag{9}$$

$$\mathcal{L}_t^{\text{SR}} = \sqrt{\|\text{I}_t^{GT} - \text{out}_t\|^2 + \varepsilon^2} \tag{10}$$

where ε is set to 1×10^{-3}. The loss function is adjusted by a certain weighting factor, and the total loss $\mathcal{L}$ is calculated as follows.

$$\mathcal{L} = 0.5 * \mathcal{L}_t^{\text{left}} + 0.5 * \mathcal{L}_t^{\text{right}} + 0.5 * \mathcal{L}_t^{\text{mid}} + \mathcal{L}_t^{\text{SR}} \tag{11}$$

4 Experiments

4.1 Datasets

In this work, our model is trained on the Vimeo-90K [22] dataset. In the training process, we randomly crop a patch region of size 256×256 from the high-resolution video sequence as the target, apply $\sigma = 1.6$ of Gaussian blur, and then perform downsampling with a scale factor of 4 to obtain the corresponding low-resolution patch of 64×64. In the testing process, we use test datasets with Vid4 [14], SPMCS [19], and Vimeo-90K-T [22] to evaluate in terms of PSNR and SSIM on the Y channel of YCbCr space.

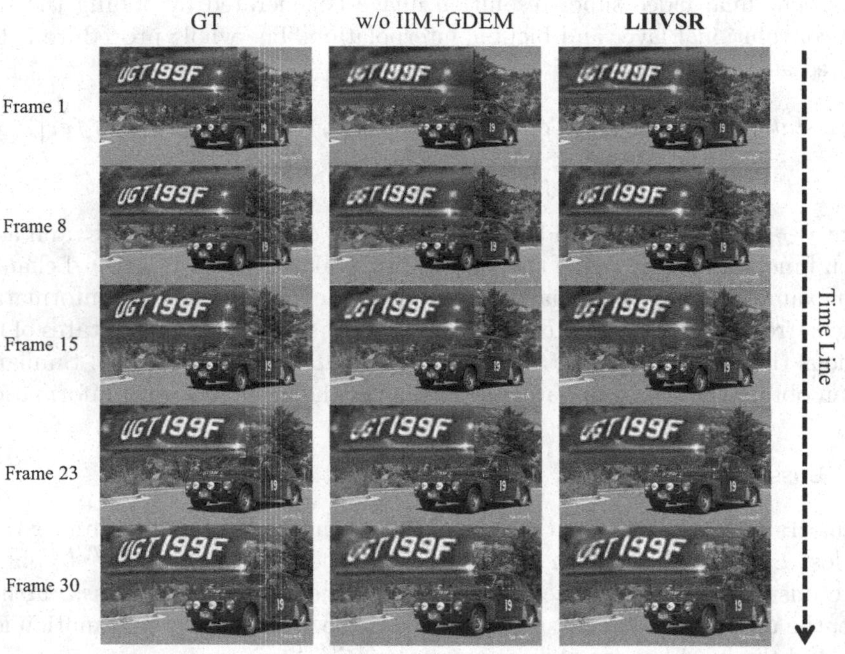

Fig. 4. Shows the visual enhancement of the SPMCS test set video sequence through the timeline, zoom in for better visualization

Table 1. Component ablation study. Each component significantly improved PSNR and validated its effectiveness

	Model A	Model B	Model C	**LIIVSR**
Baseline Frame	✓	✓	✓	✓
Gaussian Detail Enhancement Module		✓		✓
Information Initialization Module			✓	✓
PSNR(dB)	28.25	28.32	28.45	28.57

4.2 Implementation Details

The proposed LIIVSR adopts the Adam optimizer [13] and a cosine annealing scheme [15]. We adopt a pre-trained SpyNet [16] as our optical flow network for the spatial alignment of features with an initial learning rate of 2.5×10^{-5}. The number of convolution channels of the main network is 96, and the initial learning rate is 1×10^{-4}. The total number of Epochs is 150. A Charbonnier loss function is used, which can better supervise the model. To effectively enhance the robustness of the model, we use RGB channel random flipping, video frame rotation, and video frame sequence random reversal operations to enhance the data. All experiments are conducted on a server with Python 3.8.15, Pytorch 1.7.1 and NVIDIA GTX 2080TI GPU.

4.3 Ablation Study

In this section, we conduct an experimental ablation study to analyze the components of the LIIVSR framework.

By adding the GDEM module, as shown in Table 1, the method achieves a higher PSNR on the Vid4 test set with an improvement of 0.07 dB, demonstrating the method's superiority. Since the recurrent framework ensures that more useful information is received, the further the video frames are accumulated, the better the image is recovered. However, if too much useless information is accumulated, it can lead to a less accurate orientation of the model to learn features. Therefore, we investigate a module that helps the model maintain a more accurate learning direction. The information initialization module can perform aggregation and feature extraction of local information and play a crucial role in the local information interaction module. As shown in Table 1, by adding the information initialization module, the method achieves an improvement of 0.2 dB in PSNR, which proves the effectiveness of the method.

To improve the model's performance, we add the SE channel attention mechanism to the information initialization module. Since the information initialization module is run only once, the running time is unaffected even though the number of parameters increases. As shown in Fig. 4, after adding the information initialization module and the Gaussian detail enhancement module, our model LIIVSR can produce finer details and more pronounced edges, recovering a better visual effect.

Table 2. Quantitative comparison of Vid4, SPMCS, and Vimeo-90K-T (PSNR and SSIM). Red text indicates the best and the blue text indicates the suboptimal performance. Runtime is calculated from Vid4 images. 'Uni' and 'Bi' denote unidirectional and bidirectional, respectively

Method	#Frame	Runtime(ms)	Vid4	SPMCS	Vimeo-90K-T
Bicubic	1	-	21.82/0.5426	23.29/0.6385	31.30/0.8687
PFNL	7	150	27.36/0.8385	30.02/0.8804	-
EDVR	7	320	27.85/0.8503	-	-
RSDN	Uni	32	27.92/0.8505	30.14/0.8811	37.23/0.9471
BasicVSR	Bi	58	27.96/0.8553	-	37.53/0.9498
IconVSR	Bi	66	28.00/0.8570	-	37.84/0.9524
LOVSR	Uni	35	28.20/0.8612	30.34/0.8981	-
LIIVSR(ours)	Uni	37	28.57/0.8618	30.38/0.8982	37.70/0.9512

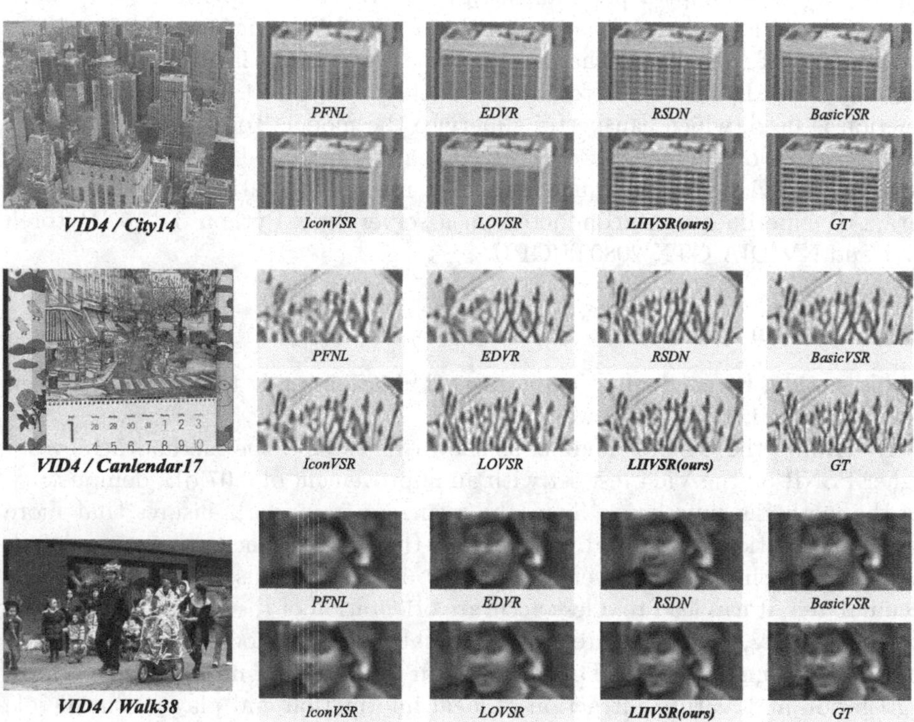

Fig. 5. Qualitative comparison of the Vid4, zoom in for better visualization

4.4 Comparisons with State-of-the-Art Methods

In this section, we compare our method with six models and the quantitative results are shown in Table 2. LIIVSR performs better than other models on the Vid4 and SPMCS datasets, achieving better performance with faster runtime. Specifically, LIIVSR outperforms LOVSR on the Vid4 test set with nearly identical runtime and higher PSNR by 0.37dB. Compared to the previous state-of-the-art IconVSR, LIIVSR runs almost 30 milliseconds faster and gains 0.57dB. This gain is considered important in VSR.

Figure 5 shows a qualitative comparison, in which our method produces higher-quality images. For example, only LIIVSR successfully recovers the clear building structure in Fig. 5. In addition, the outlines of branches, edges of roofs, and details of faces are also more successfully restored.

5 Conclusion

In this work, we propose LIIVSR, a novel unidirectional recurrent video super-resolution framework, that leverages Gaussian detail enhancement and local interaction modules to effectively recover more details of video frames. Through comprehensive experiments and evaluations on various benchmark datasets, we demonstrate that our approach outperforms other state-of-the-art VSR methods in both qualitative and quantitative assessments.

References

1. Caballero, J., et al.: Real-time video super-resolution with spatio-temporal networks and motion compensation. In: Proceedings of the IEEE Conference on Computer Vision and Pattern Recognition, pp. 4778–4787 (2017)
2. Chan, K.C., Wang, X., Yu, K., Dong, C., Loy, C.C.: BasicVSR: the search for essential components in video super-resolution and beyond. In: Proceedings of the IEEE/CVF Conference on Computer Vision and Pattern Recognition, pp. 4947–4956 (2021)
3. Chan, K.C., Zhou, S., Xu, X., Loy, C.C.: BasicVSR++: improving video super-resolution with enhanced propagation and alignment. In: Proceedings of the IEEE/CVF Conference on Computer Vision and Pattern Recognition, pp. 5972–5981 (2022)
4. Dong, C., Loy, C.C., He, K., Tang, X.: Image super-resolution using deep convolutional networks. IEEE Trans. Pattern Anal. Mach. Intell. **38**(2), 295–307 (2015)
5. Fuoli, D., Gu, S., Timofte, R.: Efficient video super-resolution through recurrent latent space propagation. In: 2019 IEEE/CVF International Conference on Computer Vision Workshop (ICCVW), pp. 3476–3485. IEEE (2019)
6. Isobe, T., Jia, X., Gu, S., Li, S., Wang, S., Tian, Q.: Video super-resolution with recurrent structure-detail network. In: Vedaldi, A., Bischof, H., Brox, T., Frahm, J.-M. (eds.) ECCV 2020. LNCS, vol. 12357, pp. 645–660. Springer, Cham (2020). https://doi.org/10.1007/978-3-030-58610-2_38
7. Isobe, T., et al.: Look back and forth: video super-resolution with explicit temporal difference modeling. In: Proceedings of the IEEE/CVF Conference on Computer Vision and Pattern Recognition, pp. 17411–17420 (2022)
8. Isobe, T., et al.: Video super-resolution with temporal group attention. In: Proceedings of the IEEE/CVF Conference on Computer Vision and Pattern Recognition, pp. 8008–8017 (2020)
9. Isobe, T., Zhu, F., Jia, X., Wang, S.: Revisiting temporal modeling for video super-resolution. arXiv preprint arXiv:2008.05765 (2020)

10. Jo, Y., Oh, S.W., Kang, J., Kim, S.J.: Deep video super-resolution network using dynamic upsampling filters without explicit motion compensation. In: Proceedings of the IEEE Conference on Computer Vision and Pattern Recognition, pp. 3224–3232 (2018)
11. Kappeler, A., Yoo, S., Dai, Q., Katsaggelos, A.K.: Video super-resolution with convolutional neural networks. IEEE Trans. Comput. Imaging **2**(2), 109–122 (2016)
12. Kim, J., Lee, J.K., Lee, K.M.: Accurate image super-resolution using very deep convolutional networks. In: Proceedings of the IEEE Conference on Computer Vision and Pattern Recognition, pp. 1646–1654 (2016)
13. Kingma, D.P., Ba, J.: Adam: a method for stochastic optimization. arXiv preprint arXiv:1412.6980 (2014)
14. Liu, C., Sun, D.: On Bayesian adaptive video super resolution. IEEE Trans. Pattern Anal. Mach. Intell. **36**(2), 346–360 (2013)
15. Loshchilov, I., Hutter, F.: SGDR: stochastic gradient descent with warm restarts. arXiv preprint arXiv:1608.03983 (2016)
16. Ranjan, A., Black, M.J.: Optical flow estimation using a spatial pyramid network. In: Proceedings of the IEEE Conference on Computer Vision and Pattern Recognition, pp. 4161–4170 (2017)
17. Sajjadi, M.S., Vemulapalli, R., Brown, M.: Frame-recurrent video super-resolution. In: Proceedings of the IEEE Conference on Computer Vision and Pattern Recognition, pp. 6626–6634 (2018)
18. Shi, W., et al.: Real-time single image and video super-resolution using an efficient sub-pixel convolutional neural network. In: Proceedings of the IEEE Conference on Computer Vision and Pattern Recognition, pp. 1874–1883 (2016)
19. Tao, X., Gao, H., Liao, R., Wang, J., Jia, J.: Detail-revealing deep video super-resolution. In: Proceedings of the IEEE International Conference on Computer Vision, pp. 4472–4480 (2017)
20. Wang, L., Guo, Y., Lin, Z., Deng, X., An, W.: Learning for video super-resolution through HR optical flow estimation. In: Jawahar, C.V., Li, H., Mori, G., Schindler, K. (eds.) ACCV 2018. LNCS, vol. 11361, pp. 514–529. Springer, Cham (2019). https://doi.org/10.1007/978-3-030-20887-5_32
21. Wang, X., Chan, K.C., Yu, K., Dong, C., Change Loy, C.: EDVR: video restoration with enhanced deformable convolutional networks. In: Proceedings of the IEEE/CVF Conference on Computer Vision and Pattern Recognition Workshops (2019)
22. Xue, T., Chen, B., Wu, J., Wei, D., Freeman, W.T.: Video enhancement with task-oriented flow. Int. J. Comput. Vision **127**, 1106–1125 (2019)
23. Yang, W., Zhang, X., Tian, Y., Wang, W., Xue, J.H., Liao, Q.: Deep learning for single image super-resolution: a brief review. IEEE Trans. Multimedia **21**(12), 3106–3121 (2019)
24. Yi, P., et al.: Omniscient video super-resolution. In: Proceedings of the IEEE/CVF International Conference on Computer Vision, pp. 4429–4438 (2021)
25. Yi, P., Wang, Z., Jiang, K., Jiang, J., Ma, J.: Progressive fusion video super-resolution network via exploiting non-local spatio-temporal correlations. In: Proceedings of the IEEE/CVF International Conference on Computer Vision, pp. 3106–3115 (2019)

Masked Scale-Recurrent Network for Incomplete Blurred Image Restoration

Jingzhou Zhu(✉), Wentao Chao, and Dong Yang

School of Artificial Intelligence, Beijing Normal University, Beijing, China
{zhujz,chaowentao,yd}@mail.bnu.edu.cn

Abstract. Muilti-scale learning has been demonstrated to be an excellent deblurring approach in image restoration according to recent studies. It makes the optimization of the function easier to achieve the global optimum. In order to restore an image that is both incomplete and blurry, we propose a Masked Scale-Recurrent Network (MSRN) in this paper, a restoration method based on multi-scale learning and an asymmetric autoencoder. It implements restoration in an end-to-end manner without any prior knowledge or other given conditions. Firstly, we process the GoPro dataset and obtain a dataset of incomplete images. And then, we perform a self-supervised reconstruction pre-training on the autoencoder, with a series of resblocks that increase the quality of the input image and improve the representation learning in the latent space. Finally, on the processed data, we train the model and finish the adjustment of the entire network. Compared with classical multi-scale learning, we introduce masks to help the model train more efficiently by focusing on essential regions of the image. It is also shown that MSRN has successful image restoration capability as well as robustness, as demonstrated in our experiments.

Keywords: image restoration · masked autoencoder · residual network · scale-recurrent network · multi-scale learning

1 Introduction

Image restoration technology is a vital component in image processing, where the input image may contain various interference. In this article, we will propose a new restoration method for incomplete blurred images. Additionally, this method can also be applied to blurry images with severe local damage. Extremely severe image interference is essentially worthless and does not contribute to image restoration or even worse. Therefore, interference that cannot be recovered by existing methods can be deleted directly and only the blurred images that can be restored should be retained. All images with irreversible interference or severe data loss should be converted into incomplete blurred images, unifying the format of the input pictures. When the input formats are unified, the first section of our task-incomplete blurry image restoration-is to reconstruct the images.

L. Iliadis et al. (Eds.): ICANN 2023, LNCS 14259, pp. 89–102, 2023.
https://doi.org/10.1007/978-3-031-44223-0_8

Image reconstruction, also known as inpainting, is a classic problem in computer vision. Popular approaches for image inpainting include foreground-aware image inpainting [2] and pluralistic image completion [4]. However, these methods have limitations when the missing parts are too large, or there is not enough labeled data. Recently, Alexey Dosovitskiy et al. [5] applied Transformer [6] from natural language processing (NLP) to computer vision (CV), opening up new possibilities for Transformer in this field. Among them, the mask reconstruction technique represented by MAE [8] (CV) and BEiT [10] (NLP) is a self-supervised training method that can effectively address the need for labeled data. The image mask reconstruction model MAE is an autoencoder with ViT [5] as its backbone. Its training efficiency is significantly higher than a simple ViT model, and its generalization ability is competitive in image reconstruction tasks.

The second section of the task is deblurring. Researchers in various fields have been conducting in-depth research to restore blurred or defocused [1] images to clear images as much as possible. The goal is to recover various details that should exist in a sharp image and facilitate subsequent picture processing. In the past five years, some methods, including conditional methods, have achieved quite remarkable results [3,9,12,15,16,18,20,21,25]. However, blurry images are usually accompanied by irreversible distortion, large-scale dense interference, and data loss due to various factors. This means the input image may change from a simple blurred image to a blurred image with several other interference, and in the worst case, it may become an incomplete blurred image. Therefore, common image restoration algorithms may only play a limited role in such circumstances. Among these algorithms, the multi-scale learning network is easy to expand and has a simple framework with a comparatively small number of parameters, making it easier to train. Therefore, we use SRN [3], which is designed based on scale-recurrent structure, as the backbone of our network and extend SRN to make the entire network more suitable for the restoration task of incomplete blurred images.

Based on the analysis above, we propose a new masked scale-recurrent network (MSRN), which is based on MAE and SRN. This network utilizes the visual representation learning ability of MAE for image reconstruction and exploits SRN's multi-scale recurrent network for fuzzy image restoration. On this basis, to adapt MSRN to new learning tasks, we have made the following three contributions:

Deep MAE. We introduce a deep masked autoencoder (DMAE) which puts a series of resblocks [22] in front of the autoencoder to preprocess the input image, resulting in a more accurate latent representation of images. This allows the autoencoder to reconstruct more valuable information on the missing parts of images for deblurring.

A New Scaling Method. We propose a new scaling method that adds a new learning scale and utilizes masks in scaling images. This approach forces the model to learn more accurate feature representation compared to training with complete photos at different scales and ensures that images learned at different scales do not exhibit pixel distortion.

Shortcut Connection. We build a shortcut connection between DMAE and SRN, which shares the position of invisible patches with the multi-scale network. With this connection, SRN learns more about the location of incomplete parts and achieves better performance in restoring those patches restored by DMAE.

2 Related Work

In this section, we will recap the background of image restoration concisely and briefly introduce related structures including their basic concepts and characteristics.

2.1 Image Deblurring

Image blur can be divided into motion blur, defocus blur, Gaussian blur, and mixed blur. Image deblurring with known fuzzy kernels is called non-blind image deblurring. The image whose fuzzy kernel is unknown is called blind image deblurring. The deep learning neural network based deblurring method, which is also a commonly used approach nowadays, has achieved quite good results on complex images with multiple unknown fuzzy kernels. After the publication of using deep learning networks to predict the direction and width of blur for deblurring [7], Su et al. [11] proposed a deep learning method for video deblurring, which uses an autoencoder with shortcut connections. Furthermore, the deep multi-scale network proposed by Nah et al. [23] obtained fruitful achievement in deblurring tasks.

In multi-scale deblurring networks, the scale-recurrent network (SRN) proposed by Tao et al. [3] is simpler and has fewer parameters. Compared to [23], it is easier to train while achieving better results. SRN is inspired by the very successful "coarse-to-fine" scheme for single-image deblurring. The input is a series of images sampled from the original image at different scales and the corresponding network outputs a intermediate image according to the given resized image. Next, the upsampled processed image and the image from the next scale are given to the network of the next scale. At the same time, there is a channel between different scales transferring hidden parameters to other scales. It is used to share implicit state parameters with other scale networks to improve convergence performance. It is precisely because of this that the total number of parameters can be significantly reduced. SRN can be described as:

$$I^i, h^i = SRN(B^i, UP(I^{i+1}), UP(h^{i+1}); \theta_{SRN}) \tag{1}$$

where i represents the index of different scales. B^i and I^i are blurry images and intermediate images at i scale. h^i is hidden state features at the i-th scale. UP is the operation that upsamples or converts input from $i+1$ to i scale. θ_{SRN} is other parameters of SRN.

Each scale's network of SRN uses a symmetric CNN architecture with skip-connections. Similar to U-net [19], the first half of the network gradually converts the input i-th scale image into latent spatial features with smaller resolution and multiple channels. The second half of the network gradually restores the features to the original i-th scale image. Encoder and decoder of the same scale are connected by a channel, which also can accelerate convergence. Based on [22,23], SRN employs ResBlocks and adds several ResBlocks between the encoding and decoding convolution layers. The loss function applied by SRN is the simple Euclidean loss and has achieved sufficiently good qualitative and quantitative results.

2.2 Image Inpainting

Image inpainting is to restore the damaged part of the image by algorithms and keep the restoration as consistent as possible with the original image. Image inpainting is not only a crucial task in computer vision but also a basic task for other subsequent processing of images. Classical image inpainting includes inpainting methods based on partial differential equations [34] and samples [32], but they usually consume a lot of computing time and have limited recovery effects. Later, with the success of deep learning in image processing, researchers tried to introduce different deep networks to achieve inpainting and proposed a large number of methods for inpainting such as autoencoder, U-Net [19], GAN [33], and Transformer [6]. Numerous experiments have shown that these methods have achieved better performance than traditional methods in inpainting.

2.3 CNN/Transformer for Image Processing

In deep learning networks, as the depth increases, the network becomes more difficult to train [17]. ResNet [22] makes training for deep networks much easier than before. It reconstructs the network and learns residual functions with reference from the output of the former layer during learning. Specifically, it creates a shortcut from input to output. This simple but effective approach prevents the model from gradient disappearing when the network is deep.

The masked autoencoder designed by He et al. [8] is a more general denoising autoencoder [14]. It is self-supervised and has two core innovations on the basis of ViT-Large/-Huge [5]. The first one is the asymmetric encoder-decoder architecture. The encoder only encodes visible patches while the decoder can see all patches. Experiments proved that this lightweight structure not only increases recovery accuracy but also drastically reduces floating point operations. The second core design is to mask the image with a high proportion, in that a small amount of masking impedes the model's attempt to acquire worthy knowledge, which will be no different from simple interpolation algorithms. Results showed that this design forces the model to learn better representations and the model achieves the best performance at a mask rate of around 75%.

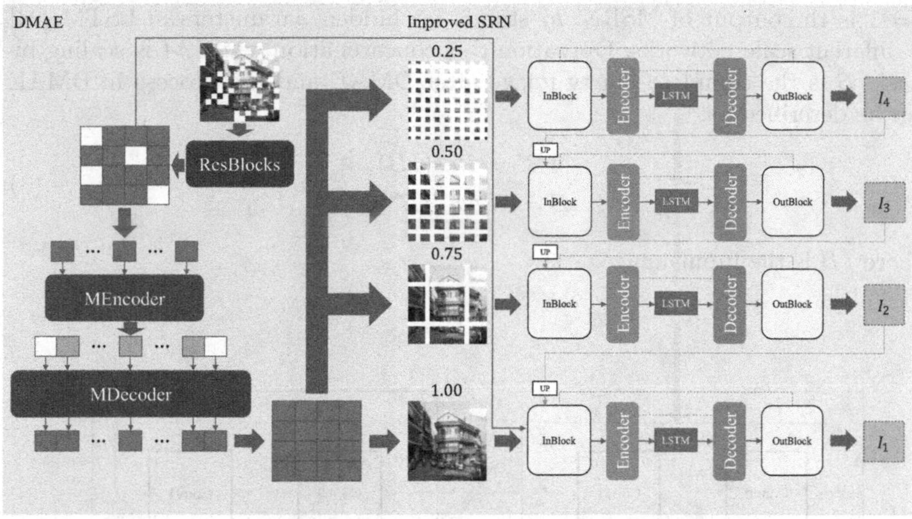

Fig. 1. The architecture of our proposed MSRN

3 Approach

Our goal is to design a universal, end-to-end network to complete the learning of incomplete blurry image restoration. Therefore, relying solely on multi-scale learning of SRN cannot complete this task. We subsequently introduced MAE and, to achieve the best recovery effect, image reconstruction should precede image deblurring. In addition, this task is more complicated than simply deblurring, so it is necessary to enhance the overall learning ability of the network. To check the effectiveness of our method, we tried to train SRN alone and MAE plus SRN to recover an incomplete and blurry image. When we were training these two networks, however, we found that neither using the SRN network alone nor simply connecting MAE and SRN can achieve good recovery results, introduced in our experiment. Our proposed MSRN is an image restoration network that combines mask reconstruction and multi-scale learning. It implements the task of using a single network to complete reconstruction and deblurring. Figure 1 illustrates the overall structure of our proposed network. It takes an incomplete blurry image as the input and completes the image inpainting through DMAE. And the reconstructed image enters the improved SRN network for deblurring. The output is a corresponding complete and unambiguous picture. Thus, our network is able to recover in an end-to-end manner. The whole network can be described as:

$$I_i = \begin{cases} ISRN[\mathcal{C}(\mathcal{M}_i(\mathcal{B}), UP(I_{i+1})), UP(h_{i+1}); \theta], & i \neq 1 \\ ISRN[\mathcal{C}(\mathcal{B}, UP(I_{i+1}), IB^*), UP(h_{i+1}); \theta], & i = 1 \end{cases} \tag{2}$$

where i denotes the scale index. IB^* represents incomplete and blurry images after ResBlocks. I_i is the intermediate representation at the i-th scale, with

$i = 1$ is the output of MSRN. h_i stands for hidden parameters in LSTM [24] of different scale networks. Operation $\mathcal{C}$ is concatenation while $\mathcal{M}$ is scaling by mask. $\mathcal{B}$ is the complete blurry image after DMAE and the process in DMAE can be described as:

$$\begin{aligned} IB^* &= Res(IB) \\ \mathcal{B} &= MAE(IB^*) \end{aligned} \tag{3}$$

where IB is the input image.

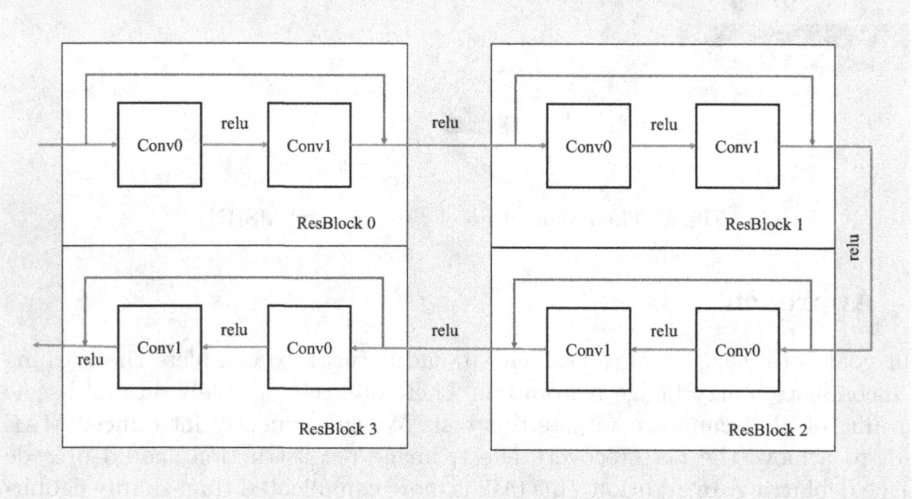

Fig. 2. The ResBlocks in DMAE

3.1 DMAE

Since MAE is a flexible autoencoder that exhibits excellent performance in representation learning on images and is suitable for multiple tasks [8], including image classification, target detection, and image segmentation, it is necessary to make some improvements on MAE to improve its performance on a single task. We use DMAE in the first half of MSRN to restore incomplete blurred images to complete blurred images. During the pre-training, we introduced a series of ResBlocks before the MAE, as shown in Fig. 1. The whole of these ResBlocks is a simple pre-trained network that improves the quality of blurry images, which allows MAE to generate clearer patches on the missing parts. We only keep the uncovered parts of the result. The structure of ResBlocks is shown in Fig. 2. Because the model will become increasingly difficult to train if the network deepens [26,28], we use residual connection [22] in each block, which skips one or more layers. It maintains the learning gradient of the network at a trainable level without additional parameters and computational complexity.

Based on [8], the image is segmented using the method in [5] that divides the image into patches. Next, we mask 75% of the image by "random sampling" [8] when training MAE. In the encoder, visible patches are mapped to the latent space through linear projection with position information. The input of the decoder consists of both visible and invisible patches. The decoder then restores the information of the incomplete parts.

3.2 Improved SRN

In the scale-recurrent network [3], each scale is composed of a symmetric and skip-connected autoencoder [27] with an LSTM in the middle of it. The output of each scale's network is the feature map learned by this scale network. After being upsampled, it will be superimposed into the image of the next scale along the depth direction and they are input to the next scale network. At the same time, the parameters in the LSTM [24,30] will also be transferred to the LSTM of the next scale. On this basis, we have made the following improvements.

The first improvement we made in SRN was the application of masks to scale images, as shown in Fig. 1. In image convolution, images are in the form of large matrices, while encoders encode discrete patches. Therefore, we have considered the following two issues when performing masking. The first is that using random sampling will cause the relative positions between various patches to be disrupted, which hinders the scaled image from presenting the correct shape. The network consequently can't learn valuable image features. The second is that the image will also exhibit significant distortion when the mask scale is too large, which can also cause the aforementioned problems. Therefore, we mask the image by grid-wise sampling [8], with a width of 16 pixels. It reduces the redundancy of the image while ensuring that the image is recognizable, allowing the network to learn more content. And this approach has been verified in subsequent experiments.

In order to improve the overall fitting ability of the network, we put forward another improvement which is the addition of a scale network. In [3] and our experiments, it has been confirmed that increasing the number of scales can improve image restoration performance. However, in our experiments, we found another issue which is the distortion on restored patches is still very distinct. We believe the reason is that there is a notable difference between the blurred portions recovered by DMAE and other blurred portions. In response to this distortion, we add the output result of ResBlocks in DMAE to the last-scale network, transferring the location of the missing patch on the original image to the back-end network. Our experiments have shown that our model with these modifications is more effective than the baseline.

3.3 Loss Function

The loss function in DMAE is the mean squared error (MSE) and we only calculate it on the missing part of the image. In the improved SRN, we use Euclidean loss [3]. The Euclidean loss on each scale network is

$$\mathcal{L}_E = \sum_{i=1}^{n} \frac{\|I_i - I_i^*\|_2^2}{\mathcal{N}_i} \tag{4}$$

where $\mathcal{N}_i$ is the total number of elements in i-th scaled image. I_i and I_i^* are the output image and sharp image respectively at the i-th scale. In fact, our loss functions are simple since we learned that the mean square error has sufficient capability to train a good network during our work.

4 Experiments

The training and testing of MAE, SRN and MSRN were completed on the GoPro [23] dataset. To reasonably shorten training time and meet MAE input requirements, we adjusted the resolution of all images from 1280×720 to 640×640 using bilinear interpolation, and the GPU in the training was RTX 3060 Ti. The incomplete ratio is 0.25. For a fair comparison, the methods in each experiment were completed under the same training images. In the experiment, we compared MSRN with other methods and tested the performance of the network under different conditions.

4.1 Dataset

The GoPro dataset is generated by the GOPRO4 Hero Black camera [23]. Blur images are obtained by averaging several consecutive latent frames and the corresponding clear images are the intermediate frames of these consecutive frames. This dataset is publicly available, with 3214 pairs of blurred and clear images with a resolution of 1280×720. There are 1111 pairs of test images, accounting for about one-third of the total dataset. Both Nah et al. and SRN tested on this dataset and successively proposed dynamic deblurring SOTA models.

4.2 Model Training

For the pre-training of ResBlocks, we used complete images for training. Because the purpose of introducing ResBlocks is only to pre-process the input image, we conducted 400 epochs during training. In the pre-training of MAE, we conduct self-supervised training for the autoencoder. The size of masks is 16×16 and other settings are the same as the default configuration in [8]. In improved SRN, the training data are original masked images, images restored by DMAE, and clear images. We did not change much in parameters. The parameters of Adam solver [29] are $\beta_1 = 0.9$, $\beta_2 = 0.999$ and $\epsilon = 1 \times 10^{-8}$. The variables in our model are initialized by Xavier method [28]. The learning rate is exponentially attenuated, with an initial value of 1×10^{-4}. The batch size is 16 while the training epoch is 3000 and it is enough in that we noticed the models had already converged very well at around the 2600th epoch.

4.3 Comparisons

To the best of our knowledge, due to the lack of a specific restoration model for incomplete blurred images in recent work, we mainly compared our methods with other applications of SRN, which is state-of-the-art in dynamic deblurring. In addition, we also compared ours with previous state-of-the-art [23] in dynamic deblurring. The results are shown in Fig. 3. Note that the images in the first row are from the training set, and the subsequent images are from the testing set.

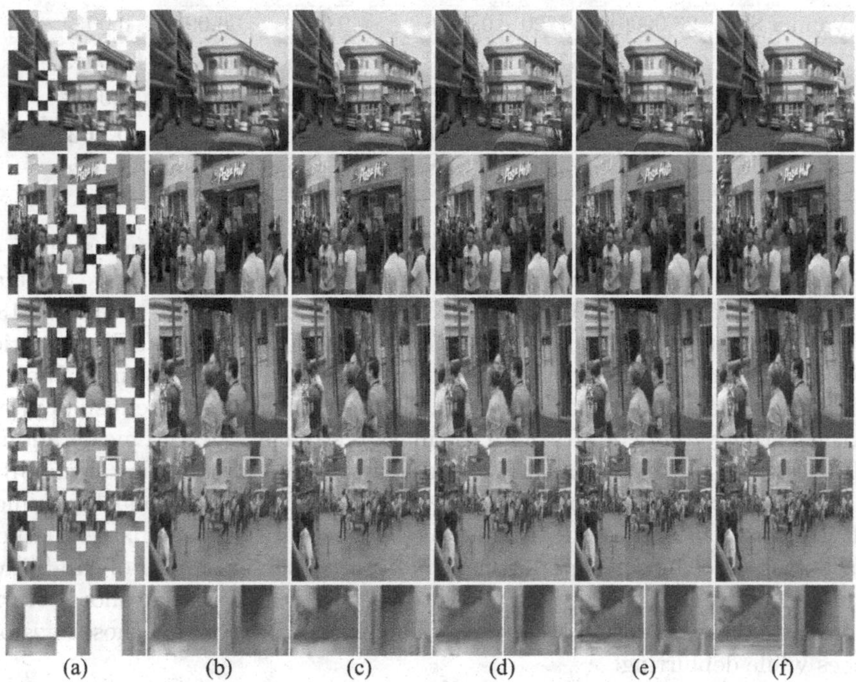

Fig. 3. Visual comparison. (a) Input. (b) Results of Nah *et al.* [24]. (c) Vanilla SRN. (d) Results of M_SRN. (e) Our results. (f) Ground Truth

Initially, we tried to use Vanilla SRN to complete reconstruction and deblurring, but, as shown in Fig. 3, SRN's learning ability is not enough and the effect of restoration is limited. Later, we used MAE for image reconstruction after SRN, but there were very obvious edges around the restored patch which means that restoration should be in front of deblurring. Based on former experiments, we decided to adopt MAE first and SRN next. However, simply connecting these two models does not have a good recovery effect on the patches restored by MAE, and even the deblurring effect on the other visible parts becomes poor. Therefore, our proposed MSRN is based on the experience above. It enhances the overall learning ability of the model and makes some improvements for the restoration of incomplete parts. In the test, MSRN achieves good results in both image deblurring and image reconstruction, as shown in Fig. 3.

Table 1. Quantitative comparison between ours and other state-of-the-art methods of dynamic scene deblurring on test data.

Methods	Metrics					
	PSNR ↑	SSIM ↑	MS-SSIM ↑	LPIPS ↓	SRER ↑	RMSE ↓
Input	10.5701	0.6696	0.5532	0.5160	52.7439	0.0185
Nah *et al.*	22.3217	0.7082	0.8347	0.4020	56.2137	0.0048
Vanilla SRN	23.0606	0.7720	0.8306	0.2534	56.0942	0.0049
Mask SRN	23.4083	0.7883	0.8479	0.2538	56.6596	0.0042
SRN_M	23.2217	0.7386	0.8682	0.3481	56.6372	0.0043
M_SRN	23.7817	0.7924	**0.8697**	0.2543	57.2761	**0.0037**
Ours	**24.4951**	**0.8004**	0.8637	**0.2383**	**57.2984**	**0.0037**

In order to verify the effectiveness of our model, we have designed a series of baseline models, among which SRN and the method of Nah et al. are popular images deblurring models. We use PSNR, SSIM, MS-SSIM [31], LPIPS [13], Signal to Reconstruction Error Ratio (SRER) and Root-MSE (RMSE) as metrics to evaluate the quality of image restoration. The results are shown in Table 1. Mask SRN is the method that scales images by grid mask and the results prove that the learning ability of SRN with the mask is stronger. SRN_M means adding MAE to the back of the original SRN. It deblurs the mask image first using SRN and then reconstructs the image using MAE. M_SRN is the model in which MAE is inserted in front of SRN, and the result indicates that the latter method has a better effect in our experiment. Finally, with the exception of MS-SSIM, our model achieves the best results. Note that in Fig. 3, we can more clearly demonstrate the excellent recovery effect of our model for restoring those invisible patches while deblurring.

4.4 Performance of Different Strategy

To verify that increasing the number of scales in our network can improve the learning ability of the network, we trained models under different scales. Similarly, we use the same data for training. The results are shown in Table 2 and they show that increasing the number of scales can improve the performance of the model. It is worth noting that when the number of scales increases from 2 to 3, the performance of the model still has a significant improvement. However,

Table 2. Results of different scales.

Number of scales	PSNR ↑	SSIM ↑	MS-SSIM ↑	LPIPS ↓	SRER ↑	RMSE ↓
1 Scale	21.3659	0.6547	0.7935	0.4669	55.8059	0.0053
2 Scales	22.1812	0.7120	0.8093	0.3909	56.0156	0.0048
3 Scales	22.7207	0.7639	0.8251	0.3423	56.2244	0.0045
4 Scales	**23.3764**	**0.7693**	**0.8357**	**0.3336**	**56.6743**	**0.0042**

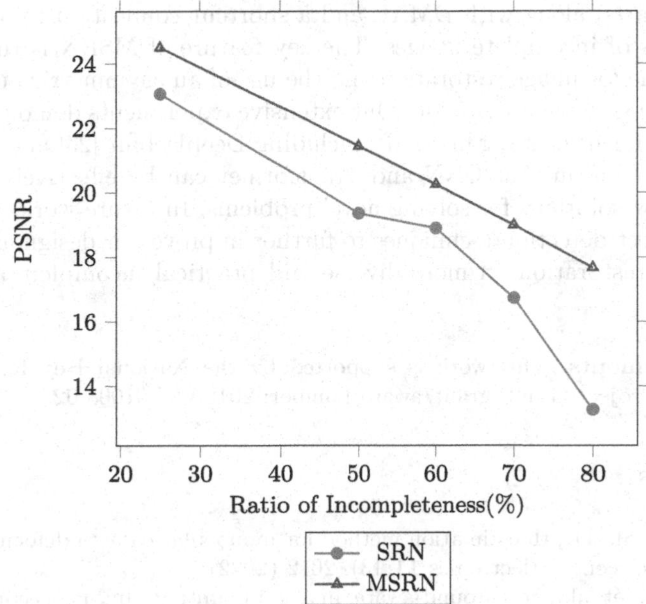

Fig. 4. Performance of MSRN and SRN under different degrees of incompleteness

as the number of scales increases from 3 to 4, the improvement of the model has become very limited.

We further examine our model in different deficiency conditions. As shown in Fig. 4, The horizontal axis is the ratio of incompleteness, and the vertical axis is the PSNR indicator of the test results. In order to explore the recovery effect of the model under a high rate of incompleteness. Besides the original 25% mask rate, we conducted experiments with mask rates of 50%, 60%, 70%, and 80% to evaluate the performance of the model under extreme conditions. When the mask rate gradually increases, our model mainly exhibits a linear decline. Significantly, when the mask rate is greater than 60%, the gap between the two gradually widens. And the downward trend of SRN shows a parabolic decline, while our model still maintains a linear decline. From this point, it shows that our model still has a certain recovery effect for severely damaged blurred images, revealing robustness. Furthermore, we have also attempted to change other parts of the network. For instance, we tried different loss functions for training and different activation function in resblocks. However, we have found that our current MSRN performs best.

5 Conclusion

In this paper, we proposed a novel and robust model, called MSRN, for restoring incomplete and blurry images without any prior knowledge. MSRN utilizes a new scaling method and adds a scale to the model to improve the restoration effect of the missing parts, along with DMAE and a shortcut connection to address the characteristics of incomplete images. The key feature of MSRN is the "coarse-to-fine" scheme for image restoration and the use of an asymmetric autoencoder structure for image reconstruction. Our extensive experiments demonstrate that MSRN outperforms existing methods, including DeepDeblur [23] and SRN. Furthermore, we confirm that CNN and Transformer can be effectively combined to provide new solutions for solving novel problems. In future work, we plan to introduce object detection techniques to further improve our design and achieve better image restoration on more diverse and practical incomplete and blurry images.

Acknowledgements. This work is supported by the National Key Research and Development Project Grant, grant/award number: 2018AAA01008-02.

References

1. Ban, Y., et al.: Depth estimation method for monocular camera defocus images in microscopic scenes. Electronics **11**(13), 2012 (2022)
2. Xiong, W., et al.: Foreground-aware image inpainting. In: Proceedings of the IEEE/CVF Conference on Computer Vision and Pattern Recognition, pp. 5840–5848 (2019)
3. Tao, X., Gao, H., Shen, X., Wang, J., Jia, J.: Scale-recurrent network for deep image deblurring. In: Proceedings of the IEEE Conference on Computer Vision and Pattern Recognition, pp. 8174–8182 (2018)
4. Zheng, C., Cham, T.J., Cai, J.: Pluralistic image completion. In: Proceedings of the IEEE/CVF Conference on Computer Vision and Pattern Recognition, pp. 1438–1447 (2019)
5. Dosovitskiy, A., et al.: An image is worth 16x16 words: transformers for image recognition at scale. arXiv preprint arXiv:2010.11929 (2020)
6. Vaswani, A., et al.: Attention is all you need. In: Advances in Neural Information Processing Systems, vol. 30 (2017)
7. Sun, J., Cao, W., Xu, Z., Ponce, J.: Learning a convolutional neural network for non-uniform motion blur removal. In: Proceedings of the IEEE Conference on Computer Vision and Pattern Recognition, pp. 769–777 (2015)
8. He, K., Chen, X., Xie, S., Li, Y., Dollár, P., Girshick, R.: Masked autoencoders are scalable vision learners. In: Proceedings of the IEEE/CVF Conference on Computer Vision and Pattern Recognition, pp. 16000–16009 (2022)
9. Wu, C., Wo, Y., Han, G., Wu, Z., Liang, J.: Non-uniform image blind deblurring by two-stage fully convolution network. IET Image Process. **14**(11), 2588–2596 (2020)

10. Bao, H., Dong, L., Piao, S., Wei, F.: BEiT: BERT pre-training of image transformers. arXiv preprint arXiv:2106.08254 (2021)
11. Su, S., Delbracio, M., Wang, J., Sapiro, G., Heidrich, W., Wang, O.: Deep video deblurring for hand-held cameras. In: Proceedings of the IEEE Conference on Computer Vision and Pattern Recognition, pp. 1279–1288 (2017)
12. Chen, L., Zhang, J., Pan, J., Lin, S., Fang, F., Ren, J.S.: Learning a non-blind deblurring network for night blurry images. In: Proceedings of the IEEE/CVF Conference on Computer Vision and Pattern Recognition, pp. 10542–10550 (2021)
13. Zhang, R., Isola, P., Efros, A.A., Shechtman, E., Wang, O.: The unreasonable effectiveness of deep features as a perceptual metric. In: Proceedings of the IEEE Conference on Computer Vision and Pattern Recognition, pp. 586–595 (2018)
14. Vincent, P., Larochelle, H., Bengio, Y., Manzagol, P.A.: Extracting and composing robust features with denoising autoencoders. In: Proceedings of the 25th International Conference on Machine Learning, pp. 1096–1103 (2008)
15. Kupyn, O., Budzan, V., Mykhailych, M., Mishkin, D., Matas, J.: Deblurgan: blind motion deblurring using conditional adversarial networks. In: Proceedings of the IEEE Conference on Computer Vision and Pattern Recognition, pp. 8183–8192 (2018)
16. Mei, J., Wu, Z., Chen, X., Qiao, Y., Ding, H., Jiang, X.: Deepdeblur: text image recovery from blur to sharp. Multimedia Tools Appl. **78**, 18869–18885 (2019)
17. Simonyan, K., Zisserman, A.: Very deep convolutional networks for large-scale image recognition. arXiv preprint arXiv:1409.1556 (2014)
18. Gong, G., Zhang, K.: Local blurred natural image restoration based on self-reference deblurring generative adversarial networks. In: 2019 IEEE International Conference on Signal and Image Processing Applications (ICSIPA), pp. 231–235. IEEE (2019)
19. Ronneberger, O., Fischer, P., Brox, T.: U-Net: convolutional networks for biomedical image segmentation. In: Navab, N., Hornegger, J., Wells, W.M., Frangi, A.F. (eds.) MICCAI 2015. LNCS, vol. 9351, pp. 234–241. Springer, Cham (2015). https://doi.org/10.1007/978-3-319-24574-4_28
20. Kupyn, O., Martyniuk, T., Wu, J., Wang, Z.: DeblurGAN-v2: deblurring (orders-of-magnitude) faster and better. In: Proceedings of the IEEE/CVF International Conference on Computer Vision, pp. 8878–8887 (2019)
21. Fan, J., Wu, L., Wen, C.: Sharp processing of blur image based on generative adversarial network. In: 2020 5th International Conference on Advanced Robotics and Mechatronics (ICARM), pp. 437–441. IEEE (2020)
22. He, K., Zhang, X., Ren, S., Sun, J.: Deep residual learning for image recognition. In: Proceedings of the IEEE Conference on Computer Vision and Pattern Recognition, pp. 770–778 (2016)
23. Nah, S., Hyun Kim, T., Mu Lee, K.: Deep multi-scale convolutional neural network for dynamic scene deblurring. In: Proceedings of the IEEE Conference on Computer Vision and Pattern Recognition, pp. 3883–3891 (2017)
24. Hochreiter, S., Schmidhuber, J.: Long short-term memory. Neural Comput. **9**(8), 1735–1780 (1997)
25. Zou, Q., Luo, L., Wang, X., Chen, D., Liu, F.: Improved image deblurring algorithm to generate antagonistic neural network. In: 2020 17th International Computer Conference on Wavelet Active Media Technology and Information Processing (ICCWAMTIP) (2020)
26. Bengio, Y., Simard, P., Frasconi, P.: Learning long-term dependencies with gradient descent is difficult. IEEE Trans. Neural Networks **5**(2), 157–166 (1994)

27. Mao, X., Shen, C., Yang, Y.B.: Image restoration using very deep convolutional encoder-decoder networks with symmetric skip connections. In: Advances in Neural Information Processing Systems, vol. 29 (2016)
28. Glorot, X., Bengio, Y.: Understanding the difficulty of training deep feedforward neural networks. In: Proceedings of the Thirteenth International Conference on Artificial Intelligence and Statistics, pp. 249–256. JMLR Workshop and Conference Proceedings (2010)
29. Kingma, D.P., Ba, J.: Adam: a method for stochastic optimization. arXiv preprint arXiv:1412.6980 (2014)
30. Shi, X., et al.: Convolutional LSTM network: a machine learning approach for precipitation nowcasting. In: Advances in Neural Information Processing Systems, vol. 28 (2015)
31. Wang, Z., Simoncelli, E.P., Bovik, A.C.: Multiscale structural similarity for image quality assessment. In The Thirty-Seventh Asilomar Conference on Signals, Systems & Computers, vol. 2, pp. 1398–1402. IEEE (2003)
32. Efros, A.A., Leung, T.K.: Texture synthesis by non-parametric sampling. In: Proceedings of the Seventh IEEE International Conference on Computer Vision, vol. 2, pp. 1033–1038. IEEE (1999)
33. Goodfellow, I., et al.: Generative adversarial networks. Commun. ACM **63**(11), 139–144 (2020)
34. Shen, J., Chan, T.F.: Mathematical models for local nontexture inpaintings. SIAM J. Appl. Math. **62**(3), 1019–1043 (2002)

Multi-fusion Recurrent Network for Argument Pair Extraction

Naixu He, Qingfeng Chen(✉), Qian Yu, and Zongzhao Han

School of Computer, Electronics and Information, Guangxi University, Nanning, China

2013301014@st.gxu.edu.cn, qingfeng@gxu.edu.cn

Abstract. Argument Pair Extraction (APE) is an extension of argument mining that focuses on identifying argument pairs from two passages that have an intrinsic interaction, such as peer review and rebuttal. Existing studies have divided this task into separate subtasks for argument mining and sentence relation classification, but they overlook the connection between the two subtasks, leading to the accumulation of errors in argument pair extraction. To address this issue, we propose the **M**ulti-fusion **C**ross-update **R**ecurrent **N**etwork (MCRN), which includes two cross-updated units: an argument mining unit and a sentence pairing unit. Specifically, we cross-update the sentence representations of both units to learn the interaction between them, allowing the acquired sentence features to contain both argumentation and sentence relation information. We also designed a recurrent structure to iteratively learn these two units, which improves the utilization of pre-trained features. To evaluate the performance of the model, we conducted extensive experiments on benchmark datasets, which demonstrated that MCRN significantly improves the APE task.

Keywords: argument pair extraction · argument mining · sentence paring · recurrent network

1 Introduction

Argument mining has significant applications in various fields, such as legal document analysis, student writing guidance, and sentiment analysis [12]. This task aims to extract structured argumentative inference components from unstructured text. Exiting studies can be divided into two categories: monological argumentation and dialogical argumentation. Monological argumentation identifies argumentative discourse structures in documents where there is only one speaker, such as persuasive essays [20,21], Wikipedia [13] and legal documents [18,19], while dialogical argumentation focuses on pairs of arguments with internal connections, which is particularly relevant in interactive texts such as online debates [10,22].

L. Iliadis et al. (Eds.): ICANN 2023, LNCS 14259, pp. 103–114, 2023.
https://doi.org/10.1007/978-3-031-44223-0_9

Argument pair extraction (APE), proposed by Cheng et al. [5], is a part of dialogical argumentation, which aims to extract argument pairs with interactivity from two argumentative passages. Argument pair extraction requires obtaining arguments in two documents and then composing the corresponding arguments into argument pairs. Early approches relied on a pipeline approach to solve the problem. Arguments are obtained by sequence labeling, and then a binary classification task is used to determine whether the arguments can form argument pairs. However, this overlooks the connection between the two tasks, which can mutually reinforce each other.

To exploit this information, recent studies have proposed some joint training models [1,6], which allow downstream tasks to obtain both sequence annotation and pair extraction results simultaneously.

Despite these advances, the APE still presents some challenges. Sequence labeling and relation classification task of APE are not two independent subtasks, and they actually depend on each other. If we want to identify argument pairs, we need to consider not only argument information but also the relation between arguments. Therefore, a significant challenge is to find appropriate ways to mutually reinforce these two tasks to improve the accuracy of predictions. Unlike most natural language processing tasks, the APE focuses on learning sentence representations with contextual information rather than word vectors or entity representations. And the learning of sentence vectors for specific downstream task is more challenging. An argument usually consists of several adjacent sentences. When determining whether a sentence belongs to an argument, we need to consider the current sentence and its neighbouring sentences only. Too much information may have a negative effect on argument prediction. How to properly introduce adjacency feature to facilitate argument extraction is another challenge.

This paper proposes a novel approach called the **M**ulti-fusion **C**ross-update **R**ecurrent **N**etwork (MCRN) to address the challenges associated with the argument pair extraction (APE). The proposed method employs a cross-updated argument mining unit and sentence pairing unit to simultaneously extract arguments and sentence relations. The cross-update mechanism allows for mutual reinforcement between argument mining and sentence relation learning. A local encoder is designed in the argument mining unit to extract argument features without introducing redundant noise. To enhance the semantic information contained in the sentence vectors, a recurrent network is incorporated to repeatedly fuse the BERT representations. Experimental results on benchmark datasets demonstrate MCRN significantly outperforms baseline methods.

2 Related Work

Argument mining aims to extract arguments from the text in order to provide structured data for the computational model of the argumentation and reasoning engine. A large amount of research in argument mining focuses on monological argumentation, such as argument component identification [14,17], argument retrieval [7,8], argument quality assessment [24], etc.

As the ultimate purpose of arguments is to be used in debates, modeling dialogical argumentation has attracted increasing attention [2,16]. Wei et al. [26] collected a dataset from online debate forum and the argument behavior was analyzed on four subtasks. Ji et al. [10] proposed discrete variational autoencoders to identify interactive arguments pairs in two posts with opposite stances. Cheng et al. [5] proposed a more challenging task, argument pair extraction, as the data to be processed are two unstructured documents and the goal of the task is both to get the arguments in them and to make them form the correct argument pairs.

From an alternative point of view, the task of APE can be considered as a form of multi-task learning. Miwa and Sasaki [15] introduced a table representation for entities and relations detection. In their tables, diagonal squares are used to predict entity types and non-diagonal lines are used to predict relationships. To solve the joint entity and relation extraction task, Wang and Lu [25] use cross-updated table encoders and sequence encoders to fill the table of entities and relations. Chen et al. [3] proposed a synchronous double-channel recurrent network for aspect-opinion pair extraction, in which a recurrently updated opinion entity extraction unit and relation detection unit are used to simultaneously extract aspects, opinions and the relations between them. However, the APE task is more complex because its extraction targets are sentences rather than words, and sentence vectors are more challenging to learn than word vectors.

3 Model

In order to address the challenges posed by the Argument Pair Extraction (APE), we propose a novel **M**ulti-fusion **C**ross-update **R**ecurrent **N**etwork (MCRN) architecture, as illustrated in Fig. 1. Following previous work [5], we conduct argument pair extraction on peer review and rebuttal datasets. The goal of APE is to extract all argument pairs in the form of $(\mathbf{arg}^{rv}, \mathbf{arg}^{rv})$, where **arg** refers to a contiguous sequence of sentences representing an argument.

3.1 Sentence Embedder

The initial stage of our proposed model entails the acquisition of sentence embeddings via a sentence embedder. It is inspired by the successful application of BERT which is used to obtain contextual semantic embeddings. Specifically, given a sentence, we obtain the token embeddings through BERT. These token embeddings are subsequently passed through a BiLSTM to obtain original sentence embeddings. As a result, for a given passage X, we can obtain the corresponding passage embedding H, which comprises the original sentence embeddings.

Note that the same model structure is employed for the passages with interaction, but with different parameters, as well as subsequent sections. For example, given two passages, a review and a rebuttal, we can obtain their respective sentence embeddings, denoted as H_{rv} and H_{rb}, by applying the sentence embedder.

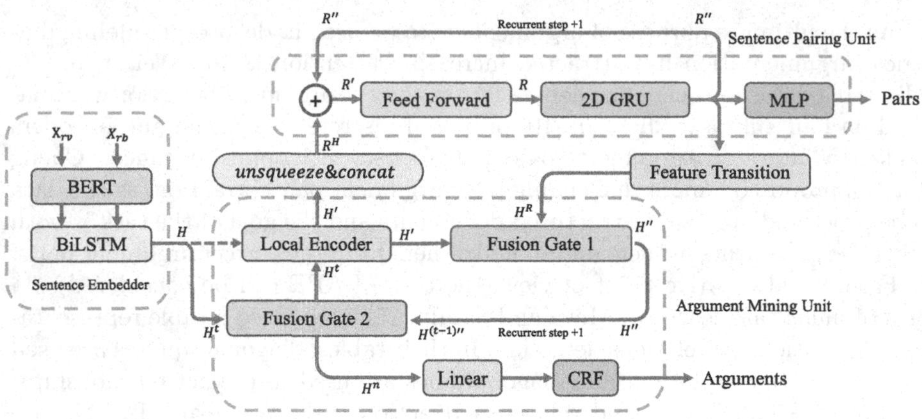

Fig. 1. The Multi-fusion Cross-update Recurrent Network - Model Architecture

3.2 Argument Mining Unit

The Argument Mining Unit (AMU) is responsible for updating sentence representations and predicting arguments. AMU, a recurrent structure, executes this task by sending updated sentence feature to the predictor while simultaneously re-fusing the feature with the original sentence feature. This integrated representation is then used as input for the next recurrent step of the argument mining process, making it an iterative and progressive process.

Local Encoder. In the context of the APE task, arguments typically consist of consecutive sentences. As a result, determining the membership of a given sentence within an argument requires only local information pertaining to itself and its immediate neighbors. For this purpose, a multihead self-attention encoder [23] with a masking mechanism is employed as a local encoder to extract the relevant features of adjacent sentences. The original sentence features, denoted as H, are initially fed as input to the local encoder during the first recurrent step. This allows us to obtain a sentence embedding H' that aggregates information from adjacent sentences.

The updated sentence features serve two primary functions: generating relation features for the sentence pairing unit, and fusing relation features for argument mining. The relation features R^H are obtained by concatenating every pair of updated sentence features H' from different passages. For instance, given review features H'_{rv} and rebuttal features H'_{rb} containing m and n sentences, respectively. The relation features are constructed by the following.

$$R^H = \{[\mathbf{h}'_{rv,i}; \mathbf{h}'_{rb,j}] | i \in \{1, 2, \ldots, m\}, j \in \{1, 2, \ldots, n\}\} \tag{1}$$

Fusion Gate. Our proposed model incorporates two fusion gates with identical structures. Specifically, a fusion gate is introduced after the local encoder to incorporate information from the other passage. This is achieved by combining the sentence features H' with H^R. Here, the sentence features H^R is described in Sect. 3.3. The fusion gate operates as follows:

$$gate = \sigma([H'; H^R]W_{gate} + b_{gate}) \tag{2}$$

$$H'' = H' \odot gate + H^R \odot (1 - gate) \tag{3}$$

where $W_{gate} \in \mathbb{R}^{2d \times d}$ and b_{gate} are learnable, and σ denotes sigmoid function.

The fused features H'' and original sentence features H will go through another fusion gate with the same structure as above to obtain the input features H^{t+1} for the argument mining unit of next recurrent step. Additionally, the sentence embeddings H^n of last recurrent will then be used to predict the arguments.

Arguments Predictor. To address the challenge of argument mining, we frame it as a sequence labeling task. Specifically, we use a conditional random field (CRF) approach [11] to perform this task. The CRF model involves a state transition matrix $T \in \mathbb{R}^{K \times K}$ and a state score matrix $S \in \mathbb{R}^{N \times K}$, where N is the number of sentences and K is the label dimension. The sentence features H'' will be used to calculate the state score S by a linear layer. Given a passage $X = \{\mathbf{s}_1, \mathbf{s}_2, \ldots, \mathbf{s}_N\}$, we predict a sequence of labels $\hat{Y} = \{\hat{y}_1, \hat{y}_1, \ldots, \hat{y}_N\}$, and its score can be defined as:

$$score(X, \hat{Y}) = \sum_{i=0}^{N} T_{\hat{y}_i, \hat{y}_{i+1}} + \sum_{i=1}^{N} S_{x_i, \hat{y}_i} \tag{4}$$

Then the probability of sequence Y will be calculated by the follow:

$$p(Y|X) = \frac{exp(score(X, Y))}{\sum_{\tilde{Y}} exp(score(X, \tilde{Y}))} \tag{5}$$

where $\tilde{Y} \in Y_X$, and Y_X denotes all possible label sequences.

3.3 Sentence Pairing Unit

Sentence Pairing Unit (SPU) is a component designed to detect the relationship between two sentences within interacted passages. The SPU is a recurrent structure that utilizes its own output features R'' and attention-based AMU features R^H to form input relation features R'. These two types of information are integrated using an element-wise summation to ensure that both forms of information are considered in the detection of sentence relationships.

In the first recurrent, $R'' \in \mathbb{R}^{|rv| \times |rb| \times 2d}$ is initialized by xavier normal [9]. Then we update the relation features R' to R using a feed-forward network:

$$R = R' + (max(0, R'W + b))W' + b' \tag{6}$$

Next, we need to incorporate contextual semantic information between different passages into the relation features. The relation feature matrix $R \in \mathbb{R}^{|rv|\times|rb|\times 2d}$ comprises $|rv|$ review sentences and $|rb|$ rebuttal sentences. The relation between the i-th review sentence and the j-th rebuttal sentence at the t-th recurrent step is denoted as $R_{i,j,t}$. Note that t here belongs to the GRU and not the MCRN. We update $R_{i,j,t}$ using a 2D-GRU [25] as follows:

$$R''_{i,j,t} = 2DGRU(R_{i,j,t-1}, R_{i-1,j,t}, R_{i,j-1,t}) \tag{7}$$

The relation feature R'' of the final recurrent step is fed into a multilayer perceptron (MLP) with three linear layers and two ReLU layers. The MLP computes the probability $p(\hat{y}^{pair}|\mathbf{s}_{rv}, \mathbf{s}_{rb})$ indicating whether sentence $\mathbf{s}_{rv}$ and sentence $\mathbf{s}_{rb}$ form a sentence pair.

Feature Transition. To enable the use of relational features in AMU, it is imperative to transform them into sentence embeddings denoted as H^R. This transformation requires reducing the dimensions of the features. To minimize computational costs, we employ an average method, where we obtain the review sentence embeddings by averaging the feature R'' row-wise, and the rebuttal sentence embeddings by averaging it column-wise. These sentence features are then updated using a linear layer, followed by layer normalization to ensure that the dimensions of H^R are consistent with the features in AMU.

3.4 Joint Learning

To establish a mutually reinforcing relationship between the argument mining unit and sentence pairing unit, we aim to maximize the probability of golden sequence $p(Y|X)$ and the probability of golden pair $p(y^{pair}|X_{rv}, X_{rb})$ simultaneously. For argument mining unit, we minimize the negative logarithm of the conditional probability of the golden label as the loss function:

$$\mathcal{L}_A = -\log p(Y|X) = \log \sum_{\tilde{Y}} \exp(score(X, \tilde{Y})) - score(X, Y) \tag{8}$$

For sentence pairing unit, the binary cross-entropy loss function is used for sentence pairing:

$$\begin{aligned} \mathcal{L}_R = -\sum_{i,j} (y^{pair} \log p(y^{pair} = 1|\mathbf{s}_{rv,i}, \mathbf{s}_{rb,j}) \\ + (1 - y^{pair}) \log p(y^{pair} = 0|\mathbf{s}_{rv,i}, \mathbf{s}_{rb,j})) \end{aligned} \tag{9}$$

where $\mathbf{s}_{rv,i}$ and $\mathbf{s}_{rb,j}$ are sentences from the passages X_{rv} and X_{rb}, respectively.

Then, the overall loss function of the model is expressed as:

$$\mathcal{L} = \mathcal{L}_A + \lambda \cdot \mathcal{L}_R \tag{10}$$

where λ is the weight of sentence pairing loss.

3.5 Inference

To extract arguments and argument pairs, an additional inference module is introduced. The sequence labeling result with the highest conditional probability, obtained through the CRF algorithm, is taken as the labeling prediction result for argument extraction.

$$\hat{Y} = \arg\max_{\tilde{Y}} p(\tilde{Y}|X) \tag{11}$$

After obtaining the sets of review arguments $A^{rv} = \{\mathbf{arg}_1^{rv}, \mathbf{arg}_2^{rv}, \dots\}$ and rebuttal arguments $A^{rb} = \{\mathbf{arg}_1^{rb}, \mathbf{arg}_2^{rb}, \dots\}$, we compute the scores $\hat{\delta}$ for each argument pair. Let $\mathbf{arg}_i^{rv}$ and $\mathbf{arg}_j^{rb}$ denote a review argument and a rebuttal argument, respectively. The score $\hat{\delta}$ is calculated as follows:

$$\hat{\delta}_{i,j} = \frac{\sum_{\mathbf{s}^{rv} \in \mathbf{arg}_i^{rv}} \sum_{\mathbf{s}^{rb} \in \mathbf{arg}_j^{rb}} \mathbb{1}_{p(\tilde{y}^{pair}=1|\mathbf{s}^{rv},\mathbf{s}^{rb})>0.5}}{|\mathbf{arg}_i^{rv}| * |\mathbf{arg}_i^{rb}|} \tag{12}$$

where $|\cdot|$ is the function to calculate the number of sentences. Given a threshold score δ, we consider two arguments $\mathbf{arg}_i^{rv}$ and $\mathbf{arg}_j^{rb}$ as an argument pair if $\hat{\delta}_{i,j} > \delta$. According to this approach, we obtain a set of argument pairs $C = \{(\mathbf{arg}_1^{rv}, \mathbf{arg}_1^{rb}), (\mathbf{arg}_2^{rv}, \mathbf{arg}_2^{rb}), \dots\}$.

4 Experiments

4.1 Dataset

To evaluate the effectiveness of MCRN, we conduct experiments on the benchmark Review-Rebuttal dataset (RR dataset) proposed by [5]. The dataset consists of 4764 pairs of peer reviews and author rebuttals collected from ICLR 2013 to ICLR 2020. The dataset has two versions: RR-passage-v1 and RR-Submission-v2. They are both divided into training, development and test sets in the ratio of 8:1:1.

4.2 Parameter Configuration

We adopt the pre-trained **BERT-base** with dimension 768 as the token embedder and we freeze it during the training process. During training, we use the Adam optimizer with a learning rate of 2e−4 and train the model for 20 epochs. The hyperparameters of our model are set as follows: batch size = 2, dropout rate = 0.5, model dimension $d = 256$, local encoder head number $N_{head} = 2$, relation loss weight $\lambda = 0.4$, argument pair threshold $\delta = 0.5$. We tuned these hyperparameters primarily based on the RR-submission-v2 dataset. To measure the performance of MCRN, we report *Precision*, *Recall* and F_1*-score* to evaluate the results on three tasks, including argument mining, sentence pairing and APE. We take the results on the test set when the model achieves optimal results on the development set.

4.3 Baselines

To demonstrate the performance of MCRN, we compare it with the following baselines:

- **PL-H-LSTM-CRF** [5] is a pipeline model that trains argument mining and sentence pair detection separately and then integrates their results for extracting argument pairs.
- **MT-H-LSTM-CRF** [5] trains two subtasks simultaneously in a multi-tasks framework, where a CRF is used to solve the argument mining task and a linear layer is used to solve the sentence matching task.
- **MLMC** [6] solves the sentence pairing problem using an attention-guided multi-cross encoding-based model. The main MLMC architecture consists of multi-layer multi-cross encoder layer.

In addition to the above three baseline models, we construct an additional baseline model, **MCRN-ML**. Which differs from MCRN in that it does not use a recurrent structure but a multi-layer stacking structure.

4.4 Experiment Results

Main Results. The comparison of our model and the baselines on argument pair extraction is shown in Table 1 and Table 2. It can be seen that the experimental results of MCRN are better than all baselines on both datasets. According to Table 1, MCRN outperforms **PL-H-LSTM-CRF** by 14.81% F_1 score on argument pair extraction, but both the pipeline model and the joint learning model exhibit comparable performance on the argument mining subtask. This indicates that there is a significant error accumulation in the pipeline model, while the joint learning model can avoid the problem as much as possible.

We also compare the MCRN with the joint learning model. According to Table 2, the results of **MCRN** are 8.81% and 2.61% inferior to **MT-H-LSTM-CRF** and **MLMC**. **MT-H-LSTM-CRF** only uses a linear layer for the sentence pairing problem, which prevents it from fully learning the relation features of sentence pairs. The results of MLMC and our approach illustrate the importance of explicitly modeling sentence pair relations. In particular, the F_1 score of **MCRN-ML** is only comparable to **MT-H-LSTM-CRF** in argument pair extraction and significantly lower than other methods in sentence pairing. This indicates that MCRN can efficiently utilize the feature representation of the pre-trained model through recurrent structure to improve the ability of learning sentence relations.

To exhibit the efficacy of our proposed approach, we also conducted experiments on the claim-evidence pair extraction (CEPE) dataset [4]. Notably, since the CEPE dataset is substantially smaller in size compared to the RR dataset, we did not implement the mask in the local encoder. Our experimental results, as demonstrated in Table 3, exhibit a performance enhancement of 1.68 when compared to the previous state-of-the-art method. Furthermore, we conducted an investigation into the influence of recurrent steps on model performance. Our

Table 1. Experiment results on RR-Passage-v1.

Models	Argument Mining			Sentence Pairing			APE		
	Prec.	Rec.	F1	Prec.	Rec.	F1	Prec.	Rec.	F1
PL-H-LSTM-CRF	**73.10**	67.65	70.27	51.34	42.08	46.25	21.24	19.30	20.23
MT-H-LSTM-CRF	71.85	71.01	**71.43**	54.28	43.24	48.13	30.08	29.55	29.81
MLMC	66.79	**72.17**	69.37	**62.69**	42.33	50.53	**40.27**	29.53	34.07
MCRN-ML	69.92	71.71	70.80	58.63	38.29	46.33	37.82	24.84	29.99
MCRN	69.27	71.39	70.32	58.50	**49.47**	**53.61**	38.20	**32.37**	**35.04**

Table 2. Experiment results on RR-Submission-v2.

Models	Argument Mining			Sentence Pairing			APE		
	Prec.	Rec.	F1	Prec.	Rec.	F1	Prec.	Rec.	F1
MT-H-LSTM-CRF	**70.74**	69.46	70.09	52.05	46.74	49.25	27.24	26.00	26.61
MLMC	69.53	**73.27**	**71.35**	60.01	46.82	52.60	37.15	29.38	32.81
MCRN-ML	69.67	69.10	69.38	59.59	38.81	47.00	36.15	24.72	29.36
MCRN	70.52	69.53	70.02	**60.13**	**48.23**	**53.53**	**39.62**	**32.03**	**35.42**

results, illustrated in Fig. 2, indicate that although there is some variability in model performance across the three datasets, overall, increasing the depth of the model leads to improved performance. Specifically, our findings demonstrate that the optimal level of performance is achieved at 3 to 4 recurrent steps, beyond which there is a decline in performance, likely due to overfitting of the model.

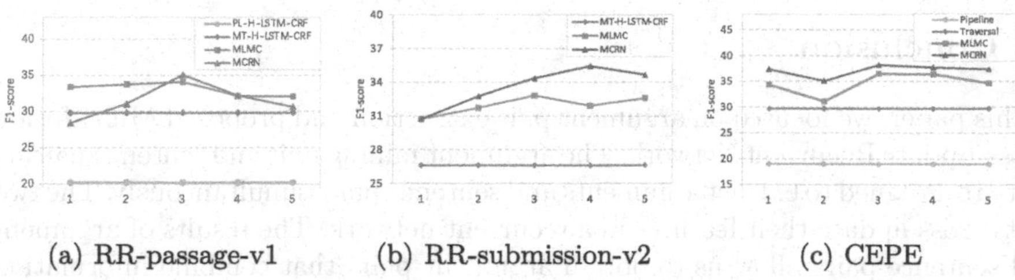

(a) RR-passage-v1 (b) RR-submission-v2 (c) CEPE

Fig. 2. Performance Comparison of Different Layer/Recurrent on Three Datasets

4.5 Ablation Study

To evaluate the effectiveness of the various modules in our proposed MCRN model, we conducted ablation experiments on the RR-submission-v2 dataset, and present the results in Table 4. Specifically, we examined the impact of removing the Local Encoder mask and replacing the Fusion Gates with mean function, as well as sharing the local encoder and CRF layers between the review and rebuttal data. The results demonstrate that the removal of Fusion Gate 1 has a marginal effect on

Table 3. Experiments on CEPE

Models	Pre.	Rec.	F_1
Pipeline	16.58	22.11	18.95
Traversal	24.06	**38.74**	29.69
MLMC*	48.92	29.08	36.48
MCRN	**54.25**	29.43	**38.16**

Table 4. Ablation Experiments

Model Settings	APE F_1	$\Delta(F_1)$
MCRN	35.42	-
w/o Fusion Gate 1	33.65	-1.77
w/o Fusion Gate 2	32.10	-3.32
w/o Local Encoder	31.81	-3.61
sharing Local Encoder	33.51	-1.91
sharing CRF	33.52	-1.90
sharing both	33.91	-1.51

performance, while the absence of Fusion Gate 2 and Local Encoder mask significantly impair the performance of our APE model. These results imply that proper fusion of pre-trained features can enhance experimental performance. Additionally, our study reveals that global attention adds excessive noise and that distant sentences are unhelpful in feature learning of target sentences. Moreover, our findings indicate that sharing the Local Encoder and CRF layers between the review and rebuttal data results in a loss of F_1 score of -1.91 and -1.90, respectively. This could be attributed to the differing data distributions between the two sets. However, sharing both modules yields a lesser F_1 score drop than sharing just one, indicating that common feature learning through sharing improves the model's performance to some extent. Nevertheless, our results suggest that customizing different encoding layers for different data distributions is more effective, as long as the data distribution is significantly different.

5 Conclusion

In this paper, we focused on argument pair extraction and proposed Multi-fusion Cross-update Recurrent Network. The argument mining unit and sentence pairing unit are designed to extract arguments and sentence pairs simultaneously. The two units cross update their features in a recurrent network. The results of argument and sentence pairs allow us to obtain argument pairs that combine information from the above two units. Extensive experiments on benchmark datasets show that MCRN has a significant improvement in contrast to baseline methods.

Acknowledgement. The work reported in this paper was partially supported by a National Natural Science Foundation of China project 61963004.

References

1. Bao, J., Liang, B., Sun, J., Zhang, Y., Yang, M., Xu, R.: Argument pair extraction with mutual guidance and inter-sentence relation graph. In: Proceedings of the 2021 Conference on Empirical Methods in Natural Language Processing, pp. 3923–3934 (2021)

2. Chalaguine, L.A., Hunter, A., Potts, H., Hamilton, F.: Impact of argument type and concerns in argumentation with a chatbot. In: 2019 IEEE 31st International Conference on Tools with Artificial Intelligence (ICTAI), pp. 1557–1562 (2019). https://doi.org/10.1109/ICTAI.2019.00224
3. Chen, S., Liu, J., Wang, Y., Zhang, W., Chi, Z.: Synchronous double-channel recurrent network for aspect-opinion pair extraction. In: Proceedings of the 58th Annual Meeting of the Association for Computational Linguistics, pp. 6515–6524. Association for Computational Linguistics, Online (2020). https://doi.org/10.18653/v1/2020.acl-main.582. http://www.aclanthology.org/2020.acl-main.582
4. Cheng, L., Bing, L., He, R., Yu, Q., Zhang, Y., Si, L.: IAM: a comprehensive and large-scale dataset for integrated argument mining tasks. In: Proceedings of the 60th Annual Meeting of the Association for Computational Linguistics (Volume 1: Long Papers), pp. 2277–2287 (2022)
5. Cheng, L., Bing, L., Yu, Q., Lu, W., Si, L.: APE: argument pair extraction from peer review and rebuttal via multi-task learning. In: Proceedings of the 2020 Conference on Empirical Methods in Natural Language Processing (EMNLP), pp. 7000–7011 (2020)
6. Cheng, L., Wu, T., Bing, L., Si, L.: Argument pair extraction via attention-guided multi-layer multi-cross encoding. In: Proceedings of the 59th Annual Meeting of the Association for Computational Linguistics and the 11th International Joint Conference on Natural Language Processing (Volume 1: Long Papers), pp. 6341–6353 (2021)
7. Dumani, L., Neumann, P.J., Schenkel, R.: A framework for argument retrieval. In: Jose, J.M., et al. (eds.) ECIR 2020. LNCS, vol. 12035, pp. 431–445. Springer, Cham (2020). https://doi.org/10.1007/978-3-030-45439-5_29
8. Ein-Dor, L., et al.: Corpus wide argument mining-a working solution. In: Proceedings of the AAAI Conference on Artificial Intelligence, vol. 34, pp. 7683–7691 (2020)
9. Glorot, X., Bengio, Y.: Understanding the difficulty of training deep feedforward neural networks. In: Proceedings of the Thirteenth International Conference on Artificial Intelligence and Statistics, pp. 249–256. JMLR Workshop and Conference Proceedings (2010)
10. Ji, L., Wei, Z., Li, J., Zhang, Q., Huang, X.J.: Discrete argument representation learning for interactive argument pair identification. In: Proceedings of the 2021 Conference of the North American Chapter of the Association for Computational Linguistics: Human Language Technologies, pp. 5467–5478 (2021)
11. Lafferty, J., McCallum, A., Pereira, F.C.: Conditional random fields: probabilistic models for segmenting and labeling sequence data. In: Proceedings of 18th International Conference on Machine Learning, pp. 282–289 (2001)
12. Lawrence, J., Reed, C.: Argument mining: a survey. Comput. Linguist. **45**(4), 765–818 (2020)
13. Levy, R., Bilu, Y., Hershcovich, D., Aharoni, E., Slonim, N.: Context dependent claim detection. In: Proceedings of COLING 2014, the 25th International Conference on Computational Linguistics: Technical Papers, pp. 1489–1500 (2014)
14. Levy, R., Bilu, Y., Hershcovich, D., Aharoni, E., Slonim, N.: Context dependent claim detection. In: Proceedings of COLING 2014, the 25th International Conference on Computational Linguistics: Technical Papers, Dublin, Ireland, pp. 1489–1500. Dublin City University and Association for Computational Linguistics (2014). http://www.aclanthology.org/C14-1141

15. Miwa, M., Sasaki, Y.: Modeling joint entity and relation extraction with table representation. In: Proceedings of the 2014 Conference on Empirical Methods in Natural Language Processing (EMNLP), pp. 1858–1869 (2014)
16. Persing, I., Ng, V.: Why can't you convince me? Modeling weaknesses in unpersuasive arguments. In: Proceedings of the Twenty-Sixth International Joint Conference on Artificial Intelligence, IJCAI 2017, pp. 4082–4088 (2017). https://doi.org/10.24963/ijcai.2017/570
17. P Petasis, G., Karkaletsis, V.: Identifying argument components through TextRank. In: Proceedings of the Third Workshop on Argument Mining (ArgMining2016), Berlin, Germany, pp. 94–102. Association for Computational Linguistics (2016). https://doi.org/10.18653/v1/W16-2811. http://www.aclanthology.org/W16-2811
18. Poudyal, P.: A machine learning approach to argument mining in legal documents. In: Pagallo, U., Palmirani, M., Casanovas, P., Sartor, G., Villata, S. (eds.) AICOL 2015-2017. LNCS (LNAI), vol. 10791, pp. 443–450. Springer, Cham (2018). https://doi.org/10.1007/978-3-030-00178-0_30
19. Poudyal, P., Šavelka, J., Ieven, A., Moens, M.F., Goncalves, T., Quaresma, P.: ECHR: legal corpus for argument mining. In: Proceedings of the 7th Workshop on Argument Mining, pp. 67–75 (2020)
20. Song, W., Song, Z., Fu, R., Liu, L., Cheng, M., Liu, T.: Discourse self-attention for discourse element identification in argumentative student essays. In: Proceedings of the 2020 Conference on Empirical Methods in Natural Language Processing (EMNLP), pp. 2820–2830 (2020)
21. Stab, C., Gurevych, I.: Identifying argumentative discourse structures in persuasive essays. In: Proceedings of the 2014 Conference on Empirical Methods in Natural Language Processing (EMNLP), pp. 46–56 (2014)
22. Tan, C., Niculae, V., Danescu-Niculescu-Mizil, C., Lee, L.: Winning arguments: interaction dynamics and persuasion strategies in good-faith online discussions. In: Proceedings of the 25th International Conference on World Wide Web, pp. 613–624 (2016)
23. Vaswani, A., et al.: Attention is all you need. In: Advances in Neural Information Processing Systems, vol. 30 (2017)
24. Wachsmuth, H., et al.: Computational argumentation quality assessment in natural language. In: Proceedings of the 15th Conference of the European Chapter of the Association for Computational Linguistics: Volume 1, Long Papers, Valencia, Spain, pp. 176–187. Association for Computational Linguistics (2017). http://www.aclanthology.org/E17-1017
25. Wang, J., Lu, W.: Two are better than one: joint entity and relation extraction with table-sequence encoders. In: Proceedings of the 2020 Conference on Empirical Methods in Natural Language Processing (EMNLP), pp. 1706–1721 (2020)
26. Wei, Z., et al.: A preliminary study of disputation behavior in online debating forum. In: Proceedings of the Third Workshop on Argument Mining (ArgMining2016), Berlin, Germany, pp. 166–171. Association for Computational Linguistics (2016). https://doi.org/10.18653/v1/W16-2820. http://www.aclanthology.org/W16-2820

Pacesetter Learning for Large Scale Cooperative Multi-Agent Reinforcement Learning

Pingqi Zhou(✉), Chao Li, Mengwei Qiu, Jun Liu, Chennan Ma, and Ming Yan

Fujian Key Lab of Sensing and Computing for Smart Cities,
School of Informatics, Xiamen University, Xiamen, China
zhoupingqi@stu.xmu.edu.cn

Abstract. In complex multi-agent reinforcement learning environments, such as Starcraft II, most existing algorithms struggle to scale up to large-scale collaboration tasks. This is partly because learning to precisely control each agent to maximize its contribution to the team becomes increasingly difficult as the number of agents and the dimensionality of the input grow. In this paper, we propose the novel **P**acesetter **LeAR**ning (PLAR) method, which builds and learns pacesetters to enable agents to consider the situation of neighboring agents and cooperate more effectively in complex, large-scale environments. By leveraging the comprehensive outlook provided by the pacesetters, agents are able to coordinate their actions more finely and achieve better overall performance. To demonstrate the effectiveness of our algorithm, we conduct experiments on both existing and newly generated scenarios. Specifically, we compare our algorithm to existing multi-agent algorithms on the existing scenarios, and we also optimize the StarCraft Multi-Agent Challenge (SMAC) from square complexity of memory to linear, enabling us to construct a larger-scale map for further evaluation. The experimental results demonstrate that PLAR outperforms existing algorithms in large-scale settings.

Keywords: Pacesetter Learning · Multi-Agent Reinforcement Learning · Large Scale

1 Introduction

Multi-agent reinforcement learning (MARL) [26] is a powerful learning method that enables multiple agents to make decisions in a complex environment to maximize the reward. It has been applied in various fields, including UAVs [14], image processing [4], and automotive [5,13]. One popular framework for improving cooperation among multiple agents is the *Centralized Training with Decentralized Execution* (CTDE) [6] approach, which addresses the challenges of local observation constraints. Recently, several CTDE-based methods have

L. Iliadis et al. (Eds.): ICANN 2023, LNCS 14259, pp. 115–126, 2023.
https://doi.org/10.1007/978-3-031-44223-0_10

derived the *Value Decomposition* (VD) paradigm to solve such as environmental instability and credit assignment problems, including VDN [21], QMIX [11], and QTRAN [17].

However, the CTDE framework exhibits limitations in its application to partially observable Markov decision processes (POMDPs) [18]. During training, agents use global state information, but during distributed execution, they only rely on their local observations, leading to information gaps between agents and hindering cooperation. This problem becomes particularly pronounced as the number of agents grows. While communication-based multi-agent reinforcement learning methods [3, 7] attempt to address this issue by enabling agents to share information, they still face challenges with transmitting and managing large amounts of communication data as the scale of the agent group increases.

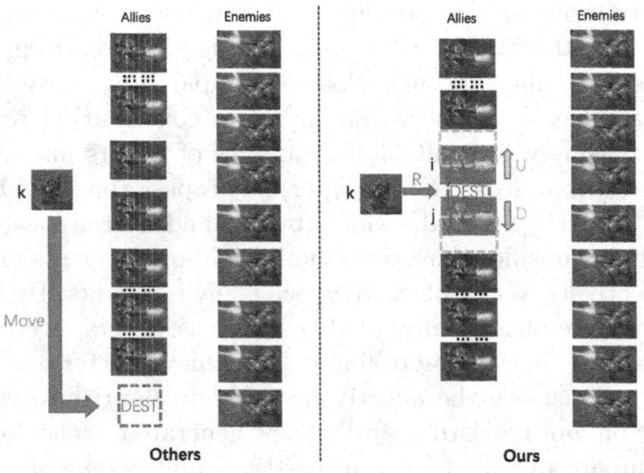

Fig. 1. A visual representation of how our algorithm distinguishes itself from others when applied to large-scale multi-agent collaboration tasks during distributed execution

Inspired by mean field multi-agent reinforcement learning (MFMARL) [25], we propose PLAR to enable multi-agent reinforcement learning to maximize overall benefits in large-scale agent collaboration. Figure 1 shows that in large-scale battles among agents, the allies are unable to arrange themselves into a battle formation simultaneously. Initially, some agents engage the enemy while agent k, arriving later and facing local observation constraints, needs to navigate to the destination using a series of predetermined moves before joining the fight. To address this challenge, our algorithm leverages the actions of neighboring agents in each agent's local observation, allowing agent k to take a direct rightward move while neighbors i and j move up and down to create space. This results in tacit cooperation that enables the team to achieve greater benefits.

Specifically, we construct a virtual agent's action by leveraging the actions of neighboring agents, which serves as the initial pacesetter in our proposed method. However, directly using the initial pacesetter's action to influence the current agent's action may lead to agents having similar actions, which can be detrimental to maximizing the overall reward. To address this, we propose defining an action-honor-value and utilizing contrastive learning [1] to maximize the mutual information between the action-honor-value and the pacesetter's action. This approach enables agents to see longer-term team benefits through the pacesetter and enrich their own action choices to the fullest extent possible. To verify the superiority of our algorithm in large-scale scenarios, we reduce the memory complexity of SMAC to linear complexity, which enables us to adapt to larger-scale maps. The modified version of SMAC is referred to as SMAC-Large. Based on the experimental results, our proposed PLAR method exhibits superior performance over existing algorithms in large-scale settings. Our main contributions can be summarized as follows:

- Our proposed PLAR method promotes agent cooperation to maximize overall rewards in large-scale multi-agent problems. Notably, this method is lightweight and does not require agents to communicate with each other.
- By reducing the memory complexity of SMAC from quadratic to linear, we develop a modified version called SMAC-Large, which enables us to adapt to larger-scale multi-agent scenarios. Using SMAC-Large, we are able to conduct experiments and evaluate the effectiveness of our proposed approach in a broader range of settings.
- Our experiments on various maps in StarCraft II demonstrate that PLAR significantly outperforms state-of-the-art competitors.

2 Related Work

Value decomposition has emerged as a popular approach for addressing multi-agent collaboration issues [2,22,27]. To ensure individual-global maximization (IGM) [17] is met during value decomposition, it is crucial to follow this constraint. VDN [21] factorizes the joint value function into the sum of each agent's value, while QMIX [11] extends this to incorporate monotonicity constraints. WQMIX [10] employs a weight function to identify the most optimal strategy for each joint action, preventing QMIX from reaching a local optimum.

To overcome the structural constraints in VDN and QMIX, QTRAN [17] converts the original global action value function into a new decomposable value function that ensures both have the same optimal actions. QPLEX [23] uses a dueling structure to improve the representation ability of the value function. ResQ [16] decomposes the joint value function into a main function and a residual function, without any representation limitations, and can be used for distributional multi-agent reinforcement learning [20]. QAtten [24] decomposes the joint value function using a multi-head attention technique to accurately consider the relationship between the total value function and the individual value function. While these value decomposition methods show great potential in general multi-agent challenge tasks, they overlook the drawbacks of CTDE's distributed execution of local observations. As the number of agents increases, this drawback becomes more pronounced and impactful, making it difficult to apply these methods to large-scale multi-agent collaborative environments.

3 Preliminaries

3.1 Dec-POMDP

A fully cooperative multi-agent task can be conceptualized as a decentralized partially observable Markov decision process (Dec-POMDP) [8]. Such a process can be modeled as a tuple $M = \langle S, U, A, P, r, O, Z, n, \gamma \rangle$. The set S represents the global state of the environment, while U denotes the joint action of all agents. At time step t, in state $s^t \in S$, each agent $i \in A := \{1, \ldots, n\}$ selects an action $u_i \in U$ based on its local observations $o_i \in O$, which are provided by the observation function $Z(s, i) : S \times A \rightarrow O$. After the joint action $\mathbf{u}^t$ is taken, the next state s^{t+1} is determined by the transition function $P(s^{t+1} \mid s^t, \mathbf{u}^t) : S \times \mathbf{U} \times S \rightarrow [0, 1]$. In Dec-POMDPs, all agents share the same reward function $r(s, \mathbf{u}) : S \times \mathbf{U} \rightarrow R$. The discount factor is denoted by γ. The goal of the agents is to learn a policy $\pi(u_i \mid o_i) : \mathbf{U} \times A \rightarrow [0, 1]$ that maximizes the discounted reward $G = \sum_{t=1}^{\infty} \gamma^t r^t$.

3.2 Mean Field Theory

Mean field theory [19] is a mathematical tool used in physics to study the behavior of large-scale statistical physical systems. In the context of stochastic games [15], MFMARL [25] introduces mean field theory to the field of multi-agent reinforcement learning in order to mitigate the curse of dimensionality that arises as the number of agents increases. Specifically, MFMARL uses the neighbors $N(i)$ of agent i to compute the average action $\bar{a}_i$ as

$$\bar{a}_i = \frac{1}{N_i} \sum_k a_k, \tag{1}$$

where k represents the neighbors of agent i. This significantly reduces the complexity of the interaction among agents. One of the methods used by MAMFRL to reduce the complexity of interaction between agents is the mean field approximation, which approximates the Q-function $Q^i(s, \boldsymbol{a})$ computed based on the joint action $\boldsymbol{a}$ to a mean field function $Q^i(s, a_i, \bar{a}_i)$ generated by each agent's action a_i and the mean action $\bar{a}_i$.

In POMDPs, our PLAR method employs mean field theory to construct the pacesetter, enabling large-scale cooperation under local observability constraints. Training the pacesetter promotes explorations while considering overall interests, facilitating tacit cooperation among agents.

4 Method

In this section, we present a novel method for learning pacesetters that enable agents to cooperate tacitly in large-scale multi-agent environments with local observations. The method consists of two steps, namely, pacesetter builder and pacesetter training, as shown in Fig. 2. Furthermore, we introduce the design approach of SMAC-Large, which reduces the original SMAC from quadratic complexity to linear complexity.

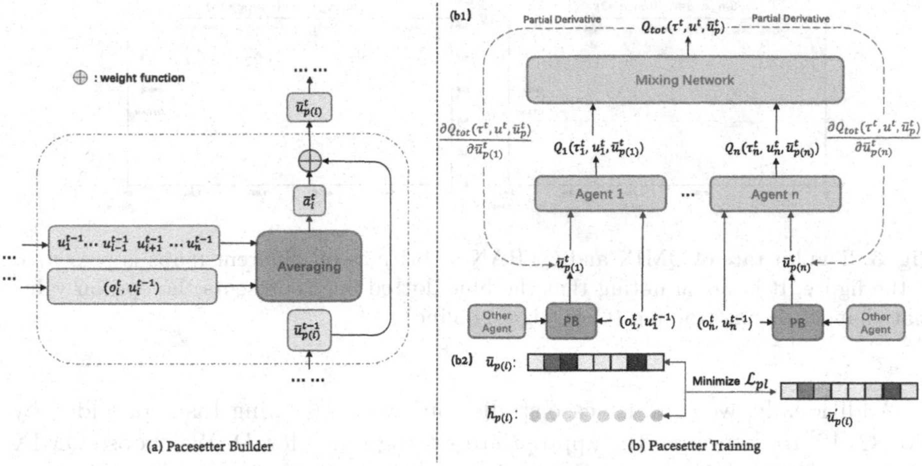

Fig. 2. An illustrative diagram of the proposed pacesetter learning (PLAR) method

4.1 Pacesetter Builder

Before discussing collaboration among a large number of agents, we need first address ways to enhance cooperation in scenarios where agents only have access to local observations. Assuming that each agent can obtain global state information during distributed execution may seem logical, but it is not ideal in real-world applications and goes against the principles of POMDPs. However, we can infer the content of global information from the local observations of each agent to improve their ability to collaborate if we approach the problem from a different perspective. By leveraging the behaviors of nearby agents that each agent has observed, we can implicitly gain global information. We refer to these agents as "pacesetters" since they possess implicit global knowledge and can assist other agents in cooperation.

Inspired by MFMARL, we have developed a pacesetter, and the specific process is presented in Fig. 2(a). The inputs to the builder include the actions of neighboring agents, as well as the local observations and actions of agent i. The centering operation calculates the average action of available neighbors $\bar{a}_i^t$ at the current moment, as shown by the equation:

$$\bar{a}_i = \frac{1}{N_{j(i)}} \sum_j u_j, \left\{ j | j \in N_{o(i)} \wedge j \in N_{d(i)}, |N_{d(i)}| = D \right\}, \quad (2)$$

where $N_{o(i)}$ represents the collection of agent indices within the local field of view of agent i, and $N_{d(i)}$ represents the collection of D recent agent indexes of agent i. Therefore, j represents the index of D neighbor agents obtained by agent i through local observation constraints. We set the size of $N_{j(i)}$ to $\mathrm{MIN}(|N_{o(i)}|, |N_{d(i)}|, 1)$, which represents the number of j.

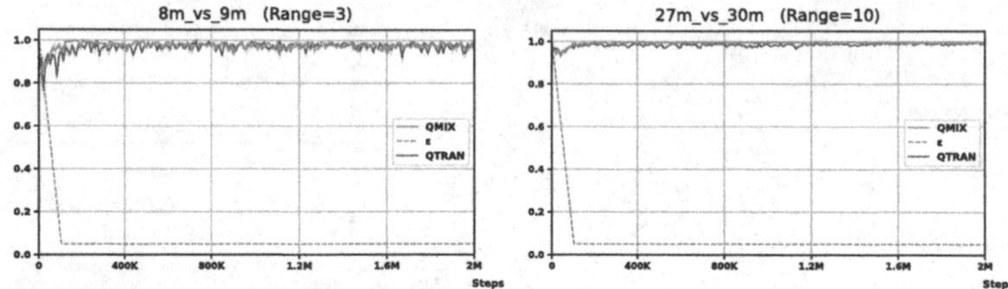

Fig. 3. The hit rate of QMIX and QTRAN algorithms on different maps is presented in the figure. It is worth noting that the blue dotted line represents the epsilon value that changes during training (Color figure online)

Additionally, we conduct case studies on two challenging tasks provided by SMAC [12] to determine the appropriate setting range for D. We choose QMIX [11] and QTRAN [17] as examples, and record the hit rate of each agent attacking the nearest three agents in the *8m_vs_9m* map and the hit rate of attacking the last ten agents in the *27m_vs_30m* map, as depicted in Fig. 3. The chart reveals that the hit rates of the two algorithms cannot reach 1 at the beginning due to the ε-greedy action, but as the algorithm is trained and the value of ε decreases, the hit rate becomes extremely close to 1. Consequently, we believe that the setting of the nearest number chosen for each map will not significantly impact the final strategy. We determine that the appropriate value range for D is $[\frac{10N_a}{27}, \frac{3N_a}{8}]$, where N_a represents the total number of ally agents.

As the number of agents increases, in order to facilitate the pacesetter to integrate additional information regarding the movements of neighboring agents, we use a weight function to include the pacesetter action from the previous instant into the creation of the pacesetter action for the following moment. This allows the agents to predict the actions of teammates and cooperate more effectively together. We set the weight function as

$$w(a, b) = a + \gamma * b, \tag{3}$$

the default value of γ is usually set to 0.1, a represents the average action $\bar{a}_i^t$ at the current moment, and b represents the pacesetter action $\bar{u}_{p(i)}^{t-1}$ at the previous moment. Certainly, the weight function is also possible to replace it with a more sophisticated function.

4.2 Pacesetter Training

After integrating the pacesetter building blocks into the VD architecture, as depicted in Fig. 2($b1$), we demonstrate that this combination adheres to the principles of IGM, which we justify as follows.

Lemma 1. *PLAR's structure adheres to the principles of IGM [17].*

Proof. Consider the mixed network of QMIX as an illustration.

$$\begin{aligned}\frac{\partial Q_{tot}\left(\tau^t, u^t, \bar{u}_p^t\right)}{\partial Q_i\left(\tau_i^t, u_i^t, \bar{u}_{p(i)}^t\right)} &= \frac{\partial (W_2^T Elu\left(W_1^T Q_i\left(\tau_i^t, u_i^t, \bar{u}_{p(i)}^t\right) + B_1\right) + B_2)}{\partial Q_i\left(\tau_i^t, u_i^t, \bar{u}_{p(i)}^t\right)} \\ &= \left(\frac{\partial Elu\left(W_1^\top Q_i\left(\tau_i^t, u_i^t, \bar{u}_{p(i)}^t\right) + B_1\right)}{\partial\left(W_1^\top Q_i\left(\tau_i^t, u_i^t, \bar{u}_{p(i)}^t\right) + B_1\right)} \cdot W_1\right)^\top W_2\end{aligned} \tag{4}$$

Considering that when $\alpha = 1$ in the Elu function, there will be $\frac{\partial Elu(\cdot)}{\partial(\cdot)} > 0$, Both W_1 and W_2 are weight parameters, after absolute value processing, so $W_1 \geq 0, W_2 \geq 0$. Based on the above, we have $\frac{\partial Q_{tot}(\tau^t, u^t, \bar{u}p^t)}{\partial Qi(\tau_i^t, u_i^t, \bar{u}p(i)^t)} \geq 0$. The IGM [17] formula is $\underset{a \in \mathcal{A}}{\arg\max} Qtot(\boldsymbol{\tau}, \boldsymbol{a}) = \left(\underset{a_1 \in \mathcal{A}}{\arg\max} Q_1(\tau_1, a_1), \ldots, \underset{a_n \in \mathcal{A}}{\arg\max} Q_n(\tau_n, a_n)\right)$. It can be observed that PLAR ensures each agent selects an action under the maximization of the global Q value function, thus following the IGM principle.

However, in order to prevent agents from solely relying on the actions constructed by the pacesetters and causing the agents' actions to become overly homogeneous, we propose training the pacesetter such that each of its actions is informed by the global Q-function, enabling the pacesetter to provide the agents with a holistic view and take useful actions while ensuring the team's interests. GBAM [1] proposes that the significance of each input in relation to the output can be determined by taking the partial derivative of the output value with respect to the input value. Based on this approach, we propose the following definition of action-honor-value.

Definition 1. *At a discrete time step t, the influence of each action in the pacesetter on the overall Q function is defined action-honor-value, and the formula is written as*

$$\bar{h}_{p(i)}^t = \frac{\partial Q_{tot}\left(\tau^t, u^t, \bar{u}_p^t\right)}{\partial \bar{u}_{p(i)}^t}. \tag{5}$$

According to CPC [9], we can minimize the InfoNCE loss to maximize the mutual information between action-honor-value and pacesetter actions, allowing each pacesetter action to have specific considerations for the team's contribution. Therefore, we construct the InfoNCE-like loss as

$$\mathcal{L}_{pl} = \underset{\left(\{\boldsymbol{h}_j\}_{j=1}^N, \boldsymbol{u}_{p(i)}\right) \sim \mathcal{D}}{\mathbb{E}}\left[-\log \frac{\exp\left(\boldsymbol{h}_i \boldsymbol{u}_{p(i)}^T\right)}{\sum_{j=1}^N \exp\left(\boldsymbol{h}_j \boldsymbol{u}_{p(i)}^T\right)}\right], \tag{6}$$

where $\boldsymbol{h}_i = [\bar{h}_{p(i)}^1, ..., \bar{h}_{p(i)}^T] \in \mathbb{R}^{A \times T}$ represents the action-honor-value of the pacesetter corresponding to agent i in the overall time step, and $\boldsymbol{u}_{p(i)} = [\bar{u}_{p(i)}^1, ..., \bar{u}_{p(i)}^T] \in \mathbb{R}^{A \times T}$, furthermore, A represents the dimension of the number of actions and T represents the total time steps.

As depicted in Fig. 2($b2$), each action in the pacesetter of agent i initially contains information about the neighboring space-time, represented by the shade of gray. After minimizing the $\mathcal{L}_{pl}$ loss, the honor value of these actions is subtly integrated into the pacesetter, allowing it to contain more information about the team's interests and providing an overall perspective to the agents to choose different actions, just as described by the colors above.

4.3 SMAC-Large Design

SMAC has become the most popular benchmark for modern multi-agent reinforcement learning algorithms. However, when it encounters a large number of agents, the required memory consumption increases quadratically. We consider this memory usage rate to be highly unreasonable and in need of further optimization.

After analyzing Fig. 3, we conclude that attacking the nearest D agents using QMIX and QTRAN results in a hit rate of nearly 1, making the remaining $N-D$ agents redundant. Additionally, observing information about the D agents closest to the current agent during training is sufficient, and observing all other agent information is redundant. This simple yet effective approach reduces the original memory complexity of SMAC from quadratic to linear.

5 Experiments

We conduct experiments to verify the effectiveness of SMAC-Large and demonstrate the superiority of our proposed PLAR method on the StarCraft II environment. Our code is available at https://github.com/junmoxiaoDake/PLAR.

5.1 Performance of SMAC-Large

We use QMIX as the core algorithm and run it on both SMAC and SMAC-Large, while progressively increasing the number of agents and recording the corresponding memory usage. The detailed results are presented in Fig. 4. As can be seen from the figure, as the number of agents increases, the memory usage of SMAC grows significantly, reaching an extremely high level when the total number of agents is over one hundred, with a maximum memory usage of 600G. In contrast, SMAC-Large exhibits a completely different behavior. As the number of agents increases, memory usage remains low and grows linearly. The maximum occupied memory shown in Fig. 4 is only about 50G. We believe that SMAC-Large greatly optimizes the memory usage of SMAC and successfully reduces its memory complexity from quadratic to linear.

5.2 Performance on StarCraft II

In the challenging StarCraft II setting, several value decomposition methods have shown remarkable performance. We combine the PLAR method with the mixing

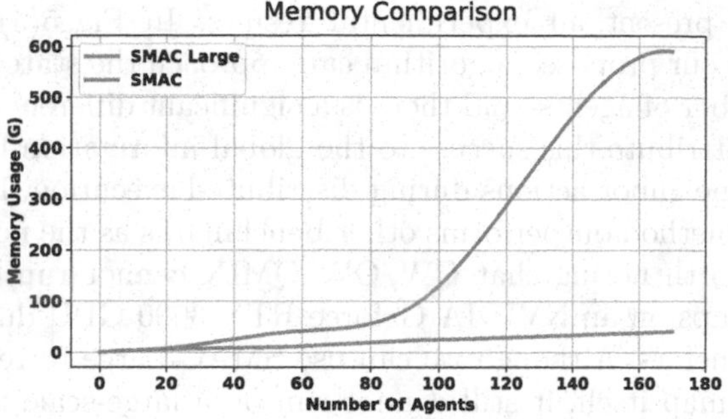

Fig. 4. Memory comparison chart of SMAC and SMAC-Large

network in QMIX [11] and evaluate its superiority against benchmarks such as QMIX, QAtten [24], QTRAN [17], QPLEX [23], OWQMIX, and CWQMIX [10]. We select the more complicated and challenging SC2.4.6.2.69232 version of the StarCraft II game. For the battle game map, we choose the **Hard** (5m_vs_6m, 8m_vs_9m) and **Super Hard** (27m_vs_30m) scenarios that are originally provided by SMAC. Furthermore, we design a **Super$^+$ Hard** (50 m) battle map based on SMAC-Large to further demonstrate the effectiveness of our algorithm on large-scale multi-agent cooperation. This map consists of a total of 100 agents.

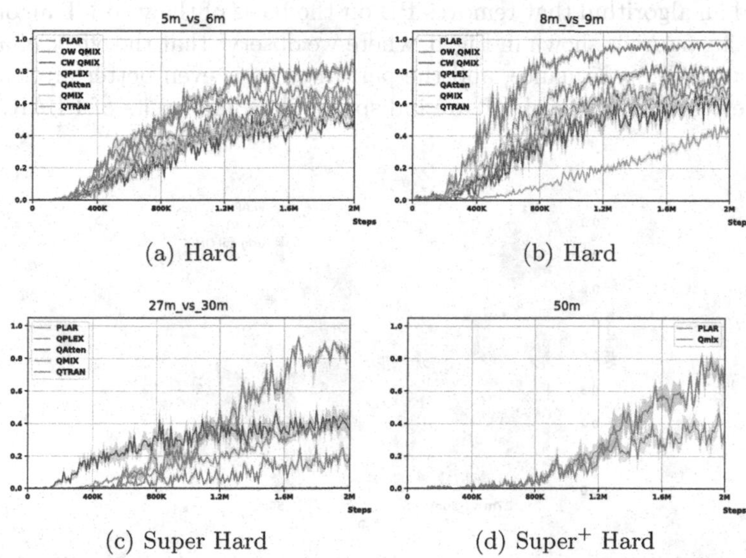

Fig. 5. The Test Win Rate of our proposed PLAR and baselines on the SMAC scenarios and SMAC-Large map. For a fair comparison, the mean and standard deviation of the performance throughout five random seeds are used to display all experimental results

In Fig. 5, we present all experimental results. In Fig. 5(a) and Fig. 5(b) demonstrate that our proposed algorithm can approach the state-of-the-art even with a small number of agents, and there is a significant difference from the original QMIX. We attribute this success to the global information being implicitly inferred through neighbor actions during distributed execution. In Fig. 5(c), our proposed PLAR method outperforms other benchmarks as the number of agents increases. It is worth noting that CW/OW QMIX cannot run on the 27 m vs 30 m and 50 m maps on an NVIDIA Geforce RTX 3090 GPU due to the size of its network parameters. Although we can use SMAC-Large to reduce the memory usage of the map itself, it still cannot run on a large-scale map due to the large parameters of the method itself. Therefore, Fig. 5(d) only compares our PLAR with the original QMIX, and other algorithms are not considered due to their parameter issues. As shown in Fig. 5(d), our proposed method outperforms QMIX by a significant margin.

As a result, the proposed PLAR algorithm is effective in handling large-scale multi-agent collaboration problems while retaining the lightweight characteristics of the original algorithm as much as possible.

5.3 Ablation Study

We conduct an ablation experiment to further evaluate the efficacy of Pacesetter Builder (PB) and Pacesetter Training (PT). We remove the PT module in the PLAR to form the w/o PT algorithm. The original QMIX algorithm can be considered an algorithm that removes PB on the basis of the w/o PT algorithm. The resulting figure is shown in Fig. 6, where we observe that the effect of adding PB improves the performance, and the performance is even better after adding PT. Therefore, both PB and PT are indispensable components of PLAR.

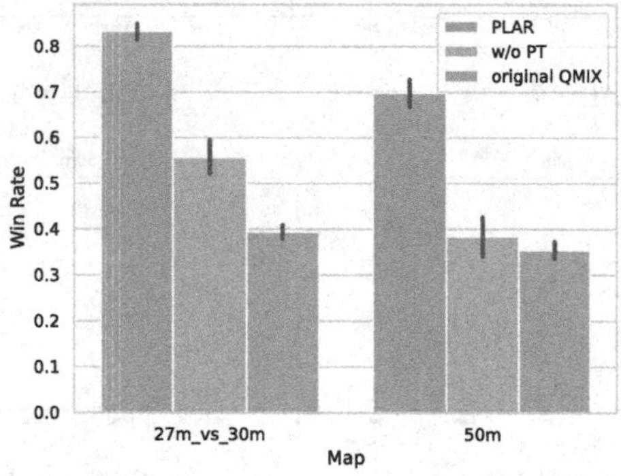

Fig. 6. Importance of Pacesetter Builder (PB) and Pacesetter Training (PT) modules. PLAR contains PB and PT modules, and w/o PT contains only PB modules. Besides, original QMIX means no PB and PT modules

6 Conclusion

In this paper, we investigate the issue of large-scale multi-agent collaboration under POMDPs. Existing algorithms face the challenge of local observation during distributed execution, and as the number of agents increases, it becomes increasingly challenging for them to coordinate and cooperate effectively. We draw inspiration from the mean field theory and propose the PLAR approach for building and training pacesetters. This enables agents to observe the pacesetters' actions and implicitly infer global information to promote cooperation and generate more diverse behaviors that improve the team's overall reward. In addition to comparing our approach to existing multi-agent algorithms on existing maps, we also improve the SMAC interface from quadratic to linear complexity, allowing us to construct larger-scale maps and further demonstrate our algorithm's performance at scale. Experimental results demonstrate that our algorithm outperforms existing algorithms in large-scale settings.

References

1. Ancona, M., Ceolini, E., Öztireli, C., Gross, M.: Towards better understanding of gradient-based attribution methods for deep neural networks. arXiv preprint arXiv:1711.06104 (2017)
2. Jeon, J., Kim, W., Jung, W., Sung, Y.: MASER: multi-agent reinforcement learning with subgoals generated from experience replay buffer. In: International Conference on Machine Learning, pp. 10041–10052. PMLR (2022)
3. Jiang, J., Lu, Z.: Learning attentional communication for multi-agent cooperation. In: Advances in Neural Information Processing Systems, vol. 31 (2018)
4. Kong, X., Xin, B., Wang, Y., Hua, G.: Collaborative deep reinforcement learning for joint object search. In: Proceedings of the IEEE Conference on Computer Vision and Pattern Recognition, pp. 1695–1704 (2017)
5. Lin, K., Zhao, R., Xu, Z., Zhou, J.: Efficient large-scale fleet management via multi-agent deep reinforcement learning. In: Proceedings of the 24th ACM SIGKDD International Conference on Knowledge Discovery & Data Mining, pp. 1774–1783 (2018)
6. Lowe, R., Wu, Y.I., Tamar, A., Harb, J., Pieter Abbeel, O., Mordatch, I.: Multi-agent actor-critic for mixed cooperative-competitive environments. In: Advances in Neural Information Processing Systems, vol. 30 (2017)
7. Mao, H., Zhang, Z., Xiao, Z., Gong, Z., Ni, Y.: Learning agent communication under limited bandwidth by message pruning. In: Proceedings of the AAAI Conference on Artificial Intelligence, vol. 34, pp. 5142–5149 (2020)
8. Oliehoek, F.A., Amato, C.: A Concise Introduction to Decentralized POMDPs. Springer, Cham (2016). https://doi.org/10.1007/978-3-319-28929-8
9. Oord, A.V.D., Li, Y., Vinyals, O.: Representation learning with contrastive predictive coding. arXiv preprint arXiv:1807.03748 (2018)
10. Rashid, T., Farquhar, G., Peng, B., Whiteson, S.: Weighted QMIX: expanding monotonic value function factorisation for deep multi-agent reinforcement learning. Adv. Neural. Inf. Process. Syst. **33**, 10199–10210 (2020)
11. Rashid, T., Samvelyan, M., De Witt, C.S., Farquhar, G., Foerster, J., Whiteson, S.: Monotonic value function factorisation for deep multi-agent reinforcement learning. J. Mach. Learn. Res. **21**(1), 7234–7284 (2020)

12. Samvelyan, M., et al.: The starcraft multi-agent challenge. arXiv preprint arXiv:1902.04043 (2019)
13. Shalev-Shwartz, S., Shammah, S., Shashua, A.: Safe, multi-agent, reinforcement learning for autonomous driving. arXiv preprint arXiv:1610.03295 (2016)
14. Shamsoshoara, A., Khaledi, M., Afghah, F., Razi, A., Ashdown, J.: Distributed cooperative spectrum sharing in UAV networks using multi-agent reinforcement learning. In: 2019 16th IEEE Annual Consumer Communications & Networking Conference (CCNC), pp. 1–6. IEEE (2019)
15. Shapley, L.S.: Stochastic games. Proc. Natl. Acad. Sci. **39**(10), 1095–1100 (1953)
16. Siqi, S., et al.: ResQ: a residual Q function-based approach for multi-agent reinforcement learning value factorization. In: Thirty-Sixth Conference on Neural Information Processing Systems (2022)
17. Son, K., Kim, D., Kang, W.J., Hostallero, D.E., Yi, Y.: QTRAN: learning to factorize with transformation for cooperative multi-agent reinforcement learning. In: International Conference on Machine Learning, pp. 5887–5896. PMLR (2019)
18. Spaan, M.T.: Partially observable Markov decision processes. In: Reinforcement Learning: State-of-the-Art, pp. 387–414 (2012)
19. Stanley, H.E.: Phase Transitions and Critical Phenomena, vol. 7. Clarendon Press, Oxford (1971)
20. Sun, W.F., Lee, C.K., Lee, C.Y.: DFAC framework: factorizing the value function via quantile mixture for multi-agent distributional Q-learning. In: International Conference on Machine Learning, pp. 9945–9954. PMLR (2021)
21. Sunehag, P., et al.: Value-decomposition networks for cooperative multi-agent learning. arXiv preprint arXiv:1706.05296 (2017)
22. Wan, L., Liu, Z., Chen, X., Lan, X., Zheng, N.: Greedy based value representation for optimal coordination in multi-agent reinforcement learning. arXiv preprint arXiv:2211.12075 (2022)
23. Wang, J., Ren, Z., Liu, T., Yu, Y., Zhang, C.: QPLEX: duplex dueling multi-agent Q-learning. arXiv preprint arXiv:2008.01062 (2020)
24. Yang, Y., et al.: Qatten: a general framework for cooperative multiagent reinforcement learning. arXiv preprint arXiv:2002.03939 (2020)
25. Yang, Y., Luo, R., Li, M., Zhou, M., Zhang, W., Wang, J.: Mean field multi-agent reinforcement learning. In: International Conference on Machine Learning, pp. 5571–5580. PMLR (2018)
26. Zhang, K., Yang, Z., Başar, T.: Multi-agent reinforcement learning: a selective overview of theories and algorithms. In: Handbook of Reinforcement Learning and Control, pp. 321–384 (2021)
27. Zohar, R., Mannor, S., Tennenholtz, G.: Locality matters: a scalable value decomposition approach for cooperative multi-agent reinforcement learning. In: Proceedings of the AAAI Conference on Artificial Intelligence, vol. 36, pp. 9278–9285 (2022)

Stable Learning Algorithm Using Reducibility for Recurrent Neural Networks

Seiya Satoh(✉)

Tokyo Denki University, Hiki-gun, Saitama 350-0394, Japan
seiya.satoh@mail.dendai.ac.jp

Abstract. A multilayer perceptron (MLP), a feedforward neural network with one hidden layer, is called reducible if a hidden unit can be removed without changing the input–output function. In the MLP's search space, the MLP is reducible in some regions, and some regions in the reducible regions have zero gradients, where learning stagnates. Nonetheless, some methods have been proposed to leverage such regions. A reducible region of an MLP with J hidden units can be generated from an MLP with $J-1$ hidden units. To begin learning from a reducible region guarantees a monotonically decreasing training error as the number of hidden units increases. The evaluation experiments reveal that the methods using reducible regions stably determine better solutions than existing methods. In addition, methods using reducible regions can stably obtain high-quality solutions not only for MLPs, but also for complex-valued MLPs, and radial basis function networks. In this study, we show that the search space of a recurrent neural network also has reducible regions. In addition, we propose a method that utilizes reducible regions to obtain higher quality solutions in a stable manner, as compared to existing methods with randomly set initial weights.

Keywords: Recurrent neural network · Reducibility · Reducible region · Hessian matrix · Eigenvector

1 Introduction

Reducibility is a crucial characteristic of multilayer perceptrons (MLPs), feedforward neural networks with one hidden layer [5,24]. In several regions, *reducible* MLPs exist in the parameter space (referred to as *reducible regions* in this study). A reducible region of an MLP may contain a continuous region with zero gradient, where learning stagnates. However, methods utilizing such regions have been proposed [18,19], where a reducible MLP with J hidden units is generated from an MLP solution with $J-1$ hidden units, and learning is started from there. As these methods use reducible regions and start learning by increasing the number of hidden units in succession, the training error decreases monotonically as the number of hidden units increases. Previous experiments in the literature have

L. Iliadis et al. (Eds.): ICANN 2023, LNCS 14259, pp. 127–139, 2023.
https://doi.org/10.1007/978-3-031-44223-0_11

obtained solutions suitable for the number of hidden units, which were of better quality than those obtained from existing methods that randomly initialize the weights.

Complex-valued MLPs, whose parameters are all complex-valued, also have reducibility [10,11,16,17]. Methods using reducible regions of a complex-valued MLP have also been proposed, and like real-valued MLPs, they exhibit better solutions than those obtained using existing methods that randomly initialize the weights [20,21]. Similarly, radial basis function networks also have reducibility, and a method using reducible regions outperformed existing methods [22]. Further, research on the reducibility of quaternionic and hyperbolic neural networks has also been performed [12,13].

Recurrent neural networks (RNNs) are used in a variety of fields, including time series forecasting, speech recognition, and human action recognition [1,6,7]. Several methods have been proposed as RNN learning methods [3,9,25,27]. Previous studies showed that a quasi-Newton method tends to outperform a steepest descent method. However, the quasi-Newton method may not obtain reasonable quality solutions depending on the initial weights.

The present study shows that reducible regions also exist in an RNN parameter space. In addition, a learning method using reducible regions for an RNN is proposed herein. This method monotonically decreases the training error as the number of hidden units increases. Further, an experiment is conducted to demonstrate that better quality solutions can be stably obtained using the proposed method than those obtained using existing methods that randomly initialize the weights.

This study is organized as follows. Section 2 describes basic definitions. Section 3 shows that reducible regions exist in an RNN parameter space. Section 4 proposes a new learning method using reducible regions. Section 5 evaluates the proposed method. Finally, Sect. 6 concludes the study and discusses future work.

2 Basic Definitions

Among the various models of RNNs, Elman RNNs are considered herein [14,23,26]. Let K be the number of input units, J be the number of hidden units, and I be the number of output units. We use the following notation.

- $\boldsymbol{w}_j^{(J)}$ Weights $\left(w_{0,j}^{(J)}, \ldots, w_{K,j}^{(J)}\right)^{\mathrm{tr}}$ from all input units to the jth hidden unit, where $w_{0,j}^{(J)}$ is the bias, and $\boldsymbol{a}^{\mathrm{tr}}$ denotes the transpose of a vector $\boldsymbol{a}$.
- $\boldsymbol{W}^{(J)}$ Weights $\left(\boldsymbol{w}_1^{(J)}, \ldots, \boldsymbol{w}_J^{(J)}\right)$ from all input units to all hidden units.
- $\boldsymbol{v}_i^{(J)}$ Weights $\left(v_{0,i}^{(J)}, \ldots, v_{J,i}^{(J)}\right)^{\mathrm{tr}}$ from all hidden units to the ith output unit, where $v_{0,i}^{(J)}$ is the bias term.
- $\boldsymbol{V}^{(J)}$ Weights $\left(\boldsymbol{v}_1^{(J)}, \ldots, \boldsymbol{v}_I^{(J)}\right)$ from all hidden units to all output units.

$\boldsymbol{r}_j^{(J)}$ Recurrent weights $\left(r_{1,j}^{(J)}, ..., r_{J,j}^{(J)}\right)^{\mathrm{tr}}$ from all hidden units to the jth hidden unit.

$\boldsymbol{R}^{(J)}$ Recurrent weights $\left(\boldsymbol{r}_1^{(J)}, ..., \boldsymbol{r}_J^{(J)}\right)$ from all hidden units to all hidden units.

$\boldsymbol{\theta}^{(J)}$ A vector of all weights $\boldsymbol{W}^{(J)}$, $\boldsymbol{V}^{(J)}$, and $\boldsymbol{R}^{(J)}$.

$\boldsymbol{x}^{(t)}$ Input signals $\left(1, x_1^{(t)}, ..., x_K^{(t)}\right)^{\mathrm{tr}}$ at time t.

$\boldsymbol{X}_{t_0,t_1}$ Input signals $\left(\boldsymbol{x}^{(t_0)}, ..., \boldsymbol{x}^{(t_1)}\right)$ from time t_0 to $t_1 (\geq t_0)$.

Given input signals $\boldsymbol{X}_{t_0,t_1}$, the output of the jth hidden unit is

$$z_j\left(\boldsymbol{X}_{t_0,t_1}; \boldsymbol{\theta}^{(J)}\right) = \begin{cases} \sigma\left(\boldsymbol{w}_j^{(J)\mathrm{tr}} \boldsymbol{x}^{(t_1)}\right), & \text{if } t_0 = t_1; \\ \sigma\left(\boldsymbol{w}_j^{(J)\mathrm{tr}} \boldsymbol{x}^{(t_1)} + \boldsymbol{r}_j^{(J)\mathrm{tr}} \boldsymbol{z}\left(\boldsymbol{X}_{t_0,t_1-1}; \boldsymbol{\theta}^{(J)}\right)\right), & \text{if } t_0 < t_1, \end{cases} \tag{1}$$

where $\boldsymbol{z}\left(\boldsymbol{X}_{t_0,t_1}; \boldsymbol{\theta}^{(J)}\right) \equiv \left(z_1\left(\boldsymbol{X}_{t_0,t_1}; \boldsymbol{\theta}^{(J)}\right), ..., z_J\left(\boldsymbol{X}_{t_0,t_1}; \boldsymbol{\theta}^{(J)}\right)\right)^{\mathrm{tr}}$, and we consider a sigmoid function $\sigma(x) = 1/(1 + e^{-x})$ as the activation function. As hidden units have recurrent weights, the outputs typically depend on the values of $\boldsymbol{x}^{(t_0)}, ..., \boldsymbol{x}^{(t_1)}$, not just $\boldsymbol{x}^{(t_1)}$.

Herein, an identity function is considered as the activation function of output units. The output of the ith output unit is

$$f_i\left(\boldsymbol{X}_{t_0,t_1}; \boldsymbol{\theta}^{(J)}\right) = \boldsymbol{v}_i^{(J)\mathrm{tr}} \tilde{\boldsymbol{z}}\left(\boldsymbol{X}_{t_0,t_1}; \boldsymbol{\theta}^{(J)}\right), \tag{2}$$

where $\tilde{\boldsymbol{z}}\left(\boldsymbol{X}_{t_0,t_1}; \boldsymbol{\theta}^{(J)}\right) \equiv \left(1, z_1\left(\boldsymbol{X}_{t_0,t_1}; \boldsymbol{\theta}^{(J)}\right), ..., z_J\left(\boldsymbol{X}_{t_0,t_1}; \boldsymbol{\theta}^{(J)}\right)\right)^{\mathrm{tr}}$. Using weights $\boldsymbol{V}^{(J)}$, the outputs $\boldsymbol{f}\left(\boldsymbol{X}_{t_0,t_1}; \boldsymbol{\theta}^{(J)}\right) \equiv \left(f_1\left(\boldsymbol{X}_{t_0,t_1}; \boldsymbol{\theta}^{(J)}\right), ..., f_I\left(\boldsymbol{X}_{t_0,t_1}; \boldsymbol{\theta}^{(J)}\right)\right)^{\mathrm{tr}}$ of the 1st to Ith output units can be calculated as:

$$\boldsymbol{f}\left(\boldsymbol{X}_{t_0,t_1}; \boldsymbol{\theta}^{(J)}\right) = \boldsymbol{V}^{(J)\mathrm{tr}} \tilde{\boldsymbol{z}}\left(\boldsymbol{X}_{t_0,t_1}; \boldsymbol{\theta}^{(J)}\right). \tag{3}$$

3 Reducible Regions

An RNN is considered *reducible* when a hidden unit can be removed such that the RNN's input-output function does not change. This Section considers the regions of a reducible RNN, referred to as *reducible regions.*

First, consider a solution for an RNN with $J - 1$ hidden units. Here all weights of such a solution are denoted by symbols with hats, such as $\widehat{w}_{K,1}^{(J-1)}$, $\widehat{\boldsymbol{v}}_i^{(J-1)}$, $\widehat{\boldsymbol{R}}^{(J-1)}$, and $\widehat{\boldsymbol{\theta}}^{(J-1)}$.

Next, consider the following region.

$$\widehat{\boldsymbol{\Theta}}_{\gamma_j}^{(J)} = \Big\{\boldsymbol{\theta}^{(J)} \Big| \boldsymbol{W}^{(J)} = \Big(\widehat{\boldsymbol{W}}^{(J-1)}, \widehat{\boldsymbol{w}}_j^{(J-1)}\Big), v_{0,i}^{(J)} = \widehat{v}_{0,i}^{(J-1)}, v_{j',i}^{(J)} = \widehat{v}_{j',i}^{(J-1)},$$
$$v_{j,i}^{(J)} = p_i \widehat{v}_{j,i}^{(J-1)}, v_{J,i}^{(J)} = (1-p_i)\widehat{v}_{j,i}^{(J-1)}, r_{j',j''}^{(J)} = \widehat{r}_{j',j''}^{(J-1)}, r_{j',J}^{(J)} = \widehat{r}_{j',j}^{(J-1)},$$
$$r_{j,j''}^{(J)} = q_{j''}\widehat{r}_{j,j''}^{(J-1)}, r_{J,j''}^{(J)} = (1-q_{j''})\widehat{r}_{j,j''}^{(J-1)}, r_{J,J}^{(J)} = (1-q_J)\widehat{r}_{j,j}^{(J-1)},$$
$$r_{j,J}^{(J)} = q_J \widehat{r}_{j,j}^{(J-1)}, j' \in \{1, ..., J-1\} \backslash \{j\}, j'' \in \{1, ..., J-1\}, i \in \{1, ..., I\}\Big\}, \quad (4)$$

where $j \in \{1, ..., J-1\}$, and $p_1, ..., p_I, q_1, ..., q_J$ are all arbitrary real numbers. Figure 1 shows an example of a region $\widehat{\boldsymbol{\Theta}}_{\gamma_j}^{(J)}$. A region $\widehat{\boldsymbol{\Theta}}_{\gamma_j}^{(J)}$ is a reducible region because it satisfies the following theorem, the proof of which can be found in the appendix.

Theorem 1. *$f(\boldsymbol{X}_{t_0,t_1}; \boldsymbol{\theta}^{(J)}) = f(\boldsymbol{X}_{t_0,t_1}; \widehat{\boldsymbol{\theta}}^{(J-1)})$ where $\boldsymbol{\theta}^{(J)} \in \widehat{\boldsymbol{\Theta}}_{\gamma_j}^{(J)}$, and $t_0 \leq t_1$.*

For MLPs, three types to generate reducible MLPs are known [5,24]. As for RNNs, other types, in addition to the aforementioned, may also generate reducible RNNs; however, the proposed method uses only the aforementioned type.

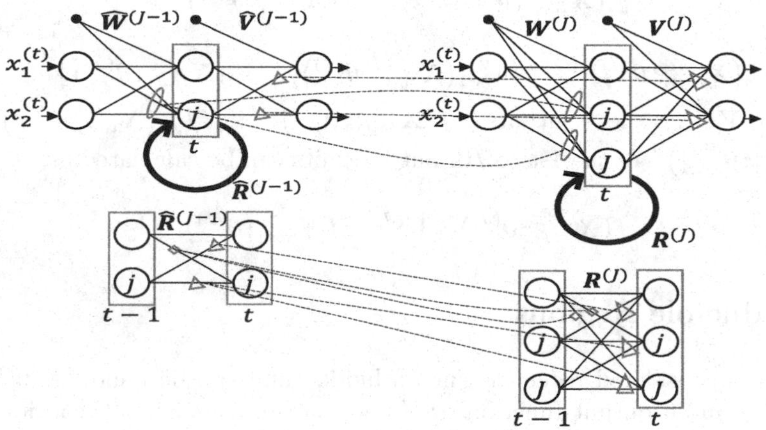

Fig. 1. Example of a region $\widehat{\boldsymbol{\Theta}}_{\gamma_j}^{(J)}$ when $K = 2, I = 2, j = 2$, and $J = 3$. The left side is the solution for an RNN with $J-1$ hidden units, whereas the right side is an RNN with J hidden units in the region $\widehat{\boldsymbol{\Theta}}_{\gamma_j}^{(J)}$. Weights across an ellipse on the right are the same as those on the left. A weight marked with a diamond on the right is the same as one marked with a diamond on the left. The sum of weights that touch a triangle is the same as one marked with a triangle on the left.

4 Reducible Region Descent

This section proposes reducible region descent (RRD), a method to start learning an RNN from a reducible region. When learning begins from a reducible region, the training error for an RNN with J hidden units becomes smaller than that of the solution with $J-1$ hidden units. Therefore, the training error monotonically decreases with increasing number of hidden units. This section explains the descent from a reducible region and the proposed method's processing flow.

4.1 Descent from a Reducible Region

Previous studies have proven that several reducible regions exist in the MLP parameter space and continuous regions with zero gradients exist in the reducible regions [5]. Similarly, points or regions with zero gradients may be in a reducible region $\widehat{\boldsymbol{\Theta}}^{(J)}_{\gamma_j}$. If the gradient is zero, learning cannot begin by a gradient-based method from the region. Therefore, herein, the eigenvalues and eigenvectors of the Hessian matrix were used, similar to the method of using reducible regions of an MLP [18]. Even if the gradient is zero, if a negative eigenvalue exists in the Hessian matrix, learning can be started in the direction of the eigenvector corresponding to the negative eigenvalue. Hence, herein, negative eigenvalues and their corresponding eigenvectors of Hessian matrices were used in the proposed method.

4.2 Procedure of the Proposed Method

Algorithm 1 shows the procedure of RRD. In addition, Fig. 2 shows a conceptual diagram of the RRD flow. In Step 1 of Algorithm 1, the initial values of the weights were randomly selected from the interval $(-1, 1)$, and the number of learning trials was set to 10 in the experiment performed herein. Further, Broyden–Fletcher–Goldfarb–Shanno (BFGS) [4], a type of quasi-Newton

Algorithm 1. RRD

1: Randomly initialize the weights of an RNN with one hidden unit and perform learning several times
2: Select a solution with the smallest training error and let the solution be denoted by $\widehat{\boldsymbol{\theta}}^{(1)}$
3: **for** $J = 2, ..., J_{\max}$ **do**
4: Generate reducible regions $\widehat{\boldsymbol{\Theta}}^{(J)}_{\gamma_1}, ..., \widehat{\boldsymbol{\Theta}}^{(J)}_{\gamma_{J-1}}$ from $\widehat{\boldsymbol{\theta}}^{(J-1)}$ and select several points on the reducible regions
5: Calculate the Hessian matrices at the selected points and calculate the eigenvalues and eigenvectors
6: Perform learning in the directions and the opposite directions of the eigenvectors corresponding to negative eigenvalues in the calculated eigenvalues
7: Let a solution with the smallest training error be $\widehat{\boldsymbol{\theta}}^{(J)}$
8: **end for**

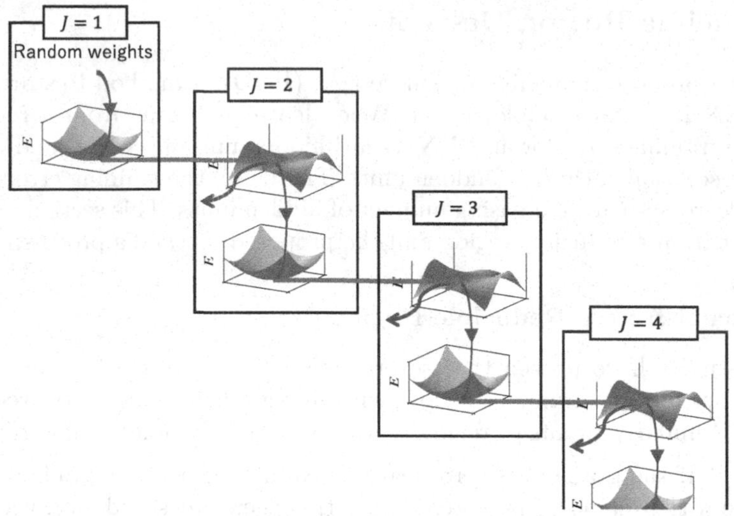

Fig. 2. Conceptual diagram of the RRD flow.

method, was used as the learning method. In BFGS, a line search was used where the initial value of the step length was set to 1. If the training error did not decrease, the step length was repeatedly halved. Learning by BFGS was stopped when the number of weight updates reached 1,000 or the step length for the line search became less than 10^{-16}. In Step 3, the maximum number $J_{\max}$ of hidden units was set to 20.

In Step 4, it is necessary to determine which points on the reducible regions will be used. In the experiment, the points where $p_1 = \cdots = p_I = q_1 = \cdots = q_J = 0.5$ and points where $p_1 = \cdots = p_I = q_1 = \cdots = q_J = 1.5$ were selected. Note that at 0.5, the signs of pair weights are the same, and at 1.5, the signs of pair weights are different. These points were selected for each $j \in \{1, ..., J-1\}$. Therefore, the number of points used in Step 4 was $2 \times (J-1)$.

The learning trials in Step 6 can be very time-consuming if numerous negative eigenvalues exist and learning trials are started in the directions of eigenvectors corresponding to all negative eigenvalues. Hence, herein, the eigenvalues were selected in order, starting with the smallest eigenvalue, and the upper limit of the number of learning trials was set to 10. In Step 6, BFGS was used after the weights were updated once in the direction (or in the opposite direction) of an eigenvector. In BFGS, the exact line search and stopping criteria were used as in Step 1.

5 Experiment

To evaluate the proposed method, an experiment was performed to predict the Lorenz attractor [15]. A computer with Ryzen 9, 3950X, and 64 GB RAM was used. Further, Julia Version 1.8.5, with DifferentialEquations Version 7.7.0, Zygote Version 0.6.55, Statistics, LinearAlgebra, and Random packages, was used as the programming language.

5.1 Settings

The Lorenz equations are $\frac{da}{dt} = \alpha(b - a)$, $\frac{db}{dt} = a(\rho - c) - b$, and $\frac{dc}{dt} = ab - \beta c$. We set ρ, α, and β to 28, 10, and 8/3, respectively, and set the initial values of a, b, and c to –10, –10, and 30, respectively. Figure 3 shows the trajectory of the a, b and c at $t = 0, \Delta t, \cdots, 499\Delta t$. Here, Δt was set to 0.05 and Tsit5 solver was used to generate the trajectory by setting the tolerance option as reltol = abstol = 10^{-6}.

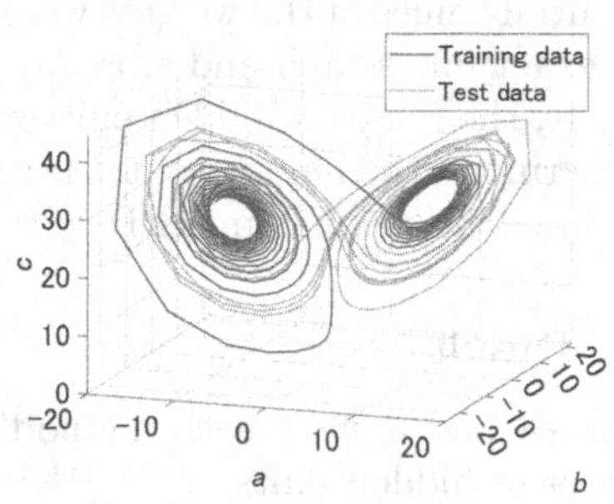

Fig. 3. Trajectory of the Lorenz attractor.

Given inputs a_t, b_t, and c_t, an RNN predicts one point ahead (Δt ahead) $a_{t+\Delta t}, b_{t+\Delta t}$, and $c_{t+\Delta t}$. Herein, 300 points were used as training data, as follows. $((a_0, b_0, c_0), (a_{\Delta t}, b_{\Delta t}, c_{\Delta t}), ..., (a_{299\Delta t}, b_{299\Delta t}, c_{299\Delta t}))$:

$$\begin{aligned} \boldsymbol{X}^{(train)}_{1,299} &= ((1, a_0, b_0, c_0)^{\text{tr}}, (1, a_{\Delta t}, b_{\Delta t}, c_{\Delta t})^{\text{tr}}, ..., \\ &\quad (1, a_{298\Delta t}, b_{298\Delta t}, c_{298\Delta t})^{\text{tr}}), \end{aligned} \tag{5}$$

$$\begin{aligned} \boldsymbol{Y}^{(train)}_{1,299} &= ((1, a_{\Delta t}, b_{\Delta t}, c_{\Delta t})^{\text{tr}}, (1, a_{2\Delta t}, b_{2\Delta t}, c_{2\Delta t})^{\text{tr}}, ..., \\ &\quad (1, a_{299\Delta t}, b_{299\Delta t}, c_{299\Delta t})^{\text{tr}}). \end{aligned} \tag{6}$$

Further, 200 points were used as test data, as follows. $((a_{300\Delta t}, b_{300\Delta t}, c_{300\Delta t}), (a_{301\Delta t}, b_{301\Delta t}, c_{301\Delta t}), ..., (a_{499\Delta t}, b_{499\Delta t}, c_{499\Delta t}))$:

$$\begin{aligned} \boldsymbol{X}^{(test)}_{1,199} &= ((1, a_{300\Delta t}, b_{300\Delta t}, c_{300\Delta t})^{\text{tr}}, (1, a_{301\Delta t}, b_{301\Delta t}, c_{301\Delta t})^{\text{tr}}, ..., \\ &\quad (1, a_{498\Delta t}, b_{498\Delta t}, c_{498\Delta t})^{\text{tr}}), \end{aligned} \tag{7}$$

$$\begin{aligned} \boldsymbol{Y}^{(test)}_{1,199} &= ((1, a_{301\Delta t}, b_{301\Delta t}, c_{301\Delta t})^{\text{tr}}, (1, a_{302\Delta t}, b_{302\Delta t}, c_{302\Delta t})^{\text{tr}}, ..., \\ &\quad (1, a_{499\Delta t}, b_{499\Delta t}, c_{499\Delta t})^{\text{tr}}). \end{aligned} \tag{8}$$

In forecasting time series data, interests are often only in predicting the future. Hence, herein, the many-to-one architecture [2,8] was used, and the following equation was considered as the objective function of the many-to-one model.

$$E_{many-to-one}(\boldsymbol{X}_{1,T}, \boldsymbol{Y}_{1,T}) = \sum_{\tau_1=h}^{T} e(\boldsymbol{X}_{\tau_1-h+1,\tau_1}, \boldsymbol{y}_{\tau_1}; \boldsymbol{\theta}^{(J)}), \tag{9}$$

where $e(\boldsymbol{X}_{\tau_0,\tau_1}, \boldsymbol{y}_{\tau_1}; \boldsymbol{\theta}^{(J)}) \equiv \left(\boldsymbol{f}(\boldsymbol{X}_{\tau_0,\tau_1}; \boldsymbol{\theta}^{(J)}) - \boldsymbol{y}_{\tau_1}\right)^{\text{tr}} \left(\boldsymbol{f}(\boldsymbol{X}_{\tau_0,\tau_1}; \boldsymbol{\theta}^{(J)}) - \boldsymbol{y}_{\tau_1}\right)$, and h is an integer greater than or equal to 1 and indicates the number of previous inputs that are reflected. In the experiment, h was set to

10. Here, we define $E_{tr} \equiv E_{many-to-one}(\boldsymbol{X}^{(train)}_{1,299}, \boldsymbol{Y}^{(train)}_{1,299})$, and $E_{test} \equiv E_{many-to-one}(\boldsymbol{X}^{(test)}_{1,199}, \boldsymbol{Y}^{(test)}_{1,199})$.

Moreover, steepest descent (SD) and BFGS with random initial weights were used as existing methods. Here, these two methods are called random initialization-SD (RI-SD) and RI-BFGS, respectively. In RI-SD and RI-BFGS, the initial values of the weights were randomly selected from the interval $(-1, 1)$. The exact line search and stopping criteria used in RRD were also used. Additionally, the range of hidden units was set to 1–20 in both RI-SD and RI-BFGS. Furthermore, the number of trials was set to 10 for each number of hidden units, matching the settings in RRD.

5.2 Results

Figures 4 and 5 show each method's smallest training and test errors for each number of hidden units.

Although the training error obtained by RI-BFGS was significantly smaller than RI-SD, the training error did not monotonically decrease with increasing number of hidden units. By contrast, the training error obtained by RRD decreased monotonically with increasing number of hidden units and was smaller than that obtained by RI-BFGS. The test error obtained by RRD was also the smallest.

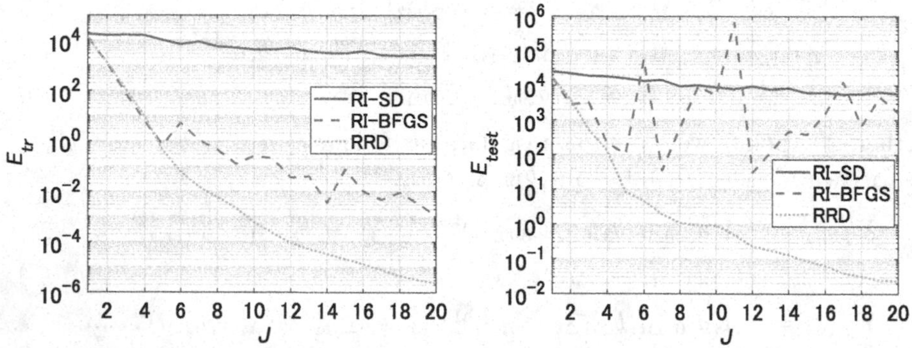

Fig. 4. Training error.

Fig. 5. Test error.

Further, the total processing times of the RI-SD, RI-BFGD, and RRD methods were 144, 51, and 65 min, respectively. RRD took more time compared with RI-BFGS, partly because RRD requires the calculation of the Hessian matrices on reducible regions. RI-SD took the longest time because the line search took a long time.

5.3 More Weight Updates for RI-BFGS

Since a solution with $J-1$ hidden units is used for learning an RNN with J hidden units in RRD, it can be interpreted that the number of weight updates

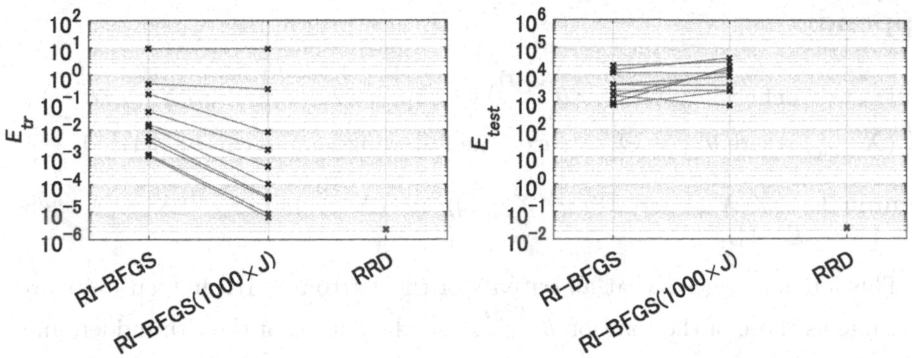

Fig. 6. Training errors when $J = 20$.

Fig. 7. Test errors when $J = 20$.

is accumulated, and the total number of weight updates is $1000 \times J$. Thus, RRD was compared with RI-BFGS, where the upper limit of weight updates was set to $1000 \times J$. Here, this method is called RI-BFGS($1000 \times J$). All other settings remained unchanged, consistent with those described in Sect. 5.1.

Figures 6 and 7 show the training and test errors when $J = 20$.

In RI-BFGS($1000 \times J$), the training error decreased with increasing number of weight updates; however, the smallest training error was still larger than an RRD training error. Interestingly, most of the test errors obtained by RI-BFGS($1000 \times J$) increased with increasing number of weight updates. By contrast, RRD enabled determining solutions with small training and test errors in a stable manner. The mean and standard deviation of the ten test errors obtained by RI-BFGS($1000 \times J$) when $J = 20$ were 1.39×10^4 and 1.35×10^4, respectively, whereas those obtained by RRD were 0.0242 and 6.93×10^{-4}, respectively.

6 Conclusion

This study shows that reducible regions exist in an RNN parameter space. In addition, a new learning method called RRD, which uses reducible regions generated from a solution, was proposed. Further, an evaluation experiment was conducted to predict the Lorenz attractor, wherein RRD stably determined quality solutions, thereby outperforming existing methods.

In the future, we plan to evaluate RRD using various datasets. We also plan to investigate the structure of reducible regions in the parameter space used in the procedure of RRD, in particular whether continuous regions exist where the gradient is zero. In addition, we plan to investigate other types to generate reducible regions.

Acknowledgements. This paper is based on results obtained from a project commissioned by the New Energy and Industrial Technology Development Organization (NEDO).

Appendix

First, we define, $z_{j''}(\boldsymbol{X}_{t_0,t_1};\widehat{\boldsymbol{\theta}}^{(J-1)}) \equiv \widehat{z}_{j''}^{(J-1)}(\boldsymbol{X}_{t_0,t_1})$, $z_{j''}(\boldsymbol{X}_{t_0,t_1};\boldsymbol{\theta}^{(J)}) \equiv z_{j''}^{(J)}(\boldsymbol{X}_{t_0,t_1})$ where $\boldsymbol{\theta}^{(J)} \in \widehat{\boldsymbol{\Theta}}_{\gamma_j}^{(J)}$. Next, the following lemma can be derived.

Lemma 1. $z_{j''}^{(J)}(\boldsymbol{X}_{t_0,t_1}) = \widehat{z}_{j''}^{(J-1)}(\boldsymbol{X}_{t_0,t_1})$, $z_J^{(J)}(\boldsymbol{X}_{t_0,t_1}) = \widehat{z}_j^{(J-1)}(\boldsymbol{X}_{t_0,t_1})$ *where* $j'' \in \{1,...,J-1\}$.

This lemma suggests that all outputs of the 1st to $J-1$th hidden units are the same as those of the solution $\widehat{\boldsymbol{\theta}}^{(J-1)}$, and the output of the Jth hidden unit is the same as that of the jth hidden unit of the solution $\widehat{\boldsymbol{\theta}}^{(J-1)}$.

Proof. Using mathematical induction, this lemme can be proven. More specifically, first, let us show that the outputs of hidden units are the same for $t_1 = t_0 + 1$. Next, assuming that the outputs are the same when $t_1 = t_0 + h$, let us show that the outputs are the same when $t_1 = t_0 + h + 1$.

To show that the outputs are the same when $t_1 = t_0 + 1$, consider the case when $t_1 = t_0$. From $\widehat{\boldsymbol{w}}_{j''}^{(J-1)} = \boldsymbol{w}_{j''}^{(J)}, j'' \in \{1,...,J-1\}$, and $\widehat{\boldsymbol{w}}_j^{(J-1)} = \boldsymbol{w}_J^{(J)}$, $\widehat{z}_{j''}^{(J-1)}(\boldsymbol{X}_{t_0,t_0}) = z_{j''}^{(J)}(\boldsymbol{X}_{t_0,t_0}), j'' \in \{1,...,J-1\}$, and $\widehat{z}_j^{(J-1)}(\boldsymbol{X}_{t_0,t_0}) = z_J(\boldsymbol{X}_{t_0,t_0})$.

When $t_1 = t_0 + 1$, the following is noted.

$$
\begin{aligned}
\widehat{z}_{j''}^{(J-1)}(\boldsymbol{X}_{t_0,t_0+1}) &= \sigma\Bigg(\widehat{\boldsymbol{w}}_{j''}^{(J-1)^{\mathrm{tr}}}\boldsymbol{x}^{(t)} + \sum_{j'=1}^{J-1}\widehat{r}_{j',j''}^{(J-1)}\widehat{z}_{j'}^{(J-1)}(\boldsymbol{X}_{t_0,t_0})\Bigg) \\
&= \sigma\Bigg(\widehat{\boldsymbol{w}}_{j''}^{(J-1)^{\mathrm{tr}}}\boldsymbol{x}^{(t)} + \sum_{j'\in\{1,...,J-1\}\backslash\{j\}}\widehat{r}_{j',j''}^{(J-1)}\widehat{z}_{j'}^{(J-1)}(\boldsymbol{X}_{t_0,t_0}) \\
&\quad + b_{j''}\widehat{r}_{j,j''}^{(J-1)}\widehat{z}_j^{(J-1)}(\boldsymbol{X}_{t_0,t_0}) + (1-b_{j''})\widehat{r}_{j,j''}^{(J-1)}\widehat{z}_j^{(J-1)}(\boldsymbol{X}_{t_0,t_0})\Bigg) \\
&= \sigma\Bigg(\boldsymbol{w}_{j''}^{(J)^{\mathrm{tr}}}\boldsymbol{x}^{(t)} + \sum_{j'\in\{1,...,J-1\}\backslash\{j\}} r_{j',j''}^{(J)} z_{j'}^{(J)}(\boldsymbol{X}_{t_0,t_0}) \\
&\quad + r_{j,j''}^{(J)} z_j^{(J)}(\boldsymbol{X}_{t_0,t_0}) + r_{J,j''}^{(J)} z_J^{(J)}(\boldsymbol{X}_{t_0,t_0})\Bigg) \\
&= z_{j''}^{(J)}(\boldsymbol{X}_{t_0,t_0+1}),
\end{aligned}
\tag{10}
$$

where $j'' \in \{1,...,J-1\}$. Moreover,

$$
\begin{aligned}
\widehat{z}_j^{(J-1)}(\boldsymbol{X}_{t_0,t_0+1}) &= \sigma\Bigg(\widehat{\boldsymbol{w}}_j^{(J-1)^{\mathrm{tr}}}\boldsymbol{x}^{(t)} + \sum_{j'=1}^{J-1}\widehat{r}_{j',j}^{(J-1)}\widehat{z}_{j'}^{(J-1)}(\boldsymbol{X}_{t_0,t_0})\Bigg) \\
&= \sigma\Bigg(\widehat{\boldsymbol{w}}_j^{(J-1)^{\mathrm{tr}}}\boldsymbol{x}^{(t)} + \sum_{j'\in\{1,...,J-1\}\backslash\{j\}}\widehat{r}_{j',j''}^{(J-1)}\widehat{z}_{j'}^{(J-1)}(\boldsymbol{X}_{t_0,t_0})
\end{aligned}
$$

$$
\begin{aligned}
&+b_J\widehat{r}_{j,j}^{(J-1)}\widehat{z}_j^{(J-1)}(\boldsymbol{X}_{t_0,t_0}) + (1-b_J)\widehat{r}_{j,j}^{(J-1)}\widehat{z}_j^{(J-1)}(\boldsymbol{X}_{t_0,t_0})\Bigg) \\
&= \sigma\Bigg(\boldsymbol{w}_J^{(J)^{\mathrm{tr}}}\boldsymbol{x}^{(t)} + \sum_{j'\in\{1,\ldots,J-1\}\setminus\{j\}} r_{j',J}^{(J)} z_{j'}^{(J)}(\boldsymbol{X}_{t_0,t_0}) \\
&\quad + r_{j,J}^{(J)} z_j^{(J)}(\boldsymbol{X}_{t_0,t_0}) + r_{J,J}^{(J)} z_J^{(J)}(\boldsymbol{X}_{t_0,t_0})\Bigg) \\
&= z_J^{(J)}(\boldsymbol{X}_{t_0,t_0+1}).
\end{aligned} \tag{11}
$$

Next, let us assume that $\widehat{z}_{j''}^{(J-1)}(\boldsymbol{X}_{t_0,t_0+h}) = z_{j''}^{(J)}(\boldsymbol{X}_{t_0,t_0+h})$, $j'' \in \{1, ..., J-1\}$, $\widehat{z}_j^{(J-1)}(\boldsymbol{X}_{t_0,t_0+h}) = z_J^{(J)}(\boldsymbol{X}_{t_0,t_0+h})$, and consider the case when $t_1 = t_0+h+1$. If the equations are transformed in the same manner as Eqs. (10) and (11), the following is obtained.

$$
\widehat{z}_{j''}^{(J-1)}(\boldsymbol{X}_{t_0,t_0+h+1}) = z_{j''}^{(J)}(\boldsymbol{X}_{t_0,t_0+h+1}), \tag{12}
$$

$$
\widehat{z}_j^{(J-1)}(\boldsymbol{X}_{t_0,t_0+h+1}) = z_J^{(J)}(\boldsymbol{X}_{t_0,t_0+h+1}), \tag{13}
$$

where $j'' \in \{1, ..., J-1\}$. From Eqs. (10), (11), (12), and (13), we obtain:

$$
\widehat{z}_{j''}^{(J-1)}(\boldsymbol{X}_{t_0,t_1}) = z_{j''}^{(J)}(\boldsymbol{X}_{t_0,t_1}), \quad \widehat{z}_j^{(J-1)}(\boldsymbol{X}_{t_0,t_1}) = z_J^{(J)}(\boldsymbol{X}_{t_0,t_1}), \tag{14}
$$

where $j'' \in \{1, ..., J-1\}$, and $t_1 \geq t_0$. □

Now, let us return to the proof of Theorem 1.

Proof. From Lemma 1, we obtain the following.

$$
\begin{aligned}
f_i(\boldsymbol{X}_{t_0,t_1};\boldsymbol{\theta}^{(J)}) &= \widehat{v}_{0,i}^{(J-1)} + \sum_{j''=1}^{J-1} \widehat{v}_{j'',i}^{(J-1)}\widehat{z}_{j''}^{(J-1)}(\boldsymbol{X}_{t_0,t_1}) \\
&= \widehat{v}_{0,i}^{(J-1)} + \sum_{j''\in\{1,\ldots,J-1\}\setminus\{j\}} \widehat{v}_{j'',i}^{(J-1)}\widehat{z}_{j''}^{(J-1)}(\boldsymbol{X}_{t_0,t_1}) \\
&\quad + p_i\widehat{v}_{j,i}^{(J-1)}\widehat{z}_j^{(J-1)}(\boldsymbol{X}_{t_0,t_1}) + (1-p_i)\widehat{v}_{j,i}^{(J-1)}\widehat{z}_j^{(J-1)}(\boldsymbol{X}_{t_0,t_1}) \\
&= v_{0,i}^{(J)} + \sum_{j''\in\{1,\ldots,J-1\}\setminus\{j\}} v_{j'',i}^{(J)} z_{j''}^{(J)}(\boldsymbol{X}_{t_0,t_1}) \\
&\quad + v_{j,i}^{(J)} z_j^{(J)}(\boldsymbol{X}_{t_0,t_1}) + v_{J,i}^{(J)} z_J^{(J)}(\boldsymbol{X}_{t_0,t_1}) \\
&= f_i(\boldsymbol{X}_{t_0,t_1};\widehat{\boldsymbol{\theta}}^{(J-1)})
\end{aligned} \tag{15}
$$

where $i \in \{1, ..., I\}$. □

References

1. Baccouche, M., Mamalet, F., Wolf, C., Garcia, C., Baskurt, A.: Sequential deep learning for human action recognition. In: Salah, A.A., Lepri, B. (eds.) HBU 2011. LNCS, vol. 7065, pp. 29–39. Springer, Heidelberg (2011). https://doi.org/10.1007/978-3-642-25446-8_4

2. Dadoun, A., Troncy, R.: Many-to-one recurrent neural network for session-based recommendation. arXiv preprint arXiv:2008.11136 (2020)
3. De Jeses, O., Hagan, M.T.: Backpropagation through time for a general class of recurrent network. In: International Joint Conference on Neural Networks, vol. 4, pp. 2638–2643. IEEE (2001)
4. Fletcher, R.: Practical Methods of Optimization, 2nd edn. John Wiley & Sons, Hoboken (1987)
5. Fukumizu, K., Amari, S.: Local minima and plateaus in hierarchical structures of multilayer perceptrons. Neural Netw. **13**(3), 317–327 (2000)
6. Graves, A., Mohamed, A.r., Hinton, G.: Speech recognition with deep recurrent neural networks. In: International Conference on Acoustics, Speech and Signal Processing, pp. 6645–6649. IEEE (2013)
7. Hewamalage, H., Bergmeir, C., Bandara, K.: Recurrent neural networks for time series forecasting: current status and future directions. Int. J. Forecast. **37**(1), 388–427 (2021)
8. Kaur, M., Mohta, A.: A review of deep learning with recurrent neural network. In: International Conference on Smart Systems and Inventive Technology, pp. 460–465. IEEE (2019)
9. Keskar, N.S., Berahas, A.S.: adaQN: an adaptive quasi-newton algorithm for training RNNs. In: Frasconi, P., Landwehr, N., Manco, G., Vreeken, J. (eds.) ECML PKDD 2016. LNCS (LNAI), vol. 9851, pp. 1–16. Springer, Cham (2016). https://doi.org/10.1007/978-3-319-46128-1_1
10. Kobayashi, M.: Exceptional reducibility of complex-valued neural networks. IEEE Trans. Neural Netw. **21**(7), 1060–1072 (2010)
11. Kobayashi, M.: Singularities of three-layered complex-valued neural networks with split activation function. IEEE Trans. Neural Netw. Learn. Syst. **29**(5), 1900–1907 (2017)
12. Kobayashi, M.: Uniqueness theorem for quaternionic neural networks. Signal Process. **136**, 102–106 (2017)
13. Kobayashi, M.: Reducibilities of hyperbolic neural networks. Neurocomputing **378**, 129–141 (2020)
14. Krichene, E., Masmoudi, Y., Alimi, A.M., Abraham, A., Chabchoub, H.: Forecasting using elman recurrent neural network. In: Madureira, A.M., Abraham, A., Gamboa, D., Novais, P. (eds.) ISDA 2016. AISC, vol. 557, pp. 488–497. Springer, Cham (2017). https://doi.org/10.1007/978-3-319-53480-0_48
15. Lorenz, E.N.: Deterministic nonperiodic flow. J. Atmos. Sci. **20**(2), 130–141 (1963)
16. Nitta, T.: Reducibility of the complex-valued neural network. Neural Inf. Process.-Lett. Rev. **2**(3), 53–56 (2004)
17. Nitta, T.: Local minima in hierarchical structures of complex-valued neural networks. Neural Netw. **43**, 1–7 (2013)
18. Satoh, S., Nakano, R.: Fast and stable learning utilizing singular regions of multilayer perceptron. Neural Process. Lett. **38**(2), 99–115 (2013)
19. Satoh, S., Nakano, R.: Multilayer perceptron learning utilizing singular regions and search pruning. In: World Congress on Engineering and Computer Science, vol. 2 (2013)
20. Satoh, S., Nakano, R.: Complex-valued multilayer perceptron search utilizing singular regions of complex-valued parameter space. In: Wermter, S., et al. (eds.) ICANN 2014. LNCS, vol. 8681, pp. 315–322. Springer, Cham (2014). https://doi.org/10.1007/978-3-319-11179-7_40

21. Satoh, S., Nakano, R.: Complex-valued multilayer perceptron learning using singular regions and search pruning. In: International Joint Conference on Neural Networks, pp. 1–6. IEEE (2015)
22. Satoh, S., Nakano, R.: A new method for learning RBF networks by utilizing singular regions. In: Rutkowski, L., Scherer, R., Korytkowski, M., Pedrycz, W., Tadeusiewicz, R., Zurada, J.M. (eds.) ICAISC 2018. LNCS (LNAI), vol. 10841, pp. 214–225. Springer, Cham (2018). https://doi.org/10.1007/978-3-319-91253-0_21
23. Şeker, S., Ayaz, E., Türkcan, E.: Elman's recurrent neural network applications to condition monitoring in nuclear power plant and rotating machinery. Eng. Appl. Artif. Intell. **16**(7–8), 647–656 (2003)
24. Sussmann, H.J.: Uniqueness of the weights for minimal feedforward nets with a given input-output map. Neural Netw. **5**(4), 589–593 (1992)
25. Tallec, C., Ollivier, Y.: Unbiasing truncated backpropagation through time. arXiv preprint arXiv:1705.08209 (2017)
26. Wang, J., Wang, J., Fang, W., Niu, H.: Financial time series prediction using elman recurrent random neural networks. Comput. Intell. Neurosci. **2016** (2016)
27. Williams, R.J., Peng, J.: An efficient gradient-based algorithm for on-line training of recurrent network trajectories. Neural Comput. **2**(4), 490–501 (1990)

t-ConvESN: Temporal Convolution-Readout for Random Recurrent Neural Networks

Matthew S. Evanusa[1,3(✉)], Vaishnavi Patil[1], Michelle Girvan[2], Joel Goodman[3], Cornelia Fermüller[1], and Yiannis Aloimonos[1]

[1] Department of Computer Science, University of Maryland, College Park, MD, USA
mevanusa@umd.edu
[2] Dept. of Physics, University of Maryland, College Park, MD, USA
[3] U.S. Naval Research Laboratory, Washington, DC, USA

Abstract. While deep neural networks have excelled at static data such as images, temporal data - the data that these networks will need to process in the real world - remains an open challenge. Handling temporal data with neural networks requires one of three options: backpropagation through time using recurrent neural networks (RNNs), treating the time series as static data for a convolutional neural network (CNNs) or attention-based transformer architectures. RNNs are an elegant autoregressive network type that naturally keep a memory of the past while performing computations. Although recurrent networks such as LSTMs have shown strong success across a multitude of fields and tasks such as natural language processing, they can be difficult to train. Transformers and 1-D CNNs, two feed-forward alternatives for temporal data, have gained popularity but in their base forms lack memory to keep track of past activations. Random recurrent networks, also known as Reservoir Computing, have shown that one need not necessarily backpropagate the error through the recurrent component. Here, we propose a novel hybrid approach that brings together the temporal memory capabilities of a random recurrent network with the powerful learning capacity of a deep temporal convolutional readout, which we call *t*-ConvESN. We experimentally verify that although the recurrent component remains random and unlearned, its combination with a deep readout achieves superior accuracy on a number of datasets from the UCR time series classification dataset collection compared to other state of the art deep learning architectures. Our experiments also show that our proposed method excels in datasets in the low-data regime.

Keywords: Recurrent Neural Network · Reservoir Computing · Deep Learning · Machine Learning · Neuromorphic Computing

1 Introduction

With the advent of multilayered/deep feed-forward networks, learning generalizable features for many tasks, such as classification, approximation the state for

L. Iliadis et al. (Eds.): ICANN 2023, LNCS 14259, pp. 140–151, 2023.
https://doi.org/10.1007/978-3-031-44223-0_12

reinforcement learning and data generation are now possible [1,2,22]. However, these networks are designed for and tend to excel at *static* tasks, such as image classification or generation. Even in cases where the state evolves, such as in RL, the network still learns a static mapping of features to approximate the state. The real world, in contrast, contains exclusively temporal data consisting of the sights, sounds, and video that constitute our daily experiences. Temporal data grows exponentially complex with time, but humans handle this overabundance by keeping a history of the past in the network as *memory*.

To this end, learning length-invariant, time-varying parametric representations of temporal data that efficiently manage a memory of past events remains an open challenge. A recent line of investigation has been opened into granting neural networks access to an explicit memory location, as in a Turing machine [35]. The mammalian brain is known to store its memory as a combination of dynamical activity [37] as well as synaptic weight changes [38]. This dynamical memory results from maintaining a *state* of the network, something lacking in feed-forward architectures. To introduce this dynamical state in a neural network, we can create cycles within the network, leading to a Recurrent Neural Network, or RNN. However, owing to the cycles in the network, training RNNs via backpropagation commonly requires an expensive and tricky unrolling of the network into a synthetic deep feed forward network before training, where the backpropagation is performed - also known as Backpropagation Through Time (BPTT) [8]. Due to the difficulty of this training, many non-recurrent methods have taken over as the state of the art for temporal data, such as Transformers [14], feed-forward convolutional autoregressive networks such as WaveNet [16] and Temporal Convolutional Networks [21]. However, it has been argued that these feed-forward architectures do not generalize well to time series whose lengths are not encountered during training [32], have restricted expressivity as compared to their recurrent counterparts [33,34], as well as issues of efficiency as well as representation learning [18]. Within the neuromorphic community who are interested in biologically realistic learning rules, BPTT in its current form is considered non-plausible. It is thus of interest to the general neural networks community - to both those interested in biologically plausible mechanisms as well as performance - to continue to investigate the benefits of recurrent neural networks. To this end, we aim to develop a model that both lends to the biological plausibility of recurrence, as well as their theoretical performative benefits.

Recently, *randomness* in neural network parameters and initialization has become an important direction of inquiry into discerning the true effectiveness of deep neural networks. Recent work on biologically-realistic backpropagation shows that randomly chosen feedback matrices are effective at training hidden layers [3]. Proposal of the *lottery ticket* hypothesis [4] argues that the true work of stochastic gradient descent is finding "winning" randomly initialized subnetworks within larger networks - that the values of the winning sub-trees did not change much even after training. Reliance on over tuning of architectures in deep learning supports the argument that it is the random initialization of the architecture (and the subsequent fine-tuning of hyperparameters) that creates the best-performing deep networks. Here, we take a step further towards demonstrating the power of randomness by merging ideas from Reservoir Computing [5,6], which has for decades rested on random, unlearned recurrent weights, with temporal convolutional deep networks, to show that random recurrent weights are sufficient for temporal learning.

We demonstrate that the temporal convolutional readout is able to more robustly learn the complex dynamics for time series classification tasks compared to other neural models both feed-forward as well as recurrent. We further demonstrate that our method significantly outperforms gradient-based BPTT-trained recurrent neural networks, and make the case that the recurrent weights need not necessarily be learned for temporal tasks. We believe this is of interest to both deep learning, as well as the neuromorphic and computational neuroscience community, as methods that do not require backpropagating through time are both more biologically realistic and more implementable in specialized neuromorphic hardware.

2 Our Proposed Method: t-ConvESN

The two main components of our architecture are an untrained, random recurrent neural network component modeled off of echo state network dynamics, and a deep temporal convolutional readout that learns multi-timescale features with a multi-layered fully connected classifier. Figure 1 shows an overview of the structure. The reservoir or random recurrent network can be seen as acting as a temporal kernel machine [20]. Another way to view the structure is that the W_I matrix is randomly expanding the input temporal sequence in data space into a much higher dimensional temporal reservoir space. Our hypothesis - following the initial reservoir hypothesis in [5] - is that this higher dimensional reservoir space is more separable than the initial data space. We replace this readout layer with a deep temporal convolutional network that learns multi-timescale features. The reservoir component effectively gives the convolutional readout access to a fading memory of the input sequence.

2.1 Standard Echo State Network Structure

In typical reservoir computing, there are three main components: an input projection, a recurrent pool, and a readout mechanism. Our proposed network consists of a randomly initialized input weight matrix and a recurrent weight matrix which together determine the *state* vector of an Echo State Network at any time step. "Neurons" in the reservoir are represented as the activity vector x_t, which is a weighted linear combination of the activity at the previous time step and the projected activity from the current time step. The activity is calculated as:

$$x_t = (1 - \alpha)x_{t-1} + \alpha f(iW_I u_t + rW_R x_{t-1}) \tag{1}$$

where x_t is the N-dimensional vector of the activity states of each reservoir neuron at time t, α is the leak rate, $f(\cdot)$ is a saturating non-linear activation

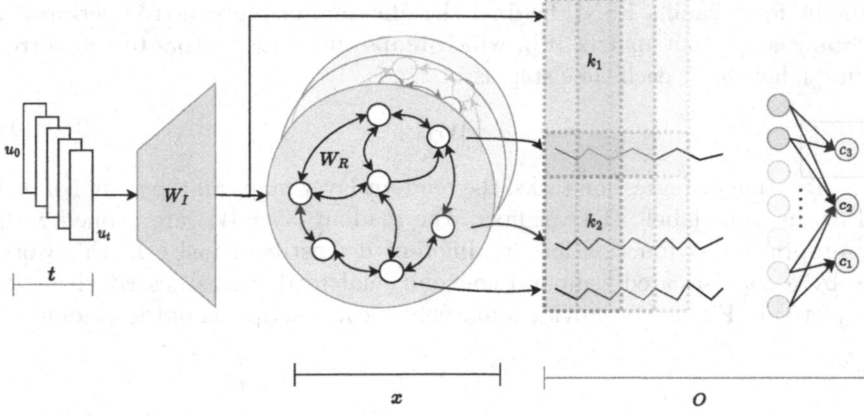

Fig. 1. The *t-ConvESN* architecture for time series classification. Each element of the input sequence $u_0...u_T$ is fed in one time step at a time to the randomly weighted recurrent neural network *(center, orange)*, where T is the maximum length of each series. At each time step (See Eq. 1), the reservoir activity is updated as a combination of the input projected by matrix W_I and the past time step's activity at $t-1$ multiplied by the recurrent weights W_R. The reservoir is instantiated in parallel with other sub-reservoirs, shown in grey (middle). All sub-reservoirs' activity are concatenated before passing into the readout. The activity of each reservoir neuron, stored as a vector x_t at each time step t, is then fed into a temporal convolutional readout (depicted here as O, taking the place of the readout W_O in the standard ESN), along with the input along a "skip connection", where multiple filters are passed across the series in *reservoir space*. Shown here are two kernels k_1 in red and k_2 in blue, as they are shifted across the time domain. Finally, per traditional convolutional architectures, the resulting feature maps are flattened and passed into a fully-connected multi-layered perceptron for final softmax classification for class value c. Not shown here is the multi-reservoir structure: shown here is one reservoir for illustrative purposes. (Color figure online)

function (here sigmoid), and W_I, W_R are the data-to-input and reservoir-to-reservoir weights, respectively. The scalars i and r act as input and recurrent weight matrix scaling constants, which reduce or increase the gain on the activity. Formally, at each time step t, a vector-valued input $u_t \in \mathbb{R}^d$ is projected into a higher dimensional reservoir space by the input weight matrix $W_I : \mathbb{R}^d \rightarrow \mathbb{R}^D$ with $(d << D)$. The $W_R : \mathbb{R}^D \rightarrow \mathbb{R}^D$, also randomly initialized, scales the state vector of the previous time step x_{t-1} such that the reservoir keeps a shallow memory of its past. This scaled previous activity is added to the projected input and this current activity is used to update the state vector x_t as per Eq. 1. The current state activity is a convex combination of the state vector of the previous time step and the current activity for smoother updates. As stated in [5], we normalize the maximum real eigenvalue of W_R, denoted the *spectral radius*, or σ, to be less than 1; this is a hyperparameter to be set. This ensures the *echo state property*, or that activity fades when there is no input.

Finally, for a vanilla ESN, the final classification or regression is performed by learning an output matrix W_O, which maps the state vectors to the corresponding labels y_t at each time step as in Eq. 1:

$$y_t = W_O x_t \tag{2}$$

For classification or regression tasks, the readout layer maps all the points of one signal to the same label. The weights of the readout layer W_O are trained with the appropriate loss function for the different downstream tasks. In this work W_O is by a sophisticated temporal convolutional readout, as described below and depicted in Fig. 1. We provide a mathematical description of the readout in Sect. 2.2.

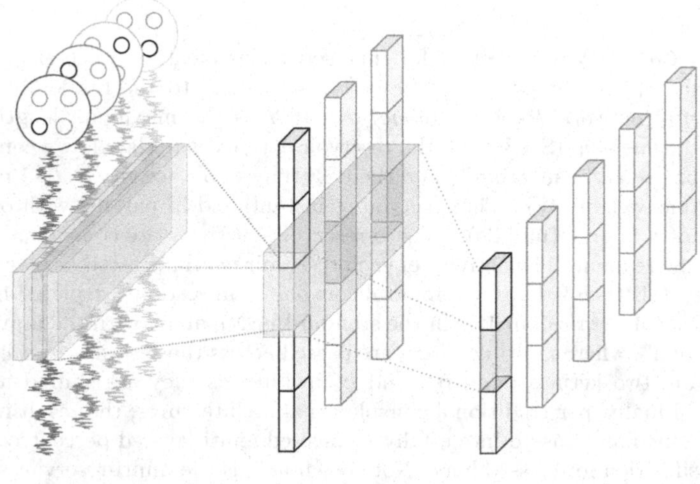

Fig. 2. A zoomed in visualization of the convolutional filters being applied to different neurons in the reservoir. As in Fig. 2, the result of this convolution (the final layer, represented by vertical bars) is passed to a fully connected readout. The neuron shading depicts that the vertical signal output corresponds to a single neuron. All of the neurons collective outputs are passed over by multi-channeled 1-dimensional convolutional kernels, which output a vector feature map. The middle and left bars represent the second and third layers, respectively, of the CNN readout - for visualization purposes, as the number of layers can be changed - and the colors correspond to the value resulting from a particular convolution channel.

Parallel Sub-reservoirs. As in [12], we use a parallelized sub-reservoir structure. Instead of one large reservoir of dimension D, we pass in the input to multiple sub-reservoirs M with each reservoir of dimension H such that $D = M * H$, which are inter-connected amongst themselves but not with other sub-reservoirs. Mathematically, this is equivalent to one large reservoir with zeroes everywhere except for small blocks of weights around the diagonal. We find this is actually more computationally stable for the readout mechanism than a large reservoir, and produces more consistent and accurate results, especially for the convolutional readout. Unlike in [12] where concatenating the sub-reservoirs for a fully connected readout forced the readout to learn alternating combinations of sub-reservoirs, for the model in this work, a parallel structure has no effect on the convolution operation. This is because the convolutions are still applied across time, and the readout learns to map neurons from sub-reservoirs in non-linear combinations across time. The parallel reservoirs are analogous to the multiple heads in the transformer attention, or the multiple channels in a CNN architecture. By increasing the number of initializations in parallel, you increase the feature space on which you can search. Figure 2 visually depicts the interaction between the sub reservoirs and the convolutional readout.

2.2 Temporal Convolutional Readout

The novelty of our work lies in using a temporal convolutional readout, also known as a Time Delay Neural Network [9], or Temporal Convolutional Neural Network [21] (without the causal convolutions, for simplicity), as the readout for a random recurrent neural network. This readout consists of filters which convolve over the state vectors of the reservoir at different time steps to extract temporal features from the data. The different reservoir state vectors x are stacked to form the time series data matrix X, which is convolved with the temporal convolutional filters across time. A filter $k = \{k^1, k^2, \cdots, k^D\}$ such that k^i slides over the activity across time of neuron x^i according to the equation:

$$f(X)[t] = (X * k)[t] = \sum_{i=1}^{D} (x^i * k^i)[t] \tag{3}$$

$$(x^i * k^i)[t] = \sum_{m=-n}^{m=n} x^i_{t-m} k^i[m]$$

Figure 2 demonstrates the movement of a the convolution filters across the output of the reservoir neurons. As for deep CNN architectures, we then stack such multiple 1d-convolution layers to extract hierarchical temporal features from the data for final classification, according to the equation:

$$\begin{aligned} f^i(X) &= \sigma \odot (f^i(X)[0], f^i(X)[1], \cdots, f^i(X)[T]) \\ y &= W_O\,(f^n \circ \cdots \circ f^2 \circ f^i(X)) \end{aligned} \tag{4}$$

where T is the number of time steps in an example of the time series, σ is the activation which is applied point-wise ($\odot$) to the output of a convolutional layer and n if the total number of 1-d convolution layers. Each convolutional layer f^i consists of multiple filters which convolve over the input to the layer in parallel, as is commonly done.

Through this, we are able to learn nonlinear combinations of the responses of individual neurons as a function of time in a much more compact way compared to all-to-all connections as in a multi-layered Perceptron. One way to view this interaction is that the readout is learning nonlinear filters of the response of the recurrent component; in this way the reservoir can be seen as acting as a random temporal kernel [20]. Due to the way convolution operates in one dimension, each channel of filters actually learns a combination of the responses of each neuron, which gives the readout more computational flexibility than being forced to learn a filter for each neuron. The convolutional kernels are stacked in layers, allowing the readout to extract hierarchical features across time. In addition, the kernels share weights, facilitating the network to learn shift-invariant features. Causal and dilated convolutions as in [16] are not used for simplicity, but are left for future work. The feature maps resulting from the convolutions are fed into a multi-layered feed forward network for final classification. While we will point out that we do train this readout with backpropagation, which is not biologically-inspired as is the reservoir; we view this as a temporary placeholder for any future biologically-adjacent nonlinear network training rule, such as Feedback Alignment [3], as the backpropagation is performed in a feed-forward manner, rather than through time.

3 Related Work

Prior work has looked into using 1-D convolutional filters for time series learning [15]. Hybrid deep learning approaches to reservoir computing have been developed in the past several years to address the inability of "vanilla" reservoir computing to scale up to complex tasks. In [12], the authors showed using a combination of a traditional reservoir with multiple sub-reservoirs, as well as a deep artificial neural network with modern regularization techniques, could outperform state of the art methods on real world data tasks. Our work can be seen as a further evolution of this work that replaces the artificial neural network readout with a more sophisticated temporal convolutional readout. In [27], the authors combined a reservoir with a complex attention and memory mechanism, that allowed the reservoir access to longer periods of memory. In [23], the authors used untrained kernels, as in a CNN [10,11], to train a reservoir to recognize image data, in order to avoid backpropagating the signal through the reservoir. Previous work in [24] also combined the reservoir with other kinds of deep learning readouts, for time series classification. A different line of research aimed to stack reservoirs in layers as a MLP stacks perceptrons in layers, leading to "deep reservoir" computing [25], and novel unsupervised ways to train them [26]. In [28], the authors use a multi-timescale convolutional readout that learns independent kernels of multi-timescale reservoirs. Our work is different in that rather than enforce multiple timescales in the collected states, we let a deep convolutional readout *learn* the multiple timescale features. Our kernels also learn to combine activity from multiple reservoirs, which aids in stability. To the best of our knowledge, our work is the first to incorporate a deep temporal convolutional readout in the time domain, for the neuron pool, that learns to combine multiple sub-reservoir activity across time as multi-channel kernels, to learn multi-timescale features.

Table 1. Comparison top-1 accuracy results of our proposed *t-ConvESN* method against four other deep neural network architectures: a standard MLP, LSTM [7], Transformer [14] encoder classifier, and a 1-d CNN (TCN) on 19 UCR datasets. All networks were run 10 times, with results posted as the mean of the runs with standard deviation to test for consistency. The top pane are univariate datasets, and the bottom pane are multivariate. All networks were trained on 1000 epochs. Our *t-ConvESN* shows surprising consistency even though the W_I and W_R weight matrices are chosen randomly, *and the 10 runs initialize a different random weight matrix each time.* The selected datasets are chosen for being more difficult, i.e., datasets that were considerably less than accuracies of 1 for most models. For consistency, the ReLU [19] activation function was used for all layers of all networks. By outperforming the TCN, we show that it is not just the convolutional readout, but the combination with the recurrent component, that performs well.

Dataset	MLP	LSTM	Transformer	TCN	**t-ConvESN**
Beef	.832 ± .02	.722 ± .04	.813 ± .03	**.967 ± .00**	**.967 ± .00**
Car	.805 ± .04	.488 ± .04	.816 ± .04	**.853 ± .01**	**.851 ± .01**
CinCECGTorso	.596 ± .03	.601 ± .03	.826 ± .03	.932 ± .01	**.968 ± .01**
ChlorineConc	.872 ± .02	.582 ± .02	.801 ± .02	**.901 ± .01**	**.901 ± .01**
Computers	.521 ± .02	.582 ± .04	.533 ± .02	.613 ± .02	**.629 ± .02**
ECG200	.862 ± .02	.710 ± .02	.882 ± .03	.932 ± .01	**.942 ± .01**
ElectricDevices	.514 ± .01	.422 ± .01	.460 ± .01	.623 ± .02	**.652 ± .01**
ItalyPowerDemand	**.964 ± .01**	.943 ± .02	.958 ± .02	.950 ± .01	**.963 ± .01**
Lightning2	.675 ± .03	.631 ± .02	.708 ± .04	.736 ± .01	**.793 ± .02**
Lightning7	.582 ± .03	.557 ± .04	.625 ± .03	.682 ± .01	**.722 ± .03**
OliveOil	.933 ± .02	.401 ± .01	.872 ± .04	.936 ± .02	**.963 ± .01**
RefrigerationDev	.353 ± .01	.477 ± .03	.361 ± .03	.490 ± .01	**.528 ± .01**
SmallKitchenApp	.368 ± .01	.623 ± .02	.371 ± .01	.586 ± .01	**.750 ± .01**
LargeKitchenApp	.400 ± .02	.532 ± .02	.521 ± .03	.543 ±.02	**.833 ± .01**
Worms	.374 ± .03	.448 ± .04	.500 ± .02	.565 ± .03	**.638 ± .02**
WormsTwoClass	.514 ± .03	.551 ± .02	.568 ± .03	.684 ± .01	**.716 ± .02**
Libras	.763 ± .02	.458 ± .02	.762 ± .03	**.884 ± .01**	**.888 ± .01**
Heartbeat	.658 ± .02	.678 ± 0.3	.667 ± .02	.687 ± .02	**.741 ± .01**
Epilepsy	.632 ± .02	.602 ± 0.03	.701 ± .02	.881 ± .01	**.958 ± .01**

4 Experiments

We compare our proposed model now against numerous state of the art methods to test its efficacy across multiple time series classification datasets in the UCR Time Series Classification dataset archive [13].

4.1 Comparison Methods and Setup

We compare against exemplar networks from the main sequential or temporal processing neural networks: Transformers, LSTMs, and Temporal Convolutional

Neural Networks along with the fully connected multi-layer perceptron. We chose specific datasets that were more challenging, which showcase our model's performance in the low-data regime, and avoided "synthetic" time series datasets that were created out of rasterizing image data. For all runs, the Rectified Linear Unit activation function [19] was used for all networks. In Table 1, we list the chosen datasets which represent more natural signal data such as electrical power, sensor readings, and ECG, and show the top accuracy results from the different methods. For different datasets, different numbers of sub-reservoirs were used: on smaller datasets, we found that four small reservoirs performed better. We perform training for the readout deep network using the AdamW [36] optimizer in pyTorch, using dropout as a regularizer in conjunction with batched training and batch normalization. Due to the large number of parameters in echo state networks, it is common to use some kind of search optimization to find optimal configurations [30]. These include α, σ, i, r, the number of sub-reservoirs, and the size of the sub-reservoir, in addition to other standard neural network hyperparameters like the learning rate. Here, we use the Optuna python library [31] to optimize said parameters. For a fair comparison, we also run the Optuna optimizer to find the best hyperparameters for the competing state-of-the-art models, such as the learning rate, dropout, number of layers, and number of heads for the Transformer. Experiments were run on the RTX A4000, A5000, and A6000 GPUs using pyTorch for the deep neural networks.

4.2 Results

Table 1 shows the top-1 accuracy across several datasets from the UCR time series classification dataset collection. For reproducibility, especially because initialization is critical for random recurrent architectures, we ran each network 10 times with different random seeds and report the mean accuracy and standard deviation. Our proposed *t-ConvESN* outperforms most other models consistently, with low standard deviation, even though the reservoir is chosen and kept random throughout training even though the reservoir is initialized randomly during each run. We hypothesize that this is empirical evidence that the random projection offers a rich set of dynamical features that are readily useable by a sophisticated readout mechanism. As in [12], we argue that standard echo state networks without a non-linear readout are not able to linearly separate some complex data. In particular, our network far outperforms the gold standard LSTM gradient-based RNN on classification tasks. We believe this is because while the datasets have lower spatial dimension, they contain long temporal sequences, and the LSTM is incapable of backpropagating far through time. On some datasets we see that fully connected models like the multilayer perceptron and Transformers outperform the sequential or temporal processing models. We believe that this is because the fully connected models have larger number of parameters and the corresponding labels for the datasets do not explicitly depend on the temporal properties. Furthermore, on some datasets we see that only the Temporal convolution network performs comparably with our t-ConvESN network. For these datasets, we speculate that the dataset does not really benefit from being projected into a higher dimensional space by the reservoir to be mapped to the corresponding labels. For some datasets which are easily separable, such as *Car* and *Beef*, our model matches the performance of the base TCN. We posit that this is because recurrence adds no additional benefit, and the class information is contained within a local window. However, for most of the other datasets, this is not the case: long-term information aids in generalizing to the test set. In addition, most of these datasets are in the extreme low-data environment, with less than 500 samples for training. We hypothesize our model particularly performs well in the low-data regime, even with a deep learning readout, because projecting the data into the random reservoir space allows the readout to learn separation planes with fewer data. However, more investigation is needed in this front. We also believe this low-data regime is the reason for the Transformer network (and the other deep learning set) relatively poor performance. While it remains to be seen if this generalizes in future work to more and more complex datasets, we believe this is a fruitful sign for neuromorphic and bio-inspired networks, that we do not have to choose between either biological inspiration or accuracy; that neuromorphic architectures can compete at the level with other state of the art methods.

5 Conclusion

In this work, we present a novel bio-inspired random recurrent neural network for temporal data, *t-ConvESN*, which projects the data into a space in such a way that gives a convolutional neural network access to a fading memory. We empirically demonstrate that the network exhibits robust and consistent performance even though the recurrent weights remain untrained, and can outperform many state of the art methods on time series. Future work can involve making the network fully biologically plausible by replacing backpropagation training of the readout with any of the newly-discovered backpropagation alternative gradient methods such as Feedback Alignment variants [3,17]. While this work employs a relatively simple CNN readout, future work can incorporate more complex convolutions such as in WaveNet [16] or attentional mechanisms.

References

1. Mnih, V., et al.: Human-level control through deep reinforcement learning. Nature **518**(7540), 529–533 (2015)
2. He, K., Zhang, X., Ren, S., Sun, J.: Deep residual learning for image recognition. In: Proceedings of the IEEE Conference on Computer Vision and Pattern Recognition, pp. 770–778 (2016)
3. Lillicrap, T.P., Cownden, D., Tweed, D.B., Akerman, C.J.: Random feedback weights support learning in deep neural networks. arXiv preprint arXiv:1411.0247 (2014)
4. Frankle, J., Carbin, M.: The lottery ticket hypothesis: finding sparse, trainable neural networks. arXiv preprint arXiv:1803.03635 (2018)

5. Jaeger, H.: The "echo state" approach to analysing and training recurrent neural networks-with an erratum note. Bonn, Germany: German Natl. Res. Center Inf. Technol. GMD Tech. Rep. **148**(34), 13 (2001)
6. Maass, W.: Liquid state machines: motivation, theory, and applications. In: Computability in Context: Computation and Logic in the Real World, pp. 275–296 (2011)
7. Hochreiter, S., Schmidhuber, J.: Long short-term memory. Neural Comput. **9**(8), 1735–1780 (1997)
8. Werbos, P.J.: Backpropagation through time: what it does and how to do it. Proc. IEEE **78**(10), 1550–1560 (1990)
9. Lang, K.J., Waibel, A.H., Hinton, G.E.: A time-delay neural network architecture for isolated word recognition. Neural Netw. **3**(1), 23–43 (1990)
10. Fukushima, K.: Neocognitron: a hierarchical neural network capable of visual pattern recognition. Neural Netw. **1**(2), 119–130 (1988)
11. LeCun, Y., Bottou, L., Bengio, Y., Haffner, P.: Gradient-based learning applied to document recognition. Proc. IEEE **86**(11), 2278–2324 (1998)
12. Evanusa, M., Shrestha, S., Patil, V., et al.: Deep-readout random recurrent neural networks for real-world temporal data. SN Comput. Sci. **3**, 222 (2022). https://doi.org/10.1007/s42979-022-01118-9
13. Bagnall, A., Lines, J., Bostrom, A., et al.: The great time series classification bake off: a review and experimental evaluation of recent algorithmic advances. Data Min. Knowl. Disc. **31**, 606–660 (2017). https://doi.org/10.1007/s10618-016-0483-9
14. Vaswani, A., et al.: Attention is all you need. Adv. Neural Inf. Process. Syst. **30** (2017)
15. Zheng, Y., Liu, Q., Chen, E., Ge, Y., Zhao, J.L.: Time series classification using multi-channels deep convolutional neural networks. In: Li, F., Li, G., Hwang, S., Yao, B., Zhang, Z. (eds.) WAIM 2014. LNCS, vol. 8485, pp. 298–310. Springer, Cham (2014). https://doi.org/10.1007/978-3-319-08010-9_33
16. Oord, A.V.D., et al.: Wavenet: a generative model for raw audio. arXiv preprint arXiv:1609.03499 (2016)
17. Evanusa, M., Fermüller, C., Aloimonos, Y.: Deep reservoir networks with learned hidden reservoir weights using direct feedback alignment. arXiv preprint arXiv:2010.06209 (2020)
18. Sundaram, S., Sinha, D., Groth, M., Sasaki, T., Boix, X.: Symmetry perception by deep networks: inadequacy of feed-forward architectures and improvements with recurrent connections. arXiv preprint arXiv:2112.04162 (2021)
19. Agarap, A.F.: Deep learning using rectified linear units (relu). arXiv preprint arXiv:1803.08375 (2018)
20. Tino, P.: Dynamical systems as temporal feature spaces. J. Mach. Learn. Res. **21**, 1649–1690 (2020)
21. Pandey, A., Wang, D.: TCNN: temporal convolutional neural network for real-time speech enhancement in the time domain. In: ICASSP 2019–2019 IEEE International Conference on Acoustics, Speech and Signal Processing (ICASSP), pp. 6875–6879. IEEE (2019)
22. Ramesh, A., et al.: Zero-shot text-to-image generation. In: International Conference on Machine Learning, pp. 8821–8831. PMLR (2021)
23. Tong, Z., Tanaka, G.: Reservoir computing with untrained convolutional neural networks for image recognition. In: 2018 24th International Conference on Pattern Recognition (ICPR), pp. 1289–1294. IEEE (2018)

24. Bianchi, F.M., Scardapane, S., Løkse, S., Jenssen, R.: Bidirectional deep-readout echo state networks. arXiv preprint arXiv:1711.06509 (2017)
25. Gallicchio, C., Micheli, A.: Deep echo state network (deepesn): a brief survey. arXiv preprint arXiv:1712.04323 (2017)
26. Ma, Q., Shen, L., Cottrell, G.W.: DeePr-ESN: a deep projection-encoding echo-state network. Inf. Sci. **511**, 152–171 (2020)
27. Ma, Q., Zheng, Z., Zhuang, W., Chen, E., Wei, J., Wang, J.: Echo memory-augmented network for time series classification. Neural Netw. **133**, 177–192 (2021)
28. Ma, Q., Chen, E., Lin, Z., Yan, J., Yu, Z., Ng, W.W.: Convolutional multitimescale echo state network. IEEE Trans. Cybern. **51**(3), 1613–1625 (2019)
29. Hendrycks, D., Gimpel, K.: Gaussian error linear units (gelus). arXiv preprint arXiv:1606.08415 (2016)
30. Maat, J.R., Gianniotis, N., Protopapas, P.: Efficient optimization of echo state networks for time series datasets. In: 2018 International Joint Conference on Neural Networks (IJCNN), pp. 1–7. IEEE (2018)
31. Akiba, T., Sano, S., Yanase, T., Ohta, T., Koyama, M.: Optuna: a next-generation hyperparameter optimization framework. In: Proceedings of the 25th ACM SIGKDD International Conference on Knowledge Discovery & Data Mining, pp. 2623–2631 (2019)
32. Dehghani, M., Gouws, S., Vinyals, O., Uszkoreit, J., Kaiser, Ł.: Universal transformers. arXiv preprint arXiv:1807.03819 (2018)
33. Hahn, M.: Theoretical limitations of self-attention in neural sequence models. Trans. Assoc. Comput. Linguist. **8**, 156–171 (2020)
34. Tran, K., Bisazza, A., Monz, C.: The importance of being recurrent for modeling hierarchical structure. arXiv preprint arXiv:1803.03585 (2018)
35. Graves, A., Wayne, G., Danihelka, I.: Neural turing machines. arXiv preprint arXiv:1410.5401 (2014)
36. Loshchilov, I., Hutter, F.: Decoupled weight decay regularization. arXiv preprint arXiv:1711.05101 (2017)
37. Cohen, J.D., et al.: Temporal dynamics of brain activation during a working memory task. Nature **386**(6625), 604–608 (1997)
38. Bear, M.F.: A synaptic basis for memory storage in the cerebral cortex. Proc. Natl. Acad. Sci. **93**(24), 13453–13459 (1996)

Adaptive Reservoir Neural Gas: An Effective Clustering Algorithm for Addressing Concept Drift in Real-Time Data Streams

Konstantinos Demertzis[1](✉), Lazaros Iliadis[2], and Antonios Papaleonidas[2]

[1] School of Science and Technology, Informatics Studies, Hellenic Open University, Patra, Greece
demertzis.konstantinos@ac.eap.gr

[2] School of Engineering, Department of Civil Engineering, Faculty of Mathematics Programming and General Courses, Democritus University of Thrace, Kimmeria, Xanthi, Greece
liliadis@civil.duth.gr

Abstracts. The concept drift phenomenon describes how the statistical properties of a data distribution change over time. In cybersecurity domain, where data arrives continuously and rapidly in a sequential manner, concept drift can be a significant challenge. Identifying concept drift, it enables security analysts to detect emerging attacks, respond promptly, and make informed decisions based on the changing nature of the data being analyzed. The Adaptive Reservoir Neural Gas (AR-NG) clustering algorithm is proposed in this paper to handle concept drift in real-time data streams. It is a novel approach that combines reservoir computing power with the neural gas algorithm, allowing the algorithm to automatically update its clustering structure as new data arrives. Furthermore, in order to effectively handle evolving data streams that significantly change over time in unexpected ways, the proposed method incorporates a density-based clustering mechanism (DBCM) to concept drift detection. Experiments on real-time data streams show that the proposed algorithm is effective at mitigating the impact of concept drift, making it a useful tool for real-time data analysis and decision-making in dynamic environments.

Keywords: Reservoir Computing · Neural Gas · Concept Drift · Data Streams

1 Introduction

The phenomenon of concept drift describes how the statistical properties of a data distribution change over time [1]. Concept drift can be a significant challenge in data stream mining, where data arrives continuously and rapidly in a sequential manner. The mean, variance, correlation, and probability distribution of the data are all statistical properties of the data distribution. When there is concept drift, these properties change, causing shifts in the underlying patterns, relationships, and structures of the data. Changes in user behavior, evolving trends, seasonality, or external factors influencing the data generation process can all cause concept drift. It can be gradual, with changes occurring gradually over time, or abrupt, with changes occurring suddenly and significantly [2].

L. Iliadis et al. (Eds.): ICANN 2023, LNCS 14259, pp. 152–166, 2023.
https://doi.org/10.1007/978-3-031-44223-0_13

Concept drift complicates data analysis and mining because models trained on historical data may become outdated and less accurate in predicting or clustering new data instances. It is critical to detect and adapt to changing data distributions in order to maintain model performance and validity in the presence of concept drift. On the other hand, in the cybersecurity domain, identifying concept drift is crucial because it can help detect and respond to evolving threats and attacks [3].

Specifically, by identifying concept drift, cybersecurity systems can adapt and learn from new patterns or behaviors that emerge over time. This enables the early detection of emerging threats that might go undetected by traditional rule-based or signature-based systems. Moreover, concept drift detection allows intrusion detection systems (IDS) to detect changes in the patterns of malicious behavior, helping to identify new attack vectors or evasion techniques [4]. Also, by dynamically adapting security controls based on concept drift, organizations can better protect their systems and networks. Also, when concept drift is detected, it may indicate a potential security breach or an ongoing attack. Rapid response can help mitigate the impact of the attack, contain the incident, and prevent further damage or data exfiltration [5]. Furthermore, by understanding how the data distribution or behavior has changed, security analysts can make more informed decisions regarding incident prioritization, resource allocation, and the selection of appropriate defensive measures [6]. Finally, concept drift detection can trigger the retraining or recalibration of machine learning cyber-defense models to adapt to new data distributions and ensure accurate and up-to-date detection [7].

The AR-NG clustering algorithm is used in this paper to present an innovative approach to effectively address concept drift in real-time data streams. AR-NG combines reservoir computing's strengths with the Neural Gas algorithm to create a powerful and adaptive clustering solution that can update its structure as new data arrives.

Reservoir computing is a computational framework that processes input data using a fixed, randomly initialized dynamic reservoir. The Neural Gas algorithm, on the other hand, is a clustering technique that divides data into groups based on similarities. AR-NG gains the ability to adaptively update its clustering structure in response to changes in the data distribution by incorporating reservoir computing into the Neural Gas algorithm.

AR-adaptive NG's nature enables it to capture the evolving patterns and relationships within the real-time data streams. AR-NG dynamically adjusts its clustering structure to reflect the current data distribution as new data points arrive, ensuring that the clusters remain accurate and up to date.

Also, by incorporating the density-based clustering mechanism, the proposed method enhances concept drift detection in evolving data streams. It is designed to discover clusters of arbitrary shape in a dataset, based on the density of data points in the feature space. This approach allows the method to effectively detect concept drift and adapt the clustering structure to handle unexpected changes in the data distribution.

The methodology of AR-NG algorithm is described in detail below.

2 Methodology

The AR-NG algorithm is designed to handle concept drift in real-time data streams by combining reservoir computing with the neural gas algorithm and incorporating a density-based clustering mechanism using DBCM. Specifically, reservoir computing is a computational framework that processes sequential data using a fixed-size dynamic reservoir. The reservoir is a network of neurons that is randomly connected and serves as a computational resource [8]. The reservoir computing approach is used in the AR-NG algorithm to deal with the dynamic nature of data streams. The reservoir computing architecture consists of the input, reservoir, and output layers. The connection and input weights are chosen at random [9]. The reservoir weights are scaled so that the Echo State Property (ESP) is maintained, which is defined as the state in which the reservoir is a "echo" of the entire input history [10]. The discrete layers are only those of input $u(n)$ and output $y(n)$ as they are defined by the problem. The hidden layers are clustered in an region, and their number is indistinguishable. The neurons $x(n)$, are connected by some percentage, which determines how sparsity the reservoir computing will be [11].

The synaptic associations that link the levels together and the reservoir computing are characterized by a value that identifies the weights [12]. In the proposed system, each input neuron is connected via $W^{in}{}_{ij}$ weights (i-input neuron, j-neuron) to each neuron from the reservoir computing. Although normalized, these weights are determined randomly before training, and their values are the final ones as they do not change during training. Also, each neuron is connected to each other neuron, via weights W_{jk} (j-neuron, k-neuron, and $j \neq k$). The respective weights, although normalized, are randomly determined before training and their values do not change. We use $x^{(l)}(t) \in R^{N_R}$ to declare the status of level l at time t. By omitting the bias conditions, the first level state transition function is defined by the following equations [13]:

$$x^{(1)}(t) = \left(1 - a^{(1)}\right)x^{(1)}(t-1) + a^{(1)} \tanh\left(W_{in}u(t) + \hat{W}^{(1)}x^{(1)}(t-1)\right)$$

For each level higher than $l > 1$ equation 1, has the following form (2) [8, 14]:

$$x^{(l)}(t) = \left(1 - a^{(l)}\right)x^{(l)}(t-1) + a^{(l)} \tanh\left(W^{l}x^{l-1}(t) + \hat{W}^{(l)}x^{(l)}(t-1)\right)$$

where $W_{in} \in R^{N_R \times N_U}$ is the input weight matrix, $\widehat{W}^{(l)} \in R^{N_R \times N_R}$ is the recurrent weight matrix for layer l, $W^{(l)} \in R^{N_R \times N_R}$ is the matrix containing the connection weights between layer l–1 and l, $a^{(l)}$ is the leaky parameter of layer l and *tanh* is the Tangent Hyperbolic function. Finally, each reservoir computing neuron is connected via $W^{out}{}_{jm}$ weights (j-neuron, m-neuron input) to the neurons in the output layer. The weights, located in the readout layer, are the only ones trained to get their final values [15, 16].

The Neural Gas algorithm is a competitive learning algorithm used for clustering. It organizes data points into clusters based on their similarity [17]. In AR-NG, the Neural Gas algorithm is combined with reservoir computing to create an adaptive clustering structure that can handle concept drift. Competitive learning neural networks include a competitive layer comprising of Competitive Neurons (CNE). Every CNE_i is characterized by a weight vector $w_i = (w_{i1,\dots,}w_{id})^T$, $i = 1,\dots, M$ and it estimates a similarity measure with the input data vector $x_i = (x_{i1,\dots,}x_{id})^T$ $x \in R$. For every input vector that is introduced to the network there is a competition between the CNE for the determination of the winning neuron. The winner is the neuron that has the higher degree of similarity between the input vector and its assigned weight vector. The output of the winning CNE is set to $o_m = 1$, whereas for the rest of the neurons the output is $o_i = 0$, $i = 1,\dots,M$,

$i \neq m$. The default similarity function used is the inverse value of the actual Euclidean distance $\|x - w_i\|$ between the input vector x^n and the weight vector w_i [18].

Initially, the algorithm initializes the clustering structure using the Neural Gas algorithm. This involves randomly selecting initial cluster centers and updating them based on the similarity between data points and cluster centers [19]. The initialization step creates an initial set of clusters to start with. These clusters are recreated with the algorithm calculating the density around each data point. This is achieved by counting the number of points in a user-defined neighborhood (*Eps-Neighbourhood*) with the definition of thresholds [20, 21]. The purpose is to locate points in the center of the areas (core), on their borders (border), and points that involve noise (noise). The extra data points are added to the center of the regions if they are densely accessible, i.e., there is a chain of core points where each one belongs to the neighborhood (*Eps-Neighborhood*) of the next point and therefore to distinguish the extreme values for each cluster.

Thus, the user can see the streams in different periods. Specifically, the neighborhood area of a point *p* is defined as the set of points for which the *Euclidean* distance between the points *p, q* is smaller than the parameter [22, 23]:

$$\mathrm{N_{Eps}(p)} = \{\mathrm{q} \in \mathrm{D} \mid \mathrm{dist(p, q)} \leq \mathrm{Eps}\}$$

provided that $p = (p1, p2)$ and $q = (q1, q2)$, the Euclidean distance is defined as:

$$\sqrt{(q_1 - p_1)^2 + (q_2 - p_2)^2}$$

So, a point p is considered to be reachable from a point q based on a density determined by the parameters *Eps, MinPts* if:

$$\mathrm{p} \in \mathrm{N_{Eps}(q)} \text{ and } \mathrm{N_{Eps}}\,(\mathrm{q}) \geq \mathrm{MinPts}$$

Having calculated the cluster density, the kernel methods' property is exploited to express several samples through a symmetric and positive definite matrix, according to the similarity of two samples in each position. Thus, the array elements are in a linear space, regardless of the space they come from. This allows the introduction of one more function in the processing stage, which exploits the nonlinear structure of the features to present them as a sparse representation problem modified to work in a *Reproducible Kernel Hilbert Space* (RKHS) [24].

Specifically, as the data is in a *Euclidean* space, the problem of the sparse representation of an *L-dimensional vector* $u \in \mathbb{R}^L$ and a basis $D = [D_1, \ldots, D_m] \in \mathbb{R}^{L \times m}$ The following relationship defines it [25]:

$$\ell(h, D) := \min_a \left\| h - \sum_{i=1}^{m} D_i a_i \right\|_2^2 + \lambda \|a\|_1$$

The sparseness of this vector is required. In the above relation, the vector $a \in \mathbb{R}^m$ Represents the sparse coefficients, and the function $\ell(h, D)$ is the optimal approximation of the problem. The above relationship between the sample distances has to be modified to a nonlinear one. For this purpose, we first define a mapping function $\varphi : \mathbb{R}^L \to \mathcal{H}$. This function maps the samples from the original space to a new Hilbert space equipped with the inner product. Therefore, using the inner product, two groups of samples, $u_i, u_j \in \mathbb{R}^L$, are mapped to a new space using the relation [26]:

$$k\left(u_i, u_j\right) = \varphi(u_i)^T \cdot \varphi\left(u_j\right) \in \mathbb{R}$$

Similarly, a set of m sequences can be expressed as a Kernel Matrix $K \in \mathbb{R}^{m\times m}$ Whose elements express the similarities between the samples. The similarity function used herein is the *Radial Basis Function* (RBF), whose variance has been estimated as the mean value of the distances of the training data [27].

But the relation of sparse coding, as presented, does not allow to work with the K register. For this reason, a modified version has been introduced, which offers the potential to work in this space based on the following equation [28]:

$$\ell(\hat{h}, \hat{D}) := \min_a \left\| \hat{h} - \hat{D}a \right\|_2^2 + \lambda \|a\|_1$$

To fully utilize the intrinsic properties of sparse representations in the above space, the proposed methodology introduces the concept of a *Spatial Pooler*, which normalizes sparse input representations by enriching the input representation with its temporal context. Specifically, the Spatial Pooler aims to prepare sparse input representations for further processing, ensuring that inputs similar to each other (have high overlap and thus high coherence) produce output vectors similar to each other. So, each input pattern is encoded by the *Spatial Pooler* into sparse representations represented as a set of A_k indices of the given pattern at iteration k. [29].

At each step, the similarity between the sparse input representations at step k and step $k + 1$ is calculated by the equation [30]:

$$s = \frac{|A_k \cap A_{k+1}|}{max(|A_k|, |A_{k+1}|)}$$

Similarity s is defined as the ratio between the number of elements (cardinality) of the same active clusters in sparse representations generated in steps k and $k + 1$ and a maximum amount of data in two comparable steps. *Spatial Pooler* is usually stable if the sparse representations of the same pattern do not change for its entire life cycle. In this case, the similarity s between all representations of the same pattern is 100%.

As the data stream arrives continuously and rapidly, the AR-NG algorithm processes each incoming data point sequentially. For each data point, the algorithm performs the following steps:

1. Neuron Activation: The reservoir neurons are activated based on the incoming data point. The activation level of each neuron in the reservoir is determined by its similarity to the current data point.
2. Competitive Learning: The activated neurons compete with each other to become the winning neuron. The winning neuron is the one with the highest activation level.
3. Clustering Initialization. Clustering initialization refers to the process of setting up the initial state of a clustering algorithm before the actual clustering procedure begins. It involves determining the initial cluster assignments or centroids for the data points being clustered. Proper initialization is important as it can significantly impact the quality and convergence speed of the clustering results.

4. Update Clustering Structure: The winning neuron and its neighboring neurons in the topological order are updated to adapt to the incoming data point. This step allows the clustering structure to dynamically evolve and adjust to concept drift.
5. Density-Based Clustering: After updating the clustering structure, a density-based clustering mechanism is employed to detect concept drift. This mechanism identifies clusters based on the density of data points. It assigns data points to clusters and identifies outliers as noise points. By analyzing the density-based clusters, the algorithm can detect significant changes in the data distribution, indicating the presence of concept drift.
6. Concept Drift Handling: If concept drift is detected, the algorithm can take appropriate actions to handle it. For example, it may merge or split clusters, update cluster centers, or adjust the clustering parameters to adapt to the new data distribution.

By combining reservoir computing, the Neural Gas algorithm, and DBCM for density-based clustering, the AR-NG algorithm provides an effective solution for handling concept drift in real-time data streams. It adapts to changing data distributions, maintains accurate clustering structures, and enables real-time analysis in dynamic environments.

The pseudocode that presented in the Appendix 1 is a high-level representation of the AR-NG algorithm. This pseudocode provides a high-level overview of the steps involved in the code, including initialization, data processing in batches, clustering, performance evaluation, concept drift detection, handling, analysis, and plotting of results.

3 Dataset and Results

Factry.io and InfluxDB were used to collect and store data about the industrial environment, such as programmable PLC controllers, SCADA systems, and construction equipment, in order to create a perfect test-bed environment for the proposed algorithm. They are created using measurements or events tracked over time, such as transactions, application performance monitoring, and server analytics [31].

The scenario was focused on collecting time series data from sensors that measure quantifiable values in an hourly manner. These sensors can be monitoring different parameters related to industrial machines' conditions and specifically to a raw water storage tank, equipped with a water level sensor and a valve. The system is configurated such that the valve opens when the water level detected by the sensor is less than or equal to 0.5 m and closes when the level is higher than 0.8 m. Additionally, included a pump that operates based on pressure levels separated by a semipermeable membrane. The pump acts as a safety device and shuts off if the water level falls below 0.25 m.

An attacker aims to manipulate the system by modifying the sensor and actuator information by creating packets to alter the sensor readings and actuator behavior. He exploits the fieldbus communication protocol to change the functionality of the devices without raising suspicions from typical detection systems that look for irregularities.

One year of data was gathered, to create a data stream that is hourly quantifiable values from the sensors, reflecting the machine's condition over time. The concept drift was related by modifying the sensor settings and actuator behavior according to the attacker's intentions. This drift can occur gradually or in sudden changes, mimicking the evolving behavior of the compromised system.

For the experiments, configured the system to send the collected data as a data stream. In the scenario described, the data stream has the following properties [32]:

1. Batch Size: The batch size refers to the number of data points collected and processed at a given time. In the provided scenario, each hour's data is considered as a batch.
2. Time Granularity: The time granularity refers to the resolution or interval at which the data is collected and recorded. In this scenario, the time granularity is specified as hourly quantifiable values from the sensors. This means that the data points are collected and recorded at hourly intervals.
3. Data Source: The data source in this scenario is industrial sensors that monitor various parameters related to machine conditions. The sensors provide quantifiable values reflecting the state of the machines and are collected using the appropriate infrastructure.
4. Data Format: Since the data is collected from sensors, it is numerical data representing measurements or readings from those sensors.
5. Concept Drift: The concept drift refers to changes or shifts in the underlying data distribution over time. In this scenario, concept drift is introduced by the attacker who modifies the sensor and actuator information. This leads to changes in the behavior of the system, which is reflected in the data stream. The concept drift is intentional and occurs gradually (medium), abruptly (high) random with very frequent changes (chaotic) depending on the attacker's actions.

After each data point is processed, the clustering performance is evaluated using several evaluation metrics. Here are the evaluation metrics used in the code:

1. Adjusted Rand Index (ARI): The adjusted Rand index measures the similarity between the true cluster assignments and the predicted cluster assignments, taking into account all pairs of samples and their respective cluster assignments. A value of 1 indicates a perfect clustering, while a value close to 0 suggests random clustering. With overlapping entries of different clusters of modeled clustering C^m and real clustering C^r, ARI can be computed as follows [22]:

$$ARI(C^r, C^m) = \frac{\Sigma_{ij}\frac{n_{ij}}{2} - \frac{\Sigma_i a_2^{a_i} \Sigma_2^{b_j}}{2}}{\frac{1}{2}\Sigma_i a_2^{a_i} + \Sigma_j a_2^{b_j} - \frac{\Sigma_i a_i \Sigma_j b_j}{n}}$$

where, n_{ij} is the number of nodes that are present in both cluster C_i^m and C_j^r, a_i is the summation of all n_{ij} corresponding to any C_j^r of C^r and all C_i^m of C^m, and b_j is the summation of all n_{ij} corresponding to any C_i^m of C^m and all C_j^r of C^r.

2. Silhouette Coefficient: The silhouette coefficient measures how well each sample in a cluster is separated from samples in other clusters. It computes the mean distance between a sample and all other points in the same cluster (a) and the mean distance between the sample and all other points in the nearest neighboring cluster (b). The silhouette coefficient ranges from –1 to 1, where a value close to 1 indicates well-separated clusters, 0 indicates overlapping clusters, and –1 indicates incorrect cluster

assignments. Specifically, silhouette score for a datapoint i is given as [22]:

$$s(i) = \begin{cases} 1 - \frac{a(i)}{b(i)} & \text{if } a(i) < b(i) \\ 0 & \text{if } a(i) = b(i) \\ \frac{b(i)}{a(i)} - 1 & \text{if } a(i) > b(i) \end{cases}$$

where bi is the inter cluster distance defined as the average distance to closest cluster of datapoint i except for that it's a part of:

$$b_i = \min_{k \neq i} \frac{1}{|C_k|} \sum_{j \in C_k} d(i,j)$$

where ai is the intra cluster distance defined as the average distance to all other points in the cluster to which it's a part of:

$$a_i = \frac{1}{|C_i| - 1} \sum_{j \in C_i, i \neq j} d(i,j)$$

3. Calinski-Harabasz Index: The Calinski-Harabasz index, also known as the variance ratio criterion, measures the ratio between the within-cluster dispersion and the between-cluster dispersion. It evaluates the compactness and separation of clusters, where a higher index value indicates better-defined clusters. The Calinski-Harabasz index is calculated as [22]:

$$CH = \frac{\frac{BGSS}{K-1}}{\frac{WGSS}{N-K}} = \frac{BGSS}{WGSS} \times \frac{N-K}{K-1}$$

where N is total number of observations, K is total number of clusters and

$$BGSS = \sum_{k=1}^{k} n_k \times \|C_k - C\|^2$$

where n_k is the number of observations in cluster k, C_k is the centroid of cluster k, C is the centroid of the dataset (barycenter) and K is the number of clusters,

$$WGSS_k = \sum_{i=1}^{n_k} \|X_{ik} - C_k\|^2$$

where n_k is the number of observations in cluster k, X_{ik} is the i-th observation of cluster k, C_k is the centroid of cluster k and then sum all individual within group sums of squares:

$$WGSS = \sum_{k=1}^{K} WGSS_k$$

where $WGSS_k$ is the within group sum of squares of cluster k and K is the number of clusters.

4. Davies-Bouldin Index: The Davies-Bouldin index measures the average similarity between each cluster and its most similar cluster, taking into account both the size and the separation between clusters. A lower index value indicates better clustering, where 0 indicates perfectly separated clusters. Calculate the Davies-Bouldin index as [22]:

$$\overline{D} = \frac{1}{N}\sum_{i=1}^{N} D_i$$

where Di chooses the worst-case scenario, and this value is equal to Ri,j for the most similar cluster to cluster i:

$$R_{ij} = \left\|A_i - A_j\right\|_p = \left(\sum_{k=1}^{n} \left|a_{k,i} - a_{k,j}\right|^p\right)^{\frac{1}{p}}$$

$R_{i,j}$ is a measure of separation between cluster C_i and cluster C_j and $a_{k,i}$ is the k th element of A_i, and there are N such elements in A for it is an n dimensional centroid.

To evaluate the method and prove its superiority, 3 different data streams with varying difficulty concept drift were used (medium, high, and chaotic) in which a comparison was made with corresponding competing algorithms, namely Density-based spatial clustering of applications with noise (DBSCAN), Online K-Means, CluStream and Balanced Iterative Reducing and Clustering using Hierarchies (BIRCH). The results are presented in the following Table 1.

These results indicate the performance of different methods in handling concept drift in Data Streams. Higher values for ARI and Silhouette indicate better clustering quality, while higher values for Calinski-Harabasz and lower values for Davies-Bouldin indicate better cluster separation.

For Data Stream 1 (medium), AR-NG method achieved the highest scores across all metrics, indicating good performance in handling concept drift. It has the highest ARI and Silhouette Score, and it also performs well in the Calinski-Harabasz and Davies-Bouldin measures. DBSCAN, Online K-Means, CluStream, and BIRCH methods also show competitive performance, but slightly lower than AR-NG in terms of ARI and Silhouette Score.

For Data Stream 2 (high), the AR-NG method maintains its relatively high performance, although the scores decrease compared to Data Stream 1. It still outperforms other methods in most metrics. DBSCAN, Online K-Means, CluStream, and BIRCH methods show comparable performance, but they exhibit significant lower scores compared to AR-NG.

For Data Stream 3 (chaotic), all methods experience a significant drop in performance across all metrics. This is likely due to the introduction of chaotic concept drift, which poses challenges for the methods to adapt and accurately cluster the data. AR-NG method still performs better than other methods, but its scores decrease substantially compared to the previous data streams. DBSCAN, Online K-Means, CluStream, and BIRCH methods also show a decrease in performance, with DBSCAN having the lowest scores among them.

Table 1. Performance Results

Data	Method	Scores			
		ARI	Silhouette	Calinski-Harabasz	Davies-Bouldin
Data Stream 1 (Medium)	AR-NG	0.82837	0.694837	1513	0.215832
	DBSCAN	0.80212	0.669901	1487	0.270023
	Online K-Means	0.79441	0.660725	1469	0.268830
	CluStream	0.79092	0.658722	1457	0.283102
	BIRCH	0.78996	0.642399	1401	0.308972
Data Stream 2 (High)	AR-NG	0.78401	0.61774	1408	0.312113
	DBSCAN	0.74392	0.55973	1251	0.360921
	Online K-Means	0.74489	0.56130	1269	0.359872
	CluStream	0.73825	0.54671	1204	0.373321
	BIRCH	0.74003	0.55682	1238	0.359283
Data Stream 3 (Chaotic)	AR-NG	0.42007	0.36093	1102	0.380049
	DBSCAN	0.32901	0.29087	857	0.499208
	Online K-Means	0.31992	0.30011	799	0.535561
	CluStream	0.33459	0.26994	865	0.523009
	BIRCH	0.35022	0.27690	888	0.501297

Overall, the results suggest that the AR-NG method demonstrates better adaptability to concept drift compared to the other methods, at least in the provided scenarios. These performance metrics suggest that the clustering algorithm is accurately capturing the underlying structure of the data, with well-separated and meaningful clusters.

4 Conclusion

Identifying concept drift in the cybersecurity domain is essential for staying ahead of evolving threats, adapting security measures, and maintaining the effectiveness of cybersecurity systems. It enables organizations to detect emerging attacks, respond promptly, and make informed decisions based on the changing nature of the data being analyzed. The Adaptive Reservoir Neural Gas algorithm presented in this paper offers a novel and effective solution for handling concept drift in real-time data streams.

By combining the power of reservoir computing and the Neural Gas algorithm, AR-NG achieves adaptive clustering that efficiently captures the evolving data distribution. Specifically, the use of reservoir computing in the clustering algorithm provides a powerful framework for efficient and parallel processing of input data streams, making it suitable for real-time or online applications. Also, the algorithm utilizes DBCM, a density-based clustering mechanism, which can effectively discover clusters of arbitrary shapes and handle noise in the data without require specifying the number of clusters in advance.

The key important is that the algorithm incorporates adaptive parameters to handle concept drift in the data stream, which can significantly impact the clustering results. By adapting the reservoir parameters based on concept drift detection, the algorithm can maintain accurate and up-to-date clustering models. This achieves by employs competitive learning to find the winning neuron among the activated reservoir neurons in order to identify the most representative neurons for each data point, leading to improved clustering accuracy and separation.

As proven experimentally the proposed streaming approach is memory-efficient since it does not require storing the entire data stream in memory. Instead, it processes data points sequentially, updating the clustering model and adapting the parameters incrementally as new data arrives. The results of this study provide evidence of its efficacy, positioning AR-NG as a valuable tool for dynamic environments requiring real-time data analysis and decision-making.

While the above algorithm has its benefits, it also has some limitations and areas for future improvement. Particularly, as the number of data points increases, the processing and memory requirements of the algorithm may become a bottleneck. Scaling up the algorithm to handle big data efficiently would be a challenge. In addition, the algorithm relies on manually setting parameters such as the size of the reservoir, DBCM parameters (epsilon and min_samples), and the number of neighbors. Finding the optimal parameter values can be a challenging task, and these values may vary depending on the characteristics of the data stream. A more automated approach for parameter tuning would enhance the algorithm's performance and applicability. From this point of view, investigating techniques to parallelize the algorithm's computations could improve its efficiency and scalability. This could involve utilizing parallel processing frameworks or distributed computing approaches to handle the processing of data points in parallel, making the algorithm more suitable for larger-scale data streams.

Appendix 1

Pseudocode of the proposed AR-NG methodology

```
# Constants
RESERVOIR_SIZE = 100
FEATURE_SIZE = 2
# Function to initialize parameters
initialize_parameters()
# Function to initialize clustering structure using Neural Gas
initialize_neural_gas()
# Function to calculate activation level based on similarity
calculate_activation_level()
# Function to activate reservoir neurons based on data point
activate_reservoir_neurons()
# Function to perform competitive learning and find the winning neuron
competitive_learning()
# Function to update clustering structure based on winning neuron and neighbors
update_clustering_structure()
# Function to update a neuron's cluster and position
update_neuron()
# Function to generate data stream
generate_data_stream()
# Function to evaluate clustering performance
evaluate_clustering_performance()
# Main function
if __name__ == '__main__':
    # Initialize parameters
    reservoir = initialize_parameters()
    initialize_neural_gas(reservoir)
    # Data stream
    data_stream = generate_data_stream(1000)
    # Initialize variables
    clusters = []
    ari_scores = []
    silhouette_scores = []
    calinski_harabasz_scores = []
    davies_bouldin_scores = []
    # Generate true labels for evaluation
    true_labels = generate_true_labels()
    # Perform online clustering
    batch_size = 100
    num_batches = length(data_stream) / batch_size
    for batch_idx in range(num_batches):
        start_idx = batch_idx * batch_size
        end_idx = start_idx + batch_size
        # Process a batch of data points
        for i in range(start_idx, end_idx):
            data_point = data_stream[i]
            # Activate reservoir neurons
            activate_reservoir_neurons(reservoir, data_point)
            # Perform competitive learning and update clustering structure
            winning_neuron = competitive_learning(reservoir)
            update_clustering_structure(winning_neuron)
```

```
        # Store cluster assignment
        clusters[i] = winning_neuron['cluster']
    # Evaluate clustering performance for the current batch
    ari, silhouette, calinski_harabasz, davies_bouldin = evaluate_clustering_performance(
        true_labels[start_idx:end_idx], clusters[start_idx:end_idx], reservoir[:end_idx]
    )
    if ari is not None:
        ari_scores.append(ari)
        silhouette_scores.append(silhouette)
        calinski_harabasz_scores.append(calinski_harabasz)
        davies_bouldin_scores.append(davies_bouldin)
    # Detect and handle concept drift for the current batch
    if detect_concept_drift(clusters[:end_idx]):
        handle_concept_drift(clusters[:end_idx])
    # Perform analysis and decision-making for the current batch
    perform_analysis(clusters[:end_idx])
    # Plot clustering result for the current batch
    plot_clusters(data_stream[:end_idx], clusters[:end_idx])
# Plot ARI scores over batches
plot_ari_scores(ari_scores)
# Plot silhouette scores over batches
plot_silhouette_scores(silhouette_scores)
# Plot Calinski-Harabasz scores over batches
plot_calinski_harabasz_scores(calinski_harabasz_scores)
# Plot Davies-Bouldin scores over batches
plot_davies_bouldin_scores(davies_bouldin_scores)
```

References

1. Lu, J., Liu, A., Dong, F., Gu, F., Gama, J., Zhang, G.: Learning under concept drift: a review. IEEE Trans. Knowl. Data Eng. **31**, 2346–2363 (2018). https://doi.org/10.1109/TKDE.2018.2876857
2. Yu, H., Liu, T., Lu, J., Zhang, G.: Automatic learning to detect concept drift. arXiv:arXiv:2105.01419 (2021). https://doi.org/10.48550/arXiv.2105.01419
3. Liu, A., Zhang, G., Lu, J.: Concept drift detection based on anomaly analysis. In: Loo, C.K., Yap, K.S., Wong, K.W., Teoh, A., Huang, K. (eds.) ICONIP 2014. LNCS, vol. 8834, pp. 263–270. Springer, Cham (2014). https://doi.org/10.1007/978-3-319-12637-1_33
4. Chauhan, R., Heydari, S.S.: Polymorphic adversarial DDoS attack on IDS using GAN. In: 2020 International Symposium on Networks, Computers and Communications (ISNCC), pp. 1–6 (2020). https://doi.org/10.1109/ISNCC49221.2020.9297264
5. Demertzis, K., Iliadis, L.: SAME: an intelligent anti-malware extension for android ART virtual machine. In: Núñez, M., Nguyen, N.T., Camacho, D., Trawiński, B. (eds.) ICCCI 2015. LNCS (LNAI), vol. 9330, pp. 235–245. Springer, Cham (2015). https://doi.org/10.1007/978-3-319-24306-1_23
6. Demertzis, K., Taketzis, D., Demertzi, V., Skianis, C.: An ensemble transfer learning spiking immune system for adaptive smart grid protection. Energies **15**(12), 4398 (2022). https://doi.org/10.3390/en15124398
7. Alhasan, S., Abdul-Salaam, G., Bayor, L., Oliver, K.: Intrusion detection system based on artificial immune system: a review. In: 2021 International Conference on Cyber Security and

Internet of Things (ICSIoT), pp. 7–14 (2021). https://doi.org/10.1109/ICSIoT55070.2021.00011

8. Hart, A.: Generalised synchronisation for continuous time reservoir computers. Rochester, NY (2021). https://doi.org/10.2139/ssrn.3987856
9. Demertzis, K., Iliadis, L., Pimenidis, E.: Geo-AI to aid disaster response by memory-augmented deep reservoir computing. Integr. Comput.-Aided Eng. **28**(4), 383–398 (2021). https://doi.org/10.3233/ICA-210657
10. Li, X., Bi, F., Yang, X., Bi, X.: An echo state network with improved topology for time series prediction. IEEE Sens. J. **22**(6), 5869–5878 (2022). https://doi.org/10.1109/JSEN.2022.3148742
11. Abu, U.A., Folly, K.A., Jayawardene, I., Venayagamoorthy, G. K.: Echo state network (ESN) based generator speed prediction of wide area signals in a multimachine power system. In: 2020 International SAUPEC/RobMech/PRASA Conference, pp. 1–5. (2020). https://doi.org/10.1109/SAUPEC/RobMech/PRASA48453.2020.9041236
12. Bala, A., Ismail, I., Ibrahim, R., Sait, S.M.: Applications of metaheuristics in reservoir computing techniques: a review. IEEE Access **6**, 58012–58029 (2018). https://doi.org/10.1109/ACCESS.2018.2873770
13. Gauthier, D.J., Bollt, E., Griffith, A., Barbosa, W.A.: Next generation reservoir computing. Nat. Commun. **12**(1), 5564 (2021). https://doi.org/10.1038/s41467-021-25801-2
14. Shao, Y., Yao, X., Wang, G., Cao, S.: A new improved echo state network with multiple output layers for time series prediction. In: 2021 6th International Conference on Robotics and Automation Engineering (ICRAE), pp. 7–11. (2021). https://doi.org/10.1109/ICRAE53653.2021.9657812
15. Demertzis, K., Iliadis, L.: Next generation automated reservoir computing for cyber Defense. In: Maglogiannis, I., Iliadis, L., MacIntyre, J., Dominguez, M. (eds.) Artificial Intelligence Applications and Innovations. AIAI 2023. IFIP Advances in Information and Communication Technology, vol. 676, pp. 16–27. Springer, Cham (2023). https://doi.org/10.1007/978-3-031-34107-6_2
16. Demertzis, K., Iliadis, L.: An autonomous self-learning and self-adversarial training neural architecture for intelligent and resilient cyber security systems. In: Iliadis, L., Maglogiannis, I., Alonso, S., Jayne, C., Pimenidis, E. (eds.) Engineering Applications of Neural Networks. EANN 2023. Communications in Computer and Information Science, vol. 1826, pp. 461–478. Springer, Cham (2023). https://doi.org/10.1007/978-3-031-34204-2_38
17. Li, J., Yao, X., Xu, K.: A comprehensive model integrating BP neural network and RSM for the prediction and optimization of syngas quality. Biomass Bioenergy **155**, 106278 (2021)
18. Alzubaidi, L., et al.: Review of deep learning: concepts, CNN architectures, challenges, applications, future directions. J. Big Data **8**(1), 53 (2021). https://doi.org/10.1186/s40537-021-00444-8
19. Aggarwal, C.C., Philip, S.Y., Han, J., Wang, J.: A framework for clustering evolving data streams. In: Freytag, J.-C., Lockemann, P., Abiteboul, S., Carey, M., Selinger, P., Heuer, A. (eds.) Proceedings 2003 VLDB Conference. Morgan Kaufmann, San Francisco, pp. 81–92 (2003). https://doi.org/10.1016/B978-012722442-8/50016-1
20. Aggarwal, C.C.: Neighborhood-based collaborative filtering. In: Aggarwal, C.C. (ed.) Recommender Systems: The Textbook, pp. 29–70. Springer International Publishing, Cham (2016). https://doi.org/10.1007/978-3-319-29659-3_2
21. Aumüller, M., Bernhardsson, E., Faithfull, A.: ANN-benchmarks: a benchmarking tool for approximate nearest neighbor algorithms. arXiv: https://doi.org/10.48550/arXiv.1807.05614 (2018)
22. Bifet, A., de Francisci Morales, G., Read, J., Holmes, G., Pfahringer, B.: Efficient online evaluation of big data stream classifiers. In: Proceedings of the 21th ACM SIGKDD International

Conference on Knowledge Discovery and Data Mining, in KDD '15, pp. 59–68. Association for Computing Machinery, New York, NY, USA (2015). https://doi.org/10.1145/2783258.2783372
23. Sabau, A.S.: Stream clustering using probabilistic data structures. arXiv: https://doi.org/10.48550/arXiv.1612.02701 (2016)
24. Stepaniants, G.: Learning partial differential equations in reproducing kernel Hilbert spaces. arXiv: https://doi.org/10.48550/arXiv.2108.11580 (2022)
25. Fujii, K., Kawahara, Y.: Dynamic mode decomposition in vector-valued reproducing kernel Hilbert spaces for extracting dynamical structure among observables. Neural Netw. **117**, 94–103 (2019). https://doi.org/10.1016/j.neunet.2019.04.020
26. Kostic, V., Novelli, P., Maurer, A., Ciliberto, C., Rosasco, L., Pontil, M.: Learning dynamical systems via Koopman operator regression in reproducing kernel hilbert spaces. arXiv: https://doi.org/10.48550/arXiv.2205.14027 (2022)
27. Hu, F., Chen, H., Wang, X.: An intuitionistic kernel-based fuzzy C-means clustering algorithm with local information for power equipment image segmentation. IEEE Access **8**(4), 4500–4514 (2020)
28. Hou, R., Tang, F., Liang, S., Ling, G.: Multi-party verifiable privacy-preserving federated k-means clustering in outsourced environment. Secur. Commun. Netw. **2021**, e3630312 (2021). https://doi.org/10.1155/2021/3630312
29. Alkathiri, M., Abdul, J., Potdar, M.B.: Kluster: Application of k-means clustering to multidimensional GEO-spatial data. In: 2017 International Conference on Information, Communication, Instrumentation and Control (ICICIC), pp. 1–7 (2017). https://doi.org/10.1109/ICOMICON.2017.8279080
30. Wielgosz, M., Pietroń, M.: Using spatial pooler of hierarchical temporal memory to classify noisy videos with predefined complexity. Neurocomputing **240**, 84–97 (2017). https://doi.org/10.1016/j.neucom.2017.02.046
31. Nguyen, Q.D., Dhouib, S., Chanet, J.P., Bellot, P.: Towards a web-of-things approach for OPC UA field device discovery in the industrial IoT. In: 2022 IEEE 18th International Conference on Factory Communication Systems (WFCS), pp. 1–4 (2022). https://doi.org/10.1109/WFCS53837.2022.9779181
32. Hahsler, M., Bolaños, M., Forrest, J.: Introduction to stream: an extensible framework for data stream clustering research with R. J. Stat. Softw. **76**, 1–50 (2017). https://doi.org/10.18637/jss.v076.i14

An Intelligent Dynamic Selection System Based on Nearest Temporal Windows for Time Series Forecasting

Gabriel Mendes Matos and Paulo S. G. de Mattos Neto(✉)

Centro de Informàtica (CIn), Universidade Federal de Pernambuco (UFPE), Recife, Pernambuco, Brazil
{gmm4,psgmn}@cin.ufpe.br

Abstract. Real-world time series present patterns that change over time, making them difficult to forecast using only one forecasting model. Dynamic selection approaches have been highlighted in literature due to their accuracy and ability to model different local patterns. These approaches select one or more models from a pool (or ensemble) to forecast each test pattern. This selection is performed based on the pool's performance in a Region of Competence (RoC), a set of samples most similar to a test pattern. The RoC definition, the pool creation, the number of selected models, and the function for combining the forecasts are critical issues for the dynamic selection approaches once their accuracy is closely related to them. This paper proposes a dynamic selection system based on a heterogeneous pool that performs a data-driven choice to determine: (i) the best RoC size, (ii) the set of the most competent forecasting models, and (iii) the most suitable combination function. The selection uses an RoC composed of the nearest antecedent windows to a test pattern. The proposal employs a heterogeneous pool comprising six forecasting models: Autoregressive Integrated Moving Average (ARIMA), Theta model, Support Vector Regression (SVR), Multilayer Perceptron (MLP), Extreme Learning Machine (ELM), and Long Short-Term Memory (LSTM). An experimental analysis performed using seven well-known data sets showed that the proposal overcame literature single and ensemble approaches, indicating that it is able to perform a better dynamic selection.

Keywords: Time Series Forecasting · Dynamic Selection · Heterogeneous Ensemble · Machine Learning · Neural Networks

1 Introduction

Time series forecasting task is present in many applications, such as finance [1], health [2], weather [3], engineering [4] and astronomy [5]. So, the development of accurate forecasting systems for real-world time series modeling has been a

L. Iliadis et al. (Eds.): ICANN 2023, LNCS 14259, pp. 167–179, 2023.
https://doi.org/10.1007/978-3-031-44223-0_14

relevant research topic [6–8]. The modeling of real application time series is challenging because the data commonly present different patterns over time [9]. Literature [10–12] supports this claim and suggests that employing a single model often leads to underperformed accuracy. This occurs because it is challenging to determine the appropriate parameters of one forecasting model for the entire data set, which can result in misspecified or biased models [13]. The multiple predictor systems (MPS) area has been highlighted in this context due to theoretical and practical results. These systems employ an ensemble of forecasters with the objective of modeling different temporal patterns of the time series [14]. MPS consist of three sequential phases: generation, selection, and combination. During the generation phase, a pool of models is created from the training set. In the selection phase, one or more forecasting models are chosen based on specific criteria. In the final phase, the selected models' outputs are combined to generate the final forecast. MPS can be classified into two categories based on their selection step [11], static and dynamic. The first class selects the models in the training phase (offline), while the second executes the model's choice in the test step (online). In the static class, one or more models are chosen to forecast the entire data set. In the dynamic class, one or more models are selected to predict each test pattern. Thus, approaches based on the dynamic selection choose a subset of models from the pool to forecast each test point. This selection strategy is more suitable for modeling the dynamic behavior commonly present in real-world time series [15].

The accuracy of a dynamic selection approach is closely related to the pool's quality, the Region of Competence (RoC) definition, the quantity of selected models to forecast a new test pattern, and the function used to combine these forecasts [11,15,16]. The forecasters that compose the pool must be able to model complementary characteristics. So, the ensemble must be accurate and diverse to model different local patterns [17]. After the pool generation, one or more models are selected based on their competence to forecast a new test pattern. The RoC definition is an important step because it determines how many and which time series patterns will be used to measure the most competent models of the pool [15]. This region is composed of the k past temporal patterns that are most similar to a given test pattern according to some criterion, e.g. Euclidean distance. After RoC creation, one or more forecasting models can be selected based on their accuracy [11]. If only one ($n = 1$) model is chosen, this model is responsible for predicting the test pattern; otherwise, forecasts of the n ($n > 1$) models need to be combined using some function to generate the final output.

This paper presents a dynamic selection system that performs a data-based search to maximize its accuracy. The proposal supposes that the nearest antecedent windows to a test pattern are more promising for RoC creation than more distant ones [11]. The proposed system employs a heterogeneous pool with two statistical techniques (Autoregressive Integrated Moving Average (ARIMA) and Theta models), and four Machine Learning models (Support Vector Regression (SVR), Multilayer Perceptron (MLP), Extreme Learning Machine (ELM), and Long Short-Term Memory (LSTM)). Finally, the proposed MPS defines how many, which, and how the models will be combined for each data set. An experimental analysis using seven real-world time series is conducted in the one-step ahead scenario. The performance of the proposed dynamic selection system is compared to single models and dynamic selection approaches of the literature in terms of three well-known metrics: Mean Squared Error (MSE), Mean Absolute Percentage Error (MAPE), and Average Relative Prediction Error Variation (ARV). The results show that the proposed system attains an overall performance superior to the single models and dynamic selection approaches with less computational cost than concurrents of the same class.

The rest of this paper is organized as follows: Sect. 2 presents related works in dynamic selection for time series forecasting. Section 3 describes the proposed dynamic selection system. Section 4 details the experiments carried out to evaluate and compare the proposed method and previous approaches. Section 5 presents and discusses the experiment results in terms of performance and computational cost. Section 6 brings final remarks and outlines future work.

2 Related Works

In [15], a heterogeneous dynamic ensemble selection approach is proposed to forecast solar irradiance time series. Its ensemble is composed of seven different literature models: ARIMA, SVR, MLP, ELM, Deep Belief Network (DBN), Random Forest (RF), and Gradient Boosting (GB). Here the RoC is defined using a local accuracy approach, where the closest patterns according to Euclidean distance are chosen to measure the competence of the models in the pool. [16] faces the concept drift adaptation issue by applying a drift detection mechanism. This technique uses a measure based on Pearsons correlation between forecasts of the base models and the target time series to dynamically prune underperforming models from the pool.

Some other approaches focus on finding the best combination weights for the models available in the pool. [17] utilizes a non-linear function based on the Gaussian complementary error to dynamically weigh and combine time series forecasts made by a heterogeneous ensemble to adapt to concept drifts. In [18], a heterogeneous ensemble composed of ten different models is proposed, where the combination settings are tuned dynamically using the Bayesian optimization algorithm (BOA). [19] introduces a method for combining forecasts through a meta-learner, which is pre-trained using a collection of time series features. Then, for a new time series, the method can extract its features and assign weights to the base models from the ensemble. [20] uses reinforcement learning to adjust the base models weights dynamically. The problem is modeled as a Markov Decision Process (MDP), where each state describes a time step of the time series, and each action represents a possible weight combination to be assigned.

The proposal stands out from other literature works by using a data-driven optimization capable of choosing the best dynamic selection parameters, such as the size of the RoC, the number of models selected from a heterogeneous pool, and the combination function to be used (if necessary). In addition, the proposal employs the most recent windows to the test pattern to create the RoC [11] to select different forecasting models that compose the pool.

3 Proposed System

The overall process is illustrated in Fig. 1, which can be divided into two phases: (I) Training and (II) Test. Phase (I) receives the training and validation sets as input data and generates the trained models and the parameters of the dynamic selection as output. The dynamic selection parameters consist of the Region of Competence (RoC) size (k), the number of models (n) to generate the final forecast, and the type of combination (mean and median) if more than one forecasting model is selected.

The first step of Phase (I) consists of creating a pool of models to forecast the time series. To increase diversity, the pool is composed of different models that are trained and validated in order to choose their best hyperparameters. This part is essential to ensure the pool will have the capability to predict different patterns.

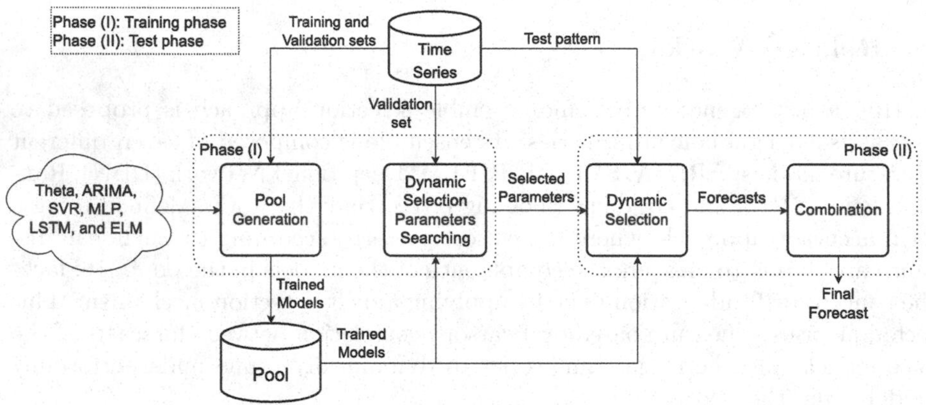

Fig. 1. Overview of the proposed approach.

In the second step of Phase (I), the trained models of the pool are used to search for the best parameters of the dynamic selection and combination steps. This step is carried out using the validation set. So, the size of the RoC (k), the number of models (n) used in the combination step, and the combination type (mean and median) are defined. After the Training phase (Phase (I)) is concluded, the proposed system can be employed to predict unseen test patterns.

Figure 1 shows that for each test pattern (x_t), Phase (II) of the proposed system receives as input the trained pool, and the parameters for steps of dynamic selection, and combination. In the first step of the Test phase, the dynamic selection step creates the RoC with k past windows (W_{t-1}, W_{t-2}, ..., W_{t-k}) regarding the current test pattern (x_t) and assesses the average performance of each pool model in these windows. Each time window W_t contains l time observations (x_{t-k}, $x_{t-(k+1)}$, $x_{t-(k+2)}$, ..., $x_{t-(k+l-1)}$). Then, each model m_j of the pool of size M generates a forecast $\hat{x}_{(t-k)+1}$ for each window W_t that composes the region of competence. The performance of a model j of the pool is measured using the average error between its forecast and the actual value for each W_t that composes the RoC. After the n models with the smallest errors are selected, the final forecast can be generated. If $n = 1$, the combination is unnecessary; otherwise, the forecasts of the $n > 1$ models are generated using the mean or median combination.

4 Experimental Protocol

A set of seven time series was used to evaluate the proposed system: Electricity, Goldman Sachs, Pollution, Star, Sunspot, Vehicle, and Wine. These data sets can be accessed at[1]. This database is composed of time series with different characteristics, such as trend, seasonality, and cycles, among others. Each time series was normalized to $[0,1]$ and divided into three sets following the temporal order: training, validation, and test, which contain 50%, 25%, and 25% of the observations, respectively. The first set was used for training the proposed and literature models, while the validation set was employed to select the best hyperparameters of the models and the dynamic selection parameters. Finally, the test set was used to evaluate the performance of the proposed model, along with other literature methods and individual models that compose the ensemble. All models were evaluated in the one-step-ahead forecasting scenario.

The proposed system employs a heterogeneous ensemble composed of six models: ARIMA, Theta model, SVR, MLP, ELM, and LSTM. These Machine Learning and Statistical models were chosen because they present distinct characteristics and are widely employed in the time series forecasting literature [2,21–28]. For the ML models (SVR, MLP, ELM, and LSTM), each series was restructured as sliding windows composed of 20 lagged observations. This way, forecasting is formulated as a supervised learning task where each lag is a feature of the input row (window), used to predict the following observation in the series. For the statistical models (ARIMA and Theta), the parameters model was updated after each new past pattern and used to predict the next one. The best configurations for the Machine Learning models composing the proposed system's heterogeneous ensemble were established using a grid search hyperparameter optimization. This selection was carried out based on validation set performance. Table 1 shows the search space used for each hyperparameter. For the ARIMA model, the stepwise algorithm described in [29] was employed. The Theta model uses a fitted Simple exponential smoothing (SES) model to estimate α and an Ordinary least squares (OLS) regression to estimate b_0 [30,31].

The parameters of the proposed system's dynamic selection were also established using the validation set performance. This search process was performed to determine the size of the RoC (k), the number of models selected to generate the final prediction (n), and the combination operator (*comb*). The k values used in the search belong to the interval $[1,20]$, while values of n belong to $[1,6]$. If $n = 1$, the forecasting of the best model according to its performance in the

[1] https://github.com/EraylsonGaldino/dataset_time_series.

Table 1. Hyperparameters of the models that compose the proposed system.

Model	Parameters	Values
ARIMA	p, d, q	Hyndman Method [29]
Theta	α	Simple Exponential Smoothing
	b_0	Ordinary Least Squares
	θ_1	0
	θ_2	2
MLP	Hidden Layer Size	20, 50, 100
	Tolerance	1E-3, 1E-4, 1E-5
	Activation Function	Sigmoid
ELM	Algorithm	Moore-Penrose pseudo-inverse
	Activation Function	Hyperbolic Tangent
	Hidden Layer Size	20, 50, 100, 200, 500
SVR	Kernel	RBF
	C	1, 10, 100, 1000
	γ	1, 1E-1, 1E-2, 1E-3
	ε	1E-1, 1E-2, 1E-3, 1E-4, 1E-5
LSTM	Units	15, 25
	Batch Size	1, 10, 100
	Epochs	50, 100
	Activation Function	ReLU, Hyperbolic tangent

region of competence is selected. Otherwise, when $n > 1$, an operator is used to combine the forecasts of the best n models. This operator is chosen between mean and median. For each time series, a configuration (k, n, *comb*) was chosen using a grid search approach based on the performance in the validation set. Table 2 shows the parameters selected for the proposed system.

Table 2. Dynamic selection parameters for the proposed system defined based on the performance of the validation set.

Time Series	k	n	comb
Electricity	3	5	Median
Goldman	6	5	Median
Pollution	12	2	Mean
Star	12	1	-
Sunspot	4	3	Median
Vehicle	14	1	-
Wine	19	1	-

The proposed system was compared against the individual models that comprise the ensemble and two dynamic selection systems: DSLA [15] and DSNAW [11]. These last two systems employ a homogeneous ensemble composed of 100 SVRs. The SVRs were trained using different samples created through the resampling (with replacement) of the original time series windows. The DSLA and DSNAW systems also employed a validation phase for choosing k, n, and *comb* parameters. In this case, n belongs to the range $[1, 20]$. After the test phase, results were assessed using three different metrics: MSE, MAPE, and ARV [15,22].

The metric ratio, defined in Eq. 1, was employed to compare the performance of the proposed system with other literature models.

$$ratio = \frac{(\varepsilon_a - \varepsilon_b)}{\varepsilon_a} \times 100, \tag{1}$$

where ε_a is the literature model performance and ε_b is the proposed system performance. MSE was used as the error measure. Oracle is a theoretic dynamic selection model that always chooses the best model for each test pattern. This model is useful to determine the superior limit of a given pool. Equation 2 quantifies how close a dynamic selection approach is to its oracle.

$$ratio_o = 100 - \frac{(MAPE_b - MAPE_o)}{MAPE_b} \times 100, \tag{2}$$

where $MAPE_b$ and $MAPE_o$ are the values of a given dynamic selection approach, and of the respective oracle. The closer to 100%, the better is the dynamic selection performed by a given approach.

5 Results

Table 3 shows the performance values in terms of MSE, MAPE, and ARV of the proposed system and literature models. The proposed system attained the best performance in most metrics in two data sets, Pollution and Wine. DSLA attained the best result in three-time series, Electricity, Star, and Vehicle. The single models, ARIMA, Theta, and MLP, achieved the best performance in Goldman, Wine, and Sunspot series, respectively. It is important to highlight that for the Wine series, the proposal was able to identify and select the best model for most of the test set samples, reaching the accuracy of the best single model. Although the proposed system attained the best performance only in two data sets, it was able to adapt to most data sets, reaching the best average result. In this way, an analysis was performed using the models' rank in each data set.

Table 4 shows the rank of the models in each data set according to MSE, MAPE, and ARV metrics. So, three rankings are created for each series. The proposed system was ranked among the three best models in 16 out of 21 cases, Theta attained the best three ranks in 10 cases, and DSLA was among the three most accurate models in 9 cases. DSNAW was ranked as the second and

Table 3. Performance results for the evaluated methods. Values in bold represent the best results for each metric and dataset pair.

Time Series	Metric	SVR	Theta	ARIMA	MLP	ELM	LSTM	DSLA	DSNAW	Proposed
Electricity	MSE	1.41E-3	2.71E-3	1.55E-2	1.91E-3	2.15E-3	6.35E-3	**1.03E-3**	1.25E-3	1.39E-3
	MAPE	4.02	5.87	13.9	4.48	4.67	9.10	**3.43**	4.05	4.01
	ARV	1.11E-1	1.95E-1	7.14E-1	1.87E-1	2.37E-1	2.75E-1	**7.21E-2**	1.01E-1	1.27E-1
Goldman	MSE	4.21E-4	**3.98E-4**	3.99E-4	6.29E-4	4.98E-4	4.92E-4	4.97E-4	4.26E-4	4.13E-4
	MAPE	9.39	8.89	**8.86**	12.2	10.1	10.3	10.4	9.32	9.23
	ARV	2.93E-2	2.73E-2	**2.73E-2**	3.72E-2	3.21E-2	3.70E-2	3.53E-2	2.91E-2	2.86E-2
Pollution	MSE	1.28E-1	1.70E-2	1.77E-2	4.52E-2	4.26E-1	1.85E-1	2.40E-2	2.48E-2	**1.68E-2**
	MAPE	57.1	**18.6**	21.4	34.7	108	68.0	22.9	24.5	21.5
	ARV	1.04	1.62	1.19	8.83E-1	9.55E-1	1.11	9.05E-1	8.74E-1	**8.46E-1**
Star	MSE	4.16E-5	4.72E-3	1.87E-4	1.17E-4	5.58E-5	1.69E-4	**2.95E-5**	5.30E-5	3.34E-5
	MAPE	1.73	20.7	4.14	3.12	3.62	3.95	**1.52**	2.05	1.81
	ARV	5.92E-4	7.24E-2	2.64E-3	1.66E-3	7.88E-4	2.41E-3	**4.18E-4**	7.50E-4	4.74E-4
Sunspot	MSE	2.14E-2	2.14E-2	1.59E-2	**1.37E-2**	2.61E-2	1.78E-2	1.77E-2	1.43E-2	1.50E-2
	MAPE	58.1	82.7	61.6	52.8	117	68.3	53.6	**52.4**	54.3
	ARV	5.81E-1	3.11E-1	2.87E-1	**2.51E-1**	3.66E-1	3.09E-1	4.29E-1	2.90E-1	2.82E-1
Vehicle	MSE	1.46E-2	**1.33E-2**	2.10E-2	1.62E-2	4.39E-2	3.09E-2	1.51E-2	1.43E-2	1.49E-2
	MAPE	13.5	13.8	17.0	14.6	23.3	18.2	**13.5**	14.2	14.7
	ARV	8.01E-1	1.01	1.79	9.26E-1	1.00	8.41E-1	**6.50E-1**	8.35E-1	1.01
Wine	MSE	5.28E-3	**1.04E-3**	5.43E-3	3.18E-3	2.09E-3	5.37E-3	6.98E-3	1.71E-3	**1.04E-3**
	MAPE	124	**47.3**	123	102	58.9	132	92.5	62.3	**47.3**
	ARV	7.51E-1	**3.77E-1**	1.58	7.87E-1	4.91E-1	7.66E-1	6.08E-1	4.69E-1	**3.77E-1**

third-best model 5 and 3 times, respectively. The proposed system achieved the best average and median ranks by analyzing the overall performance. This result shows that although the proposal had not attained the best performance in most cases, it is able to adapt to different scenarios.

Table 5 shows the ratio metric calculated according to Eq. 1. The ratio corresponds to the percentage difference regarding MSE between the proposed system and the literature single and ensembles. The proposed system reached a consistent advantage in all datasets over most literature models. For Pollution and Wine series, the proposal overcame all literature models. On average, the proposed system beat all other literature models in this metric.

Table 6 shows the count (in percentage) of each base model of the ensemble in the predictions of the proposed system. The most frequently selected models were Theta, SVR, and MLP, respectively. Theta was the only model chosen for the whole Wine test set. It is possible to note that the selection is related to the performance of the models in each data set (Table 3).

Figure 2 shows the metric $ratio_o$ described in Eq. 2 to compare the dynamic selection performed by the proposed system, DSLA, and DSNAW. The closer is $ratio_o$ to 100% (oracle performance), the better the dynamic selection performed by the model. It can be seen that the proposed system, which is based on a heterogeneous ensemble, gets closer to its oracle than the DSLA and DSNAW. Both models are based on a homogeneous ensemble in all scenarios. A reason-

Table 4. Ranking of the evaluated approaches based on error metrics.

Time Series	Metric	SVR	Theta	ARIMA	MLP	ELM	LSTM	DSLA	DSNAW	Proposed
Electricity	MSE	4	7	9	5	6	8	**1**	2	3
	MAPE	3	7	9	5	6	8	**1**	4	2
	ARV	3	6	9	5	7	8	**1**	2	4
Goldman	MSE	4	**1**	2	9	8	6	7	5	3
	MAPE	5	2	**1**	9	6	7	8	4	3
	ARV	5	2	**1**	9	6	8	7	4	3
Pollution	MSE	7	2	3	6	9	8	4	5	**1**
	MAPE	7	**1**	2	6	9	8	4	5	3
	ARV	6	9	8	3	5	7	4	2	**1**
Star	MSE	3	9	8	6	5	7	**1**	4	2
	MAPE	2	9	8	5	6	7	**1**	4	3
	ARV	3	9	8	6	5	7	**1**	4	2
Sunspot	MSE	7	8	4	**1**	9	6	5	2	3
	MAPE	5	8	6	2	9	7	3	**1**	4
	ARV	9	6	3	**1**	7	5	8	4	2
Vehicle	MSE	3	**1**	7	6	9	8	5	2	4
	MAPE	2	3	7	5	9	8	**1**	4	6
	ARV	2	7	9	5	6	4	**1**	3	8
Wine	MSE	6	**1**	8	5	4	7	9	3	**1**
	MAPE	8	**1**	7	6	3	9	5	4	**1**
	ARV	6	**1**	9	8	4	7	5	3	**1**
Average		4.76	4.76	6.10	5.38	6.57	7.14	3.90	3.38	**2.86**
Median		5	6	7	5	6	7	4	4	**3**

Table 5. Performance difference (% MSE) according to Eq. 1.

Time Series	SVR	Theta	ARIMA	MLP	ELM	LSTM	DSLA	DSNAW
Electricity	1.88	48.78	91.06	27.35	35.61	78.15	−35.07	−10.97
Goldman	1.82	−3.94	−3.62	34.30	17.01	16.06	16.87	3.03
Pollution	86.82	1.03	5.26	62.82	96.05	90.92	29.94	32.09
Star	19.78	99.29	82.11	71.45	40.14	80.24	−13.33	36.98
Sunspot	29.73	29.79	5.83	−9.74	42.39	15.84	15.03	−5.37
Vehicle	−2.49	−12.31	28.75	7.53	65.92	51.55	1.23	−4.71
Wine	80.29	0.00	80.84	67.35	50.35	80.65	85.10	39.11
Average	31.12	23.23	41.46	37.30	49.64	59.06	14.25	12.88

able explanation is that choosing the best model in the homogeneous ensemble is much more challenging since it has 100 forecasters. At the same time, the proposal employs a heterogeneous ensemble with only six models. Even with a small pool size, the proposed approach performed better overall than the DSLA and DSNAW, which shows the employment of a heterogeneous ensemble can deliver better accuracy more efficiently. Figure 3 shows the sum of execution times for all time series in each approach's training and test phases. The dynamic selection approaches' training time comprises the ensemble models' training and the search for the dynamic selection parameters. The test time of a dynamic selection approach consists of the spent forming the RoC and generating forecasts for each individual model. The proposal ran much faster in the training phase than the other dynamic selection approaches based on larger homogeneous ensembles. The latter not only spent more time training each model but also much slower finding the best dynamic selection parameters due to the number of forecasting models to be evaluated. In the test phase, the proposal had a slower execution due to Theta and ARIMA models since they are adjusted at each test input, impacting the final test time.

Table 6. Percentage (%) of test patterns where a base model was chosen to generate the final prediction.

Time Series	SVR	Theta	ARIMA	MLP	ELM	LSTM
Electricity	100.00	98.36	26.23	100.00	97.54	77.87
Goldman	95.24	99.47	100.00	52.38	75.66	77.25
Pollution	12.12	42.42	75.76	60.61	0.00	9.09
Star	60.00	0.00	0.00	0.00	40.00	0.00
Sunspot	48.10	22.78	63.29	75.95	26.58	63.29
Vehicle	31.75	68.25	0.00	0.00	0.00	0.00
Wine	0.00	100.00	0.00	0.00	0.00	0.00
Average	49.60	61.61	37.90	41.28	34.25	32.50

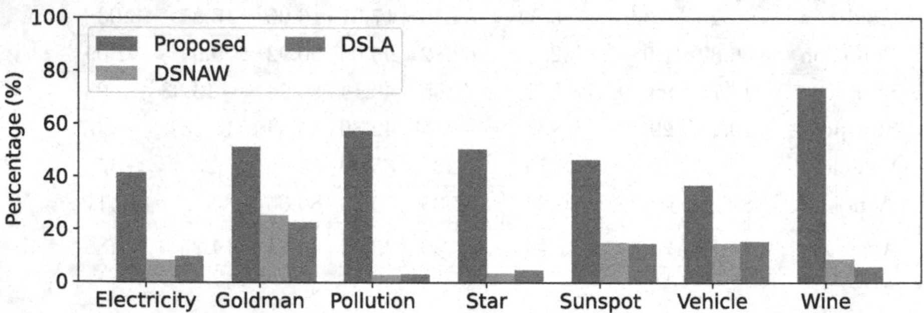

Fig. 2. Performance ratio between each DSNAW approach and its oracle in terms of Eq. 2.

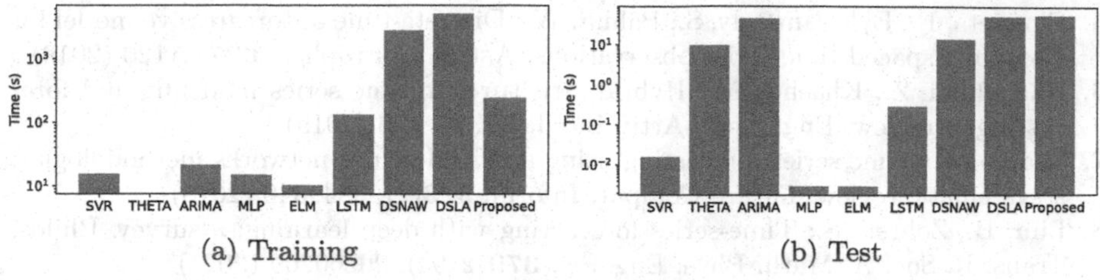

(a) Training (b) Test

Fig. 3. Execution times in log scale.

6 Conclusion

This paper proposed an intelligent dynamic selection system that searches for the most suitable RoC size, the most competent model set, and the best combination function to maximize its accuracy. The ensemble is composed of six different models: ARIMA, Theta, SVR, MLP, ELM, and LSTM.

The experimental evaluation was conducted with seven well-known time series using three metrics (MSE, MAPE, and ARV). The proposed system achieved the best overall results compared to single and dynamic selection approaches, ranking among the top three in 16 out of 21 combinations considering the performance metrics and time series. This result shows that using a diverse ensemble increased the generalization capacity, requiring less computational cost in the training phase. This led to greater robustness and stability of the proposed system when dealing with different time series.

Regarding future works, using trainable combinations is a promising alternative to increase the proposal's accuracy [12]. Searching for the best parameters dynamically is another relevant guideline since the number of well-performing models, the best combination operator, and the most suitable RoC size may change over time. Furthermore, using different combination approaches, and state-of-the-art forecasting models, may also increase accuracy and provide better robustness.

References

1. Sezer, O.B., Gudelek, M.U., Ozbayoglu, A.M.: Financial time series forecasting with deep learning: A systematic literature review: 2005–2019. Appl. Soft Comput. **90**, 106181 (2020)
2. Kaushik, S., et al.: AI in healthcare: time-series forecasting using statistical, neural, and ensemble architectures. Front. Big Data **3**, 4 (2020)
3. Karevan, Z., Suykens, J.A.: Transductive LSTM for time-series prediction: an application to weather forecasting. Neural Netw. **125**, 1–9 (2020)
4. Pierros, I., Vlahavas, I.: Architecture-agnostic time-step boosting: a case study in short-term load forecasting. In: Pimenidis, E., Angelov, P., Jayne, C., Papaleonidas, A., Aydin, M. (eds.) Artificial Neural Networks and Machine Learning. ICANN 2022. LNCS, vol. 13531, pp. 556–568. Springer, Cham (2022). https://doi.org/10.1007/978-3-031-15934-3_46

5. Elorrieta, F., Eyheramendy, S., Palma, W.: Discrete-time autoregressive model for unequally spaced time-series observations. Astron. Astrophys. **627**, A120 (2019)
6. Hajirahimi, Z., Khashei, M.: Hybrid structures in time series modeling and forecasting: a review. Eng. Appl. Artif. Intell. **86**, 83–106 (2019)
7. Tealab, A.: Time series forecasting using artificial neural networks methodologies: a systematic review. Future Comput. Inform. J. **3**(2), 334–340 (2018)
8. Lim, B., Zohren, S.: Time-series forecasting with deep learning: a survey. Philos. Trans. R. Soc. A. Math. Phys. Eng. Sci. **379**(2194), 20200209 (2021)
9. Cheng, C., et al.: Time series forecasting for nonlinear and nonstationary processes: a review and comparative study. IIE Trans. **47**, 1053–1071 (2015)
10. Makridakis, S., Spiliotis, E., Assimakopoulos, V.: The M4 competition: 100,000 time series and 61 forecasting methods. Int. J. Forecast. **36**, 54–74 (2019)
11. Silva, E.G., De Mattos Neto, P.S.G., Cavalcanti, G.D.C.: A dynamic predictor selection method based on recent temporal windows for time series forecasting. IEEE Access. **9**, 108466–108479 (2021)
12. Neto, P.S.D.M., Firmino, P.R.A., Siqueira, H., Tadano, Y.D.S., Alves, T.A., De Oliveira, J.F.L., Marinho, M.H.D.N., Madeiro, F.: Neural-based ensembles for particulate matter forecasting. IEEE Access **9**, 14470–14490 (2021)
13. Qi, M., Zhang, G.P.: An investigation of model selection criteria for neural network time series forecasting. Eur. J. Oper. Res. **132**(3), 666–680 (2001)
14. Oliveira, M., Torgo, L.: Ensembles for time series forecasting. In: Asian Conference on Machine Learning, pp. 360–370. PMLR (2015)
15. Santos, D., et al.: Solar irradiance forecasting using dynamic ensemble selection. Appl. Sci. **12**, 3510 (2022)
16. Saadallah, A., Priebe, F., Morik, K.: A drift-based dynamic ensemble members selection using clustering for time series forecasting. In: Brefeld, U., Fromont, E., Hotho, A., Knobbe, A., Maathuis, M., Robardet, C. (eds.) ECML PKDD 2019. LNCS (LNAI), vol. 11906, pp. 678–694. Springer, Cham (2020). https://doi.org/10.1007/978-3-030-46150-8_40
17. Cerqueira, V., Torgo, L., Oliveira, M., Pfahringer, B.: Dynamic and heterogeneous ensembles for time series forecasting. In: 2017 IEEE International Conference on Data Science and Advanced Analytics (DSAA), pp. 242–251 (2017)
18. Du, L., Gao, R., Suganthan, P., Wang, D.: Bayesian optimization based dynamic ensemble for time series forecasting. Inf. Sci. **591**, 155–175 (2022)
19. Montero-Manso, P., Athanasopoulos, G., Hyndman, R.J., Talagala, T.S.: FFORMA: feature-based forecast model averaging. Int. J. Forecast. **36**(1), 86–92 (2020)
20. Fu, Y., Wu, D., Boulet, B.: Reinforcement learning based dynamic model combination for time series forecasting. Proc. AAAI Conf. Artif. Intell. **36**(6), 6639–6647 (2022)
21. Siami-Namini, S., Tavakoli, N., Siami Namin, A.: A comparison of ARIMA and LSTM in forecasting time series. In: 2018 17th IEEE International Conference on Machine Learning and Applications (ICMLA), pp. 1394–1401 (2018)
22. de O. Santos Jùnior, D.S., de Oliveira, J.F., de Mattos Neto, P.S.: An intelligent hybridization of ARIMA with machine learning models for time series forecasting. Knowl. Based Syst. **175**, 72–86 (2019)
23. Chen, J.L., Li, G.S.: Evaluation of support vector machine for estimation of solar radiation from measured meteorological variables. Theoret. Appl. Climatol. **115**, 627–638 (2013)

24. Valente, J.M., Maldonado, S.: SVR-FFS: a novel forward feature selection approach for high-frequency time series forecasting using support vector regression. Expert Syst. Appl. **160**, 113729 (2020)
25. Borghi, P.H., Zakordonets, O., Teixeira, J.P.: A COVID-19 time series forecasting model based on MLP ANN. Proc. Comput. Sci, **181**, 940–947 (2021)
26. Song, G., Dai, Q.: A novel double deep ELMs ensemble system for time series forecasting. Knowl. Based Syst. **134**, 31–49 (2017)
27. Thomakos, D.D., Nikolopoulos, K.: Forecasting multivariate time series with the theta method. J. Forecast. **34**(3), 220–229 (2015)
28. Elsworth, S., Güttel, S.: Time Series Forecasting Using LSTM Networks: A Symbolic Approach (2020)
29. Hyndman, R., Khandakar, Y.: Automatic time series forecasting: the forecast package for R. J. Statist. Softw. **26**, 1–22 (2008)
30. Assimakopoulos, V., Nikolopoulos, K.: The theta model: a decomposition approach to forecasting. Int. J. Forecast. **16**, 521–530 (2000)
31. Fiorucci, J., Pellegrini, T., Louzada, F., Petropoulos, F.: The Optimised Theta Method (2015)

Generating Sparse Counterfactual Explanations for Multivariate Time Series

Jana Lang[1], Martin A. Giese[1], Winfried Ilg[1], and Sebastian Otte[2,3](✉)

[1] Section for Computational Sensomotorics, Department of Cognitive Neurology, Centre for Integrative Neuroscience and Hertie Institute for Clinical Brain Research, University Clinic Tübingen, Tübingen, Germany

[2] Neuro-Cognitive Modeling, Deparment of Computer Science, University of Tübingen, Tübingen, Germany

sebastian.otte@uni-tuebingen.de

[3] Institute for Robotics and Cognitive Systems, University of Lübeck, Lübeck, Germany

Abstract. Since neural networks play an increasingly important role in critical sectors, explaining network predictions has become a key research topic. Counterfactual explanations can help to understand why classifier models decide for particular class assignments and, moreover, how the respective input samples would have to be modified such that the class prediction changes. Previous approaches mainly focus on image and tabular data. In this work we propose SPARCE, a generative adversarial network (GAN) architecture that generates SPARse Counterfactual Explanations for multivariate time series. Our approach provides a custom sparsity layer and regularizes the counterfactual loss function in terms of similarity, sparsity, and smoothness of trajectories. We evaluate our approach on real-world human motion datasets as well as a synthetic time series interpretability benchmark. Although we make significantly sparser modifications than other approaches, we achieve comparable or better performance on all metrics. Moreover, we demonstrate that our approach predominantly modifies salient time steps and features, leaving non-salient inputs untouched.

Keywords: Explainable Artificial Intelligence · Counterfactual Explanations · Multivariate Time Series · Generative Adversarial Networks · Long Short-Term Memorys

1 Introduction

With the advent of machine learning for decision making in critical sectors like healthcare, predictive maintenance, or traffic, serious concerns have been raised about the trustworthiness of these algorithms. In recent years, the field of explainable artificial intelligence (XAI) has therefore gained increasing popularity. While manifold techniques for explaining tabular data and image classifiers have been proposed, temporal data has largely been neglected. In contrast to

L. Iliadis et al. (Eds.): ICANN 2023, LNCS 14259, pp. 180–193, 2023.
https://doi.org/10.1007/978-3-031-44223-0_15

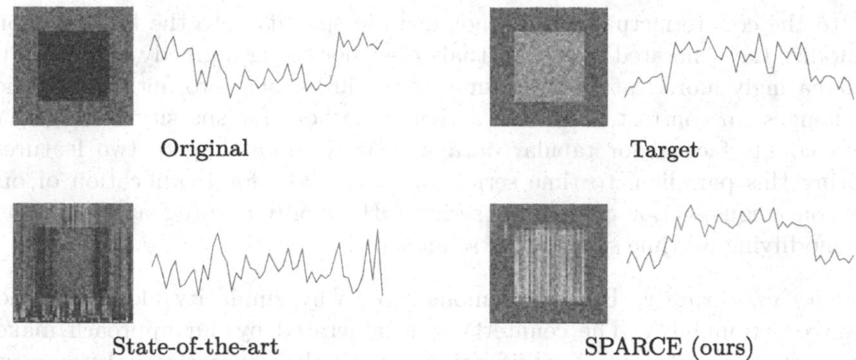

Fig. 1. Counterfactuals generated using a state-of-the-art approach [16] and our approach for a multivariate time series. Columns represent features and rows represent time steps. The curves arranged right to the boxes depict respective sequences for one of the center features.

image data, time series interpretability poses manifold challenges, including the presence of distinct time and space dimensions and an increased difficulty of visualizing information in a meaningful way. Recent work has raised strong concerns about the adaptability of prevalent XAI methods to multivariate time series [7].

Counterfactual Explanations. Derived from philosophical reasoning, *counterfactual explanations* try to find modifications to an input query so that the classification changes to a desired class [18]. Features of the input query can be mutable, i.e. the values can and may be modified, or immutable. A valid counterfactual should only modify mutable input features [8]. Meaningful counterfactual explanations can guide users towards a better understanding of decisions made by a system. If a classifier predicts a certain disease risk based on a patient's medical record, it is helpful to understand not only what factors led to the decision, but also what factors would have to change and in which way to minimize the risk.

1.1 Objectives for Counterfactual Explanations

Precision, Similarity & Realism. A valuable counterfactual explanation is close to the original data point, looks plausible and realistic and suggests actionable modifications [2,9]. The choice of distance functions to measure the actionability of a counterfactual has been a topic of discussion. The original approach by [18] iteratively minimizes the distance between the predicted class for the counterfactual and the target class (via $\mathcal{L}_2$ norm) as well as the distance between query and counterfactual (via $\mathcal{L}_1$ norm) using gradient descent. [2] additionally assess realism of the generated counterfactual by measuring how likely it is that the counterfactual stems from the observed data distribution.

Sparsity. [2] implement sparsity as the $\mathcal{L}_0$ norm between query and counterfactual, that measures how many features were changed to go from the original data point to the counterfactual. [14] do not include sparsity into the loss function, but modify the generated counterfactuals post-hoc using a greedy algorithm to set increasingly more features with smaller modifications zero until the prediction changes. In contrast, [9] define a rigid threshold for sparsity stating that a good counterfactual for tabular data may only modify up to two features. Adapting this paradigm to time series, [3] only allow for modification of one single contiguous section of the time series. Others only ensure feature sparsity, while modifying all time steps of the sequence [1].

Similarity vs. Sparsity. Figure 1 demonstrates why similarity alone does not guarantee actionability. The counterfactual generated by our approach makes sparse, but more substantial modifications, while the counterfactual generated using a state-of-the-art approach makes minor changes in all time steps and features. If solely regularized by the $\mathcal{L}_1$ norm (i.e. the similarity constraint), the latter would be preferred. Taking the actionability of the counterfactual into account, one would most likely prefer the counterfactual generated by SPARCE despite the higher $\mathcal{L}_1$ loss. As a consequence, sparsity plays a central role in our approach.

1.2 Generative Approaches

To generate more realistic and plausible counterfactuals, while overcoming high computational costs of iterative optimization methods, generative adversarial networks (GANs) have recently been introduced for the generation of counterfactual explanations [16,17]. GANs have become popular for generating realistic looking fake images by training a generator to create fake samples that a discriminator would erroneously perceive as real samples [4]. GAN-based architectures for counterfactual search add a classifier to the standard GAN approach. In this way, the generator learns to produce realistic looking counterfactuals that change the classifier's prediction to a target class.

While [16] only evaluate their model on image and tabular data, [17] also assess their approach on univariate time series. Both approaches use $\mathcal{L}_1$ or $\mathcal{L}_2$ norms as regularization terms that act on the generator's loss function. Particularly for multivariate time series, this formulation is problematic, since it creates proximate, but not sparse counterfactuals. Indeed, sample counterfactuals generated by [17] modify every single time step of the query sequence. In some domains, this might be necessary. However, it is questionable whether such a counterfactual explanation would have any explanatory power. Besides, it is unclear whether these modifications could actually be acted upon in reality. Our approach is thus designed to create truly sparse counterfactual explanations for multivariate time series without compromising other important objectives of counterfactuals, including realism, similarity, and plausibility.

2 Method

Motivated by the insufficient adaptation of counterfactual approaches to multivariate time series, we propose SPARCE: a novel framework to efficiently generate SPARse Counterfactual Explanations for multivariate time series data. Our approach aims to change the class label of an original time series to a target class (*precision*). Generated counterfactuals should be within the distribution of the original data points (*realism*) and stay as close as possible to the query sequence (*similarity*). In contrast to related approaches for multivariate time series, we postulate that counterfactuals are time- and feature-sparse, i.e. that only a subset of features and time steps is modified (*sparsity*). Finally, for applications where time series evolve smoothly over time, we aim to modify the original data point in a temporally plausible manner (*smoothness*).

2.1 Generating Counterfactual Explanations

Basing our approach on a generator-discriminator architecture, we ensure realism of the generated samples. In line with [16] we define a modified generator $\mathcal{G}$ which learns to generate residuals $\delta = \mathcal{G}(\mathbf{x}_q)$ from the input sample $\mathbf{x}_q$. In contrast to standard GANs, the generator does not use a random seed, but real samples as inputs. Thus, original samples are first divided into queries $\mathbf{x}_q$ and targets $\mathbf{x}_t$. Targets are samples labeled as the target class $\mathbf{c}_t$ and are used as real examples for the discriminator $\mathcal{D}$. The query subset contains all other samples and is presented as inputs to the generator $\mathcal{G}$. Residuals created by the generator are added to the query to produce a counterfactual ($\mathbf{x}_{cf} = \mathbf{x}_q + \delta$). A pre-trained classifier $\mathcal{C}$ determines the class prediction for the generated counterfactual. At the same time, the counterfactual is presented to the discriminator as a fake sample. In combination with real target samples, the discriminator tries to distinguish between real and fake (i.e. generated) samples. The realism of the generated counterfactual examples increases as the generator learns to fool the discriminator. The classifier prevents the generator from producing zero-residuals, i.e. from learning the identity function (Fig. 2).

$$\mathcal{L}_{adv} = -\log(\mathcal{D}(\mathbf{x}_q + \mathcal{G}(\mathbf{x}_q))) \tag{1}$$

$$\mathcal{L}_{cls} = -\mathbf{c}_t \log(\mathcal{C}(\mathbf{x}_q + \mathcal{G}(\mathbf{x}_q))) \tag{2}$$

$$\mathcal{L}_{sim} = \|\mathbf{x}_q - \mathbf{x}_{cf}\|_1 \tag{3}$$

$$\mathcal{L}_{sparse} = \|\mathbf{x}_q - \mathbf{x}_{cf}\|_0 \tag{4}$$

$$\mathcal{L}_{jerk} = \sum_{t=0}^{T-1} \|\delta^{t+1} - \delta^t\|_2 \tag{5}$$

$$\mathcal{L}_G = \mathbb{E}_{\mathbf{x}_q}\left[\lambda_1\mathcal{L}_{adv} + \lambda_2\mathcal{L}_{cls} + \lambda_3\mathcal{L}_{sim} + \lambda_4\mathcal{L}_{sparse} + \lambda_5\mathcal{L}_{jerk}\right] \tag{6}$$

$$\mathcal{L}_D = \frac{1}{2}\,\mathbb{E}_{\mathbf{x}_q}\left[-\log(\mathcal{D}(\mathbf{x}_q))\right] - \mathbb{E}_{\mathbf{x}_q}\left[\log(1 - (\mathcal{D}(\mathbf{x}_q + \mathcal{G}(\mathbf{x}_q))))\right] \tag{7}$$

Generator. The generator is realized with a many-to-many sequence prediction model trained to generate modifications to a query sequence. To capture temporal dependencies in the input, different types of sequence models can be chosen,

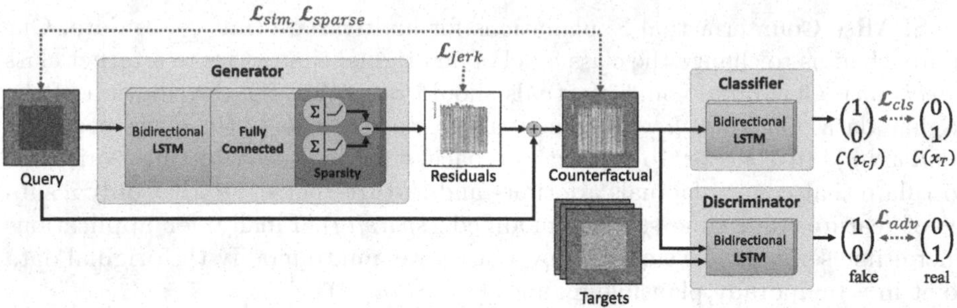

Fig. 2. Schematic illustration of our GAN-based approach for counterfactual search. Inputs are divided into query and target time series (displayed as heatmaps) according to the desired target class. A recurrent generator with sparsity activation generates residuals for each query. Residuals are added to the corresponding query to create a counterfactual explanation. A pretrained sequence classifier predicts the class label of the counterfactual. A recurrent discriminator tries to distinguish counterfactuals from real targets.

including long short-term memories (LSTMs), gated recurrent units, or temporal convolutional neural networks. Input and output of the generator are of the same shape. Loss functions for generator and discriminator derive from the minimax loss suggested by [4]. The generator maximizes the discriminator's estimate that the counterfactual is real (Eq. 1). One important aspect of the generator is the subtractive dual ReLU [15] output in the sparsity layer. Instead of a single linear output the two contrastive outputs allow the network to produce positive and negative residuals while it is still easy to generate exact zero-residuals ($\delta = ReLU(\delta_{pos}) - ReLU(\delta_{neg})$).

Immutable Features. In case of immutable features in the original dataset, the generator only produces residuals for all mutable features. In this specific case, the input to the generator is larger than its output. Generated residuals for the mutable features are then likewise added to the respective mutable features in the query sequence. All immutable features of the query instance remain untouched.

Discriminator. The discriminator takes on the role of distinguishing between real samples (i.e. samples from the original dataset) and fake samples (i.e. generated counterfactuals). It aims to maximize its estimate that the counterfactual is fake and the query is real (Eq. 7). It is implemented as a binary many-to-one sequence classification model with sigmoid activation that takes in a multivariate time series and produces a probability between 0 and 1, indicating whether the given sample looks like a real or fake sample. As the counterfactuals begin to look more realistic, the discriminator's accuracy drops towards 50% (chance).

Classifier. Unlike vanilla GANs, a counterfactual GAN needs a third neural network, the classifier. In our approach the classifier is realized with a many-to-one sequence classification model. The classifier is pretrained on the original dataset and learns to classify the label of a sequence. In contrast to [16], our classifier does not only distinguish between samples which belong and samples that do not belong to the target class. Instead, we train a full classifier which learns to distinguish all classes in the original dataset. That said, our classifier can either be binary (with sigmoid activation) or multi-class (with softmax activation) in case of two or multiple original class labels, respectively. This property allows us to flexibly alter the desired target class for the generated counterfactuals without retraining the classifier. Moreover, our approach could also simultaneously be trained on all target classes. In this case, generating counterfactuals for different target classes would not require retraining of any network element of our approach.

Regularization. The combination of adversarial loss $\mathcal{L}_{adv}$ and classification loss $\mathcal{L}_{cls}$ loss ensures that the generated counterfactual changes the class label, while resembling a sample from the original data distribution. The classification loss between the predicted class for the counterfactual and the target class is derived from the cross-entropy loss (Eq. 2). In line with other counterfactual approaches, we apply the $\mathcal{L}_1$ norm as a similarity regularization term $\mathcal{L}_{sim}$ on the generator loss (Eq. 3). Importantly, we also use the $\mathcal{L}_0$ norm as a real sparsity constraint $\mathcal{L}_{sparse}$ which ensures that the number of modifications stays low (Eq. 4). It was shown that $\mathcal{L}_0$ regularization effectively fosters sparse hidden state updates in RNNs [5]. To address the sequentiality of time series, we introduce another regularization term, the *jerk* constraint $\mathcal{L}_{jerk}$. This term ensures that changes are evenly distributed over time by penalizing large differences between modifications in consecutive time steps (Eq. 5). Additional weighting factors λ_{1-5} allow each component of the generator loss to be switched on or off to meet the specific needs of individual datasets. A more fine-grained weighting with weighting factors between 0 and 1 enables a direct influence on the loss balance (Eq. 6).

On the Sparsity of Generated Counterfactuals. One key difference of our model in comparison with other counterfactual approaches is the clear distinction between similarity and sparsity. The combination of the sparsity constraint $\mathcal{L}_{sparse}$ and the sparsity layer as part of the generator architecture produces truly sparse counterfactuals with zero-residuals in a number of time steps and features. Importantly, we let the system inherently learn the trade-off between realism, precision, similarity, sparsity and smoothness during the training process. As a consequence, unlike other counterfactual approaches for time series, there is no need to define a fixed number of time steps and features that which may be changed. On the same lines, there is not only one specific section of the series which can be modified. Instead, we demonstrate that our approach identifies and modifies salient time steps and features while leaving most non-salient time steps and features untouched.

3 Experiments

Our approach is evaluated on three different multivariate time series datasets in comparison with three related counterfactual methods. The evaluated tasks comprise two movement datasets for multi-class classification and one synthetic time series interpretability benchmark for binary classification. Human motion datasets are anonymized and cannot be mapped back to individual subjects.

3.1 Datasets

MotionSense: The human motion dataset *MotionSense* [13] (Open Database License ODbL) provides multivariate time series collected by accelerometer and gyroscope sensors of a smartphone stored in a subject's pocket as they perform different actions. Actions include walking downstairs, walking upstairs, sitting, standing, walking and jogging. For this work, we only used active movement sequences and thus excluded sitting and standing trials which yielded a total number of 11194 samples. Each time series was truncated to a length of 100 time steps. All twelve features describing attitude, gravity, rotation and user acceleration are treated as mutable.

Catching: The *Catching* dataset [11] (provided by personal permission) contains multivariate two-dimensional movement trajectories of healthy and pathological ball catching trials over 60 time steps. At each time step, 20 features capture the catcher's arm position as well as the position of the ball. Each of the 1975 catching trials is assigned a label indicating the subject's disease status: healthy control, patient with Autism Spectrum Disorder or patient with Spinocerebellar Ataxia. All features specifying the catcher's body posture are defined as mutable features, while the two features describing the ball position are treated as immutable.

Moving Box: The synthetic *Moving Box* dataset was introduced to benchmark interpretability in time series predictions [7]. It portrays a wide range of temporal and spatial properties commonly found in multivariate time series. Each time series spans 50 time steps and 50 features of which only a subset is salient. Samples are assigned a binary label (0: negative class, 1: positive class) and have a defined start and end point of salient time steps and features per sample. In this dataset, all features are mutable. We used a representative subset containing 13950 samples with boxes of different sizes and at varying positions as well as a variety of generating time series processes.

3.2 Approaches

ICS: We loosely follow [18] for an implementation of an iterative counterfactual search algorithm. Each counterfactual is initialized with a random uniform distribution between the minimum and maximum values of the query sequence. The class of the generated counterfactual is predicted using a pretrained classifier. We use the $\mathcal{L}_2$ distance to measure the classification loss and the unweighted $\mathcal{L}_1$ norm to enforce similarity.

All following approaches are based on GANs combined with a pretrained classifier. To account for temporal dependencies in the data, generator and discriminator are implemented as bidirectional LSTMs [6]. The generator is a two-layer many-to-many bidirectional LSTM with 256 hidden neuron and dropout of 0.4. The discriminator is built up as a one-layer many-to-one bidirectional LSTM with 16 hidden neurons, sigmoid output activation and dropout of 0.4. For both networks, the final LSTM layer is followed by a fully-connected output layer.

GAN: This approach consists of a counterfactual LSTM-GAN producing complete counterfactuals based on query sequences. The fully-connected output layer of the generator is followed by a tanh activation. The generator loss is regularized using the $\mathcal{L}_1$ norm to optimize the distance between counterfactual and query.

CounteRGAN: This approach is a time series specific implementation of [16] and implements an LSTM generator that produces residuals based on query sequences. All other aspects of the implementation are equal to the GAN approach.

SPARCE: Our approach likewise generates residuals instead of complete counterfactuals. In comparison to CounteRGAN, we additionally regularize the generator loss via sparsity and smoothness constraints (cf. Section 2.1). Moreover, we add weighting factors λ_{1-5} to enable the (de-)activation of single regularization constraints if required. Most importantly, the LSTM generator implemented in our approach does not conclude with a linear or tanh activation layer, but instead uses a custom sparsity layer of two interoperating ReLU activations (cf. Section 2.1).

3.3 Evaluation Metrics

Realism: In line with [19], we use *t-distributed stochastic neighbor embedding* (*t-SNE*) for a visual assessment of the in-distributionness of the generated counterfactuals [12]. We separately plot query and target samples of the original dataset along with the counterfactuals generated by each approach to determine whether the generated counterfactuals rather resemble queries or targets.

Precision: Classification error of generated counterfactuals is measured by the $\mathcal{L}_2$ norm between the classifier's prediction for a counterfactual sequence and the target class. The metric is indicated as the average distance across all test samples. The lower the metric, the higher the precision of the counterfactual approach. A precision value of 0.0 means that all generated counterfactuals were correctly classified as the target class.

Similarity: The $\mathcal{L}_1$ distance between each query and the corresponding counterfactual is used to assess similarity. The metric is averaged over all test samples and normalized using the number of time steps and features in the dataset. Lower values indicate higher mean proximity of the generated counterfactuals to the corresponding queries.

Sparsity: Generated counterfactuals of each approach are evaluated on the number of modified time steps and features to transform the query into the coun-

Table 1. Quantitative results for all datasets

Dataset	Measure	ICS	GAN	CounteRGAN	SPARCE (Ours)
Catching	Precision	0.24 ± .05	**0.00** ± .00	**0.00** ± .00	0.01 ± .01
	Similarity	1.66 ± .04	0.22 ± .02	0.12 ± .01	**0.09** ± .04
	Sparsity	1.00 ± .00	1.00 ± .00	1.00 ± .00	**0.27** ± .10
	Smoothness	0.55 ± .01	0.07 ± .01	**0.01** ± .01	**0.01** ± .01
MotionSense	Precision	0.37 ± .07	**0.00** ± .00	**0.00** ± .01	0.04 ± .06
	Similarity	1.32 ± .01	0.71 ± .21	0.33 ± .09	**0.22** ± .13
	Sparsity	1.00 ± .00	1.00 ± .00	1.00 ± .00	**0.22** ± .14
	Smoothness	0.58 ± .00	0.09 ± .01	**0.03** ± .02	0.04 ± .03
Moving Box	Precision	0.99 ± .00	**0.00** ± .00	0.01 ± .01	**0.00** ± .00
	Similarity	1.32 ± .00	0.87 ± .17	0.59 ± .05	**0.40** ± .06
	Sparsity	1.00 ± .00	1.00 ± .00	1.00 ± .00	**0.30** ± .05
	Smoothness	0.29 ± .00	0.12 ± .01	0.03 ± .00	**0.02** ± .00

terfactual using the $\mathcal{L}_0$ norm between queries and corresponding counterfactual examples. Values are averaged and normalized in the same way as the similarity metric. Here lower values represent higher average sparsity, i.e. fewer modifications in the time and feature dimensions. In the case of immutable features in the dataset, the sparsity metric is only computed on all mutable features. As a consequence, the maximum sparsity value equals 1.0 indicating that all features in all time steps have been modified in each counterfactual.

Smoothness: This time series specific metric is assessed with the $\mathcal{L}_2$ distance between modifications of consecutive time steps. High values indicate large differences between modifications in subsequent steps. Lower values represent modifications that are more smoothly distributed over the course of the sequence. This metric is likewise averaged across all samples and normalized using the number of time steps and features.

4 Results

4.1 Quantitative Evaluation

All results are reported on the held-out subsets for testing (20% of each dataset). Unless otherwise stated, results are averaged over five repetitions with random seeds. The target class for counterfactuals is healthy control for *Catching*, walking upstairs for *MotionSense* and class 1 for *Moving Box*. ICS is performed for 100 steps ($\lambda_{init} = 1.0$, max. λ steps $= 10$). The loss is minimized with Adam [10] optimization ($lr = 0.4, \beta_1 = 0.9, \beta_2 = 0.999$). All GAN-based approaches are trained for 100 epochs in batches of 32 samples using Adam optimization ($lr = 0.0002, \beta_1 = 0.5, \beta_2 = 0.999$). For all quantitative metrics, lower values represent better performance. The best value for each metric is printed in bold numbers.

Fig. 3. t-SNE plots for *Moving Box* dataset. Queries are plotted in red, targets in green and generated counterfactuals in blue. (Color figure online)

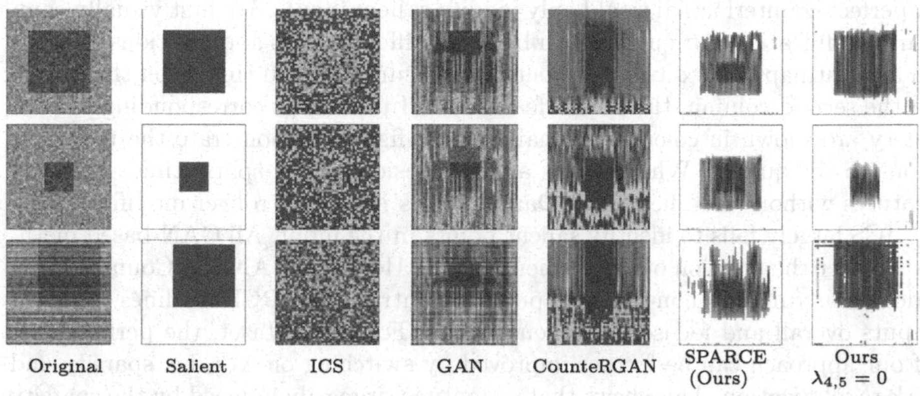

Fig. 4. Predefined salient inputs vs. counterfactual modifications for the *Moving Box* dataset.

Considering the *Catching* dataset, GAN and CounteRGAN achieve a precision of 100%, however closely followed by our approach (Table 1). SPARCE outperforms ICS, GAN and CounteRGAN on the similarity and sparsity of generated counterfactuals and shares the best smoothness value with the CounteRGAN approach. It can be seen that no tested approach besides ours can generate sparse counterfactuals. This observation also holds for the *MotionSense* and *Moving Box* datasets. SPARCE reaches the best or second-best performance on each metric in spite of making considerably sparser modifications than the other approaches.

4.2 Realism

We qualitatively assess the in-distributionness of generated counterfactuals for the synthetic *Moving Box* dataset via t-SNE visualization (*components* = 2, *perplexity* = 4.4, *iterations* = 300). In Fig. 3, the first subplot illustrates the distribution of queries and targets in the original dataset. The remaining subplots additionally show the distribution of counterfactuals generated by the respective approaches. While counterfactuals generated by ICS lie within but also largely out of the original distribution, those generated by GAN form separate groups next to queries and targets. Since the task of counterfactual search is to find samples that modify a query sample to look like a target, counterfactuals generated by CounteRGAN and SPARCE show the most promising distributions. Indeed, counterfactuals of both approaches modify queries in a way that the resulting sequences approximate and even overlap with target samples.

4.3 Saliency

Since salient features and time steps are known upfront for the synthetic *Moving Box* dataset, we compare the overlap with time steps modified by each approach. A perfect counterfactual would only modify salient inputs. We first visually compare modifications for queries with boxes of different sizes and positions (Fig. 4). In all heatmaps, the x-axis represents the feature axis and time is on the y-axis. In the second column, the salient features and time steps corresponding to each query are shown in color. All remaining sub-figures demonstrate the modifications to the queries. White spaces are zero-residuals (i.e. sparse time steps and features without modifications). Darker colors indicate stronger modifications.

ICS largely fails to identify salient points in the input. All GAN-based methods detect the position of most salient inputs. However, GAN and CounteRGAN additionally modify non-salient inputs. In contrast, SPARCE modifies far fewer inputs overall and focuses on salient inputs. For this dataset, the performance of our approach can be further improved by switching off $\lambda_{4,5}$, i.e. sparsity and jerk regularization. This shows that sparsity is primarily induced by the sparsity layer. It also demonstrates that the application of the jerk constraint depends on the problem. Here, a clear value increase marks the transition from non-salient to salient inputs. In human motion datasets, in contrast, smooth movements are natural and desired.

We furthermore assess the salience overlap in a quantitative manner via the receiver operating characteristic (ROC) curve in combination with the area under the curve (AUC) score. Higher AUC scores indicate better discrimination performance between salient and non-salient inputs. Figure 5 visualizes mean ROC curves over five repetitions for both target classes. In both cases, we see that our approach produces counterfactuals that show a substantially higher overlap with predefined salient inputs than other approaches. Visual and quantitative evaluation therefore demonstrates that our approach creates sparse counterfactual explanations and is also suitable for the identification of salient inputs in multivariate time series.

4.4 Geometric Plausibility

To assess geometric plausibility of the *Catching* dataset, we compute the Euclidean distances between body parts for the original dataset and the generated counterfactuals (Fig. 6). ICS is excluded from the figure, since the corresponding values lie outside of the displayed area. Counterfactuals generated by our approach most closely resemble the body-part distances found in the original data. This can indicate higher geometric plausibility of our generated counterfactuals. In order to fully inspect geometric plausibility, however, the angles at which the joints are positioned in relation to one another would also have to be examined.

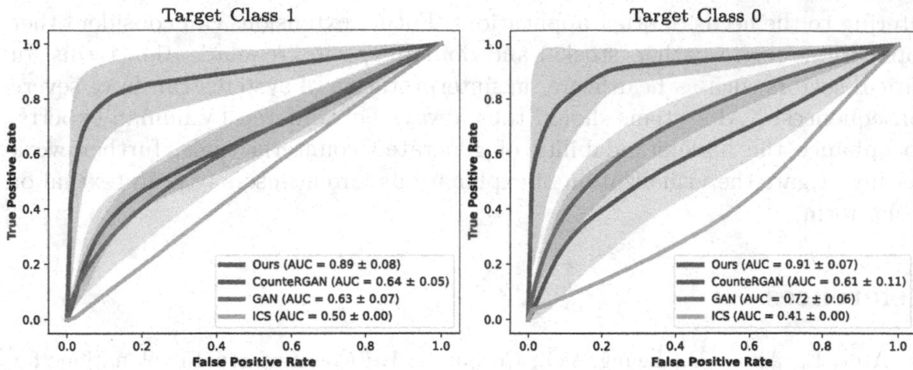

Fig. 5. Mean ROC curve measuring the overlap between predefined salient inputs and counterfactual modifications for the *Moving Box* dataset. Shaded areas describe one standard deviation of the mean ROC.

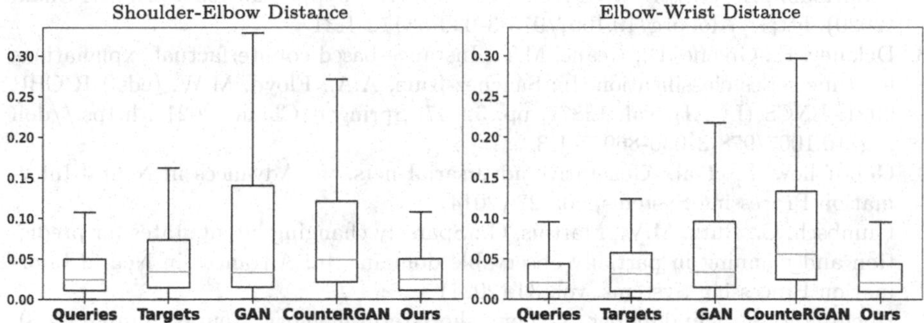

Fig. 6. Measured distances between body parts for originals and counterfactuals for the *Catching* dataset. Orange horizontal lines denote the median distance. Boxes contain all values between lower and upper quartiles. (Color figure online)

5 Conclusions

We proposed GAN architecture for generating time- and feature-sparse counterfactual explanations for multivariate time series. Our approach extends previous methods by a custom sparsity layer and additional loss regularization for sparsity and smoothness. In extensive experiments, we demonstrate that in spite of making substantially sparser modifications SPARCE achieves comparable or superior performance on common metrics for counterfactual search. Benchmarking our approach on a synthetic interpretability dataset, we show that it can also be used for feature attribution. The application to real-world human motion datasets demonstrates that our approach generates sparser and more plausible counterfactuals than related approaches.

The design of our approach allows for a flexible change of the desired target class, as well as an easy adaptation of the counterfactual value function catering to the needs of other applications. Future extensions can consider other applications (e.g. weather, stocks) and domain-specific regularization terms. In critical sectors such as healthcare, misinterpretation of systems can have severe consequences. XAI systems should thus always be validated by human experts. To enhance the understandability of generated counterfactuals, further work can investigate the visualization of explanations for end-users (e.g. in textual or visual form).

References

1. Ates, E., Aksar, B., Leung, V.J., Coskun, A.K.: Counterfactual explanations for multivariate time series. In: 2021 International Conference on Applied Artificial Intelligence (ICAPAI), pp. 1–8. IEEE (2021)
2. Dandl, S., Molnar, C., Binder, M., Bischl, B.: Multi-objective counterfactual explanations. In: Bäck, T., Preuss, M., Deutz, A., Wang, H., Doerr, C., Emmerich, M., Trautmann, H. (eds.) PPSN 2020. LNCS, vol. 12269, pp. 448–469. Springer, Cham (2020). https://doi.org/10.1007/978-3-030-58112-1_31
3. Delaney, E., Greene, D., Keane, M.T.: Instance-based counterfactual explanations for time series classification. In: Sánchez-Ruiz, A.A., Floyd, M.W. (eds.) ICCBR 2021. LNCS (LNAI), vol. 12877, pp. 32–47. Springer, Cham (2021). https://doi.org/10.1007/978-3-030-86957-1_3
4. Goodfellow, I., et al.: Generative adversarial nets. In: Advances in Neural Information Processing Systems, vol. 27 (2014)
5. Gumbsch, C., Butz, M.V., Martius, G.: Sparsely changing latent states for prediction and planning in partially observable domains. In: Advances in Neural Information Processing Systems, vol. 34 (2021)
6. Hochreiter, S., Schmidhuber, J.: Long short-term memory. Neural Comput. **9**(8), 1735–1780 (1997)
7. Ismail, A.A., Gunady, M., Corrada Bravo, H., Feizi, S.: Benchmarking deep learning interpretability in time series predictions. Adv. Neural. Inf. Process. Syst. **33**, 6441–6452 (2020)
8. Karimi, A.H., Schölkopf, B., Valera, I.: Algorithmic recourse: from counterfactual explanations to interventions. In: Proceedings of the 2021 ACM Conference on Fairness, Accountability, and Transparency, pp. 353–362 (2021)
9. Keane, M.T., Smyth, B.: Good counterfactuals and where to find them: a case-based technique for generating counterfactuals for explainable AI (XAI). In: Watson, I., Weber, R. (eds.) ICCBR 2020. LNCS (LNAI), vol. 12311, pp. 163–178. Springer, Cham (2020). https://doi.org/10.1007/978-3-030-58342-2_11
10. Kingma, D.P., Ba, J.: Adam: a method for stochastic optimization. In: International Conference on Learning Representations (2015)
11. Lang, J., Giese, M.A., Synofzik, M., Ilg, W., Otte, S.: Early recognition of ball catching success in clinical trials with RNN-based predictive classification. In: Farkaš, I., Masulli, P., Otte, S., Wermter, S. (eds.) ICANN 2021. LNCS, vol. 12894, pp. 444–456. Springer, Cham (2021). https://doi.org/10.1007/978-3-030-86380-7_36
12. Van der Maaten, L., Hinton, G.: Visualizing data using t-SNE. J. Mach. Learn. Res. **9**(11), 1–27 (2008)

13. Malekzadeh, M., Clegg, R.G., Cavallaro, A., Haddadi, H.: Mobile sensor data anonymization. In: Proceedings of the International Conference on Internet of Things Design and Implementation, pp. 49–58. IoTDI 2019, ACM, New York, NY, USA (2019)
14. Mothilal, R.K., Sharma, A., Tan, C.: Explaining machine learning classifiers through diverse counterfactual explanations. In: Proceedings of the 2020 Conference on Fairness, Accountability, and Transparency, pp. 607–617 (2020)
15. Nair, V., Hinton, G.E.: Rectified linear units improve restricted Boltzmann machines. In: ICML (2010)
16. Nemirovsky, D., Thiebaut, N., Xu, Y., Gupta, A.: CounterGAN: generating realistic counterfactuals with residual generative adversarial nets. arXiv preprint arXiv:2009.05199 (2020)
17. Van Looveren, A., Klaise, J., Vacanti, G., Cobb, O.: Conditional generative models for counterfactual explanations. arXiv preprint arXiv:2101.10123 (2021)
18. Wachter, S., Mittelstadt, B., Russell, C.: Counterfactual explanations without opening the black box: automated decisions and the GDPR. Harv. JL & Tech. **31**, 841 (2017)
19. Yoon, J., Jarrett, D., Van der Schaar, M.: Time-series generative adversarial networks. In: Advances in Neural Information Processing Systems, vol. 32 (2019)

Graph Neural Network-Based Representation Learning for Medical Time Series

Zhuzi Zheng[1], Changchun Guo[2], Jianyong Chen[1](✉), and Jianqiang Li[1]

[1] College of Computer Science and Software Engineering, Shenzhen University, Shenzhen 518000, China
jychen@szu.edu.cn

[2] Shenzhen Pingshan People's Hospital, Shenzhen 518000, China

Abstract. The ability to analyze and predict medical time series data is crucial for enhancing healthcare decision-making and improving patient outcomes. Currently, the algorithms used for classification and prediction of medical time series data are limited in their capabilities and may not be reliable enough to meet the demands of practical applications. The purpose of this paper is to promote the representation learning of complex data primarily comprised of medical time series, in order to facilitate various downstream tasks. Under the framework of graph neural networks (GNN), we present indegree regularized neural message passing to reflect the dependencies between different sequences. Our approach also leverages representation learning to convert multivariate time series (MTS) and static features into nodes of GNN. Moreover, we propose a dynamic loss function to encourage the consistent learning of sensor dependency graphs across models. Based on these proposals, our method can effectively capture not only the temporal dependencies among variables, but also the multidimensional dependencies among MTS and static features. We classify time series on two medical challenge and a human activity datasets. The results show that our approach can significantly improve downstream task performance across various metrics. Code is available at https://github.com/Zzzoptimus/GICG.

Keywords: Graph neural network · Medical time series · Regularized neural message passing · Time series classification

1 Introduction

The significance of classification and prediction related to multiple medical time series lies in their ability to assist medical professionals in making informed decisions about patient care. By analyzing and predicting medical time series data, healthcare providers can identify patterns and trends that may be indicative of certain conditions or diseases, and take appropriate action to mitigate or treat those conditions. For example, the early detection of certain diseases

L. Iliadis et al. (Eds.): ICANN 2023, LNCS 14259, pp. 194–205, 2023.
https://doi.org/10.1007/978-3-031-44223-0_16

can allow for timely intervention and improve treatment outcomes. Overall, the ability to classify and predict medical time series data can lead to more accurate diagnoses, earlier detection of health issues, and better treatment outcomes for patients. However, the current state of algorithms utilized for classifying and predicting medical time series data is limited in terms of its abilities and may not be dependable enough to fulfill practical application requirements.

The dataset we use mainly consists of medical time series. In medical scenarios, the various physiological indicators of the human body, such as heart rate, blood pressure, and oxygen saturation, are interdependent time series. Changes in heart rate can impact blood pressure, while high blood pressure can cause harm to heart function, elevating the risk of cardiovascular events like myocardial infarction and stroke in individuals with rapid heartbeat. Additionally, the static characteristics of the human body, including age and weight, can also influence these indicators. Moreover, if the influence between two physiological indicators in the human body changes, it can also indicate that there are problems in certain parts of the body. The changes in the influence between these sensors can be represented using message passing in graph neural networks (GNN).

The message passing neural network [5] was proposed in 2017. Each node and edge in the graph is associated with a learnable feature vector. The network iteratively passes messages between the nodes in a graph structure, updating their feature vectors based on the information received from neighboring nodes. This iterative process allows the information to be shared and aggregated across the graph, enabling GNN to model complex relationships and dependencies between nodes. It have been successfully applied to a wide range of tasks, including molecule property prediction, social network analysis, and protein structure prediction. They are particularly useful for problems where the input data has an inherent graph structure and traditional neural networks cannot be directly applied. We improve the message passing in GNN to make it more suitable for our task. In summary, the main contributions of this paper are as follows:

- We propose a regularized message passing strategies. A technique is proposed to apply indegree regularized constraint on the message passing of nodes.
- We propose global graph node representation learning. The static and the time series features can be kept in a consistent feature space after representation.
- A dynamic loss function is proposed that can promote consistent learning of sensor dependency graphs by establishing the similarity between two self-connections graphs.
- We conduct experimental analysis on three public large-scale datasets. The performance of our proposed model is significantly improved compared to the other baselines.

2 Related Works

In this chapter, we will demonstrate the relevant work from two perspectives: the data analysis about multivariate time series (MTS) and the development of GNN.

2.1 Multivariate Time Series

MTS are a crucial and ubiquitous type of data that represent multiple time-varying variables or signals recorded over time. They are widely used in a diverse range of domains, such as finance to analyze stock prices, meteorology to forecast weather patterns, medicine to monitor vital signs of patients, and many others. Irregularity in a multivariate case can create challenges for models that expect well-aligned and fixed-size inputs. Observations can be misaligned across different sensors and the number of observations can also vary considerably across samples due to a multitude of sampling frequencies and varying time intervals [24]. These characteristics can further complicate the analysis. An intuitive way to deal with irregular time series is to impute missing values and process them as regular time series [4]. However, imputation methods can distort the underlying distribution and lead to unwanted distribution shifts.

Historically, linear regression [6], random forest [9], and support vector machines [25] have been widely adopted for modeling and predicting MTS in academic research. Thanks to the advancement of computing power, state-of-the-art deep learning architectures have been developed to analyze MTS in various domains. In particular, these models have shown remarkable performance in analyzing and forecasting medical MTS. Recurrent neural networks (RNNs) [2], auto-encoders (AE) [11], and generative adversarial networks (GANs) [23] have demonstrated remarkable performance in medical data imputation and prediction, leveraging their powerful learning and generalization capabilities achieved through complex nonlinear transformations. Recent advancements in the field have led to the development of models that can directly learn from irregularly sampled time series. For instance, Che et al. developed a decay mechanism based on gated recurrent units (GRU-D) [1] and binary masking to capture long-range temporal dependencies. SeFT [8] takes a set-based approach and transforms irregularly sampled time series datasets into sets of observations modeled by set functions insensitive to misalignment. mTAND [16] leverages a multi-time attention mechanism to learn temporal similarity from non-uniformly collected measurements and produce continuous-time embeddings. IP-Net [14] adopt imputation to interpolate irregular time series against a set of reference points using a kernel-based approach.

2.2 Graph Neural Network

GNN are a type of deep learning model that can capture the structural and relational information of graphs [22,27]. It is an optimizable transformation on all attributes of the graph (nodes, edges, global-context) that preserves graph symmetries (permutation invariances) [20]. The graph's description is in a matrix format that is permutation invariant. All nodes, edges and global-context can be represented by vectors. This type of representation can be used for various applications, such as predicting molecular properties, reasoning with graphs and relations, and many others.

Recently, GNN have emerged as a successful approach to model complex patterns in structured graph data and a variety of improved GNNs have been reported. Graph convolutional networks (GCN) model node feature representations by aggregating representations of their one-step neighbors. Building upon this, graph attention networks (GAT) [19] use attention functions to compute different weights for different neighbors during aggregation. GNN-based models have shown success in time-related tasks, such as traffic prediction [21]. Applications of GNN in recommendation systems [10] and related domains have demonstrated their effectiveness in modeling large-scale, multi-relational data. Raindrop [26] is introduced as a graph-guided network for irregularly sampled time series and cases where sensor data is missing.

3 Method

In order to efficiently capture the relationships between various types of data and provide reference for medical decision-making, we propose a novel architecture named global indegree consistency GNN(GICG), which takes each sample (In clinical data, a patient's health status is recorded at irregular time intervals using different sensors) as input, where each sample is represented as a weighted directed graph (see Fig. 1). In each graph, nodes are formed by the irregularly recorded observations of each sensor, while the edge weights of the message passing between these nodes are learned during training. GICG aims to learn a fixed-dimensional embedding vector for a given sample and predict relevant labels based on this vector. Previous research [3,26] has represented MTS as feature vectors of nodes, and then through message passing, resulted in a global feature vector for the graph. Then it is concatenated with the static features of each sample to form a combined feature vector for downstream tasks. However, this concatenation approach is not a good choice because the processed time series feature vectors and the static features have undergone different mappings and transformations, and they reside in different high-dimensional feature spaces with potentially different data scales. In fact, the static features are similar with the time series data with little or no temporal variation. Therefore, we have adopted a consistent approach to process both types of data as time series data and represent them as different nodes (see Fig. 1 "Static" and "Active") in GNN.

3.1 Global Graph Node Representation

In order to construct sensor dependency graphs, consider a dataset $D = \{(S_i, y_i) \mid i = 1, \ldots, N\}$ consisting of N labeled samples, where each sample S_i is an irregular MTS with a corresponding label $y_i \in \{1, \ldots, C\}$. The label y_i denotes the class membership of the sample S_i among C istinct classes. Each sample contains M_a uniformly sampled sensors and M_s static features, resulting in M nodes ($M = M_a + M_s$) denoted as u, v, and so on. Each node is represented by a time-sorted observation sequence, with static features having a constant observation value at every timestamp. And d_k is denoted as cardinality

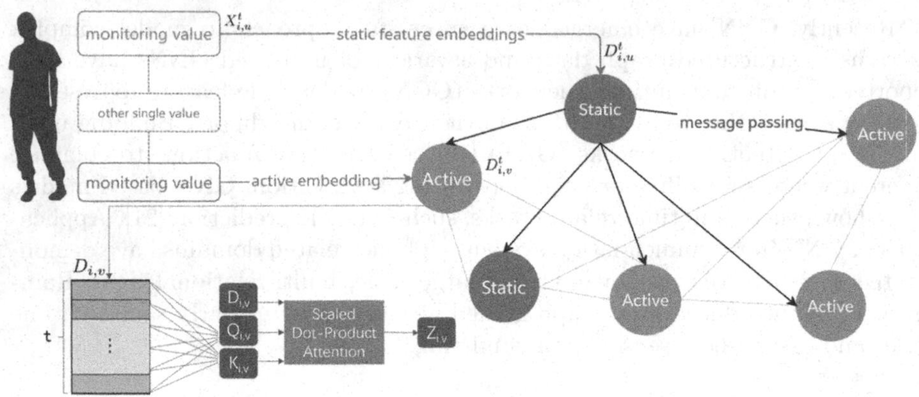

Fig. 1. The overview architecture of our model. Based on observed single value $X_{i,u}^t$, we generates the sensor embedding $Z_{i,u}$. The "Static" node represents the static feature representation, while the "Active" nodes represent the original time series data. The graph is updated through message passing to obtain the feature matrix $D_{i,v}$ of a node at all timestamps. Finally, the sensor embedding $Z_{i,v}$ is obtained through the attention mechanism. For simplicity, we have omitted the time information and the layer index of multi-layer message passing in the graph.

of the set comprising all timestamps included in the time series. For a node u in sample S_i, a single observation is represented as a tuple $(t, X_{i,u}^t)$, where the value $X_{i,u}^t \in \mathbb{R}$ is recorded for the node u at timestamp $t \in \mathbb{R}^+$. For nodes representing time series, the observation values are irregularly recorded, meaning that the time intervals between consecutive observation values may vary across nodes.

In order to map observations from both active sensors and static features to a high-dimensional space, we apply a nonlinear transformation. Due to the possibility of different distributions being followed by recorded values at different sensors, this is achieved through a trainable weight vector W_u, which depends on different nodes but is shared across samples and time dimensions. W_u transforms observations X from different nodes into a fixed-length vector of d, which is then mapped to a high-dimensional space through a nonlinear transformation using the following formula:

$$D_{i,u}^t = Sigmoid(X_{i,u}^t W_u) \tag{1}$$

3.2 Regularized Message Passing

Regularized message passing strategies are used to improve the consistent learning of sensor dependency graphs across different samples. They generate embeddings for inactive neighboring sensors, enhancing the quality and robustness of the learned embeddings. (see Fig. 1 "message passing"). These techniques aim to promote similarity between two self-connection graphs and ensure that the learning process remains stable and accurate. Following the previous step shown in Eq. (1), we now have fixed-length embeddings for each sensor at every timestamp. To update the weights of node v, we consider its dependencies with other nodes. This approach enables us to provide reasonable values for nodes with missing data at a particular timestamp, leveraging the inter dependency among nodes. Let us consider nodes u and v as an example to calculate the proportion of the information propagated from u to v with the following equation:

$$P_{i,uv}^{t} = Sigmoid(D_{i,u}^{t} W[r_u || p_i^t]^T), \tag{2}$$

where r_u refers to the outdegree vector of node v. It enables the model to learn different attention weights for distinct edges from various sensors. Moreover, $P_i^t \in \mathbb{R}^+$ represents time by mapping the 1-dimensional timestamp t to a multi-dimensional vector using trigonometric functions. We use P_i^t to compute attention weights that are sensitive to time. And W is a trainable weight matrix that is used for dimension mapping. The calculation result $P_{i,uv}^t \in [0, 1]$ is attention weight from u to v. Combining all these components, we can compute the embedding $D_{i,v}^t$ with the neighbor v of node u as follows:

$$D_{i,v}^{t} = Gelu(D_{i,u}^{t} W_u W_v^T P_{i,uv}^{t} c_{i,uv}) \tag{3}$$

The edge weight vector $c_{i,uv}$ is shared across all timestamps. Moreover, it will be updated in the following sections to achieve more efficiency in regularized message passing. We utilize regularized message passing by updating the edge weight vector $c_{i,uv}$. Firstly, we calculate the exponential sum of in-degrees $c_{i,v}$ of node v: $c_{i,v} = \sum_{u=1}^{M} (e^{c_{i,uv}/T})$. Then we use an activation function with distillation temperature to obtain the weight propagated to node v. The formula is shown as follows:

$$c_{i,uv} = \frac{e^{c_{i,uv}/T}}{\sum_{u=1}^{M} (e^{c_{i,uv}/T})}, \qquad \text{for} \quad u = 1, 2, \ldots, M \tag{4}$$

In the above equation, T is the distillation temperature [7], which controls the smoothness of the connections to node v. A higher T leads to a smoother result. For each outgoing node u and incoming node v, we traverse all M nodes in the graph and update the weights of all edges connecting them.

3.3 Sensor Embedding

After performing the previous operations, we obtained the high-dimensional vector $D_{i,v}$ for node v across all timestamps. Utilizing the time attention weights introduced in this section, we compressed $D_{i,v}$ along its dimensions to obtain the sensor embedding $S_{i,v}$(see Fig. 1). It is noteworthy that the impact of different timestamps on vector $S_{i,v}$ varies. To be specific, we compute in parallel the significance of node v at each timestamp using the following formula:

$$A_{i,v} = softmax(\frac{Q_{i,v} K_{i,v}^T}{\sqrt{d_k}} W_s) D_{i,v}, \tag{5}$$

where $Q_{i,v}, K_{i,v}$ are mapped by the formula: $Q_{i,v} = D_{i,v}W_Q, K_{i,v} = D_{i,v}W_K$. d_k is the dimension of unique timestamps in all time series. The equation is divided by $\sqrt{d_k}$ in order to maintain the dimensionality of attention weights within a more favorable range of numerical values, where $W_s \in \mathbb{R}^{d\times 1}$ is introduced to facilitate the dimension reduction operation. We will generate a temporal attention weight vector instead of self-attention matrix. Subsequently, we perform residual connections and transformations on the temporal embedding with the following formula:

$$S_{i,u} = \sum_{i=1}^{t}(A_i^t||[W_p p_i^t]W_a), \tag{6}$$

where W_p is a linearly mapped matrix. After the mapping process, we concatenate the resulting matrices and A_i^t to form a single matrix, where W_p and W_a are two linear projector shared by all samples and sensors.

3.4 Graph Embedding

The values of node embeddings are highly informative to some extent, and the concatenation of all node vectors results in a vector of only thousands of dimensions. Therefore, there is no need to further compress information, and we can directly use the concatenated vector S_i as the feature vector for the sample i. Good performance can be achieved by adding a simple fully connected layer. This approach works perfectly fine when the number of nodes is small, but for cases with a large number of nodes, it is necessary to use some feature extraction methods.

3.5 Dynamic Loss Function

In order to promote consistent learning of sensor dependency graphs, we employ the following loss function: $L = L_{CE} + pL_s$, where L_{CE} is cross entropy loss. The dissimilarity L_s is computed for identical sensors across different graphs (samples). L_s is calculated with the following formula:

$$L_s = \frac{\sum_{i=1}^{N}\sum_{j=1}^{N}\sum_{v=1}^{M}||S_{i,v} - S_{j,v}||_2}{(N-1)^2 M}, \tag{7}$$

where N denotes the total number of samples and M denotes the number of nodes in each sample. p is calculated with formula: $p = \sqrt{M/T}/2$, where T is the length of sequences. As the number of samples (N) can be large, L_s is typically computed only for samples within a batch to improve efficiency.

4 Experiments

4.1 Datasets

These datasets are all related to healthcare and human activity. The purpose of them is to enable early disease screening or advance prediction of ICU mortality in patients. Here, we provide a brief overview of the datasets used in the following experiments.

(1) P19: PhysioNet Sepsis Early Prediction Challenge 2019. P19 dataset includes 40,336 patients and each patient contains MTS by 34 irregularly sampled sensors. Each patient has a binary label representing occurrence of sepsis in the next 6 h. The dataset is imbalanced with 4% positive samples [13].

(2) P12: PhysioNet Predicting Mortality Challenge 2012. P12 dataset contains 12, 000 patients. Each patient contains MTS with 36 sensors. Each sample has a static vector with 9 elements including age, gender, etc. Each patient is associated with a binary label indicating length of stay in ICU. P12 is imbalanced with only 7% negative samples [17].

(3) PAM: PAMAP2 Physical Activity Monitoring. PAM dataset measures daily living activities of 9 subjects with 3 inertial measurement units. PAM dataset contains 5, 333 samples. Each sample is measured by 17 sensors and contains 600 continuous observations. PAM does not include static attributes and the samples are approximately balanced across all 8 categories [12].

We divide the dataset randomly into training (80%), validation (10%), and test (10%) sets. We split the dataset in five random ways according to the above ratio, then we performed five independent experiments.

4.2 Baselines

For comparison, we consider several models including decay mechanism based on GRU-D and binary masking, SeFT's set-based modeling, and the transformer-based method trans-mean. We will also compare our approach to mTAND's multi-time attention mechanism, as well as graph-guided network Raindrop. Additionally, we will evaluate IP-Net imputation-based methods, which interpolate irregular time series using kernel-based techniques against a set of reference points.

4.3 Evaluation Metrics

In binary classification (P19 and P12), we will use classification Accuracy, AUROC (Area Under the Receiver Operating Characteristic Curve), and AUPRC (Area Under the Precision-Recall Curve) as evaluation index. AUROC measures the ability of a model to distinguish between positive and negative classes by calculating the area under the curve of the receiver operating characteristic (ROC) curve, which plots the true positive rate (sensitivity) against the false positive rate (1-specificity) at various threshold settings. AUPRC, on the other hand, measures the trade-off between precision and recall of a model by calculating the area under the curve of the precision-recall curve, which plots the precision against the recall at various threshold settings.

We use both AUROC and AUPRC metrics simultaneously because while AUROC is useful for binary classification with balanced or imbalanced class distribution, it may not be optimal for imbalanced datasets. On the other hand, AUPRC is particularly useful for imbalanced classification problems, but can be less sensitive to false negatives and challenging to optimize precision and recall simultaneously.

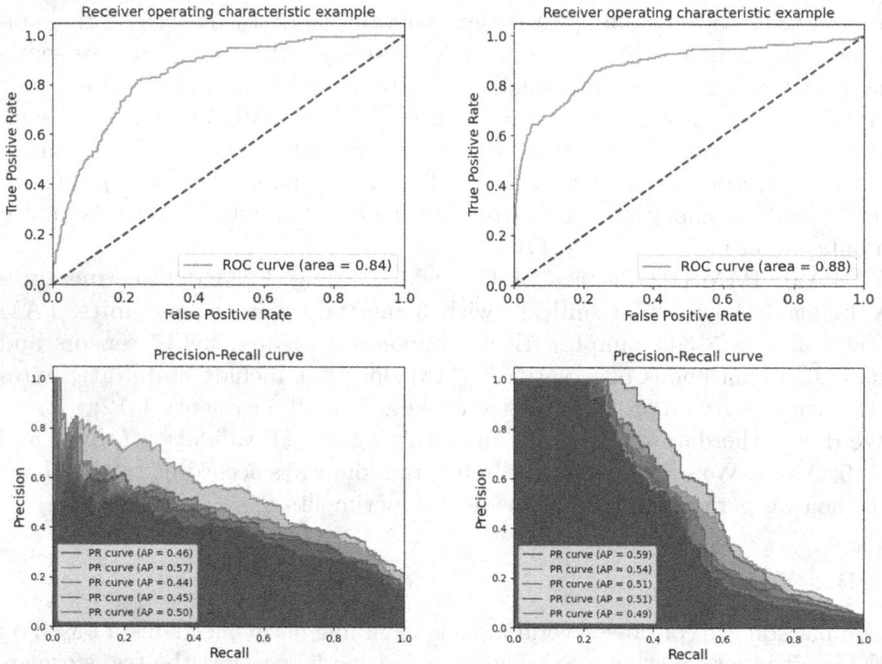

Fig. 2. The ROC curves and PRC curves of GICG tests on binary classification datasets, with the P12 dataset on the left and the P19 dataset on the right. On the PRC curves, average precision (AP) is the area under the curve, and the five curves represent five independent tests.

As shown in Fig. 2, the AUROC of GICG on the P12 and the P19 datasets reached 0.84 and 0.88, respectively. The average AUPRC of five experiments on the P12 and the P19 datasets reached 0.48 and 0.53, respectively.

4.4 Experimental Comparison Results

We conducted experiments on the aforementioned three datasets and identified optimal experimental settings and hyperparameter optimization for each dataset. Our experimental results are compared with multiple baselines on all the three datasets, demonstrating the superiority of our proposed approach.

Table 1. Comparison with the state-of-the-art methods on the datasets P12 and P19. It is the average of 5 experiments. Values with bold fonts indicate the best performance of all results.

Models	P12			P19		
	ACC	AUROC	AUPRC	ACC	AUROC	AUPRC
GRU-D [1]	0.763	0.672	0.460	0.785	0.839	0.469
Transformer [18]	0.752	0.651	0.429	0.778	0.832	0.476
Trans-mean [15]	0.764	0.668	0.449	0.802	0.841	0.474
SeFT [8]	0.719	0.668	0.361	0.786	0.787	0.311
mTAND [16]	0.731	0.653	0.403	0.780	0.804	0.324
Raindrop [26]	0.759	0.722	0.453	0.831	0.862	0.516
IP-Net [14]	0.765	0.725	0.441	0.813	0.846	0.381
GICG	**0.795**	**0.836**	**0.485**	**0.868**	**0.876**	**0.525**

In accordance with Table 1, our method GICG has achieved the highest performance on the binary classification datasets P12 and P19. This indicates that GICG can better capture the interrelationships between different variables and has stronger capabilities to aggregate information over the time dimension. To further substantiate our idea, We conducted further experiments on the eight-class classification dataset PAM.

Table 2. Comparison with the state-of-the-art methods on the PAM dataset. For every value, its left-hand side displays the average of 5 experiments, while its right-hand side represents the standard deviation.

PAM	Accuracy	Precision	Recall	F1 score
GRU-D [1]	0.833 ± 0.02	0.846 ± 0.01	0.852 ± 0.02	0.848 ± 0.01
Transformer [18]	0.835 ± 0.02	0.848 ± 0.02	0.860 ± 0.01	0.850 ± 0.01
Trans-mean [15]	0.837 ± 0.02	0.849 ± 0.03	0.864 ± 0.02	0.851 ± 0.02
SeFT [8]	0.671 ± 0.02	0.700 ± 0.02	0.682 ± 0.02	0.685 ± 0.02
mTAND [16]	0.746 ± 0.04	0.743 ± 0.04	0.795 ± 0.03	0.768 ± 0.03
Raindrop [26]	0.870 ± 0.01	0.889 ± 0.02	0.886 ± 0.02	0.886 ± 0.01
IP-Net [14]	0.843 ± 0.04	0.756 ± 0.02	0.779 ± 0.02	0.766 ± 0.03
GICG	**0.889 ± 0.01**	**0.902 ± 0.01**	**0.906 ± 0.01**	**0.903 ± 0.01**

As show in Table 2, We compare the performance of different models for the classification of irregularly sampled time series, and provide a summary of the average accuracy, precision, recall, and F1 score across five experiments. GICG has demonstrated the best performance on all evaluation measures. The performance has the lowest standard deviation from the average value, as implies high stability of the performance. Therefore, our approach can be regarded as the better choice for irregularly sampled time series classification tasks.

5 Conclusion

In this paper, we propose GICG, an improved approach based on GNN for handling medical MTS data. GICG utilizes representation learning to capture the temporal and multidimensional dependencies in medical MTS data and static features with time-invariant properties. This is achieved through the integration of global regularized message passing. GICG provides a flexible and robust solution for various downstream tasks of complex time series data. We demonstrate the effectiveness of our approach through experiments on two healthcare and a human activity datasets, showing significant improvements in downstream task performance across various metrics. This can lead to better performance and more reliable results in a wide range of applications.

Acknowledgements. This work was supported in part by the National Key R&D Program of China under Grant 2020YFA0908700, in part by the National Nature Science Foundation of China under Grant U2013201 and in part by the Pearl River Talent Plan of Guangdong Province under Grant 2019ZT08X603.

References

1. Che, Z., Purushotham, S., Cho, K., Sontag, D., Liu, Y.: Recurrent neural networks for multivariate time series with missing values. Sci. Rep. **8**(1), 6085 (2018)
2. Cui, R., Liu, M., Initiative, A.D.N., et al.: RNN-based longitudinal analysis for diagnosis of Alzheimer's disease. Comput. Med. Imaging Graph. **73**, 1–10 (2019)
3. Deng, A., Hooi, B.: Graph neural network-based anomaly detection in multivariate time series. In: Proceedings of the AAAI Conference on Artificial Intelligence. vol. 35, pp. 4027–4035 (2021)
4. Du, W., Côté, D., Liu, Y.: SAITS: self-attention-based imputation for time series. Expert Syst. Appl. **219**, 119619 (2023)
5. Gilmer, J., Schoenholz, S.S., Riley, P.F., Vinyals, O., Dahl, G.E.: Neural message passing for quantum chemistry. In: International Conference on Machine Learning, pp. 1263–1272. PMLR (2017)
6. Godfrey, K.: Simple linear regression in medical research. N. Engl. J. Med. **313**(26), 1629–1636 (1985)
7. Hinton, G., Vinyals, O., Dean, J.: Distilling the knowledge in a neural network. arXiv preprint 1503.02531 (2015)
8. Horn, M., Moor, M., Bock, C., Rieck, B., Borgwardt, K.: Set functions for time series. In: International Conference on Machine Learning, pp. 4353–4363. PMLR (2020)
9. Khalilia, M., Chakraborty, S., Popescu, M.: Predicting disease risks from highly imbalanced data using random forest. BMC Med. Inform. Decis. Mak. **11**, 1–13 (2011)

10. Kumar, I., Hu, Y., Zhang, Y.: EFLEC: efficient feature-leakage correction in GNN based recommendation systems. In: Proceedings of the 45th International ACM SIGIR Conference on Research and Development in Information Retrieval, pp. 1885–1889 (2022)
11. Lee, J., Sun, S., Yang, S.M., Sohn, J.J., Park, J., Lee, S., Kim, H.C.: Bidirectional recurrent auto-encoder for photoplethysmogram denoising. IEEE J. Biomed. Health Inform. **23**(6), 2375–2385 (2018)
12. Reiss, A., Stricker, D.: Introducing a new benchmarked dataset for activity monitoring. In: 2012 16th International Symposium on Wearable Computers (2012). https://doi.org/10.1109/iswc.2012.13
13. Reyna, M., et al.: Early prediction of sepsis from clinical data: the physionet/computing in cardiology challenge 2019. In: 2019 Computing in Cardiology Conference (CinC), Computing in Cardiology Conference (CinC) (2020). https://doi.org/10.22489/cinc.2019.412
14. Shukla, S.N., Marlin, B.M.: Interpolation-prediction networks for irregularly sampled time series. arXiv preprint arXiv:1909.07782 (2019)
15. Shukla, S.N., Marlin, B.M.: A survey on principles, models and methods for learning from irregularly sampled time series. arXiv preprint arXiv:2012.00168 (2020)
16. Shukla, S.N., Marlin, B.M.: Multi-time attention networks for irregularly sampled time series. arXiv preprint arXiv:2101.10318 (2021)
17. Silva, I., Moody, G., Scott, D.J., Celi, L.A., Mark, R.G.: Predicting in-hospital mortality of ICU patients: the physionet/computing in cardiology challenge 2012. In: 2012 Computing in Cardiology, pp. 245–248. IEEE (2012)
18. Vaswani, A., et al.: Attention is all you need. In: Advances in Neural Information Processing Systems, vol. 30 (2017)
19. Velickovic, P., Cucurull, G., Casanova, A., Romero, A., Lio, P., Bengio, Y., et al.: Graph attention networks. Stat **1050**(20), 10–48550 (2017)
20. Wang, C., Qiu, Y., Gao, D., Scherer, S.: Lifelong graph learning. In: Proceedings of the IEEE/CVF Conference on Computer Vision and Pattern Recognition, pp. 13719–13728 (2022)
21. Wang, X., et al.: Traffic flow prediction via spatial temporal graph neural network. In: Proceedings of the Web Conference 2020, pp. 1082–1092 (2020)
22. Wu, Z., Pan, S., Chen, F., Long, G., Zhang, C., Philip, S.Y.: A comprehensive survey on graph neural networks. IEEE Trans. Neural Netw. Learn. Syst. **32**(1), 4–24 (2020)
23. Yan, B., Wang, H., Wang, X., Zhang, Y.: An accurate saliency prediction method based on generative adversarial networks. In: 2017 IEEE International Conference on Image Processing (ICIP), pp. 2339–2343. IEEE (2017)
24. Zerveas, G., Jayaraman, S., Patel, D., Bhamidipaty, A., Eickhoff, C.: A transformer-based framework for multivariate time series representation learning. In: Proceedings of the 27th ACM SIGKDD Conference on Knowledge Discovery & Data Mining, pp. 2114–2124 (2021)
25. Zhang, G.: A modified SVM classifier based on RS in medical disease prediction. In: 2009 Second International Symposium on Computational Intelligence and Design, vol. 1, pp. 144–147. IEEE (2009)
26. Zhang, X., Zeman, M., Tsiligkaridis, T., Zitnik, M.: Graph-guided network for irregularly sampled multivariate time series. arXiv preprint arXiv:2110.05357 (2021)
27. Zhou, J., et al.: Graph neural networks: a review of methods and applications. AI Open **1**, 57–81 (2020)

Knowledge Forcing: Fusing Knowledge-Driven Approaches with LSTM for Time Series Forecasting

Muhammad Ali Chattha[1,2,3(✉)], Muhammad Imran Malik[3], Andreas Dengel[1,2], and Sheraz Ahmed[2]

[1] Rheinland-Pfälzische Technical University Kaiserslautern-Landau, RPTU, Kaiserslautern 67663, Germany
muhammad_ali.chattha@dfki.de

[2] German Research Center for Artificial Intelligence, DFKI, Kaiserslautern 67663, Germany

[3] National University of Science and Technology, NUST, Islamabad 44000, Pakistan

Abstract. Long Short-Term Memory (LSTM) typically relies solely on historical data for training and although, they excel at modelling sequential series and finding hidden patterns in the data, they are unable to utilize expert knowledge. Knowledge-driven systems (KDS), on the other hand, rely on domain knowledge and consist of rules explicitly defined by human experts. Both LSTM and KDS offer unique advantages, hence relying on a single approach can be suboptimal. However, currently there is a lacking of frameworks that can concurrently utilize explicit information in the KDS and hidden features in the data. In this paper, we propose a novel fusion mechanism, knowledge-forced LSTM (KF-LSTM), that combines knowledge-driven approaches with LSTM for time series forecasting. KF-LSTM employs LSTM in an encoder-decoder setting, where the decoder utilizes KDS predictions in a residual connection. This enables the decoder to utilize sequential relations in the historical data passed on by the encoder as well as information present in KDS in a complementary manner. We tested KF-LSTM on 4 real-world datasets in a multi-horizon forecasting setting. Even with utilizing relatively shallow single layered LSTM, KF-LSTM achieves State-of-the-Art (SotA) performance on almost all of the datasets, highlighting the information fusion capabilities of the framework. On average, knowledge forcing improves over previous SotA by **20%**.

Keywords: Time series forecasting · Knowledge fusion · Knowledge-driven system · Neural Networks · Hybrid Systems

1 Introduction

Time series forecasting is an important problem as it has great impact on many crucial domains such as demand prediction, financial forecasts, traffic flow prediction, weather forecasts, etc. Having an accurate estimate of future prospects

L. Iliadis et al. (Eds.): ICANN 2023, LNCS 14259, pp. 206–217, 2023.
https://doi.org/10.1007/978-3-031-44223-0_17

allows for better planning, which is pivotal for efficient resource management and profit generation. As a result, a great deal of importance is laid on time series forecasting and any improvements in forecasting approaches are highly sort after.

Time series forecasting approaches can be broadly categorized into two main categories: Knowledge-driven and data-driven approaches. Knowledge-Driven Systems (KDS) consists of explicitly defined rules that are made up by human experts who have substantial domain knowledge about the problem. These rules make up the knowledge base of the KDS and are used in a predefined manner for inference. As a result, KDS system can utilize the knowledge of human experts when performing the forecasting task. These expert rules are typically in the form of logical expressions such as first order logic [18,32], or mathematical expressions such as statistical methods [2,9]. Statistical methods normally consist of mathematical operations predefined by human experts and have shown great performance [16,17]. In contrast, data-driven methods rely on historical data from which they learn to extract hidden patterns that are useful for the solution. Long Short-Term Memory (LSTM) have shown considerable efficacy in modelling time series and sequential data. Both of the approaches, although used for the same goal, operate on very different underlying information. Both KDS and LSTM have different and unique strengths, and relying on a single approach can be suboptimal.

However, there is a severe lacking of frameworks that can combine the strengths of both KDS and LSTM. Current hybrid methods, for forecasting problem, mostly rely on ensemble methods, where two or more methods are combined after the inference by taking the average of their individual predictions. While ensemble methods do improve the overall result in some scenarios, they are limited by the accuracy of individual models [26]. Any inaccurate model can negatively impact the performance of the overall ensemble since, regardless of their accuracy, every model contributes to the final prediction. We believe that in an ideal fusion mechanism, the framework should be aware of the strengths of constituent models and should utilize these strengths accordingly, rather than simply taking an average.

Based on the above motivation, we propose a novel fusion framework, knowledge-forced LSTM (KF-LSTM), that fuses knowledge-driven approaches with LSTM in a way where their strengths are combined, and individual inaccuracies are catered for. KF-LSTM framework accesses the efficacy of predictions given by KDS and the utilizes information present in the historical data to offset any missing or incorrect information. This is achieved by using an encoder-decoder LSTM architecture, where KDS predictions are connected in a residual connection setting with the decoder. As a result, the decoder takes in information from KDS via the skip connection and information from historical data via the internal states of the encoder. Since the decoder calculates the residual function, it can offset and correct any missing or inaccurate information in the KDS, which current ensemble based hybrid methods are incapable of. We test knowledge forced LSTM on 4 real world forecasting datasets in a multi-horizon forecasting setting. Although, we utilized a single layered LSTM model, the proposed framework outperformed recent transformer based forecasting models and achieved SotA performance across most of the datasets. On average, knowledge forcing framework improved over previous SotA by **20%**. In particular contribution of this paper are as follows:

- We introduce a novel fusion framework, KF-LSTM, that combines knowledge-driven approaches with LSTMs in a constructive manner.
- KF-LSTM achieves **20%** relative performance improvement over previous SotA on 4 real-world benchmark datasets.
- We show that KF-LSTM is agnostic to underlying KDS and can work with wide array KDS approaches.
- We show that KF-LSTM dynamically combines information from constituent models based on their individual efficacy.
- We show that KF-LSTM outperforms current ensemble based hybrid frameworks, highlighting its superior information fusion capabilities.

2 Related Work

In the context of time series forecasting, Hybrid schemes mostly revolve around ensemble-based methods. Syml et al. [22] utilized ensemble of DNN models with different parameters to obtain final forecast. Similarly, Larrea et.al. and Kaushik et. al. [10,13] also employed ensemble technique for the forecasting task. Ensemble technique combines different models in time series forecasting, but issues such as model diversity and accuracy can affect overall predictions. Highly inaccurate models can negatively effect the accuracy of the overall ensemble. Recently, attention-based models such as transformer networks, have gained interest for better forecasting performance [14,27,28]. The attention mask is computed by utilizing covariates in the dataset, which can be considered as knowledge from an additional source. Graph-based forecasting network aims to capture spatial dependencies among different time series in the dataset along with temporal modelling [6]. Both attention maps and spatial information can be considered as additional information that improve the overall forecasts; however, such techniques suffer when dealing with data that lacks mutual dependence or spatial information among time series.

Incorporating logic rules directly into neural network architecture has also been proposed [24,25]. Here, elements of the rule-set are considered as a unit in the neural network and their weights are pre-computed using relations defined in the rule-set. Some additional units that are not part of the logic rule-set are also used in the neural network to learn relations from the data as well. Such methods incorporate the knowledge base directly into the model, but this also limits flexibility and requires strong hierarchical coherence between the rule base and neural network layers. Although knowledge distillation is not directly applicable to the forecasting problem, it is still worth mentioning as a knowledge sharing framework [7,29]. Knowledge distillation is used for knowledge transfer, specifically in classification tasks. The method involves training a smaller model (student network) to mimic the predictions of a larger, more complex model (teacher network). Although it improves the classification capabilities of student model, however, scenarios when teacher network is inaccurate is not catered.

3 Multi Horizon Forecasting

The main objective of a forecasting framework is to learn a parametric function that maps $\boldsymbol{X_w}$ values from the past to $\hat{\boldsymbol{Y}}_{\boldsymbol{h}}$, where w and h represents input window size and the output size, horizon, respectively. $\boldsymbol{X_w}$ represents list of values $x_t, x_{t-1}, ..., x_{t-w}$ and $\hat{\boldsymbol{Y}}_{\boldsymbol{h}}$ represents list containing h predicted values $\hat{x}_{t+1}, \hat{x}_{t+2}, ..., \hat{x}_{t+h}$. This can be mathematically expressed as:

$$[\hat{x}_{t+1}, \hat{x}_{t+2}, ..., \hat{x}_{t+h}] = \Phi([x_t, x_{t-1}, ..., x_{t-w}]; \mathcal{W}) \tag{1}$$

$$\hat{\boldsymbol{Y}}_{\boldsymbol{h}} = \Phi(\boldsymbol{X_w}; \mathcal{W}) \tag{2}$$

where $\mathcal{W} = \{W_l, b_l\}_{l=1}^{L}$ encapsulates the parameters of the network comprised of L layers and $\Phi : \mathbb{R}^{w+1} \mapsto \mathbb{R}^h$ defines the mapping from the input space to the output space. The optimal parameters of the mapping function $\mathcal{W}^*$ are computed by optimizing over the loss curve using gradient descent. Typically, Mean Squared Error (MSE) is used as a loss function, and hence, the optimization problem for regression can be mathematically stated as:

$$\mathcal{W}^* = \arg\min_{\mathcal{W}} \frac{1}{h} \sum_{i=1}^{h} \|Y_{t+i} - \Phi([x_t, ..., x_{t-w}]; \mathcal{W})\|_2^2 \tag{3}$$

$$\mathcal{W}^* = \arg\min_{\mathcal{W}} \frac{1}{h} \sum_{i=1}^{h} \|Y_{t+i} - \hat{Y}_{t+i}\|_2^2 \tag{4}$$

where Y_{t+i} and $\hat{Y}_{t+i}$ denotes the ground truth and the predicted value at time $t+i$ respectively.

4 Knowledge Forcing Framework

Figure 1 shows the overall architecture of the knowledge forcing framework. The input sequence is first passed to KDS, which comes up with forecasts according to the rules defined in its knowledge base. The input sequence is also passed on to the LSTM encoder, which computes a fixed latent representation, v of the input sequence. This encoded representation given by the last hidden state of the LSTM is used to initialize the internal state of the decoder. Instead of sequentially using the output of the decoder at the previous time step as an input for the next time step, we utilize predictions given by KDS as input to the decoder. These KDS predictions are also added to the output of the decoder, making a residual connection. This enables the knowledge forcing framework to encapsulate information from both KDS and LSTM in a complementary manner. In the following subsections, we further elaborate on the constituent KDS and LSTM architecture, along with the knowledge fusion mechanism.

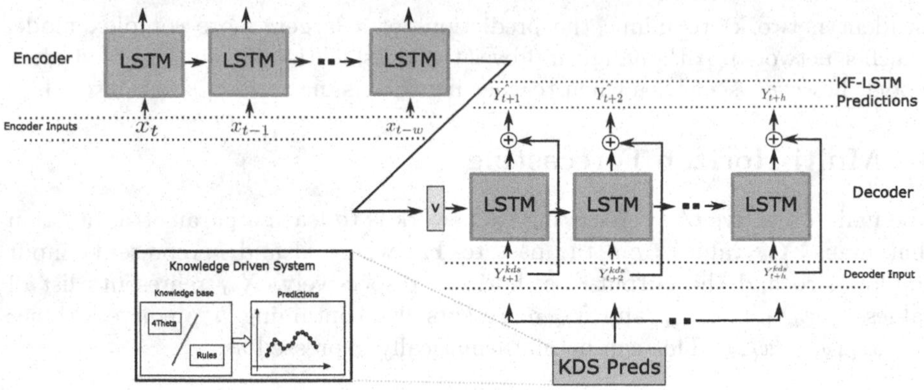

Fig. 1. KF-LSTM framework architecture.

4.1 Constituent KDS and LSTM Models

Knowledge forcing framework is agnostic to the underlying KDS model, however, for evaluations we utilize statistical methods 4Theta [23]. 4Theta is based on the original Theta [1] method, which models time series by decomposing it into theta lines. The theta lines are obtained by utilizing a parameter θ, which controls the curvature of theta lines. $0 < \theta < 1$ leads to less fluctuating lines, modeling the long term linear dependencies in the time series and higher-order $\theta > 1$ models the fluctuation, modeling the short-term attributes of the time series. For simplicity, we mathematically present a theta estimator using two theta lines in Eq. 5

$$Y_t = \omega_{\theta_1} Y_t^{\theta_1} + \omega_{\theta_2} Y_t^{\theta_2} \tag{5}$$

where ω_{θ_1} and ω_{θ_2} are the weights of the two theta lines. θ_1 and θ_2 model the long- and short-term characteristics of the original data, respectively. $Y_t^{\theta_1}$ represents the theta line at point t and can be obtained by the following equation Eq. 6

$$Y_t^{\theta} = \theta Y_t^{''} = \theta(Y_t - 2Y_{t-1} + Y_{t+2}) = \theta Y_t + (1 - \theta)(b + at) \tag{6}$$

where $Y^{''}$ is the second difference of the data and b and a are the intercept and slope of simple linear regression in time Y^0.

We employ a single layered LSTM model with 64 hidden units as our data-driven model. LSTM employs gating mechanism namely: input i_t, forget f_t, and output o_t gate which determines which long-term information to store and which short-term memory is to be read from the memory cell. This allows LSTMs to retain key information in the input sequence while ignoring less important parts. These long- and short-term information are preserved using internal state vectors C_t and h_t respectively. This can be represented mathematically by

$$C_t = f_t.C_{t-1} + i_t.C_t', h_t = o_t.\Phi(C_t) \tag{7}$$

where Φ represents tangent function i,e., $tanh$.

4.2 Knowledge Fused Optimization

The input $\boldsymbol{X}_w$ is first given to KDS that makes an inference about future h values based on information explicitly defined in its knowledge base. The same input is also passed to the encoder of the KF-LSTM that encodes long- and shot-term information in the historical data in its latent representations. We represent this vector containing latent representations as v, which consists of vector C_t and h_t from Eq. 7. The main difference of KF-LSTM from vanilla LSTM is in the decoder, In KF-LSTM, the KDS predictions are given as input to the decoder instead of giving the output of previous time stamp as an input to the decoder of the next time stamp. In addition to this, the predictions given by KDS are also added to the output given by the decoder, This makes a residual connection, where the decoder is connected in the residual connection whereas the KDS is connected via the skip connection. This changes the objective function learned by the decoder. The decoder now learns the residual function instead of learning input sequence to output sequence mapping. The residual function basically offsets any information that is either missing or incorrect in KDS predictions. This not only allows information to flow from KDS but enables KF-LSTM to correct inaccuracies in KDS predictions by utilizing hidden information contained in the historical data. As a result, KF-LSTM combines information in KDS and in historical data in a complementary and constructive way, where inaccuracies are suppressed and corrected. Let $\boldsymbol{Y}_h^{LSTM}$ is the output of the LSTM decoder. Mathematically, this is calculated by

$$\boldsymbol{Y}_h^{LSTM} = \Phi(p(Y_t|v, Y_h^{KDS})) \tag{8}$$

where Y_h^{KDS} are the predictions given by the KDS. Since the final output of KF-LSTM is a summation of $\boldsymbol{Y}_h^{LSTM}$ and Y_h^{KDS}. The optimization Eq. 4 can now be written as

$$\begin{aligned} \mathcal{W}^* &= \arg\min_{\mathcal{W}} \sum_{x\in\mathcal{Y}} \|\mathcal{Y} - (Y_h^{KDS} + Y_h^{LSTM})\|_2^2 \\ &= \arg\min_{\mathcal{W}} \sum_{x\in\mathcal{Y}} \|(\mathcal{Y} - Y_h^{KDS}) - Y_h^{LSTM}\|_2^2 \\ &= \arg\min_{\mathcal{W}} \sum_{x\in\mathcal{Y}} \|\xi_{KDS} - Y_h^{LSTM}\|_2^2 \end{aligned} \tag{9}$$

where $\mathcal{Y}$ is the ground truth and ξ_{KDS} represents error in KDS predictions. As evident from the Eq. 9, KF-LSTM modifies the objective learned by the underlying LSTM, which is to minimize the error contained in KDS predictions. This is done by information contained in the historical data, which is encoded in vector v and is passed to the decoder and is used to initialize the internal states of the decoder. As a result, the overall KF-LSTM framework tries to combine the best of both world, which is not the case in other hybrid schemes.

5 Experiments and Results

5.1 Datasets

We evaluate knowledge forcing framework on 4 benchmark datasets belonging to different real-world applications. The datasets utilized are as follows: (1) *PeMSD7(M)* [31] dataset contains vehicular traffic information of District 7 of California containing data of 228 sensors from May to June 2012, (2) *Nasdaq* [21] dataset contains stock price (NASDAQ 100 index) information of 81 corporations, recorded every minute for 105 days, (3) *Energy* [3] dataset is made up of 26 different attributes related to energy consumption of different appliances in a single household, (4) *ETTm2* [28] datasets contains readings of electrical transformers like load and oil temperature, recorded every 15 min from July 2016 to July 2016.

5.2 Baseline Methods

We compare knowledge forcing framework against more than 8 baseline methods including recent transformer based methods: ETSformer [27], Autoformer [28], Spatial-Temporal Transformer Networks (STTN) [30], Informer [33], Reformer [11], LogTrans [14], graph-based networks: Graph-Wavenet [20], Spatio-Temporal Graph Convolutional (STGCN) [31], Convolutional and Recurrent Neural Networks: LSTM [8], Diffusion Convolutional Recurrent Neural Network (DCRNN) [15], Long- and Short-term time series network (LSTNet) [12], Multi-level Construal Neural Network (MLCNN) [5], Neural basis expansion (N-BEATS) [19]. However, we only report the results claimed by the authors of individual methods and do not reproduce results except for ETSformer [27], Autoformer [28] and Nbeats [19].

Table 1. Results of KF-LSTM framework along with baseline methods on all the datasets. A lower MSE and MAE value represents better forecasts. Best results are written with green, while second best are written with blue color.

Methods		KF-LSTM		ETSformer [27]		Autoformer [28]		Informer [33]		LSTnet [12]		Nbeats [19]		MLCNN [5]		STTN [30]	
Metrics		MSE	MAE	MSE	MAE	MSE	MAE	MSE	MAE	MSE	MAE	MSE	MAE	MSE	MAE	MSE	MAE
PeMSD7(M)	3	13.26	1.96	21.34	2.78	19.27	2.72	-	-	-	-	23.04	3.71	-	-	16.32	2.14
	6	25.17	2.63	28.52	3.24	31.36	3.41	-	-	-	-	40.20	4.54	-	-	28.84	2.70
	9	19.94	2.37	25.10	2.91	32.26	3.21	-	-	-	-	64.80	5.22	-	-	36.60	3.03
Nasdaq	3	0.011	0.029	2.22	0.780	1.85	0.45	-	-	0.134	0.093	10.18	1.11	0.133	0.091	-	-
	6	0.022	0.041	3.03	0.830	3.50	0.53	-	-	0.272	0.135	10.76	1.13	0.266	0.130	-	-
	12	0.052	0.061	3.06	0.850	1.93	0.46	-	-	0.569	0.195	6.864	0.78	0.546	0.186	-	-
Energy	3	174.0	2.70	209.38	2.42	259.85	3.86	-	-	240.56	1.82	236.85	2.76	228.92	1.88	-	-
	6	188.40	1.43	234.09	2.82	289.00	4.00	-	-	249.64	2.39	258.57	3.02	255.68	2.38	-	-
	12	251.30	2.03	262.44	3.32	314.71	4.35	-	-	285.27	3.11	291.38	3.12	281.57	3.04	-	-
ETTm2	96	0.187	0.301	0.189	0.28	0.255	0.34	0.365	0.45	3.142	1.37	-	-	-	-	-	-
	192	0.251	0.355	0.253	0.32	0.281	0.34	0.533	0.56	31.54	1.37	-	-	-	-	-	-
	336	0.746	0.582	0.314	0.36	0.339	0.37	1.363	0.89	3.160	1.37	-	-	-	-	-	-

5.3 Results

Table 1 shows results obtained by knowledge forced LSTM along with baseline methods. Knowledge forced LSTM consistently achieves SotA results on all the datasets except ETTm2, where it achieves second-best result on MAE metric but still manages SotA result on MSE metric except for the horizon of 336. Averaging across all the prediction lengths, knowledge forced LSTM achieves **23%** reduction in MSE and **22%** reduction in MAE compared to previous SotA on PeMSD7(M) dataset. **91%** reduction in MSE and **68%** reduction in MAE on Nasdaq dataset and **14%** and **10%** reduction on MSE and MAE on Energy dataset. On ETTm2 dataset, knowledge forced LSTM achieves **9%** reduction in MSE for horizon 96 and 192, while it achieves second-best results on MAE metric except for the forecasting horizon of 336, where knowledge forced LSTM achieves third-best result overall. We believe that this is due to an extremely long forecasting horizon, which a shallow LSTM was unable to model properly. Nevertheless, average across all the dataset and evaluation metrics, knowledge forced LSTM achieves **20%** improvement over the previous SotA.

Figure 2 shows plots of forecasts made by KF-LSTM and recent transformer-based methods, Autoformer [28] and ETSformer [27]. KF-LSTM not only follows the trend more accurately, but also models subtle variations and extremas more accurately, which is of real importance in domains such as finance.

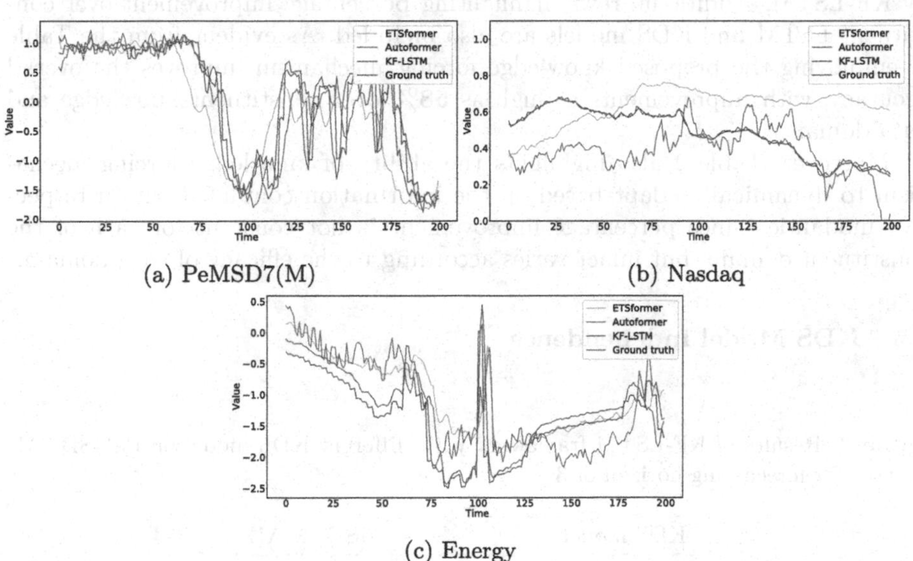

Fig. 2. Prediction of KF-LSTM, Autoformer and ETSformer on PeMSd7(M), Nasdaq, and energy dataset for horizon 3

5.4 Ablation Study

Table 2. Comparison of MSE and MAE metrics of vanilla LSTM and KDS without the fusion mechanism for PeMSD7(M) dataset. Percentage improvement given by the KF-LSTM over the vanilla LSTM and KDS is also given.

Metric (Horizon)	Vanilla LSTM	KDS	KF-LSTM
MSE (3/ 6/ 9)	14.44/ 30.7/ 35.4	15.9/ 30.7/ 47.5	**13.26/ 25.17/ 19.94**
Percentage Improvement in MSE (3/ 6/ 9)	**8%/ 18%/ 44%**	**16%/ 18%/ 58%**	-
MAE (3/ 6/ 9)	2.24/ 2.73/ 3.50	2.13/ 2.90/ 3.44	**1.96/ 2.63/ 2.37**
Percentage Improvement in MAE (3/ 6/ 9)	**13%/ 4%/ 32%**	**8%/ 9%/ 31%**	-

In this section, we study the impact of knowledge forcing by evaluating the underlying KDS and LSTM models in isolation without the fusion mechanism. Table 2 shows the result of LSTM and KDS model along with the results obtained by KF-LSTM. Additional rows highlighting percentage improvement over constituent LSTM and KDS models are also included. As evident from the Table 2, employing the proposed knowledge forcing mechanism improves the overall accuracy, with improvements as high as **58%** over constituent knowledge and data domains.

Moreover, Table 2 also highlights the ability of knowledge forcing mechanism to dynamically adapt based on the information contained within respective modalities since percentage improvement is not constant for each of the constituent domain, but infact varies according to the efficacy of each domain.

5.5 KDS Model Independence

Table 3. Results of KF-LSTM framework with different KDS model on PeMSD7(M) dataset for forecasting horizon of 3

KDS model	MSE	MAE
Rule-based KDS	13.36	2.04
Statistical method as KDS	13.26	1.96

In this section, we verify the agnostic nature of the knowledge forcing mechanism towards the underlying KDS model. This is important because the knowledge base of KDS can take different forms like rule-based relations, mathematical formulations etc., and it is desirable that the knowledge fusion framework is flexible enough to incorporate different KDS models. For this, we change the underlying KDS from a statistical based method to a rule-based model. The rules for forecasting are made from the scheme proposed in [4], which borrows concepts from graph-based network by considering each time series observations as a node of the graph and calculating relations between the nodes with correlation functions. Table 3 shows the results of knowledge forcing with a rule-based KDS model.

5.6 Comparison with Ensemble Methods

In this section, we evaluate the knowledge forced LSTM framework against the ensemble technique, that is a commonly used method in the literature for combining predictions of two or more models. Table 4 shows the comparison of KF-LSTM with the ensemble method. For every dataset, KF-LSTM gives substantially superior performance compared to the ensemble. This is primarily due to the error correction capabilities of KF-LSTM that in a way mitigate some of the inaccuracies in the final output.

Table 4. Comparison of ensemble methods with KF-LSTM on all the datasets.

Dataset	Horizon	MSE		MAE	
		Ensemble	KF-LSTM	Ensemble	KF-LSTM
PeMSD7(M)	3	13.70	**13.26**	2.04	**1.96**
	6	24.90	**25.17**	2.64	**2.63**
	9	30.01	**19.94**	3.00	**2.37**
Nasdaq	3	0.032	**0.011**	0.052	**0.029**
	6	0.035	**0.022**	0.054	**0.041**
	12	0.107	**0.052**	0.086	**0.061**
Energy	3	208.83	**174.00**	2.75	**2.70**
	6	245.50	**188.40**	1.76	**1.43**
	12	272.58	**251.30**	2.40	**2.03**
ETT	96	0.32	**0.19**	0.31	**0.30**
	192	0.35	**0.25**	0.36	**0.36**
	336	0.76	**0.75**	0.60	**0.58**

6 Conclusion

In this paper, we present a novel hybrid framework, KF-LSTM, that combines KDS approaches with LSTM in a way, where not only useful information contained in the constituent domains are integrated but their inaccuracies and shortcomings are also catered for in the final output. We evaluate KF-LSTM against recent SotA baseline methods on 4 time series benchmark forecasting datasets. Despite being a relatively shallow network, KF-LSTM outperforms recent transformer and graph-based models handsomely and establishes new SotA on almost every dataset. This highlights the effectiveness of the proposed fusion framework. We also show that KF-LSTM in flexible towards different KDS models. This will prove useful in applicability of KF-LSTM in real-world applications, where KDS may comprise of different and diverse knowledge bases. We also compare KF-LSTM with current ensemble based hybrid schemes. KF-LSTM significantly outperforms ensemble technique in terms of overall accuracy. The ability of KF-LSTM to constructively utilize knowledge and data domain will prove useful in unlocking the true potential of artificial intelligence especially in critical applications where domain knowledge is also crucial.

References

1. Assimakopoulos, V., Nikolopoulos, K.: The theta model: a decomposition approach to forecasting. Int. J. Forecast. **16**(4), 521–530 (2000)
2. Box, G.E., Jenkins, G.M., Reinsel, G.: Time series analysis: forecasting and control Holden-day San Francisco. BoxTime Series Analysis: Forecasting and Control Holden Day 1970 (1970)
3. Candanedo, L.M., Feldheim, V., Deramaix, D.: Data driven prediction models of energy use of appliances in a low-energy house. Energy Build. **140**, 81–97 (2017)
4. Chattha, M.A., van Elst, L., Malik, M.I., Dengel, A., Ahmed, S.: KENN: enhancing deep neural networks by leveraging knowledge for time series forecasting. arXiv preprint arXiv:2202.03903 (2022)
5. Cheng, J., Huang, K., Zheng, Z.: Towards better forecasting by fusing near and distant future visions. In: AAAI, pp. 3593–3600 (2020)
6. Han, H., et al.: STGCN: a spatial-temporal aware graph learning method for poi recommendation. In: 2020 IEEE International Conference on Data Mining (ICDM), pp. 1052–1057. IEEE (2020)
7. Hinton, G., Vinyals, O., Dean, J.: Distilling the knowledge in a neural network. arXiv preprint arXiv:1503.02531 (2015)
8. Hochreiter, S., Schmidhuber, J.: LSTM can solve hard long time lag problems. In: Advances in Neural Information Processing Systems, pp. 473–479 (1997)
9. Hunter, J.S.: The exponentially weighted moving average. J. Qual. Technol. **18**(4), 203–210 (1986)
10. Kaushik, S., et al.: Ai in healthcare: time-series forecasting using statistical, neural, and ensemble architectures. Front. Big Data **3**, 4 (2020)
11. Kitaev, N., Kaiser, Ł., Levskaya, A.: Reformer: the efficient transformer. arXiv preprint arXiv:2001.04451 (2020)
12. Lai, G., Chang, W.C., Yang, Y., Liu, H.: Modeling long-and short-term temporal patterns with deep neural networks. In: The 41st International ACM SIGIR Conference on Research & Development in Information Retrieval, pp. 95–104 (2018)
13. Larrea, M., Porto, A., Irigoyen, E., Barragán, A.J., Andújar, J.M.: Extreme learning machine ensemble model for time series forecasting boosted by PSO: application to an electric consumption problem. Neurocomputing **452**, 465–472 (2021)
14. Li, S., et al.: Enhancing the locality and breaking the memory bottleneck of transformer on time series forecasting. Adv. Neural. Inf. Process. Syst. **32**, 5243–5253 (2019)

15. Li, Y., Yu, R., Shahabi, C., Liu, Y.: Diffusion convolutional recurrent neural network. In: Data-driven Traffic Forecasting, ICLR 2018 Conference, pp. 1–16 (2017)
16. Makridakis, S., Hibon, M.: The M3-competition: results, conclusions and implications. Int. J. Forecast. **16**(4), 451–476 (2000)
17. Makridakis, S., Spiliotis, E., Assimakopoulos, V.: The m4 competition: results, findings, conclusion and way forward. Int. J. Forecast. **34**, 802–808 (2018)
18. Moghram, I., Rahman, S.: Analysis and evaluation of five short-term load forecasting techniques. IEEE Trans. Power Syst. **4**(4), 1484–1491 (1989)
19. Oreshkin, B.N., Carpov, D., Chapados, N., Bengio, Y.: N-beats: neural basis expansion analysis for interpretable time series forecasting. arXiv preprint arXiv:1905.10437 (2019)
20. Pan, Z., Liang, Y., Wang, W., Yu, Y., Zheng, Y., Zhang, J.: Urban traffic prediction from spatio-temporal data using deep meta learning. In: Proceedings of the 25th ACM SIGKDD International Conference on Knowledge Discovery & Data Mining, pp. 1720–1730 (2019)
21. Qin, Y., Song, D., Chen, H., Cheng, W., Jiang, G., Cottrell, G.: A dual-stage attention-based recurrent neural network for time series prediction. arXiv preprint arXiv:1704.02971 (2017)
22. Smyl, S.: A hybrid method of exponential smoothing and recurrent neural networks for time series forecasting. Int. J. Forecast. **36**(1), 75–85 (2020)
23. Spiliotis, E., Makridakis, S., Assimakopoulos, V.: The m4 competition in progress. In: 38th International Symposium on Forecasting (2018)
24. Towell, G.G., Shavlik, J.W.: Knowledge-based artificial neural networks. Artif. Intell. **70**(1–2), 119–165 (1994)
25. Tran, S.N., Garcez, A.S.d.: Deep logic networks: inserting and extracting knowledge from deep belief networks. IEEE Trans. Neural Netw. Learn. Syst. 29(2), 246–258 (2018)
26. Wang, W.: Some fundamental issues in ensemble methods. In: 2008 IEEE International Joint Conference on Neural Networks (IEEE World Congress on Computational Intelligence), pp. 2243–2250. IEEE (2008)
27. Woo, G., Liu, C., Sahoo, D., Kumar, A., Hoi, S.: ETSformer: exponential smoothing transformers for time-series forecasting. arXiv preprint arXiv:2202.01381 (2022)
28. Wu, H., Xu, J., Wang, J., Long, M.: Autoformer: Decomposition transformers with auto-correlation for long-term series forecastingIn: Advances in Neural Information Processing Systems, vol. 34 (2021)
29. Xie, Q., Hovy, E., Luong, M.T., Le, Q.V.: Self-training with noisy student improves Imagenet classification. arXiv preprint arXiv:1911.04252 (2019)
30. Xu, M., Dai, W., Liu, C., Gao, X., Lin, W., Qi, G.J., Xiong, H.: Spatial-temporal transformer networks for traffic flow forecasting. arXiv preprint arXiv:2001.02908 (2020)
31. Yu, B., Yin, H., Zhu, Z.: Spatio-temporal graph convolutional networks: a deep learning framework for traffic forecasting. arXiv preprint arXiv:1709.04875 (2017)
32. Zhang, R., Ashuri, B., Deng, Y.: A novel method for forecasting time series based on fuzzy logic and visibility graph. Adv. Data Anal. Classif. **11**(4), 759–783 (2017)
33. Zhou, H., et al.: Informer: beyond efficient transformer for long sequence time-series forecasting. In: Proceedings of AAAI (2021)

MAGNet: Muti-scale Attention and Evolutionary Graph Structure for Long Sequence Time-Series Forecasting

Zonglei Chen, Fan Zhang, Tianrui Li, and Chongshou Li(✉)

School of Computing and Artificial Intelligence, Southwest Jiaotong University, Chengdu 611756, China
czlei@my.swjtu.edu.cn, {trli,fan.zhang,lics}@swjtu.edu.cn

Abstract. Long sequence time-series forecasting (LSTF) has been widely applied in various fields, such as electricity usage planning and financial long-term strategic guidance. However, LSTF faces challenges in capturing two different types of information: the temporal dependencies of individual features and the interdependencies among multiple features in multivariate time series forecasting. Graph neural networks (GNNs) are commonly used to reveal the correlations among feature variables using graph structures in multivariate forecasting. However, in LSTF, the interdependencies among variables are often dynamic and evolving. Therefore, in this paper, we propose a Multi-scale Attention and Evolutionary Graph Structure (MAGNet) framework to address these challenges. To capture the dynamic changes in interdependencies among variables, we design an evolutionary graph learning layer that constructs an adjacency matrix for each time step and uses gated recurrent units to model the changing correlations, thus learning dynamic feature graph structures. We also utilize graph convolutional modules to capture the dependencies in the learned feature graph structure. Furthermore, to capture the two types of information that the temporal dependencies of individual features and the interdependencies among multiple features, we propose a multi-scale temporal capturing module that incorporates channel attention and spatial attention. Finally, we compare and analyze our proposed method against several high-performance models on 6 real-world datasets. Experimental results demonstrate the efficiency of the proposed method. Code is available at this repository: https://github.com/Masterleia/MAGNet.

Keywords: Time Series Forecasting · Long Time Series Forecasting · GNN · Attention · Deep Learning

Supported by the National Natural Science Foundation of China (Grant Nos. 62202395, 62176221), Natural Science Foundation of Sichuan Province (Grant No. 2022NSFSC0930), Fundamental Research Funds for the Central Universities (Grant No. 2682022CX067, 2682023CF012), Science and Technology Project of Sichuan Province (No. 2022JDRC0067), and Natural Science Foundation of Hebei Province (Grant No. F2022105033).

L. Iliadis et al. (Eds.): ICANN 2023, LNCS 14259, pp. 218–230, 2023.
https://doi.org/10.1007/978-3-031-44223-0_18

1 Introduction

Time series forecasting (TSF) is a classical forecasting task that predicts the future trend changes of time series, and has been widely used in real-world applications such as energy [3], transportation [11], and meteorology [13]. With the development of technology, a task gradually opens to using more historical data to predict the longer-term future, which is noted as *long sequence time-series forecasting (LSTF)* problem [2,16,17].

LSTF has become increasingly popular in various applications, such as electricity usage planning [4] and long-term financial strategic guidance [7]. However, algorithms like LSTM are susceptible to significant declines in inference performance and predictive accuracy as the sequence length grows. In order to efficiently capture long-term dependencies, there are two challenges to be resolved as follows:

(a) The temporal dependencies within a single feature and the correlations between multiple features. With the increase of predict horizons, the input steps also increase, leading to the increase of trend and periodicity information contained within a single feature. Moreover, multiple feature variables are interrelated, such as the rise in temperature often affects humidity changes. Transformer-based models, such as [14,17], have demonstrated their effectiveness for addressing these challenges in LSTF. The parallel computing approach in the Transformer-based architecture speeds up the inference in LSTF, and the self-attention mechanism enables the model to handle long series data by capturing long-term dependencies between the data. However, these methods do not distinguish between the two types of information mentioned above, but instead use the attention module to capture the dependencies uniformly.

(b) Different inter-feature correlations exhibit significant changes with the increase of prediction horizons. Recently, GNNs have achieved remarkable performance in multivariate time series forecasting by revealing the correlations among input features through graph structures. However, in long sequence multivariate time-series forecasting, the hidden topological graph structure usually changes as the prediction horizon increases. Researchers have proposed adaptive and dynamic graph structures to address this issue. For example, Han et al. [5] designed DMSTGCN using a dynamic graph convolution module to predict traffic speed, and MTGNN [15] proposed a graph learning module to adaptively extract a sparse graph adjacency matrix. However, the dynamic graph structures in these models only change the graph structure between samples, while different time steps within a sample still share the same graph structure. Figure 1 shows the dynamic graph structure in a sample. In LSTF, the input and prediction time steps can reach 96 or even more in a forecasting task, leading to significant changes in the graph structure within a sample. Therefore, constructing a single adjacency matrix A for each sample may miss the graph changes within a sample.

In this paper, we propose a MAGNet network based on Multi-scale Attention and Evolutionary Graph Structure to address the aforementioned challenges. Specifically, we propose an evolutionary graph learning layer that builds

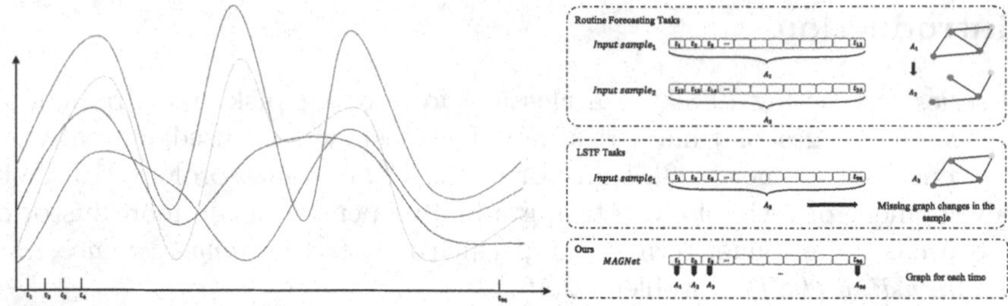

Fig. 1. Graph problems. There may be interactions between features in multivariate forecasting. Most existing works adopt a fixed graph structure for a given sample, while the graph structure among samples is evolving. However, in LSTF tasks, the graph structure within a sample may be evolving continuously.

a dynamic adjacency matrix for each time step, which simulates the continuously changing correlations using gated recurrent units. We also use graph convolution modules to capture the dependencies in the feature graph structure. Additionally, to capture different types of information, i.e., temporal dependency within a single feature and correlations among multiple features, we propose a multi-scale temporal capturing layer, which utilizes channel attention and spatial attention in conjunction with dilated convolutions. Channel attention is employed to extract correlations among different features, while spatial attention is used to extract temporal dependencies among different time steps. In summary, our main contributions are as follows:

1. We propose an evolutionary graph learning layer that addresses the problem of missing graph changes in LSTF when using GNNs, by constructing an adjacency matrix for each time step using gated recurrent units to model changing correlations, and capturing feature dependencies with graph convolution modules.
2. We introduce a multi-scale temporal capture layer that targets both the temporal dependencies of individual features and the correlations between different features, using channel attention and spatial attention in conjunction with dilated convolutions to capture these different types of information.
3. Experimental results on six real-world datasets not only demonstrate the accuracy of our proposed approach in LSTF, but also show the effectiveness of evolutionary graph learning in LSTF.

2 Related Work

In recent years, deep learning has made rapid progress in the field of time series, greatly improving its nonlinear modeling capabilities. LSTF has received extensive attention from researchers. To address the problem of capturing long-term dependencies in LSTF, Log Trans [8] reduces the time complexity to $O(L(logL)^2)$ through convolutional self-attention, while Informer [17] proposes a ProbSparse self-attention to drastically reduce the spatial complexity of model computations with the self-attention distillation operation. In contrast, Autoformer [14] proposes sequence decomposition and the Auto-Correlation mechanism. Pyraformer [9] reduces computational time complexity through pyramidal attention by keeping the maximum length of the signal traversal path constant with respect to the sequence length L. FEDformer [18] proposes a frequency enhanced decomposed Transformer based on frequency domain mapping. Quatformer [1] introduces learnable cycle and phase information to describe complex periodic patterns through learning-to-rotate attention (LRA). Muformer [16] enhances features through a multi-perception domain (MPD) processing mechanism. SCINet [10] preserves the trend and seasonal components of data by recursively downsampling the time series into sub-sequences.

3 Preliminary

The time series with N features can be represented as a set of T samples denoted by $\hat{X} = \{X_1, X_2, ..., X_T | X_i \in \mathbb{R}^{N \times T \times C}\}$, where X_i denotes the values of the variables at each time step t, and C represents the feature dimension of a single variable.The forecasting problems needs to capture the sequence of the series data to grasp the future trend of the sequence data. According to the different number of predict horizons, we can classify the forecasting tasks into single-step, and multi-step forecasting. In this paper, we focus on multivariate multi-step forecasting. In the N-th group time series with i sample data $X_{N,t-i:t}$. We take the historical data of this time series to predict a sequence of future values $X_{N,t+1:t+h+1}$:

$$\hat{X}_{N,t+1:t+h+1} = \mathcal{F}(X_{N,t-i:t}) \tag{1}$$

where i denotes the historical input time step, t is the current time step, $\mathcal{F}$ denotes the mapping function, and h denotes the predicted horizons.

4 Methodology

In this section, we offer a detailed description of the MAGNet framework that we have proposed, providing a comprehensive exposition of its architecture and design principles.

4.1 Overview

As depicted in Fig. 2, We introduce the overall network framework and computation process of MAGNet. MAGNet is composed of three modules: Evolutionary Graph Learning Module, Graph Convolution Module, and Multi-scale Temporal Capturing Module. Firstly, the input $x \in \mathbb{R}^{B \times N \times T_{in}}$, where B represents batch size, N represents the number of features, and T_{in} represents the input time steps, is first passed through a 1×1 Conv2D to obtain the result ξ_1, which is then fed into the multi-scale temporal capturing module to generate the output

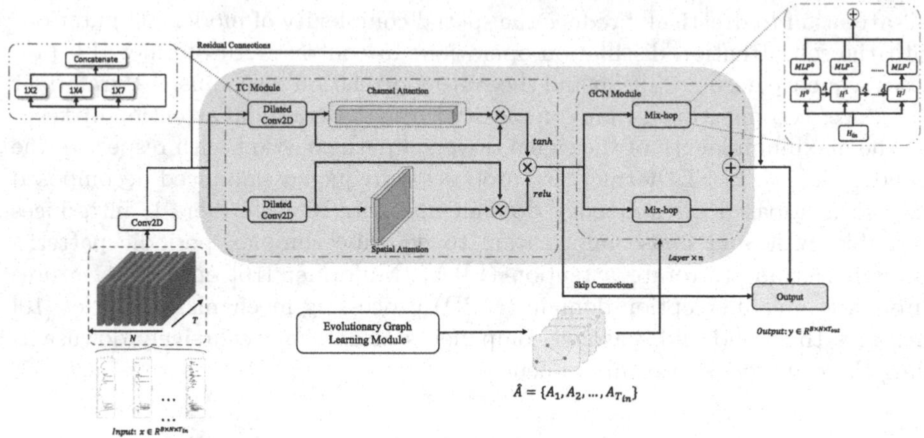

Fig. 2. MAGNet Framework

$\mathcal{TC}$. The evolutionary graph learning module generates a set of adjacency matrices $\hat{A}$ for each sample and each time step, representing the associations between features. The graph convolution module takes the output $\mathcal{TC}$ from the multi-scale temporal capturing module and $\hat{A}$ from the evolutionary graph learning module to further capture the correlations between features, and passes the output $\mathcal{GC}$ to the next *Layer*. A multi-scale temporal capturing module and a graph convolution module together form a *Layer*, and multiple layers can be stacked up to n layers. Finally, to mitigate the issue of gradient vanishing, we have also incorporated residual connections and skip connections into the framework. The overall framework can be defined as follows.

$$\mathcal{TC}_n = \mathcal{F}_{tc}(\xi_n) \tag{2}$$

$$\hat{A}_n = \mathcal{F}_{egc}(\hat{A}_{n-1}) \tag{3}$$

$$\mathcal{GC}_n = \xi_{n+1} = \mathcal{F}_{gc}(\mathcal{TC}_n, \hat{A}_n) \tag{4}$$

where ξ_n represents the Input of the n-th layer, $\mathcal{TC}_n$ represents the output of the multi-scale temporal capturing module $\mathcal{F}_{tc}$ of the n-th layer, $\hat{A}_n$ represents the set of adjacency matrices generated by the evolutionary graph learning module $\mathcal{F}_{egc}$ for the n-th layer, and $\mathcal{GC}_n$ represents the output of the multi-scale temporal capturing module $\mathcal{F}_{gc}$ of the n-th layer. The residual connection is used to directly pass the initial input to the next layer, while the skip connection is used to propagate information to the final output. MAGNet is trained end-to-end. The following sections will provide detailed explanations of the evolutionary graph learning module, temporal capture module, and graph convolution module.

4.2 Evolutionary Graph Learning Module

The evolutionary graph learning module adaptively learns the evolving graph structure in the data and generates a set of adjacency matrices to model the interrelationships among features. In this paper, we adopt a sampling-based approach to only compute pairwise relationships among nodes in a subset of nodes, mitigating the high computational and spatial complexity when considering similarity among all nodes. Furthermore, in this study, we focus more on how one feature influences the changes in another feature. Therefore, the designed graph learning layer learns the similarity relationships among features. The evolutionary graph learning module incorporates a Gate Recurrent Unit (GRU) and sets a separate GRU for each layer of the GC module, which receives the adjacency matrix set from the $(n-1)$-th layer and generates the adjacency matrix $\hat{A}_n$ for the n-th layer. The calculation process can be defined as follows.

$$M_{n,1} = tanh(\alpha GRU_1(\hat{A}_{n-1})) \tag{5}$$

$$M_{n,2} = tanh(\alpha GRU_2(\hat{A}_{n-1})) \tag{6}$$

$$\hat{A}_n = ReLU(tanh(\alpha(M_{n,1}M_{n,2}^T - M_{n,2}M_{n,1}^T))) \tag{7}$$

$$idx = argtopk(\hat{A}_n[:, i, :]) \tag{8}$$

$$\hat{A}_n[:, i, -idx] = 0, i \in (1, 2, ..., N) \tag{9}$$

where, the adjacency matrix collection for the $(n-1)$-th layer, denoted as $\hat{A}_{n-1}$, and the hyperparameter α, which controls the *tanh* saturation rate, are used in GRU_1 and GRU_2 to learn the evolving graph structure in the samples and generate the adjacency matrix for the current layer. During the initial stages of training, the collection of adjacency matrices between features is initialized using embedding. The subtraction expression in Eq. 7 introduces asymmetry in the adjacency matrices. *ReLU* and *tanh* activation functions are used to regularize the adjacency matrices. In scenarios with a large number of features, such as in the case of the electricity dataset with 321 predictive variables, we adopt a strategy of parsing the adjacency matrices in Eqs. 8 and 9. For each feature, we select the top k most correlated features. While retaining the weights of connected features, we set the weights between non-connected features to zero. The description of the multi-scale temporal capturing module follows next.

4.3 Multi-scale Temporal Capture Module

The Multi-scale Temporal Capture Module addresses two types of information in the features, namely temporal dependencies within a single feature and inter-feature correlations among multiple features. To achieve this, we design channel attention and spatial attention modules that are combined with dilated convolutions. Dilated convolutions are used to extract deep features from the data, while channel attention is employed to capture the correlations between different features, and spatial attention is used to capture the temporal dependencies between different time steps. Finally, the outputs of these two parts are multiplied after being activated by $ReLU$ and $tanh$ activation functions, resulting in the output $\mathcal{TC}_n$ of this module. The following sections provide detailed explanations of dilated convolution, channel attention, and spatial attention, respectively.

Dilated Convolution. The dilated convolutional layer is used in this study to extract deep features of different long-term and short-term dependency patterns in the data. We have designed multiple dilated convolutional with different kernel sizes, as illustrated the purple dashed box in Fig. 2.

In this study, we utilized convolutional kernels with sizes of 1×1, 1×2, 1×4, and 1×7. By combining these kernels, we can effectively capture inherent cycles in time series data, such as 7, 12, 24, 28, and 60, and extract deep features of different long-term and short-term dependency patterns. The formulation of this approach is as follows.

$$D_n = concat(c_{1\times1} * \xi_n, c_{1\times2} * \xi_n, c_{1\times4} * \xi_n, c_{1\times7} * \xi_n) \tag{10}$$

where, $c_{1\times1} \in \mathbb{R}^1$, $c_{1\times2} \in \mathbb{R}^2$, $c_{1\times4} \in \mathbb{R}^4$, and $c_{1\times7} \in \mathbb{R}^7$ represent the different convolutional filters with various kernel sizes as mentioned. $concat$ denotes the concatenation operation, and D_n represents the deep features extracted from the dilated convolutional in the n-th TC module, which includes different long-term and short-term dependency patterns. These features are then fed into the subsequent channel attention and spatial attention modules, as described below.

Channel Attention. The channel attention aims to capture the channel-wise dependencies in the input feature map D_n with dimension N, in order to identify meaningful features and assign different weights to each feature. First, a global max pooling and average pooling are applied separately to the spatial dimensions of the input feature map. The pooled results are then fed into a two-layer MLP, where the two layers are shared. Finally, the outputs from the two MLP layers are added together and passed through a *sigmoid* activation function to obtain the weight coefficients $\mathcal{CA}$.

$$\mathcal{CA}(D_n) = \sigma(MLP(AvgPool(D_n)) + MLP(MaxPool(D_n))) \tag{11}$$

Spatial Attention. The spatial attention calculates correlation based on the time step dimension T of the input data, in order to identify which time steps are more important and assign different weights to each time step. Similar to the channel attention module, we first apply max pooling and average pooling separately along the channel dimension, and then concatenate the pooled results together. Next, a 7×7 convolutional layer with *sigmoid* activation function is applied to obtain the weight coefficients $\mathcal{SA}$.

$$\mathcal{SA}(D_n) = \sigma(c_{7\times7} * ([AvgPool(D_n), MaxPool(D_n)])) \tag{12}$$

Lastly, the weight coefficients $\mathcal{CA}$ and $\mathcal{SA}$ obtained from the channel attention and spatial attention modules are multiplied element-wise with the deep features D_n extracted by the dilated convolutional, and then passed through *tanh* and *relu* activation functions respectively before being outputted to the GC Module. The following section provides a detailed introduction to the GC Module.

4.4 Graph Convolution Module

The graph convolutional module can integrates node information with neighboring node information. In this paper, mixhop propagation layers are used to process horizontal and vertical connections separately and then sum them up. The structure of the mixhop propagation layer is shown in Fig. 2.

Mixhop consists of two parts, information propagation and information update, information propagation are calculated using Eq. 13.

$$H^j = \beta H_{in} + (1 - \beta)\tilde{A}H^{j-1} \tag{13}$$

where β is a hyperparameter representing the proportion of original node information used, j denotes the depth of the propagation layer. H^j denotes the output of the current hidden layer and H_{in} denotes the input of the current hidden layer. $\tilde{A} = \tilde{D}^{-1}(\hat{A}+I)$, where $\hat{A}$ is the adjacency matrix of the graph, $\tilde{D}$ is the diagonal degree matrix, and I is the identity matrix.

The information propagation step involves recursive propagation of node information along the given graph structure, while retaining a proportion of the node's original states during the propagation process. This approach allows the propagated node states to preserve locality while also exploring the deeper neighborhood, thus mitigating the problem of over-smoothing to some extent. The formula for information update is as follows:

$$\mathcal{GC}_n = \xi_{n+1} = \sum_{i=0}^{j} H^j W^j \tag{14}$$

The parameter matrix W^j is used for information update, and when the given graph structure has no spatial dependencies, W^j is set to zero, which retains only the initial node information. In addition, skip connections and residual connections are incorporated into the model to effectively alleviate the problem of gradient vanishing.

5 Experiments

In this section, we conducted experiments on six real-world datasets and compared our proposed method with several state-of-the-art models to demonstrate its superiority. In-depth analysis was also performed to validate the effectiveness of our approach.

5.1 Datasets and Setup

The six datasets utilized in the experiments are described below.

ETTh1[1]: The ETTh1 dataset encompasses data obtained from electricity transformers, comprising load and oil temperature measurements recorded at 15-minute intervals from July 2016 to July 2018.

Electricity[2]: The Electricity dataset comprises hourly electricity consumption data obtained from 321 customers, spanning the period from 2012 to 2014.

Exchange[3]: The Exchange dataset records the daily exchange rates of eight countries over a period spanning from 1990 to 2016.

Traffific[4]: The Traffific dataset comprises hourly data obtained from the California Department of Transportation, capturing road occupancy rates as measured by various sensors on San Francisco Bay area freeways from July 2016 to July 2018.

Weather[5]: The Weather dataset comprises meteorological data recorded every 10 min throughout the year 2020, including 21 indicators such as air temperature, humidity, etc.

ILI[6]: The ILI dataset comprises CDC-recorded data on influenza-like illness (ILI) patients from 2002 to 2021, providing the ratio of ILI patients to the total number of patients.

Implementation Details. We adopt the MSE as the loss function and use the ADAM optimizer, where the initial learning rate is 10–4, the early stopping mechanism is used as the termination condition of the model training process, and the patience is 3. The Z-score normalization method is used for all datasets. The input len is set to 96 for the ETTh1, ECL, Exchange, Traffic, and WTH datasets and 36 for the COVID19 dataset. The settings of predict horizon are {96, 192, 336, 720, 768} for the ETTh1, ECL, Exchange, Traffic, and WTH, {24, 36, 48, 60} for ILI. The training set, validation set, and test set of each dataset are divided according to a ratio of 7:1:2. The hyperparameter settings of each model are determined based on the settings of their source works. All our models are implemented based on PyTorch, the open-source codes of each original paper are collected and experimented with, and all experiments are repeated 5 times and trained on dual NVIDIA TITAN X pascal 12-GB-GPU workstations. MAE and MSE were used as evaluation metrics.

[1] ETTh1: https://github.com/zhouhaoyi/ETDataset.

[2] Electricity: https://archive.ics.uci.edu/ml/datasets/ElectricityLoadDiagrams20112014.

[3] Exchange: https://drive.google.com/drive/folders/1ZOYpTUa82_jCcxIdTmyr0LXQfvaM9vIy.

[4] Traffific: http://pems.dot.ca.gov.

[5] Weather: https://www.bgc-jena.mpg.de/wetter/.

[6] ILI: https://gis.cdc.gov/grasp/fluview/fluportaldashboard.html.

5.2 Baselines

We selected six high-performance methods from the field of LSTF, including Pyformer [9], FEDformer [18], Informer [17], Autoformer [14], Reformer [6] and Transformer [12], which have been proposed in recent years.

Table 1. Multivariate experimental forecasting results. The MAE and MSE mark the top models with the best forecasting results under each horizon, and a lower MAE and MSE indicates a better prediction effect.

Models		**MAGNet**		FEDformer		Pyraformer		Autoformer		Informer		Reformer		Transformer	
Metric		MAE	MSE	MAE	MSE	MAE	MSE	MAE	MSE	MAE	MSE	MAE	MSE	MAE	MSE
ETTh1	96	**0.416**	**0.376**	0.452	0.458	0.749	0.972	0.444	0.437	0.568	0.682	0.654	0.826	0.526	0.530
	192	**0.445**	**0.442**	0.472	0.484	0.893	1.253	0.532	0.554	0.628	0.734	0.699	0.901	0.586	0.624
	336	**0.462**	**0.447**	0.482	0.497	0.945	1.321	0.533	0.562	0.842	1.132	0.737	0.985	0.751	0.969
	720	**0.489**	**0.471**	0.501	0.502	0.959	1.365	0.627	0.687	0.843	1.241	0.779	1.087	0.863	1.232
Electricity	96	**0.293**	**0.180**	0.302	0.187	0.374	0.275	0.312	0.198	0.412	0.325	0.384	0.294	0.351	0.251
	192	**0.303**	**0.186**	0.309	0.195	0.382	0.281	0.325	0.215	0.441	0.359	0.411	0.333	0.365	0.266
	336	0.326	0.223	**0.324**	**0.212**	0.386	0.284	0.352	0.258	0.436	0.353	0.418	0.348	0.371	0.273
	720	**0.353**	**0.263**	0.357	0.251	0.398	0.294	0.412	0.348	0.445	0.380	0.488	0.411	0.381	0.294
Exchange	96	**0.261**	**0.134**	0.288	0.157	0.751	0.847	0.543	0.488	0.785	0.911	0.944	1.391	0.659	0.735
	192	**0.383**	**0.276**	0.416	0.332	0.841	1.014	0.786	0.998	0.856	1.141	0.963	1.406	0.821	1.171
	336	**0.493**	**0.441**	0.494	0.448	0.966	1.386	0.807	1.096	1.001	1.535	1.085	1.773	0.977	1.538
	720	**0.823**	**1.154**	0.867	1.308	0.975	1.353	1.027	1.626	1.228	2.319	1.155	1.909	1.376	2.796
Traffic	96	**0.341**	**0.624**	0.357	0.578	0.357	0.634	0.387	0.628	0.401	0.716	0.381	0.694	0.367	0.661
	192	**0.358**	**0.639**	0.375	0.607	0.364	0.650	0.397	0.642	0.419	0.753	0.375	0.697	0.352	0.649
	336	**0.364**	**0.652**	0.378	0.618	0.368	0.662	0.382	0.614	0.478	0.846	0.379	0.701	0.359	0.663
	720	**0.370**	**0.671**	0.381	0.628	0.373	0.687	0.385	0.634	0.563	1.001	0.373	0.687	0.371	0.674
Weather	96	**0.256**	**0.182**	0.338	0.256	0.293	0.216	0.331	0.253	0.354	0.281	0.371	0.333	0.462	0.442
	192	**0.291**	**0.227**	0.342	0.283	0.414	0.365	0.307	0.362	0.447	0.417	0.461	0.445	0.544	0.574
	336	**0.331**	**0.277**	0.407	0.367	0.450	0.422	0.391	0.355	0.565	0.526	0.601	0.757	0.608	0.717
	720	**0.378**	**0.343**	0.406	0.391	0.591	0.647	0.446	0.439	0.747	1.031	0.643	0.831	0.743	0.992
ILI	24	**1.258**	**3.226**	1.305	3.560	1.315	3.978	1.840	6.647	1.605	5.451	1.181	3.946	1.525	5.014
	36	**1.054**	**2.601**	1.126	2.844	1.446	4.67	1.909	7.025	1.575	5.229	1.229	4.131	1.528	5.123
	48	**1.066**	**2.577**	1.141	2.957	1.437	4.525	1.920	7.104	1.565	5.158	1.344	4.263	1.509	5.024
	60	1.148	2.827	**1.111**	**2.792**	1.471	4.718	1.917	7.094	1.596	5.316	1.399	4.474	1.546	5.209

5.3 Main Results and Analysis

The main experimental results are presented in Table 1. In the multivariate forecasting task, we observe that: (1) MAGNet outperforms most of the models on all six datasets, achieving significant improvements on some datasets. For example, compared to FEDformer, MAGNet achieves a 8.2% improvement (at 96) in MSE on the ETTh1 dataset, and 18.6% (at 336) and 6.8% (at 720) improvements in MSE on the Weather dataset. (2) In addition, MAGNet demonstrates significant advantages in prediction accuracy compared to some baseline methods, such as Transformer and Reformer. These results demonstrate the effectiveness of MAGNet in improving LSTF prediction accuracy. We conduct ablation experiments to further verify the effectiveness of the proposed modules.

5.4 Ablation Study

In order to validate the effectiveness of the framework, we conducted ablation experiments on the Electricity dataset in this section, with a prediction horizon set to 336, and named different components after removal as follows.

- MAGNet: refers to the complete framework proposed in this paper.
- MAGNet§: refers to MAGNet with the evolutionary graph learning module removed and a fixed graph structure used instead.
- MAGNet†: refers to MAGNet with the channel attention module removed, and the output of the dilated convolution in this branch is directly passed to the next module.
- MAGNet‡: refers to MAGNet with the spatial attention module removed, and the output of the dilated convolution in this branch is directly passed to the next module.
- MAGNet$^{\pounds}$: refers to MAGNet with both the channel attention and spatial attention modules removed.

As shown in Table 2, after removing different parts, MAGNet performance has declined to varying degrees. Through comparison, it can be found that the evolutionary graph learning module is effective and superior to the static graph form. Therefore, modeling the dynamic evolution process of the graph is necessary in LSTF for multivariate forecasting. In addition, we have also removed channel attention and spatial attention separately, and the model's performance has shown varying degrees of decline. After removing both, the model's performance has dropped significantly. It can be seen that using channel attention and spatial attention to capture two types of information separately is an highly effective method.

Table 2. Ablation Results.

Models	Metric	Horizons			
		96	192	336	720
MAGNet	MAE	0.293	0.303	0.326	0.353
	MSE	0.180	0.186	0.223	0.263
MAGNet§	MAE	0.413	0.445	0.447	0.452
	MSE	0.324	0.366	0.370	0.379
MAGNet†	MAE	0.313	0.326	0.355	0.416
	MSE	0.202	0.218	0.263	0.358
MAGNet‡	MAE	0.376	0.385	0.389	0.401
	MSE	0.277	0.284	0.289	0.301
MAGNet$^{\pounds}$	MAE	0.752	0.843	0.967	0.979
	MSE	0.849	1.016	1.395	1.412

6 Conclusion

In this paper, we propose a MAGNet framework based on multi-scale attention and evolutionary graph structure to address the challenges of single-feature temporal dependencies and inter-feature correlations in long sequence time series multi-variable forecasting, as well as the significant changes in correlation among different features with the increase of predict horizons. In this framework, we design an evolutionary graph learning module to construct an adjacency matrix for each time step and simulate changing correlations. We also use graph convolutional modules to capture dependency relationships in feature graph structures. Furthermore, we propose a multi-scale temporal capture module to capture two different types of information. We verify the superiority and effectiveness of the proposed method by comparing it with several state-of-the-art models on multiple real-world datasets and long sequence time series forecasting tasks.

References

1. Chen, W., Wang, W., Peng, B., Wen, Q., Zhou, T., Sun, L.: Learning to rotate: quaternion transformer for complicated periodical time series forecasting. In: Proceedings of the 28th ACM SIGKDD Conference on Knowledge Discovery and Data Mining, pp. 146–156 (2022)
2. Cirstea, R.G., Guo, C., Yang, B., Kieu, T., Dong, X., Pan, S.: Triformer: triangular, variable-specific attentions for long sequence multivariate time series forecasting-full version. In: International Joint Conference on Artificial Intelligence (2022)
3. Edwards, R.D., Magee, J., Bassetti, W.C.: Technical Analysis of Stock Trends. CRC Press, Boca Raton (2018)
4. Fu, C., Nguyen, T.: Models for long-term energy forecasting. In: 2003 IEEE Power Engineering Society General Meeting (IEEE Cat. No. 03CH37491), vol. 1, pp. 235–239. IEEE (2003)
5. Han, L., Du, B., Sun, L., Fu, Y., Lv, Y., Xiong, H.: Dynamic and multi-faceted spatio-temporal deep learning for traffic speed forecasting. In: Proceedings of the 27th ACM SIGKDD Conference on Knowledge Discovery & Data Mining, pp. 547–555 (2021)
6. Kitaev, N., Kaiser, L., Levskaya, A.: Reformer: the efficient transformer. In: Proceedings of the 8th International Conference on Learning Representations, ICLR. OpenReview.net (2020)
7. Lefrancois, R., Mamidipudi, P., Li, J.: Expectation risk: a novel short-term risk measure for long-term financial projections. Available at SSRN 3715727 (2020)
8. Li, S., et al.: Enhancing the locality and breaking the memory bottleneck of transformer on time series forecasting. Adv. Neural. Inf. Process. Syst. **32**, 5244–5254 (2019)
9. Liu, S., et al.: Pyraformer: low-complexity pyramidal attention for long-range time series modeling and forecasting. In: International Conference on Learning Representations (2021)
10. Minhao, L., et al.: SCINet: time series modeling and forecasting with sample convolution and interaction. In: Advances in Neural Information Processing Systems (2022)

11. Qu, L., Li, W., Li, W., Ma, D., Wang, Y.: Daily long-term traffic flow forecasting based on a deep neural network. Expert Syst. Appl. **121**, 304–312 (2019)
12. Vaswani, A., et al.: Attention is all you need. Adv. Neural. Inf. Process. Syst. **30**, 5998–6008 (2017)
13. Ward, S.N.: Area-based tests of long-term seismic hazard predictions. Bull. Seismol. Soc. Am. **85**(5), 1285–1298 (1995)
14. Wu, H., Xu, J., Wang, J., Long, M.: Autoformer: decomposition transformers with auto-correlation for long-term series forecasting. Adv. Neural. Inf. Process. Syst. **34**, 22419–22430 (2021)
15. Wu, Z., Pan, S., Long, G., Jiang, J., Chang, X., Zhang, C.: Connecting the dots: multivariate time series forecasting with graph neural networks. In: Proceedings of the 26th ACM SIGKDD International Conference on Knowledge Discovery & Data Mining, pp. 753–763 (2020)
16. Zeng, P., Hu, G., Zhou, X., Li, S., Liu, P., Liu, S.: Muformer: a long sequence time-series forecasting model based on modified multi-head attention. Knowl. Based Syst. **254**, 109584 (2022)
17. Zhou, H., et al.: Informer: beyond efficient transformer for long sequence time-series forecasting. In: Proceedings of the AAAI Conference on Artificial Intelligence, vol. 35, pp. 11106–11115 (2021)
18. Zhou, T., Ma, Z., Wen, Q., Wang, X., Sun, L., Jin, R.: Fedformer: frequency enhanced decomposed transformer for long-term series forecasting. In: International Conference on Machine Learning, ICML, vol. 162, pp. 27268–27286. PMLR (2022)

MIPCE: Generating Multiple Patches Counterfactual-Changing Explanations for Time Series Classification

Hiroyuki Okumura(✉) and Tomoharu Nagao

Yokohama National University, Yokohama, Kanagawa, Japan
okuhiro.8765@gmail.com, nagao@ynu.ac.jp

Abstract. In the development of AI and deep neural networks (DNNs), a growing concern has emerged regarding not only accuracy, but explainability. The corresponding field of research, known as eXplainable AI (XAI), is important because interpreting the predictions of AI helps users make decisions in critical areas such as medicine. XAI has recently gained popularity particularly for counterfactual explanations from a psychological perspective. However, despite recent progress in XAI, few existing methods focus on explaining time series data. We therefore propose Multiple Patches Counterfactual-changing Explanations (MIPCE) for fully convolutional networks (FCNs), which focuses on subsequences of time series, showing the process of change to the counterfactual. First, MIPCE obtains subsequences from features appearing in the FCN, and divides the time series data into patches. Using GPLVM, it then generates the interpretable process of counterfactual change in each patch. We compared our method with other counterfactual methods in terms of proximity, plausibility, and substitutability. These quantitative results indicate that MIPCE outperforms existing methods. In addition, our user test shows that our explanations are useful in helping users understand the decision-making processes of DNNs.

Keywords: XAI · Time Series Classification · Counterfactual Explanations

1 Introduction

Recent years have witnessed a surge of interest in DNNs, particularly in the field of image recognition. Research on time series classification using DNNs has likewise progressed, with FCNs having demonstrated competitive performance, making them promising candidates for real-world applications [10,26]. However, the inner workings of DNNs are a black box, making it difficult for end users to trust model output. To address this problem, researchers have been actively exploring the field of XAI. Methods such as LIME [21], SHAP [19] and CAM [28] have been proposed to provide transparent explanations of model predictions. One approach within XAI is counterfactual explanation, which shows how a

L. Iliadis et al. (Eds.): ICANN 2023, LNCS 14259, pp. 231–242, 2023.
https://doi.org/10.1007/978-3-031-44223-0_19

query can be altered to the counterfactual instance in order to change the model's prediction result. Counterfactual explanation not only presents important components of the query that contributed to the prediction, but also suggests the user's next action to change the result. From this perspective, it is said to be psychologically effective [4], with many methods having been proposed [8,13,18]. Although counterfactual explanation has become an increasingly popular XAI field in recent years [20], most existing methods focus on image and tabular data, and few methods have been developed for time series data [7,9,12].

In the field of time series, certain subsequences within the data are considered to have significance [27]. Just as DNNs learn semantic concepts in the image domain [3], they are likely to learn subsequences in time series. To improve end-user understanding and satisfaction, it is effective to present explanations based on these subsequences, in addition to changing the model classification results. Actually, research in the image domain has shown that presenting the meaningful concepts learned by DNNs as explanations has led to increased user satisfaction [1]. Furthermore, in the case of time series data, multiple subsequences contribute to classification [10]. To fully interpret a model's predictions, it is therefore necessary to treat all of these subsequences simultaneously.

Our proposed method, MIPCE, obtains subsequences (referred to as patches) learned by the FCN, and divides the corresponding query into patches. Aside from generating counterfactuals, MIPCE also provides the process of each patch's continuous change to the counterfactual. This is because presenting changes to the counterfactual has been shown to have a positive effect on user understanding and satisfaction [23].

2 Related Works

As mentioned previously, LIME, SHAP, and CAM are widely recognized XAI methods. They provide visual explanations by highlighting the regions that contribute to the classification. In the case of counterfactuals, Watcher proposed a baseline method (W-CF) [25] that generates the counterfactual within a small distance from the query. As extensions of W-CF, many methods in the image domain use generative models, such as generative adversarial networks (GANs), to obtain the counterfactuals [11,17,23]. Furthermore, methods that use features appearing in DNNs along with GANs have also been proposed [13]. These methods are designed to satisfy proximity, which measures the similarity between the query and counterfactual, and plausibility, which determines whether the counterfactual is following the data distribution or is out of distribution (OOD). In addition, counterfactuals must be generated in a form that is recognizable to humans from an XAI perspective [20]. Some methods jointly present the process of change to the counterfactual [11,17]. One such method has demonstrated the effectiveness of its interpretation through expert evaluations [23]. However, it should be noted that these methods do not specifically focus on time series data.

In the field of time series XAI, one popular approach is to focus on time series subsequences known as shapelets [27], and a method has been developed to explain random forest classification models that are trained with shapelets [12]. Our approach also focus on subsequences, but it differs in terms of the target models and the procedures for obtaining subsequences. Another method is Native-Guide [7], which modifies the results of any classification model by changing part of the query to the nearest-neighbor instance of a different class (denoted as NUN, short for nearest-unlike-neighbor). This method can be applied to DNNs classification models such as FCNs, but there are difficulties in accurately capturing subsequences. It should also be noted that these methods do not have the capability to generate continuous changes to the counterfactual.

3 MultIple Patches Counterfactual-Changing Explanations(MIPCE)

MIPCE divides time series data into subsequences using Gaussian mixture models (GMM), and generates continuous changes from the query to the counterfactual (see Fig. 1). It is necessary for the process of change to follow the principle of proximity in order to provide more interpretable explanations for users. Ideally, continuous changes would gradually approach the counterfactual in the range between the query and counterfactual. In addition, sparsity, defined as the idea of not changing anything except the necessary parts of the query, is also important for interpretability. To generate these ideal explanations, MIPCE uses Gaussian process latent variable models (GPLVM) [14] for each patch.

3.1 Setup and Notation

Assume a two-class FCN classification model [26] (denoted as M) as a black-box model. We represent the input data as $\mathbf{y} \in \mathbb{R}^{T_\mathbf{y}}$, latent variable of the $\mathbf{y}$ as

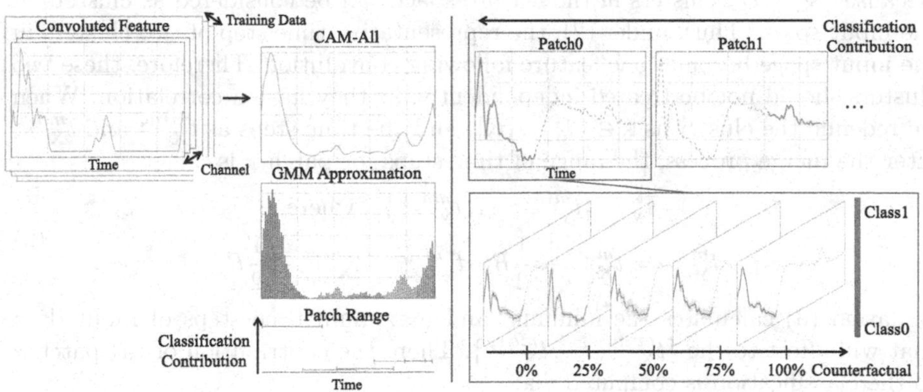

Fig. 1. MIPCE overview. (Left) Time series patch division. (Right) Change to the counterfactual. Green shows the original query, others show changes from the query. (Color figure online)

$\mathbf{z}$, and the feature extracted by the convolution as $\mathbf{X} \in \mathbb{R}^{T_{\mathbf{X}} \times S}$. S denotes the number of channels in the last convolutional layer. $\{\mathbf{x}_s\}_{s=1}^{S} \geq \mathbf{0}$ by using ReLU activations, and $T_{\mathbf{X}}$ and $T_{\mathbf{y}}$ are equal by setting the strides of all convolutional layers to 1. Let R denote the convolutional receptive field. For the query (denoted as q), the classified class by the FCN is represented as c, and the classification probability is represented as $M_c(\mathbf{y})$. For the counterfactual, the classified class and the probability is similarly represented as $c', M_{c'}(\mathbf{y})$. Let $\mathbf{v}_{scaled}$ denote the min-max normalized value for $\mathbf{v}$, and $v_{\arg \text{scaled}_{\mathbf{z}}}$ denote the scaled v by applying min-max normalization to the set $\mathbb{v}$ ($v \in \mathbb{v}$) obtained by varying $\mathbf{z}$ in its defined range.

3.2 Algorithm

Divide the Time Series Data into Patches (Algorithm 1). Using the features of all N_D training data $\{\mathbf{X}^n\}_{n=1}^{N_D}$, compute a variant of CAM (CAM-All $\in \mathbb{R}^{T_{\mathbf{X}}}$) that retrieves all features contributing to the classification together:

$$\text{CAM-All} = \Big(\sum_{c\in\{1,2\}} \frac{1}{N_D S} \sum_{n=1}^{N_D} \sum_{s=1}^{S} |w_{s,c}|\mathbf{x}_s^n\Big)_{scaled} \tag{1}$$

$w_{s,c}$ is a weight that connects the s channel's output of the convolution layer to the class c input of the softmax layer in the FCN. The GMM, which uses Dirichlet process [2] (referred to as DPGMM), is then fit to the sampled data points via rejection sampling [5] from the CAM-All. This allows the CAM-All to be divided into clusters in the temporal direction.

Let the minimum, maximum, and mean time steps of each cluster $\Bbbk \in \{\mathbb{1}, \ldots, \mathbb{K}\}$ be denoted as $t_{\mathbf{X}}^{min_{\Bbbk}}, t_{\mathbf{X}}^{max_{\Bbbk}}$, and $t_{\mathbf{X}}^{mean_{\Bbbk}}$ respectively. When $\Bbbk$ is in ascending order, $\Bbbk$ and $\Bbbk + \mathbb{1}$ are merged into a single cluster if:

$$t_{\mathbf{X}}^{mean_{\Bbbk+\mathbb{1}}} - t_{\mathbf{X}}^{mean_{\Bbbk}} \leq R \tag{2}$$

Because $T_{\mathbf{X}} = T_{\mathbf{y}}$, clusters in the feature space can be considered as clusters in the input space. Thus, under (2), the representative time step of two clusters in the input space becomes one feature following convolution. Therefore, these two clusters should not be treated independently, as they have a correlation. When we redefine the cluster as $\Bbbk \in \{\mathbb{1}, \ldots, \mathbb{K}\}$, and the time steps as $t_{\mathbf{X}}^{min_{\Bbbk}}$ and $t_{\mathbf{X}}^{max_{\Bbbk}}$ after the merge process, the range of time steps for patch $\Bbbk$ is:

$$\begin{gathered} \mathbb{T}_{\mathbf{y}}^{\Bbbk} = \{t_{\mathbf{y}}^{min_{\Bbbk}}, \ldots, t_{\mathbf{y}}^{max_{\Bbbk}}\}, \text{ where} \\ t_{\mathbf{y}}^{min_{\Bbbk}} = t_{\mathbf{X}}^{min_{\Bbbk}} - \frac{1}{2}R, \; t_{\mathbf{y}}^{max_{\Bbbk}} = t_{\mathbf{X}}^{max_{\Bbbk}} + \frac{1}{2}R \end{gathered} \tag{3}$$

Equation (3) calculates the mininum and maximum time steps of input data that will affect to the $\{t_{\mathbf{X}}^{min_{\Bbbk}}, \ldots, t_{\mathbf{X}}^{max_{\Bbbk}}\}$. Then, the contribution of the patch $\Bbbk$ to the classification is computed via:

$$\text{Contrib}_{\Bbbk} = \sum_{t\in\mathbb{T}_{\mathbf{y}}^{\Bbbk}} \text{CAM-All}_t \tag{4}$$

where CAM-All_t is a t time step value of the CAM-All.

Algorithm 1. Patch Division and Contribution to Classification

Input: $\{\mathbf{X^n}\}_{n=1}^{N_D}$: Convoluted features of all training data, $\mathbf{W}$: Weight matrix with $w_{s,c}$ as its (s,c) element, R: Convolutional receptive field of FCN
1. Compute the CAM-All with (1).
2. Run rejection sampling from the CAM-All.
3. Fit DPGMM to sampled points and obtain $t_{\mathbf{X}}^{min_{\mathbb{k}}}, t_{\mathbf{X}}^{max_{\mathbb{k}}}$ and $t_{\mathbf{X}}^{mean_{\mathbb{k}}}$ of a cluster $\mathbb{k}$.
4. Merge clusters based on (2), and obtain $\mathbb{T}_{\mathbf{y}}^{\mathbb{k}}$ with (3).
5. Compute Contrib$_{\mathbb{k}}$ of each patch $\mathbb{k}$ with (4).

return: $\mathbb{T}_{\mathbf{y}}^{\mathbb{k}}$ and Contrib$_{\mathbb{k}}$ of each patch.

Generate Counterfactual Changing (Algorithm 2). When representing latent variables and observational data as $\mathcal{D} = \{(\mathbf{z}_1, \mathbf{y}_1), (\mathbf{z}_2, \mathbf{y}_2), \ldots\}$, the GPLVM's expected value of the predictive distribution for the unknown latent variable $\mathbf{z}^*$ is defined as:

$$\begin{aligned} \mathbb{E}[p(\mathbf{y}^* \mid \mathbf{z}^*, \mathcal{D})] &= \mathbf{k}_*^T \mathbf{K}^{-1} \mathbf{Y} \\ \mathbf{k}_* = (k(\mathbf{z}^*, \mathbf{z}_1), k(\mathbf{z}^*, \mathbf{z}_2), \ldots)^T &, \mathbf{Y} = (\mathbf{y}_1, \mathbf{y}_2, \ldots)^T \end{aligned} \tag{5}$$

k represents the kernel function and $\mathbf{K}$ represents covariance matrix. As GPLVM is commonly used for dimensionality reduction, it is possible to divide the latent space into clusters. Considering three clusters – $\mathbb{c}1$, $\mathbb{c}2$ and $\mathbb{c}3$ – case, (5) can be:

$$\mathbb{E}[p(\mathbf{y}^* \mid \mathbf{z}^*, \mathcal{D})] = (\mathbf{k}_{*,\mathbb{c}1}, \mathbf{k}_{*,\mathbb{c}2}, \mathbf{k}_{*,\mathbb{c}3}) \mathbf{K}^{-1} (\mathbf{Y}_{\mathbb{c}1}, \mathbf{Y}_{\mathbb{c}2}, \mathbf{Y}_{\mathbb{c}3})^T \tag{6}$$

If we want to obtain $\mathbf{y}^*$ that exists between $\mathbf{Y}_{\mathbb{c}1}$ and $\mathbf{Y}_{\mathbb{c}2}$, this case is difficult to realize due to the influence of $\mathbf{Y}_{\mathbb{c}3}$. The same argument can be applied to the case where we want to obtain the ideal continuous change to the counterfactual. Therefore, it is necessary to select one cluster of each class in advance.

Data Selection. Prepare the query patch $\mathbf{y}^q_{\mathbb{T}_{\mathbf{y}}^{\mathbb{k}}}$ and N_{sim} similar patches of each class c and c' with Euclidean distance. Then, train Bayesian GPLVM [24] with the patches, and apply DPGMM to obtain the latent variable $\mathbf{z}_q$ of the query, class c latent variable clusters $\mathbb{z}_c \in \{\mathbb{1}, \ldots, \mathbb{Z}_c\}$ and so is class c'. When we denote the mean of the $\mathbb{z}_c$ as $\mathbf{z}_{\mathbb{z}_c}$, and the number of elements as $|\mathbb{z}_c|$, score clusters with:

$$\text{Score-}\mathbb{z}_c = \frac{1}{|\mathbb{z}_c|} \sum_{\mathbf{z} \in \mathbb{z}_c} M_c(\mathbb{E}[G_B(\mathbf{z})]) + \alpha_1(1 - (\|\mathbf{z}_q - \mathbf{z}_{\mathbb{z}_c}\|_2^2)_{\text{arg scaled}_{\mathbf{z}_{\mathbb{z}_c}}}) + \alpha_2 |\mathbb{z}_c| \tag{7}$$

In (7), Bayesian GPLVM is represented as G_B, and $G_B(\mathbf{z})$ denotes the predictive distribution of $\mathbf{z}$. The first term represents the average patch classification probability of cluster $\mathbb{z}_c$. The second and the third terms are constraints to satisfy proximity and plausibility, as the cluster's elements size reflects the data distribution. Finally, the cluster $\hat{\mathbb{z}}_c$ can be selected with $\arg\max_{\mathbb{z}_c}\{\text{Score-}\mathbb{1}_c, \ldots, \text{Score-}\mathbb{Z}_c\}$. Similarly, we can find $\hat{\mathbb{z}}_{c'}$ for class c'.

We assume a small value of N_{sim}. It is therefore necessary to increase the number of data points in the latent space prior to DPGMM clustering. Bayesian

Algorithm 2. Generate Changes to the Counterfactual Using GPLVM

Input: M: FCN, $\mathbf{y}^q_{\mathbb{T}^k_{\mathbf{y}}}$: The query patch, N_{sim}: The number of similar patches to use

1. Prepare N_{sim} similar patches from class c and c' of $\mathbf{y}^q_{\mathbb{T}^k_{\mathbf{y}}}$.
2. Train Bayesian-GPLVM and obtain latent Gaussian distributions of the query patch, class c and c' patches.
3. Fit DPGMM and obtain $\hat{\mathbb{z}}_c, \hat{\mathbb{z}}_{c'}$ by scoring clusters with (7).
4. Train GPLVM (G) with $\hat{\mathbb{z}}_c, \hat{\mathbb{z}}_{c'}$ patches and explore $(\mathbf{z}_{cf}, \mathbf{z}_{sf})$ with (8) and (9).
5. Obtain $\mathbb{z}_{q\to sf}$ and $\mathbb{z}_{sf\to cf}$ with (10).

return: $G(\mathbb{z}_{q\to sf})$ and $G(\mathbb{z}_{sf\to cf})$

GPLVM is an appropriate choice because it allows sampling from the Gaussian distribution of the latent variable, while having equivalent properties to GPLVM.

Counterfactual Changing. Train GPLVM with the query patch, as well as patches of the clusters $\hat{\mathbb{z}}_c$ and $\hat{\mathbb{z}}_{c'}$. This allows us to obtain the latent variables $\mathbf{z}_q$ of the query, $\{\mathbf{z}^n\}_{n=1}^N$ of the class c and $\{\mathbf{z}^{n'}\}_{n'=1}^{N'}$ of the class c', where $N = |\hat{\mathbb{z}}_c|$ and $N' = |\hat{\mathbb{z}}_{c'}|$. Then, select a $\mathbf{z}_{cf}$ to generate a counterfactual patch:

$$\begin{aligned} \mathbf{z}_{cf} &= \underset{\mathbf{z}^{n'}}{\arg\max}\{\text{Score-}\mathbf{z}^{1'}, \ldots, \text{Score-}\mathbf{z}^{N'}\}, \quad \text{where} \\ \text{Score-}\mathbf{z}^{n'} &= M_{c'}(\mathbb{E}[G(\mathbf{z}^{n'})]) + \alpha_3(1 - (\|\mathbf{z}_q - \mathbf{z}^{n'}\|_2^2)_{\text{arg scaled}_{\mathbf{z}^{n'}}}) \end{aligned} \tag{8}$$

In (8), GPLVM is represented as G as well as Bayesian GPLVM in (7). Using $\mathbf{z}_q$ and $\mathbf{z}_{cf}$, explore the latent space $\mathcal{Z}$ to find $\mathbf{z}_{sf}$ to generate a semifactual patch:

$$\begin{aligned} \mathbf{z}_{sf} = \underset{\mathbf{z}\in\mathcal{Z}}{\arg\max}(1 - |0.5 - M_c(\mathbb{E}[G(\mathbf{z})])|_{\text{arg scaled}_{\mathbf{z}}}) \\ + \alpha_4(1 - (\|\mathbf{z} - \mathbf{z}_q\|_2^2 + \|\mathbf{z} - \mathbf{z}_{cf}\|_2^2)_{\text{arg scaled}_{\mathbf{z}}}) \end{aligned} \tag{9}$$

The semifactual is the instance when the classification result changes. Equation (9) constrains that $\mathbf{z}_{sf}$ is within the $\mathbf{z}_q$ and $\mathbf{z}_{cf}$ while the classification probability of the patch is 0.5. After acquiring $(\mathbf{z}_q, \mathbf{z}_{sf}, \mathbf{z}_{cf})$, we can obtain the set of internal latent variables $\mathbb{z}_{q\to sf}$ and $\mathbb{z}_{sf\to cf}$ by linearly varying β in (10), where $0 \le \beta \le 1$:

$$\mathbb{z}_{q\to sf} = \beta\mathbf{z}_q + (1-\beta)\mathbf{z}_{sf}, \quad \mathbb{z}_{sf\to cf} = \beta\mathbf{z}_{sf} + (1-\beta)\mathbf{z}_{cf} \tag{10}$$

Then, generate the continuously changing patch from the query to the semifactual and from the semifactual to the counterfactual, by $G(\mathbb{z}_{q\to sf})$ and $G(\mathbb{z}_{sf\to cf})$. Using the linear kernel with an RBF kernel for the GPLVM allows us to generate continuous changes that gradually increase the distance from the query.

The Whole Algorithm. Based on Algorithm 1, divide the query into patches and then generate counterfactual changes in the order of the patches with the highest contribution to the classification using Algorithm 2. By iterating this process until the classification result changes, the final explanation can be obtained.

The end user is presented with the expected value and a 95% confidence interval. During the iterative process, overlapping patches may be used for explanation. In such cases, Algorithm 2 is applied to them as a single patch.

4 Experiments

We verified the effectiveness of MIPCE with five time series datasets from UCR Archive [6]: ECG200, Strawberry, GunPoint, ProximalPhalanxOutlineCorrect (Proximial), and Wafer. Although the Wafer dataset has a test size of 6164, we randomly selected 50 samples from each class in the interest of conserving computational time. In Experiment 1, we compared MIPCE with several existing methods. Experiment 2 was conducted to evaluate continuous changes, whereas Experiment 3 investigated whether users could understand the decision processes of DNNs from explanations.

FCN Settings. The model consists of three convolutional layers with ReLU activations, a global average pooling layer, and a softmax layer. Batch normalization was applied before input to the ReLU. The number of channels in the convolution, and the kernel size, were set in the order of $(128, 256, 128)$ and $(7, 5, 3)$ from the input layer, respectively. This refers to [26] where high accuracy is achieved.

MIPCE Settings. For the GPLVM and Bayesian GPLVM, we set the latent variable dimensions to 2, and used the results of PCA as initial values. Models were trained with Normal$(0, 1)$, Gamma$(3, 1)$ and Gamma$(1, 1)$ as the prior distributions of latent variables, corresponding to parameters of the linear and RBF kernels respectively. Training was conducted over 1000 iterations and optimized with L-BFGS-B [15]. $(\alpha_1, \alpha_2, \alpha_3, \alpha_4)$ in the algorithm were all set to 0.1 and $N_{sim} = 15$. We explored the $\mathbb{Z}$ in (9) via grid search, and changed β in (10) so that $\mathbb{z}_{q\rightarrow sf}$ and $\mathbb{z}_{sf\rightarrow cf}$ were 50 steps each.

4.1 Experiment 1: Counterfactuals

We compared MIPCE with W-CF and Native-Guide in qualitative and quantitative metrics, specifically in terms of proximity, plausibility, and substitutability.

Proximity evaluates the relative distance between the query (q) and counterfactual (CF) by $\frac{d(q,\text{CF})}{d(q,\text{NUN})}$. We employed the L1 norm, L2 norm, and L∞ (L-Inf) norm as d.

Plausibility evaluates whether the counterfactual is OOD with OCSVM [22] and Isolation Forest (IForest) [16]. In addition, we used interpretable metrics called IM1 and IM2, which use an autoencoder [13]. OCSVM and IForest detect OOD based on distance, whereas IM1 and IM2 do so based on features.

Substitutability evaluates whether sufficient classification accuracy is achieved when using counterfactuals as training data [13]. Prepare a k-nearest neighbor classifier k-NN$_{\text{orig}}$ trained on the original data, and k-NN$_{\text{CF}}$ trained on the counterfactuals. Then calculate the accuracy in classifying the test dataset and obtain the following ratio: R%-Sub $\equiv \frac{k\text{-NN}_{\text{CF}}\text{ Acc.}}{k\text{-NN}_{\text{orig}}\text{ Acc.}} \times 100$.

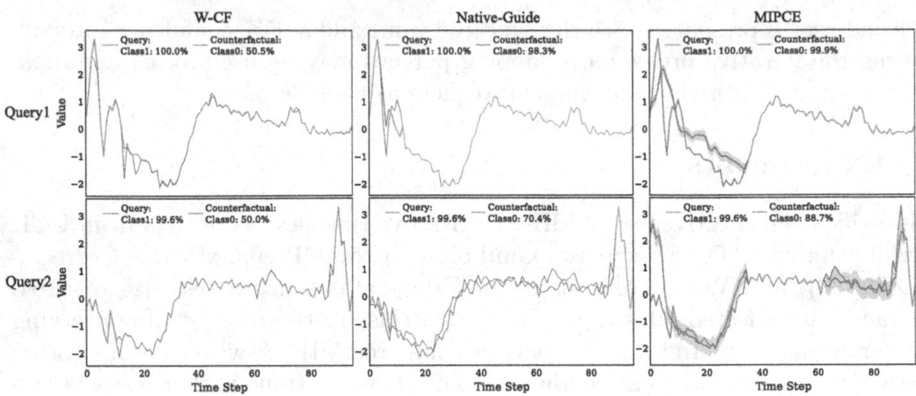

Fig. 2. Counterfactuals of the ECG200. MIPCE shows expected values as a solid line and 95% confidence intervals as fill. The color is the same as Fig. 1 right.

Table 1. Evaluation results of counterfactuals.

		L1	L2	L_Inf	OCSVM	IForest	IM1	IM2	R%-Sub
ECG200	W-CF	**0.08**	**0.25**	**0.62**	0.265	0.266	1.781	0.969	0.136
	Native-Guide	0.2	0.48	0.86	0.22	0.261	1.215	0.533	0.2
	MIPCE	0.66	0.98	1.3	**0.15**	**0.225**	**0.626**	**0.296**	**0.556**
Strawberry	W-CF	**0.11**	**0.4**	1.43	0.017	0.116	1.286	0.018	0.082
	Native-Guide	0.54	0.69	**0.81**	0.005	0.05	1.54	0.008	0.111
	MIPCE	0.83	1.06	1.44	**0.003**	**0.04**	**1.095**	**0.007**	**0.287**
GunPoint	W-CF	**0.06**	**0.18**	**0.56**	0.174	0.228	1.263	**0.035**	0.023
	Native-Guide	0.27	0.56	0.85	0.113	0.155	1.029	0.061	0.321
	MIPCE	1.4	1.65	1.79	**0.04**	**0.129**	**0.622**	0.038	**0.901**
Proximal	W-CF	**0.07**	**0.26**	**0.65**	0.014	0.064	1.185	0.013	0.204
	Native-Guide	0.31	0.54	0.83	0.003	0.057	1.208	0.011	0.247
	MIPCE	1.27	1.32	1.28	**0.0**	**0.021**	**1.016**	**0.008**	**0.692**
Wafer	W-CF	**0.01**	**0.03**	**0.08**	**0.13**	0.441	2.809	1.048	0.014
	Native-Guide	0.36	0.55	0.85	0.25	0.63	1.636	1.169	0.02
	MIPCE	0.75	0.85	1.01	0.37	**0.62**	**1.199**	**0.769**	**0.242**

Results. Figure 2 shows the counterfactuals generated by each method, along with corresponding queries, which belong to the same class. We observe that in the case of query2, MIPCE generated sparse explanations. In addition, if we examine query1 and query2 together, we can clearly interpret the important subsequences.

From a quantitative perspective, W-CF obtained the best results in terms of proximity (see Table 1). However, as seen in Fig. 2, good proximity does not necessarily correlate with high human interpretability. In addition, W-CF exhibited poor results in terms of plausibility, as it generated counterfactuals that do not exist in the real world. Conversely, our method obtained better plausibility and substitutability scores. This suggests that MIPCE captures subsequences that are critical for classification, and generates counterfactuals that follow the data distribution.

4.2 Experiment 2: Change to the Counterfactual

In the process of continuous change, we evaluated the proximity and plausibility of instances that change the query to the counterfactual $r\%$ ($r \in \{0, 25, 50, 75, 100\}$). We used the same metrics as in Experiment 1. From a proximity perspective, it is desirable for the distance between the query and instance to increase with the changing rate of the counterfactual. From a plausibility perspective, it is desirable for instances with a change rate of approximately 50% to be OOD. These evaluations were inspired by [13].

Results. The distance from the query was observed to increase with the rate of change to the counterfactual (see Fig. 3 and Fig. 4a). Therefore, it can be said that the process of continuous change is an ideal one. In terms of plausibility, OCSVM and IForest exhibited smaller changes in their evaluation values compared to IM1 and IM2. This indicates that distance-based metrics cannot detect intermediate counterfactual instances that would not follow the data distribution. Conversely, the autoencoder's metrics judge instances close to the 50% ratio to be OOD.

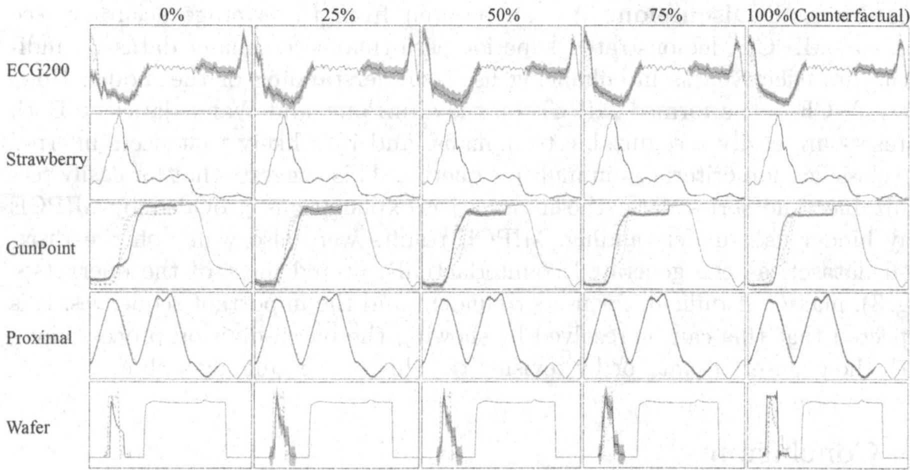

Fig. 3. Counterfactual changing of each dataset. The solid line represents the corresponding percentage, and the dashed line shows instances for other percentages. The color is the same as in Fig. 1 right.

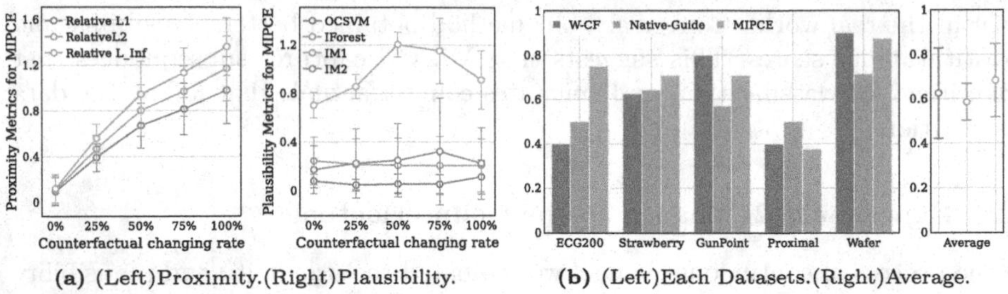

(a) (Left)Proximity.(Right)Plausibility. **(b)** (Left)Each Datasets.(Right)Average.

Fig. 4. (a) Counterfactual change evaluation of the mean and standard deviation of the five datasets. (b) Results of user test.

4.3 Experiment 3: User Test

Present explanations generated by specific methods from W-CF, Native-Guide, and MIPCE to assess the user's understanding of the DNN decision process. Effectiveness was evaluated by measuring the ability of users to correctly predict the DNN's classification result of an unknown query. Our participants, all college students with prior knowledge of machine learning, were divided among 3 groups of approximately 6 students each. Each group was presented with 8 examples of explanations, and subsequently tested with 4 unknown queries. The results determined which explanation method is the most conducive for the user's understanding of the DNN. This experiment was inspired by [1].

Results and Discussion. As can be seen from the average accuracy (see Fig. 4b), MIPCE demonstrated superior performance on many datasets, indicating its effectiveness in enhancing user's understanding of the model. However, W-CF outperformed MIPCE on the GunPoint and Wafer datasets. Both datasets are easily recognizable to humans, and it is likely that users inferred the classification criteria from multiple queries. This suggests that for easily recognizable time series data, the informative explanations provided by MIPCE may hinder user understanding. MIPCE results were also worse on the Proximal dataset, as the generated counterfactuals altered most of the query (see Fig. 3), making it difficult for users to understand the important sequences. It is expected that this can be resolved by showing the patch division process along with the counterfactuals, or by revising the cluster merging algorithm.

5 Conclusion

For counterfactual explanations in time series classification, we propose MIPCE, which takes subsequences from an FCN and presents the counterfactual changes of the patches that contribute to classification. Quantitative evaluation results indicate that MIPCE generates more plausible counterfactuals consistent with the data distribution compared to conventional methods. In addition, our approach is able to retrieve features that contribute to classification, indicating the potential of using them for data augmentation. Furthermore, user testing has shown the effectiveness of our method.

In the future, we will improve our method to present more effective explanations based on user feedback. One idea for improvement is to show the patch division, as well as the contribution of each patch to classification, along with the current explanation. Another direction is data augmentation. In the continuous changes of MIPCE, it is possible to obtain the classification probability and confidence level of the generated instance, which serve as indicators of how well the instance follows the data distribution. This could be used for data augmentation, and we will explore the possibility of applying our method therein.

Acknowledgements. This paper is based on results obtained from a project commissioned by the New Energy and Industrial Technology Development Organization (NEDO).

References

1. Akula, A., Wang, S., Zhu, S.C.: Cocox: generating conceptual and counterfactual explanations via fault-lines. In: Proceedings of the AAAI Conference on Artificial Intelligence, vol. 34, pp. 2594–2601 (2020)
2. Blei, D.M., Jordan, M.I.: Variational inference for Dirichlet process mixtures. Bayesian Anal. **1**(1), 121–143 (2006)
3. Bolei, Z., Khosla, A., Lapedriza, A., Oliva, A., Torralba, A.: Object detectors emerge in deep scene cnns. In: International Conference on Learning Representations (2015)
4. Byrne, R.M.: Counterfactuals in explainable artificial intelligence (xai): evidence from human reasoning. In: IJCAI, pp. 6276–6282 (2019)
5. Casella, G., Robert, C.P., Wells, M.T.: Generalized accept-reject sampling schemes. In: Lecture Notes-Monograph Series, pp. 342–347 (2004)
6. Dau, H.A., et al.: The ucr time series archive. IEEE/CAA J. Automatica Sinica **6**(6), 1293–1305 (2019)
7. Delaney, E., Greene, D., Keane, M.T.: Instance-based counterfactual explanations for time series classification. In: Sánchez-Ruiz, A.A., Floyd, M.W. (eds.) ICCBR 2021. LNCS (LNAI), vol. 12877, pp. 32–47. Springer, Cham (2021). https://doi.org/10.1007/978-3-030-86957-1_3
8. Dhurandhar, A., et al.: Explanations based on the missing: towards contrastive explanations with pertinent negatives. Adv. Neural Inf. Process. Syst. **31**, 1–12 (2018)
9. Guidotti, R., Monreale, A., Spinnato, F., Pedreschi, D., Giannotti, F.: Explaining any time series classifier. In: 2020 IEEE Second International Conference on Cognitive Machine Intelligence (CogMI), pp. 167–176 (2020)
10. Ismail Fawaz, H., Forestier, G., Weber, J., Idoumghar, L., Muller, P.A.: Deep learning for time series classification: a review. Data Min. Knowl. Disc. **33**(4), 917–963 (2019)
11. Joshi, S., Koyejo, O., Vijitbenjaronk, W.D., Kim, B., Ghosh, J.: Towards realistic individual recourse and actionable explanations in black-box decision making systems. ArXiv arXiv:1907.09615v1 (2019)

12. Karlsson, I., Rebane, J., Papapetrou, P., Gionis, A.: Explainable time series tweaking via irreversible and reversible temporal transformations. In: 2018 IEEE International Conference on Data Mining (ICDM), pp. 207–216. IEEE (2018)
13. Kenny, E.M., Keane, M.T.: On generating plausible counterfactual and semi-factual explanations for deep learning. In: Proceedings of the AAAI Conference on Artificial Intelligence, vol. 35, pp. 11575–11585 (2021)
14. Lawrence, N.: Gaussian process latent variable models for visualisation of high dimensional data. Adv. Neural Inf. Process. Syst. **16**, 1–8 (2003)
15. Liu, D.C., Nocedal, J.: On the limited memory bfgs method for large scale optimization. Math. Program. **45**(1), 503–528 (1989)
16. Liu, F.T., Ting, K.M., Zhou, Z.H.: Isolation forest. In: 2008 Eighth IEEE International Conference on Data Mining, pp. 413–422. IEEE (2008)
17. Liu, S., Kailkhura, B., Loveland, D., Han, Y.: Generative counterfactual introspection for explainable deep learning. In: 2019 IEEE Global Conference on Signal and Information Processing (GlobalSIP), pp. 1–5. IEEE (2019)
18. Van Looveren, A., Klaise, J.: Interpretable counterfactual explanations guided by prototypes. In: Oliver, N., Pérez-Cruz, F., Kramer, S., Read, J., Lozano, J.A. (eds.) ECML PKDD 2021. LNCS (LNAI), vol. 12976, pp. 650–665. Springer, Cham (2021). https://doi.org/10.1007/978-3-030-86520-7_40
19. Lundberg, S.M., Lee, S.I.: A unified approach to interpreting model predictions. Adv. Neural Inf. Process. Syst. **30**, 1–10 (2017)
20. Mark T Keane, Eoin M Kenny, E.D., Smyth, B.: If only we had better counterfactual explanations: five key deficits to rectify in the evaluation of counterfactual xai techniques. In: Proceeding of the 30th International Joint Conference on Artificial Intelligence, IJCAI, pp. 4466–4474 (2021)
21. Ribeiro, M.T., Singh, S., Guestrin, C.: "why should i trust you?" explaining the predictions of any classifier. In: Proceedings of the 22nd ACM SIGKDD International Conference on Knowledge Discovery and Data Mining, pp. 1135–1144 (2016)
22. Schölkopf, B., Platt, J.C., Shawe-Taylor, J., Smola, A.J., Williamson, R.C.: Estimating the support of a high-dimensional distribution. Neural Comput. **13**(7), 1443–1471 (2001)
23. Singla, S., Pollack, B., Chen, J., Batmanghelich, K.: Explanation by progressive exaggeration. In: International Conference on Learning Representations (2020)
24. Titsias, M., Lawrence, N.D.: Bayesian gaussian process latent variable model. In: Proceedings of the Thirteenth International Conference on Artificial Intelligence and Statistics, pp. 844–851. JMLR Workshop and Conference Proceedings (2010)
25. Wachter, S., Mittelstadt, B., Russell, C.: Counterfactual explanations without opening the black box: automated decisions and the gdpr. Harv. JL Tech. **31**, 841 (2017)
26. Wang, Z., Yan, W., Oates, T.: Time series classification from scratch with deep neural networks: a strong baseline. In: 2017 International Joint Conference on Neural Networks (IJCNN), pp. 1578–1585. IEEE (2017)
27. Ye, L., Keogh, E.: Time series shapelets: a novel technique that allows accurate, interpretable and fast classification. Data Min. Knowl. Disc. **22**(1), 149–182 (2011)
28. Zhou, B., Khosla, A., Lapedriza, A., Oliva, A., Torralba, A.: Learning deep features for discriminative localization. In: Proceedings of the IEEE Conference on Computer Vision and Pattern Recognition, pp. 2921–2929 (2016)

Multi-Timestep-Ahead Prediction with Mixture of Experts for Embodied Question Answering

Kanata Suzuki[1,2], Yuya Kamiwano[1], Naoya Chiba[1,3], Hiroki Mori[1], and Tetsuya Ogata[1,4,5](✉)

[1] Faculty of Science and Engineering, Waseda University, Tokyo, Japan
ogata@waseda.jp

[2] Artificial Intelligence Laboratories, Fujitsu Limited, Minato City, Kanagawa, Japan

[3] OMRON SINIC X Corporation, Tokyo, Japan

[4] Waseda Research Institute for Science and Engineering (WISE) at Waseda University, Tokyo, Japan

[5] National Institute of Advanced Industrial Science and Technology, Tokyo, Japan

Abstract. In this study, we propose a method that integrates visual field predictions with different time scales and investigates its effectiveness for embodied question answering (EQA). In EQA, it is desirable to be able to automatically select a prediction time scale according to the situation, as the path to the target object depends on the instructions provided. However, previous studies have only investigated subtask learning with a limited prediction timescale and target. We propose a mixed expert model in which multiple expert networks predict future images at different time steps, and a higher-level gating network estimates the distribution of each experts output. By sequentially adjusting the output of the expert network, the proposed method enables robot navigation considering multi-timestep-ahead prediction. Comparison experiments on the EQA MP3D dataset show that the proposed method improves the prediction accuracy of the model regardless of the distance to the target.

Keywords: Embodied Question Answering · Mixture of Experts · Multi-step Ahead Prediction

1 Introduction

In this study, we investigate the prediction time scale and prediction target in the subtask when learning an autonomous mobility task using deep neural networks (DNNs). In recent years, robots that can operate in human living environments have garnered significant attention [1]. Among them, studies on embodied question answering (EQA) task in which a robot receives instructions

K. Suzuki and Y. Kamiwano—The starred authors are contributed equally.

L. Iliadis et al. (Eds.): ICANN 2023, LNCS 14259, pp. 243–255, 2023.
https://doi.org/10.1007/978-3-031-44223-0_20

from a human and searches for a target object, have been actively conducted [4, 5, 24, 26]. The EQA task requires exploring the simulator environment close to the real one [16, 18] from a first-person perspective and navigating to a target object directed by natural language. Therefore, previous studies have proposed techniques regarding the integration among different domains to obtain useful feature representations [17, 24, 26]. It is also known that in studies using DNNs as described, it is effective to design the model to solve 'subtasks" in addition to the main task [5, 7, 13]. Subtasks often predict sensor information that is separate from the robot's action sequence, and in this study, we focus on image information, which plays a particularly important role in the EQA task.

In contrast, it is important to consider the prediction scale on the time series because the autonomous movement task needs to predict a sequence of actions comprising multiple timesteps. Hermann et al. showed that designing a subtask that predicts image information at time $t+1$ from the action generated at time t and the input image improves the prediction performance of the main task [7]. However, the study did not discuss whether the prediction scale of time $t+1$ is appropriate. Because the path to arrival in EQA tasks varies depending on the provided objective, it would be desirable to be able to automatically select a prediction time scale appropriate for the situation.

In this study, we worked on multi-timestep-ahead image prediction using the mixture of experts (MoE) method [10]. By preparing a gating network that allocates the prediction results for each time scale, it is possible to prioritize appropriate sub-networks (experts) according to the situation without having to set the prediction timesteps in detail. In addition, we use multiple types of images (RGB and semantic segmentation images) as prediction targets for subtasks, and we examine the impact on the overall model performance.

2 Related Work

2.1 Subtask Prediction

The robot navigation task [2, 8, 12, 14, 23, 27] requires various skills such as visual recognition, language comprehension, motion prediction, and long-term memory. Particularly in visual recognition, it is important to extract better feature representations from high-dimensional image information. [4] proposed a motion prediction model comprising a vision module, language module, and navigation module, and validated it with an EQA task. The vision module used an encoder-decoder model to extract three types of features: reconstructed RGB, depth, and semantic segmentation images. [24] extended the EQA task to a photorealistic environment and proposed a method with RGB images, three-dimensional (3D) point clouds, or a combination of them as input and output of DNNs. The study showed that spatial information from 3D point clouds is effective in learning obstacle avoidance. It can be said that these studies demonstrated the effectiveness of designing subtasks for image prediction.

In addition, the importance of time-series prediction in subtasks has been recognized. The study described in the previous section used an RNN, which has recursive coupling to predict image features at time $t+1$ [7]. By integrating motion and image information and training the RNN with them, time-series prediction that also considers the task context is possible. [13] increased the number of variations of images to be predicted as subtasks and studied their optimal combination, based on the aforementioned study. In contrast, [20] proposed an error recovery function by combining learning- and model-based controllers by predicting past motion sequences. Thus, the internal state of the RNN has embedded dynamics that are useful for the robot task, and various task extensions are possible by designing time-series predictions with different prediction scales as subtasks.

2.2 Combine Multiple Prediction Models

While the studies described in the previous section used single subtask prediction results, it is generally known that combining multiple prediction models improves overall model performance [6,10]. [10] proposed the an MoE method that combines multiple neural networks. In the aforementioned study, four experts are provided that are responsible for a vowel identification task, and a GN is trained to weigh the output of each expert. [17] constructed MoE models with experts for multiple types of image prediction. In [9], a series of robot motions were divided into multiple parts, and the motion models for each part were switched by triggering errors in the predicted images. The combination of prediction models is not limited to learning-based controllers. [11] and [15] showed that using a model-based controller as support in reinforcement learning can improve the efficiency of learning.

Against the background of the aforementioned previous studies, this study aims to construct an MoE model that integrates subtask predictions that have multi-timesteps. We also aim to verify the effectiveness and validity of the proposed method in the EQA task. The contributions of this study are as follows:

1. We propose an MoE model with the multi-timestep-ahead prediction for an EQA task.
2. Comparative validation of the proposed method using EQA MP3D dataset [24].
3. Comparative validation of subtask prediction images effective for EQA task.

3 Method

An overview of the proposed model is shown in Fig. 2. The model has a perception module comprising a variational auto-encoder (VAE) and a navigation module comprising the MoE model using multiple LSTMs. The perception module is a feature extractor of the input image, and the navigation module is a controller that outputs the next action of the robot. We train the proposed model using navigation episodes $\{(i_1, a_1), \cdots (i_T, a_T)\}$ of sequence length T, comprising images i and actions a. In the training phase, the VAE is trained first, and

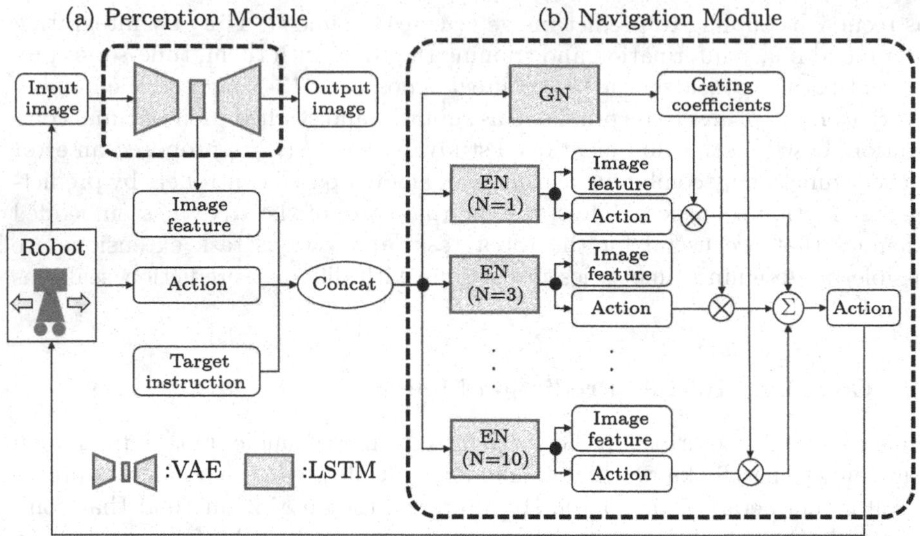

Fig. 1. Overview of the proposed method. The proposed method comprises (a) a perceptual module including VAE and (b) a navigation module including MoE using multiple LSTMs. The five expert networks (ENs) used in the MoE are integrated by a GN.

the MoE model is subsequently trained using the navigation episodes including image features extracted by the VAE. The details of the dataset used in the experiments are described in Sect. 4. This section describes the feature extraction process using VAE and thereafter explains the details of the MoE model.

3.1 Perception Module

In the perception module, the VAE is first trained with the acquired image data i to extract image features f for the training phase of MoE (Fig. 1a). The VAE is able to extract abstract features of the input image by fitting them into a probability distribution assumed in advance for latent variables. It is also suitable for representing the robot's movement transitions by capturing the robot state represented by the image in a probabilistic representation.

The VAE used in the proposed method comprises an encoder, which comprises convolutional (Conv) and fully-connected (FC) layers, and a decoder, which comprises deconvolutional (Deconv) and FC layers. The model is trained such that the input and output images are equal. If the VAE can successfully reconstruct the input image, the image features are considered to be well embedded in the output of the intermediate layer. In this study, we used RGB images as input to the VAE and reconstructed RGB images and semantic segmentation images as output (details are provided in Sect. 4).

3.2 Navigation Module

An overview of the MoE model used in the navigation module is shown in Fig. 1b. The MoE is a method of combining multiple neural networks with a hierarchical structure. The model has some ENs that predict the next state and a GN to allocate the output of the ENs.

Expert Network. The proposed model has multiple ENs, each of which predicts the desired main task and subtask, respectively. We allow each EN to predict image features of different timesteps ahead, thereby providing variation in the prediction ability of the model. We use LSTMs as ENs. ENs have as input the action a_t at time t, the image features f_t extracted by VAE, and the language instruction l_t. The model predicts the action a_{t+1} at time $t+1$ and the image features f_{t+N} at time $t+N$ (Eq. 1) as follows:

$$a_{t+1}^E, f_{t+N}^E, u_{t+1}^E = LSTM(a_t, f_t, l_t, u_t^E), \tag{1}$$

where u denotes the internal state that is the recursive input of LSTM and $\bullet^E$ is the input and output of the EN. The action a comprises vectors representing discretized commands. N represents the prediction time scale of subtasks of each EN. In this study, we set $N = \{1, 3, 5, 7, 10\}$, and a total of five ENs were used.

Gating Network. The GN determines the ENs that are important to the target of the main task. The GN has the same inputs as the ENs and predicts a gating coefficient g_k that represents the weight of the output of the k-th EN (Eqs. 2 and 3) as follows:

$$h_{t+1}^G, u_{t+1}^G = LSTM(a_t, f_t, i_t, u_t^G), \tag{2}$$

$$g_{t+1,k} = \frac{e^{h_{t+1,k}^G}}{\sum e^{h_{t+1}^G}}, \tag{3}$$

where e denotes the exponential function and $\bullet^G$ denotes the input/output of the GN. As shown in Eq. 3, g is expressed as a probability distribution by multiplying the output h_k^G of the GN corresponding to the k-th EN by the softmax function. After multiplying the predicted g by the output a^E of each EN, all are added together to obtain the next robot action a of the entire network (Eq. 4) as follows:

$$a_{t+1} = \sum_{k=1}^{K=5} g_{t+1,k} a_{t+1,k}^E, \tag{4}$$

where $\bullet_{t+1,k}$ denotes the value corresponding to the k-th EN at time $t+1$.

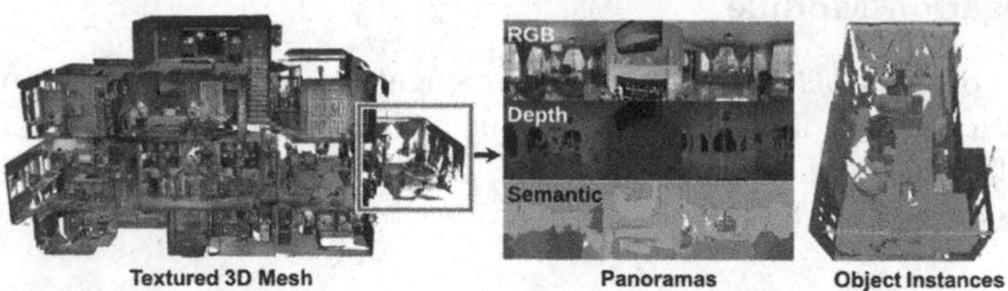

Fig. 2. Matterport 3D shimulator [3]. The simulator is a photorealistic environment and various annotations are available.

The EN and GN parameters are learned to minimize the loss function L defined in Eq. 5 as follows:

$$L = \frac{1}{T-1}\left[\sum_{t=1}^{T-1}\sum_{k=1}^{K=5}(\|\hat{a}_t - a_{t,k}^E\|_2^2 + \|\hat{f}_{t,k} - f_{t,k}^E\|_2^2) + \sum_{t=1}^{T-1}\|\hat{a}_t - a_t\|_2^2\right], \quad (5)$$

where $\hat{\bullet}$ denotes the teaching signal. When the teaching signals of future images do not exist in the data series, the error is set to 0. By training ENs and GN simultaneously, the GN predicts the dynamic gating coefficient corresponding to each EN. Consequently, the proposed model can consider multiple prediction time scales by enhancing the output of the appropriate EN.

4 Experiments

4.1 Dataset

In our experiments, we used the EQA MP3D dataset [24] generated from Matterport 3D [3], a simulator environment for indoor scenes. As shown in Fig. 2, the EQA MP3D dataset provides surface reconstruction, camera pose, and 2D/3D semantic segmentation as annotations. We used 83 buildings and 1136 target instructions from the dataset to generate a total of 11796 episodes in which a robot moved the shortest distance from the starting position to the target. Each episode is a sequence of sensorimotor information comprising an image i and an action a of a successful navigation task. The patterns of target instruction were "What room is the < OBJ> located in?," "What color is the < OBJ>?," and "What color is the < OBJ> in the < ROOM> ?." Table 1 lists the full pattern of < OBJ> and < ROOM> included in the target instructions. For the training and test phase, we divided the dataset as summarized in Table 2.

4.2 Hyperparameter

The parameters of VAE and LSTM are listed in Table 3. VAE has 256×256×3 pixel RGB images as input and predicts reconstructed RGB images or semantic

Table 1. Word vocabulary used in the target instruction

OBJ (25)	shelf, picture, sink, clothes, electrical appliance, door, chair, bathtub, plant, furniture, fireplace, chest of drawers, seat, sofa, stool, bed, table, curtain, shower, towel, cushions, blinds, counters, toilet, cabinet
ROOM (18)	family room, closet, spa, dining room, lounge, gym, garage, TV room, living room, office, foyer, bedroom, laundry room, meeting room, hallway, bathroom, kitchen, rec room,

Table 2. Data division

Dataset	Seens	Episodes
Train	57	9024
Validation	24	2747
Test	2	25

Table 3. Structure of DNNs

Network	Dims
VAE[1,2]	input@3chs - convs@(32-64-128)chs - full@1024 - full@32 - full@1024 - dconvs@(128-64-32)chs - output@3chs
EN(LSTM)	*I/O*@40/36 - *hidden&cell*@128 (2 layer)
GN(LSTM)	*I/O*@40/5 - *hidden&cell*@128 (2 layer)

segmentation images. GN and EN have as input 32-dimensions image feature f, 4-dimensions action a, and 4-dimensions target instruction l, for a total of 40-dimensions. Action a represents the four types of robot commands {Go Front, Turn Left, Turn Right, Stop}. The ENs have as outputs the image features and actions of the next timestep, and the GNs have as outputs the gating coefficients corresponding to the outputs of the five ENs. We trained the VAE for 20 epochs and the LSTM for 4 epochs with an Adam optimizer.

4.3 Evaluation

At the test phase, the target instructions described in the Sect. 4.1 are initially input to the model, and it predicts the next action in the sequence. The test episode starts at a fixed timestep away from the target object. The test episode is terminated after a specified number of timesteps that are sufficient to reach the target. We evaluated the proposed method from two perspectives: success rate and approach distance. For the success rate, the success criterion is the presence or absence of the target object in the last frame of the navigation task. The robot must select the command "Stop" when it reaches the target object. For the approach distance, we measure the distance to the target at the end of the episode and consider the closer distance to be closer to the correct navigation.

We conducted two learning experiments. In experiment A, the following three models were used for comparison to verify the effectiveness of the proposed method; (A-i) the vanilla LSTM with no subtasks, (A-ii) the LSTM with a subtask to predict only image features at time $t+1$, and (A-iii) the MoE model with multiple prediction scales (proposed method). By comparing these models, we verify whether multiple prediction scales are effective for the EQA task.

In experiment B, we compare models trained using (B-i) reconstructed RGB images and (B-ii) semantic segmentation images as VAE prediction targets. To limit the consideration to the subtask prediction target, only the VAE prediction target is changed based on the model in (A-ii). This allows us to examine the types of prediction images that are effective as subtasks of the EQA task.

5 Results and Discussion

5.1 Experiment A: Comparison by Prediction Time Scale

In our experiments, two navigation tasks with different distances from the initial position to the target were used. One initial position was 30 timesteps away from the target (Case 1), and the other was 50 timesteps away from the target (Case 2). The success rates of 25 trials for each are shown in Fig. 3. The success rates at the initial position 30 timesteps away from the target object were (A-i) 54% for no subtask, (A-ii) 64% with a single expert network, and (A-iii) 80% with the MoE model (proposed method). The success rates at the initial location 50 timesteps away from the target were 36%, 56%, and 64% for (A-i), (A-ii), and (A-iii), respectively. These results indicate that training the model with image prediction as a subtask improves navigation performance. In addition, the proposed method for image prediction with multiple time scales performed better.

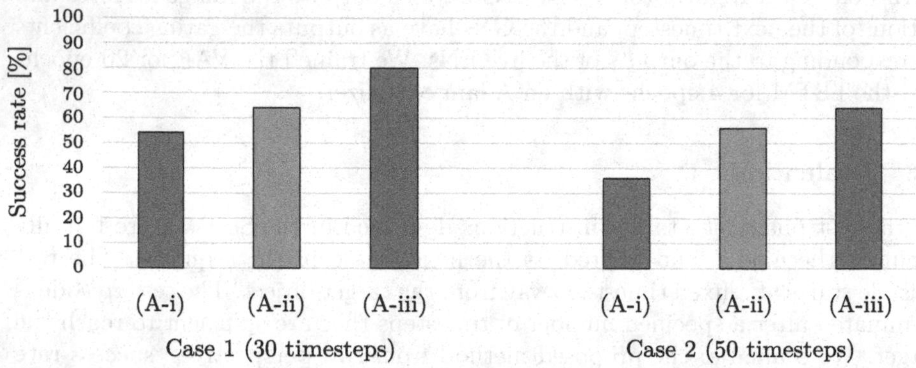

Fig. 3. Success rates by prediction scale in the cases with different distances from the initial position to the target object. (A-i) indicates vanilla LSTM, (A-ii) indicates LSTM with one expert, and (A-iii) indicates the proposed method. The proposed method exhibited the best performance among the three methods.

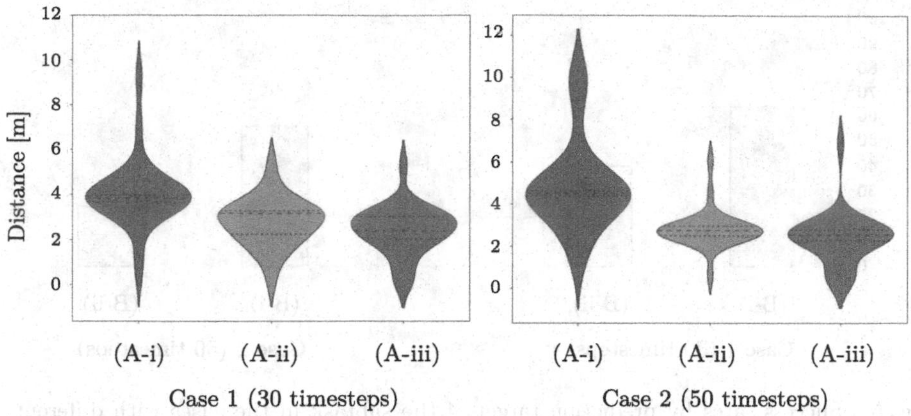

Fig. 4. Approach distance by prediction scale in experiment A. The approach distance represents the distance between the robot and the target in the last frame of the test episode.

Next, the results of the mean and distribution of the violin plots for each approach distance are shown in Fig. 4. Similar to the previous results, it was shown that the final approach distance to the target became closer in the order of (I-i)→(I-ii)→(I-iii) for both initial positions 30, or 50 timesteps away from the target. We checked the generated navigation trajectories, and there were two main types of failure scenarios. One is the case that the robot navigated to a completely different location, and the other is the case of the same location as the target, but not viewed in the acquired image. Because most of the failure cases in the models with subtasks were the latter, there was no significant difference between (A-ii) and (A-iii) in terms of approach distance. Therefore, in combination with the results of Fig. 3, it can be said that the proposed method improves the prediction accuracy regardless of the distance to the target.

5.2 Experiment B: Comparison by Subtask Prediction Target

In experiment B, we compared the models by changing the prediction images for the subtasks. We verified two models; (B-i) a model in which the image predicted by the VAE was a reconstructed RGB image, and (B-ii) a model in which the output was a semantic segmentation image. The training of each VAE was terminated when the validation error was sufficiently converged. Figure 5 shows the success rate for 25 trials of 30 timesteps and 50 timesteps away from the target, respectively. The success rate at the initial position 30 timesteps away from the target was 64% for (B-i) and 40% for (B-ii), an the success rate at the initial position 50 timesteps away from the target was 56% for (B-i) and 24% for (B-ii). These results indicate that reconstructed RGB images are more suitable than semantic segmentation images for the target of subtask prediction.

The input image, reconstructed RGB image, and predicted semantic segmentation images are shown in Fig. 6. The predicted semantic segmentation images

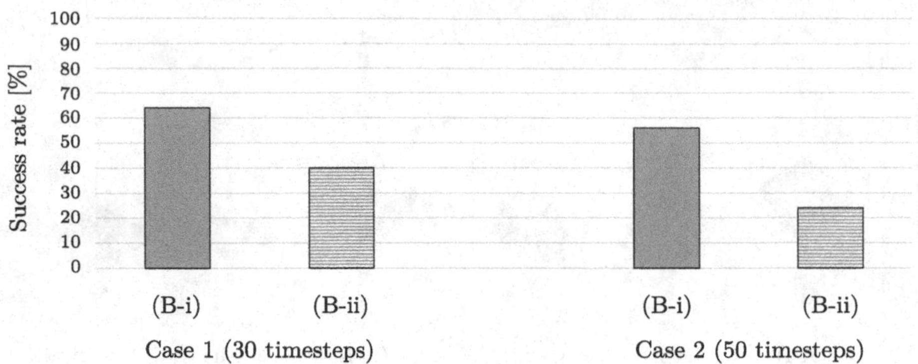

Fig. 5. Success rates by prediction target of the subtask in the cases with different distances from the initial position to the target object. (B-i) indicates the model with RGB image prediction and (B-ii) indicates the model with semantic segmentation image prediction.

are able to recognize some large objects such as floors and windows, but are not able to recognize detailed objects. This is presumably because segmentation prediction assigns a label or category to each object in the image. Owing to the this, there is a possibility of missing important object information in complex scenes such as moving between rooms. In fact, most of the failures in (B-ii) were cases involving room movement. In contrast, the reconstructed RGB images showed the overall visual field in a hazy manner; however, the environment could be understood to some extent. This indicates that although the RGG image features are redundant to the navigation task, they contain information necessary to perform the task.

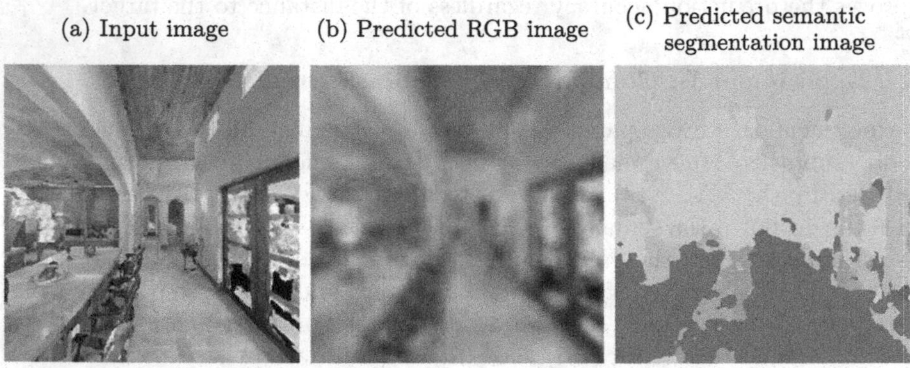

Fig. 6. Examples of (a) input image, predicted (b) RGB, and (c) semantic segmentation images. The reconstructed RGB image vaguely reconstructs the entire image while the semantic segmentation fails to capture detailed features.

5.3 Limitation

The proposed method has two concerns. The first is scalability. Because our method automatically combines multi-timestep outputs, some ENs must be prepared in advance. This may increase the number of ENs and the computational cost when the task becomes more complex and long-term. One possible solution is to embed dynamics on multiple time scales in the internal state of the RNN [25]. Self-organization through learning reduces the need for pre-design.

The second is the scarcity of language reception. The proposed method was validated with only a limited pattern of language instructions. Some previous studies have extended the acceptance of input instructions to robots by utilizing large language models [1,2], and we plan to incorporate them into our model. In addition, extending the model to include dialogue [19,27] may reduce the number of failure cases such as those listed in Sect. 5.1. Our learning framework is easy to extend with reference to previous studies [21,22].

6 Conclusion

In this study, we proposed the MoE model that integrates five ENs predicting image features at different timesteps by a GN to improve the prediction performance in the EQA task. We conducted learning experiments using the EQA MP3D dataset and evaluated the navigation task from different initial positions to a destination in terms of success rate and approach distance. Experimental results confirmed that the proposed method improves the prediction accuracy of the model regardless of the distance to the goal. In future work, we will study the diversification of subtask prediction targets and the application of the proposed method to real robots.

Acknowledgement. This work was supported by JST [Moonshot R&D][Grant Number JPMJMS2031].

References

1. Brohan, A., et al.: Rt-1: robotics transformer for real-world control at scale. arXiv preprint arXiv:2212.06817 (2022)
2. Brohan, A., et al.: Do as i can, not as i say: grounding language in robotic affordances. In: Proceedings of the Conference on Robot Learning (2022)
3. Chang, A., et al.: Matterport3d: learning from rgb-d data in indoor environments. In: Proceedings of the International Conference on 3D Vision (2017)
4. Das, A., Datta, S., Gkioxari, G., Lee, S., Parikh, D., Batra, D.: Embodied question answering. In: Proceedings of the IEEE/CVF Conference on Computer Vision and Pattern Recognition, pp. 1–10 (2018)
5. Das, A., Gkioxari, G., Lee, S., Parikh, D., Batra, D.: Neural modular control for embodied question answering. In: Proceedings of the Conference on Robot Learning, pp. 53–62 (2018)
6. Haruno, M., Wolpert, D.M., Kawato, M.: Mosaic model for sensorimotor learning and control. Neural Comput. **13**(10), 2201–2220 (2001)

7. Hermann, K.M., et al.: Grounded language learning in simulated 3d world. arXiv preprint arXiv:1706.06551 (2017)
8. Hong, Y., Wang, Z., Wu, Q., Gould, S.: Bridging the gap between learning in discrete and continuous environments for vision-and-language navigation. In: Proceedings of the IEEE/CVF Conference on Computer Vision and Pattern Recognition, pp. 15439–15449 (2022)
9. Ito, H., Yamamoto, K., Mori, H., Ogata, T.: Efficient multitask learning with an embodied predictive model for door opening and entry with whole-body control. Sci. Rob. **7**(65), eaax8177 (2022)
10. Jacobs, R.A., Jordan, M.I., Nowlan, S.J., Hinton, G.E.: Adaptive mixtures of local experts. Neural Comput. **3**(1), 79–87 (1991)
11. Johannink, T., et al.: Residual reinforcement learning for robot control. In: Proceedings of the International Conference on Robotics and Automation, pp. 6023–6029 (2019)
12. Kurita, S., Cho, K.: Generative language-grounded policy in vision-and-language navigation with bayes' rule. arXiv preprint arXiv:2009.07783 (2020)
13. Li, Z., Motoyoshi, T., Sasaki, K., Ogata, T., Sugano, S.: Rethinking self-driving: multi-task knowledge for better generalization and accident explanation ability. arXiv preprint arXiv:1809.11100 (2018)
14. Nguyen, K., Dey, D., Brockett, C., Dolan, B.: Vision-based navigation with language-based assistance via imitation learning with indirect intervention. In: Proceedings of the IEEE/CVF Conference on Computer Vision and Pattern Recognition, pp. 12527–12537 (2019)
15. Okawa, Y., Sasaki, T., Iwane, H.: Control approach combining reinforcement learning and model-based control. In: Proceedings of the 12th Asian Control Conference, pp. 1419–1424 (2019)
16. Savva, M., et al.: Habitat: a platform for embodied AI research. In: Proceedings of the IEEE/CVF International Conference on Computer Vision, pp. 9339–9347 (2019)
17. Shen, W.B., Xu, D., Zhu, Y., Guibas, L.J., Fei-Fei, L., Savarese, S.: Situational fusion of visual representation for visual navigation. In: Proceedings of the IEEE/CVF International Conference on Computer Vision, pp. 2881–2890 (2019)
18. Shridhar, M., et al.: Alfred: a benchmark for interpreting grounded instructions for everyday tasks. In: Proceedings of the IEEE/CVF Conference on Computer Vision and Pattern Recognition, pp. 10740–10749 (2020)
19. Singh, K.P., Weihs, L., Herrasti, A., Choi, J., Kemhavi, A., Mottaghi, R.: Ask4help: learning to leverage an expert for embodied tasks. arXiv preprint arXiv:2211.09960 (2022)
20. Suzuki, K., Mori, H., Ogata, T.: Compensation for undefined behaviors during robot task execution by switching controllers depending on embedded dynamics in rnn. IEEE Rob. Autom. Lett. **6**(2), 3475–3482 (2021)
21. Toyoda, M., Suzuki, K., Hayashi, Y., Ogata, T.: Bidirectional translation between descriptions and actions with small paired data. IEEE Rob. Autom. Lett. **7**(4), 10930–10937 (2022)
22. Toyoda, M., Suzuki, K., Mori, H., Hayashi, Y., Ogata, T.: Embodying pre-trained word embeddings through robot actions. IEEE Rob. Autom. Lett. **6**(2), 4225–4232 (2021)
23. Wang, X., et al.: Reinforced cross-modal matching and self-supervised imitation learning for vision-language navigation. In: Proceedings of the IEEE/CVF Conference on Computer Vision and Pattern Recognition, pp. 6629–6638 (2019)

24. Wijmans, E., et al.: Embodied question answering in photorealistic environments with point cloud perception. In: Proceedings of the IEEE/CVF Conference on Computer Vision and Pattern Recognition, pp. 6652–6661 (2019)
25. Yamashita, Y., Tani, J.: Emergence of functional hierarchy in a multiple timescale neural network model: a humanoid robot experiment. PLoS Comput. Biol. **4**(11), e000220-1–e1000220-18 (2008)
26. Yu, L., Chen, X., Gkioxari, G., Bansal, M., Berg, T.L., Batra, D.: Multi-target embodied question answering. In: Proceedings of the IEEE/CVF Conference on Computer Vision and Pattern Recognition, pp. 6309–6318 (2019)
27. Zhu, Y., et al.: Self-motivated communication agent for real-world vision-dialog navigation. In: Proceedings of the IEEE/CVF International Conference on Computer Vision, pp. 1594–1603 (2021)

Rethink the Top-u Attention in Sparse Self-attention for Long Sequence Time-Series Forecasting

Xiangxu Meng[1], Wei Li[1,2](✉), Tarek Gaber[3], Zheng Zhao[1], and Chuhao Chen[1]

[1] College of Computer Science and Technology, Harbin Engineering University, Harbin 150001, China
{mxx,wei.li,zhaozheng,chenchuhao}@hrbeu.edu.cn

[2] Modeling and Emulation in E-Government National Engineering Laboratory, Harbin Engineering University, Harbin 150001, China

[3] School of Science, Engineering and Environment, University of Salford, Manchester, UK
t.m.a.gaber@salford.ac.uk

Abstract. Long time-series forecasting plays a crucial role in production and daily life, covering various areas such as electric power loads, stock trends and road traffic. Attention-based models have achieved significant performance advantages based on the long-term modelling capabilities of self-attention. However, regarding the criticized quadratic time complexity of the self-attention mechanism, most subsequent work has attempted to improve on it from the perspective of the sparse distribution of attention. In the main line of these works, we further investigate the position distribution of Top-u attention in the long-tail distribution of sparse attention and propose a two-stage self-attention mechanism, named ProphetAttention. Specifically, in the training phase, ProphetAttention memorizes the position of Top-u attention, and in the prediction phase, it uses the recorded position indices of Top-u attention to directly obtain Top-u attention for sparse attention computation, thereby avoiding the redundant computation of measuring Top-u attention. Results on four widely used real-world datasets demonstrate that ProphetAttention improves the prediction efficiency of long sequence time-series compared to the Informer model by approximately 17%–26% across all prediction horizons and significantly promotes prediction speed.

Keywords: Time-series · Top-u Attention · Long-tailed distribution · Sparse self-attention

1 Introduction

Transformer [21] has led a revolution in time-series analysis because of its extraordinary talent for modeling sequential data with long-term dependencies. Its supremacy over conventional approachs [7,15,17], such as convolution

L. Iliadis et al. (Eds.): ICANN 2023, LNCS 14259, pp. 256–267, 2023.
https://doi.org/10.1007/978-3-031-44223-0_21

neural networks (CNNs)-based [6,25] and recurrent neural networks (RNNs)-based [14,20] can be attributed to the employment of self-attention mechanism that efficiently collects information at each time step while overcoming the issue of vanishing gradients.

Given the remarkable effectiveness of Transformer [21], many subsequent improvements have been proposed in recent years, particularly in the application area of time-series analysis and prediction, such as Informer [26], Reformer [10], Linformer [22], and Sparseformer [3]. These studies have made various improvements and optimizations to Transformer, enriching the "Transformer family" with many excellent members and covering many practical applications [5,8,11]. It is worth noting that among the various techniques proposed in these works, the most impressive one is the unique self-attention mechanism they proposed. For example, Linformer [22] uses linear mapping to reduce the length of $\mathbf{Q}$ and $\mathbf{K}$, limiting the time complexity of self-attention to $O(n)$. Sparseformer [3] discovers the sparsity of self-attention and used a few attention points with larger weights to provide a more focused attention score. Informer [26] defines a KL-divergence-based measurement and uses a small number of computation to obtain Top-u $\mathbf{Q}$ with a high self-attention score, followed by dot product operations with Top-u $\mathbf{Q}$ and $\mathbf{K}$ to obtain the self-attention score. Although these studies all noted the sparse distribution in self-attention and achieved significant results by exploiting this phenomenon, it is evident that they focused only on the overall distribution of attention and did not finely consider the scores of individual attention, leaving much space for improvement. For instance, Sparseformer only heuristically constrains each sequence point to be relevant only to the surrounding k points and to itself. There is no theoretical analysis or empirical discussion of this approach, only effectiveness assessments from a performance perspective. Informer selects the active Top-u $\mathbf{Q}$ from the overall $\mathbf{Q}$ for self-attention calculation, without any further analysis of that Top-u $\mathbf{Q}$, for instance, *what is the distribution pattern of the Top-u $\mathbf{Q}$? Do the Top-u $\mathbf{Q}$ in different attention layers have the same distribution?*

Based on a recent study of the "Transformer family", we study the specific distribution of active Top-u attention in detail and derive two important observations:

- After stable training, the position of Top-u attention is relatively constant within a single attention layer.
- There are significant differences in Top-u attention across different attention layers.

On the basis of these observations, we propose a novel self-attention, called ProphetAttention. Specifically, ProphetAttention consists of two distinct execution phases. In the training phase, ProphetAttention adopts the same process as Informer to select Top-u attention, but marks the Top-u attention positions of different attention layers. In the prediction phase, since Top-u attention (more popularly interpreted as Top-u index) has already been labeled, the different attention layers use the previous position markings for attention calculation, thus avoiding a repetitive Top-u measurement processes. We embed ProphetAttention into Informer and replace the sparse-attention of Informer to verify the effectiveness of ProphetAttention. The results on four widely used datasets show that ProphetAttention can achieve comparable performance and significantly improve the prediction speed of the model. In summary, our work makes the following contributions:

1. We further explore the long-tail distribution of attention and identify the specific layer-wise and epoch-wise distribution patterns of attention in the long-tail distribution.
2. Based on aforementioned two observations, we propose a novel self-attention mechanism, called ProphetAttention, which can reduce the redundant computation of sparse attention in the prediction phase by reusing previously active attention positions.
3. We embed ProphetAttention into the latest sparse-attention model, Informer, to validate its effectiveness. Experiments on four widely used time-series forecasting datasets demonstrate that our model outperforms the baseline of all 80 comparisons by a factor of 64 and significantly improves prediction efficiency.

The rest of this paper is organized as follows. First, we use Informer as an example to present how to calculate Top-u $\mathbf{Q}$ in Sect. 2.1. Then, Sect. 2.2 shows our investigation on the specific distribution and position of Top-u attention. Third, Sect. 2.3 describes our proposed ProphetAttention and the implementation steps to apply it to sequence prediction. Section 3 presents detailed results of embedding ProphetAttention into Informer and applying it to four datasets. Finally, we draw several conclusions in Sect. 4.

2 Methodology

2.1 How is Top-u Q Calculated?

The canonical self-attention mechanism introduced in Transformer [21] is defined by a set of tuple inputs, namely query, key, and value, which execute a scaled dot-product operation, denoted as

$$\mathcal{A}(\mathbf{Q},\mathbf{K},\mathbf{V}) = \mathrm{Softmax}\left(\mathbf{Q}\mathbf{K}^{\top}/\sqrt{d}\right)\mathbf{V} \tag{1}$$

where $\mathbf{Q} \in \mathbb{R}^{L_Q \times d}, \mathbf{K} \in \mathbb{R}^{L_K \times d}$, $\mathbf{V} \in \mathbb{R}^{L_V \times d}$ and d is the input dimension.

The canonical self-attention is conventionally known for its quadratic time complexity, which requires high computational resources. Informer [26] solves this problem using a KL-divergence-based approach that chooses the Top-u $\mathbf{Q}$ to compute the self-attention score. This approach significantly enhances the overall computational efficiency. However, upon closer inspection of the operational procedure of the Informer compared to the Transformer (see Fig. 1), it is clear that the former has the distinguishing feature of selecting $\mathbf{K}$. Consequently, Informer needs to perform a calculation each time to determine the location of the

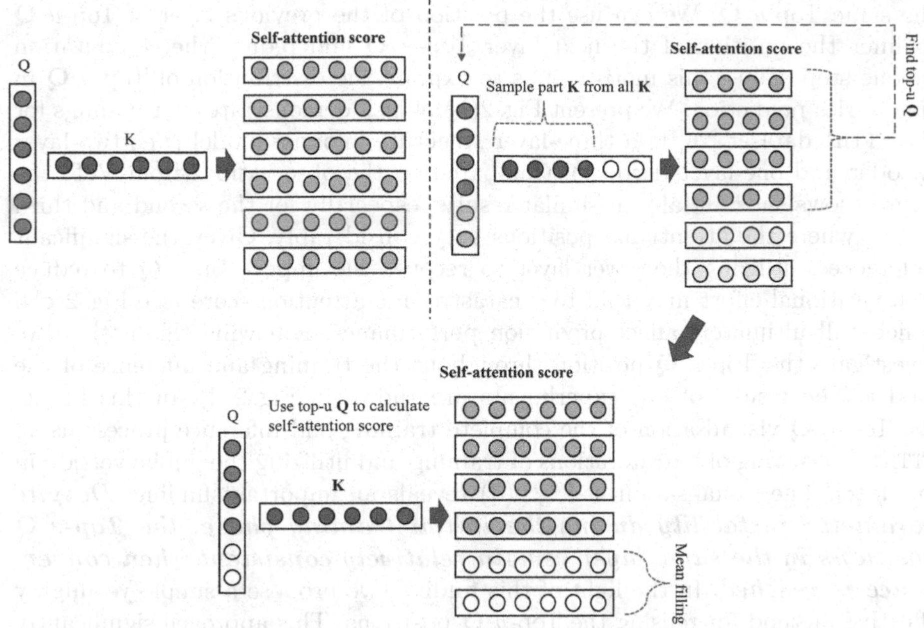

Fig. 1. (Left) Detailed process: Informer uses self-attention score to search for active **Q**, and uses the active **Q** to calculate self-attention output. (Right) Distinct self-attention score and indistinct self-attention score.

Top-u **Q**. This, in turn, naturally raises a question: *Is it possible to determine the position of the Top-u* **Q** *in advance to avoid the need for extra calculations?* To answer this question, we conducted extensive experiments and detailed analysis of Top-u **Q**.

2.2 Investigate the Top-u Distribution Explicitly

Although the positioning of individual Top-u **Q** in the "Transformer family" of the time-series forecasting community [10,22,26] has not been investigated in detail. Similar studies have been conducted in the computer vision community, which directly inspired our work. In Vision Transformer (ViT) [4], they found how the span of between pixels in an image varies with the depth of the network. Figure 2(a) illustrates their findings, showing two key observations.

- The variation in attention between adjacent layers at different pixel locations is minimal in computer vision tasks.
- The average attention span between pixels converges to a relatively fixed range with increasing depth.

To address the above question, if there are similar patterns in Top-u **Q** in each layer of a time-series prediction task, where each layer has approximately the same Top-u **Q**. We can use the position of the previous layer of Top-u **Q** to infer the position of the next layer Top-u **Q** and reduce the computation by one step. Thus, this motivates us to explore the distribution of Top-u **Q** in time-series prediction. We present Fig. 2(b), which demonstrates our findings for the ETTh1 dataset [26] in a three-layer structure Informer model (*i.e.*, two-layer encoder and one-layer decoder). Compared to the observations from ViT, the figure shows substantially dissimilar results, especially for the second and third layers, where the attentional positions vary considerably. Given the significant differences, utilizing the lower layer to recover the upper Top-u **Q** to reduce computational effort may lead to a catastrophic attention score (see Fig. 2(c)), which will ultimately affect prediction performance. Following this notion, we investigate the Top-u **Q** position throughout the training and inference of the model. The results of our experiments are shown in Fig. 2(d). In this figure, the Top-u **Q** visualisation of the complete training and inference process using ETTh1 (consisting of four iterations of training and utilizing the public version in Informer). The visualisation in Fig. 2(d) reveals an important finding: ***Despite parameter instability during the initial training phase, the Top-u Q positions in the same layer remain relatively consistent when convergence is reached.*** In the light of this finding, we propose a simple yet highly effective method for reusing the Top-u **Q** positions. This approach significantly reduces the computational overhead while preserving prediction accuracy. The detailed implementation steps are presented in the next subsection.

2.3 Implementation Details

Our approach consists of two distinct phases. The first stage involves identifying the positions of Top-u **Q** in the training phase, while the second stage involves reusing the positions of Top-u **Q** in the inference phase.

Specifically, in the training phase, we randomly select a subset of **K** and gather all **Q** from the selected subset for the self-attention computation. We then use a measurement based on KL-divergence [26] to identify the **Q** with the highest self-attention score, *i.e.*, Top-u, $u = logL_Q$. The specific criteria used to measure attention scores are as follows:

$$\bar{M}(\mathbf{q}_i, \mathbf{K}) = \max_j \left\{ \frac{\mathbf{q}_i \mathbf{k}_j^\top}{\sqrt{d}} \right\} - \frac{1}{L_K} \sum_{j=1}^{L_K} \frac{\mathbf{q}_i \mathbf{k}_j^\top}{\sqrt{d}} \tag{2}$$

where $\mathbf{q}_i$ and $\mathbf{k}_j$ denote each component of **Q** and **K**, respectively, and d denotes the dimensional constant used to regularize the self-attention score.

Subsequently, we store the computed position indices of Top-u **Q** and calculate its average position indices using a particular procedure:

$$\text{Top-u Index}_{return} = \frac{1}{\text{Length}_{Top-uIndex}} \sum_{i=1}^{Epoch} \text{Top-u Index}_i \tag{3}$$

where $\text{Length}_{Top-uIndex}$ represents the total number of Top-u Index.

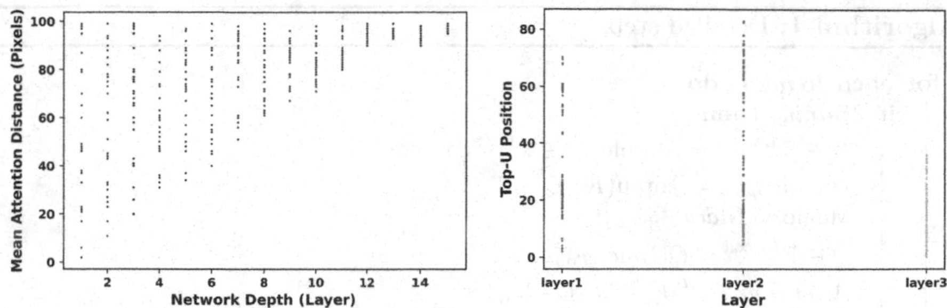

(a) Visualization of Vision Transformer attention.

(b) Layer-wise Distribution of Top-u Attention.

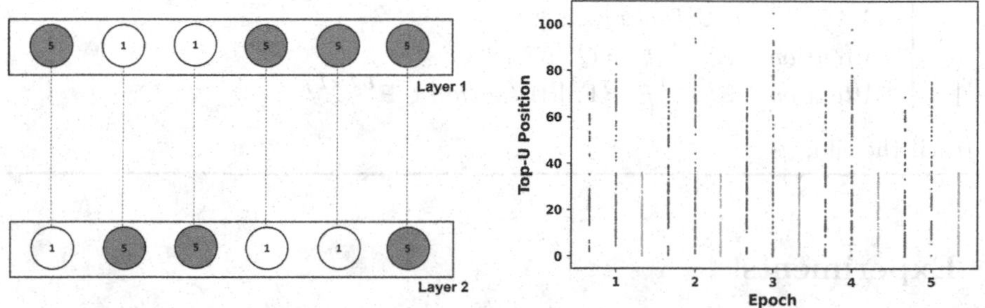

(c) Clear differences in the location of Top-u attention between adjacent layers.

(d) Layer-wise and epoch-wise distribution of Top-u attention in Informer.

Fig. 2. Visualization of Attention in Vision Transformer (ViT) and temporal Transformer.

In the prediction phase, we utilize the Top-u Index$_{return}$ to eliminate the need for redundant calculations when selecting Top-u **Q**. Instead, we can directly leverage the previous index positions to identify Top-u **Q** for self-attention score calculation. To clarify the distinction between the inference and training phases, we outline the entire process in Algorithm 1.

To ensure that the effectiveness of our proposed ProphetAttention is fully validated, we incorporate it into Informer, and test it on four widely used datasets.

Algorithm 1: Detailed steps

for each *Iteration* **do**
  if *Training* **then**
    $\hat{K} \in \mathbb{R}^{\hat{L_K} \times d} = \text{Sample}(K \in \mathbb{R}^{L_K \times d})$;
    $Index_{Top-u} = \text{Top-u}(\hat{K} \cdot Q)$;
    $\text{Memory}(Index_{Top-u})$;
    $\hat{Q} \in \mathbb{R}^{\hat{L_Q} \times d} = Q[Index_{Top-u}]$;
    $Attention \in \mathbb{R}^{L_{\hat{Q}} \times L_K} = \hat{Q} \cdot K$;
    $Attention \in \mathbb{R}^{L_Q \times L_K} = \text{Fill}(Attention \in \mathbb{R}^{L_{\hat{Q}} \times L_K})$;
  if *Prediction* **then**
    $Index_{Top-u} = \text{Return}(\text{Memory}(Index_{Top-u}))$;
    $\hat{Q} \in \mathbb{R}^{\hat{L_Q} \times d} = Q[Index_{Top-u}]$;
    $Attention \in \mathbb{R}^{L_{\hat{Q}} \times L_K} = \hat{Q} \cdot K$;
    $Attention \in \mathbb{R}^{L_Q \times L_K} = \text{Fill}(Attention \in \mathbb{R}^{L_{\hat{Q}} \times L_K})$;
until the end;

3 Experiments

3.1 Experimental Setup

Dataset. We use four datasets in our experiments, *i.e.*, *Electricity Transformer Temperature* (ETTh1, ETTh2, ETTm1) and *Weather* (WTH). ETTh1 and ETTh2 both consist of six-variable time series that record power load features every hour. ETTm1 records data every 15 min, but it is similar to ETTh1 and ETTh2. WTH provides climatological data for almost 1,600 locations in the United States from 2010 to 2013. The data is taken hourly and consists of 11 climate features and the target variable 'wet bulb'. To ensure a fair comparison with Informer [26], our train/validation/test data covers 12/4/4 months for ETTh1, ETTh2, and ETTm1, and 28/10/10 months for WTH.

Settings. To train our model, we adopt the Adam [9] optimizer with an initial learning rate of $1e^{-4}$ which is gradually reduced by a factor of 0.5 each epoch. We employ a batch size of 32 and perform early stopping with a patience of 3, stopping the training process after a maximum of 8 epochs. Notably, our experimental settings are kept identical to those of Informer [26] to ensure a fair comparison. All models are trained/tested using a single NVIDIA V100 GPU.

3.2 Performance Comparison and Analysis

To merge our proposed ProphetAttention, we replace the self-attention layer in Informer. We then compared the obtained new model against Informer [26], Reformer [10], LSTMa [2], LogTrans [12], DeepAR [18], ARIMA [1], and Prophet

Table 1. Univariate long sequence time-series forecasting results on four datasets (five cases).

Methods		Ours		Informer		LogTrans		Reformer		LSTMa		DeepAR		ARIMA		Prophet	
Metric		MSE	MAE	MSE	MAE	MSE	MAE	MSE	MAE	MSE	MAE	MSE	MAE	MSE	MAE	MSE	MAE
ETTh1	24	**0.088**	**0.237**	0.098	0.247	0.103	0.259	0.222	0.389	0.114	0.272	0.107	0.280	0.108	0.284	0.115	0.275
	48	**0.125**	**0.315**	0.158	0.319	0.167	0.328	0.284	0.445	0.193	0.358	0.162	0.327	0.175	0.424	0.168	0.330
	168	**0.151**	**0.272**	0.183	0.346	0.207	0.375	1.522	1.191	0.236	0.392	0.239	0.422	0.396	0.504	1.224	0.763
	336	**0.118**	**0.293**	0.222	0.387	0.230	0.398	1.860	1.124	0.590	0.698	0.445	0.552	0.468	0.593	1.549	1.820
	720	**0.137**	**0.281**	0.269	0.435	0.273	0.463	2.112	1.436	0.683	0.768	0.658	0.707	0.659	0.766	2.735	3.253
ETTh2	24	**0.083**	**0.222**	0.093	0.240	0.102	0.255	0.263	0.437	0.155	0.307	0.098	0.263	3.554	0.445	0.199	0.381
	48	**0.152**	**0.307**	0.155	0.314	0.169	0.348	0.458	0.545	0.190	0.348	0.163	0.341	3.190	0.474	0.304	0.462
	168	0.286	0.430	**0.232**	**0.389**	0.246	0.422	1.029	0.579	0.385	0.514	0.255	0.414	2.800	0.595	2.145	1.068
	336	0.290	0.436	**0.263**	**0.417**	0.267	0.437	1.668	1.228	0.558	0.606	0.604	0.607	2.753	0.738	2.096	2.543
	720	**0.261**	**0.416**	0.277	0.431	0.303	0.493	2.030	1.721	0.640	0.681	0.429	0.580	2.878	1.044	3.355	4.664
ETTm1	24	**0.022**	**0.114**	0.030	0.137	0.065	0.202	0.095	0.228	0.121	0.233	0.091	0.243	0.090	0.206	0.120	0.290
	48	**0.046**	**0.166**	0.069	0.203	0.078	0.220	0.249	0.390	0.305	0.411	0.219	0.362	0.179	0.306	0.133	0.305
	96	**0.168**	**0.347**	0.194	0.372	0.199	0.386	0.920	0.767	0.287	0.420	0.364	0.496	0.272	0.399	0.194	0.396
	228	**0.292**	**0.465**	0.401	0.554	0.411	0.572	1.108	1.245	0.524	0.584	0.948	0.795	0.462	0.558	0.452	0.574
	672	**0.356**	**0.522**	0.512	0.644	0.598	0.702	1.793	1.528	1.064	0.873	2.437	1.352	0.639	0.697	2.747	1.174
WTH	24	**0.113**	**0.246**	0.117	0.251	0.136	0.279	0.231	0.401	0.131	0.254	0.128	0.274	0.219	0.355	0.302	0.433
	48	0.191	0.326	**0.178**	**0.318**	0.206	0.356	0.328	0.423	0.190	0.334	0.203	0.353	0.273	0.409	0.445	0.536
	168	**0.256**	**0.381**	0.266	0.398	0.309	0.439	0.654	0.634	0.341	0.448	0.293	0.451	0.503	0.599	2.441	1.142
	336	**0.290**	**0.407**	0.297	0.416	0.359	0.484	1.792	1.093	0.456	0.554	0.585	0.644	0.728	0.730	1.987	2.468
	720	**0.326**	**0.426**	0.359	0.466	0.388	0.499	2.087	1.534	0.866	0.809	0.499	0.596	1.062	0.943	3.859	1.144
Count		34		6		0		0		0		0		0		0	

[19]. Table 1 and 2 summarize the univariate/multivariate evaluation results of all the methods on 4 datasets, with the best performing models highlighted in **bold**.

As can be seen from Table 1, our model achieves high prediction performance in the univariate prediction setting. It obtain the best results in 34 out of 40 comparison indicators, while Informer obtains the best results in remaining 6 indicators. In particular, when the prediction length is extended, our model achieves better prediction performance compared to Informer. For example, with a prediction length of 720 steps in ETTh1, our model reduces the prediction MSE from 0.269 to 0.137, which is a decrease of approximately 49.44% compared to Informer.

As seen in Table 2, ProphetAttention also obtains the best prediction performance in the multivariate prediction setting, obtaining the best results in 30 out of 40 comparison indicators, while Informer obtains the best results in 12 indicators. It is worth noting that the suboptimal results of ProphetAttention are mainly concentrated in the ETTh1 and ETTh2 datasets, due to the coarse granularity of the features in these two datasets (1 h record interval). The coarse-grained records lead to little difference in numerical values between different points, resulting in insufficient distinction in self-attention scores. Although ProphetAttention does not show significant performance improvements in this case, it can be verified that ProphetAttention is effective given the significant improvement in prediction efficiency and the combined consideration of the four datasets.

Table 2. Multivariate long sequence time-series forecasting results on four datasets (five cases).

Methods		Ours		Informer		LogTrans		Reformer		LSTMa		LSTnet	
Metric		MSE	MAE	MSE	MAE	MSE	MAE	MSE	MAE	MSE	MAE	MSE	MAE
ETTh1	24	**0.560**	**0.546**	0.577	0.549	0.686	0.604	0.991	0.754	0.650	0.624	1.293	0.901
	48	**0.683**	**0.623**	0.685	0.625	0.766	0.757	1.313	0.906	0.702	0.675	1.456	0.960
	168	1.082	0.827	**0.931**	**0.752**	1.002	0.846	1.824	1.138	1.212	0.867	1.997	1.214
	336	1.233	0.887	**1.128**	**0.873**	1.362	0.952	2.117	1.280	1.424	0.994	2.655	1.369
	720	1.380	0.950	**1.215**	**0.896**	1.397	1.291	2.415	1.520	1.960	1.322	2.143	1.380
ETTh2	24	**0.550**	**0.576**	0.720	0.665	0.828	0.750	1.531	1.613	1.143	0.813	2.742	1.457
	48	**1.314**	**0.894**	1.457	1.001	1.806	1.034	1.871	1.735	1.671	1.221	3.567	1.687
	168	4.814	1.862	**3.489**	**1.515**	4.070	1.681	4.660	1.846	4.117	1.674	3.242	2.513
	336	**2.448**	**1.280**	2.723	1.340	3.875	1.763	4.028	1.688	3.434	1.549	2.544	2.591
	720	**3.384**	1.604	3.467	**1.473**	3.913	1.552	5.381	2.015	3.963	1.788	4.625	3.709
ETTm1	24	**0.317**	**0.369**	0.323	**0.369**	0.419	0.412	0.724	0.607	0.621	0.629	1.968	1.170
	48	**0.476**	**0.472**	0.494	0.503	0.507	0.583	1.098	0.777	1.392	0.939	1.999	1.215
	96	**0.511**	**0.511**	0.678	0.614	0.768	0.792	1.433	0.945	1.339	0.913	2.762	1.542
	228	**0.922**	**0.746**	1.056	0.786	1.462	1.320	1.820	1.094	1.740	1.124	1.257	2.076
	672	**0.953**	**0.770**	1.192	0.926	1.669	1.461	2.187	1.232	2.736	1.555	1.917	2.941
WTH	24	**0.330**	**0.380**	0.335	0.381	0.435	0.477	0.655	0.583	0.546	0.570	0.615	0.545
	48	**0.383**	**0.422**	0.395	0.459	0.426	0.495	0.729	0.666	0.829	0.677	0.660	0.589
	168	**0.603**	0.571	0.608	**0.567**	0.727	0.671	1.318	0.855	1.038	0.835	0.748	0.647
	336	**0.681**	**0.620**	0.702	**0.620**	0.754	0.670	1.930	1.167	1.657	1.059	0.782	0.683
	720	**0.667**	**0.608**	0.831	0.731	0.885	0.773	2.726	1.575	1.536	1.109	0.851	0.757
Count		30		12		0		0		0		0	

In addition, we perform an efficiency analysis of proposed ProphetAttention, considering that Informer achieves the highest efficiency through sparse attention, and our efficiency comparison is mainly with Informer. As can be observed in Fig. 3, the prediction time of our model increases slightly as the prediction horizon increases, indicating that our model is able to maintain a high prediction efficiency when dealing with longer time-series. In contrast, the prediction time of Informer model increases significantly with increasing prediction horizon, which may be due to the complexity of the model leading to a bottleneck in processing long time-series. The results show that our model is approximately 17%–26% more efficient in prediction across all prediction horizons compared to the Informer model.

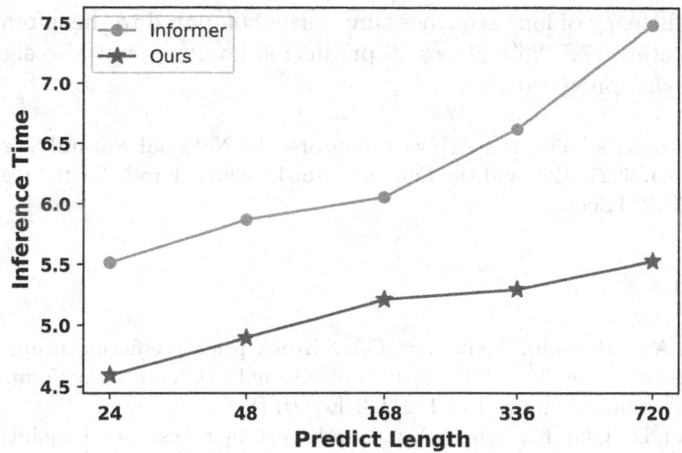

Fig. 3. Comparison of Inference Time

3.3 Does ProphetAttention only Work Effectively on Informer?

To fully verify whether ProphetAttention is only applicable to the structure of Informer, we replace the FullAttention in PatchTST [16] with ProphetAttention for validation. The compared models include the current state-of-the-art baselines DLinear [24], FEDformer [27], Autoformer [23] and Pyraformer [13]. As shown in Table 3, PatchTST embedded with ProphetAttention (Ours), achieves the best performance in six out of eight test results, demonstrating the effectiveness of ProphetAttention.

Table 3. Multivariate long sequence time-series forecasting results (four cases).

Methods		Ours		PatchTST		DLinear		FEDformer		Autoformer		Pyraformer	
Metric		MSE	MAE	MSE	MAE	MSE	MAE	MSE	MAE	MSE	MAE	MSE	MAE
ETTh1	96	**0.372**	**0.396**	0.375	0.399	0.375	0.399	0.376	0.415	0.435	0.446	0.664	0.612
	192	0.406	**0.416**	0.414	0.421	**0.405**	**0.416**	0.423	0.446	0.456	0.457	0.790	0.681
	336	0.432	**0.433**	**0.431**	0.436	0.439	0.443	0.444	0.462	0.486	0.487	0.891	0.738
	720	**0.442**	**0.459**	0.449	0.466	0.472	0.490	0.469	0.492	0.515	0.517	0.963	0.782

4 Conclusion

In this paper, we conduct a detailed study of the long-tail distribution of self-attention scores and discover a pattern of relatively fixed active attention positions. Based on this finding, we propose a novel method for calculating self-attention that reuses the active attention positions. Experimental results show that our novel self-attention mechanism, ProphetAttention, not only improves the prediction efficiency of long sequence time-series compared to the Informer model by approximately 17%–26% across all prediction horizons, but also significantly increases prediction speed.

Acknowledgments. This research was sponsored by National Natural Science Foundation of China, 62272126, and the Fundamental Research Funds for the Central Universities, 3072022TS0605.

References

1. Ariyo, A.A., Adewumi, A.O., Ayo, C.K.: Stock price prediction using the arima model. In: 2014 UKSim-AMSS 16th International Conference on Computer Modelling and Simulation, pp. 106–112. IEEE (2014)
2. Bahdanau, D., Cho, K., Bengio, Y.: Neural machine translation by jointly learning to align and translate. arXiv preprint arXiv:1409.0473 (2014)
3. Child, R., Gray, S., Radford, A., Sutskever, I.: Generating long sequences with sparse transformers. arXiv preprint arXiv:1904.10509 (2019)
4. Dosovitskiy, A., et al.: An image is worth 16×16 words: transformers for image recognition at scale. arXiv preprint arXiv:2010.11929 (2020)
5. Gong, M., Zhao, Y., Sun, J., Han, C., Sun, G., Yan, B.: Load forecasting of district heating system based on informer. Energy **253**, 124179 (2022)
6. Hewage, P., et al.: Temporal convolutional neural (tcn) network for an effective weather forecasting using time-series data from the local weather station. Soft Comput. **24**, 16453–16482 (2020)
7. Huang, P.H., Hsiao, T.C.: Intrinsic entropy: a novel adaptive method for measuring the instantaneous complexity of time series. IEEE Signal Process. Lett. **30**, 160–164 (2023)
8. Jiang, Y., et al.: Very short-term residential load forecasting based on deep-autoformer. Appl. Energy **328**, 120120 (2022)
9. Kingma, D.P., Ba, J.: Adam: a method for stochastic optimization. arXiv preprint arXiv:1412.6980 (2014)
10. Kitaev, N., Kaiser, Ł., Levskaya, A.: Reformer: the efficient transformer. arXiv preprint arXiv:2001.04451 (2020)
11. Lee, H.J., Lee, D.S., Yoon, Y.D.: Unified power flow controller based on autotransformer structure. Electronics **8**(12), 1542 (2019)
12. Li, S., et al.: Enhancing the locality and breaking the memory bottleneck of transformer on time series forecasting. Adv. Neural Inf. Process. Syst. **32** (2019)
13. Liu, S., et al.: Pyraformer: low-complexity pyramidal attention for long-range time series modeling and forecasting. In: International Conference on Learning Representations (2021)
14. Luo, Y., Chen, Z., Yoshioka, T.: Dual-path rnn: efficient long sequence modeling for time-domain single-channel speech separation. In: ICASSP 2020–2020 IEEE International Conference on Acoustics, Speech and Signal Processing (ICASSP), pp. 46–50. IEEE (2020)
15. Money, R., Krishnan, J., Beferull-Lozano, B., Isufi, E.: Online edge flow imputation on networks. IEEE Signal Process. Lett. **30**, 115–119 (2022)
16. Nie, Y., Nguyen, N.H., Sinthong, P., Kalagnanam, J.: A time series is worth 64 words: long-term forecasting with transformers. arXiv preprint arXiv:2211.14730 (2022)

17. Rahman, M.M., et al.: A comprehensive study and performance analysis of deep neural network-based approaches in wind time-series forecasting. J. Reliable Intell. Environ. **9**, 1–18 (2022)
18. Salinas, D., Flunkert, V., Gasthaus, J., Januschowski, T.: Deepar: probabilistic forecasting with autoregressive recurrent networks. Int. J. Forecast. **36**(3), 1181–1191 (2020)
19. Taylor, S.J., Letham, B.: Forecasting at scale. Am. Stat. **72**(1), 37–45 (2018)
20. Tokgöz, A., Ünal, G.: A rnn based time series approach for forecasting Turkish electricity load. In: 2018 26th Signal Processing and Communications Applications Conference (SIU), pp. 1–4. IEEE (2018)
21. Vaswani, A., et al.: Attention is all you need. Adv. Neural Inf. Process. Syst. **30** (2017)
22. Wang, S., Li, B.Z., Khabsa, M., Fang, H., Ma, H.: Linformer: self-attention with linear complexity. arXiv preprint arXiv:2006.04768 (2020)
23. Wu, H., Xu, J., Wang, J., Long, M.: Autoformer: decomposition transformers with auto-correlation for long-term series forecasting. Adv. Neural Inf. Process. Syst. **34**, 22419–22430 (2021)
24. Zeng, A., Chen, M., Zhang, L., Xu, Q.: Are transformers effective for time series forecasting? arXiv preprint arXiv:2205.13504 (2022)
25. Zheng, Z., Zhang, Z., Wang, L., Luo, X.: Denoising temporal convolutional recurrent autoencoders for time series classification. Inf. Sci. **588**, 159–173 (2022)
26. Zhou, H., et al.: Informer: beyond efficient transformer for long sequence time-series forecasting. In: Proceedings of the AAAI Conference on Artificial Intelligence, vol. 35, pp. 11106–11115 (2021)
27. Zhou, T., Ma, Z., Wen, Q., Wang, X., Sun, L., Jin, R.: Fedformer: frequency enhanced decomposed transformer for long-term series forecasting. In: International Conference on Machine Learning, pp. 27268–27286. PMLR (2022)

Temporal Attention Signatures for Interpretable Time-Series Prediction

Alexander Katrompas(✉) and Vangelis Metsis

Texas State University, San Marcos, TX 78666, USA
{amk181,vmetsis}@txstate.edu

Abstract. Deep neural networks have become a staple in time-series prediction due to their remarkable accuracy. However, their internal workings often remain elusive. Significant advancements have been made in the interpretability of these networks, with attention mechanisms and feature maps being notably effective for image classification by highlighting the crucial data points. While human observers can readily confirm the significance of features in image classification, the interpretability of time-series data and its modeling remains challenging. To address this, we put forth an innovative approach that unifies temporal attention and visualization as a blend of recurrent neural networks, self-attention, and general attention. This synergy results in the generation of *temporal attention signatures*, akin to image attention heat maps. Temporal attention not only enhances prediction accuracy beyond that of recurrent networks alone but also demonstrates that varying label classes yield distinct attention signatures. This observation indicates that neural networks focus on different sections of time-series sequences contingent on the prediction target. We conclude with a discussion on the practical implications of this novel approach, including its applicability to model interpretation, sequence length selection, and model validation. This leads to more accurate, robust, and interpretable models, instilling greater confidence in their results.

Keywords: Neural Networks · Deep Learning · Attention Mechanisms · Time-Series · Model Interpretability

1 Introduction

Recurrent neural network models (RNNs) have a long, successful history in time-series modeling [13]. Recent advancements in the combination of attention mechanisms with Long Short-Term Memory (LSTM) networks, a type of RNN, have demonstrated that LSTMs can achieve improved performance, surpassing both RNNs and attention-only models (i.e., transformers) [9,20]. As a result, RNNs, particularly LSTMs, remain competitive for modeling complex time-series data, particularly in hybrid models [13,20].

Attention mechanisms have been successfully used in text processing [3,11, 18] and in image classification. Attention has also led to advances in model interpretability, wherein image attention heat maps validate the network's

L. Iliadis et al. (Eds.): ICANN 2023, LNCS 14259, pp. 268–280, 2023.
https://doi.org/10.1007/978-3-031-44223-0_22

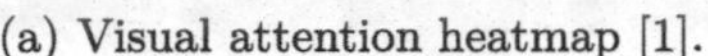

(a) Visual attention heatmap [1].

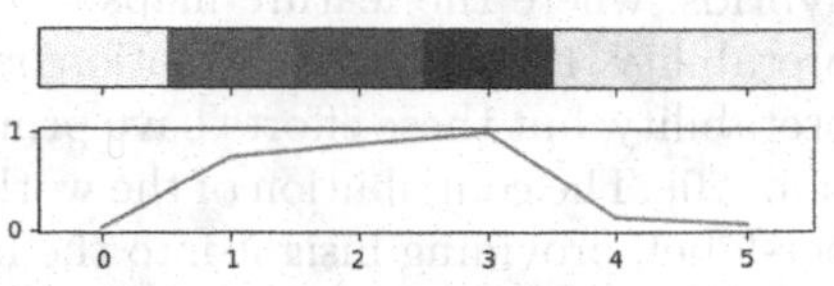

(b) Temporal attention signature sequence length 6.

Fig. 1. Examples of self-attention visualization demonstrating which parts of a sequence are important to the classification decision.

attention [7,10]. Inspired by both the accuracy of RNN-attention models and image attention interpretability, we introduce a novel RNN-attention time-series model, which we refer to as *temporal attention*, used to achieve state-of-the-art accuracy and interpretability via *temporal attention signatures.*

For comparison to image classification, Fig. 1a shows an image attention heat map, which reveals what the classification network identifies as significant [1]. The visualization is easily validated through observation, providing credibility to the model [1]. Time-series data and models are typically more challenging to interpret. Therefore, despite their accuracy, time-series models may be viewed with some skepticism [16]. In the work, we develop temporal attention signatures, providing a method of interpretation and validation for time-series models which is conceptually comparable but computationally innovative. For illustration, Fig. 1b shows an attention signature displaying a six-step time-series sequence, wherein it can easily be seen that the middle of the sequence significantly influences the prediction of the specific label.

Temporal attention signatures demonstrate that the network consistently focuses on specific segments of a time-series sequence on a per-label basis. This will enable human observers to understand the RNN's decision-making process, distinguishing data sequences into classes through attention. Attention signatures help demystify the black box, providing another tool to fine-tune, interpret, and validate time-series models.

2 Background

2.1 Related Work

Recently, progress has been made toward comprehending the internal mechanisms of neural networks, however, neural networks predominantly remain "black boxes." For text and image processing, interpretability research involves presenting the text and images in an intuitive format which can be easily verified by human observers [1,10]. In the domain of deep learning time-series models, much of the interpretability research involves analyzing the network's internal structures (e.g., neural activations), and visualizing and performing statistical analyses of input/output [5,16]. Work has also employed visualizations of RNN-CNN hybrids, where the feature maps of the CNN layers can be visualized for interpretability [19]. Similarly, attention has been utilized with RNNs to enhance interpretability, but these efforts have primarily been in the area of feature interpretation [20]. The contribution of the work is in time-step importance interpretability per-label, providing insight into the influence of time on time-series model accuracy, giving both model builders and users further confidence in model predictions.

2.2 Recurrent Neural Networks

RNNs excel in preserving temporal information through the recurrence mechanism, which feeds the previous recurrent layer's output back into the current input. The mechanism constructs a temporal chain of causality, creating a network "memory." The memory enables the RNN to model time-series data more effectively than most other networks. Although RNNs encompass various network architectures, in the study we focus on the LSTM, which has demonstrated itself to be one of the most robust RNN variants [4,8].

Previous work has shown that attention mechanisms can significantly enhance RNN accuracy in various time-series modeling [9,14,20]. The improvement in time-series modeling arises from a RNN's inherent tendency to assign more weight to nearer time-steps than older ones. While the smooth weighting in time may be desirable in some cases, it may not be in others. Attention mitigates the issue and allows the RNN to construct possibly better representations of sequences by enabling the network, if advantageous, to attend to data "out of order" [3,9,11,18].

2.3 Attention Mechanisms

Attention mechanisms, originally created for text prediction in sequence-to-sequence models, allow the network to focus on particular portions of a sequence, highlighting the importance of one token or another within the sequence to create a more accurate representation of the sequence for output [3,11]. Attention can be broadly described as a weight or context vector of importance within a sequence [3,17].

2.4 General Attention Mechanism

The general attention mechanism creates a weight vector, known as a context vector, which captures the importance of each output step of the RNN to the prediction outcome. With access to the hidden states of the entire input sequence, the attention mechanism selects specific elements from the sequence to improve the output. In this way, the context vector enables the model to concentrate more on the relevant portions of the input sequence, as needed. See Formulas 1 through 3 [3,11].

2.5 Self-attention Mechanism

Unlike general attention, self-attention directly calculates the importance of sequence portions relative to other portions, generating a context matrix. The context matrix enables the computation of a better representation of each sequence, allowing subsequent layers to model more effectively. Formulas 4 through 6 provide additional details on the self-attention mechanism used in the work [17,18].

3 Temporal Attention

Temporal attention in the work refers to the use of both of the aforementioned attention mechanisms in conjunction with a LSTM network in time-series modeling. We employ both self-attention and general attention (in the form of global-soft attention) to develop models that achieve both high accuracy and high interpretability. Self-attention, when added to a LSTM network, enhances accuracy by establishing relationships between different time steps [9], while general attention both further enhances accuracy (see Sect. 5.2) and also allows us to produce interpretable results through novel temporal attention signatures.

Temporal general attention operates by capturing the full LSTM output (i.e., "hidden layer"), typically denoted H_t^T, from within a sequence and training a separate layer to "attend" to some parts of the LSTM output more than others. Equations 1 through 3 define temporal general attention [3,11], where H is the output of the LSTM layer (i.e., input to the attention layer), and x is model input ((i.e., input to the LSTM layer).

Temporal General Attention Equations

$$e_i = \tanh(W_a H^T + b_a) \qquad [\text{ similarity score }] \qquad (1)$$
$$a_i = softmax(e_i) \qquad [\text{ attention weights }] \qquad (2)$$
$$y = \Sigma_i a_i H^T \qquad [\text{ output vector }] \qquad (3)$$

Temporal self-attention closely follows traditional self-attention [17,18], with minor but notable changes. The "value matrix," a projection of input, is used as-is. In the case of quantitative time-series data, there is no purpose to a transformation of the input data. Another difference is dot-product attention is used, rather than scaled dot-product. The purpose of scaling is to avoid the vanishing gradient problem. Since LSTM networks avoid this inherently, there is no purpose to scaling in the attention layer. Equations 4 through 6 describe temporal self-attention.

Temporal Self-Attention Equations

$$E = \tanh(W_a H^T + b_a) \qquad [\text{ similarity score }] \qquad (4)$$
$$A = softmax(W_e E) \qquad [\text{ attention weights }] \qquad (5)$$
$$Y = AH \qquad [\text{ output matrix }] \qquad (6)$$

4 Data

The data sets used are as follows and chosen with the following rationale; time-series prediction/classification tasks; comparison to similar studies [9]; sufficiently different classification tasks; a mix of data sizes and sequence lengths; both binary and multi-label classification.

- *ECG Heartbeat Categorization* (multi-label classification): ECG readings[1],[2]. Sequence size 187.
- *SmartFall* (binary classification): Raw (x, y, z) accelerometer readings of activities of daily life (ADL), predicting falls [12]. Sequence size 40.
- *Air Quality Time-Series data UCI* (binary prediction): Detecting CO levels will rise/fall tomorrow [15]. Sequence size 8.
- *Dissolved Oxygen Levels* (multi-label classification): Classifying levels of dissolved oxygen in natural bodies of water [6]. Sequence size 6.
- *Australian BOM Observations* (binary prediction): Prediction of rain/no-rain tomorrow [2]. Sequence size 5.

Larger data sets were split into train, validation, and test 60/20/20. Smaller sets are split into train and test 80/20 and run with 5-fold cross-validation.

5 Model and Methodology

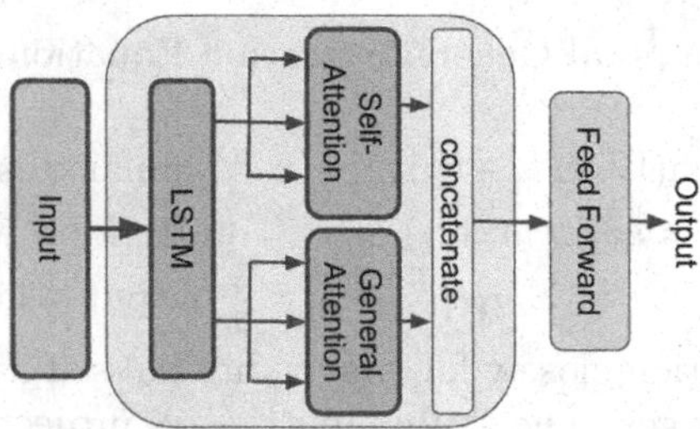

Fig. 2. Temporal attention architecture.

5.1 Architecture

The temporal attention model[3] is designed to model sequences through time while attending to portions of a time sequence in which some time-steps are more important to one another (self-attention) or to output (general attention). The combination of attention mechanisms allows for both higher accuracy (see

[1] ECG source 1.
[2] ECG source 2.
[3] Source code of the project.

Sect. 5.2) and uniquely interpretable results through the use of temporal attention signatures. The architecture is illustrated in Fig. 2.

The use of self-attention is motivated by the desire to achieve maximal accuracy [9]. However, general attention, when used in conjunction with self-attention, further improves accuracy (see Sect. 5.2). Furthermore, general attention is used to generate attention signatures, which is central to the work. The choice of general attention for signature generation is based on the theoretical behavior of each type of attention. Self-attention provides information about the relative importance of different time-steps with respect to one another, effectively adding new "features" to the input and improving sequence representation. In contrast, general attention calculates absolute attention scores between input and output. Since our goal in signature generation is to determine the absolute importance of each time-step in the sequence relating to output, thereby yielding interpretable insight to the model's choices, temporal attention signatures are generated using the general attention mechanism. Self-attention was also investigated for interpretability, but did not yield per-label interpretable insights. The investigation is omitted for brevity, as it did not contribute to the study other than to further validate the theoretical choice of general attention signatures.

Table 1. Ablative study, showing temporal attention (TempAtt), removing general attention (SelfAtt), removing self-attention (GenAtt), removing both (LSTM).

Data	TempAtt	SelfAtt	GenAtt	LSTM
ECG	**0.990**	0.990	0.962	0.941
SmartFall	0.960	**0.961**	0.956	0.939
Air Quality	**0.987**	0.962	0.924	0.912
Diss Oxy	**0.976**	0.970	0.945	0.937
AUS BOM	**0.939**	0.923	0.894	0.853

5.2 Accuracy and Ablative Study

Prior work has shown that LSTMs with self-attention can achieve higher accuracy and more robust time-series models than either LSTMs alone, or self-attention alone [9]. Temporal attention as presented here uses a combination of both self-attention and general attention to further enhance accuracy. Presented in Table 1 is an ablative study demonstrating the enhanced accuracy of temporal attention over either type of single attention RNN combination and no attention (i.e., LSTM alone).

5.3 Signature Generation

Rank Matrix: The first step in signature generation is to present test sequences to a fully trained model, and to generate an attention rank matrix, which is

Table 2. Example rank matrix, label 0, Australian BOM weather prediction.

step	low	med-low	med	med-high	high	total	confidence
0	23	105	97	**6732**	87	7044	0.96
1	**6450**	139	172	159	124	7044	0.92
2	201	173	**6302**	146	222	7044	0.89
3	108	**6589**	203	92	52	7044	0.94
4	47	71	13	11	**6902**	7044	0.98

then used to generate a confidence measure. For illustration, we use the shortest sequence length of 5 (Australian BOM data) to step through the generation and interpretation of temporal attention signatures. For each test sequence presented, attention values corresponding to Eq. 2 are recorded (a vector of length sequence size). The vector is normalized using min-max scaling in the range [0, 1], on a *per-sequence* basis. Normalization is performed on a per-sequence basis to facilitate relative importance assessment within the sequence and for comparison between different sequences. Normalized scores are ranked in order of importance (lowest importance 0 to highest important 4). The rankings of all normalized attention vectors per-label are compiled into a rank matrix. The matrix represents the per-label frequency in which a time-step per sequence occurs at each importance ranking (see Table 2). Reading the matrix row-wise determines the per-label frequency of each time-step at each importance ranking. For example, in Table 2, the rank matrix for label 0 of the Australian BOM data shows time-step 0 is of medium-to-high importance most of the time (6,732/7,044 or 96%), while time-step 1 is of low importance most of the time (6,450/7,044 or 90%), and so on.

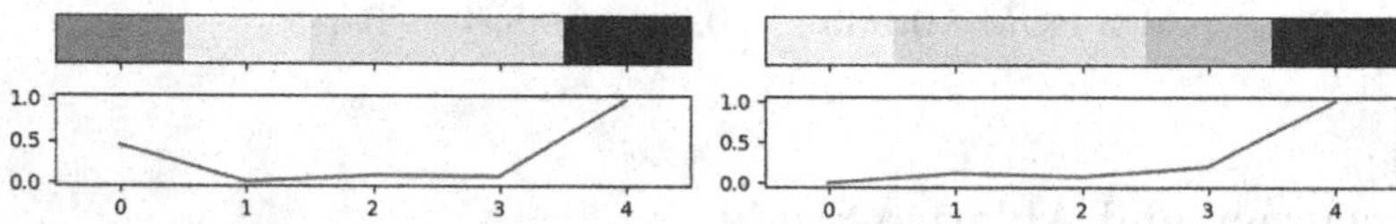

Fig. 3. Sample signatures (labels [0,1]) for the Australian BOM rain prediction.

Confidence Measure: Using the rank matrix, a confidence vector is calculated as shown in Table 2's *confidence* column. If the average of the vector is 90% or higher (determined empirically), the time-steps' rankings are considered "confident." For example, in Table 2, the confidence is 0.94. Once judged confident, the normalized attention scores on a per-label basis are averaged to calculate a single normalized attention vector per-label. These single vectors represent each label's *attention signature.* Figure 3 displays the attention signatures for the "no rain" (left) and "rain" (right) prediction labels for the Australian BOM weather data.

6 Experiments and Results

Each data set was trained repeatedly until 20 models with both high accuracy (> 0.92) and confidence (> 0.90) were obtained. All models were processed as described in Sect. 5.3 and the stability and repeatability of the signatures were verified for each data set (see next paragraph), producing a set of per-label temporal attention signatures per data set. Each of these signature sets is then be analyzed for interpretability insights (see Sect. 7.1).

To validate that attention signatures are similar across models, we calculate the Euclidean distances between per-label signatures per-model. Since signature values for each time step are scaled to $[0, 1]$, the maximum possible Euclidean distances between signatures is known. Therefore, along with visual inspection of the graphical signatures, average Euclidean distances between models may be used as a validation measure to ensure signatures are stable and repeatable. Table 3 shows these averages and maximums across experiments and demonstrates that signatures across models are similar, stable, and repeatable. Figures 3 through 7 detail the temporal signatures of each of the data sets.

Table 3. Euclidean distances summaries for all data sets.

data set	average e-dist	max e-dist	sequence length	percent max
Australian BOM	0.128	2.24	5	05.7%
Air Quality	0.581	4.47	20	13.0%
SmartFall	0.771	6.32	40	12.2%
Dissolved O2	0.185	2.45	6	07.5%
ECG	1.631	10.0	187	16.3%

7 Applications

7.1 Interpretability

Visualizations of temporal attention signatures enable the identification of important time intervals within a sequence, providing insight into the most relevant factors for classification. This helps both validate the model and also enhances our understanding of critical data points that may require attention when making human decisions. For instance, the Australian BOM weather signatures (see Fig. 3) clearly demonstrate that step 5 is of high importance to both labels. This is intuitive, since yesterday's weather is a major factor in predicting today's weather. However, the "no rain" label signature also indicates that weather five days ago carries some importance. This provides insight that, further into the past, there may be information that could aid in the prediction of one case versus another.

To further analyze our findings, we select two more complex data sets, the SmartFall ADL data (multivariate, binary label) and ECG data (univariate, multi-label), for more in-depth discussion (see Figs. 6 and 7 respectively). In each case, a typical input sequence for each label is overlaid with the attention signature (dotted blue line). In the SmartFall data set, the orange, green, and red lines represent the x, y, and z accelerometer scores. In the ECG data set, the single-channel ECG reading is in orange.

In the case of the SmartFall data, label 1 (fall) exhibits the network attending to data immediately preceding the fall and the fall itself (steps 20–35). In contrast, for label 0 (no fall), the network attends to the majority of the input data (steps 5–40). Both results are intuitive and demonstrate that the network attends to a fall much in the same way a human would. When observing a non-fall ADL, a human would tend to observe most things equally. However, when a fall is observed, human attention immediately narrows to the fall and the time immediately preceding the fall to detect "what happened?" This clearly indicates that the network can distinguish between "fall" and "no fall" similarly to human observation (Fig. 6).

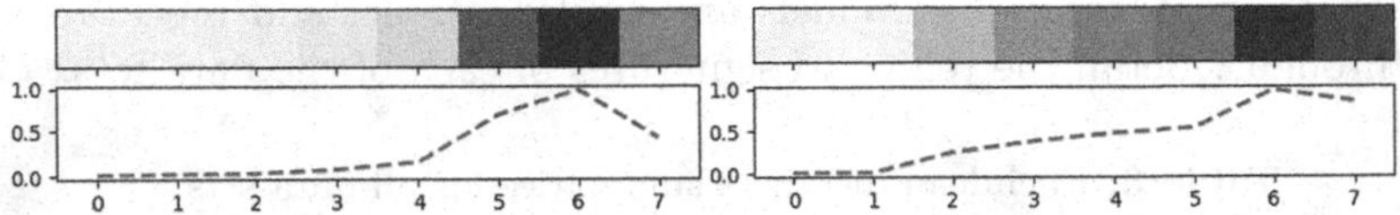

Fig. 4. Air quality data. Label 0: CO levels fall (left), and label 1: CO levels rise (right).

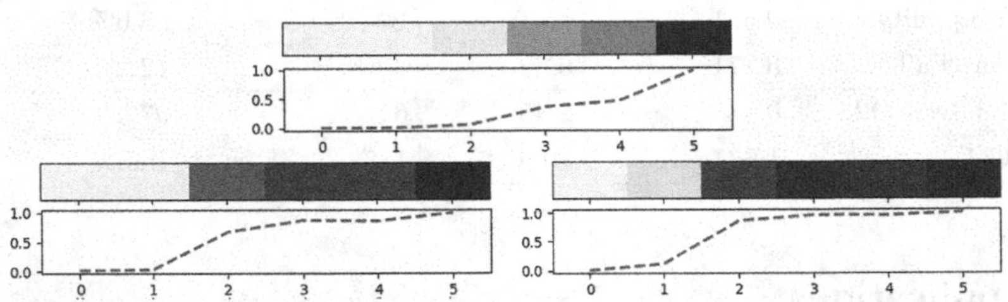

Fig. 5. Dissolved oxygen data. Label 0: toxic (top), label 1: inhospitable (bottom-left), label 2: supports life (bottom-right).

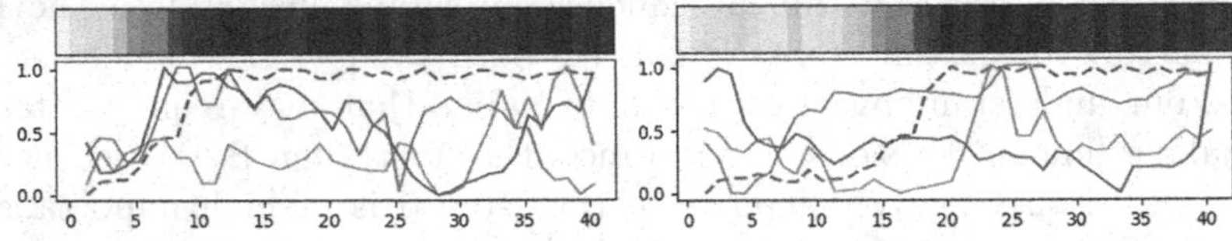

Fig. 6. SmartFall data. Label 0: no fall (left), and label 1: fall (right). Line graphs show temporal attention signature (dotted blue) and x, y, z signals (orange, green, red). (Color figure online)

In the case of ECG data (Fig. 7), for label 1, which corresponds to superventricular ectopic beats (i.e., premature and/or narrow beats), the network attends

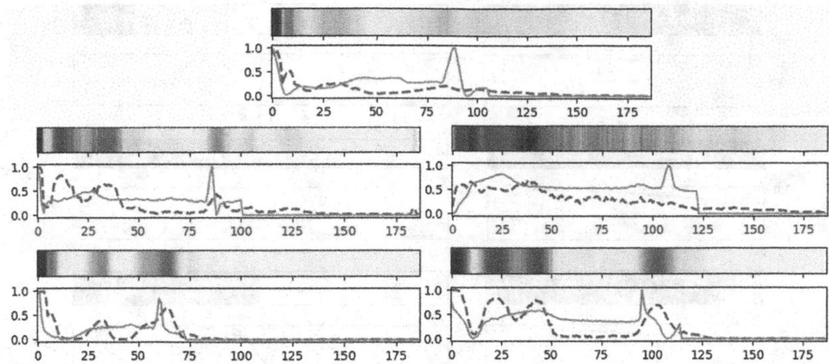

Fig. 7. ECG data. Label 0: Non-Ectopic (top), label 1: Superventrical Ectopic (mid-left), label 2: Ventricular Ectopic (mid-right), label 3: Fusion (btm-left), label 4: Unknown (btm-right). Lines show temporal attention (dotted blue) with ECG signal. (Color figure online)

to the early portion of the cycle as expected. For label 2, which corresponds to ventricular ectopic beats (i.e., small changes in normal heartbeats leading to extra or skipped beats), the network pays more general attention throughout the cycle due to its complex nature. For label 3, which corresponds to fusion beats (i.e., supraventricular and ventricular impulses coincide), the network attends to the fusion portions as expected. For label 0, which corresponds to normal beats, the network attention is low throughout most of the cycle, indicating nothing noteworthy. Lastly, for label 4, which corresponds to unknown beats, we observe temporal attention attending with a strong correlation to the beat cycle itself, indicating that the shape of the beat is noteworthy and may require further investigation by a domain expert.

These observations provide two valuable insights. First, we can validate our intuition by correlating network attention with domain expert knowledge, thereby increasing confidence in the model. Secondly, we can use temporal attention to gain new insight into unknown states by investigating data portions that the networks indicate are important.

Not discussed for brevity, the two remaining signature sets, dissolved oxygen and air quality data, show similar results; clearly distinguishable temporal attention signatures which domain experts may examine for validation and insight.

7.2 Sequence Length

In the context of time-series modeling, selecting optimal sequence length is not always straightforward, especially when the data does not possess a natural fixed sequence length. Typically, sequence length selection is based on intuition, trial-and-error, or grid search. By generating temporal attention signatures, a relationship between sequence length and prediction becomes clearly evident, which provides insight into both selecting and empirically validating sequence length.

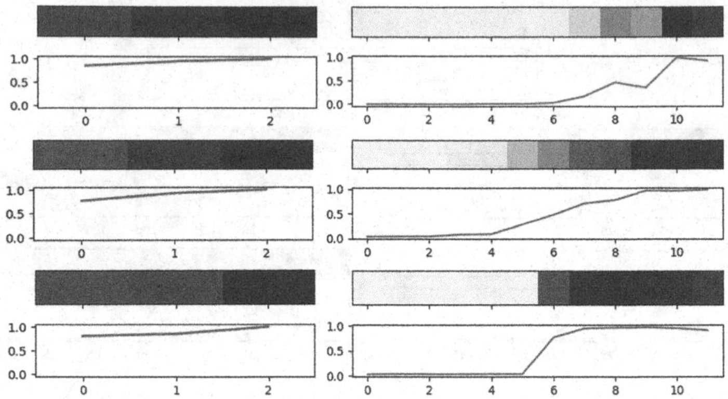

Fig. 8. Dissolved oxygen data set signatures (labels 0, 1, 2) for sequence size 3 (left) and sequence size 12 (right).

Based on the observations made by temporal attention signatures thus far, it should be expected that selecting a sequence length that is too long will yield a signature with very little importance toward the beginning of the sequence. Similarly, selecting a sequence length that is too short will yield a signature with most steps showing high importance. Therefore, temporal attention signatures can be used to reduce the guesswork and cost associated with obtaining the optimal sequence length, as well as to validate the final sequence length selection, regardless of how it was chosen.

As empirical evidence, we examine the dissolved oxygen data set, where an optimal sequence size of 6 was obtained through grid search. Figure 8 illustrates training using size 3 (left) and size 12 (right). When the sequence size is low (3), all time steps are heavily weighted, indicating that there is more relevant information further into the past. At sequence size 12, almost all weighting is assigned to the six most recent time steps. Furthermore, the model accuracies are as follows: size 6: 0.98, size 3: 0.91, size 12: 0.95.

For brevity, demonstration with other data sets is omitted, however extensive sequence length experimentation validates the result. This demonstrates that visual inspection of temporal attention signatures can be employed to quickly narrow the field of sequence size choices, and can also be used to validate sequence length, regardless of the selection method.

8 Conclusion

The work presents a novel and practical approach for simultaneously increasing accuracy in time-series modeling and analyzing time-series data through temporal attention. Temporal attention signatures allow for the identification of important events or patterns within the data that contribute to the final prediction or classification. By analyzing attention signatures, one can validate or challenge prior assumptions, providing confidence in the model. Additionally, the technique can reveal new insights previously unknown to the analyst. Furthermore, attention signatures can aid in the determination of optimal sequence length, reducing the need for costly trial-and-error methods. Ultimately, the approach inherently improves accuracy and also leads to further improvements by facilitating the fine-tuning of sequence length through visual inspection.

References

1. An, J., Joe, I.: Attention map-guided visual explanations for deep neural networks. Appl. Sci. **12**, 3846 (2022)
2. Australian Bureau of Meteorology (BOM): Australia, Rain Tomorrow. Australian BOM National Weather Observations
3. Bahdanau, D., Cho, K., Bengio, Y.: Neural machine translation by jointly learning to align and translate. ArXiv arXiv:1409.0473 (2014)
4. Cheng, J., Dong, L., Lapata, M.: Long short-term memory-networks for machine reading. In: Proceedings of the 2016 Conference on Empirical Methods in Natural Language Processing, pp. 551–561 (2016)
5. Davel, M., Theunissen, M., Pretorius, A., Barnard, E.: Dnns as layers of cooperating classifiers. In: Proceedings of the AAAI Conference on Artificial Intelligence, vol. 34, pp. 3725–3732 (2020)
6. Durell, L., Scott, J.T., Hering, A.S.: Replication data for: functional forecasting of dissolved oxygen in high-frequency vertical lake profiles (2022)
7. Guo, H., Fan, X., Wang, S.: Human attribute recognition by refining attention heat map. Pattern Recogn. Lett. **94**, 38–45 (2017)
8. Hewamalage, H.: Recurrent neural networks for time series forecasting: current status and future directions. Int. J. Forecast. **37**, 388–427 (2020). https://doi.org/10.1016/j.ijforecast.2020.06.008
9. Katrompas, A., Ntakouris, T., Metsis, V.: Recurrence and self-attention vs the transformer for time-series classification: a comparative study. In: Artificial Intelligence in Medicine, pp. 99–109. Springer, Heidelberg (2022). https://doi.org/10.1007/978-3-031-09342-5_10
10. Liang, Y., Li, M., Jiang, C.: Generating self-attention activation maps for visual interpretations of convolutional neural networks. Neurocomputing **490**, 206–216 (2021)
11. Luong, M.T., Pham, H., Manning, C.: Effective approaches to attention-based neural machine translation (2015)
12. Mauldin, T., Canby, M., Metsis, V., Ngu, A., Rivera, C.: Smartfall: a smartwatch-based fall detection system using deep learning. Sensors **18**, 3363 (2018)
13. McClarren, R.: Recurrent neural networks for time series data, pp. 175–193 (2021)
14. Qin, Y., Song, D., Cheng, H., Cheng, W., Jiang, G., Cottrell, G.: A dual-stage attention-based recurrent neural network for time series prediction (2017)
15. De Vito, S., et al.: On field calibration of an electronic nose for benzene estimation in an urban pollution monitoring scenario. Sens. Actu. B: Chem. **129**(2), 750–757 (2008)
16. Siddiqui, S., Mercier, D., Munir, M., Dengel, A., Ahmed, S.: Tsviz: demystification of deep learning models for time-series analysis. IEEE Access **7**, 67027–67040 (2019)

17. Vaswani, A., et al.: Attention is all you need. In: 31st Conference on Neural Information Processing Systems (NIPS 2017) (2017)
18. Vaswani, P., Uszkoreit, J., Shaw, A.: Self-attention with relative position representations, pp. 464–468 (2018)
19. Wang, J., Yang, Y., Mao, J., Huang, Z., Huang, C., Xu, W.: Cnn-rnn: a unified framework for multi-label image classification. 2016 IEEE Conference on Computer Vision and Pattern Recognition (2016)
20. Zhang, X., Liang, X., Li, A., Zhang, S., Xu, R., Wu, B.: At-lstm: an attention-based lstm model for financial time series prediction. In: IOP Conference Series: Materials Science and Engineering, vol. 569, p. 052037 (2019)

Time-Series Prediction of Calcium Carbonate Concentration in Flue Gas Desulfurization Equipment by Optimized Echo State Network

Shunsuke Takagaki[1](✉), Koki Tateishi[1], and Hiroyasu Ando[2]

[1] Mitsubishi Heavy Industries, Ltd., Tokyo, Japan
{shunsuke.takagaki.qp,koki.tateishi.wd}@mhi.com
[2] Tohoku University, Sendai, Japan
hiroyasu.ando.d1@tohoku.ac.jp

Abstract. As an example of an application of machine learning to industrial problems, there has been active research and development of soft sensors that replace hardware sensors with time-series prediction models, thereby enabling to sensor cost reduction and application to model predictive control. However, the training costs of neural networks (NNs) as a machine learning algorithm are very high due to the gradient descent method. As this paper shows, a prediction model with higher accuracy and about 1600 times higher speed than existing NN-based methods and very low training costs can be implemented for predicting calcium carbonate concentrations in flue gas desulfurization equipment. That performance can be achieved by appropriate setting of the network structure and parameters of the Echo State Network (ESN). Ablation studies of several approaches to improve ESN performance show that it is particularly effective to select an appropriate activation function and to design an appropriate objective function for optimization of the regularization coefficient in ridge regression.

Keywords: Echo State Network · Reservoir Computing · time-series prediction · soft sensor

1 Introduction

Attempts to solve time-series prediction tasks using machine learning techniques are being actively applied to industrial problems. For instance, in process industries, including the plant sector, data-driven time-series prediction models constructed by machine learning methods using operating data measured and collected in the past are called "soft sensors" [1]. Installation of soft sensors enables the real-time prediction of state quantities that are difficult to measure in real-time. They can not only provide lower sensor installation and maintenance costs by replacing hardware sensors but also enable applications such as anomaly detection [2] and model predictive control [3].

L. Iliadis et al. (Eds.): ICANN 2023, LNCS 14259, pp. 281–292, 2023.
https://doi.org/10.1007/978-3-031-44223-0_23

As an example of plant products, flue gas desulfurization (FGD) equipment, which removes sulfur dioxide (SO_2) from flue gas, is installed in coal-fired power plants and other facilities to reduce environmental effects of exhaust gases. The limestone-gypsum method [4] is used widely for this equipment. Because the calcium carbonate concentration in the slurry affects the desulfurization performance and the gypsum byproduct quality, the calcium carbonate concentration has been monitored or controlled by a hardware sensor. However, these sensors are typically expensive and difficult to maintain. From the plant user's perspective, a need exists to reduce costs by substituting soft sensors. In such applications to plant products, the key is adequate representation of the dynamics of the target to be predicted. Therefore, applying algorithms that are suitable for time-series prediction is important.

Support Vector Regression (SVR), Feed Forward Neural Network (FFNN), Recurrent Neural Network (RNN), and other methods are used widely as time-series prediction algorithms. Particularly, methods based on RNN, a type of deep learning, are known for their superior performance. An RNN has a network structure that can flexibly represent the dynamics of a time-series by recursively connecting neurons. However, RNNs optimize all the enormous network weights by Back Propagation Through Time (BPTT). For that reason, issues such as increased training costs and gradient explosion become apparent because of multilayering [5]. Among these, gradient explosion causes instability in time-series prediction, which has been solved by installing architectures such as Gated Recurrent Unit (GRU) [6] and Long Short-Term Memory (LSTM) [7], which have structures that retain memories. In the context of FFNN, ResNet [8] solved gradient explosion using residual connections, furthermore, a method has been proposed called Neural Ordinal Differential Equations (NODE) [9]. It was inspired by the approach to serialize multilayered and discrete structures in ResNet. However, the optimization (training) of weights in these methods is performed by gradient descent-based methods. Their high training costs have persisted as an open issue.

A method called Echo State Network (ESN) [10], a type of Reservoir Computing (RC) technology, has been developed in recent years as an alternative to this gradient descent-based training method. It reduces training costs considerably. A typical ESN consists of an input layer, a reservoir layer, and an output layer, of which the weights of the input and reservoir layers are fixed after random initialization. The output layer weights are then obtained directly from the input-output relation in the output layer by linear regression or other methods. Fundamentally, ESN avoids the difficulty of gradient explosion and enables extremely fast training. Therefore, although industrial applications of ESN are anticipated in the future, there are still few examples. Practical design guidelines that will be effective at improving accuracy have not yet been organized sufficiently.

Based on the discussion presented above, this paper specifically examines the problem of predicting calcium carbonate concentration in FGD equipment as an example of the application of ESN to industrial problems. While referring to existing accuracy improvement approaches, we also attempt to train a highly accurate and fast time-series prediction model. Analysis of the trial results can demonstrate the effectiveness of time-series prediction model building with ESN to satisfy the needs of calcium carbonate concentration soft sensors and can provide guidelines for generic accuracy improvement for other applications as well. The remainder of this paper is organized as explained below.

Section 2 presents a description of the principle of ESN and several approaches to improve its accuracy. Section 3 explains the trial conditions for the application of ESN to the problem of predicting calcium carbonate concentration using actual plant operating data. Section 4 describes the results of the experiments and demonstrates the method's effectiveness through comparisons with other methods and an ablation study of the approaches described in Sect. 2. Finally, in Sect. 5, we conclude the paper.

2 Methods

2.1 ESN Structure and Training Method

A typical ESN comprises an input layer, a reservoir layer, and an output layer. The reservoir layer has numerous sparsely connected neurons, including self-connections. It can be regarded as a type of RNN in the context of machine learning. Letting $\boldsymbol{u}(t) \in \mathbb{R}^{D\times 1}$ be the input value at time t in the time-series, $\boldsymbol{x}(t) \in \mathbb{R}^{N\times 1}$ be the state of the reservoir, and $\boldsymbol{y}(t) \in \mathbb{R}^{M\times 1}$ be the output value, then the state transition equation in ESN is expressed as

$$\boldsymbol{x}(t) = f(\boldsymbol{W}_{\text{in}}[\mathbf{1}; \boldsymbol{u}(t)] + \boldsymbol{W}\boldsymbol{x}(t-1)) \text{ and} \tag{1}$$

$$\boldsymbol{y}(t) = \boldsymbol{W}_{\text{out}}[\mathbf{1}; \boldsymbol{u}(t); \boldsymbol{x}(t)], \tag{2}$$

where $\boldsymbol{W}_{\text{in}} \in \mathbb{R}^{N\times(1+D)}$, $\boldsymbol{W} \in \mathbb{R}^{N\times N}$, $\boldsymbol{W}_{\text{out}} \in \mathbb{R}^{M\times(1+D+N)}$ respectively represent the connection weights of the input, reservoir and output layer, $\mathbf{1} \in \mathbb{R}^{1\times 1}$ denotes bias term, and $[\cdot;\cdot]$ denotes vector concatenation. In addition, $f(\cdot)$ is the activation function which performs the nonlinear transformation. It is generally a sigmoidal function such as tanh. The first Eq. (1) has the important shortcoming that the speed of the dynamics of the state update cannot be adjusted. A structure called Leaky-Integrator ESN [10], which allows adjustment by introducing a parameter α and modifying it as shown below, is now used widely.

$$\boldsymbol{x}(t) = (1-\alpha)\boldsymbol{x}(t-1) + \alpha f(\boldsymbol{W}_{\text{in}}[\mathbf{1}; \boldsymbol{u}(t)] + \boldsymbol{W}\boldsymbol{x}(t-1)) \tag{3}$$

In that equation, α is called the leakage rate. The smaller it is, the slower the dynamics. It is also possible to add an output feedback connection to the ESN structure. Although Eq. (2) represents the output of the network from the input and reservoir states, the left side can be $\boldsymbol{y}(t+\tau)$ for tasks that predict $\tau(\geq 1)$ steps ahead. As described in this paper, we study one-step-ahead prediction by a Leaky-Integrator ESN plus this feedback connection $\boldsymbol{W}_{\text{fb}} \in \mathbb{R}^{N\times M}$, i.e., an ESN structure (Fig. 1) with state update by

$$\boldsymbol{x}(t) = (1-\alpha)\boldsymbol{x}(t-1) + \alpha f(\boldsymbol{W}_{\text{in}}[\mathbf{1}; \boldsymbol{u}(t)] + \boldsymbol{W}\boldsymbol{x}(t-1) + \boldsymbol{W}_{\text{fb}}\boldsymbol{y}(t)), \tag{4}$$

$$\boldsymbol{y}(t+1) = \boldsymbol{W}_{\text{out}}[\mathbf{1}; \boldsymbol{u}(t); \boldsymbol{x}(t)]. \tag{5}$$

It is noteworthy that the weight matrix should generally be a sparse matrix. As described hereinafter, we sparsified $\boldsymbol{W}_{\text{in}}$ and $\boldsymbol{W}_{\text{fb}}$ by constraining each reservoir neuron to be connected to only one of the input and feedback dimensions (corresponding to setting the number of nonzero elements in each column of $[\boldsymbol{W}_{\text{in}}^{\top}; \boldsymbol{W}_{\text{fb}}^{\top}]$ to 1), referring to [11], and also by setting the nonzero element ratio of $\boldsymbol{W}$ as 0.1.

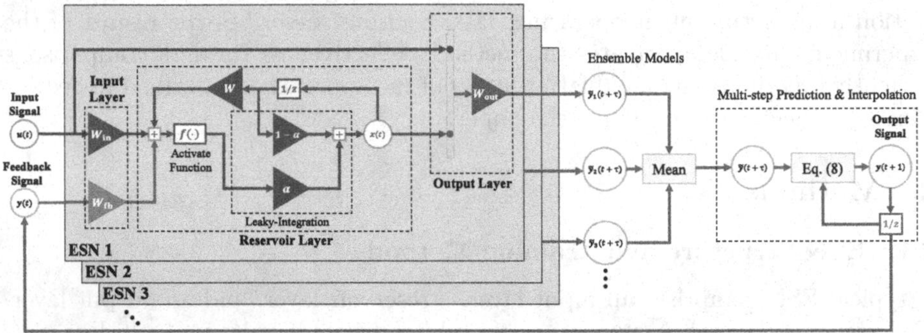

Fig. 1. Overall architecture of ESN in this paper.

The ESN is trained using the following steps.

1. Initialize the ESN by setting the leakage rate α, generating a random weight matrices ($\boldsymbol{W}, \boldsymbol{W}_{\text{in}}$, and $\boldsymbol{W}_{\text{fb}}$), and setting the initial reservoir state value $\boldsymbol{x}(0)$.
2. Sequentially generate time-series data $\boldsymbol{x}(t)$ in the reservoir state according to (4). Because $\boldsymbol{W}_{\text{out}}$ is untrained, the true value of $\boldsymbol{y}(t)$ is used (so-called "Teacher Forcing").
3. Train $\boldsymbol{W}_{\text{out}}$ so that the error on both sides of (5) becomes small.

Scaling of weight matrices $\boldsymbol{W}, \boldsymbol{W}_{\text{in}}$, and $\boldsymbol{W}_{\text{fb}}$ is an important factor affecting the dynamics of the ESN. Particularly for $\boldsymbol{W}$, the spectral radius ρ (the maximum absolute value of the eigenvalues) is an important parameter for satisfying the Echo State Property [10]. Let ρ_0 be the spectral radius of the random matrix $\boldsymbol{W}_0$, a random matrix $\boldsymbol{W}$ with a desired spectral radius ρ is obtainable by computing $\boldsymbol{W} = \boldsymbol{W}_0/\rho_0 \times \rho$.

The reservoir state immediately after the start of ESN drive might take undesirable values because of transient effects, which might adversely affect the training of $\boldsymbol{W}_{\text{out}}$. In this case, it is conceivable to exclude the state quantity in the initial period from the training of $\boldsymbol{W}_{\text{out}}$, but this is undesirable from a practical standpoint because the ESN trained in this way is forced to discard the initial predicted value even during prediction. As described in this paper, as a countermeasure, $\boldsymbol{u}(0)$ and $\boldsymbol{y}(0)$ are given without updating the step at $t = 0$. They are initialized by updating $\boldsymbol{x}(0)$ a certain number of times to reduce the influence of transient effects.

It is noteworthy that $\boldsymbol{W}_{\text{out}}$ can be trained very rapidly using least-squares method with the MSE in (5) as the objective function, but it is common to use ridge regression to avoid overfitting. Let $\boldsymbol{X}$ and $\boldsymbol{Y}$ be the matrices of the time-series data in $[\mathbf{1}; \boldsymbol{u}(t); \boldsymbol{x}(t)]$ and $\boldsymbol{y}(t+1)$ in (5), concatenated in the column direction, respectively, then $\boldsymbol{W}_{\text{out}}$ is obtainable as

$$\boldsymbol{W}_{\text{out}} = \boldsymbol{Y}\boldsymbol{X}^{\top}(\boldsymbol{X}\boldsymbol{X}^{\top} + \lambda \boldsymbol{I})^{-1}, \tag{6}$$

where λ is a parameter that determines the strength of regularization, and $\boldsymbol{I} \in \mathbb{R}^{(1+D+N)\times(1+D+N)}$ is an identity matrix.

2.2 Design Guidelines for Improving ESN Accuracy

Although ESN is a method with a simple structure and fast training speed, it is important to design it appropriately to meet the desired accuracy in practical use. This section describes organization of the design guidelines by referring to some methods for improving accuracy that have been examined in earlier studies.

Hyperparameter Optimization. As explained in Sect. 2.1, ESN requires the setting of structural parameters such as the scales of $\boldsymbol{W}_{\text{in}}$ and $\boldsymbol{W}_{\text{fb}}$ (denoted as w_{in} and w_{fb}), the spectral radius ρ of $\boldsymbol{W}$ and leakage rate α, and the strength of regularization λ of the ridge regression when training $\boldsymbol{W}_{\text{out}}$. The optimal values of these hyperparameters must be adjusted according to the task, and it has been demonstrated that adjustment through Bayesian optimization is effective [11]. However, the optimality of the regularization strength λ of ridge regression depends on the relation between $[\mathbf{1}; \boldsymbol{u}(t); \boldsymbol{x}(t)]$ and $\boldsymbol{y}(t+1)$ in (5). Moreover, it is affected by the randomness of the weight matrices that generate $\boldsymbol{x}(t)$. Therefore, it must be distinguished clearly from the structural parameters in the optimization. As described herein, the structural parameters are adjusted by Bayesian optimization with accuracy as the objective function. Also, λ is optimized by grid search when training the $\boldsymbol{W}_{\text{out}}$ of ESN at each iteration. The optimality of λ can be expressed in two ways: 1. the training accuracy of (5) using reservoir state data generated by Teacher Forcing (TF); or 2. the prediction accuracy when the ESN is driven (called Generative Mode (GM)) with feedback of output predictions after training (5). The latter is more important in practical use. Optimization based on the latter is desirable. For the discussions presented here, optimization based on accuracy in GM is used as a baseline. Then the two are compared.

Selection of Activation Function. The tanh function is commonly used as the activation function $f(\cdot)$ in a typical ESN. In contrast, the use of an even function, especially the Sinc function ($y = \sin(x)/x$), has been reported to improve accuracy [12]. However, ESN with this Sinc function was used to evaluate only common benchmark problems (Mackey-Glass or NARMA). As described herein, we will examine the effectiveness of ESN using a real-world dataset with this Sinc function as the activation function.

Ensemble Models. Even after the hyperparameters have been adjusted, ESNs can be affected by the randomness of the weight matrices and initial reservoir values when training ESNs with those parameters, thereby yielding models that exhibit unstable behavior. To stabilize the prediction results and to ensure the robustness of the ESN, the effectiveness of ensemble models used widely in the machine learning field has been reported [11]. In the example of an ESN model with feedback connections presented in Fig. 1, the output $\boldsymbol{y}_n(t)(n = 1, 2, \ldots)$ of each model is averaged as the output $\boldsymbol{y}(t)$ of the entire model and then fed back to the reservoir layer.

Multi-step Prediction and Interpolation. When the step width is small with respect to the dynamics of the prediction target, the change in one step of the prediction target is small. Therefore, the prediction is more susceptible to noise components when training with a real-world dataset. In contrast, it is expected that the influence of noise can be avoided by performing τ-steps-ahead prediction, where $\boldsymbol{y}(t+1)$ in (5) is replaced by $\boldsymbol{y}(t+\tau)$, and then by obtaining the one-step-ahead prediction by interpolation. In the case of linear interpolation, the calculation can be performed as shown in the following equation:

$$\tilde{\boldsymbol{y}}(t+\tau) = \boldsymbol{W}_{\text{out}}[\boldsymbol{1}; \boldsymbol{u}(t); \boldsymbol{x}(t)], \tag{7}$$

$$\boldsymbol{y}(t+1) = \frac{\tau - 1}{\tau}\boldsymbol{y}(t) + \frac{1}{\tau}\tilde{\boldsymbol{y}}(t+\tau). \tag{8}$$

Related Works. Based on the above, this paper focuses on a model structure that combines an ensemble of multiple ESNs and a mechanism for interpolating predictions, as shown in Fig. 1, in order to deal with instability caused by randomness and the influence of noise components in real-world dataset. Examples of research on extensions or function sharing of such ESN models include Assembly ESN [13], which integrates multiple sub-ESNs with separated components of high-dimensional inputs, and WSALR [14], which replaces some of the sigmoid neurons with wavelet neurons in SALR [15], a method for improving ESNs. However, these methods do not focus primarily on the presence of randomness or noise, and are not a direct approach to industrial applications of ESN. Also, to our knowledge, there have been no practical studies on the validation of the selection of activation functions by real-world dataset, or on regularization factor optimization method.

3 Experimental Setup

3.1 Datasets

As described in this paper, we validate the design guidelines presented in Sect. 2 using the two datasets presented in Table 1: the toy dataset and real-world dataset.

First, a dataset of a spring-mass-damper model with one-dimensional control inputs was used as the toy dataset. This dataset consists of five batches of time-series data $y(t)$ of displacements for different boundary conditions ($y(0)$, $\dot{y}(0)$, and $u(t)$) according to (9), generated by the ODE solver. As described in this paper, the spring coefficient $k = 10$, mass $m = 1$, damping coefficient $c = 1$, and time $t = 0$–10 are set.

$$\frac{\mathrm{d}}{\mathrm{dt}}\begin{bmatrix} y \\ \dot{y} \end{bmatrix} = \begin{bmatrix} 0 & 1 \\ k/m & -c/m \end{bmatrix}\begin{bmatrix} y \\ \dot{y} \end{bmatrix} + \begin{bmatrix} 0 \\ 1/m \end{bmatrix} u \tag{9}$$

As a real-world dataset, an actual operating dataset of the FGD equipment in a coal-fired power plant was used. This dataset consists of 12 batches of continuous time-series data of different lengths, with an objective variable of calcium carbonate concentration and with eight explanatory variables, such as SO_2 concentration at the FGD equipment inlet-outlet. For the discussions presented herein, the variables and time scales are non-dimensionalized.

Table 1. Toy and real-world datasets used for this study.

Dataset	Explanatory variables	Samples	Batches
spring-mass-damper (toy)	1	505	5
FGD equipment (real-world)	8	35218	12

3.2 Experiment Procedure

Toy Dataset. For the ESN with the number of neurons in the reservoir layer fixed at 100, the activation function was the Sinc function. The number of ensembles was set as 10, we evaluate the accuracy of the one-step-ahead predicting mass displacement y. The evaluation procedure is the following.

First, $w_{\text{in}}, w_{\text{fb}}, \rho$, and α were adjusted by LA-MCTS [16], a type of Bayesian optimization. For each iteration of the optimization, λ was ascertained for each randomly generated ESN structure by grid search; then the ESN training and objective functions were evaluated. We adjusted the hyperparameter without ensemble. Next, with the optimized hyperparameter, we trained 100 ESNs with different random seeds and evaluated the distribution of the accuracy (RMSE and maximum error) of the objective variable in cross-validation. The objective function of LA-MCTS was RMSE in the cross-validation divided into batches. The maximum value of accuracy in four trials was used to reduce the influence of randomness. In addition, RMSE in the cross-validation when driving the ESN in Generative Mode was used as the evaluation metric for grid search of λ.

To verify the effectiveness of the design guideline simply, we compared the baseline [Model A] under the conditions above with [Model B] in which λ was optimized by RMSE on both sides of (5) when $\boldsymbol{W}_{\text{out}}$ was trained by Teacher Forcing without ensemble of the ESN models.

Real-World Dataset. The number of neurons in the reservoir layer was fixed at 100. The activation function was the Sinc function. The number of ensembles was set as 10. The accuracy of the prediction of calcium carbonate concentration one-step-ahead was evaluated by linear interpolation from the 15-steps-ahead prediction value for the ESN. The evaluation method is the same as that used for the toy dataset.

In addition to detailed verification of the effectiveness of the design guidelines, we compared the accuracy and training time with existing time-series prediction algorithms: LSTM and NODE. The latter is a method that computes the gradient of the weight parameters for the loss function using an ODE solver. For LSTM, we used a network of two stacked LSTM blocks with 100 neurons in the hidden layer and 50000 epochs of training with an Adam optimizer with a learning rate of 10^{-4}. For NODE, we used a two-layer fully connected FFNN with 20 neurons in the hidden layer and tanh as the activation function, and trained 500 epochs each with Adam optimizers with learning rates of 10^{-3} and 10^{-4}. We also conducted an ablation study under the conditions presented in Table 2.

Table 2. Cases for Ablation Study.

Case	Optimization Metrics for λ	Activation Function f	Number of Ensembles	Prediction Step
[base]	RMSE@GM*1	Sinc	10	15
[TF]	**RMSE@TF*2**	Sinc	10	15
[fixed-λ]	**N/A*3**	Sinc	10	15
[tanh]	RMSE@GM	**tanh**	10	15
[w/o Ens.]	RMSE@GM	Sinc	**1**	15
[1step]	RMSE@GM	Sinc	10	**1**

*1 RMSE on predicted and true values when ESN is driven in GM.
*2 RMSE on both sides of (5) when $\boldsymbol{W}_{\text{out}}$ is trained by TF.
*3 Fixed to $\lambda = 10^{-3}$.

4 Results and Discussion

4.1 Toy Dataset

The findings from 100 evaluations of RMSE and maximum error in the toy dataset with optimized ESN hyperparameters are presented in Fig. 2. [Model A] is more robust and accurate than [Model B], thereby confirming the effectiveness of λ optimization in Generative Mode and the ensemble of models.

4.2 Real-World Dataset

Figure 3 portrays a scatter plot of the prediction results for ESN[base], NODE, and LSTM. Table 3 presents a comparison of the accuracy and training time. It can be seen that the accuracy of ESN[base] far exceeds that of NODE and LSTM (about 50% error reduction over LSTM), and the training time is also reduced to

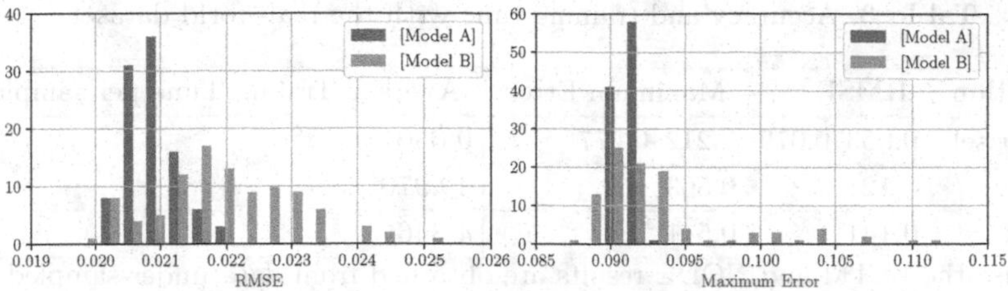

Fig. 2. Evaluation results obtained with toy dataset.

about one-1600 of that for NODE, which shows that ESN can achieve fast and accurate model building even on a real-world dataset. In this study, we compare these methods with fixed model structures. Therefore, LSTM and NODE are expected to approach ESN in terms of accuracy by making the structure more complex, but conversely, the training time is expected to increase further relative to ESN.

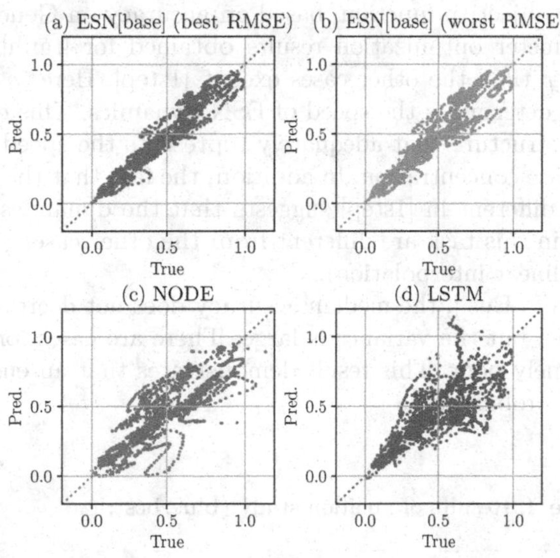

Fig. 3. Scatter plot of predicted results with the real-world dataset. Because the LSTM and NODE results are obtained from data undersampled at 15 point intervals, this figure shows the undersampled plots, including ESN[base], for fair comparison.

The ablation study results are presented in Table 4, and Fig. 4 and 5. From these results, the following points were clarified.

– In each case, RMSE, the objective function, is improved greatly during the hyperparameter optimization process. This finding demonstrates the validity of hyperparameter adjustment using Bayesian optimization.

Table 3. Accuracy and training time with the real-world dataset.

Algorithm	RMSE	Maximum Error	Average Trainig Time per sample [s]*
ESN[base]	0.063–0.079	0.212–0.277	0.030
NODE	0.121	0.563	49.970
LSTM	0.141	0.541	4.346

* Because the LSTM and NODE results are obtained from data under-sampled at 15 point intervals,they are normalized by data length, for fair comparison.

- Actually, [base] shows the best performance as an accuracy distribution. Each of the design guidelines presented in Sect. 2 works well not only for the toy dataset but also for the real-world dataset.
- The performance is degraded in the case of [tanh] compared to [base], indicating that the choice of an appropriate activation function is important.
- The next case that considerably degrade accuracy is [TF] or [fixed]. Considering that the performance of both is almost equal, it is not enough to simply optimize the regularization factor λ of ridge regression, but it is effective to properly design objective function, based on accuracy on Generative Mode.
- The hyperparameter optimization results obtained for [tanh] have a larger spectral radius ρ than the other cases except [1step]. Here, ρ (and α) is the parameter that determines the speed of ESN dynamics. This case is likely to have no model structure that adequately represents the speed of response of calcium carbonate concentration. In addition, the fact that the optimal values of ρ and α are different in [1step] suggests that the dynamics that the ESN should acquire in this task are different from the other cases (15-steps-ahead prediction and linear interpolation).
- In the case of [w/o Ens.], the median accuracy does not decrease significantly relative to [base], but the variance is large. There are cases for which performance is extremely poor. This result demonstrates that an ensemble of ESN models improves robustness.

Table 4. Results of ablation study (blue, best; red, worst).

Case	Optimized hyperparameters				RMSE			Maximum Error		
	w_{in}	w_{fb}	ρ	α	Min.	Med.	Max.	Min.	Med.	Max.
[base]	0.687	1.132	0.200	0.771	0.063	**0.072**	**0.079**	0.212	**0.225**	**0.277**
[TF]	0.555	0.668	0.230	0.932	0.081	0.085	0.092	0.234	0.258	0.304
[fixed-λ]	0.371	0.668	0.110	0.762	0.084	0.089	0.094	0.241	0.262	0.287
[tanh]	1.418	1.260	0.696	0.805	0.089	0.096	0.112	0.251	0.300	0.571
[w/o Ens.]	0.687	1.132	0.200	0.771	**0.061**	0.079	0.420	**0.210**	0.258	1.454
[1step]	1.096	1.216	0.421	0.056	0.066	0.077	0.094	0.214	0.262	0.386

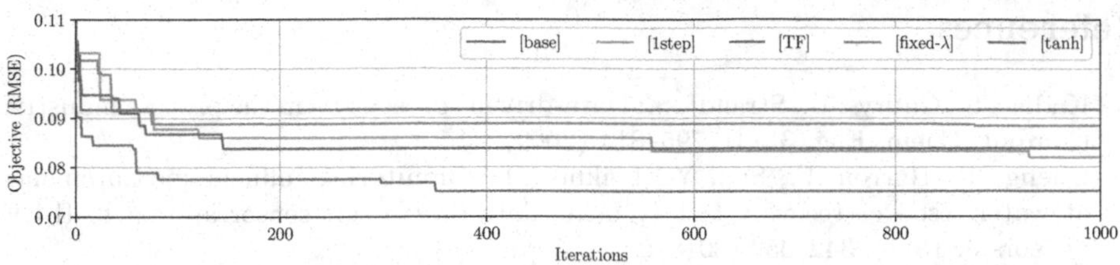

Fig. 4. Hyperparameter optimization process in each ablation study case.

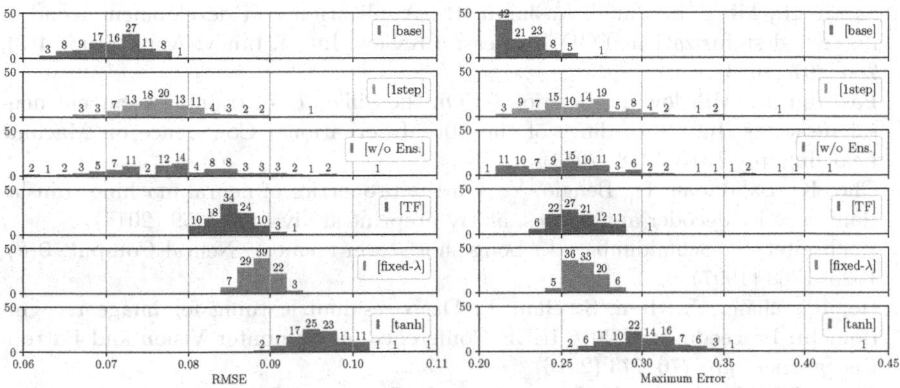

Fig. 5. Results of an ablation study of the RMSE and maximum error distribution (without outliers).

5 Conclusions

When applying ESN to real-world dataset, we organized design guidelines for the improvement of accuracy. Then, as an example, we conducted a trial and evaluation of ESN on a calcium carbonate concentration prediction problem. Results demonstrated that ESN can construct a highly accurate model extremely quickly compared to existing methods, with about 50% error reduction over LSTM and about one-1600 of the training time for NODE. The ablation study results demonstrate that the selection of an appropriate activation function and the appropriate design of the objective function in the optimization of the regularization factor λ are particularly effective for improving the accuracy of the ESN. These results increase the practicality of ESN-based soft sensors for calcium carbonate concentration, help reduce environmental impact, and provide useful ESN design guidelines for other applications.

Although not specifically discussed in this paper, ESN has intrinsic accuracy variability due to the randomness of the fixed weight matrices. Suppressing this and improving robustness are considered important future issues to further improve its practicality.

References

1. Kadlec, S., Gabrys, B., Strandt, S.: Data-driven soft sensors in the process industry. Comput. Chem. Eng. **33**(4), 795–814 (2009)
2. Cheng, T., Harrou, F., Sun, Y., Leiknes, T.: Monitoring influent measurements at water resource recovery facility using data-driven soft sensor approach. IEEE Sensors J. **19**(1), 342–352 (2018)
3. Yang, S.H., Wang, X.Z., McGreavy, C., Chen, Q.H.: Soft sensor based predictive control of industrial fluid catalytic cracking processes. Chem. Eng. Res. Des. **76**(4), 499–508 (1998)
4. Jamil, R., Ming, L., Jamil, I., Jamil, R.: Application and development trend of flue gas desulfurization (FGD) process: a review. Int. J. Innov. Appl. Stud. **4**(2), 286–297 (2013)
5. Pascanu, R., Mikolov, T., Bengio, Y.: On the difficulty of training recurrent neural networks. In: Proceedings of the 30th International Conference on Machine Learning, pp. 1310–1318 (2013)
6. Cho, K., Bahdanau, D., Bengio, Y.: On the properties of neural machine translation: encoder-decoder approaches. arXiv preprint arXiv:1409.1259 (2014)
7. Hochreiter, S., Schmidhuber, J.: Long short-term memory. Neural Comput. **9**(8), 1735–1780 (1997)
8. He, K., Zhang, X., Ren, S., Sun, J.: Deep residual learning for image recognition. In: Proceedings of 2016 IEEE Conference on Computer Vision and Pattern Recognition, pp. 770–778 (2016)
9. Chen, T.Q., Rubanova, Y., Bettencourt, J., Duvenaud, D.K.: Neural ordinary differential equations. Adv. Neural Inf. Process. Syst. **31**, 6572–6583 (2018)
10. Jaeger, H.: The "echo state" approach to analysing and training recurrent neural networks. German National Research Center for Information Technology Report 148 (2001)
11. Racca, A., Magri, L.: Robust optimization and validation of echo state networks for learning chaotic dynamics. Neural Netw. **142**, 252–268 (2021)
12. Chang, H., Nakaoka, S., Ando, H.: Effect of shapes of activation functions on predictability in the echo state network. arXiv preprint arXiv:1905.09419 (2019)
13. Iinuma, T., Nobukawa, S., Yamaguchi, S.: Assembly of echo state networks driven by segregated low dimensional signals. In: Proceedings of 2022 International Joint Conference on Neural Networks, pp. 1–8 (2022)
14. Zhou, Y., Zhang, M., Lin, L.P.: Time series forecasting by the novel Gaussian process wavelet self-join adjacent-feedback loop reservoir model. Expert Syst. Appl. **198**(15), 116772 (2022)
15. Zhang, M., Wang, B., Zhou, Y.: Prediction of chaotic time series based on SALR model with its application on heating load prediction. Arab. J. Sci. Eng. **46**, 8171–8187 (2021)
16. Wang, L., Fonseca, R., Tian, Y.: Learning search space partition for black-box optimization using monte carlo tree search. Adv. Neural Inf. Process. Syst. **33**, 19511–19522 (2020)

WAG-NAT: Window Attention and Generator Based Non-Autoregressive Transformer for Time Series Forecasting

Yibin Chen[1], Yawen Li[2], Ailan Xu[3], Qiang Sun[1(✉)], Xiaomin Chen[1], and Chen Xu[1]

[1] School of Information Science and Technology, Nantong University, Nantong 226019, China
1910110082@stmail.ntu.edu.cn, {sunqiang,chenxm,xuchen}@ntu.edu.cn
[2] Shanghai Academy of Environmental Sciences, Shanghai 200235, China
[3] Jiangsu Province Nantong Environmental Monitoring Centre, Nantong 226019, China

Abstract. Time series forecasting plays a crucial part in many real-world applications. Recent studies have proven the power of Transformer to model long-range dependency for time series forecasting tasks. Nevertheless, the quadratic computational complexity of self-attention is the major obstacle to application. Previous studies focus on structural adjustments of the attention mechanism to achieve more efficient computation. In contrast, local attention has better performance than full attention in feature extraction and computation simplification due to the sparsity of the attention mechanism. Besides, in practice, the speed of inference is more significant, which is also a key factor. In response to these, we develop a novel non-autoregressive Transformer model based on window attention and generator, namely **WAG-NAT**. The generator allows one-step-forward inference. The window attention module contains a window self-attention layer to capture local patterns and a window interaction layer to fuse information among different windows. Experimental results show that WAG-NAT has a distinct improvement in prediction accuracy compared with RNNs, CNNs, and other previous Transformer-based models across various benchmarks. Our implementation is available at https://github.com/cybisolated/WAG-NAT.

Keywords: Time series forecasting · Non-autoregressive Transformer · Window attention · Deep learning

1 Introduction

By conveniently predicting future events or indicators, deep learning-based time series forecasting effectively improves the quality of decision-making. Therefore, time series forecasting plays a significant role in many fields, such as weather forecasting [6,9,17], logistics management [18], and economics [16].

L. Iliadis et al. (Eds.): ICANN 2023, LNCS 14259, pp. 293–304, 2023.
https://doi.org/10.1007/978-3-031-44223-0_24

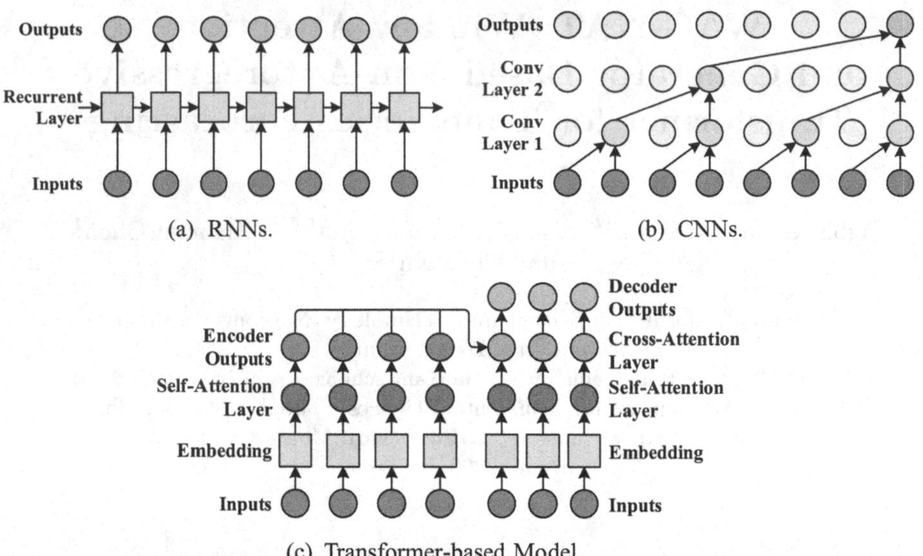

(a) RNNs.

(b) CNNs.

(c) Transformer-based Model.

Fig. 1. Three typical models for time series forecasting.

Figure 1 shows three mainstream deep learning models for time series forecasting based on sequence modeling as follows: (1) recurrent neural networks (RNNs), (2) convolutional neural networks (CNNs), and (3) Transformer-based networks.

RNNs are widely applied for time series forecasting and are developed into new variants, e.g., LSTM and GRU. RNNs can model complex temporal relationships within sequential data, therefore taking advantages in occasions emphasizing the importance of time order. Nevertheless, it is challenging for RNNs to train deep networks and model long-range dependency due to the vanishing gradient problem [15]. Moreover, RNNs' weakness of modeling complicated dynamic patterns could result in the underfitting of intricate data.

CNNs have been applied to the task of time series forecasting because of their ability to extract features from sequential data [12]. CNNs capture local patterns and extract relevant features from time series data. These characteristics elevate the suitability of CNNs in the local-pattern-dominated data processing. The emergency of temporal convolutional network (TCN) [4] is one of the milestones facilitating CNNs to shine in time series forecasting. TCN couples residual connections and dilated causal convolutions to model time series data, thus achieving significant results in various tasks. However, CNNs' capture of long-term dependency is not as effective as other models, e.g., LSTM. As a result, the prediction accuracy is relatively low for data with long-term dependency.

Transformer was originally developed for natural language processing (NLP), and now it has become the most popular and powerful tool for time series forecasting. A few fundamental studies have applied time series forecasting with

Transformer-based models. [13] proposed the first Transformer model with only a decoder for time series forecasting, which introduces causal convolution to produce queries and keys before the attention layer. The model incorporates local and global patterns, and outperforms the RNN-based models across various benchmarks. [19] has developed a novel paradigm that employs a vanilla Transformer to predict time series data. The historical sequential data is utilized as the input for the encoder, while training and inference procedures are similar to that of NLP. However, this approach preserves the autoregressive decoder architecture in NLP, resulting in large cumulative errors especially when predicting long sequences. The work in [20] extends the start token technique of NLP's "dynamic decoding" into a generative way. This generates an output sequence of a specified length and solves the problem of cumulative errors to a certain extent. Besides, the Informer model [20] has effectively reduced the computational complexity of the self-attention mechanism and has broken the memory bottleneck in stacking layers for long inputs. However, the start token technique requires a shift of partial encoder inputs to the decoder and filling the prediction position with zeros. This sacrifices the prediction capacity of the decoder and the padded zeros contribute little to prediction accuracy.

In this work, to overcome the challenges mentioned above, we build a novel generator between the encoder and decoder inspired by the work of [5,8]. This generator incorporates an embedded encoder sequence and a learnable positional encoding vector to create the required input sequences, therefore predict sequences without the restriction of the length. In addition, under the precondition that temporal effects might not correspond significantly with the increasing time intervals [1], a particular point in a time series does not attend to another point that is far away from it. We do not think it is necessary to perform attention computation to the whole sequence due to the sparsity of attention weights [13,20]. Therefore, we adopt the window attention mechanism [14] and use group convolution [10] to merge the information from different windows. The experimental result shows that the computational complexity of attention is effectively reduced. To sum up, our main contribution are as follows:

1. We design a novel non-autoregressive Transformer-based architecture for time series forecasting, including an encoder, a generator, and a decoder. The model generates the predicted sequences of specific length within one step forward regardless of training or inference.
2. We refine the structure of the generator to effectively combine location and future-known information, thus generating optimal sequences.
3. We introduce the window attention technique with complexity $\mathcal{O}(L)$ to enhance locality for time series forecasting. Different windows interact through group convolution to fully integrate information.

2 Problem Definition

We take multi-step forecasting as a scenario, and suppose y_t^i is the ground truth value of entity i at time t. Each entity denotes a logical grouping, such as measurements from items for sale, or data from different weather stations. For given observations of target $y^i_{t-k:t} = \{y^i_{t-k}, \cdots, y^i_t\}$ and covariates $\boldsymbol{x}^i_{t-k:t} = \{\boldsymbol{x}^i_{t-k}, \cdots, \boldsymbol{x}^i_t\}$ over a look-back window of size k, future known exogenous inputs $\boldsymbol{z}^i_{t-k:t+\tau} = \{\boldsymbol{z}^i_{t-k}, \cdots, \boldsymbol{z}^i_{t+\tau}\}$ and static metadata $\boldsymbol{s}^i_{t-k:t+\tau} = \{\boldsymbol{s}^i_{t-k}, \cdots, \boldsymbol{s}^i_{t+\tau}\}$ associated with the entity (e.g., meteorological station number) over the mentioned look-back window and forecasting horizon of size τ, time series forecasting model predicts future values of τ steps $\hat{y}^i_{t+1:t+\tau} = \{\hat{y}^i_{t+1}, \cdots, \hat{y}^i_{t+\tau}\}$, which can be formulated as

$$\hat{y}^i_{t+1:t+\tau} = f(y^i_{t-k:t}, \boldsymbol{x}^i_{t-k:t}, \boldsymbol{z}^i_{t-k:t+\tau}, \boldsymbol{s}^i_{t-k:t+\tau}), \tag{1}$$

where $f(\cdot)$ represents the learnt prediction function by the model. We note $\boldsymbol{x}^i_t$, $\boldsymbol{z}^i_t$ and $\boldsymbol{s}^i_t$ as a set of variables, and these variables are either real or categorical. To be simplified, the entity index i is omitted from formulas below unless necessary.

3 Proposed Model

In this section, we discuss the proposed WAG-NAT model in detail. WAG-NAT is a Transformer-based model, which adopts an encoder-decoder architecture. As shown in Fig. 2(b), we improve the canonical Transformer architecture on the encoder and the decoder to realize WAG-NAT. Meanwhile, a plug-and-play generator is introduced to produce decoder inputs, which allows the generation of long predicted sequences within one step forward.

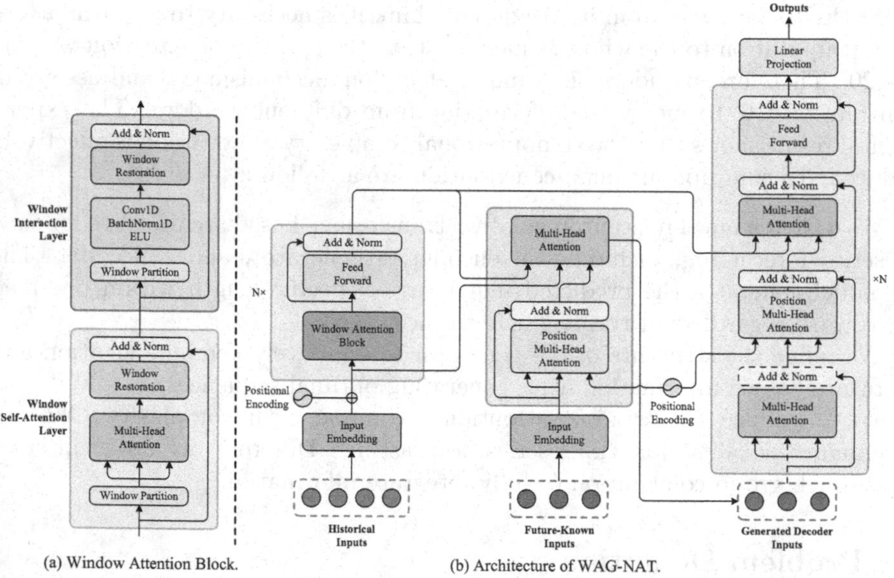

Fig. 2. (a) The detailed architecture of a window attention block; (b) the architecture of WAG-NAT.

3.1 Encoder: Reinforcing Computing Power with Window Attention Mechanism

The encoder is used to extract the long-range dependency, similar to its extraction of semantic information from source language text in translation tasks. The encoder accepts the historical sequence as inputs, i.e., the look-back window. We denote $\boldsymbol{X}_{t-k:t} = \{\boldsymbol{y}_{t-k:t} \circ \boldsymbol{x}_{t-k:t} \circ \boldsymbol{z}_{t-k:t} \circ \boldsymbol{s}_{t-k:t}\}$ as the encoder inputs, where $\circ$ represents the concatenation operation across feature dimension.

Feature Representation. Regarding feature representations of the Transformer-based models, most only allow input of real variables, therefore categorical variables are not utilized. However, those categorical variables could be crucial to the prediction (e.g., wind direction for weather forecasting). Here we apply entity embeddings [7] as feature representations for categorical variables, and add those to the embedded real variables. Besides, the sinusoidal positional encoding technique is used, then we get the representation of $\boldsymbol{X}_{t-k:t}$, denoted by $\mathcal{X}_{t-k:t} \in \mathbb{R}^{k \times d_m}$, where d_m is the embedding dimension.

Window Attention Block. A canonical self-attention module multiplies the input sequence with three different weight tensors to generate queries, keys and values, denoted by Q, K and V. Then, the scaled dot-product is performed, and can be formulated as

$$\mathcal{A}(Q, K, V) = \frac{\text{Softmax}(QK^\top)}{\sqrt{d_m}} V \tag{2}$$

According to the above formula, each query attends to all the keys, which causes quadratic time complexity over the length of queries. Generally speaking, if the selected lagged features have a large distance to the predicted point, these features may not contribute effectively to the accuracy of prediction. Therefore, we propose a *window attention block*, as presented in Fig. 2(a). Specifically, we divide the input sequence into multiple windows equidistantly. The window self-attention layer performs a self-attention operation within each window, and each query only attends to the keys from the same window. After that, various windows interact through the window interaction layer, where the information from different windows is fully integrated.

Window Self-Attention Layer. Denoting L the length of input sequence and w the length of input sequence in each window, called by window size, we attain $M = L/w$ windows. Then we get queries, keys and values of each window, thus obtaining M output sequences $\omega_i = \mathcal{A}(Q_i, K_i, V_i)$, where $i = 1, \cdots, M$ and $Q_i, K_i, V_i \in \mathbb{R}^{w \times d_m}$. The computational complexity of a canonical multi-head self-attention (MSA) module is $\mathcal{O}(\text{MSA}) = 4Ld_m^2 + 2L^2 d_m$, and that for a window multi-head self-attention (WMSA) module is

$$\begin{aligned} \mathcal{O}(\text{WMSA}) &= M(4wd_m^2 + 2w^2 d_m) \\ &= 4Ld_m^2 + 2wLd_m, \end{aligned} \tag{3}$$

where the latter term is linear to L when window size w is fixed. That is to say, the length of sequences is the bottleneck for a MSA module, but are totally affordable for a WMSA module.

Window Interaction Layer. Local information is sufficiently extracted within each window through the window self-attention layer. However, window self-attention lacks connections across windows and limits itself to local modeling. The group convolution technique is introduced to interact across windows and keep a temporal order, without affecting the efficient computing capacity. Supposing the outputs of window self-attention layer $\boldsymbol{\Omega} = \{\omega_i, \cdots, \omega_M\} \in \mathbb{R}^{M \times w \times d_m}$ and stacking features for each ω_i, a new set of windows $\boldsymbol{\mathcal{W}} \in \mathbb{R}^{(w \times d_m) \times M}$ can be obtained. Then, features are divided into w groups with respect to channels, and 1-D convolution is performed over each group, which achieves full interaction among windows and efficient computation at the same time.

Finally, a fully-connected layer is applied to produce the final outputs. We note that encoder layers can be stacked, as illustrated in Fig. 2(b), to fulfill further feature extraction depending on the forecasting task.

3.2 Generator: Producing Sequential Outputs Full of Fused Information with Position and Future-Known Covariates

A vanilla Transformer model predicts $\hat{y}_{t+1:t+\tau}$ in an autoregressive manner when inferring [19]. That is to say, τ-step forward is required, leading to large cumulative error and exorbitant cost of computation resources when the forecasting horizon increases. Since the forecasting horizon could be known in advance, we generate the inputs of the decoder within one step forward, and make the parallel inference feasible. The generator accepts future-known features $\boldsymbol{G}_{t+1:t+\tau} = \{\boldsymbol{x}_{t+1:t+\tau} \circ \boldsymbol{z}_{t+1:t+\tau} \circ \boldsymbol{s}_{t+1:t+\tau}\}$ as inputs. Adopting the same embedding strategy as the encoder, we attain the embedded sequences, denoted by $\boldsymbol{\xi}_{t+1:t+\tau} \in \mathbb{R}^{\tau \times d_m}$. In addition, we bring in a position multi-head attention (PMA) module, exactly operating as a canonical attention module despite of adopting positional encoding tensors as queries. Therefore, the positional information is successfully incorporated into the attention procedure. Plus, attended keys and values are position-sensitive, so more temporal information is preserved. Next, a multi-head attention is performed. In this case, queries, keys and values are outputs of the PMA module, outputs of the encoder, and embedded inputs of the encoder, respectively. To explain that, we aim to use sufficiently fused features with position and covariate information (corresponding to the queries) to query the appropriate encoder input features (corresponding to the values) to serve as the input for the decoder. Besides, after the adequate encoding procedure, the encoder output has integrated sufficient local and global information, and could be used as keys to improve query quality (corresponding to the keys). Subsequently, the decoder inputs $\boldsymbol{\phi}_{t+1:t+\tau} \in \mathbb{R}^{\tau \times d_m}$ are generated, which can be directly fed to the decoder without embedding.

3.3 Decoder: Generating Predictions Through One-Step Forward Process

The generated sequence $\phi_{t+1:t+\tau}$ is actually the weighted-sum representation of encoder inputs over length dimension with sufficient feature selection and information fusion. Also, the sequence is the most suitable decoder input. Consequently, the embedding layer is eliminated in the decoder. Unlike the decoder in a vanilla Transformer, WAG-NAT introduces a PMA module between two attention modules, as demonstrated in Fig. 2(b). The PMA module inherits the operation in the generator. With all the required sequential inputs, prediction sequence of length τ can be obtained through a one-step forward procedure, which is impressively time-saving compared with the autoregressive model. Note that the decoder layers are also the same stackable as encoder layers.

4 Experiment

4.1 Datasets

We conduct experiments on several datasets, namely *Electricity Transformer Temperature* [20] (namely {ETTh1, ETTh2} and ETTm1)[1] and *Beijing Multi-Site Air-Quality* (BMSAQ)[2]. The BMSAQ dataset includes hourly air pollutants data from 12 nationally controlled air quality monitoring sites in Beijing, ranging from 1 March 2013 to 28 February 2017. We take "ozone concentration" as the predictive target and the rest as covariates. A brief description of these datasets is listed in Table 1.

4.2 Experimental Settings

Baselines. We select five deep learning-based time series forecasting methods as baselines and divided them into four groups, namely (1) RNNs: {LSTMa [3]}, (2) CNNs: {TCN [4]}, (3) autoregressive Transformers: {vanilla Transformer [19]} and (4) non-autoregressive Transformers: {LogTrans [13], Informer [20]}.

Table 1. A brief depiction of datasets.

Datasets	Number of Variants	Number of Samples	Granularity	Task Type	Data Split (Training/Validation/Testing)
{ETTh1, ETTh2}	7	17,420	1 h	Multivariate	12/4/4 months[a]
ETTm1	7	69,680	15 min		
BMSAQ	13	420,768	1 h	Univariate	38/5/5 months

[a] We follow the data split method of [20].

[1] The ETT dataset was collected from https://github.com/zhouhaoyi/ETDataset.
[2] We obtained the BMSAQ dataset from https://archive.ics.uci.edu/ml/datasets/Beijing+Multi-Site+Air-Quality+Data.

Metrics. For all the benchmarks, two metrics including MSE $= \frac{1}{n}\sum_{i=1}^{n}(y_i - \hat{y}_i)^2$ and MAE $= \frac{1}{n}\sum_{i=1}^{n}|y_i - \hat{y}_i|$ are adopted to evaluate the performance of models over the test set, where n is the size of prediction window, y_i and $\hat{y}_i$ are the actual and estimated values of predictive target respectively. For multivariate forecasting task, we take the average over different targets.

Training and Tuning Details. We conduct training, testing and tuning procedures on a 12 GB Nvidia RTX 3060 GPU. The normalization technique is adopted to simplify model convergence. For the ETT dataset, we apply z-score normalization, consistent with [20]. For the BMSAQ dataset, we apply min-max normalization and label encoding for both real and categorical inputs respectively to each monitoring site, which is recognized as an independent entity.

Table 2. Ranges of hyperparameters for WAG-NAT on all the datasets.

Datasets	{ETTh1, ETTh2}	BMSAQ	ETTm1
Encoder Length (k)	{24, 48,168, 336}		{24, 48, 96, 288}
d_m	{32, 64, 128, 256, 512}		
Number of Heads	{1, 2, 4, 8}		
Number of Encoder Layers	{1, 2, 3}		
Number of Decoder Layers	{1, 2, 3}		
Window Size	{4, 6, 8, 12}		
Conv Kernel Size	{3, 5, 7}		
Learning Rate (log domain)	$[10^{-4}, 10^{-2}]$		
Dropout	{0.05, 0.1, 0.15, 0.2, 0.3}		

We use *Pytorch Lightning* as the training framework. We select MSE as the loss function and apply the Adam optimizer [11] during the training of the model. For hyperparameter tuning, we define the ranges of different hyperparameters and adopt *Optuna* [2] to optimize parameters automatically. After tuning, we use the optimal parameters for evaluation. For illustration, Table 2 presents the ranges of hyperparameters for our WAG-NAT model.

4.3 Results and Analysis

Table 3 lists the experimental results of all methods on four datasets over test set. We define a short-term forecasting task when $\tau \leq 48$, otherwise a long-term forecasting task. Our WAG-NAT model wins most benchmarks in short- and long-term forecasting.

Short-Term Forecasting. As for short-term forecasting, we conclude that (1) Transformer outperforms WAG-NAT on ETTh1 and BMSAQ datasets, and is less effective than WAG-NAT on other datasets. (2) WAG-NAT shows significant

Table 3. Performance comparison of different models on test set of the 4 datasets. The best results across various benchmarks are **bolded**.

Model		WAG-NET		Informer†		LogTrans		TCN		Transformer		LSTMa	
Metric		MSE	MAE	MSE	MAE	MSE	MAE	MSE	MAE	MSE	MAE	MSE	MAE
ETTh1	24[a]	0.473	0.479	0.577	0.549	0.686	0.604	0.472	0.501	**0.449**	**0.479**	0.650	0.624
	48	0.467	**0.486**	0.685	0.625	0.766	0.757	0.525	0.539	**0.466**	0.497	0.702	0.675
	168	**0.653**	**0.601**	0.931	0.752	1.002	0.846	0.743	0.670	0.714	0.633	1.212	0.867
	336	**0.857**	**0.731**	1.128	0.873	1.362	0.952	0.981	0.792	0.932	0.805	1.424	0.994
ETTh2	24	**0.261**	**0.384**	0.720	0.665	0.828	0.750	0.696	0.678	0.424	0.501	1.143	0.813
	48	**0.650**	**0.648**	1.457	1.001	1.806	1.034	0.836	0.964	1.522	0.949	1.671	1.221
	168	1.722	1.112	3.489	1.515	4.070	1.681	2.456	1.247	**1.622**	**0.973**	4.117	1.674
	336	**2.019**	**1.180**	2.723	1.340	3.875	1.763	3.096	1.496	2.662	1.219	3.434	1.549
ETTm1	24	**0.274**	**0.346**	0.323	0.369	0.419	0.412	0.598	0.504	0.315	0.389	0.621	0.629
	48	**0.334**	**0.387**	0.494	0.503	0.507	0.583	0.590	0.548	0.445	0.462	1.392	0.939
	96	**0.413**	**0.448**	0.678	0.614	0.768	0.792	0.468	0.497	0.464	0.482	1.339	0.913
	288	**0.547**	**0.551**	1.056	0.786	1.462	1.320	0.721	0.663	0.681	0.631	1.740	1.124
BMSAQ[b]	24	2.858	3.710	3.526	4.187	3.590	4.779	3.026	**3.376**	**2.735**	3.686	3.690	4.693
	48	3.338	4.357	3.557	4.455	3.900	4.679	3.710	4.529	**3.237**	**4.187**	4.147	5.174
	168	**3.595**	**4.651**	3.854	5.013	4.075	4.874	3.729	4.743	3.739	4.976	4.348	4.865
	336	**3.816**	**4.957**	4.168	5.235	4.245	5.010	4.184	5.191	4.250	5.059	5.214	5.454

†To be fair, we reimplement Informer to support entity embeddings for categorical inputs, as mentioned in Sect. 3.1.

[a] This column represents the forecasting horizon τ.

[b] Due to the diversity of normalization methods, the scale of metrics on BMSAQ dataset varies from other datasets. To align the numerical format, the scale of metrics is 10^{-3}.

improvement compared to the RNN-based model LSTMa with an average MSE decrease of 45.69% ($\tau = 24$) and 47.52% ($\tau = 48$), which means the attention mechanism extracts global information better, and is less likely to lose memories temporally as found in the case of RNNs. (3) Compared to the CNN-based model, namely TCN, WAG-NAT also displays better results, indicating local and global information is integrated efficiently with the window attention mechanism, and hence the effect is better than only extracting local information. (4) WAG-NAT surpasses the generative Transformers, i.e., Informer and LogTrans, which reveals that the proposed generator can decide optimal sequences as decoder inputs. Besides, it justifies the choice of queries, keys, and values of the multi-head attention module in the generator.

Long-Term Forecasting. With regard to long-term forecasting, we suggest (1) the RNN-based LSTMa achieves the worst results across benchmarks, revealing that long-range dependency is lost when the memory path gets longer substantially. (2) Concerning the vanilla Transformer, the cumulative error enlarges as τ increases, and thus becomes a bottleneck of the autoregressive Transformer. (3) Compared with generative Transformers, WAG-NAT gains an MSE decrease of 31.91% ($\tau = 168$) and 25.56% ($\tau = 336$) on the ETTh1, ETTh2 and BMSAQ datasets on average, demonstrating the mechanism of the proposed generator is more capable and aligned.

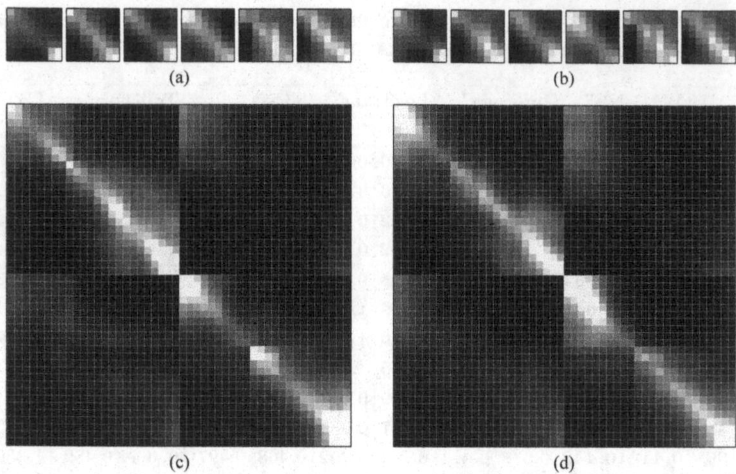

Fig. 3. Heatmaps of attention scores of WMSA and MSA after softmax activation at encoder layer 1. (a) and (b) represents attention scores of WMSA from window 1 to 6 at head 1 and 2 respectively. In the same way, (c) and (d) denotes attention scores of MSA at head 1 and 2. The brighter the square, the greater the corresponding attention score.

4.4 Effectiveness of Window Attention Mechanism

To illustrate the effectiveness of the window attention mechanism, we construct a WAG-NAT model with two encoder layers on the ETTh1 dataset where $k = 48$ and $w = 8$. Meanwhile, we replace the WMSA module of the encoder in WAG-NAT with MSA to investigate the distribution of different attention scores. Figure 3 presents the attention scores of {head 1, head 2} at encoder layer 1. From Fig. 3(c) and (d), we could observe that areas around the diagonal are brighter, which means most queries are prone to attend to neighboring keys. Besides, inactive queries suggest that redundant information is extracted, resulting in a waste of computing resources. Nevertheless, the attention scores of the WMSA module reveal that most queries in each window are active, which eliminates the capture of redundant information and further proves the rationality of the window attention mechanism.

4.5 Sensitivity Analysis

We perform the sensitivity analysis of the proposed WAG-NAT model on the ETTh1 dataset.

Window Size. Figure 4a presents the effect of window size $w \in \{4, 6, 8, 12\}$ on prediction accuracy at different encoder lengths $k \in \{24, 48, 96, 168, 240, 336\}$. The MSE tends to rise as k increases. Besides, a larger window size ($w = 8, 12$) performs worse prediction than a small window size, especially when input

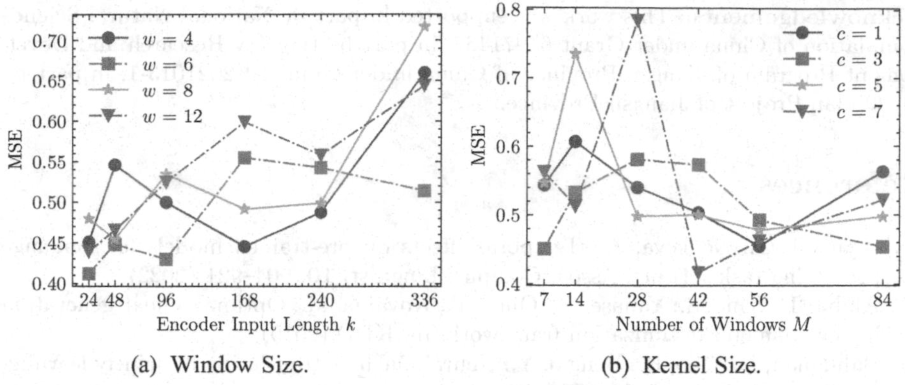

(a) Window Size. (b) Kernel Size.

Fig. 4. Results of parameter sensitivity benchmarks.

sequence are long. Instead, $w = 6$ is a preferred value, whether for short-term or long-term forecasting tasks.

Kernel Size. Furthermore, to investigate the most efficient approach to interacting among windows under different window numbers M, we carry out several sets of experiments with different kernel sizes $c \in \{1, 3, 5, 7\}$. Specifically, we fix $k = 336$ and gradually increase $w \in \{4, 6, 8, 12, 24, 48\}$, then we get $M \in \{84, 56, 42, 28, 14, 7\}$. From Fig. 4b, we observe that MSE tends to decrease when M grows, which indicates that better results could be achieved when more windows are involved in the interaction. In addition, we find that the smaller the kernel size becomes, the greater accuracy of the prediction results. To conclude, local information is fully extracted, and compact window interaction yields better results. Surprisingly, even if $c = 1$, it works very well in most cases, which may indicate that adequate capture of the local patterns is a more important factor for time series forecasting.

5 Conclusion

In this work, we proposed a novel non-autoregressive Transformer model WAG-NAT, featuring a generator and window attention mechanism. The proposed window attention mechanism contains a window self-attention layer to achieve locality improvement and a window interaction layer to fuse local and global information from different windows. In addition, the one-step-forward prediction of WAG-NAT elevates the speed of inference. Results of various benchmarks on diverse real-world datasets demonstrate the capability and advancement of our model. Furthermore, extensive experiments were conducted to prove the effectiveness of the window attention mechanism and offer insights into parameter selection.

Acknowledgements. This work was supported in part by National Natural Science Foundation of China under Grant 61971467, in part by the Key Research and Development Program of Jiangsu Province of China under Grant BE2021013-1, in part by the Qinlan Project of Jiangsu Province.

References

1. Agarwal, O., Nenkova, A.: Temporal effects on pre-trained models for language processing tasks. Trans. Assoc. Comput. Linguist. **10**, 904–921 (2022)
2. Akiba, T., Sano, S., Yanase, T., Ohta, T., Koyama, M.: Optuna: a next-generation hyperparameter optimization framework. In: KDD (2019)
3. Bahdanau, D., Cho, K., Bengio, Y.: Neural machine translation by jointly learning to align and translate. In: ICLR (2015)
4. Bai, S., Kolter, J.Z., Koltun, V.: An empirical evaluation of generic convolutional and recurrent networks for sequence modeling. arXiv:1803.01271 (2018)
5. Chen, K., Chen, G., Xu, D., Zhang, L., Huang, Y., Knoll, A.: NAST: non-autoregressive spatial-temporal transformer for time series forecasting. arXiv preprint arXiv:2102.05624 (2021)
6. Chen, Y., Chen, X., Xu, A., Sun, Q., Peng, X.: A hybrid CNN-transformer model for ozone concentration prediction. Air Qual. Atmos. Hlth. **15**(9), 1533–1546 (2022)
7. Gal, Y., Ghahramani, Z.: A theoretically grounded application of dropout in recurrent neural networks. In: NIPS (2016)
8. Gu, J., Bradbury, J., Xiong, C., Li, V.O.K., Socher, R.: Non-autoregressive neural machine translation. In: ICLR (2018)
9. Hewage, P., Trovati, M., Pereira, E., Behera, A.: Deep learning-based effective fine-grained weather forecasting model. Pattern Anal. Appl. **24**(1), 343–366 (2021)
10. Ioannou, Y., Robertson, D., Cipolla, R., Criminisi, A.: Deep roots: improving CNN efficiency with hierarchical filter groups. In: ICCV (2017)
11. Kingma, D.P., Ba, J.: Adam: a method for stochastic optimization. In: ICLR (2015)
12. Koprinska, I., Wu, D., Wang, Z.: Convolutional neural networks for energy time series forecasting. In: IJCNN (2018)
13. Li, S., et al.: Enhancing the locality and breaking the memory bottleneck of transformer on time series forecasting. In: NIPS (2019)
14. Liu, Z., et al.: Swin transformer: hierarchical vision transformer using shifted windows. In: ICCV (2021)
15. Noh, S.H.: Analysis of gradient vanishing of RNNs and performance comparison. Information **12**(11), 442 (2021)
16. Nosratabadi, S., et al.: Data science in economics: comprehensive review of advanced machine learning and deep learning methods. Mathematics **8**(10), 1799 (2020)
17. Salman, A.G., Kanigoro, B., Heryadi, Y.: Weather forecasting using deep learning techniques. In: ICACSIS (2015)
18. Woschank, M., Rauch, E., Zsifkovits, H.: A review of further directions for artificial intelligence, machine learning, and deep learning in smart logistics. Sustainability **12**(9), 3760 (2020)
19. Wu, N., Green, B., Ben, X., O'Banion, S.: Deep transformer models for time series forecasting: the influenza prevalence case. arXiv preprint arXiv:2001.08317 (2020)
20. Zhou, H., et al.: Informer: beyond efficient transformer for long sequence time-series forecasting. In: AAAI (2021)

A Novel Encoder and Label Assignment for Instance Segmentation

Huiyong Zhang, Lichun Wang(✉), Shuang Li, Kai Xu, and Baocai Yin

Beijing Key Laboratory of Multimedia and Intelligent Software Technology, Beijing Artificial Intelligence Institute, Beijing University of Technology, Beijing 100124, China
{zhyzhy,shuangli,xukai}@emails.bjut.edu.cn, {wanglc,ybc}@bjut.edu.cn

Abstract. SparseInst, a recent lightweight instance segmentation network, achieves better balance between efficiency and precision. However, the information contained in the single-layer features output by the encoder is not rich enough and the label assignment strategy leads to imbalance between positive and negative samples. In order to further improve the instance segmentation performance, we propose LAIS network including a novel feature encoding module and a Multi-Step Hungarian matching strategy (MSH). By combining multi-scale feature extraction and inter-layer information fusion, the encoder outputs features with more detailed and comprehensive information. By performing multiple rounds of one-to-one Hungarian matching, MSH eliminates the imbalance and duplication during the sample allocation. Experiments show that LAIS is more accurate than SparseInst without significantly increasing parameters and GFLOPs. In particular, LAIS reached 33.8% AP on the COCO val, 1.0% higher than SparseInst when using the same ResNet-50 Backbone.

Keywords: Instance Segmentation · Single-Output · Feature Extraction · Label Assignment

1 Introduction

Instance segmentation, not only classifies each pixel in the image, but also distinguishes different instances of the same category, which is a very challenging task in the field of computer vision. As an essential link in the environment perception process of robots, unmanned vehicles and other agents, instance segmentation consuming less computation resources is more practical.

Same with the other computer vision tasks, convolution is widely used to obtain features in different instance segmentation frameworks [4,8,23]. Usually, different convolution kernels are learned to obtain features with different attributes from an image. With the deepening of the network, the receptive field of the convolution kernel is gradually enlarged. So single feature map cannot include the semantic information from different scales at the same time, because

L. Iliadis et al. (Eds.): ICANN 2023, LNCS 14259, pp. 305–316, 2023.
https://doi.org/10.1007/978-3-031-44223-0_25

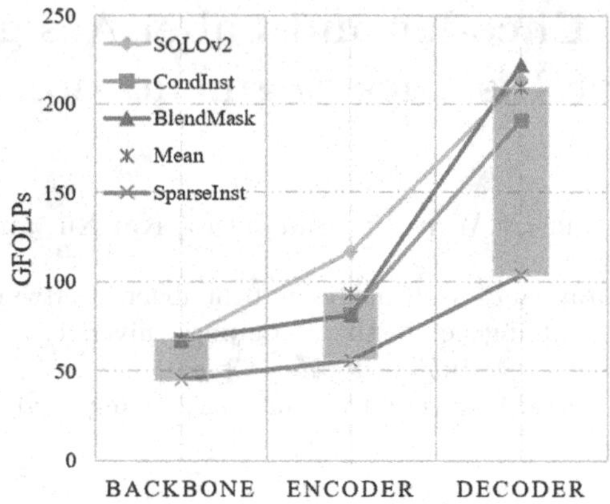

Fig. 1. Comparison of cumulative GFLOPs of instance segmentation models. The blue lines correspond to models using multi-output encoder, and the orange line corresponds to model having single-output encoder. The green bar shows the average gap of GFLOPs between instance segmentation models with different structures. (Color figure online)

the semantic information of small-scale objects lies in lower layer feature map and the semantic information of large-scale objects lies in higher layer feature map. As a result, the output features of the last layer of the backbone cannot fully represent objects of all scales. By adopting multi-output structure, feature pyramid network (FPN) [12] allows each level of features to represent objects within a specific scale range, and enables information fusion between layers to solve the problem of under-expression and inadequate fusion of features. When used in instance segmentation models, the multi-output structure expands the whole network, which increases the memory burden and GFLOPs, as shown in Fig. 1. For achieving a balance between accuracy and performance, recent researches developed single-output structure [3,4,33]. But these methods cannot take into account the extraction and fusion of features completely. In order to improve the quality of single-output feature, we design an encoder based on the FPN strategy, which can fully extracts semantic information and fuses detail information.

In order to train the instance segmentation model efficiently, an effective label assignment strategy for computing the matching relationship between predicted mask and ground truth (GT) is necessary. Earlier instance segmentation networks obtain the matching by setting an IoU threshold. When a GT is small-scale, its intersection with a prediction is usually small. On the contrary, when a GT is large-scale, its intersection with a prediction is usually large. So, the IoU threshold based methods allocate fewer positive samples to small objects, resulting in unbalanced distribution of training samples between small and large objects. Hungarian [21] assigns one prediction for each GT, achieving balance but the number of positive samples is far less than the number of negative samples when an image includes fewer instances. The imbalance between positive samples and negative samples will make the model training suboptimal. To solve this problem, Uniform Matching strategy [3] assigns same number of predictions to each GT, but one predication may be repeatedly assigned to several GTs. The duplicated assignment will lead to inaccurate model learning. In order to achieve non-duplicate and balanced assignment, we propose Multi-Step Hungarian Matching (MSH) strategy, which performs multiple rounds of Hungarian assignment.

Our contributions are mainly as follows:

1. We design a simple and effective plug-and-play multi-scale feature extraction and fusion structure, which can extract the deep semantic features of objects with different sizes while retaining detailed information.
2. We design a general label assignment strategy MSH, which achieves non-duplicate and balanced assignment between predictions and GTs.
3. We propose a simple instance segmentation framework, which has high efficiency and achieves considerable accuracy. Experiments show that the proposed framework is effective.

2 Related Works

2.1 Encoder Structure

Multi-output Encoder. The widely used multi-output structure is FPN which greatly promotes the feature extraction effect. PANet [15] enhances the entire feature hierarchy and boosts information flow by adding an additional bottom-up pathway to FPN. ssFPN [18] extracted a new scale sequence feature of FPN to strengthen feature information of small objects. EfficientDet [22] proposed a weighted bi-directional FPN, which achieves easy and fast multi-scale feature fusion. LibraRCNN [17] strengthened each level of features of FPN with the integrated balanced features.

Single-output Encoder. In order to achieve higher computation efficiency, some networks adopted encoder with single-output structure, such as YOLOF [3] and SparseInst [4]. The single-output encoder outputs one feature map to the decoder, and basically has the same feature expression ability as FPN, which greatly reduces the memory consumption and model complexity.

2.2 Label Assignment

One-to-many Assignments. Max-IoU [13] determined positive and negative samples based on the IoU of predictions and GTs. ATSS [32] dynamically selected positive and negative samples according to the statistical characteristics of objects. By defining the GT and background as supplier and the anchor as demander, OTA [6] regarded the allocation problem as Optimal Transport (OT) problem to obtain a globally optimal allocation strategy. Uniform Matching [3] allocated K samples to each GT regardless of the size of object, which maintains the relative balance among samples.

One-to-one Assignments. POTO [24] dynamically allocates foreground samples according to the quality of classification and regression simultaneously. Hungarian algorithm [4] assigned the most suitable unique candidate for each GT, so the number of positive samples is equal to the number of GT.

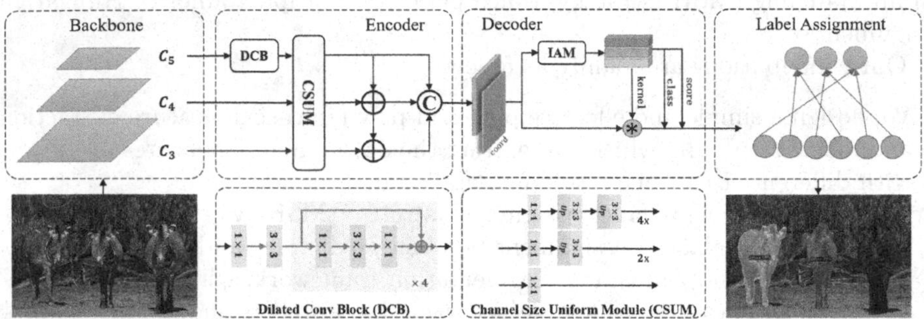

Fig. 2. The overall pipeline of model. Encoder (Discussed in Sect. 3.1) extracts and fuses features. Decoder performs prediction task. Label Assignment (Discussed in Sect. 3.2) assign masks to GTs during training phase.

3 Proposed Approach

Current instance segmentation methods, such as CondInst [23] and SOLO [25, 26], have achieved considerable accuracy, but when training the model, the FPN-based structure and label allocation strategy need a lot of memory and a long time.

SparseInst [4] replaced the multi-output structure of encoder with single-output structure, reducing the calculation and memory burden. In addition, the network predicted a fixed number of proposals, making the network more lightweight, and used the Hungarian algorithm to match proposals and GTs, improving inference speed of the model by avoiding NMS during the inference process. At the same time, SparseInst [4] innovatively proposed the concept of instance activation map (IAM). Each instance activation map represents an instance in the image. However, we argue that the structure of encoder and the label assignment strategy can be further improved to make the network more efficient. The pipeline of our model is shown in Fig. 2, and the following sections describe the details.

3.1 Encoder Using Multi-scale Extraction and Fusion

Pei et al. [19] has proved that the combination of C3-C5 could achieve strong performance with the lowest number of parameters and training memory. Therefore, we only use C3-C5 as the input of Encoder. In order to make the feature output by encoder contain multi-scale information, we apply the dilated convolution block (DCB) [3] to extract feature, as shown in Fig. 3a. Since the information

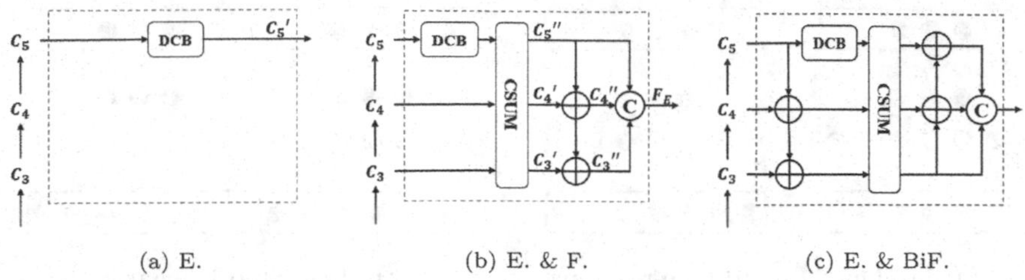

(a) E. (b) E. & F. (c) E. & BiF.

Fig. 3. Different Encoder Structure. (a) Only Multi-scale Feature Extraction Module. (b) Multi-scale Feature Extraction and One-way Fusion Module . (c) Multi-scale Feature Extraction and BiFusion Module.

of C_5 is enough to recover multi-scale information [11], we only perform feature extraction on C_5, which can be expressed as:

$$C_5' = \mathrm{DCB}(C_5) \tag{1}$$

where $\mathrm{DCB}(\cdot)$ denotes the dilated convolution block, which is used to further extract the semantic information C_5' on the basis of C_5. DCB set different dilation coefficients to extract semantic information under different receptive fields.

In order to fully fuse semantic information and detail information, we design a new structure for feature fusion. Figure 3b depicts the one-way fusion structure, the feature fusion process can be expressed as:

$$\begin{aligned} C_5'', C_4', C_3' &= \mathrm{CSUM}(C_5', C_4, C_3), \\ C_4'' &= f(C_5'' + C_4'), \\ C_3'' &= f(C_4'' + C_3'), \\ F_E &= \mathrm{Concat}(C_3''; C_4''; C_5'') \end{aligned} \tag{2}$$

$\mathrm{CSUM}(\cdot)$ is the channel and size uniform module, which transforms the channels and sizes of C_5', C_4, C_3 to be uniform. The structure of CSUM is shown in Fig. 2. Through addition operation, features C_4' and C_3' are sequentially fused with higher layer features to further promote the flow of different types of feature information in the network. The feature mapping function $f(\cdot)$ consists of a 3×3 convolution, mapping the features into a new feature space. F_E is concatenation of the fused features and the output of encoder.

In order to allow different types of feature information to flow more fully in network, we design a bidirectional fusion structure as shown in Fig. 3c. Its performance is slightly better than one-way fusion, but it costs more training time.

3.2 Label Assignment Using Multi-step Hungarian

In order to achieve balanced and non-duplicated assignment between predictions and GTs, we propose MSH strategy as shown in Algorithm 1, which equals decomposing the one-to-many matching process (Fig. 4b) into multiple one-to-one matching (Fig. 4a) procedures, and each step is optimal.

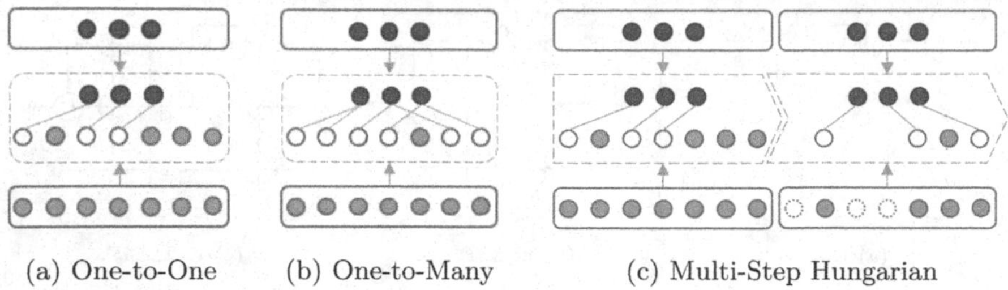

(a) One-to-One (b) One-to-Many (c) Multi-Step Hungarian

Fig. 4. Comparison of processes with different label assignment strategies. Green circles represent GT set, blue circles represent prediction set, and empty circles represent matched predictions.

Specifically, in each round of allocation, Hungarian algorithm is used to select the optimal matching predictions M_m^t. The matched predictions M_m^t are added to the candidate list M_m and deleted from the prediction set M_p, then the next round of allocation is performed on the remaining predictions and the GTs. This ensures that the optimal one-to-one assignment is achieved for each allocation and avoids to repeatedly assign same prediction to the different GTs.

In addition, the matching costs C_g^p follow the pairwise dice-based matching scores $C(i,k)$ in SparseInst, which is the cost between the i-th prediction and the k-th ground-truth. The matching score ensures that the prediction and GT of each pair of assignments are considered from the perspective of global optimization.

After several rounds, MSH ensures that all GTs, regardless of size, can match the same number of positive samples without duplication. The balanced and no-duplicate assignment makes the network converge more easily during training. The MSH matching process is shown in Fig. 4c. It can be expressed as follows,

$$\mathrm{OTM}_{MSH}(P,G) = \bigcup_{t=1}^{T} \mathrm{OTO}_H(P_t, G) \tag{3}$$

Algorithm 1: Multi-Step Hungarian Matching

Input: The set of prediction masks M_p; the set of ground truth masks M_g; The times the Hungarian algorithm was executed T.

Output: The matched predictions masks M_m

Initialize: $M_m = \varnothing$;

while t = *1, ..., T* **do**

  Compute matching costs C_g^p between M_p and M_g;

  M_m^t, M_g = HungarianMatch(M_p,M_g,C_g^p);

  $M_m = M_m \cup M_m^t$;

  $M_p = M_p - M_m^t$;

end

return M_m

---

where $\mathrm{OTO_H}(\cdot, \cdot)$ represents the one-to-one allocation process using the Hungarian algorithm, $\mathrm{OTM_{MSH}}(\cdot, \cdot)$ represents the allocation using MSH algorithm, and T is the number of rounds of allocation. $P_t \in R^N$ is the subset of predictions. G is the set of GTs.

4 Experiments

In this section, we evaluate LAIS on MS COCO, and perform ablation study for each component.

Dataset and Evaluation Metrics. All of our experiments are conducted on the large-scale dataset MS COCO [14] with 80 different categories and different annotation forms, which can be used for object detection, instance segmentation, keypoint detection and other tasks. Specifically, we train LAIS on train2017(118k images) and evaluate it on val2017(5k images), and take MS COCO AP as the main evaluation metrics.

Training Details. Unless specifically emphasized, the training process of LAIS follows the SparseInst training scheme, and uses the standard model ResNet-50 [9] pre-trained on ImageNet [5] as the backbone. Based on the Detectron2 [27] framework, we adopt AdamW [16] optimizer to carry out 90k iterations on 3090 GPUs. The training batch size is 48 and the initial learning rate is 0.0001. Xavier initialization [7] is applied to initialize newly defined network layers. The learning rate is divided by 10 at 60k and 80k iterations respectively, and the weight decay is 0.05. The loss coefficients are consistent with the SparseInst. In addition, we set the default number (N) of instance activation maps as 300.

Inference Details. During the inference stage, when an image is input, the model outputs the predicted masks and corresponding confidence scores. Since MSH outputs multiple predictions for one GT, a Non-Maximum Suppression (NMS) was used to remove duplicate predictions, which is different from SparseInst.

4.1 Main Result

Table 1 shows the accuracy comparison between LAIS and other instance segmentation methods. The experimental results show that LAIS achieves competitive performance on the COCO dataset. Specifically, with the same ResNet-50 backbone and 12 epochs, our method achieves a gain of 3.2% AP over the SparseInst. Especially on AP_{75} and $\mathrm{AP_L}$ metrics, LAIS achieves 4.0% and 4.7% improvement respectively. After training for 36 epochs, the accuracy is further improved to 33.8 AP. It should be noted that the SparseInst compared with our method uses Basic-IAM and without data augmentation, which is different from the setting reported in the original paper but consistent with our method. In addition, the multi-output methods predict separately according to the features at different scales. The representation ability of multi-output models is stronger than single-output methods, which leads to most of the multi-output methods are better than single-output methods. We compare the parameters and GFLOPs of SparseInst and LAIS, the specific results are shown in Table 2.

Table 1. Instance segmentation performance comparison of different models on MS COCO val (%). † means the model is trained with Basic-IAM and has no data augmentation, which is consistent with LAIS.

Encoder	Methods	Backbone	Epochs	AP	AP_{50}	AP_{75}	AP_S	AP_M	AP_L
MultiOutput	MaskRCNN [8]	R-50	12	34.6	56.5	36.6	15.4	36.3	49.7
	MEInst [31]	R-50	12	32.2	53.9	33.0	13.9	34.4	48.7
	BlendMask [2]	R-50	12	34.3	55.4	36.6	14.9	36.4	48.9
	CenterMask-Lite [10]	R-50	48	32.9	-	-	12.9	34.7	48.7
	PolarMask [28]	R-50	12	29.1	49.5	29.7	12.6	31.8	42.3
	YOLACT-550 [1]	R-50	12	28.2	46.6	29.2	9.2	29.3	44.8
	PointINS [20]	R-50	12	32.2	51.6	33.4	13.4	34.4	48.4
	BorderPointsMask [30]	R-50	12	31.4	52.0	32.8	16.3	34.4	42.8
	PolarMask++ [29]	R-50	12	30.2	52.6	30.8	14.4	32.5	43.1
SingleOutput	SparseInst† [4]	R-50	12	28.7	47.7	29.7	10.7	30.4	44.5
	SparseInst† [4]	R-50	36	32.8	53.1	34.2	15.1	35.3	48.3
	LAIS	R-50	12	**31.9**	**51.0**	**33.7**	**12.7**	**33.7**	**49.2**
	LAIS	R-50	36	**33.8**	**53.1**	**35.8**	**14.2**	**35.9**	**50.7**

Table 2. Comparison of parameters and GFLOPs on MS COCO using ResNet-50 as the backbone.

Model	Epochs	#param(M)	GFLOPs	AP
SparseInst	12	31.584M	90.8 ± 8.2	28.7
LAIS	12	32.045M	94.8 ± 8.6	31.9

4.2 Ablation Study

In this section, we separately conduct multiple experiments to analyze and prove the effectiveness of individual modules. Unless otherwise specified, the settings of ablation experiments use ResNet-50 as Backbone and 1× training schedule.

Ablation on Different Structures of Encoder. The number of instance activation maps (N) is set as 100, which aims to make a fair comparison with the SparseInst. The results are shown in Table 3a. Specifically, only using the feature extraction module DCB in the encoder, the model accuracy is close to (in AP) or even exceeds (in AP_L) SparseInst, which demonstrates that the features extracted by LAIS are more sufficient. When the cross-layer method similar to FPN is added in the structure, the model accuracy is 30.2 AP, which has a large improvement in AP_S (+3.9%). When adding FPN-style fusion before CSMU, the performance has slight improvement but more training time is required. We ultimately adopt one-way fusion structure in the Encoder.

Number of Instance Activation Maps. More activation maps help to find suitable instances. The experimental results in Table 3b show that the accuracy improves as the number of action maps increases, and the performance tends to saturate at 400. When setting the number of action maps as 400, more training time is required, so we set the number of instance activation maps as 300.

Table 3. Ablation experiments on different components of LAIS on MS COCO val. The model uses ResNet-50 as backbone. Pos. means positive.

(a) Encoder Structures.

Structures	AP	AP_S	AP_M	AP_L
SparseInst	28.7	10.7	30.4	44.5
E.	27.4	7.7	28.1	45.7
E. & F.	30.2	11.6	**31.9**	**47.2**
E. & BiF.	**30.3**	**12.3**	31.8	45.7

(b) Number of IAM.

N	AP	AP_S	AP_M	AP_L
100	28.7	10.7	30.4	44.5
200	29.4	**11.3**	**31.0**	45.1
300	**29.5**	10.4	30.9	**46.2**
400	29.4	**11.3**	30.8	44.6

(c) Number of Pos. Samples.

Multi-T	AP	AP_S	AP_M	AP_L
Multi-1	29.5	10.4	30.9	46.2
Multi-2	**30.6**	**11.7**	32.3	46.4
Multi-3	30.2	11.3	31.6	**47.2**
Multi-4	30.4	**11.7**	**32.4**	47.1

(d) Different Matching Strategies.

Matching Strategy	AP	AP_S	AP_M	AP_L
Hungarian Matching [21]	29.5	10.4	30.9	46.2
Uniform Matching [3]	30.6	11.4	**32.5**	**48.1**
MSH Matching	**30.6**	**11.7**	32.3	46.4

(e) Ablation of Proposed Components.

Encoder	MSH	AP	AP_S	AP_M	AP_L
		29.5	10.4	30.9	46.2
✓		30.2	11.6	31.9	47.2
	✓	30.6	11.7	32.3	46.4
✓	✓	**31.9**	**12.7**	**33.7**	**49.2**

Table 4. Time-consuming comparison of two matching strategies.

Matching Strategy	total time(s)	iters	time/iter
Uniform Matching	0.282239	20	0.0141 s
Multi-Step Hungarian	0.019552	20	0.0009 s

Number of Assigned Positive Samples. Theoretically, when the number of positive samples assigned to each GT increases, the regression of instance activation locations becomes easier. Table 3c shows the experimental results when assigning different numbers of predictions to one GT, and the accuracy is the highest when assigning two predictions to one GT. Considering the time complexity of the algorithm and the accuracy of the model, the number of assigned positive samples is set to 2.

Comparison of Different Matching Strategies. Table 3d shows experiment results when using different strategies for matching predictions and GTs. The number of instance activation maps in this experiment is 300. Considering the AP, MSH exceeds Hungarian Matching and achieves same 30.6% as Uniform Matching. When the same AP is obtained, MSH assigns two positive samples to each GT, while Uniform Matching assigns four positive samples to each GT. This means MSH is more efficient.

Ablation of Proposed Components. The contribution of different components to the whole model is evaluated through ablation experiments. The results in Table 3e show that the proposed encoder structure and MSH strategy are both reasonable and effective.

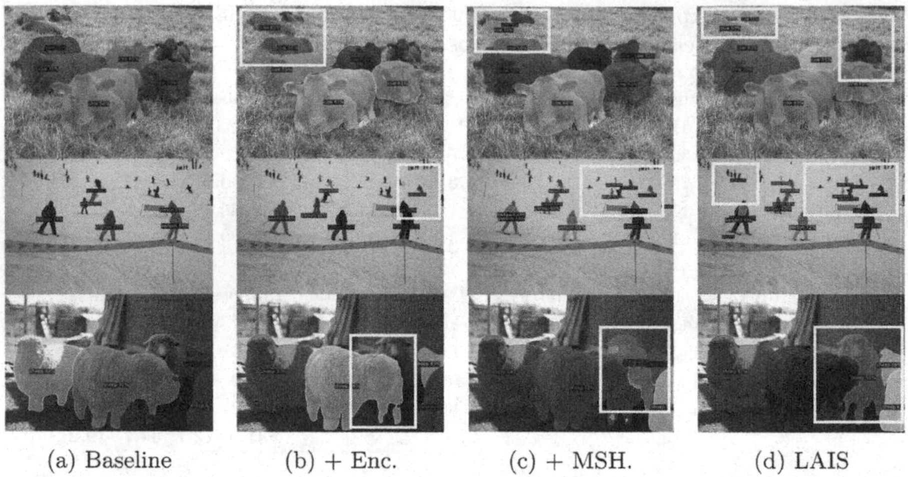

(a) Baseline (b) + Enc. (c) + MSH. (d) LAIS

Fig. 5. Visualization of Instance Segmentation Results for Ablation of Different Components.

4.3 Visualization

We give the visualization results of SparseInst, LAIS only using our Encoder design, LAIS only using MSH Matching, and the complete LAIS, as shown in Fig. 5. Taking the second row as an example, it can be seen that using our encoder structure (Fig. 5b) and MSH (Fig. 5c) can further improve the instance segmentation effect. This conclusion is consistent with the results of the ablation experiments in Table 3e. In addition, as far as the last column is concerned, LAIS performs well in the face of different sizes objects.

4.4 Further Analysis

With the same accuracy, MSH consumes less time and allocates fewer samples than Uniform Matching. We measured the time spent for 20 iterations of each strategy, and then calculated the average time of each matching strategy, the results are shown in Table 4. Under the same experimental condition, the speed of MSH is 14 times faster than that of Uniform Matching, and the experiment proves that MSH is more efficient.

5 Conclusion

In this paper, we design an efficient feature extraction fusion structure, which obtains better feature representation for single-output instance segmentation. Furthermore, we propose a new label assignment strategy named Multi-Step Hungarian matching, which can eliminate imbalance and duplication problem. Equipped with our module and strategy, the accuracy of network is improved, demonstrating its effectiveness. In future research, we will further explore efficient instance expression of decoder.

Acknowledgments.. This work is supported by The National Key R&D Program of China (No. 2021ZD0111902), NSFC (U21B2038, 61876012), Foundation for China university Industry-university Research Innovation (No. 2021JQR023).

References

1. Bolya, D., Zhou, C., Xiao, F., Lee, Y.J.: YOLACT: real-time instance segmentation. In: CVPR (2019)
2. Chen, H., Sun, K., Tian, Z., Shen, C., Huang, Y., Yan, Y.: BlendMask: top-down meets bottom-up for instance segmentation. In: CVPR (2020)
3. Chen, Q., Wang, Y., Yang, T., Zhang, X., Cheng, J., Sun, J.: You only look one-level feature. In: CVPR (2021)
4. Cheng, T., et al.: Sparse instance activation for real-time instance segmentation. In: CVPR (2022)
5. Deng, J., Dong, W., Socher, R., Li, L.J., Li, K., Fei-Fei, L.: ImageNet: a large-scale hierarchical image database. In: CVPR (2009)
6. Ge, Z., Liu, S., Li, Z., Yoshie, O., Sun, J.: Ota: optimal transport assignment for object detection. In: CVPR (2021)
7. Glorot, X., Bengio, Y.: Understanding the difficulty of training deep feedforward neural networks. In: AISTATS (2010)
8. He, K., Gkioxari, G., Dollár, P., Girshick, R.: Mask R-CNN. In: ICCV (2017)
9. He, K., Zhang, X., Ren, S., Sun, J.: Deep residual learning for image recognition. In: CVPR (2016)
10. Lee, Y., Park, J.: CenterMask: real-time anchor-free instance segmentation. In: CVPR (2020)
11. Li, Y., Mao, H., Girshick, R., He, K.: Exploring plain vision transformer backbones for object detection. arXiv preprint arXiv:2203.16527 (2022)
12. Lin, T.Y., Dollár, P., Girshick, R., He, K., Hariharan, B., Belongie, S.: Feature pyramid networks for object detection. In: CVPR (2017)
13. Lin, T.Y., Goyal, P., Girshick, R., He, K., Dollár, P.: Focal loss for dense object detection. In: ICCV (2017)
14. Lin, T.Y., et al.: Microsoft coco: common objects in context. In: ECCV (2014)
15. Liu, S., Qi, L., Qin, H., Shi, J., Jia, J.: Path aggregation network for instance segmentation. In: CVPR (2018)
16. Loshchilov, I., Hutter, F.: Decoupled weight decay regularization. In: ICLR (2019)
17. Pang, J., Chen, K., Shi, J., Feng, H., Ouyang, W., Lin, D.: Libra R-CNN: towards balanced learning for object detection. In: CVPR (2019)
18. Park, H.J., Choi, Y.J., Lee, Y.W., Kim, B.G.: ssFPN: scale sequence (s^2) feature based feature pyramid network for object detection. arXiv preprint arXiv:2208.11533 (2022)
19. Pei, J., Cheng, T., Fan, D.P., Tang, H., Chen, C., Van Gool, L.: OSFormer: one-stage camouflaged instance segmentation with transformers. In: ECCV (2022)
20. Qi, L., et al.: PointINS: point-based instance segmentation. IEEE TPAMI **44**(10), 6377–6392 (2021)
21. Stewart, R., Andriluka, M., Ng, A.Y.: End-to-end people detection in crowded scenes. In: CVPR (2016)
22. Tan, M., Pang, R., Le, Q.V.: EfficientDet: scalable and efficient object detection. In: CVPR (2020)
23. Tian, Z., Shen, C., Chen, H.: Conditional convolutions for instance segmentation. In: ECCV (2020)

24. Wang, J., Song, L., Li, Z., Sun, H., Sun, J., Zheng, N.: End-to-end object detection with fully convolutional network. In: CVPR (2021)
25. Wang, X., Kong, T., Shen, C., Jiang, Y., Li, L.: Solo: Segmenting objects by locations. In: ECCV (2020)
26. Wang, X., Zhang, R., Kong, T., Li, L., Shen, C.: Solov2: dynamic and fast instance segmentation. In: NIPS (2020)
27. Wu, Y., Kirillov, A., Massa, F., Lo, W.Y., Girshick, R.: Detectron2. https://github.com/facebookresearch/detectron2 (2019)
28. Xie, E., et al.: PolarMask: single shot instance segmentation with polar representation. In: CVPR (2020)
29. Xie, E., Wang, W., Ding, M., Zhang, R., Luo, P.: Polarmask++: enhanced polar representation for single-shot instance segmentation and beyond. IEEE TPAMI **44**(9), 5385–5400 (2021)
30. Yang, H., Zheng, L., Barzegar, S.G., Zhang, Y., Xu, B.: BorderPointsMask: one-stage instance segmentation with boundary points representation. Neurocomputing **467**, 348–359 (2022)
31. Zhang, R., Tian, Z., Shen, C., You, M., Yan, Y.: Mask encoding for single shot instance segmentation. In: CVPR (2020)
32. Zhang, S., Chi, C., Yao, Y., Lei, Z., Li, S.Z.: Bridging the gap between anchor-based and anchor-free detection via adaptive training sample selection. In: CVPR (2020)
33. Zhao, H., Shi, J., Qi, X., Wang, X., Jia, J.: Pyramid scene parsing network. In: CVPR (2017)

A Transformer-Based Framework for Biomedical Information Retrieval Systems

Karl Hall[1(✉)], Chrisina Jayne[1], and Victor Chang[2]

[1] School of Computing, Engineering and Digital Technologies, Teesside University, Middlesbrough, UK
{K.Hall,C.Jayne}@tees.ac.uk

[2] Aston Business School, Aston University, Birmingham, UK
V.Chang1@aston.ac.uk

Abstract. With the increasing amount of electronic biomedical research available, it is becoming difficult for scientists and researchers to effectively access and process this information. In this study, a framework is proposed for biomedical information retrieval using state-of-the-art transformer-based natural language processing methods, focusing on discovering genetic relationships and mechanisms that contribute to diseases and other health conditions. Data processing, model evaluation and algorithm transparency through the use explainable artificial intelligence are proposed as the key components of the methodology. The framework is explained and demonstrated in the context of COVID-19 in a topical and systematic manner, and is designed so that it can be adapted for use in other biomedical settings.

Keywords: Information retrieval systems · Natural language processing · Document ranking · Transformer models · Explainable AI

1 Introduction

In the age of Big Data, a vast amount of information is becoming readily available, especially in the healthcare sector. Efforts have been made to collect and store this information in large repositories to increase availability for effective access and processing. However, due to the volume of the information, a suitable solution is difficult to find. Academic researchers and medical practitioners would benefit greatly from a streamlined information retrieval (IR) framework that can support systematic research and critical development of medical interventions.

From the lay perspective, traditional search engines provide an easy way for users to search for required information. Similarly, from a scientific perspective, question answering (QA) and other IR systems have been developed, allowing more effective access to biomedical data. IR systems for biomedical research papers can be developed by implementing artificial intelligence (AI), and natural

L. Iliadis et al. (Eds.): ICANN 2023, LNCS 14259, pp. 317–331, 2023.
https://doi.org/10.1007/978-3-031-44223-0_26

language processing (NLP) techniques. Generalised biomedical IR systems, such as [11] have been developed using such methods. More recently, QA systems such as [22,31], were developed to retrieve information on COVID-19 at the start of the pandemic.

One of the primary areas of biomedical research is concerned with the biological and genetic mechanisms of viruses, bacteria and other pathogens and the interactions between them. Understanding the role genetics plays in this regard can provide crucial insights that can be used to reduce the impacts of medical conditions. One well-known example is that the SARS-CoV-2 spike protein is known to bind to and downregulate (cause a lower level of production of) the angiotensin-converting enzyme 2 (ACE2). ACE2 downregulation, when combined with COVID-19 infection, is known to increase the likelihood of multiple organ damage or failure, including the brain, lungs, heart, liver and kidneys [23]. This is just one such example, with many more lesser or unknown interactions between COVID-19, genetic mechanisms and other diseases. Understanding these genetic impacts and interactions can help develop effective treatments for diseases [21].

In this study, an IR framework is proposed allowing for rapid and easy access to biomedical research information. In particular, the focus is on developing a framework for the development of genetic IR systems. To achieve this, the effectiveness of a wide range of approaches is explored by assessing NLP and document ranking (DR) techniques. Consequently, this makes it easier for researchers, biomedical professionals and others to more easily process the large amount of genetic information available. In particular, utilising document ranking ensures that the most relevant information is easily accessible.

Technical NLP approaches to this problem have varied over the years. More traditional methods focused on the frequency of search terms. Both classical machine learning models and deep learning models have also been used in this regard. At the forefront of NLP research is the transformer model [33]. Transformer models offer a modern approach, typically showing better performance at NLP tasks than more traditional methods. New transformer models with state-of-the-art language processing capabilities are being developed on a regular basis and advancements in this area are expected to continue. Therefore, this study proposes a transformer-based IR system.

While a large amount of research has been done by biomedical scientists and bioinformatics experts, no current up-to-date transformer-based state-of-the-art IR system exists primarily focusing on the genetic issues and impacts surrounding COVID-19. Biomedical scientists are typically advancing their research in this area more quickly than computer scientists. Additionally, the issue of the COVID-19 pandemic is fresh and topical in the minds of everyone, given its impact over the past three years. Therefore, in this study, a biomedical IR framework is clearly presented in the context of COVID-19.

The main contributions of the framework are as follows. Firstly, it provides a way for developing effective genetic IR systems featuring transformer models. This begins by exploring the best approaches for data selection and model evaluation. The framework also focuses on being expansible and designed in such a way that it can be applied to other areas of biomedical research. Ultimately, the goal of the framework is to provide a more effective approach to biomedical professionals, allowing for more effective and timely interventions.

The structure of the paper is as follows. Firstly, related research is reviewed (Sect. 2), focusing on data selection (Sect. 2.1), IR systems (Sect. 2.2), and IR system evaluation (Sect. 2.3) in the context of COVID-19. The framework is then presented (Sect. 3), and each component of the framework is explained: data processing (Sect. 3.1), models considered (Sect. 3.2), model evaluation metrics (Sect. 3.3) and explainability (Sect. 3.4). Experiments are conducted in Sect. 4 to justify the model selection for the framework. Finally, the adoption of the framework, limitations and future work perspectives are discussed.

2 Related Work to the Case Study

2.1 COVID-19 Literature Datasets

A large number of COVID-19 data sets are derived from research publication databases, showcasing scientific findings and discussion about the impacts of COVID-19. CORD-19 and LitCovid are the two most commonly utilised databases used in COVID-19 research analysis, especially when NLP techniques are involved.

The COVID-19 Open Research Dataset (CORD-19) [34] is both the largest and the most well-known example. CORD-19 is a joint collaboration between many key institutions, such as the US government, various national health organisations and the Allen Institute for AI.

LitCovid [8] is another similar database providing access to over 325,000 publications through PubMed which are related to COVID-19 research. LitCovid has been used for a wide range of NLP applications, such as text summarisation [16], document search [13] and question answering systems [4].

2.2 COVID-19 Information Retrieval Systems

Several academic search engines have developed special features to help users find COVID-19 related research. For instance, Google Scholar has recently created a specific COVID-19 research category. Users can easily search and filter results based on their preferences.

Moreover, independent research groups have used machine learning algorithms to develop COVID-19 specific search engines. One such engine is the COVID-19 Search Engine (CO-SE) [24], which implements transformer-based models and natural language processing to improve search results. It allows users to search COVID-19 literature with more precise keywords to obtain the most relevant results.

Another notable COVID-19 IR system is the COVID-19 Literature Surveillance Team. This team uses artificial intelligence to screen literature and filter out irrelevant information. It also helps researchers to access the most relevant and up-to-date information about COVID-19.

While these IR systems are accelerating the progress of COVID-19 research, they focus on the general landscape of COVID-19 research rather than narrowing their efforts in a more precise manner. The groundwork these systems have put in place has opened the door for researchers to start targeting more domain-specific applications of IR systems for COVID-19 research.

2.3 TREC-COVID Challenge

The TREC-COVID challenge [25] was a scientific IR challenge that was organised in response to the COVID-19 pandemic. The challenge aimed to develop effective search and retrieval strategies for COVID-19 research literature. The primary goal of the challenge was to assist researchers, healthcare professionals, and policymakers in their efforts to combat the pandemic. The challenge involved developing algorithms and systems to retrieve relevant scientific literature related to COVID-19 from a large collection of research articles.

The TREC-COVID data set consisted of more than 200,000 articles related to COVID-19, including preprints and published articles. Participants in the challenge were provided with a set of information queries related to COVID-19, and they were tasked with developing IR models and algorithms that could effectively identify relevant articles from the data set. The challenge was divided into several tracks, including ad-hoc retrieval, question answering, and document similarity.

In particular, a range of different algorithms was explored to optimise performance, such as ensemble models combining transformer-based models such as BERT with other model components [5]. In addition, approaches such as continuous active learning and utilising document set processing [35] and neural ranking models [38] were explored.

The TREC-COVID challenge has been a significant event in the development of IR systems and has led to the development of new algorithms for COVID-19 research. It has also highlighted the importance of effective search and retrieval strategies for scientific literature in response to a rapidly evolving public health crisis.

3 Framework Architecture and Methodology

The framework architecture can be divided into components as shown in Fig. 1. The subsections in this section correspond to each of the individual components of the framework architecture.

3.1 Data Collection

The first step in the data collection component is to identify and obtain the most suitable data set. For the case study, the CORD-19 database has been

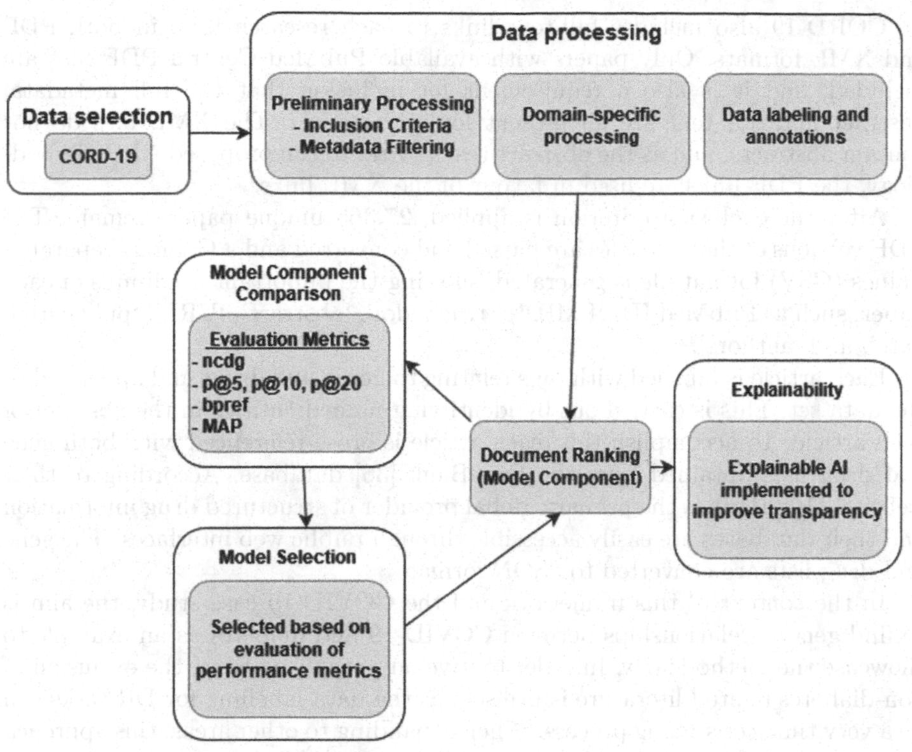

Fig. 1. Proposed framework architecture.

determined to be the best data set by the majority of COVID-19 researchers and is outlined in Sect. 2.1.

The original version of the CORD-19 data set was initially made available on March 16, 2020. The final version from June 2022 consists of over 1 million articles and is the version used in this study. It includes articles from a range of other biomedical-focused article repositories, such as medRxiv, arXiv, Medline, PMC and the World Health Organisation's COVID-19 database.

In this study, a purpose-built data set based on CORD-19 is prepared by collecting an up-to-date version of CORD-19. In order to ensure consistency and accuracy of data, preliminary data processing is then conducted.

3.2 Data Processing

Firstly, each article is assessed and cross-referenced to systematic inclusion criteria to ensure only the most relevant data is included. There are many papers within the database published before 2020. These papers mostly focus on research on historical coronaviruses and not COVID-19. Therefore, only research published between January 1, 2020 and June 2, 2022 is included. Only papers published in peer-reviewed research journals and conferences are included.

CORD-19 also includes full-text links to each research item in both PDF and XML formats. Only papers with available PubMed Central PDF files are included, and it is also a requirement for inclusion that the full metadata, abstract and full text are all present for each article. The XML files do not contain abstracts, and as the abstract text is vital to the proposed NLP methodology, the PDF links are used in favour of the XML links.

After the exclusion criterion is applied, 27,363 unique papers remain. The PDF versions of these articles are parsed and converted and a Comma-Separated Values (CSV) format file is generated, showing the important attributes of each paper, such as PubMed ID ('PMID'), 'title', 'doi', 'abstract', 'URL', 'publication date', and 'authors'.

Each article is labelled with tags relating to genes and drugs and appended to the data set. This is carried out by identifying named entities in the abstract of each article. To accomplish this, each article is cross-referenced with both gene and drug lists obtained from the DrugBank [36] database. According to their website, DrugBank is the primary global provider of structured drug information and their databases are easily accessible through public web interfaces. The gene and drug lists are converted to JSON format.

In the context of this framework and the COVID-19 case study, the aim is to find genetic relationships between COVID-19 and diabetes as an example to showcase the methodology. In order to save on processing time, the exclusion of non-diabetes related literature is utilised, as the data labelling for DR tasks can be a very time-consuming process. When expanding to other areas, this approach is recommended in order to both streamline the data being used and focus on the domain-specific area. The latter is especially important as it has been shown to improve DR performance. Finally, the data needs to be labelled in order to evaluate the system's document ranking performance.

3.3 Model Component

The model is a crucial component of the framework, as it heavily contributes towards the effectiveness of any IR system. A wide range of transformer models are explored and evaluated to gain insight into the optimal characteristics of the system's model component.

BERT [12] is a pre-trained deep learning model for natural language processing (NLP) tasks. It uses a transformer architecture that was introduced in the seminal proposal [33], which laid the groundwork for more complex transformer-based models. BERT is most frequently used as a benchmarking tool with which to compare the effectiveness of other models, as it has proven to be a robust and reliable model.

BERT can be used for document ranking by first encoding the query and each document separately using BERT's pre-trained transformer layers. The resulting vectors are then used to compute a relevance score for each document, which is used to rank the documents. To compute the relevance score, a dot product is used between the query vector and each document vector. This produces a score that measures the similarity between the query and the retrieved document.

The advantage of using BERT transformer-based modelling for document ranking is its ability to capture the context and meaning of words in a query and document. This can lead to a more accurate ranking compared to traditional bag-of-words or lexical matching approaches.

RoBERTa [19] is a larger variation of the BERT model. It is based on the same transformer architecture as BERT, but it incorporates a number of modifications that improve its performance on NLP tasks, including document ranking.

There are several reasons for this. Firstly, RoBERTa uses a larger pre-training corpus than BERT. Secondly, it employs a longer training schedule [19], implementing dynamic masking to improve the ability to generalise to new tasks. Finally, it uses an improved training objective that results in better learning of sentence representations.

Past research [29,32] has clearly shown that RoBERTa offers an improvement over BERT across a range of NLP tasks. Furthermore, the same conclusion was reached in this case study.

DistilBERT in contrast to RoBERTa, Distilled BERT, or DistilBERT [27] is a smaller and faster variation of BERT. Its smaller size and faster speed are achieved by using knowledge distillation [6], thereby compressing the original BERT model while retaining most of its performance and preserving the original BERT architecture.

As a result of this, DistilBERT typically offers slightly lower performance than other transformer-based models, but DistilBERT still has a valuable place. When lower amounts of computational power are available, or when computational speed is a priority in the training process, DistilBERT tends to offer approximately a 50% reduction in this regard.

BioBERT [18] is a variant of the BERT model that has been pre-trained on biomedical text. As such, it has been shown to be exceptionally effective across various biomedical natural language processing tasks. The key factor contributing to the performance of BioBERT is domain specificity as it was trained on biomedical data. As a result, it performs better when processing biomedical literature compared to BERT [9].

In this study, BioBERT was shown to perform better on document ranking tasks than any of the models not trained on domain-specific data. Therefore, as expected we can hypothesise that a domain-specific approach is likely to be the optimal solution for document ranking COVID-19 literature.

BioLinkBERT [37], like BioBERT, is a variant of BERT pre-trained on biomedical text. It was specifically designed to capture biomedical concepts and relationships from structured knowledge graphs, including gene ontology.

Because of this, BiolinkBERT is more specific for the domain of the case study than BioBERT and it performs better on document ranking tasks as a result.

RankingSVM [7] is a classical ML model popular for use in document ranking. It is based on Support Vector Machines and it learns by using a margin-based ranking function. This method has historically been shown to be effective in IR and DR tasks. However, it has fallen behind in effectiveness when combined with newer state-of-the-art transformer-based models.

In this study, RankingSVM was primarily used as a benchmark as a means to explore approaches outside of those using transformer architecture and to verify the hypothesis that transformer-based models would be better models to recommend for the framework.

3.4 Model Component Evaluation

In order to evaluate the IR system, evaluation metrics were selected that were also used in the TREC-COVID shared task evaluation. These metrics are Normalized Discounted Cumulative Gain (NDCG), precision at different cutoffs of the ranking ($p@n$), mean average precision (MAP), and Bpref (a preference-based IR measure).

Normalized Discounted Cumulative Gain. NDCG is a performance metric for document ranking quality often used to evaluate the effectiveness of IR systems. More specifically, it evaluates the correctness of the order (ranking) of the returned results. A higher NDCG score indicates more effective document ranking results. Similarly to the TREC-COVID challenge evaluation, the top 20 returned results are considered for NDCG evaluation ($NDCG@20$). NDCG is computed as:

$$NDCG_p = \frac{DCG_p}{IDCG_p} \tag{1}$$

where DCG is $DCG_p = \sum_{i=1}^{p} \frac{rel_i}{log_2(i+1)}$, rel_i is the relevance value of the ith article in the ranking, and $IDCG$ is the DCG that an ideal ranking an article would have at position p.

Precision at n. Precision is the proportion of the returned results relevant to the search query $(TP + FP)$ that are successfully retrieved (TP). For IR systems, precision performance is evaluated with regard to different ranges of numbers of documents. For example, the precision with regards to the top n number of search results is often evaluated, where n could be 1, 5, 10, 20, or other numbers. Precision is computed as follows:

$$\frac{TP}{TP + FP} \tag{2}$$

where TP = true positives and FP = false positives.

Similarly, precision at n is typically expressed as $p@n$, where p is precision and n is the number of articles considered in the evaluation, from the highest-ranked article down to n inclusive.

Bpref. The *bpref* [26] evaluation metric is a measure of ranking quality in information retrieval. It was introduced as a modification of the traditional precision and recall metrics used in information retrieval.

Bpref stands for binary preference and is designed to measure the effectiveness of a ranking algorithm based on the order in which documents are presented to a user. This metric considers both the number of relevant documents retrieved and their position in the ranked list.

In *bpref*, each relevant document is assigned a preference score of 1, while irrelevant documents are assigned a preference score of 0. The score is calculated as the maximum difference between the proportion of relevant documents that are ranked higher than the current position and the proportion of irrelevant documents that are ranked higher than the current position. More specifically, *bpref* is defined as:

$$bpref = \frac{1}{R}\sum_{r}\left(1 - \frac{min(number\ of\ n\ above\ r, R)}{min(N, R)}\right) \quad (3)$$

where R is the number of relevant judgments per topic.

The final *bpref* score is calculated as the average preference score across all relevant documents. The metric provides a useful measure of how effectively a ranking algorithm orders relevant documents, regardless of the number of irrelevant documents in the ranked list.

Mean Average Precision is a commonly used evaluation metric for measuring the effectiveness of IR systems, evaluating the effectiveness of ranking algorithms with respect to a given query. MAP can be utilized to assess the relevance of IR systems' returned search results by comparing them against a matching annotated list of related documents for a particular query. One drawback of this approach is that this often requires expert human input.

MAP is calculated by computing the average precision (AP) for the relevant documents contained within the ranked list. AP is a measure of the precision of the algorithm at a particular rank in the list. It considers both the number of documents retrieved, their individual relevance, and also their position within the ranked list of returned results.

The AP for a given search query is then calculated as the average of the AP scores for all documents returned. The MAP score is the mean of the AP scores across all search queries used. AP is defined as:

$$AP = \sum_{n}(R_n - R_{n-1})P_n \quad (4)$$

with MAP being the mean of all APs, where R_n and P_n are the precision and recall respectively at the nth threshold [2].

MAP is a widely used evaluation metric to measure the effectiveness of IR systems, particularly for tasks such as document retrieval and web search. It provides a useful summary of the overall effectiveness of a ranking algorithm across a data set, taking into account both precision and recall. A higher MAP score indicates that the ranking algorithm is more effective at retrieving relevant documents.

3.5 Model Selection

After evaluating the range of suitable models available, a decision needs to be made on which model the model component in the system architecture should be based.

By most evaluation metrics, such as the Biomedical Language Understanding and Reasoning Benchmark (BLURB) [15], BiolinkBERT is currently the most effective transformer-based model. It currently sits at the top of the BLURB leaderboard, which is used for comparing the performance of transformer models for NLP tasks. The experiments in this case study confirm this, with BioLinkBERT achieving the highest scores across all evaluation metrics of the models tested. Additionally, it is the most domain-specific to our study. Therefore this model is the most relevant and most effective model for IR systems designed for extracting genetic relationships from biomedical literature.

3.6 Explainability

Explainable AI (XAI) refers to the ability of an AI system to explain the reasoning behind its decisions or predictions in a way that can be easily understood by humans. One challenge with transformer-based models is that they can be difficult to interpret and understand, especially when they are making complex predictions based on large amounts of data. XAI can help address this issue by providing ways to explain the reasoning behind the model's outputs.

As AI models become more complex, their capabilities become higher. However, it also becomes more difficult to explain more complex models and their outputs. XAI tools such as LIME [14] and SHAP [30] seek to address this problem by providing solutions to better explain how the model component works. Incorporating explainability in the framework can enable biomedical practitioners to use AI in a more effective manner while also increasing both their understanding and trust in such approaches. One recent study [20] suggests that LIME is a more stable algorithm and well-suited for explainability of results when compared to SHAP. This is particularly true when high-importance attributes exist within the model component for document ranking. LIME is also much more time efficient than most other XAI models, making it ideal for use when computational power and infrastructure are important.

XAI can provide explanations of how biomedical documents are ranked in document ranking systems based on the input query with a high level of detail. Approaches such as Rank-LIME [10] have been developed specifically as an XAI tool for document ranking and IR systems. Rank-LIME provides local model-agnostic explanations for document ranking algorithms. As an example, consider the query "What are the genetic links between COVID-19 and diabetes?". Rank-LIME can show for the top n results which keywords, phrases, and named entities contributed to the ranking of each document. This may include highlighting specific genes or other biomedical terms related to the input query that were identified to determine the rankings for each document. Another approach is to use visualisation techniques such as heat maps to highlight the most relevant parts of the input text.

The explainability of transformer models is a significant problem, as their complexity makes this difficult. However, XAI techniques for transformer models have recently been successfully developed. For example, feature attribution [1] involves identifying the features or inputs that had the biggest impact on the model's output, and counterfactual explanations, which involve generating alternative inputs that would have resulted in different outputs from the model. Other examples of XAI approaches for transformer models include Layer-wise Relevance Propagation [17], Gradient-Input [28], and more recently, the use of attention rollouts [3].

In conclusion, XAI techniques are becoming increasingly important, especially as these models are used in more critical applications where the ability to explain model predictions is essential for building trust and ensuring transparency and accountability. XAI can be a useful tool to highlight the key terminology in the documents and how they contribute to document ranking in biomedical IR systems. Future work will focus on experiments testing and evaluating different XAI approaches for explaining the document ranking component of the proposed framework.

4 Experiments, Discussion and Future Work

4.1 Experiments

Each of the models are evaluated on their performance in document ranking. To evaluate the document ranking performance of the models, an experiment is conducted based on calculating the relevance scores of retrieved documents. The model component gives each retrieved document a relevance score with regard to a number of pre-defined search queries. Relevance scores are given for each document based on how relevant they are to each search query. The relevance scores are used to rank the retrieved documents from the most relevant to the least relevant and are generated in JSON format. For each query, the document rankings are cross-referenced with an annotated data set developed by domain experts to determine the effectiveness of the document ranking lists provided by each model. The results for each model are then evaluated and compared using the evaluation metrics in the model component evaluation component (NDCG, p@n, *bpref* and MAP) outlined and explained in Sect. 3.4.

Of the models evaluated, BiolinkBERT achieved the best results across all evaluation metrics (Table 1). This can be attributed to a number of factors.

Table 1. Document ranking performance evaluation.

Model	ndcg@20	p@5	p@10	p@20	bpref	MAP
BERT	0.2177	0.3301	0.2605	0.2200	0.1506	0.0653
RoBERTa	0.2528	0.3620	0.2953	0.2555	0.1730	0.0923
DistilBERT	0.2120	0.3196	0.2492	0.2072	0.1444	0.0603
BioBERT	0.3371	0.3988	0.3763	0.3451	0.2132	0.1267
BiolinkBERT	**0.4012**	**0.4527**	**0.4333**	**0.4183**	**0.2420**	**0.1692**
RankingSVM	0.1493	0.2146	0.1988	0.1644	0.1294	0.0416

BiolinkBERT has the highest domain specificity with regards to the biomedical domain, additionally providing an emphasis on genetics when compared to other models. It excels in finding genetic relationships through the use of IR systems. Therefore, this suggests that BiolinkBERT is the most suitable for adoption in the context of the proposed framework. In a more general sense, we can determine that domain specificity is one of the primary factors when deciding what approach to take for the design of IR systems. This is further confirmed by the other heavily domain-specific model, BioBERT, which performs significantly better than any of the models which are not domain-specific.

Another reason for BiolinkBERT excelling in information retrieval, and in particular, document ranking lies in its training methods. It takes a novel approach to incorporate document link knowledge by also training on hyperlinks between documents (for example, by pretraining on Wikipedia hyperlinks and PubMed citation links). It is understandable, therefore, that a better understanding of relationships between documents results in higher levels of performance on information retrieval and document ranking tasks.

While transformer-based models are relatively new, advances in this area have been rapidly improving. New state-of-the-art models are being developed quickly and often. In computer science, one year is a very long time with regard to state-of-the-art performance. BiolinkBERT is one of the most recently developed transformer-based models at this time, with the most recent official release coming in December 2022. Therefore, it is crucial for researchers to utilise the latest approaches and advances in this area in order to ensure the best possible performance in information retrieval systems.

4.2 Discussion

One of the goals of this project was to develop an easy-to-follow framework methodology that is easy to adopt and extended for use in other areas. While the proposed framework is showcased through the lens of a more topical application in COVID-19 research, it has been designed in such a way that it can be extended for use in other areas of biomedical research. Each component of the framework can be extended to other biomedical domains and utilised in a similar manner. In particular, with the exception of CORD-19, many data repositories are not specific to one particular disease. PubMed, for example, extends across the entirety of the biomedical and life sciences domain and is suitable for use in any biomedical NLP research setting.

With that in mind, the goal is that this framework, or individual components of the framework, can be adopted by biomedical researchers to improve the efficiency of their working methodologies. With time this becomes more important as both the size and complexity of the data available increases.

As the framework is designed at the conceptual level, additional steps be taken with regard to its usability. For example, it is suggested that this approach is supplemented with either a web interface for public access or a private program interface for use in private healthcare or research settings. Additionally, implementing a data analysis pipeline will help with producing data visualisation in a way that makes the findings of any conducted study to be explained.

4.3 Limitations and Future Work

Two main limitations of the framework proposal have been identified to be addressed and improved through future research.

Firstly, the number of experiments conducted to validate the proposed framework is one such limitation. The document ranking performance evaluation is conducted on one dataset in one highly specific domain. More extensive experiments need to be conducted with a wider range of datasets and across a wider range of domains. The latter in particular can demonstrate that the framework can be replicated successfully for use in other biomedical areas outside of what was presented in the COVID-19 case study.

Secondly, the validation and use of XAI is a key component of the framework methodology. The document ranking performance was validated through performance evaluation experiments. Experiments with different XAI techniques will be conducted to validate the inclusion of XAI as part of the framework. This aspect will be explored more thoroughly in future work to provide a better understanding of how XAI can help explain complex predictions made by transformer-based models in biomedical IR systems.

5 Conclusion

As the amount and complexity of available data increases across all domains, it becomes increasingly important that biomedical research can be conducted in a structured and coherent manner. IR systems are also suffering from the increase in Big Data approaches. As such, efficient access and analysis of this information is needed to accelerate developments in biomedical applications. Furthermore, any algorithms used for analysis should be transparent and explainable in an efficient manner. In such a time-sensitive environment as biomedical science, the value of efficient research cannot be understated. The COVID-19 pandemic has recently shown the importance of acting in a timely manner when lives are at stake on a global scale. Preparation for such an event is particularly important.

Indeed, one of the reasons why the pandemic had such a devastating impact is due to how unprepared both global and national healthcare systems were for such an event. By proposing a standardized framework, such an approach can help research organisations be more prepared for health crises and efficient IR systems are crucial when addressing such issues in a timely fashion.

References

1. Abhishek, K., Kamath, D.: Attribution-based XAI methods in computer vision: a review. arXiv preprint arXiv:2211.14736 (2022)
2. Agafonova, Y., Gaidel, A., Surovtsev, E., Kapishnikov, A.: Segmentation of meningiomas in MRI of the brain using deep learning methods. In: 2021 International Conference on Information Technology and Nanotechnology (ITNT), pp. 1–4. IEEE (2021)
3. Ali, A., Schnake, T., Eberle, O., Montavon, G., Müller, K.R., Wolf, L.: XAI for transformers: better explanations through conservative propagation. In: International Conference on Machine Learning, pp. 435–451. PMLR (2022)
4. Alzubi, J.A., Jain, R., Singh, A., Parwekar, P., Gupta, M.: COBERT: COVID-19 question answering system using BERT. Arab. J. Sci. Eng., 1–11 (2021)
5. Bendersky, M., Zhuang, H., Ma, J., Han, S., Hall, K., McDonald, R.: RRF102: meeting the TREC-COVID challenge with a 100+ runs ensemble. arXiv preprint arXiv:2010.00200 (2020)
6. Buciluă, C., Caruana, R., Niculescu-Mizil, A.: Model compression. In: Proceedings of the 12th ACM SIGKDD international conference on Knowledge Discovery and Data Mining, pp. 535–541 (2006)
7. Cao, Y., Xu, J., Liu, T.Y., Li, H., Huang, Y., Hon, H.W.: Adapting ranking SVM to document retrieval. In: Proceedings of the 29th Annual International ACM SIGIR Conference on Research and Development in Information Retrieval, pp. 186–193 (2006)
8. Chen, Q., Allot, A., Lu, Z.: LitCovid: an open database of COVID-19 literature. Nucleic Acids Res. **49**(D1), D1534–D1540 (2021)
9. Choi, D., Lee, H.: Extracting chemical-protein interactions via calibrated deep neural network and self-training. arXiv preprint arXiv:2011.02207 (2020)
10. Chowdhury, T., Rahimi, R., Allan, J.: Rank-lime: local model-agnostic feature attribution for learning to rank. arXiv preprint arXiv:2212.12722 (2022)
11. Demner-Fushman, D., Antani, S., Simpson, M., Thoma, G.R.: Design and development of a multimodal biomedical information retrieval system. J. Comput. Sci. Eng. **6**(2), 168–177 (2012)
12. Devlin, J., Chang, M.W., Lee, K., Toutanova, K.: BERT: pre-training of deep bidirectional transformers for language understanding. arXiv preprint arXiv:1810.04805 (2018)
13. Esteva, A., et al.: Covid-19 information retrieval with deep-learning based semantic search, question answering, and abstractive summarization. NPJ Digit. Med. **4**(1), 68 (2021)
14. Garreau, D., Luxburg, U.: Explaining the explainer: a first theoretical analysis of lime. In: International Conference on Artificial Intelligence and Statistics, pp. 1287–1296. PMLR (2020)
15. Gu, Y., et al.: Domain-specific language model pretraining for biomedical natural language processing. ACM Trans. Comput. Healthcare (HEALTH) **3**(1), 1–23 (2021)

16. Kieuvongngam, V., Tan, B., Niu, Y.: Automatic text summarization of COVID-19 medical research articles using BERT and GPT-2. arXiv preprint arXiv:2006.01997 (2020)
17. Komorowski, P., Baniecki, H., Biecek, P.: Towards evaluating explanations of vision transformers for medical imaging. In: Proceedings of the IEEE/CVF Conference on Computer Vision and Pattern Recognition, pp. 3725–3731 (2023)
18. Lee, J., et al.: BioBERT: a pre-trained biomedical language representation model for biomedical text mining. Bioinformatics **36**(4), 1234–1240 (2020)
19. Liu, Y., et al.: Roberta: a robustly optimized BERT pretraining approach. arXiv preprint arXiv:1907.11692 (2019)
20. Man, X., Chan, E.P.: The best way to select features? Comparing MDA, LIME, and SHAP. J. Financ. Data Sci. **3**(1), 127–139 (2021)
21. Mei, M., Tan, X.: Current strategies of antiviral drug discovery for COVID-19. Front. Mol. Biosci. **8**, 671263 (2021)
22. Ngai, H., Park, Y., Chen, J., Parsapoor, M.: Transformer-based models for question answering on covid19. arXiv preprint arXiv:2101.11432 (2021)
23. Ni, W., et al.: Role of angiotensin-converting enzyme 2 (ACE2) in COVID-19. Crit. Care **24**(1), 1–10 (2020)
24. Raza, S.: A COVID-19 search engine (CO-SE) with transformer-based architecture. Healthcare Anal. **2**, 100068 (2022)
25. Roberts, K., et al.: Searching for scientific evidence in a pandemic: an overview of TREC-COVID. J. Biomed. Inform. **121**, 103865 (2021)
26. Robertson, S., Zaragoza, H.: On rank-based effectiveness measures and optimization. Inf. Retrieval **10**, 321–339 (2007)
27. Sanh, V., Debut, L., Chaumond, J., Wolf, T.: DistilBERT, a distilled version of BERT: smaller, faster, cheaper and lighter. arXiv preprint arXiv:1910.01108 (2019)
28. Shrikumar, A., Greenside, P., Kundaje, A.: Learning important features through propagating activation differences. In: International Conference on Machine Learning, pp. 3145–3153. PMLR (2017)
29. Staliūnaitė, I., Iacobacci, I.: Compositional and lexical semantics in RoBERTa, BERT and DistilBERT: a case study on CoQa. arXiv preprint arXiv:2009.08257 (2020)
30. Sundararajan, M., Najmi, A.: The many shapley values for model explanation. In: International Conference on Machine Learning, pp. 9269–9278. PMLR (2020)
31. Tang, R., et al.: Rapidly bootstrapping a question answering dataset for COVID-19. arXiv preprint arXiv:2004.11339 (2020)
32. Tarunesh, I., Aditya, S., Choudhury, M.: Trusting RoBERTa over BERT: insights from checklisting the natural language inference task. arXiv preprint arXiv:2107.07229 (2021)
33. Vaswani, A., et al.: Attention is all you need. In: Advances in Neural Information Processing Systems, vol. 30 (2017)
34. Wang, L.L., et al.: CORD-19: the COVID-19 open research dataset. ArXiv (2020)
35. Wang, X.J., Grossman, M.R., Hyun, S.G.: Participation in TREC 2020 COVID track using continuous active learning. arXiv preprint arXiv:2011.01453 (2020)
36. Wishart, D.S., et al.: DrugBank: a comprehensive resource for in silico drug discovery and exploration. Nucl. Acids Res. **34**(suppl_1), D668–D672 (2006)
37. Yasunaga, M., Leskovec, J., Liang, P.: LinkBert: pretraining language models with document links. arXiv preprint arXiv:2203.15827 (2022)
38. Zhang, E., et al.: Covidex: neural ranking models and keyword search infrastructure for the covid-19 open research dataset. arXiv preprint arXiv:2007.07846 (2020)

A Transformer-Based Method for UAV-View Geo-Localization

Ping Wang, Zheyu Yang, Xueyang Chen, and Huahu Xu(✉)

School of Computer Engineering and Science, Shanghai University, Shanghai, China
huahuxu@163.com

Abstract. The geo-localization is the task of matching a query image depicting the ground-view of an unknown location with a group of satellite-view images with GPS tags. UAV-view can mitigate the large visual differences between images from different viewpoints. CNN-based approaches have achieved great success in cross-view geo-localization, but they rely on polar transform and have limited receptive field of convolution. Therefore, we investigate the geo-localization in terms of both feature representation and viewpoint transformation, design an end-to-end multitask jointly trained network model, introduce an efficient Transformer-based lightweight structure, use the strengths of transformer related to global information modeling and explicit position information encoding, and propose an end-to-end geo-localization architecture integrating a geo-localization module and a cross-view synthesis module, called Transformer-Based for UAV-View Geo-Localization (TUL). The geo-localization module combines feature segmentation and region alignment to achieve cross-view image matching. The cross-view synthesis module synthesizes maps close to real satellite images by conditional generative adversarial networks (cGAN). Image matching and synthesis are also considered, using the network to match images over two input domains so that the network is biased to learn potential feature representations that are useful for image synthesis. Furthermore, an image augmentation strategy is proposed for data enhancement to address the problem of sample imbalance due to the difference in the number of satellite images and images from other sources in University-1652 dataset. Experiments show that our method has significant performance improvement and reaches the state-of-the-art application level.

Keywords: UAV-view geo-localization · Cross-view image synthesis · CGAN · Transformer

1 Introduction

The cross-view geo-localization [15] can be applied to several fields such as aerial photography, self-driving cars and drone navigation [20]. The intervention of drone views will expand its application, which can be classified into drone localization and drone navigation. CNN-based methods are difficult to mine

L. Iliadis et al. (Eds.): ICANN 2023, LNCS 14259, pp. 332–344, 2023.
https://doi.org/10.1007/978-3-031-44223-0_27

the semantic information of the global context, and down-sampling operations will reduce image resolution, while Transformer is more adapted to the above scenarios. Since Vision Transformer (ViT) [5] requires an excessively large training dataset, this paper uses Data-efficient image Transformers (DeiT) [16] that can counteract CNNs on ImageNet-1K with similar parameters and inference throughput, which outperforms CNN-based methods in terms of performance.

This paper proposes the first end-to-end joint multitask training approach based on the DeiT architecture: **(1) Geo-localization module**: we use different convolutional kernels for the drone branch and the same convolutional kernel for the satellite branch when position embedding, and then automatically divide the feature map according to its heat distribution to segment the patch-level instances, and finally align multiple specific regions in different views one by one. **(2) The cross-view synthesis module**: The cGAN reads in the UAV-view image, passes it through a generator composed of UAV Transformer Encoder & Decoder, generates a pseudo-satellite view image, and synthesizes a map close to the real satellite image by a discriminator reading in the real satellite image.

As satellite view images from the University-1652 [20] dataset are very sparse, we propose an image enhancement strategy to extend the satellite images. Comparing and analyzing KLLoss [19] and TripletLoss, we improve TripletLoss to further improve the performance of the model.

In summary, the main contributions of this paper are as follows:

1. We propose a Transformer-based strong baseline cross-view matching for image geo-localization that outperforms CNN-based methods.
2. We design a geo-localization module and a cross-view synthesis module to cross-view image matching and synthesize maps close to real satellite images.
3. We propose an image augmentation strategy to improve the accuracy without adding additional inference costs.
4. TUL achieves state-of-the-art performance on both tasks of drone view target localization and drone navigation in the University-1652.

2 Related Work

The main challenge of cross-view geo-localization is the difference in appearance and viewpoints of different view images [10]. The current research mainly focuses on either directly extracting viewpoint invariant features from the input image, or applying explicit viewpoint transformation to the inputs.

Domain-invariant Features: Most current researchers [1,7] have used two-way CNNs to extract different features from different views separately for feature mapping and similarity metrics. To alleviate the visual differences between different views, University-1652 [20] introduced the drone view, Wang et al. [17] proposed a square division strategy. However, none of these methods establish spatial correspondence between the two views to reduce the visual gap.

Viewpoint Transformation: To alleviate visual disparity, recent research work has moved away from focusing solely on the feature representation of the image and has added view-transformation pre-processing operations to the input image, either using polar transformations to transform the view as in the study by Shi et al. [14] or adding additional generative adversarial network model branches to synthesize new images as in the study by Regmi et al. [12].

Vision Transformer: Transformer was originally a large-scale pre-trained network model used in NLP. In the field of computer vision, ViT solves a large number of vision tasks by segmenting each input image into k $\times$ k small blocks and then feeding each block to multiple transformer encoders as a token for position embedding. L2LTR [18] was applied in the field of cross-view geolocation and is a hybrid CNN+Transformer approach. A common ViT is used on top of ResNet, where CNNs are used to extract features, and self-attention and position embedding are only used for high-level CNN features, which also do not fully utilize the global modeling capability and position information from the first layer, in contrast to CNN-based methods, which require a larger GPU memory and pre-training dataset [18], while our approach improves the GPU memory efficiency and saves computational resources.

3 Method

An overview of the complete network architecture is shown on Fig. 1.

3.1 Vision Transformer for Geo-Localization

Based on the University-1652 benchmark [20], we constructed a transformer-based strong baseline for multitasking joint training, consisting of a geo-localization module and a cross-view synthesis module, as shown in Fig. 1.

3.2 Geo-Localization Module

Linear Projection. We improve the linear projection layer (LP) by using multiple different convolution kernels for linear projection of the drone image according to the distance when position embedding, and using the same convolution kernel for the same distance, which improves the cross-view matching performance.Our strategy is to group patches by distance. In the picture we consider that targets with the same x-axis have the same distance to the camera and targets with different y-axis have different distances to the camera, so we group 16×16 patches into 16 groups according to the y-axis, each group being 16 patches with the same x-axis.This works better than setting up a fixed projection matrix.

Segmentation. The model divides the area according to the distribution of the different categories in the heatmap drawn by Grad-CAM [13]. We can get all the outputs $\mathcal{L} \in \mathbb{R}^{B \times N \times S}$ as follows:

$$\mathcal{L} = \left[\mathbf{F}\left(\mathbf{x_p^1}\right); \mathbf{F}\left(\mathbf{x_p^2}\right); \cdots; \mathbf{F}\left(\mathbf{x_p^N}\right)\right] \tag{1}$$

where B represents the batch size, N represents the ~~patch size~~ and S represents the length of the feature vector corresponding to each patch.

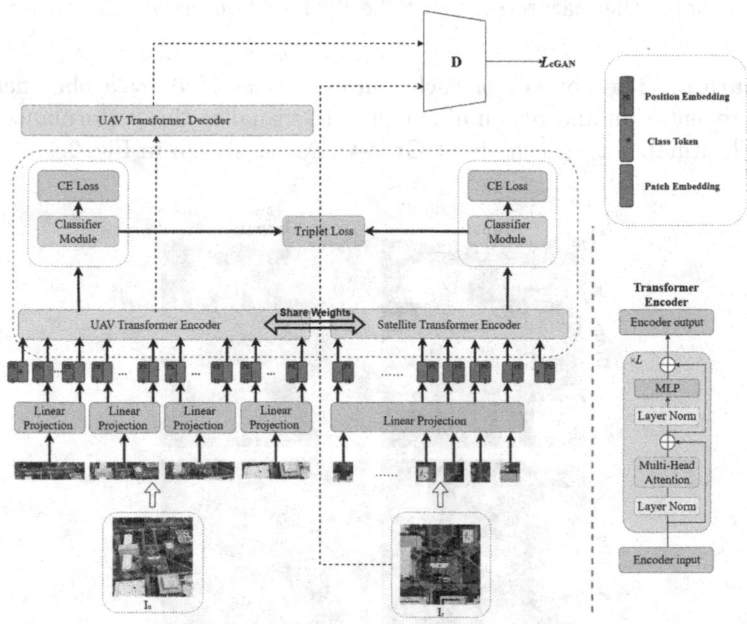

Fig. 1. The proposed TUL framework.

The heat value of each patch can be expressed as follows:

$$P^c = \frac{1}{S}\sum_{i=1}^{S} M^i \quad c = \{1, 2, \cdots, N\} \tag{2}$$

where P^c denotes the heat value of the cth patches. M^i denotes the cth value of the feature vector corresponding to the ith patch.

We sort the value of P^{1-N} in descending order and split the patches into n equal parts. The number of patches for each region is determined as follows:

$$N^i = \begin{cases} \left\lfloor \frac{N}{n} \right\rfloor & i = \{1, 2, \cdots, n-1\} \\ N - (n-1) \times \left\lfloor \frac{N}{n} \right\rfloor & i = n \end{cases} \tag{3}$$

where N^i denotes the number of patches in the ith region, $\lfloor\rfloor$ is the floor function and n defaults to 3 (buildings, roads, and trees).

Alignment. After segmentation, we divide all patches into n regions and align the feature content corresponding to the different regions. After sorting by token module length, tokens from different views are matched in order.Then their feature vectors are obtained as followed using the averaging pooling operation:

$$V^i = \frac{1}{N^i} \sum_{j=1}^{N^i} f_i^j \quad \in \mathbb{R}^{B \times N^i \times S} \qquad i = \{1, 2, \cdots, n\} \tag{4}$$

where f_i^j denotes the feature vector of the ith block of the jth instance region.

Visualisation. The content of each feature is classified by a classifier after feature segmentation and region alignment. To visualise the performance of the model, a heatmap was drawn about Grad-CAM, as shown in Fig. 2.

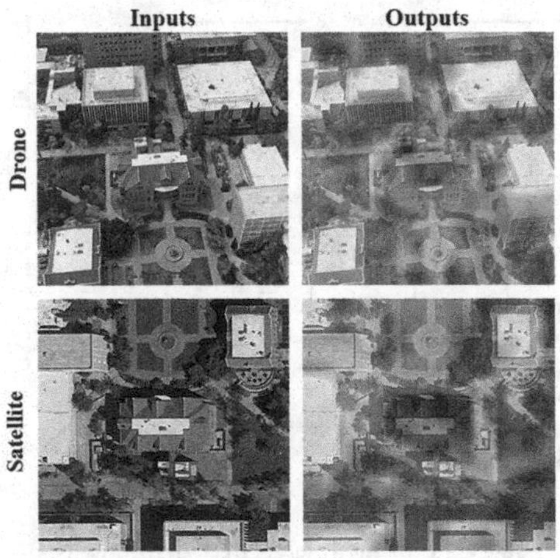

Fig. 2. The images on the left column are the input images from the drone view and the satellite view. The image in the right column is the heatmap output from our Transformer-based geo-localization module.

3.3 Cross-View Synthesis Module

We make full use of the drone image features obtained by the geo-localization module, which are fed into the cross-view synthesis module to achieve the mapping of the target building. Generative adversarial networks (GANs) [6] contain two main adversarial networks trained by adversarial training, namely the generator G and the discriminator D.

We use the drone images I_u as the condition to generate realistic pseudo-satellite images $G_{(I_u)}$, which are then fed into the discriminator D with real satellite images and scored for authenticity, and this feedback motivates the generator to synthesize images that more closely resemble the real image.

We use a cGAN architecture with the generator G consisting of the UAV Transformer Encoder & Decoder and the discriminator D consisting of the PatchGAN classifier [8]. In addition, we use a patch-wise strategy that facilitates the synthesis of pseudo-satellite view images consisting of repeated patterns of buildings, roads and trees.

3.4 Loss Function

An Improved Loss Function $\mathcal{L}_{cGAN}$ Based on Image Synthesis. We add traditional regularisation $\mathcal{L}_1$ to calculate the absolute value of the pixel-by-pixel difference between the real and false images generated by generator G, to optimise the objectives of the GAN, which helps the network to capture low-level image features and induce convergence of the image synthesis.

$$G^* = arg \min_G \max_D \mathcal{L}_{cGAN}(G, D) + \lambda \mathcal{L}_{L1}(G) \tag{5}$$

During training, the weights of the two components of G and D are updated by means of generative adversarial.

$$\ell = \lambda_{cGAN} \mathcal{L}_{cGAN} + \lambda_{L_1} \mathcal{L}_{L_1} \tag{6}$$

$$\mathcal{L}_{cGAN}(G, D) = E_{I_u, I_s}\left[\log D(I_u, I_s)\right] + E_{I_u}\left[\log\left(1 - D(I_u, G(I_u))\right)\right] \tag{7}$$

$$\mathcal{L}_{L1}(G) = E_{I_s, I_u}\left[\|I_s - G(I_u)\|_1\right] \tag{8}$$

TripletLoss. We use Euclidean distance to determine the similarity between samples and TripletLoss to narrow the distance between identical targets from different domains, expressed as follows:

$$TL = \|d(a, p) - d(a, n) + M\|_+ \tag{9}$$

$$d(a, x) = \|a - x\|_2 \tag{10}$$

where $\|\cdot\|_+$ denotes the operation $max(\cdot, 0)$. $\|\cdot\|_2$ denotes a 2-parametric operation. M is the value of margin. Equation 10 represents the Euclidean distance used to measure the distance between vectors. In Eq. 9 we use $M = 0.3$ to calculate TripletLoss.

3.5 An Image Augmentation Strategy

During the experiments, we found some instability in the training process of the Transformer-based model, probably mainly due to the sample imbalance: there is only one satellite image per category, but it corresponds to 54 drone images with different heights and angles, which leads to an imbalance of the sample size. In response, we propose an image augmentation strategy: obtaining images from the University-1652 dataset in satellite view and generating multiple enhanced satellite images to expand the data volume. The image augmentation method mainly uses random flipping, cropping, padding, rotation, and ColorJitter.

4 Experiment

4.1 Datasets and Evaluation Protocol

University-1652 is a multi-view multi-source benchmark for drone-based geo-localization, which is suitable for drone view target localization (drone→satellite) and drone navigation (satellite→drone). Its result of statistic is shown in Table 1. The column of classes indicates the number of buildings, and the column of university indicates the number of universities included in the sample. The dataset collected 1,652 buildings from 72 universities in the world. The training set and the testing set have no overlap between the buildings.

Table 1. Statistics on the type and number of University-1652.

split		views	images	classes	university
Train		Drone	37854	701	33
		Satellite	701	701	
		Street	11640	701	
Test	Query	Drone	37855	701	39
		Satellite	701	701	
		Street	2579	701	
	Gallery	Drone	51355	951	
		Satellite	951	951	
		Street	2921	793	

We evaluate model performance using Recall@K (R@K) and Average Precision (AP). The K nearest reference neighbours in the embedding space are retrieved based on the cosine similarity of each query. A true reference image is considered correct if it appears in the top K retrieved images.

4.2 Implementation Details

Training Strategy. For training, we resized the input image to a size of 256 × 256, using 12 transformer encoders with 12 heads for multi-head attention block. The model was initialized on ImageNet-1K using non-pre-trained weights. For the optimiser, we adopted stochastic gradient descent (SGD) with momentum 0.9 and weight decay 0.0005 with a mini-batch of 8. For the initial learning rate setting, the backbone parameter was set to 0.00003 and the remaining learnable parameters were set to 0.0001. The model was trained for a total of 120 epochs.

Loss Function. We used CrossEntropy loss as the classification loss function, TripletLoss to reduce the distance from the same target to different domains.

Test. The models were written using the PyTorch framework, and the network was trained using an NVIDIA GeForce 2080Ti.

4.3 Comparison with Existing Methods

This paper uses DeiT as the backbone. On the University-1652 [20] dataset, we compare the proposed TUL with existing competing methods, as shown in Table 2, the TUL recall was 83.37% for the Drone→Satellite task and 86.24% for the AP, and 89.72% for the TUL and 90.31% for the AP in the Satellite→Drone task, which indicates that the model performance has outperformed the state-of-the-art method FSRA. Considering fairness issues, we replicated FSRA in our own experimental environment to achieve a comparison of model performance in the same environment. Finally, for qualitative assessment as shown in Fig. 4, we can see that the TUL can find relevant images from different perspectives.

Table 2. Comparison with state-of-art results reported from University-1652.

Method	Backbone	Drone→Satellite		Satellite→Drone	
		R@1	AP	R@1	AP
Contrastive Loss [3]	VGG16	52.39	57.44	63.91	52.24
Soft Margin TripletLoss [7]	VGG16	53.21	58.03	65.62	54.47
TripletLoss (M = 0.3) [9]	ResNet-50	55.18	59.97	63.62	53.85
Instance Loss+GeM [11]	ResNet-50	65.32	69.61	79.03	65.35
Instance Loss [20]	ResNet-50	58.23	62.91	74.47	59.45
LCM (ResNet-50) [4]	ResNet-50	66.65	70.82	79.89	65.38
LPN [17]	ResNet-50	75.93	79.14	86.45	74.79
FSRA [2]	Vit-S	82.25	84.82	87.87	81.53
FSRA	Vit-S	81.40	84.13	87.59	88.45
Ours	DeiT-B	83.37	86.24	89.72	90.31

4.4 Ablation Studies

This section verifies the effectiveness of each component of the network model.

Effect of the Linear Projection Layer (LP). Assuming that S denotes the cross-view synthesis branch and G denotes the geo-localization branch in TUL, we use G with the LP removed as W.

As can be seen from Table 3, removing the LP component, the performance drops significantly and is 3% lower than the state-of-the-art method. With the addition of the cross-view synthesis branch, the performance does not improve significantly, indicating that cGAN can be used as an extended application of the model for synthesizing maps of target buildings.

Table 3. Effect of LP.

Method	Drone→Satellite		Satellite→Drone	
	R@1	AP	R@1	AP
W	79.93	83.14	86.45	87.79
G	83.23	86.43	89.69	90.45
G+S	83.37	86.24	89.72	90.31

Effect of the Transformer in Cross-View. Regarding accuracy and speed we compared the performance of the Transformer-based and ResNet-based networks as shown in Table 4. We visualise the DeiT-B attention graph and observe the heatmap distribution for our approach, as shown in Fig. 3. The attention mechanism allows the network to focus on global contextual information.

Effect of the Loss Function. As shown in Table 5, only using KLLoss increases by 0.82%/1.06% AP on the Drone→Satellite/Satellite→Drone mission. Only using TripletLoss increased by 2.92%/4.44% AP. When we used both KLLoss and TripletLoss, the accuracy of AP did not improve significantly. Therefore, we did not use KLLoss in our model, but TripletLoss. We speculate that TripletLoss and KLLoss are consistent in the same network fitting direction.

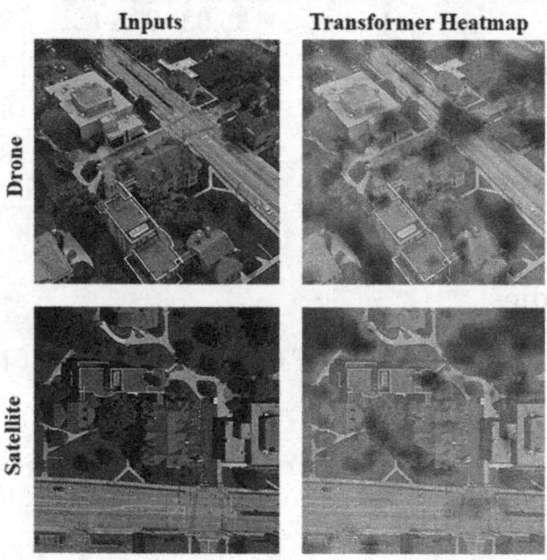

Fig. 3. The left is the original image, and the right is the heatmap of the last layer of DeiT-B.

Table 4. Comparison of ResNet and Vision Transformer.

Backbone	Inference Time	Drone→Satellite		Satellite→Drone	
		R@1	AP	R@1	AP
ResNet-50	1x	60.93	65.31	75.61	61.69
ResNet-101	1.48x	65.33	68.32	79.44	65.43
Vit-S/16	1.21x	71.04	74.62	83.31	84.08
Vit-B/16	1.79x	73.32	76.88	84.74	85.72
DeiT-S/16	1.12x	75.51	78.24	83.17	84.29
DeiT-B/16	1.36x	78.82	81.63	86.37	87.74

Table 5. Ablation studies to verify the effects of some other tricks.

KLLoss	TripletLoss	AP(%)	
	(M = 0.3)	D→S	S→D
		83.32	85.87
✓		84.14	86.93
✓	✓	86.23	90.33
	✓	86.24	90.31

Effect of the Input Image Size. Large images require great memory and run-time while small images destroy the features of original image. The experimental results are shown in Table 6. For a balance, we observed that as the input image size increased from 224 to 512, the Recall@K and AP become better; when the image size ranges from 512 to 1024, the performances get worse. TUL has the best matching accuracy when the image size is 512, and shows the lowest matching accuracy when the image size is set to 1024.

Table 6. Ablation study on the impact of different input sizes on University-1652.

Image Size	Drone→Satellite		Satellite→Drone	
	R@1	AP	R@1	AP
224	80.71	83.63	87.23	88.02
256	83.37	86.24	89.72	90.31
384	84.72	87.13	87.49	88.97
512	85.50	88.93	90.73	92.04

4.5 Visualization of Qualitative Result

For the two basic tasks of the University-1652 dataset: drone view target localization and drone navigation, we visualise some of the retrieved results in Fig. 4.

For both tasks, we randomly selected three drone and satellite images from each of the test datasets. For each input image, we take out the top five similar images from the gallery set and TUL obtained exactly correct results.

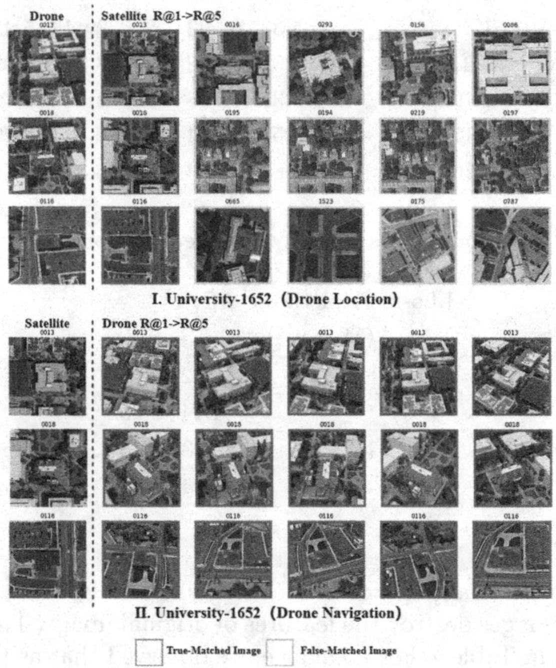

Fig. 4. Qualitative image retrieval results.

5 Conclusion

In this paper, we study the problem of cross-view image matching based on geo-localization and propose a TUL model for drone localization and navigation. We take full account of the spatial geometric correspondence between different views to reduce domain disparity, and different convolutional kernels are used for UAV images the same convolutional kernel is used for satellite images, making the model independent of polar coordinate transformations for generality and flexibility. The training processes for cross-view synthesis and geolocation are not only end-to-end, but they are integrated in a single architecture.

We apply the transformer's architecture to the field of cross-view geo-localization and obtain state-of-the-art cross-view geo-localization performance with high matching accuracy on the standard University-1652 dataset. The geo-localization module achieves patch-level semantic segmentation and region-level feature alignment. The increased inference time of the DeiT-B backbone approach compared to Resnet-50 would be considered a drawback of the method. In addition, we have used an image augmentation strategy to adapt the model to a better state, making TUL stronger using an improved TripletLoss. TUL can not only better serve image localization and drone navigation, but can also be used for cross-view image synthesis to generate maps of target buildings. In the future, we will continue to explore how to further improve the matching accuracy of drone images with satellite images and propose a new dense drone cross-view geo-localization dataset to meet the requirements of practical applications.

References

1. Cai, S., Guo, Y., Khan, S., Hu, J., Wen, G.: Ground-to-aerial image geo-localization with a hard exemplar reweighting triplet loss. In: Proceedings of the IEEE/CVF International Conference on Computer Vision, pp. 8391–8400 (2019)
2. Dai, M., Hu, J., Zhuang, J., Zheng, E.: A transformer-based feature segmentation and region alignment method for UAV-view geo-localization. IEEE Trans. Circuits Syst. Video Technol. **32**(7), 4376–4389 (2021)
3. Deng, W., Zheng, L., Ye, Q., Kang, G., Yang, Y., Jiao, J.: Image-image domain adaptation with preserved self-similarity and domain-dissimilarity for person re-identification. In: Proceedings of the IEEE Conference on Computer Vision and Pattern Recognition, pp. 994–1003 (2018)
4. Ding, L., Zhou, J., Meng, L., Long, Z.: A practical cross-view image matching method between UAV and satellite for UAV-based geo-localization. Remote Sens. **13**(1), 47 (2020)
5. Dosovitskiy, A., et al.: An image is worth 16x16 words: transformers for image recognition at scale. arXiv preprint arXiv:2010.11929 (2020)
6. Goodfellow, I., et al.: Generative adversarial nets in advances in neural information processing systems (nips), pp. 2672–2680. Curran Associates, Inc., Red Hook, NY, USA (2014)
7. Hu, S., Feng, M., Nguyen, R.M., Lee, G.H.: CVM-Net: cross-view matching network for image-based ground-to-aerial geo-localization. In: Proceedings of the IEEE Conference on Computer Vision and Pattern Recognition, pp. 7258–7267 (2018)
8. Li, C., Wand, M.: Precomputed real-time texture synthesis with Markovian generative adversarial networks. In: Leibe, B., Matas, J., Sebe, N., Welling, M. (eds.) ECCV 2016. LNCS, vol. 9907, pp. 702–716. Springer, Cham (2016). https://doi.org/10.1007/978-3-319-46487-9_43
9. Liu, H., Feng, J., Qi, M., Jiang, J., Yan, S.: End-to-end comparative attention networks for person re-identification. IEEE Trans. Image Process. **26**(7), 3492–3506 (2017)
10. Liu, L., Li, H.: Lending orientation to neural networks for cross-view geo-localization. In: Proceedings of the IEEE/CVF Conference on Computer Vision and Pattern Recognition, pp. 5624–5633 (2019)
11. Radenović, F., Tolias, G., Chum, O.: Fine-tuning CNN image retrieval with no human annotation. IEEE Trans. Pattern Anal. Mach. Intell. **41**(7), 1655–1668 (2018)
12. Regmi, K., Borji, A.: Cross-view image synthesis using geometry-guided conditional GANs. Comput. Vis. Image Underst. **187**, 102788 (2019)
13. Selvaraju, R.R., Cogswell, M., Das, A., Vedantam, R., Parikh, D., Batra, D.: Grad-CAM: visual explanations from deep networks via gradient-based localization. In: Proceedings of the IEEE International Conference on Computer Vision, pp. 618–626 (2017)

14. Shi, Y., Liu, L., Yu, X., Li, H.: Spatial-aware feature aggregation for image based cross-view geo-localization. In: Advances in Neural Information Processing Systems 32 (2019)
15. Tian, X., Shao, J., Ouyang, D., Shen, H.T.: UAV-satellite view synthesis for cross-view geo-localization. IEEE Trans. Circuits Syst. Video Technol. **32**(7), 4804–4815 (2021)
16. Touvron, H., Cord, M., Douze, M., Massa, F., Sablayrolles, A., Jégou, H.: Training data-efficient image transformers & distillation through attention. In: International Conference on Machine Learning, pp. 10347–10357. PMLR (2021)
17. Wang, T., et al.: Each part matters: local patterns facilitate cross-view geo-localization. IEEE Trans. Circuits Syst. Video Technol. **32**(2), 867–879 (2021)
18. Yang, H., Lu, X., Zhu, Y.: Cross-view geo-localization with layer-to-layer transformer. Adv. Neural. Inf. Process. Syst. **34**, 29009–29020 (2021)
19. Yim, J., Joo, D., Bae, J., Kim, J.: A gift from knowledge distillation: fast optimization, network minimization and transfer learning. In: Proceedings of the IEEE Conference on Computer Vision and Pattern Recognition, pp. 4133–4141 (2017)
20. Zheng, Z., Wei, Y., Yang, Y.: University-1652: a multi-view multi-source benchmark for drone-based geo-localization. In: Proceedings of the 28th ACM International Conference On Multimedia, pp. 1395–1403 (2020)

Cross-Graph Transformer Network for Temporal Sentence Grounding

Jiahui Shang, Ping Wei(✉), and Nanning Zheng

Institute of Artificial Intelligence and Robotics,
Xi'an Jiaotong University, Xi'an, China
pingwei@xjtu.edu.cn

Abstract. Temporal sentence grounding aims to retrieve moments associated with the given sentences in untrimmed videos, which is a multimodal problem and needs the adequate understanding of the sentence and video structure as well as the accurate interaction of the two modals. In this paper, we propose a cross-graph Transformer network (CGTN) model to address this problem, where the sentence is taken as a dependency tree and the video as a graph, according to their non-linear structures. Based on the graph structures, we design the self-graph attention and cross-graph attention to model the relationship between the nodes in the graph and cross the graphs. We test the proposed model on two challenging datasets. Extensive experiments demonstrate the strength of our method.

Keywords: Temporal grounding · Cross-modal · Graph attention

1 Introduction

Temporal sentence grounding (TSG) is temporal action localization with natural language, which needs to consider the unique sentence and video structure, as well as the interactions between the language and vision modals. Over the past decades, a remarkable progress has been made in TSG and numerous advanced approaches have sprung up [4,11,17,29], from simple operation [11] of video and language features to complex interactions [4,17,29]. However, the current methods often ignore the unique structural information of the language and video, which is crucial to fully understand the sentence and video information.

Adequate understanding of the sentence and video structures and effective modeling their interaction are key issues for TSG. Firstly, understanding the fine-grained structure of the input query is the basis to analyze the semantic information. Ignoring the local dependence between the words in the sentence makes it hard to fully understand the sentence content. As shown in Fig. 1, each word in the sentence contacts with other words with non-linear relationships. The sentence can be organized into a semantic dependency tree, where the predicate verb is regarded as the root node [19]. Each word is organized as a tree node. The relationship between the words is modeled by the edges. Secondly, different

L. Iliadis et al. (Eds.): ICANN 2023, LNCS 14259, pp. 345–356, 2023.
https://doi.org/10.1007/978-3-031-44223-0_28

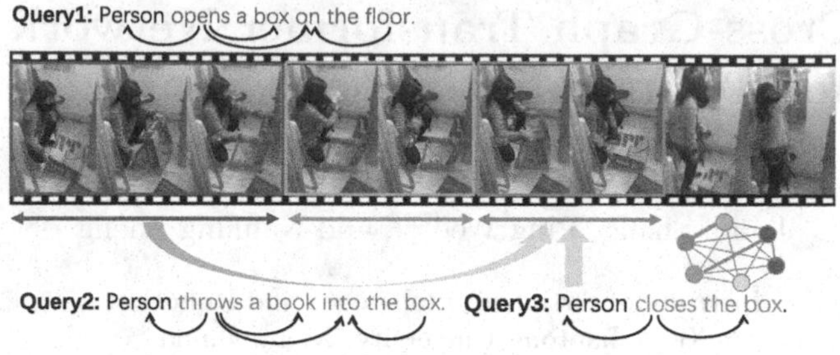

Fig. 1. Non-linearity in videos and sentences.

action instances in videos also have the nonlinear dependence. As shown in Fig. 1, the action 'opens a box on the floor' shares information with the action 'closes the box', but they are separated by the other action 'throws a book into the box'. Due to this sorting relationship, when we locate the query 'Person closes the box', linear modeling of the video may fail to capture the visual information related to 'opens a box'. The video can be organized into a graph to model the nonlinear dependence of action instances. Each video clip feature is regarded as a graph node, and the graph edges model their relationship.

In this paper, we propose a cross-graph Transformer network (CGTN) model to represent the query as the dependency tree and the video as graph considering their respective structural characteristics. Using the attention mechanism in Transformer [25], we design a graph-based attention mechanism to model the fine-grained interaction between the constructed nonlinear structures, where self-graph attention used in one graph models the relationship itself and cross-graph attention used between two graphs models their interaction. It explores the fine-grained and nonlinear interactions between two graph structures by characterizing the degree of mutual influence between the nodes in graphs. We tested our method on two challenging datasets: TACoS [21] and ActivityNet Caption [13]. The experiments show the effectiveness of the proposed methods.

2 Related Work

Temporal sentence grounding in videos aims to retrieve moments in videos corresponds to an given text [11]. Recent studies mainly address this problem from two aspects: cross-modal interaction and accurate moment retrieval. For video-language cross-modal interaction, the early work used direct operation [11] and later studies gradually considered the interaction between the video and language [4,5,16,17,29], such as word-by-frame fine-grained interaction [4,5], multi-stage interaction [12,31]. For accurate moment retrieval, there are mainly two types: proposal-based and proposal-free. Proposal-based methods divide the candidate moment set, and then predict the offsets of the candidates relative to the ground truth as well as score them [15,31,35]. Proposal-free methods directly predict the start and end time of moments [2,22,28]. We adopt the proposal-based pipeline and model the interaction between videos and languages.

The Transformer [25] was initially proposed for machine translation. Recently it has been widely used in language and visual tasks [3,14,18,23]. DETR [3] designs an end-to-end efficient Transformer for object detection. For the high efficiency and accuracy of Transformer, some methods apply it to the vision-language cross-modal tasks [8,9]. TransVG [8] uses visual Transformer and linguistic Transformer to separately model the visual and linguistic features. The concatenation features and the predefined learnable tokens are fed into the visual-linguistic Transformer. The learnable tokens of the output are used for the spatial coordinate regression. VGTR [9] encodes the visual and linguistic features separately in encoders, and designs text-guided visual self-attention mechanism in the decoder to model the visual-linguistic interaction. Transformers can be used on graphs [10,30,33] and have been proven to be effective in many tasks. We apply the standard multi-head attention mechanism in Transformer [25] to the graph structures for temporal sentence grounding.

3 Approach

For a given untrimmed video V and a query Q, TSG aims to predict the start and end time positions of the moment associated with the query in video. As shown in Fig. 2, the proposed cross-graph Transformer network is composed of three major components: Feature Extraction and Graph Construction, Cross-Graph Transformer and Moment Retrieval. We extract the features of the input video and the query to learn their semantic and contextual graph-based representation. The self-graph and cross-graph attention are used to model the graphs and their fine-grained interaction. The moment retrieval module is carried out based on the rich graph structure features.

3.1 Feature Extraction and Graph Construction

We divide the input untrimmed video V into n short overlapping clips and use the pretrained C3D network [24] to extract features for each clip. The video-level feature V is the stack of all the clip features and represented as $V = (v^1, v^2, ..., v^n)$. For the input query sentence Q with w words, we use the pretrained GloVe model [20] to obtain each word embedding, and Bi-GRU [7] to model the context of words in the sentence. The final word-level feature at each position is obtained by the stack of the hidden states in both directions. We obtain the query sentence representation as $Q = (q^1, q^2, ..., q^w)$.

After extracting the linear features of the video and query, we organize them into nonlinear graph structures. Specifically, for query, we use the dependency parsing [19] in NLP to model the dependency between the words in the sentence. The predicate verb is the center of a sentence, and other elements in the sentence are directly or indirectly related to the verb. Therefore, the sentence can be organized into a syntax tree with the predicate verb as the root node, and other words as tree nodes. The edge weight in the tree represents the dependency between the words. The video is organized as a non-linear graph structure with

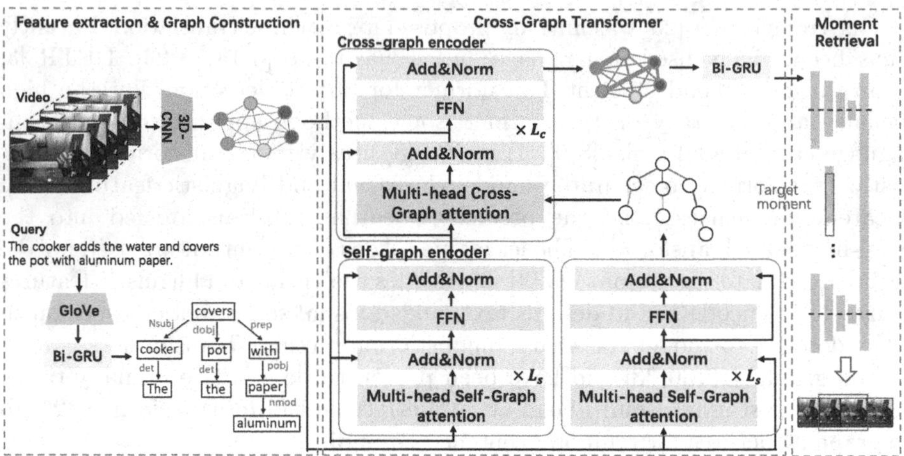

Fig. 2. The architecture of our CGTN model.

each clip feature as the graph node. The video graph $G = (g^1, g^2, ..., g^n)$ is initialized with the video-level feature V and g^i is for the ith node ($i \in \{1, ..., n\}$). The sentence tree $T = (t^1, t^2, ..., t^w)$ is initialized with the sentence-level feature Q and t^i is the ith node ($i \in \{1, ..., w\}$).

3.2 Cross-Graph Transformer

We apply the standard multi-head attention [25] to graph structures. We design a self-graph encoder to model the relationship between nodes within each graph, to effectively capture the video and sentence information. We propose a cross-graph encoder that captures the nuanced interactions between the graphs, enabling the identification of specific moments in video features that match the query description. The cross-graph Transformer component outputs the semantically enhanced video features for subsequent moment retrieval.

Self-Graph Encoder. For the video, we input the initialized video graph G into the self-graph encoder. For the non-linearity of the graph, we use the learnable position encoding as the position information instead of the fixed position encoding in traditional Transformer. We expresses the relationship between the nodes as the edge weight in the graph. For sentence, similarly, we input the initialized sentence tree T into the self-graph encoder. We expressed the dependence between words in sentence as the weight in the sentence tree. Since the sentence tree and video graph employ the same attention calculation process, we use the video graph to explain the proposed attention mechanism. The proposed self-graph encoder consists of L_s same layers and each layer consists of a self-graph attention followed by a feed forward network. The input is the initialized graph $G = [g^1, g^2, ..., g^n]$ with n nodes, and the output is the informative graph $\hat{G} = [\hat{g}^1, \hat{g}^2, ..., \hat{g}^n]$, where $\hat{g}^i$ is the ith node. We use the same mechanism for the sentence tree to continuously learn the relationship between nodes.

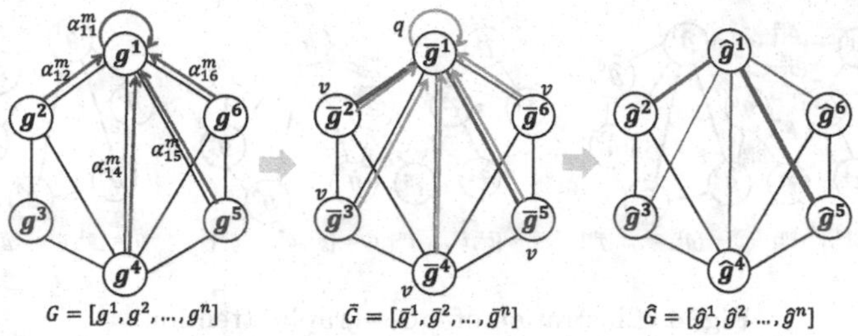

Fig. 3. Illustration of self-graph attention.

Self-Graph Attention. Given $G = [g^1, g^2, ..., g^n]$ with n nodes, for each node g^i, as shown in Fig. 3, we first enhance the features of node g^i with nodes g^j adjacent to node g^i as GAT [26]:

$$\bar{g}^i = g^i + \biguplus_{m=1}^{M} \sigma\left(\sum\nolimits_{j \in N_i} \alpha_{ij}^m W^m g^j\right), \tag{1}$$

where $m = 1, 2, ..., M$ indexes the m-th attention head and $\biguplus_{m=1}^{M}$ denotes the concatenation of M heads. $\overline{G} = [\overline{g}^1, ..., \overline{g}^n]$ is the output. $j \in N_i$ and N_i is the adjacent node set of node g^i in the same graph. W^m is the learnable transformation weight matrix, α_{ij}^m is the self-attention coefficient of the m-th head between node g^i and node g^j, which represents the affinity of node g^i and node g^j:

$$\alpha_{ij}^m = \frac{\exp\left(\text{LeakyReLU}\left(W_a^{\mathrm{T}}\left[W_m g^i \,||\, W_m g^j\right]\right)\right)}{\sum_{j \in N_i} \exp\left(\text{LeakyReLU}\left(W_a^{\mathrm{T}}\left[W_m g^i \,||\, W_m g^j\right]\right)\right)}, \tag{2}$$

where T represents a transpose operator. W_a and W_m are two learnable matrices. After enhancement using the adjacent nodes, as shown in Fig. 3, we apply the multi-head self attention [3,36] in Transformer to enhance the feature of node $\bar{g}^i$ using all the nodes in graph:

$$MultiHeadAttn(\bar{g}^i, \overline{G}) = \biguplus_{m=1}^{M} (\overline{W}_m [\sum\nolimits_{k \in n} A_{imk} \cdot \widehat{W}_m \bar{g}^k]), \tag{3}$$

where i and k index a query element and a key element, respectively. The representations of query and key element are $\bar{g}^i, \bar{g}^k \in \mathbb{R}^C$, which are embedded with position. It means that each node $\bar{g}^i$ is regarded as a query element to interact with the whole graph $\overline{G}$. $\widehat{W}_m \in \mathbb{R}^{C_v \times C}$ and $\overline{W}_m \in \mathbb{R}^{C \times C_v}$ are learnable and used to adjust dimensions, where C_v is equal to C/M. The attention weights $A_{imk} \propto \exp\left\{\frac{(U_m \bar{g}^i)^{\mathrm{T}} (V_m \bar{g}^k)}{\sqrt{C_v}}\right\}$ are normalized as $\sum_{k=1}^{n} A_{imk} = 1$. $U_m, V_m \in \mathbb{R}^{C_v \times C}$ are learnable weights.

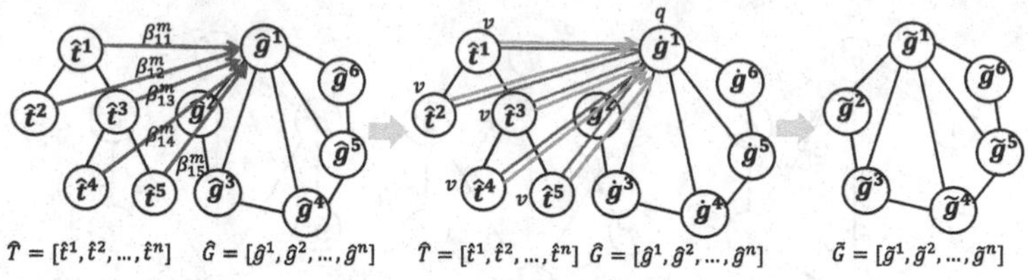

Fig. 4. Illustration of cross-graph attention.

After L_s layers of propagation, the information of each node has been enhanced. Similarly, we apply the same attention learning process to the sentence tree. After the self-graph encoder applied in the video graph and sentence tree, each node in graph is effectively enhanced. The encoded video graph and sentence tree are denoted as $\widehat{G}$ and $\widehat{T}$, respectively.

Cross-Graph Encoder. The cross-graph encoder aims to learn the interaction between two different graphs referred as source and target graph. Here we use the encoded video graph $\widehat{G}$ as target graph and the encoded sentence tree $\widehat{T}$ as source graph. Similarly, the proposed cross-graph encoder contains L_c layers, where one layer consists of a cross-graph attention followed by a feed forward network. The inputs are two different graphs: source graph $\widehat{T} = \left[\hat{t}^1, \hat{t}^2, ..., \hat{t}^w\right]$ with w nodes, target graph $\widehat{G} = \left[\hat{g}^1, \hat{g}^2, ..., \hat{g}^n\right]$ with n nodes.

Cross-Graph Attention. As shown in Fig. 4, for each node $\hat{g}^i$ in target graph, we enhance the features of node $\hat{g}^i$ with nodes $\hat{t}^j$ adjacent to $\hat{g}^i$ in source graph:

$$\dot{g}^i = \hat{g}^i + \biguplus_{m=1}^{M} \sigma\left(\sum\nolimits_{j \in N_i} \beta_{ij}^m \widetilde{W}^m \hat{t}^j\right), \tag{4}$$

where $m = 1, 2, ..., M$ indexes the mth attention head and $\biguplus_{m=1}^{M}$ denotes the concatenation of M heads. N_i is the adjacent node set of node $\hat{g}^i$ in source graph. Other variables share the same definitions in self-graph attention, and $\widetilde{W}^m$ is the learnable transformation weight matrix. β_{ij}^m is the cross-attention coefficient of m-th head between node $\hat{g}^i$ and node $\hat{t}^j$, which represents the affinity of them:

$$\beta_{ij}^m = \frac{\exp\left(\text{LeakyReLU}\left(W_c\left[W_t^m \hat{g}^i \,||\, W_s^m \hat{t}^j\right]\right)\right)}{\sum_{j \in N_i} \exp\left(\text{LeakyReLU}\left(W_c\left[W_t^m \hat{g}^i \,||\, W_s^m \hat{t}^j\right]\right)\right)}. \tag{5}$$

After feature enhancement with the adjacent nodes, we also apply the multi-head attention to enhance node $\dot{g}^i$ using all the nodes from source graph:

$$MultiHeadAttn(\dot{g}^i, \widehat{T}) = \biguplus_{m=1}^{M} (W_t[\sum\nolimits_{k \in w} A_{imk} \cdot W'_m \hat{t}^k]). \tag{6}$$

Finally, by L_c layer passing, the output of the cross-graph attention is fed to a Bi-GRU layer to model the video context, and the result is denoted as $\widetilde{G} = \left[\tilde{g}^1, \tilde{g}^2, ..., \tilde{g}^n\right]$ with rich semantic information, which is used to conduct subsequent moment retrieval.

3.3 Moment Retrieval

We retrieve the moments in the same way with the work CMIN [35]. By self-graph and cross-graph modeling, we obtain the semantically rich video graph representation $\widetilde{G} = [\tilde{g}^1, \tilde{g}^2, ..., \tilde{g}^n]$. We conduct the time moment retrieval based on $\widetilde{G}$. We generate a set of candidate moments with multi-scale windows $\{(\hat{s}_{ik}, \hat{e}_{ik})\}_{k=1}^{K}$ at each time step i, where K is the number of window widths. $(\hat{s}_{ik}, \hat{e}_{ik}) = \left(\frac{i-w_k}{2}, \frac{i+w_k}{2}\right)$ are the start and end times of the kth candidate moment at time i, $i = 1, 2, ..., n$. w_k is the width of the kth candidate moment. The confidence scores for the candidate moments at the ith time step are:

$$cs_i = f_1\left(\tilde{g}^i\right), \tag{7}$$

where $cs_i \in \mathbb{R}^K$ represents the confidence scores of K moments at time step i and cs_{ik} corresponds to the kth moment. f_1 is a conv1d layer with sigmoid function. The predicted offsets are obtained by:

$$\hat{o}_i = f_2\left(\tilde{g}^i\right), \tag{8}$$

where $\hat{o}_i \in \mathbb{R}^{2K}$ represents the predicted offsets of K moments at time i. $\hat{o}_{ik} = (\hat{o}_{ik}^s, \hat{o}_{ik}^e)$ indexs the k-th moment. f_2 is a conv1d layer with sigmoid function.

3.4 Loss Function

Following the method CMIN [35], we use the overlap loss and the boundary loss to constrain the training process of the overall network.

Overlap Loss. For each candidate moment $(\hat{s}_{ik}, \hat{e}_{ik})$, we calculate its IoU score IoU_{ik} with the ground truth (s, e). If IoU_{ik} is larger than a correct threshold λ, we reset it to 1, otherwise 0. The higher the IoU score, the higher the confidence score. Thus we use the IoU score to constrain the confidence score of candidate moments in the overlap loss:

$$\mathcal{L}_{over} = -\frac{1}{nK}\sum\nolimits_{i=1}^{n}\sum\nolimits_{k=1}^{K}(1 - IoU_{ik}) \cdot log(1 - cs_{ik}) + IoU_{ik} \cdot log(cs_{ik}), \tag{9}$$

where we consider all the candidates in the overlap loss and K is the number of window widths. n is the number of time step.

Boundary Loss. We compute the localization offsets for the positive candidate moments that IoU scores are larger than a positive threshold γ. Suppose there are N_{pos} positive candidate moments corresponding to ground truth (s, e). For each positive candidate $(\hat{s}_j, \hat{e}_j)$, we calculate the start and end offsets as:

$$(o_j^s, o_j^e) = (s - \hat{s}_j, e - \hat{e}_j), \tag{10}$$

where (o_j^s, o_j^e) are the ground truth offsets. Thus, for N_{pos} positive candidate moments, the boundary loss is:

$$\mathcal{L}_{boun} = \frac{1}{N_{pos}}\sum\nolimits_{j=1}^{N_{pos}} \left\|\hat{o}_j^s - o_j^s\right\|_1 + \left\|\hat{o}_j^e - o_j^e\right\|_1, \tag{11}$$

where the $(\hat{o}_j^s, \hat{o}_j^e)$ are the predicted offsets. $\|\cdot\|_1$ denotes the smooth L1 operation.

We combine the overlap loss and boundary loss with a hyper-parameter α:

$$\mathcal{L} = \mathcal{L}_{over} + \alpha\mathcal{L}_{boun}. \tag{12}$$

4 Experiments

4.1 Datasets and Setup

We test the proposed method on two datasets. The ActivityNet Caption dataset [13] contains videos of human daily outdoor activities. Following the standard split, we use 37417 video-query pairs for training, 17505 pairs for validation, and 17031 pairs for testing. The TACoS dataset [21] contains videos of human cooking scenes. Following the standard split, we use 10146 video-query pairs for training, 4589 pairs for validation, and 4083 pairs for testing.

We use 'R@n, IoU@m' (denoted as R_n^m) as the evaluation metric. It denotes the percentage of top-n retrieved moments where at least one moment has an IoU larger than m with the ground truth. We use $n \in \{1, 5\}$, $m \in \{0.5, 0.7\}$ for ActivityNet Caption, and $m \in \{0.3, 0.5\}$ for TACoS.

Following previous studies, we use the pretrained C3D [24] for video feature extraction, and set the length of video feature as 200. For the query, we use the pretrained GloVe word2vec [20] for word embedding with 300-d features, and the hidden state dimension in Bi-GRU is set to 512. In our self and cross graph encoder, the number of head is set to 4, and the number of layer is set to 2. In the moment retrieval module, we set the window widths as $[8, 16, 32, 64]$ on TACoS, and $[16, 32, 64, 96, 128, 160, 196]$ on ActivityNet Caption. We set the correct threshold λ as 0.3, the positive threshold γ as 0.7, and the loss coefficient α as 1×10^{-3}. During training, we adopt an Adam optimizer with learning rate 2×10^{-4} for TACoS and 4×10^{-4} for ActivityNet Caption. The batch size is set to 64 and 32 respectively. During inference, we first rank all the candidates based on their confidence scores, and then use non-maximum suppression (NMS) to select the top-ranked candidates as the final prediction.

4.2 Comparison with Other Methods

We compare our CGTN method with other methods on ActivityNet Caption dataset and TACoS dataset. The results are shown in Table 1 and Table 2 respectively. The results show that our method outperforms other approaches. These results demonstrate the effectiveness and strength of our method.

Figure 5 illustrates some qualitative results of the moments retrieved by our CGTN model on the TACoS dataset. We observe that our CGTN can generate the accurate time boundaries of moments.

Table 1. Comparison on ActivityNet Caption dataset, measured by $R_n^m(\%)$.

Method	$R_1^{0.3}$	$R_1^{0.5}$	$R_1^{0.7}$	$R_5^{0.3}$	$R_5^{0.5}$	$R_5^{0.7}$
MCN [1]	39.35	21.36	6.43	68.12	53.23	29.70
CTRL [11]	47.43	29.01	10.34	75.32	59.17	37.54
ACRN [16]	49.70	31.67	11.25	76.50	60.34	38.57
QSPN [29]	52.13	33.26	13.43	77.72	62.39	40.78
SCDM [31]	54.80	36.75	19.86	77.29	64.99	41.53
ABLR [32]	55.67	36.79	–	–	–	–
GDP [6]	56.17	39.27	–	–	–	–
CMIN [35]	63.61	43.40	23.88	80.54	67.95	50.73
Our CGTN	**66.80**	**48.52**	**27.32**	**83.11**	**69.67**	**57.41**

Table 2. Comparison on TACoS dataset, measured by $R_n^m(\%)$.

Method	$R_1^{0.1}$	$R_1^{0.3}$	$R_1^{0.5}$	$R_5^{0.1}$	$R_5^{0.3}$	$R_5^{0.5}$
ABLR [32]	34.70	19.50	9.40	–	–	–
ACRN [16]	24.22	19.52	14.62	47.42	34.97	24.88
QSPN [29]	25.31	20.15	15.23	53.21	36.72	25.30
CMIN [35]	32.48	24.64	18.05	62.13	38.46	27.02
GDP [6]	39.68	24.14	13.50	–	–	–
TGN [4]	41.87	21.77	18.90	53.40	39.06	31.02
SCDM [31]	–	26.11	21.17	–	40.16	32.18
CBP [27]	–	27.31	24.79	–	43.64	37.40
VSLNet [34]	–	29.61	24.27	–	–	–
Our CGTN	**42.01**	**32.38**	**25.69**	**68.04**	**52.86**	**38.91**

4.3 Ablation Studies

We explore the component effects of our CGTN by removing each of them from CGTN individually. The ablation studies are list as the following.

w/o DT. The semantic dependency tree (DT) adopted in the graph construction of the sentence is removed. Instead, a fully connected graph is used as the initialization.

w/o VSG: The self-graph encoder for video (VSG) is removed. The extracted video features are directly used for the subsequent modules.

w/o QSG: The self-graph encoder for sentence (QSG) is removed. We directly use the extracted sentence features for the subsequent modules.

w/o CG: The cross-graph attention (CG) is removed. We directly use the video graph after the self-graph encoder for moment retrieval.

The ablation results are shown in Table 3. We observe that the removal of each component of the model leads to decrease in performance. These results show the effectiveness of the different components.

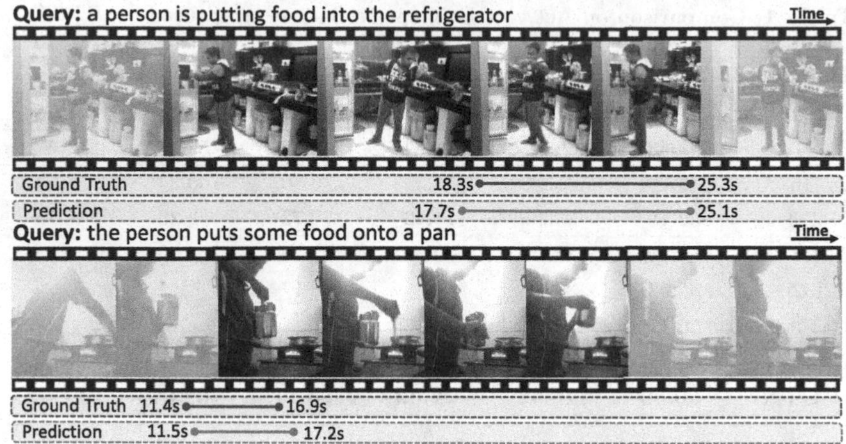

Fig. 5. Some examples of the predicted moments on TACoS dataset.

Table 3. Ablation study on TACoS dataset, measured by $R_n^m(\%)$.

Method	$R_1^{0.1}$	$R_1^{0.3}$	$R_1^{0.5}$	$R_5^{0.1}$	$R_5^{0.3}$	$R_5^{0.5}$
w/o DT	39.55	29.71	23.08	64.59	50.11	35.76
w/o VSG	39.09	29.68	21.74	63.87	50.02	34.91
w/o QSG	38.70	27.99	22.85	62.74	49.21	34.31
w/o CG	38.23	29.12	21.92	62.54	49.63	35.01
Full CGTN	**42.01**	**32.38**	**25.69**	**68.04**	**52.86**	**38.91**

5 Conclusion

In this paper, we propose a cross-graph Transformer network for temporal sentence grounding. The query and video are represented as graph structures which characterize the non-linear relations. Based on the standard multi-head attention in Transformer, we design the customized self and cross graph attention to model the fine-grained dependence of the video and query as well as their interactions. We test our method on two public datasets and the extensive experiments demonstrate the effectiveness of the method. Our future work will investigate new graph attention methods in multi-modal tasks.

Acknowledgement. This research was supported by the grants National Natural Science Foundation of China (No.62088102), the Youth Innovation Team of Shaanxi Universities, and the Fundamental Research Funds for the Central Universities.

References

1. Anne Hendricks, L., Wang, O., Shechtman, E., Sivic, J., Darrell, T., Russell, B.: Localizing moments in video with natural language. In: IEEE International Conference on Computer Vision, pp. 5803–5812 (2017)
2. Cao, M., Chen, L., Shou, M.Z., Zhang, C., Zou, Y.: On pursuit of designing multi-modal transformer for video grounding. arXiv preprint (2021)
3. Carion, N., Massa, F., Synnaeve, G., Usunier, N., Kirillov, A., Zagoruyko, S.: End-to-end object detection with transformers. In: Vedaldi, A., Bischof, H., Brox, T., Frahm, J.-M. (eds.) ECCV 2020. LNCS, vol. 12346, pp. 213–229. Springer, Cham (2020). https://doi.org/10.1007/978-3-030-58452-8_13
4. Chen, J., Chen, X., Ma, L., Jie, Z., Chua, T.S.: Temporally grounding natural sentence in video. In: Conference on Empirical Methods in Natural Language Processing, pp. 162–171 (2018)
5. Chen, J., Ma, L., Chen, X., Jie, Z., Luo, J.: Localizing natural language in videos. In: AAAI Conference on Artificial Intelligence, vol. 33, pp. 8175–8182 (2019)
6. Chen, L., et al.: Rethinking the bottom-up framework for query-based video localization. In: AAAI Conference on Artificial Intelligence, vol. 34, pp. 10551–10558 (2020)
7. Chung, J., Gülçehre, Ç., Cho, K., Bengio, Y.: Empirical evaluation of gated recurrent neural networks on sequence modeling. CoRR abs/1412.3555 (2014)
8. Deng, J., Yang, Z., Chen, T., Zhou, W., Li, H.: TransVG: end-to-end visual grounding with transformers. In: IEEE/CVF International Conference on Computer Vision, pp. 1769–1779 (2021)
9. Du, Y., Fu, Z., Liu, Q., Wang, Y.: Visual grounding with transformers. In: 2022 IEEE International Conference on Multimedia and Expo, pp. 1–6 (2022)
10. Dwivedi, V.P., Bresson, X.: A generalization of transformer networks to graphs. arXiv preprint arXiv:2012.09699 (2020)
11. Gao, J., Sun, C., Yang, Z., Nevatia, R.: TALL: temporal activity localization via language query. In: IEEE International Conference on Computer Vision (ICCV), pp. 5277–5285 (2017)
12. Hou, Z., Ngo, C.W., Chan, W.K.: CONQUER: contextual query-aware ranking for video corpus moment retrieval. In: ACM International Conference on Multimedia, pp. 3900–3908 (2021)
13. Krishna, R., Hata, K., Ren, F., Fei-Fei, L., Carlos Niebles, J.: Dense-captioning events in videos. In: IEEE International Conference on Computer Vision (2017)
14. Li, H., Wei, P., Li, J., Ma, Z., Shang, J., Zheng, N.: Asymmetric relation consistency reasoning for video relation grounding. In: Avidan, S., Brostow, G., Cissé, M., Farinella, G.M., Hassner, T. (eds.) ECCV 2022. LNCS, vol. 13695, pp. 125–141. Springer, Cham (2022). https://doi.org/10.1007/978-3-031-19833-5_8
15. Liu, D., Qu, X., Liu, X.Y., Dong, J., Zhou, P., Xu, Z.: Jointly cross-and self-modal graph attention network for query-based moment localization. In: ACM International Conference on Multimedia, pp. 4070–4078 (2020)
16. Liu, M., Wang, X., Nie, L., He, X., Chen, B., Chua, T.S.: Attentive moment retrieval in videos. In: The 41st international ACM SIGIR Conference on Research & Development in Information Retrieval, pp. 15–24 (2018)
17. Liu, M., Wang, X., Nie, L., Tian, Q., Chen, B., Chua, T.S.: Cross-modal moment localization in videos. In: ACM International Conference on Multimedia, pp. 843–851 (2018)

18. Ma, Z., Wei, P., Li, H., Zheng, N.: HOIG: end-to-end human-object interactions grounding with transformers. In: IEEE International Conference on Multimedia and Expo (ICME), pp. 1–6 (2022)
19. Marcheggiani, D., Titov, I.: Encoding sentences with graph convolutional networks for semantic role labeling. arXiv preprint (2017)
20. Pennington, J., Socher, R., Manning, C.D.: GloVe: global vectors for word representation. In: Conference on Empirical Methods in Natural Language Processing, pp. 1532–1543 (2014)
21. Regneri, M., Rohrbach, M., Wetzel, D., Thater, S., Schiele, B., Pinkal, M.: Grounding action descriptions in videos. Trans. Assoc. Comput. Linguist. **1**, 25–36 (2013)
22. Rodriguez, C., Marrese-Taylor, E., Saleh, F.S., Li, H., Gould, S.: Proposal-free temporal moment localization of a natural-language query in video using guided attention. In: IEEE/CVF Winter Conference on Applications of Computer Vision, pp. 2464–2473 (2020)
23. Shang, J., Wei, P., Li, H., Zheng, N.: Multi-scale interaction transformer for temporal action proposal generation. Image Vis. Comput. **129**, 104589 (2023)
24. Tran, D., Bourdev, L., Fergus, R., Torresani, L., Paluri, M.: Learning spatiotemporal features with 3d convolutional networks. In: IEEE International Conference on Computer Vision, pp. 4489–4497 (2015)
25. Vaswani, A., et al.: Attention is all you need. In: 31st International Conference on Neural Information Processing Systems, pp. 6000–6010 (2017)
26. Veličković, P., Cucurull, G., Casanova, A., Romero, A., Lio, P., Bengio, Y.: Graph attention networks. arXiv preprint (2017)
27. Wang, J., Ma, L., Jiang, W.: Temporally grounding language queries in videos by contextual boundary-aware prediction. In: AAAI Conference on Artificial Intelligence, vol. 34, pp. 12168–12175 (2020)
28. Wu, J., Li, G., Liu, S., Lin, L.: Tree-structured policy based progressive reinforcement learning for temporally language grounding in video. In: AAAI Conference on Artificial Intelligence, vol. 34, pp. 12386–12393 (2020)
29. Xu, H., He, K., Plummer, B.A., Sigal, L., Sclaroff, S., Saenko, K.: Multilevel language and vision integration for text-to-clip retrieval. In: AAAI Conference on Artificial Intelligence, vol. 33, pp. 9062–9069 (2019)
30. Yu, C., Ma, X., Ren, J., Zhao, H., Yi, S.: Spatio-temporal graph transformer networks for pedestrian trajectory prediction. In: Vedaldi, A., Bischof, H., Brox, T., Frahm, J.-M. (eds.) ECCV 2020, Part XII. LNCS, vol. 12357, pp. 507–523. Springer, Cham (2020). https://doi.org/10.1007/978-3-030-58610-2_30
31. Yuan, Y., Ma, L., Wang, J., Liu, W., Zhu, W.: Semantic conditioned dynamic modulation for temporal sentence grounding in videos. IEEE Trans. Pattern Anal. Mach. Intell. **44**, 2725–2741 (2020)
32. Yuan, Y., Mei, T., Zhu, W.: To find where you talk: temporal sentence localization in video with attention based location regression. In: AAAI Conference on Artificial Intelligence, vol. 33, pp. 9159–9166 (2019)
33. Yun, S., Jeong, M., Kim, R., Kang, J., Kim, H.J.: Graph transformer networks. In: Advances in Neural Information Processing Systems, vol. 32 (2019)
34. Zhang, H., Sun, A., Jing, W., Zhou, J.T.: Span-based localizing network for natural language video localization. arXiv preprint (2020)
35. Zhang, Z., Lin, Z., Zhao, Z., Xiao, Z.: Cross-modal interaction networks for query-based moment retrieval in videos. In: 42nd International ACM SIGIR Conference on Research and Development in Information Retrieval, pp. 655–664 (2019)
36. Zhu, X., Su, W., Lu, L., Li, B., Wang, X., Dai, J.: Deformable DETR: deformable transformers for end-to-end object detection. arXiv:2010.04159 (2020)

EGCN: A Node Classification Model Based on Transformer and Spatial Feature Attention GCN for Dynamic Graph

Yunqi Cao, Haopeng Chen(✉), and Jinteng Ruan

Shanghai Jiao Tong University, Shanghai, China
{caoyunqi,chen-hp,rejector}@sjtu.edu.cn

Abstract. Node classification is an important area in graph data-related research and has attracted the attention of many researchers. Graph structure data can be divided into static graphs and dynamic graphs. Due to the temporal characteristics of dynamic graphs, dynamic graphs have higher information density and richer data features than static graph data. In order to better complete the extraction of the features for dynamic graphs, we design a comprehensive feature extraction module and then create the dynamic graph node classification model EGCN. The introduced time dimension in the dynamic graph not only brings the temporal feature but also brings the implicit spatial feature, which is mostly ignored in related research. So we propose a method for modeling implicit spatial features and combine it with GCN to introduce SAGCN for implicit spatial feature attention. We also introduce a temporal feature extraction module called TEncoder based on the transformer and combine them to design the dynamic graph node classification model EGCN. EGCN has two variants, EGCN-S and EGCN-T, which differ in their temporal and spatial characteristics of attention. Experiments show that EGCN achieves state-of-the-art performance. EGCN-S and EGCN-T achieved 1% and 5% improvement over the main baseline DS-TAGCN on dataset DBLP.

Keywords: dynamic graph · node classification · graph convolutional network

1 Introduction

Graph node classification is an important direction in various research areas for graphs. Graph node classification aims at predicting the class of unknown nodes from the attribute features of known classes of nodes in the graph and their topological relationships with their neighbors. This research has many application scenarios in reality, including the prediction and classification of user-group attributes in social networks [11], knowledge graph building [8], finding identification of abnormal accounts in the transaction flow, and so on. In recent years, due to the advantages of graph neural networks on graph data [24], there are

L. Iliadis et al. (Eds.): ICANN 2023, LNCS 14259, pp. 357–368, 2023.
https://doi.org/10.1007/978-3-031-44223-0_29

many works proposing node classification methods based on GNN like GPN [20] and GraphSAGE [8]. Not only that, networks such as GAT [5,23] and GCN [1,21] have also been applied in graph node classification tasks.

Existing graph node classification models mainly focus on static graphs but ignore dynamic graphs, which are composed of a series of static graphs representing data at different timestamps. Compared to static graphs, dynamic graphs have higher information dimension and density, showing temporal characteristics that enable more precise modeling of real-world problems. They have many applications, such as traffic [4] and limb prediction [18,25]. Our focus is on node classification in dynamic graphs.

Dynamic graphs have a stronger feature representation density and modeling capability compared to static graphs, thus enabling dynamic graph-based node classification models to have stronger feature extraction capability, higher classification prediction accuracy, and a wider range of application scenarios. The features of dynamic graphs can be divided into temporal and spatial domain features, i.e. feature evolution in the time dimension and static features at each timestamp. Existing work on dynamic graph node classification has taken these features into account and extracted them accordingly. However, the introduction of the time dimension not only adds temporal features but also introduces implicit spatial features. With time changes, the spatial features of the graph data at a certain timestamp are actually influenced by the corresponding spatial features of other timestamps, which means the features at each timestamp are no longer independent but are associated with the features of the data at other times. Therefore, this implicit feature needs to be considered when performing feature extraction.

Based on the above problems, this paper proposes a dynamic graph node classification model EGCN with implicit feature attention. We tackle three main problems: implicit feature modeling, extraction of temporal features, and extraction of spatial features. For the first problem, we divide the implicit spatial features into two parts: implicit node features and implicit topological features, and propose a unified modeling method for both; for the second problem, based on the powerful feature extraction ability of transformer [22], we combine transformer with dynamic graph data to complete the extraction of temporal features; for spatial feature extraction, we add an implicit feature modeling module on the basis of GCN [10] to achieve a GCN with implicit feature attention. Finally, we combine the above-mentioned modules and propose a complete dynamic graph node classification model EGCN. The main contributions of this paper are as follows.

1. We introduce the implicit spatial feature concept and its modeling method, and combine it with the GCN model to create SAGCN, a module for extracting spatial features with implicit feature attention.
2. We propose TEncoder based on transformer for temporal feature extraction in dynamic graph scenarios.
3. We propose EGCN (TEncoder-SAGCN), a dynamic graph node classification model that captures the evolution of node features with changes in spatial features and achieves node classification tasks.

2 Related Work

In recent years, researchers have proposed graph node classification models specifically for dynamic graphs due to their strong feature representation capabilities.

The existing dynamic graph node classification methods can be divided into two main branches.

Graph embedding is one popular method for handling dynamic graphs as it reduces their dimensionality while preserving temporal and spatial features. This simplifies feature extraction, allowing for easy input into the network. By embedding temporal features directly into the low-dimensional vector, the structure and form of dynamic features become similar to static graph features, eliminating the need to reconstruct the feature extraction network. Recent studies have successfully implemented some graph embedding for dynamic graphs [6,13,16,19]. These methods simplify the problem of dynamic graph feature extraction and allow for the reuse of the static graph feature extraction network.

Another approach for dynamic graph feature extraction is to separately extract temporal and spatial features using different networks. LSTM [9] and GRU [3] are commonly used for temporal feature extraction, while GCN is used for spatial feature extraction. For example, EvolveGCN [14] extracts temporal features through RNN and spatial features through GCN, while WD-GCN and CD-GCN [12] combine LSTM and GCN. There are also many approaches to modeling structured sequence data through different network structures [2,17]. This approach offers better modularity and extensibility compared to direct feature embedding, as it decouples the modeling approach from the data.

Both of the above methods focus only on explicit data in dynamic graphs and ignore the possibility of implicit spatial features. However, the DS-TAGCN model [15] addresses this issue by incorporating implicit topological features using GCN. While the model has shown promising results in dynamic graph node classification, there is still room for improvement. Firstly, the implicit topological features considered are only a part of the implicit spatial features. Secondly, the feature extraction network used by the model can be enhanced. Therefore, the DS-TAGCN model has the potential for further development in both its temporal and spatial feature extraction modules.

3 Problem Formulation

This paper addresses the dynamic graph node classification problem, which involves classifying unknown nodes based on known classes in a dynamic graph. The dynamic graph data is composed of static graph data arranged in chronological order, with each timestamp representing the state of the dynamic graph at that time. Figure 1 illustrates the features of dynamic graph data. A formal description of the dynamic graph node classification problem is given below.

$$D = \{G_1, G_2, \cdots, G_n\} \tag{1}$$

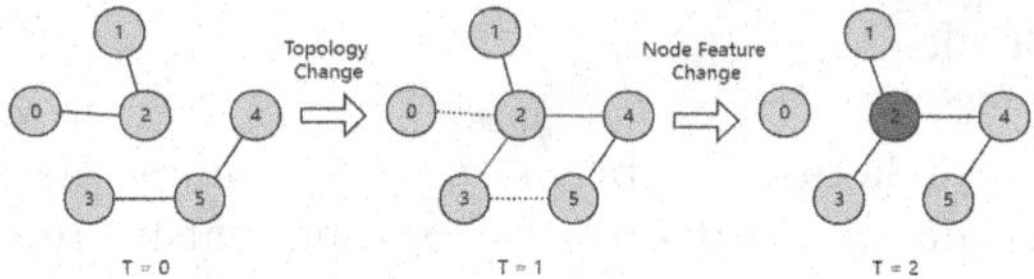

Fig. 1. Dynamic Graph Structure

D represents the dynamic graph, which consists of a set of static graphs combined under different timestamps, and G_i represents the static graphs under timestamp i in the dynamic graph.

$$G_i = \{V, A, X\} \tag{2}$$

In G_i, nodes are represented by the set of nodes V. For each node, its features form the node feature matrix X. The edges between nodes are described by an adjacency matrix A. In the dynamic graph classification problem, the nodes are divided into the set of classified nodes V_C and unclassified nodes V_U.

$$V = V_C \cup V_U \tag{3}$$

Each node of the dynamic graph belongs to a class that does not change with the timestamp. We use L to denote the set of all the classes for nodes. The dynamic graph node classification task is to classify the nodes in the unclassified node set V_U by the classified nodes in V_C and the overall features of the dynamic graph D, then find a class for it in L.

4 Spatial Feature Module

We categorize dynamic graph features into temporal and spatial. Temporal features evolve with time while spatial features relate to node features and topology at each timestamp. This subsection focuses on our spatial feature modeling method. The traditional spatial feature extraction modules only increase data features compared to static graph data, ignoring the connection between data at different times. However, the introduction of the time dimension affects the spatial features of graph data and introduces an implicit spatial feature, representing the overall spatial feature of the whole dynamic graph independent of individual timestamps.

4.1 Implicit Spatial Feature

The implicit spatial feature is unique to dynamic graphs and cannot be directly obtained from data, but it has a significant impact on the spatial feature of dynamic graph data. Extracting and modeling this feature can improve dynamic graph spatial feature modeling and enable the construction of a more capable dynamic graph node classification model.

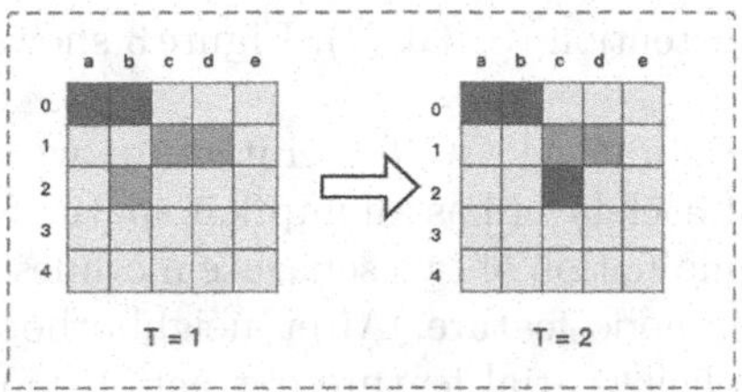

Fig. 2. An Example of Node Feature Evolution

The implicit spatial feature is composed of the implicit topological feature and the implicit node feature. Ruan et al. [15] introduced the implicit topological features in dynamic graphs. In a dynamic graph, the edges between nodes change at different times, resulting in an indirect connection between nodes. For example, in Fig. 1, node 0 and node 3 have no edges connecting them in all three timestamps, but they have a common neighbor node 2 at different timestamps, thus there is actually an indirect topological connection between the two nodes throughout the time dimension. We call this implicit relationship an implicit topological relationship. In addition to the implicit topological features described above, we propose that there are implicit node features in dynamic graphs. In dynamic graph data, nodes may have vastly different static node features at different times. Modeling static node features at each timestamp independently ignores the potential influence of features from other times and may not capture the complete node features. These features, which are independent of the exact timestamp, are referred to as implicit node features. By incorporating implicit node features, the feature extraction module can better capture the overall features of dynamic graph nodes, resulting in more comprehensive feature extraction.

Figure 2 depicts the evolution of dynamic graph node features, corresponding to the data at timestamps T_1 and T_2 in Fig. 1. The vertical axis shows the nodes, the horizontal axis shows the node feature dimensions and different colors represent different feature values. It is evident that node 2 experiences significant feature changes at T_1 and T_2, with features on dimensions b and c being particularly prominent. However, solely considering the static node features would fail to capture the overall feature performance of node 2 over time. Thus, the introduction of implicit node features is crucial to focus on the global node features and enhance the feature extraction process.

4.2 Spatial-Feature Attention GCN

This subsection introduces the specific method of implicit spatial feature modeling. In this paper, we use the GCN model as the base architecture for data spatial feature modeling and realize the extraction of complete spatial features by adding an implicit spatial feature modeling module. We refer to it as a GCN with implicit spatial feature attention (SAGCN). Figure 3 shows the overall design of the SAGCN model.

SAGCN follows the standard GCN architecture with two SAGCN layers stacked sequentially, but each layer has an implicit spatial feature modeling module. This module is a combination of two separate modules: the implicit topology feature and the implicit node feature. After neighborhood feature extraction, data is fed into the implicit spatial feature extraction module. Here, two independent implicit feature extraction modules model the implicit spatial features and incorporate them into the feature module for the next operation. The modeling method for implicit spatial features is explained in detail below. In the original GCN implementation, the operation in each GCN layer is:

$$X^{l+1} = LX^lW \tag{4}$$

where $L = \tilde{D}^{-\frac{1}{2}}\tilde{A}\tilde{D}^{-\frac{1}{2}}$, $\tilde{A} = A + I$, and $\tilde{D} = \sum_j \tilde{A}_{ij}$. The X^{l+1} and X^l correspond to the output of the two GCN layers. The L is the normalized Laplacian matrix, W is the weight matrix, and I is the identity matrix. The original GCN layer only captures the dynamic graph data features of the current timestamp. Still, we enhance it by adding implicit spatial features, including implicit topological and node features. We introduce implicit topological features first, the resulting GCN layer with added features can be calculated as follows:

$$X^{l+1} = (L + W_A)X^lW \tag{5}$$

W_A characterizes the learnable matrix of the implicit topology. For the implicit topological feature modeling, $W_A \in R^{N\times N}$ would introduce too large parameters and may also lead to over-fitting problems. Therefore, we replace W_A with LW_1, where W_1 is the learnable topological attention matrix. Further, we denote X^lW by W_2 and define $W_T = W_1W2$, then the Eq. 5 can be statutorily expressed as:

$$X^{l+1} = LX^lW + LW_T \tag{6}$$

where W_T is the topological attention matrix for implicit topological feature extraction.

For the implicit node feature modeling part, we introduce the modeling module of implicit node features for GCN. By adopting a similar reduction approach, the following calculation results are obtained:

$$X^{l+1} = LX^lW + X_0W_N \tag{7}$$

where W_N is the overall feature attention matrix of the nodes used for implicit node feature extraction. To fully consider the implicit node features independently from the time dimension, we model the computation with the overall features X_0 of the dynamic graph over the entire time scale, and in this paper, we use the mean values of the corresponding features at all timestamps for the initialization of X_0.

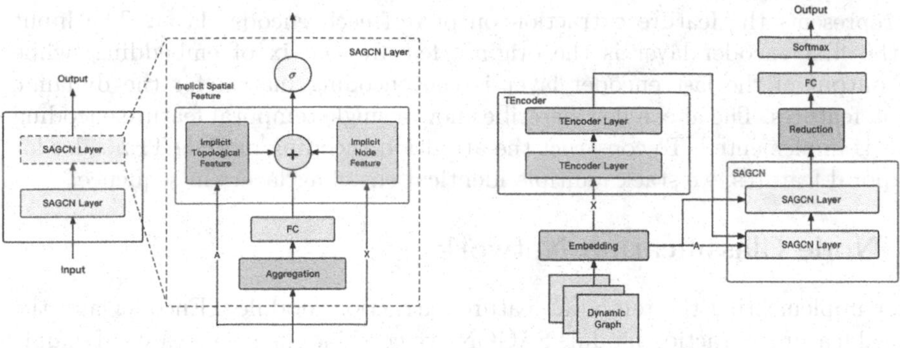

Fig. 3. Architecture of SAGCN

Fig. 4. Architecture of EGCN

We obtain the complete implicit spatial feature modeling method by combining Eq. 6 with Eq. 7. Therefore, the specific computation in the SAGCN layer can be expressed as follows.

$$X^{l+1} = LX^lW + LW_T + X_0W_N \tag{8}$$

SAGCN consists of two SAGCN layers arranged according to the above equation.

5 Temporal Feature Module

In this subsection, we propose the implementation of the temporal feature extraction module, TEncoder. It is a transformer-based attention network designed for extracting temporal node features from dynamic graph data. TEncoder is based on the encoder component of the transformer model and uses multi-head attention computation to extract the features.

The TEncoder model comprises multiple encoder layers that are stacked with the same structure. Each encoder layer's computation process is as follows. First, $Q = XW_Q, K = XW_K, V = XW_V$ where W_Q, W_K, W_V are randomly initialized weight matrices.

$$Z_i = Softmax(\frac{QK^T}{\sqrt{W}})V \tag{9}$$

Z_i is the output of a single self-attentive module, and the output of all single self-attentive modules is combined and transformed to obtain the final output Z_O of the attention module. Finally, the final output of the feature extraction encoding is obtained by the residual layer and the fully connected layer.

$$L_1 = Norm(Z_O + X) \tag{10}$$

$$F_1 = ReLU(L_1W_1 + B_1) \tag{11}$$

$$F_2 = F_1W_2 + B_2 \tag{12}$$

$$L_2 = Norm(F_2 + L_1) \tag{13}$$

L_2 represents the feature extraction output of each encoder layer. The input to the first encoder layer is the original feature matrix of embedding, while the output of the last encoder layer is the encoding matrix for the dynamic graph features. The above flow describes how a single temporal feature encoding layer is implemented. To construct the attention encoding module TEncoder for temporal features, we stack multiple identical encoding layers in sequence.

6 Node Classification Network

After implementing the temporal feature extraction module TEncoder and the spatial feature extraction module SAGCN, we combine them to create a dynamic graph spatiotemporal feature extraction module, which enables us to develop the dynamic graph node classification model TEncoder-SAGCN (EGCN).

Figure 4 shows the overall design of EGCN. First, the embedding module transforms the input into a low-dimensional vector. The feature extraction model completes the extraction of features through the separate spatial module SAGCN and temporal module TEncoder. In particular, the spatial feature extraction module introduces the modeling strategy of implicit spatial features. The reduction module aggregates the overall features into a single dimension for classification and finally performs the classification task.

We assume that for dynamic graph data, temporal features should receive more attention than spatial features, so we adopt a feature extraction model with a priority on temporal features. Following this idea, EGCN model adopts the temporal feature extraction by TEncoder first and then use SAGCN to model the spatial feature approximately.

The modular implementation of the spatiotemporal feature extraction model allows for changing the focus of the node classification model by altering the order of the modules. Based on the origin EGCN design, we implement EGCN-S (Spatial) where SAGCN extracts spatial features first and EGCN-T (Temporal) where TEncoder extracts temporal features first. EGCN-T is a better choice in scenarios where features change significantly over time, but EGCN-S may achieve better results in scenarios where spatial features are more obvious.

7 Experiments

7.1 Experiment Setup

This experiment utilized the DBLP dataset, obtained from the bibliography website dblp[1]. It is a dynamic graph representation of a co-author network, where nodes correspond to authors, edges represent relationships between authors, and timestamps correspond to real-world years. We constructed this dataset using data from the past ten years. Each node in the dataset belongs to one of five research fields, determined by their ten most recent publications. At each timestamp, node features are generated based on the content of the papers published by the authors in that year. Table 1 shows the specific information.

[1] https://dblp.uni-trier.de.

Table 1. Basic Information of Dataset DBLP

Node	Edge	Node Feature	Timestamp	Class
6606	21408	100	10	5

Table 2. Comparison of Different SAGCN

Model	Accuracy	AUC	F1	Implicit Topological Feature	Implicit Node Feature
SAGCN1	0.429	0.683	0.274	✗	✗
SAGCN2	0.453	0.684	0.313	✓	✗
SAGCN3	0.785	0.940*	0.783	✗	✓
SAGCN4	0.798*	0.935	0.792*	✓	✓

7.2 Evaluation of Implicit Spatial Feature Modeling

In this subsection, we verify the effect of the introduction of implicit spatial features and the SAGCN model. We design the following ablation experiments to verify. Equation 8 depicts the SAGCN operation, where LW_T and X_0W_N correspond to modeling implicit topological and node features, respectively. To evaluate the impact of implicit spatial and topological features, we conduct four experiments by varying two implicit spatial features. We only use SAGCN as the feature extraction module to eliminate the impact of other modules. We evaluate the model's performance using relevant metrics for node classification and present the results in Table 2.

The original GCN is referred to as SAGCN1. Table 2 shows that SAGCN with implicit spatial feature modeling achieves better classification results than the original GCN, particularly SAGCN3 with implicit node feature extraction modules, which improved accuracy by over 0.3. These results demonstrate the powerful role of implicit node feature modeling in dynamic graph spatial feature extraction. SAGCN2, which focuses on implicit topological relations, only shows a small improvement on the original GCN, possibly due to the sparsity of the dataset. Implicit topological features may not significantly impact overall feature modeling in sparse datasets. SAGCN3, which focuses on implicit node features, significantly outperforms the original GCN. SAGCN4, which focuses on all implicit spatial features, achieves the best results in most metrics. These results confirm the effectiveness of the proposed implicit spatial feature modeling method.

7.3 Evaluation of Temporal Feature Modeling

In this section, we validate the temporal feature extraction module TEncoder proposed in this paper. To do so, we implement a dynamic graph node classification model using only the temporal feature extraction module. We use LSTM as

Table 3. Comparison of Different Baseline Models

Model	Temporal Modeling	Spatial Modeling	Implicit Topological Modeling	Implicit NodeFeature Modeling	Accuracy	AUC	F1
node2vector	✗	✓	✗	✗	0.369	0.642	0.272
GraphSAGE	✗	✓	✗	✗	0.710	0.907	0.697
GCN	✗	✓	✗	✗	0.429	0.683	0.274
SAGCN	✗	✓	✓	✓	0.798	0.935*	0.792
LSTM	✓	✗	✗	✗	0.768	0.907	0.755
TEncoder	✓	✗	✗	✗	0.797	0.916	0.784
DGCN	✓	✓	✗	✗	0.411	0.701	0.304
TAGCN-LSTM	✓	✓	✓	✗	0.754	0.901	0.745
LSTM-TAGCN	✓	✓	✓	✗	0.765	0.902	0.765
EGCN-S	✓	✓	✓	✓	0.761	0.912	0.747
EGCN-T	✓	✓	✓	✓	0.817*	0.927	0.802*

the baseline and evaluate the classification results. The results of the experiment are recorded in rows 5 and 6 of Table 3. It can be seen that the TEncoder model outperforms the LSTM model in all parameters, demonstrating the effectiveness of the proposed transformer-based temporal feature extraction module.

7.4 Evaluation of Node Classification Model

In this subsection, we validate the effectiveness of our proposed node classification model EGCN, using both EGCN-S and EGCN-T models. To assess its performance, we compared it with several baseline models, including LSTM-TAGCN and TAGCN-LSTM [15] which add implicit topological modeling, GynGEM [6] which is based on spatiotemporal feature modeling using embedding process, and DGCN [12] which combines LSTM and GCN. We also considered static graph-based node classification models such as node2vector [7], GraphSAGE [8], and GCN. Since these models do not account for temporal features, we extracted spatial features for each dynamic graph slice at each timestamp and combined them into a complete feature matrix to apply them in the dynamic graph node classification scenario.

Table 3 summarizes the characteristics of baseline models used in the experiments. The table is divided into three parts, these three components also form the ablation experiment. The first four rows represent models that only model spatial features. These methods generally have poor feature extraction abilities on dynamic graphs. However, SAGCN outperforms other models in each classification metric, indicating the effectiveness of its implicit spatial feature modeling strategy. The result shows that temporal feature modeling is crucial for dynamic graph data, and the lack of it can impact the overall classification ability. Even though SAGCN does not model temporal features directly, its implicit spatial features serve as an indirect representation of temporal features, resulting in the strongest feature extraction capability among the spatial models. The second part is rows 5 and 6, they are described in Sect. 7.3.

The last part (rows 7-11) presents complete feature extraction and classification models proposed for dynamic graphs. TAGCN-LSTM and LSTM-TAGCN include an implicit topological feature modeling module, which improves classification ability compared to DGCN. Rows 9 and 10 present the EGCN models proposed in this paper, where LSTM-TAGCN corresponds to EGCN-T (temporal feature-first) and TAGCN-LSTM corresponds to EGCN-S (spatial feature-first). The cross-sectional comparison indicates that EGCN outperforms LSTM-TAGCN on this node classification task while EGCN-T achieved a global optimum in both accuracy and F1 particularly. It illustrates the effectiveness of the implicit node feature modeling proposed in this paper and the proposed dynamic graph node classification model.

8 Conclusion

We introduce EGCN, a node classification model for dynamic graphs based on spatiotemporal feature extraction. Our approach extracts temporal features using a transformer-based module TEncoder, and introduces SAGCN, a dynamic graph spatial feature extraction module, to model spatial features with attention to implicit spatial features. We combine these modules to create EGCN, which achieves state-of-the-art performance on node classification tasks on our dataset DBLP. Our experiments show that the introduction of implicit spatial features improves GCN's feature extraction capabilities, while our complete EGCN model significantly outperforms the baseline DS-TAGCN [15] in both feature extraction ability and classification accuracy. Overall, EGCN expands the ways in which we can model temporal features and improves the modeling strategy for spatial features.

References

1. Abu-El-Haija, S., Kapoor, A., Perozzi, B., Lee, J.: N-GCN: multi-scale graph convolution for semi-supervised node classification. In: Uncertainty in Artificial Intelligence, pp. 841–851. PMLR (2020)
2. Louis-Pascal, X., Meng, Q., Jian, T.: Continuous graph neural networks. In: ICML, pp. 10432–10441 (2020)
3. Chung, J., Gulcehre, C., Cho, K., Bengio, Y.: Empirical evaluation of gated recurrent neural networks on sequence modeling. arXiv preprint arXiv:1412.3555 (2014)
4. Dai, R., Xu, S., Gu, Q., Ji, C., Liu, K.: Hybrid spatio-temporal graph convolutional network: Improving traffic prediction with navigation data. In: Proceedings of the 26th ACM SIGKDD International Conference on Knowledge Discovery & Data Mining, pp. 3074–3082 (2020)
5. Gong, L., Cheng, Q.: Exploiting edge features for graph neural networks. In: Proceedings of the IEEE/CVF Conference on Computer Vision and Pattern Recognition, pp. 9211–9219 (2019)
6. Goyal, P., Kamra, N., He, X., Liu, Y.: DynGEM: deep embedding method for dynamic graphs. arXiv:1805.11273. Social and Information Networks (2018)

7. Grover, A., Leskovec, J.: node2vec: scalable feature learning for networks. In: Proceedings of the 22nd ACM SIGKDD International Conference on Knowledge Discovery and Data Mining, pp. 855–864 (2016)
8. Hamaguchi, T., Oiwa, H., Shimbo, M., Matsumoto, Y.: Knowledge transfer for out-of-knowledge-base entities: a graph neural network approach. arXiv preprint arXiv:1706.05674 (2017)
9. Hochreiter, S., Schmidhuber, J.: Long short-term memory. Neural Comput. **9**(8), 1735–1780 (1997)
10. Kipf, T.N., Welling, M.: Semi-supervised classification with graph convolutional networks. arXiv preprint arXiv:1609.02907 (2016)
11. Li, J., Rong, Y., Cheng, H., Meng, H., Huang, W., Huang, J.: Semi-supervised graph classification: a hierarchical graph perspective. In: The World Wide Web Conference, pp. 972–982 (2019)
12. Manessi, F., Rozza, A., Manzo, M.: Dynamic graph convolutional networks. In: Pattern Recognition, p. 107000 (2020)
13. Nguyen, H.G., Lee, B.J., Rossi, A.R., Ahmed, K.N., Koh, E., Kim, S.: Continuous-time dynamic network embeddings. In: WWW 2018: The Web Conference 2018 Lyon France April, 2018, pp. 969–976 (2018)
14. Pareja, A., et al.: EvolveGCN: evolving graph convolutional networks for dynamic graphs. arXiv:1902.10191. Learning(2019)
15. Ruan, J., Chen, H., Wang, Z., Chen, S.: DS-TAGCN: a dual-stream topology attentive GCN for node classification in dynamic graphs. In: 2021 International Joint Conference on Neural Networks (IJCNN), pp. 1–7. IEEE (2021)
16. Sankar, A., Wu, Y., Gou, L., Zhang, W., Yang, H.: DySAT - deep neural representation learning on dynamic graphs via self-attention networks. In: WSDM 2020: The Thirteenth ACM International Conference on Web Search and Data Mining Houston TX USA February, 2020, pp. 519–527 (2020)
17. Seo, Y., Defferrard, M., Vandergheynst, P., Bresson, X.: Structured sequence modeling with graph convolutional recurrent networks. In: Cheng, L., Leung, A.C.S., Ozawa, S. (eds.) ICONIP 2018. LNCS, vol. 11301, pp. 362–373. Springer, Cham (2018). https://doi.org/10.1007/978-3-030-04167-0_33
18. Shi, L., Zhang, Y., Cheng, J., Lu, H.: Two-stream adaptive graph convolutional networks for skeleton-based action recognition. In: Proceedings of the IEEE/CVF Conference on Computer Vision and Pattern Recognition, pp. 12026–12035 (2019)
19. Singer, U., Guy, I., Radinsky, K.: Node embedding over temporal graphs. In: IJCAI, pp. 4605–4612 (2019)
20. Stadler, M., Charpentier, B., Geisler, S., Zügner, D., Günnemann, S.: Graph posterior network: Bayesian predictive uncertainty for node classification. In: Advances in Neural Information Processing Systems 34 (2021)
21. Vashishth, S., Sanyal, S., Nitin, V., Talukdar, P.: Composition-based multi-relational graph convolutional networks. arXiv preprint arXiv:1911.03082 (2019)
22. Vaswani, A., et al.: Attention is all you need. In: Advances in Neural Information Processing Systems 30 (2017)
23. Veličković, P., Cucurull, G., Casanova, A., Romero, A., Lio, P., Bengio, Y.: Graph attention networks. arXiv preprint arXiv:1710.10903 (2017)
24. Xu, K., Hu, W., Leskovec, J., Jegelka, S.: How powerful are graph neural networks? arXiv preprint arXiv:1810.00826 (2018)
25. Yan, S., Xiong, Y., Lin, D.: Spatial temporal graph convolutional networks for skeleton-based action recognition. In: Thirty-second AAAI Conference on Artificial Intelligence (2018)

Enhance Representational Differentiation Step by Step: A Two-Stage Encoder-Decoder Network for Implicit Discourse Relation Classification

Yuxiang Lu, Yu Hong(✉), Zujun Dou, and Guodong Zhou

School of Computer Science and Technology, Soochow University, Suzhou, China
tianxianer@gmail.com , gdzhou@suda.edu.cn

Abstract. We tackle implicit discourse relation classification (abbr., IDRC). The current neural IDRC models still suffer from the unbalanced data distributions and one-to-many equivocal correspondence. Different classes of instances have hard-to-distinguish representations in a semantic space, which hurts the classification process. We propose a new encoder-decoder network to improve the representational differentiation in encoding and decoding, by two cold-start and hot-start learning phases. We use metric learning and self-generation for constrained differentiation. We also use a KNN-based discriminator with confidence-based sampling. It improves the distribution-sensitive relation classification. The results show that our model, in PDTB 2.0 and PDTB 3.0 benchmarks, outperforms the state-of-the-art methods in most cases. We will share the models and codes for reproducible research (https://github.com/Destiny-Lu/HCS-KNN).

Keywords: Discourse relation classification · Metric learning · Refine distribution

1 Introduction

task of discourse relation analysis is to recognize the semantic relations between arguments [1], such as A_i and A_j in case 1), which appear as two successively-occurred text spans in a document. The current study tackles it in the way of text classification, dividing pairs of arguments into different classes of relations, such as the ones we considered in this paper, including `Expansion` (EXP.), `Contingency` (CON.), `Comparison` (COM.) and `Temporality` (TEM.).

Recently, a variety of neural encoders have been developed to enhance the distributed representation learning, so as to differentiate the distributions of various relation-types of argument pairs in a unified semantic space. They significantly contribute to the effective relation classification during decoding. Nevertheless, it is still difficult to obtain entirely distinguishable distributions because of the following data characteristics in The Penn Discourse TreeBank (PDTB) [13].

L. Iliadis et al. (Eds.): ICANN 2023, LNCS 14259, pp. 369–381, 2023.
https://doi.org/10.1007/978-3-031-44223-0_30

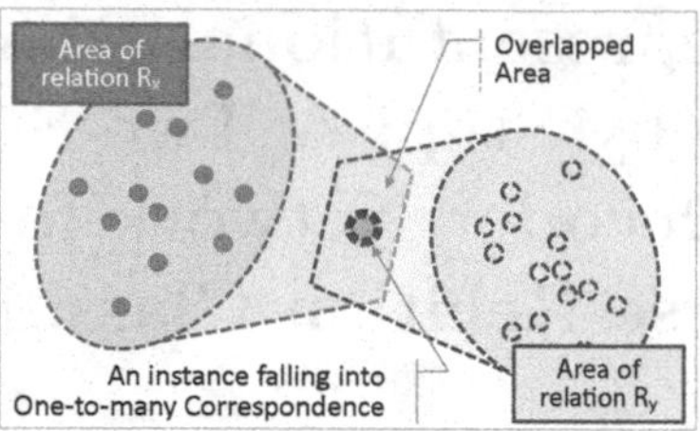

Fig. 1. The enlarged range of overlapped distribution areas between different relation-types of argument pairs.

1) $\mathbf{A}_i$ *For South Gardens, the grid was to be a 3-D network of masonry or hedge walls with real plants inside them.*
   $\mathbf{A}_j$ *In a letter to the BPCA, Kelly/Varnell called this "arbitrary and amateurish".*
   $\mathbf{A}_k$ *Landscape architects were expelled from the garden in July.*

   Relations between A_i and A_j: **CON.**, **EXP**.
   Relations between A_j and A_k: **CON.**, **TEM**.

First of all, a large number of argument pairs have the same arguments, but different relations. For example, two argument pairs from case 1) have the same argument A_j, but different relations. The shareable arguments make the argument pairs hard to distinguish in distribution. Second, many argument pairs have more than one type of relation. For example, A_i and A_j in case 1) have both EXP and CON relations. The ambiguous relation correspondence enlarges the overlapped distribution areas between different relation-types of argument pairs (see Fig. 1). This makes it hard to project argument pairs into the areas with clear class boundaries. Finally, the existing studies still suffer from unbalanced data distributions. The rare temporally-related arguments (5% in all) are not "stripped" from the common instances of EXP relation (54%), by their representations. The data characteristics (argument sharing, one-to-many correspondence and unbalanced data distribution) worsen each other.

In this paper, we intend to enhance representational differentiation step by step, using a two-stage encoder-decoder network.

The first stage stands for a cold-start phase, where the hybrid data of implicit and explicit is used for initially fine-tuning the pretrained RoBERTa [9] encoder. In addition, the constrained representation differentiation is conducted at this stage, using metric learning and self-generation. Metric learning [22] is utilized to distance the distributions of a specific relation-type of argument pairs from other types. Self-Generation is applied for imposing constraints on the distributional data migration. It prevents severe variation of distributed representations, so as to avoid confusion in distribution among all classes of instances and enhance the encoder's ability to extract information from argument pairs.

The second stage stands for a hot-start phase, where pure implicit IDRC data is used to fine-tune the encoder obtained in the first stage, with the goal of enhancing representational differentiation on task-specific data. KNN [1] coupled with confidence-based sampling is used as the decoder. It determines relations conditioned on few high-confidence instances instead of all available ones.

Ideally, in the first stage, we intend to address the issue of indistinguishable distributions caused by argument sharing and one-to-many correspondence. In the second stage, we tackle unbalanced data distribution and close the gap between hybrid data and pure data. The experiments on the benchmark PDTB 2.0 demonstrate that the models in both stages produce considerable improvements. In addition, compared to the state of the art, our method yields the improvements of about 5.0% and 7.2% F1-scores for the binary classification of rarely-occurred COM and TEM relations, with minor performance degradation for the frequently-occurred EXP relation.

2 Related Work

Information interaction and fusion between arguments help to enhance context-aware semantic encoding. This is proven in recent research [14,24]. Zhang et al. [24] (2019) construct a cross-argument connection graph, and use GCN to implement information convergence over the graph. Ruan et al. [14] (2020) develop a two-channel interactively-propagative attention network, where interactive and self attention are used for encoding. Ruan et al. [14] (2020)'s model is similar to Lan et al. [6] (2017)'s interaction model, but Lan et al. [6] (2017) build two encoder-decoder channels for multi-task learning over the argument pair, and use gated interaction between the channels. Other advanced interaction-based approaches include multi-grained [2] and multi-perspective [8] bidirectional interaction, global-to-local interaction learning by BERT [15], and penalty-based confrontation with smooth interactive attention [8].

Data sparsity is a challenge for obtaining reliable encoders for IDRC. Previous study expands IDRC corpus using explicit instances by connective elimination [11]. Recently, back translation between explicit and implicit instances is used for data expansion [16]. Besides, multi-task learning is used. Some scholars [6,12,19] build auxiliary tasks to enhance the IDRC-specific encoder, by sharing the knowledge from different tasks. They use external datasets for auxiliary tasks, such as BLLIP corpus [6] and bilingually-constrained synthetic data [19]. The common auxiliary tasks are the prediction and/or classification of explicit connectives. Similarly, Xu et al. [23] (2018) design a self-supervised active learning loop to learn from both internal and external datasets. By contrast, Dou et al. [3] (2021) use CVAE to generate the variant embeddings of observable instances in encoding, to achieve data augmentation without external data.

Unbalanced data distributions in PDTB may cause biases in classifying instances based on distributed representations. The common solution for this problem is downsampling. Li et al. [7] (2014) examine the effects of various methods, including upsampling, downsampling, feature sharping, etc.

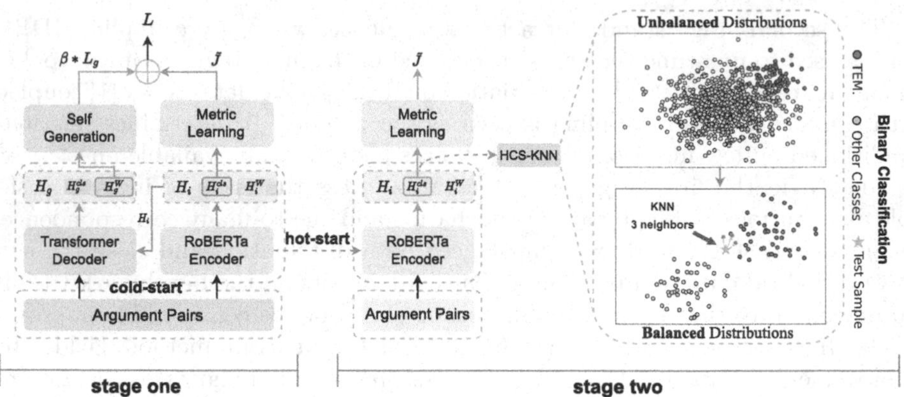

Fig. 2. The architecture of our two-stage encoder-decoder network for IDRC. (Color figure online)

3 Approach

We construct a two-stage encoder-decoder network towards IDRC, where representational differentiation is performed in both the encoding and decoding processes, step by step. We denote the network as "scratcher" from here on. Figure 2 shows the overall architecture of "scratcher". It utilizes the pretrained RoBERTa encoder to produce distributed representations for pairwise arguments, and fine-tunes it twice in the cold-start and hot-start encoding phases respectively.

In the code-start phase, the hybrid IDRC data is used to fine-tune the encoder. Specifically, constrained representational differentiation is done, using metric learning and self-generation in a multi-task framework. The goal of metric learning is to make the representations of argument pairs distinct for different relation-types. In contrast, self-generation prevents too much variation.

In the hot-start phase, the pure IDRC data is used for fine-tuning. The encoder is connected with a statistical KNN discriminator instead of any fully-connected layers. Confidence-based sampling is used to determine the relation on high-confidence K-nearest neighbors. This enhances representational differentiation. The discriminator is not involved in fine-tuning. Fine-tuning is done within metric learning (metric learning is done twice in the two phases).

3.1 Hybrid and Pure Datasets

We train the scratcher" network with two datasets, hybrid and pure. The pure dataset is the benchmark IDRC corpus in PDTB, where all the argument pairs have no explicit connectives (the annotated relations depend on the understanding of argument semantics). The hybrid dataset is made by combining IDRC and EDRC corpora in PDTB. EDRC has a large-scale argument pairs, each with an explicit connective (e.g., *because*) that signals the relation type. We follow the previous work [11,16,23] to delete explicit connectives from EDRC instances before combination.

2) $\mathbf{A}_1$ *The seniority-list controversy, along with the job-classification dispute, has been turned over to the mediator,*
$\mathbf{A}_2$ ***Meanwhile*** *the company is operating with two separate pilot groups and seniority lists.*

The hybrid dataset has more instances and richer semantic information, but it also has EDRC noises after connective deletion. See the case in 2), where the EDRC instance is annotated with TEM relation because of the connective "*meanwhile*", but it is EXP relation when the connective is masked. So, we use the hybrid dataset to fine-tune RoBERTa encoder in the code-start phase, to improve the encoder in perceiving domain-related semantic knowledge. The pure dataset is used for fine-tuning in the hot-start phase, to strengthen the encoder using exact task-specific instances, without noises.

3.2 Stage 1: Constrained Differentiation

We segment every argument into tokens before use, and consider an argument as the token sequence. Given a pair of arguments A_1 and A_2, we concatenate the corresponding token sequences in terms of the regular input pattern of pretrained RoBERTa:

$$S = [CLS]A_1[SEP]A_2[SEP] \tag{1}$$

where, CLS denotes the aggregated feature as usual, while SEP is the special token that labels the sequence boundaries. The maximum length of both A_1 and A_2 is set to 128. We use the pretrained RoBERTa encoder to compute the hidden state H_i: $H_i = \text{RoBERTa}(S)$, where H_i has the representation $H_i^{cls} \in \mathbb{R}^d$ of CLS and the representations $H_i^W \in \mathbb{R}^{128\times d}$ of all the tokens in A_1 and A_2 (i.e., $H_i = [H_i^{cls}, H_i^W]$). We use H_i^{cls} for metric learning to get distinguishable representations (see the blue channel in Fig. 2). We use H_i^W for self-generation (see the green channel in Fig. 2), which prevents too much variation of H_i.

We see that, in the cold-start phase, there is no neural layer or unit connected with an IDRC decoder. Both metric learning and self-generation run in self-supervised learning, and they alternate and compete during training. The main effect we want is to improve the shareable RoBERTa encoder, i.e., the one shared by both channels. In the rest of this section, we explain the two channels.

Metric Learning. Metric learning is done during training. It improves the encoder in migrating instances by refining their representations, by grouping positive instances and separating negative ones. Usually, the lifted structure loss $\tilde{J}$ [17] is used to evolve the encoder with back-propagation. It is computed based on Euclidean distance d between instances:

$$J = \sum_{i\in\mathcal{C}} \left(\log \sum_{k\in\mathcal{C}_o} e^{(\alpha - d_{i,k})} + \sum_{j\in\mathcal{C}_p} d_{i,j} \right) \tag{2}$$

$$\tilde{J} = J/(\mathcal{N}_p + \mathcal{N}_o) \tag{3}$$

where, $\mathcal{C}_p$ denotes the positive set which contains $\mathcal{N}_p$ positive instances, while $\mathcal{C}_o$ denotes the negative set which contains $\mathcal{N}_o$ negative instances. Specially, $\mathcal{C}$ is the union of $\mathcal{C}_p$ and $\mathcal{C}_o$, containing all instances in a mini-batch. Besides, $e^{(*)}$ is the exponential function, and α is a hyperparameter. Euclidean distance d is computed using the embedding H^{cls} output by RoBERTa. In our experiments, the argument pairs holding the consistent relation are specified as positive instances of each other. On the contrary, the argument pairs holding inconsistent relations are considered as negative instances.

According to Eq. (2), increasing di, k and decreasing di, j reduce loss $\tilde{J}$. That means, if an encoder produces different representations for different relation-types of argument pairs, di, k and $\tilde{J}$ will decrease. If the encoder produces similar representations for the same relation-type of argument pairs, di, j and $\tilde{J}$ will decrease. So, fine-tuning the RoBERTa encoder by metric learning helps to produce distinguishable representations for different types of instances, i.e., differentiating relation classes in distribution.

A possible drawback of metric learning is Chained Chaotic Redistribution (CCR). CCR means that migration of a class of instances causes their invasion into the areas of other types of instances. See Fig. 3-(a), for example, when the instances of relation EXP are migrated from the area of relation CON, they may invade the area of relation TEM. Worse, it may be a chained form when different classes of instances are migrated cyclically.

CCR may happen when different classes of instances are organized in a series of batches, and used for minimize the loss $\tilde{J}$ during training. There are two main reasons. First, our loss function $\tilde{J}$ pulls the same relation embedding close and pushes away the different within a batch. But we cannot ensure that the different relation embeddings are pushed to a right position. For example, we can close the distance between Con within a batch and push away the distance between Con and Exp. But Exp may be pushed into the space of Tem, and then more Exp will be pulled into Tem when the distance between Exp is closed. This can cause a chain effect and interaction between batches. Second, many argument pairs have more than one type of relation. This can affect the class boundaries (Fig. 1) and even cause spatial invasion (Fig. 3-(a)), which unbalanced data distributions can worsen.

Self-generation. To prevent too much CCR, we build a self-generation based learning channel to limit representational differentiation (i.e., finite migration). The channel has RoBERTa encoder and transformer decoder, acting as a Seq2Seq generation model. The decoding accuracy of the generation task depends on the encoding performance, so self-generation can improve the encoding capability. The generation task also constrains the encoding process so that it doesn't rely only on metric learning but also on its semantic representation. It drives the encoder to produce the representations that help to revive the input argument pair. This helps to reduce dramatic representational changes (see Fig. 3-(b)).

Specifically, given the hidden state H_i output by RoBERTa encoder, we feed it into the transformer decoder (abbr., $Tran$), along with the token sequence S

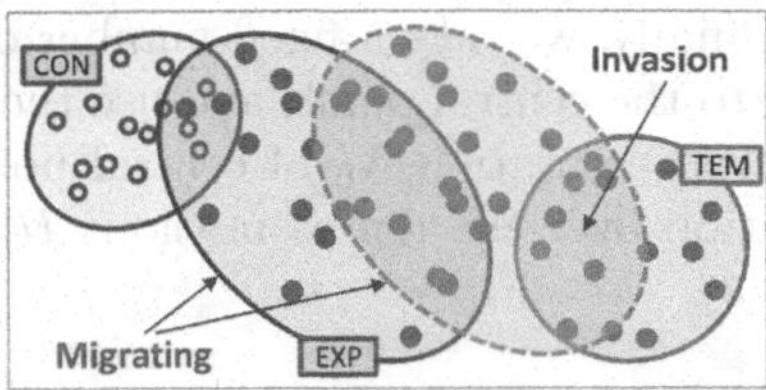

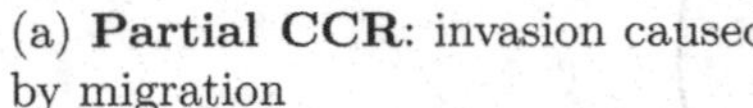
(a) **Partial CCR**: invasion caused by migration

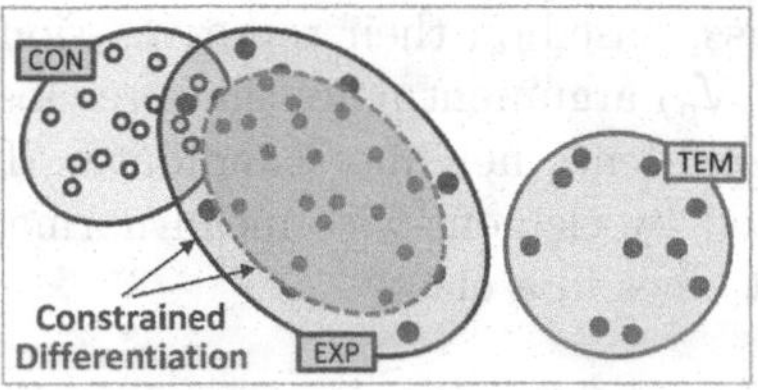

(b) **Impose** constraint on differention

Fig. 3. Diagrams of partial CCR as well as constrained differentiation (by self-generation).

of argument pair. This allows the decoder state H_g to be estimated by $Tran$, which includes both the decoder state H_g^{cls} of CLS and the states H_g^W of possible tokens in the output sequence:

$$H_g = Tran(H_i, S) \tag{4}$$

The generation of argument pair is performed by sequence prediction conditioned on H_g^W. We couple the transformer decoder with a fully-connected layer and softmax layer, so as to predict the output sequence. Cross entropy L_g between the input arguments and self-generation result is used as the loss for back propagation during training.

Multi-task Learning. The metric learning and self-generation channels share the RoBERTa encoder. The shareable parameters in RoBERTa are fine-tuned when supervised learning is conducted for both channels. Towards every batch of training data, metric learning is conducted and supervised for learning first, and then self-generation. The overall loss used for back propagation is calculated by combining $\tilde{J}$ and L_g with a trade-off coefficient β:

$$\mathcal{L} = \tilde{J} + \beta L_g \tag{5}$$

3.3 Stage 2: Task-Specific Differentiation

We transfer the RoBERTa encoder to the pure IDRC data in the hot-start phase, where fine-tuning is done again. The goal is to improve the encoder's adaptability to IDRC task. Representational differentiation is done in this phase. But it not only happens in a single-channel metric learning process, but also in the statistics-based relation determination process.

Confidence-based sampling helps KNN. It ensures the selection of neighbors that have distinguishable representations. We call them high-confidence neighbors. Confidence-based sampling has three steps: first, we find the central point of distribution area for each relation-type of argument pairs; second, for a class, we calculate Euclidean distance to the central point for each argument pair in the class, based on their representations; Finally, we take a fixed number of $\mathcal{N}_c$ ($\mathcal{N}_c < \mathcal{N}_p$) argument pairs that are closest to the central point, and use them as high-confidence neighbor candidates. The representation X_0 of central point is obtained by element-wise mean normalization over the representations H_i^{cls} of all instances in a class:

$$X_0 = \left(\sum_{i=1}^{\mathcal{N}_p} H_i^{cls} \right) / \mathcal{N}_p \tag{6}$$

The hyperparameter $\mathcal{N}_c$ is the same for all the classes during sampling. This helps to reduce the negative effects of unbalanced data distribution when KNN is used. The sampled neighbor candidates are in the core area of a class (see Fig. 2). Differentiation is improved by that.

Metric learning is used as in stage one. But it is done separately, without self-generation. So there is no constraint on representational differentiation in the hot-start phase. It assumes that a global mutually-exclusive relationship among all classes of instances has been learned on the hybrid data. Doing metric learning again on the pure dataset (a subset of hybrid data) only influences the representations of IDRC instances slightly. Also, those ambiguous samples in the middle of the relation space will be filtered a lot during the confidence-based sampling process. More importantly, location discrimination should be the only goal in the second stage of training, and self-generation will hurt the model's performance instead.

4 Experimentation

4.1 Dataset and Evaluation Metrics

We experiment on the benchmark corpus of PDTB 2.0. We follow the common practice [5] to split the corpus, taking sections 02-20 as the training set, sections 00-01 as the development set (abbr., Dev), and sections 21-22 as the test set. Table 3 (in Appendix) show the statistics of argument pairs in different relation classes (Rel.) and datasets. We follow the previous work to evaluate all IDRC models using $F1$-score and accuracy (*Acc.*), for both binary and 4-way IDRC.

4.2 Hyperparameter Settings

In the training process, we set the learning rate to 2e−5 for the first stage, while 1e−5 for the second stage. We conduct 100 steps of warm-up and 0.01 decay of L2 weights. The batch size is set to 32. The epochs are set to 20 and 10 in the first and second stages. AdamW [10] is used as the optimizer at all stages. We use wordpieces [20] for segmentation. The input length of encoder is set to 256, while that of 3-layer transformer decoder is set to 128. Truncation is used. We set α and β to 1 and 0.1.

Table 1. Performance (%) comparison to state of the art in PDTB2.0 (the top half) and PDTB3.0 (the bottom half). Our "scratcher" is considered for comparison.

Model	COM.	CON.	EXP.	TEM.	4-way F1	*Acc.*
Nguyen et al. [12]	48.44	56.84	73.66	38.60	53.00	-
Varia et al. [18]	44.10	56.02	72.11	44.41	50.20	59.13
He et al. [4]	47.98	55.62	69.37	38.94	51.24	59.94
Liu et al. [8]	59.44	60.98	77.66	50.26	63.39	69.06
Dou et al. [3]	55.72	63.39	**80.34**	44.01	**65.06**	70.17
Ours ("scratcher")	**60.74**	**63.55**	77.90	**51.21**	63.76	**70.84**
Xiang et al. [21]	35.83	66.77	70.00	42.13	56.63	64.04
Ours ("Scratcher")	**58.00**	**73.48**	**77.01**	**54.47**	**65.57**	**72.05**

4.3 Main Results

We compare our "scratcher" model with the state-of-the-art IDRC models. Table 1 shows the results.

For binary classification, our model improves COM, CON and TEM. These classes have fewer instances than EXP (see Table 3), and previous work fails to improve them except Liu et al. [8] (2020)'s multi-perspective model. Our method achieves the best performance without external corpora. Our method outperforms Liu et al. [8] (2020)'s model for both binary and 4-way IDRC. The advantage is 2.57% (for CON) at best. Dou et al. [3] (2021)'s CVAE-based data augmentation method has a higher $F1$-score for EXP. The model is self-supervised like ours. But Dou et al. [3] (2021) augments data for all classes equally. It fails to address unbalanced data distributions. So its performance is uneven over the classes (e.g., higher $F1$ for EXP but lower for TEM). Xiang et al. [21] (2022)'s MANF uncovers semantic and linguistic evidence and its Tem and Com performance is also affected by the data characteristics.

Our "scratcher" is trained to differentiate representations under the constraint of preventing disordered migration. It also alleviates unbalanced data distributions by classifying high-confidence neighbor candidates. The performance of "scratcher" is smooth, with significant improvements for COM and TEM (7.2% at best), and minor degradation for EXP (2.4%), in PDTB 2.0. Our performance in 4-way is mediocre, because the CCR phenomenon is more severe in 4-way than binary. The 4-way task needs to consider the space of four categories, while the binary only needs positive and negative ones. Our "scratcher", in PDTB v3.0 corpus, outperforms the state-of-the-art system in every case.

4.4 Ablation Experiments

We carry out ablation experiments to examine the neural components of representational differentiation step by step, where **Baseline** is constructed with RoBERTa encoder and linear decoder, **KNN** replaces the linear decoder by

Table 2. Ablation experiment results (%), where "scratcher" is constructed by expanding the baseline step by step.

Method	Data	COM.	CON.	EXP.	TEM.	4-way F1	*Acc.*
Baseline	Pure	53.71	59.30	75.90	32.46	50.97	62.24
+ML	Pure	54.08	59.80	77.26	33.23	59.70	67.40
+KNN+ML	Pure	55.04	60.95	76.51	32.56	60.13	68.24
+HCS&KNN+ML	Pure	60.51	61.04	76.45	42.23	60.87	68.33
+HCS&KNN+ML+Trans	Hybrid	59.26	62.88	77.01	48.21	61.81	70.26
Ours ("Scratcher")	Hybrid	60.74	63.55	77.90	51.21	63.76	70.84

KNN; **HCS&KNN** denotes the situation that high-confidence samples (i.e., distinguishable neighbors) are used for KNN; **ML** denotes the use of metric learning; **Trans** refers to the utilization of the two-stage learning framework (transferring from cold-start phase to hot-start); **SG** is the situation that self-generation is used for imposing constraints. Since few studies are based on PDTB v3.0, for comparison, all the following experiments are based on PDTB 2.0.

The experimental results are shown in Table 2. First of all, it can be observed that ML, KNN and HCS yield significant improvements when pure IDRC is used for training. In addition, the separately-implemented two-stage learning on hybrid data (Trans) enhances the encoder further, yielding improvements for most IDRC scenarios. Though it can be found that the binary IDRC performance of COM degrades. Such degradation results from CCR, i.e., disordered migration caused by unconstrained ML. The problem is avoided when self-generation (SG) is used for imposing constraints.

4.5 KNN Versus Perceptron for Decoding

Our "scratcher" doesn't use any neural decoder. Instead, the statistics-based KNN is used for IDRC. It acts as a decoder, but it isn't involved in the learning during training. We test the performance of "scratcher" when a one-layer perceptron is used as the decoder, where perceptron is trained with the other neural components (i.e., ML, Trans and SG). Figure 4-(a) shows the performance of "scratcher" on hybrid data with and without perceptron.

We see that perceptron causes performance degradation, even though it is compatible with other neural units. The reason is that it cannot work with HCS to reduce the negative effects of unbalanced data distribution. In Appendix, we report the effects of using Multi-Layer Perceptron (MLP) for decoding.

4.6 Additional Hyperparameter Due to KNN

Replacing MLP with HCS&KNN is effective and less time-consuming, but it adds an extra hyperparameter to the development process. The hyperparameter is the number $\mathcal{N}_c$ of high-confidence neighbor candidates and K neighbors.

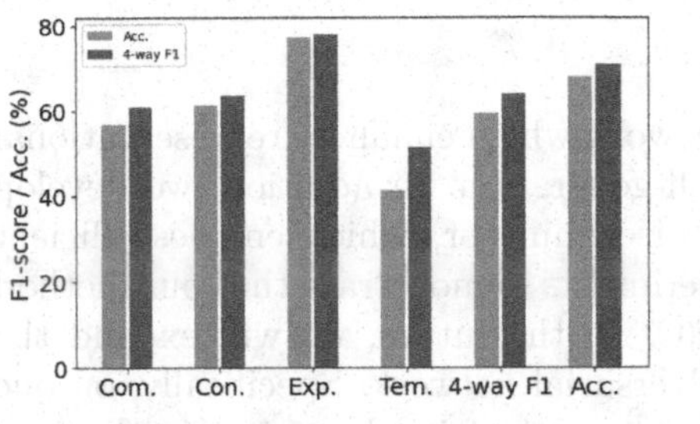

(a) Perceptron versus HCS&KNN.

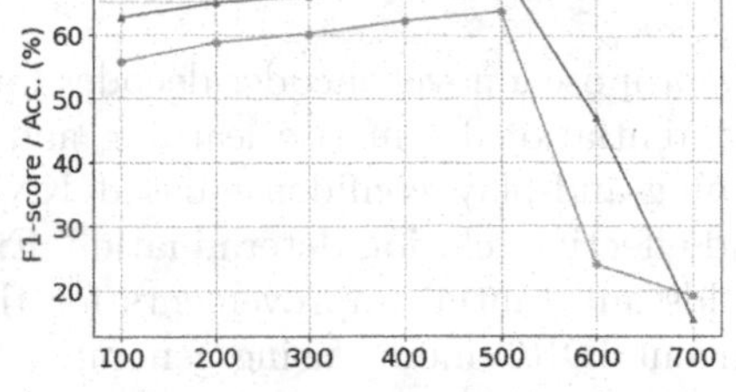

(b) Setting $\mathcal{N}_c$ for HCS&KNN

Fig. 4. Decoder selection and number of high-confidence neighbor candidates

We fine-tune $\mathcal{N}_c$ from 100 to 700, and get different IDRC performance for different $\mathcal{N}_c$. The performance curves of $F1$-score and Acc are in Fig. 4-(b). We see that IDRC performance increases slowly when $\mathcal{N}_c$ is in [100, 500], and it drops sharply when $\mathcal{N}_c$ is larger than 500. We set $\mathcal{N}_c$ to 500. $\mathcal{N}_c$ is a task-specific hyperparameter because it depends on the scale of neighbor candidates. It needs to be reset for other tasks or datasets. Also, if we don't use confidence-based sampling, K will affect the performance a lot. For example, Tem's F1 will change from 30.67 to 34.39 when we search for K from 5 to 40. But performance is stable when we use confidence-based sampling and doesn't change during the search. This shows the CCR and the validity of our method.

Table 3. Statistics in PDTB v3.0 (left) and PDTB 2.0 (right).

Rel.	Train.	Dev.	Test.	Rel.	Train.	Dev.	Test.
TEM.	1,447	136	148	TEM	704	48	55
COM.	1,937	190	154	COM	2,104	189	145
CON.	5,916	529	529	CON	3,622	281	273
EXP.	8,645	748	643	EXP	7,394	638	538
Total	17,945	1,653	1,474	Total	13,824	1,156	1,011

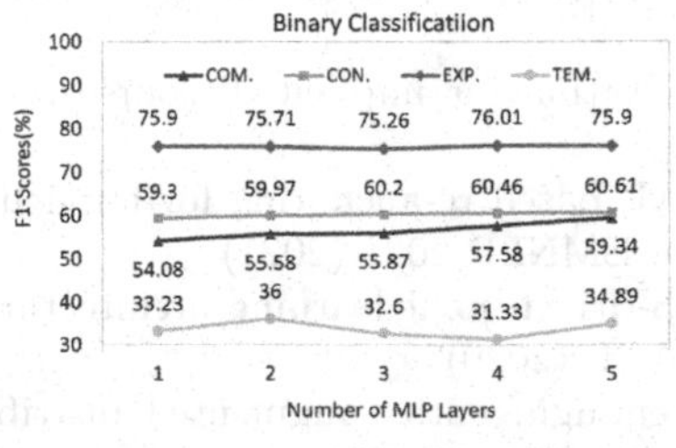

(a) Perceptron versus HCS&KNN.

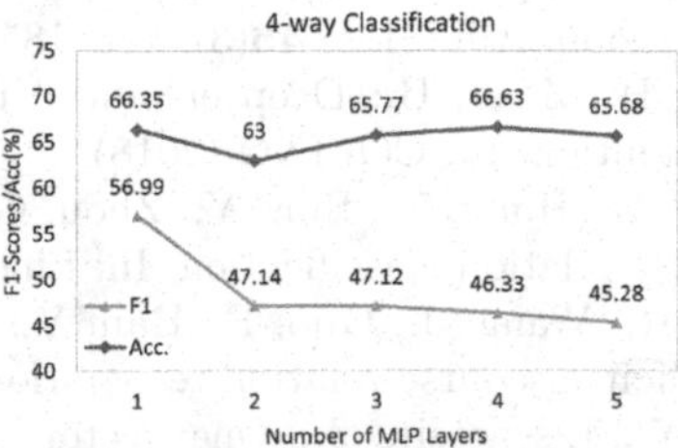

(b) Setting $\mathcal{N}_c$ for HCS&KNN

Fig. 5. Decoder selection and number of high-confidence neighbor candidates

5 Conclusion

We propose a novel encoder-decoder framework which enhances representational differentiation by metric learning and self-generation. In addition, we develop a plug-and-play confidence-based KNN discriminator, which enables efficient and effective relation determination. Experiments demonstrate that our method yields substantial improvements for IDRC. In the future, we will expand the current IDRC model using generative adversarial network. Specifically, on one hand, we will generate distracting instances (counterfeits) by rewriting the ones holding other types of relations. On the other hand, we utilize the generated instances to challenge IDRC discriminators for distinguishing true instances from counterfeits. This will be the first work in exclusively enhancing IDRC decoder.

Acknowledgements. The research is supported by National Key R&D Program of China (2020YFB1313601) and National Science Foundation of China (62076174).

Appendix

We replace HCS&KNN with MLP to reconstruct "scratcher", and retrain the whole model for IDRC. The goal is to verify whether deeper neural layers produce more significant improvements, and outperform HCS&KNN. There are five MLPs taken into consideration in this experiment, which possess different numbers of hidden layers.

Figure 5-(a) shows the performance curves for binary IDRC, and Fig. 5-(b) gives that of 4-way IDRC. Both are obtained on pure IDRC data. Each curve corresponds to performance variation when the number of hidden layers is changed from 1 to 5. It can be observed that most curves fall in a smooth trend in the binary classification scenario. More seriously, the 4-way performance shows a declining trend. The performance fails to surpass that of HCS&KNN. This demonstrates that simply increasing the perceptual depth is ineffective.

References

1. Altman, N.S.: An introduction to kernel and nearest-neighbor nonparametric regression. Am. Stat. **46**(3), 175–185 (1992)
2. Bai, H., Zhao, H.: Deep enhanced representation for implicit discourse relation recognition. In: COLING (2018)
3. Dou, Z., Hong, Y., Sun, Y., Zhou, G.: CVAE-based re-anchoring for implicit discourse relation classification. In: Findings of EMNLP 2021 (2021)
4. He, R., Wang, J., Guo, F., Han, Y.: TransS-driven joint learning architecture for implicit discourse relation recognition. In: ACL (2020)
5. Ji, Y., Eisenstein, J.: One vector is not enough: entity-augmented distributed semantics for discourse relations. TACL **3**, 329–344 (2015)
6. Lan, M., Wang, J., Wu, Y., Niu, Z.Y., Wang, H.: Multi-task attention-based neural networks for implicit discourse relationship representation and identification. In: EMNLP (2017)

7. Li, J.J., Nenkova, A.: Addressing class imbalance for improved recognition of implicit discourse relations. In: Proceedings of the 15th Annual Meeting of the Special Interest Group on Discourse and Dialogue, pp. 142–150 (2014)
8. Liu, X., Ou, J., Song, Y., Jiang, X.: On the importance of word and sentence representation learning in implicit discourse relation classification. In: IJCAI, pp. 3830–3836 (2020)
9. Liu, Y., et al.: RoBERTa: a robustly optimized BERT pretraining approach (2019), cite arxiv:1907.11692
10. Loshchilov, I., Hutter, F.: Decoupled weight decay regularization. In: ICLR (2018)
11. Marcu, D., Echihabi, A.: An unsupervised approach to recognizing discourse relations. In: ACL, pp. 368–375 (2002)
12. Nguyen, L.T., Van Ngo, L., Than, K., Nguyen, T.H.: Employing the correspondence of relations and connectives to identify implicit discourse relations via label embeddings. In: ACL (2019)
13. Prasad, R., et al.: The Penn discourse TreeBank 2.0. In: LREC 2008 (2008)
14. Ruan, H., Hong, Y., Xu, Y., Huang, Z., Zhou, G., Zhang, M.: Interactively-propagative attention learning for implicit discourse relation recognition. In: COLING (2020)
15. Shi, W., Demberg, V.: Next sentence prediction helps implicit discourse relation classification within and across domains. In: EMNLP (2019)
16. Shi, W., Yung, F., Rubino, R., Demberg, V.: Using explicit discourse connectives in translation for implicit discourse relation classification. In: Proceedings of the Eighth International Joint Conference on Natural Language Processing, pp. 484–495 (2017)
17. Song, H.O., Xiang, Y., Jegelka, S., Savarese, S.: Deep metric learning via lifted structured feature embedding. In: CVPR, pp. 4004–4012 (2016)
18. Varia, S., Hidey, C., Chakrabarty, T.: Discourse relation prediction: revisiting word pairs with convolutional networks. In: SIGdial (2019)
19. Wu, C., Shi, X., Chen, Y., Huang, Y., Su, J.: Bilingually-constrained synthetic data for implicit discourse relation recognition. In: EMNLP, pp. 2306–2312 (2016)
20. Wu, Y., et al.: Google's neural machine translation system: bridging the gap between human and machine translation. arXiv preprint arXiv:1609.08144
21. Xiang, W., Wang, B., Dai, L., Mo, Y.: Encoding and fusing semantic connection and linguistic evidence for implicit discourse relation recognition. In: Findings ACL 2022 (2022)
22. Xing, E., Jordan, M., Russell, S.J., Ng, A.: Distance metric learning with application to clustering with side-information. In: Becker, S., Thrun, S., Obermayer, K. (eds.) NIPS, vol. 15. MIT Press (2002)
23. Xu, Y., Hong, Y., Ruan, H., Yao, J., Zhang, M., Zhou, G.: Using active learning to expand training data for implicit discourse relation recognition. In: EMNLP (2018)
24. Zhang, Y., Jian, P., Meng, F., Geng, R., Cheng, W., Zhou, J.: Semantic graph convolutional network for implicit discourse relation classification. arXiv preprint arXiv:1910.09183

FPTN: Fast Pure Transformer Network for Traffic Flow Forecasting

Junhao Zhang, Juncheng Jin, Junjie Tang, and Zehui Qu(✉)

College of Computer and Information Science, Southwest University, Chongqing, China
{superblack,arieldong522,swu645867768}@email.swu.edu.cn, quzehui@swu.edu.cn

Abstract. Traffic flow forecasting is challenging due to the intricate spatio-temporal correlations in traffic flow data. Existing Transformer-based methods usually treat traffic flow forecasting as multivariate time series (MTS) forecasting. However, too many sensors can cause a vector with a dimension greater than 800, which is difficult to process without information loss. In addition, these methods design complex mechanisms to capture spatial dependencies in MTS, resulting in slow forecasting speed. To solve the abovementioned problems, we propose a Fast Pure Transformer Network (FPTN) in this paper. First, the traffic flow data are divided into sequences along the sensor dimension instead of the time dimension. Then, to adequately represent complex spatio-temporal correlations, three types of embeddings are proposed for projecting these vectors into a suitable vector space. After that, to capture the complex spatio-temporal correlations simultaneously in these vectors, we utilize Transformer encoder and stack it with several layers. Extensive experiments are conducted with 4 real-world datasets and 13 baselines, which demonstrate that FPTN outperforms the state-of-the-art on two metrics. Meanwhile, the computational time of FPTN spent is less than a quarter of other state-of-the-art Transformer-based models spent, and the requirements for computing resources are significantly reduced.

Keywords: Traffic flow forecasting · Transformer · Spatio-temporal data

1 Introduction

Traffic flow forecasting attempts to predict the future traffic flow in road networks based on historical traffic conditions, which have been widely studied in recent years. It plays a significant role in improving the service quality of Intelligent Transportation Systems (ITS) [10]. Commonly, traffic flow prediction relies on traffic flow sensors distributed in the road network to count the passage of vehicles. The sensor's traffic records have been processed to an equal frequency(e.g., every 5 min) sequence over time. Therefore, the data utilized for traffic flow prediction is inherently spatio-temporal, encapsulating not only historical traffic flow information but also spatial elements like the geographical positioning of traffic sensors and the construction of the road network [14,21].

L. Iliadis et al. (Eds.): ICANN 2023, LNCS 14259, pp. 382–393, 2023.
https://doi.org/10.1007/978-3-031-44223-0_31

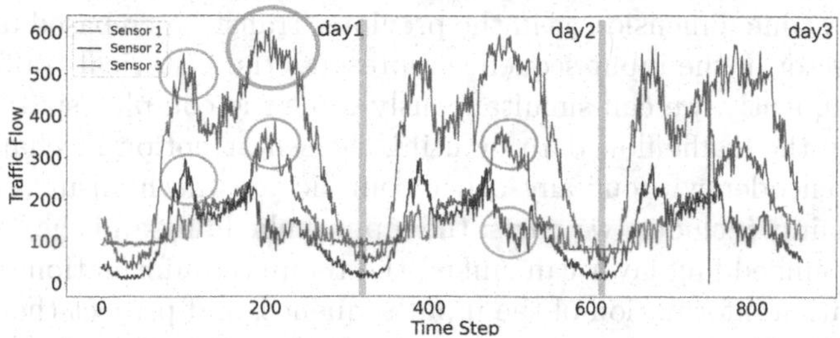

Fig. 1. The traffic flow of different sensors has diverse patterns. Sensor 3 has two peaks in one period while Sensor 1 has only one. Sensor 1 and Sensor 2 have different peak times.

This task is complex, attributed to the intricate and long-range spatio-temporal interrelationships that exist within traffic networks. As Fig. 1 shows, diversified patterns excited in different traffic sensors, which means the spatio-temporal dependencies are non-linear, dynamic, and shifting long-range [14]. Numerous past research efforts have aimed to tackle this challenge. Earlier conventional studies, such as [13], employed time series models to extract correlations from traffic data using statistical tools and conventional machine learning techniques. However, these approaches only take temporal information into consideration, spatial features have been ignored. Not long after that, deep learning techniques have been widely used to capture prominent spatio-temporal patterns. These approaches typically model temporal dependencies with variants of Recurrent Neural Networks (RNN) [1], and model spatial dependencies with Convolutional Neural Networks (CNN) [24] or Graph Convolutional Networks (GCN) [11]. Some methods [10,14,21] further combined these spatial and temporal models to capture spatio-temporal correlations from traffic data jointly. However, these methods extract temporal features and spatial features separately and then fuse them, which could lose the interlaced spatial and temporal information. Additionally, GCN mainly uses man-made predefined graphs to represent the spatial topological relationship between sensors, which cannot fully portray the complex spatio-temporal dependencies between sensors. Recently, Transformer [20] has achieved great success in NLP and CV. Thus researchers began to use Transformer for traffic flow forecasting. However, they regarded traffic flow forecasting as multivariate time series forecasting and designed other complex mechanisms (e.g., GCN) to capture the spatial correlation in the sequence. That results in (1) hard sequence embedding due to a large number of sensors, and the dimension of the vector in the multivariate time series could be too long. (2) Limited spatio-temporal feature extraction in traffic flow data due to GCN. (3) Significant time overhead in making predictions.

To remedy the above problems, we propose a novel framework, termed as Fast Pure Transformer Network (FPTN), which utilizes pure Transformer architecture to extract complex spatio-temporal correlations simultaneously. Specifically, We divide the traffic flow data along the sensor dimension instead of dividing the data along the time dimension as in the previous Transformer-based methods. In this way, a vector in the input sequence represents the historical traffic flow of a sensor. Consequently, we can simultaneously mine the complex spatio-temporal information in the traffic flow data by using the self-attention mechanism in the Transformer encoder without any other complicated mechanism (e.g., GCN). Our model mainly includes two parts: the input embedding and the Transformer encoder. The embedding layer can embed the temporal information of the data, learn the location information of the input sequence, and project the traffic flow data into a suitable vector space for representation. The Transformer encoder uses the self-attention mechanism to extract complex spatio-temporal relationships from sequences partitioned along the sensor dimension.

The main contributions of this work are concluded as follows:

(1) We divide the traffic flow data along the sensor dimension and utilize the Transformer encoder to extract complex spatio-temporal correlations simultaneously.
(2) We propose the FPTN, which uses pure Transformer architecture to capture spatio-temporal dependencies without using other complex mechanisms, which significantly speeds up the forecasting speed.
(3) Comprehensive experimental results reveal that our methodology surpasses other state-of-the-art (SOTA) techniques.

2 Related Work

Traffic Flow Forecasting. In previous traditional methods, researchers often use statistical time-series models or machine learning models to capture temporal correlations of time series from traffic flow data [25]. After that, deep learning techniques have been widely adopted. CNN was utilized to capture spatial correlations in STResNet [24]. ConvLSTM [19] integrated CNN and LSTM to jointly model spatial and temporal dependencies. Some variants of RNN models combine traffic graphs to capture long-range spatio-temporal dependencies [5,14]. Recent studies formulate traffic flow prediction on graphs and utilize GCN models for spatio-temporal forecasting [7,17,18]. GraphWaveNet [21] combined GCN and gated temporal convolution to process traffic conditions. STFGNN [10] created a spatio-temporal fusion graph. FOGS [16] proposed a learning graph to extract spatial correlation adaptively.

Transformer. Motivated by its strong capability of capturing global spatio-temporal information, Transformer-based models have been applied to spatio-temporal data mining [8] and traffic flow forecasting [4,6,9,12,22,25]. GMAN [25] proposed spatial and temporal attention mechanisms with gated fusion to capture the complex spatio-temporal dependencies. STTN [22] designed spatial Transformer and temporal Transformer to model various scales of spatial dependencies and capture long-range temporal dependencies. Bi-STAT [4] proposed a Bidirectional Spatial-Temporal Transformer, which further utilizes the past recollection of past traffic conditions. ST-TIS [9] used a novel region sampling strategy to reduce the computation complexity of canonical Transformer.

3 Problem Formulation

A traffic network can be characterized as an undirected graph $\mathcal{G} = (S, E_{road})$, where S signifies the set of sensors, $|S| = N$, N is the quantity of sensors, and E_{road} represents the road segments connecting these sensors. We denote the recorded traffic flow as $X_\mathcal{G} \in \mathbb{R}^{N\times T\times C}$ indicating the observations taken from traffic network $\mathcal{G}$ over T continuous time steps, where each element corresponds to C observed traffic features such as speed, volume. In this study, our focus lies on predicting traffic volume, thus $C = 1$. Consequently, the recorded traffic flow is reshaped as $X_\mathcal{G} \in \mathbb{R}^{N\times TC}$. The speed and density are computed in a manner analogous to the traffic volume.

Previous Works. Previous works treat traffic flow forecasting as multivariable time series forecasting. They denote the observed traffic conditions on $\mathcal{G}$ at the t-th time step as a vector $X_\mathcal{G}^{(t)} \in \mathbb{R}^N$, where the i-th element of $X_\mathcal{G}^{(t)}$ is the traffic condition observed by the i-th sensor at the t-th time step. The aim of traffic flow forecasting is to find a function f to forecast the next K steps multivariable time series based on the past T steps multivariable time series.

$$\left(X_\mathcal{G}^{(t-T+1)}, ..., X_\mathcal{G}^{(t)}\right) \xrightarrow{f} \left(X_\mathcal{G}^{(t+1)}, ..., X_\mathcal{G}^{(t+K)}\right) \tag{1}$$

However, it's hard to embed multivariable time series into the Transformer model without information loss when N is large, for example, in PeMSD7 dataset $N = 883$, which means $X_\mathcal{G}^{(t)} \in \mathbb{R}^{883}$, the existing Transformer-based model commonly needs to compress the vector to a suitable dimension such as 256 and then input it into the Transformer.

Our Work. We denote the observed traffic conditions on $\mathcal{G}$ at the n-th sensor as a vector $X_\mathcal{G}^{(n)} \in \mathbb{R}^{TC} (C = 1)$, where the i-th element of $X_\mathcal{G}^{(n)}$ is the traffic condition observed by the n-th sensor at the i-th time step, and T is the number of steps in the observed time interval. Traffic flow forecasting aims to find a function f to forecast the next K steps traffic conditions of N sensors $\hat{X}_\mathcal{G} \in \mathbb{R}^{N\times KC}$ based on the past T steps traffic conditions of N sensors $X_\mathcal{G} \in \mathbb{R}^{N\times TC}$

$$\left(X_\mathcal{G}^{(1)}, X_\mathcal{G}^{(2)}, X_\mathcal{G}^{(3)}, ..., X_\mathcal{G}^{(N)}\right) \xrightarrow{f} \left(\hat{X}_\mathcal{G}^{(1)}, \hat{X}_\mathcal{G}^{(2)}, \hat{X}_\mathcal{G}^{(3)}, ..., \hat{X}_\mathcal{G}^{(N)}\right) \tag{2}$$

4 Proposed Model

We present the framework of FPTN in Fig. 2. It consists of (1) an input embedding layer, (2) stacked Transformer encoders and (3) an output layer.

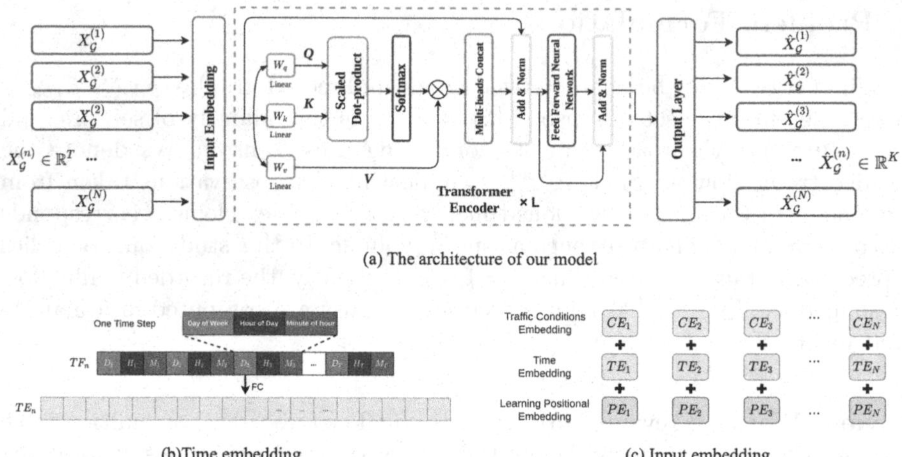

Fig. 2. (a) The architecture of the proposed Fast Pure Transformer Network (FPTN). $X_{\mathcal{G}}^{(n)} \in \mathbb{R}^T$ is the vector of the traffic flow data decomposed along the sensor dimension, which represents the observation value of the traffic conditions in T time steps at the n-th sensor. Then $X_{\mathcal{G}}^{(n)}$ is processed by the (c) input embedding layer and fed into the Transformer Encoder. (b) is the process of time embedding in FPTN.

4.1 Input Embedding

Traffic Conditions Embedding. The historical traffic conditions observed by all sensors is $X_{\mathcal{G}} \in \mathbb{R}^{N \times TC}$. Thus, in FPTN the traffic conditions is a vector $X_{\mathcal{G}}^{(n)} \in \mathbb{R}^T$ $(C = 1)$ for one sensor. To represent the complex spatio-temporal relationship, we project the vector $X_{\mathcal{G}}^{(n)} \in \mathbb{R}^T$ to the dimension d_{model} and $d_{model} > T$ (e.g., $T = 12$ and $d_{model} = 256$):

$$S = X_{\mathcal{G}} \cdot W^s + b^s \tag{3}$$

where $S \in \mathbb{R}^{N \times d_{model}}$ is the embedding of traffic conditions observed by N sensors, $W^s \in \mathbb{R}^{T \times d_{model}}$ and $b^s \in \mathbb{R}^{d_{model}}$ are the weight and bias of traffic conditions embedding.

Temporal Embedding. In order to capture the dynamic relationships across temporal dimensions, we have constructed a time embedding that encodes the timestep of each sensor's traffic conditions into a vector, as illustrated in Fig. 2(b). Specifically, we first normalize three time characteristics: day of the week (D), hour of the day (H), and minute of the hour (M) into $\mathbb{R}^3$ using min-max scaling for each time step, then concatenate them to form a vector $TF_n \in \mathbb{R}^{3T}$ along the temporal dimension. Following this, a one-layer fully-connected neural network is utilized to transform the time feature $TF_n \in \mathbb{R}^{3T}$ into a time embedding vector $TE_n \in \mathbb{R}^{d_{model}}$:

$$TE_n = TF_n \cdot W^t + b^t \tag{4}$$

Here, $W^t \in \mathbb{R}^{3T \times d_{model}}$ and $b^t \in \mathbb{R}^{d_{model}}$ denote the weight and bias of the Time Embedding, respectively. Hence, we obtain the Time Embedding, expressed as:

$$TE = TF \cdot W^t + b^t \tag{5}$$

where $TE \in \mathbb{R}^{N \times d_{model}}$, $TF \in \mathbb{R}^{N \times 3T}$.

Learning Positional Embedding. In contrast to NLP and time series tasks, the input sequence of FPTN does not adhere to a strict order as it pertains to the N sensors, and the N vectors are not ordered. This leads us to favor a learned positional embedding over the unchanging sinusoidal positional embedding. In more precise terms, we apply a learnable parameter matrix $PE \in \mathbb{R}^{N \times d_{model}}$ for positional embedding, making each sensor's positional embedding $PE_n \in \mathbb{R}^{d_{model}}$. Consequently, FPTN is capable of adaptively adjusting positional embeddings during the learning phase, enabling the model to autonomously grasp the positional correlation amongst the N vectors and aiding it in uncovering the spatial correlations within traffic conditions.

Finally, as shown in Fig. 2(c), we add time embedding $TE \in \mathbb{R}^{N \times d_{model}}$ and learning positional embedding $PE \in \mathbb{R}^{N \times d_{model}}$ to the traffic conditions embedding $S \in \mathbb{R}^{N \times d_{model}}$:

$$E = S + TE + PE \tag{6}$$

$E \in \mathbb{R}^{N \times d_{model}}$ is the input sequence of Transformer encoder.

4.2 Transformer Encoder

Since the traffic data is spatio-temporal data [14,21], it is crucial to extract the intertwined and complex spatio-temporal correlations from $E \in \mathbb{R}^{N \times d_{model}}$. In FPTN, we use the Transformer's encoder to capture the spatio-temporal relationships in the traffic data simultaneously. Specifically, the attention mechanism in Transformer's encoder can extract the correlations among each vector in each encoder layer, which means the temporal and spatial correlations among N sensors can be calculated simultaneously. Therefore, our model does not need to design some additional complex mechanisms to extract spatial and temporal correlations separately and then integrate them. Consequently, FPTN can significantly reduce the computational costs of the model with a pure Transformer structure. In addition, FPTN avoids the loss of information caused by separate feature extraction and fusion.

As shown in Fig. 2, the Transformer encoder we used for FPTN is similar to the conventional Transformer [20] model, mainly composed of three parts: multi-head attention, feed-forward neural network, and residual-link & normalization. Multi-head attention mechanism can learn complex and diverse spatio-temporal patterns in traffic flow data. Formally, the multi-head attention function combines queries Q, keys K, and values V with h heads as follows:

$$MultiHead(Q, K, V) = Concat(Head_1, ..., Head_h)W^O \tag{7}$$

$$Head_i = Attention(QW_i^Q, KW_i^K, VW_i^V) \tag{8}$$

Here W_i^Q, W_i^K, $W_i^V \in \mathbb{R}^{d_{model} \times \frac{d_{model}}{h}}$, and $W^O \in \mathbb{R}^{d_{model} \times d_{model}}$. In addition, the attention function is scaled dot-product attention as follows:

$$Attention = softmax(\frac{QK^T}{\sqrt{D}})V \tag{9}$$

where D is the dimension of Q, K.

Feed-forward network consists of two linear transformations with a GELU activation in between as follows:

$$FFN\left(x\right) = GELU(xW_1 + b_1)W_2 + b_2 \tag{10}$$

The dimensionality of input and output is d_{model}, and the inner-layer has dimensionality $d_{ff} = 4d_{model}$.

Since the input sample length of the data we use here is fixed and there is no extreme length variation, we use batch normalization instead of layer normalization [23].

4.3 Output Layer

In FPTN, the input and output vector space is the same, which is the traffic flow data of N sensors. Therefore, our model framework does not use decoder and cross-attention. As shown in Fig. 2(a), we use a fully connected layer network directly after the Transformer encoder to get the output $\hat{X}_{\mathcal{G}}^{(n)} \in \mathbb{R}^K$:

$$\hat{X}_{\mathcal{G}}^{(n)} = Z_n \cdot W_o + b_o \tag{11}$$

where $Z_n \in \mathbb{R}^{d_{model}}$ is the final vector representation of Transformer encoder, $W_o \in \mathbb{R}^{d_{model} \times K}$, $b_o \in \mathbb{R}^K$ are output layer parameters. Finally, the predictions of next K time steps traffic flow denoted as $\hat{Y} = (\hat{X}_{\mathcal{G}}^{(1)}, \hat{X}_{\mathcal{G}}^{(2)}, ..., \hat{X}_{\mathcal{G}}^{(N)}) \in \mathbb{R}^{N \times K}$.

We choose the mean absolute error (MAE) loss function to train FPTN:

$$\mathcal{L}\left(\Theta\right) = \frac{1}{N \times K} \sum_{n=1}^{N} \sum_{i=1}^{K} \left| Y_{n,i} - \hat{Y}_{n,i} \right| \tag{12}$$

where Θ represents all learnable parameters in FPTN, $Y_{n,i}$ is the ground-truth of sensor n at time step i.

5 Experiments

In this section, we describe our experimental environments and results. Our software and hardware environments are as follows: PYTHON 3.9.7, PYTORCH 1.12.0, NUMPY 1.19.2, PANDAS 1.4.3 and CUDA 11.3, Intel(R) Core(TM) i5-11400 CPU @2.6 GHz, 32 GB RAM and one NVIDIA RTX 3090 GPU, which is a personal computer configuration. We use 4 datasets and 13 baseline models.

Table 1. The summary of the datasets used in our work

Dataset	Sensors	Time Steps	Time Range	Sample Rate
PeMSD3	358	26,208	09/2018 – 11/2018	5 mins
PeMSD4	307	16,992	01/2018 – 02/2018	5 mins
PeMSD7	883	28,224	05/2017 – 08/2017	5 mins
PeMSD8	170	17,856	07/2016 – 08/2016	5 mins

5.1 Datasets

During the experiment, we employed four authentic traffic datasets: PeMSD3, PeMSD4, PeMSD7, and PeMSD8. These datasets were sourced from [10], and a statistical breakdown of the four sets can be seen in the Table 1.

5.2 Experimental Procedure

Each of the four datasets is consolidated into 5-minute intervals, thereby generating 12 data entries (time steps) per hour, and subsequently, 288 entries per day. The upcoming $K = 12$ step traffic conditions are forecasted based on the preceding $T = 12$ steps. Z-score normalization is utilized for the traffic data to ensure a more stable training process. The datasets are divided using a 6:2:2 and 7:1:2 ratio into training, validation, and testing subsets, respectively. The performance of varying models is evaluated using the mean absolute error (MAE), the mean absolute percentage error (MAPE), and the root mean squared error (RMSE), with the optimal outcome of our model being documented.

Implementation Details. In the case of FPTN, we explore the following set of hyperparameters: Training is performed for 400 epochs using the RAdam [15] optimizer, with a universal batch size of 64 across all datasets. The learning rate lr across all methods is within $\{5 \times 10^{-3}, 1 \times 10^{-3}, 5 \times 10^{-4}, 1 \times 10^{-4}\}$. The dimension of input embedding d_{model} is varied among {64, 128, 256, 512, 1024}. The number of successive Transformer encoder layers L is in the set {2, 3, 4, 5, 6}. The heads h for the multi-head attention mechanism range from {4, 8, 16, 32}. To optimize performance, an early stop approach is employed with a patience of 40 iterations on the training dataset.

Baseline Methods. In order to assess the comprehensive effectiveness of our research, FPTN is juxtaposed with a broad range of baseline methods and SOTA models, which include: **ARIM-A**, **GraphWaveNet** [21], **GMAN** [25], **Traffic-Transformer** [3], **STTN** [22], **STF-GNN** [10], **STG-NCDE** [5], **GMSDR** [14], **FOGS** [16], **Bi-STAT** [4]. Some of them have already been introduced in the Sect. 2.

Table 2. The computation time on the PeMSD4 dataset.

Metric	DCRNN	AGCRN	GMAN	Bi-STAT	FPTN
MAE	21.22	19.83	19.36	18.74	**18.49**
RMSE	33.44	32.26	31.06	30.31	**30.29**
Training (s/epoch)	377.09	249.54	237.31	229.01	**23.62**
Inference (s)	26.78	25.28	11.01	11.56	**2.69**

5.3 Experimental Result

Evaluation of Algorithmic Efficiency. Primarily, we assess the computational time efficiency of FPTN in relation to AGCRN [2], DCRNN [11], GMAN, and Bi-STAT, utilizing the PeMSD4 dataset, as presented in Table 2. It is discernible that AGCRN and DCRNN exhibit a slower operational pace compared to Transformer-oriented models such as GMAN, Bi-STAT, and FPTN, which can be attributed to the time-intensive nature of the recurrent structure employed in RNNs. Furthermore, FPTN necessitates considerably less computational time for both training and inference compared to GMAN and Bi-STAT, a result of the adoption of a non-decoder Transformer structure within FPTN, in tandem with the absence of auxiliary processing mechanisms like GCN or RNN. Specifically, FPTN's training phase clocks in at 23.62 s/epoch, amounting to a mere 10.31% of Bi-STAT's 229.01 s/epoch. In a similar vein, the inference duration for FPTN, registered at 2.69 s, is significantly more expedited compared to Bi-STAT's 11.56 s, reflecting a ratio of 76.73%.

Evaluation of Forecasting Performance. The empirical findings, derived from an examination of the four publicly accessible datasets, are detailed in Table 3. On a broader scale, our proposed methodology, known as FPTN, exceeds the performance of all baseline methods on all four datasets, as evaluated by two critical metrics: Mean Absolute Error (MAE) and Root Mean Square Error (RMSE). Specifically, when applied to the PeMSD7 dataset and evaluated using the MAE metric, FPTN distinctly surpasses FC-LSTM, STSGCN, and STFGNN, with performance enhancement ratios of 33.49%, 17.81%, and 15.00% respectively. The reason might be that the Transformer Encoder used in our model can better capture spatio-temporal information than RNN and GNN.

In comparison to Transformer-based models such as GMAN, STTN, and Traffic-Transformer, our model, FPTN, exhibits superior performance with enhancement ratios of 6.30%, 10.98%, and 10.98%, respectively, as per the RMSE metric on the PeMSD3 dataset. Concurrently, FPTN requires significantly less time for training and inference than GMAN, as previously mentioned. Overall, FPTN not only achieves a higher performance but also operates at a markedly faster pace than the baseline models. A plausible explanation for this is our adoption of a pure Transformer architecture, which effectively extracts complex spatio-temporal correlations without the necessity of incorporating additional mechanisms.

Table 3. Forecasting error on PeMSD3, PeMSD4, PeMSD7 and PeMSD8.

Datasets	Metric	ARIMA	FC-LSTM	Graph WaveNet	STSGCN	AGCRN	STFGNN	GMAN	Traffic-Transformer	STTN	STG-NCDE	GMSDR	FOGS	Bi-STAT	**FPTN**
PeMSD3	MAE	35.41	21.33	19.12	17.48	15.98	16.77	16.49	16.39	16.11	15.57	15.78	15.13	15.29	**14.62**
	RMSE	47.59	35.11	32.77	29.21	28.25	28.34	26.48	27.87	27.87	27.09	26.82	24.98	27.54	**24.81**
	MAPE(%)	33.78	23.33	18.89	16.78	15.23	16.30	17.13	15.84	16.19	15.06	15.33	**14.37**	15.19	14.61
PeMSD4	MAE	33.73	26.77	24.89	21.19	19.83	20.48	19.36	19.16	19.32	19.21	-	19.35	18.74	**18.49**
	RMSE	48.80	40.65	39.66	33.65	32.26	32.51	31.06	30.57	30.79	31.09	-	31.33	30.31	**30.29**
	MAPE(%)	24.18	18.23	17.29	13.90	12.97	16.77	13.55	13.70	13.15	12.76	-	12.71	**12.59**	13.10
PeMSD7	MAE	38.17	29.98	26.39	24.26	22.37	23.46	21.48	23.90	21.05	20.53	-	20.62	20.64	**19.94**
	RMSE	59.27	45.94	41.50	39.03	36.55	36.60	34.55	36.85	33.77	33.84	-	33.96	34.03	**32.49**
	MAPE(%)	19.46	13.20	11.97	10.21	9.12	9.21	9.01	10.90	8.94	8.80	-	**8.58**	8.88	8.77
PeMSD8	MAE	31.09	23.09	18.28	17.13	15.95	16.94	14.51	15.37	15.28	15.45	16.36	14.92	14.07	**13.98**
	RMSE	44.32	35.17	30.05	26.80	25.22	26.25	23.68	24.21	24.25	24.81	25.58	24.09	23.45	**23.30**
	MAPE(%)	22.73	14.99	12.15	10.96	10.09	10.60	9.45	10.09	9.98	9.92	10.28	9.42	**9.27**	10.06

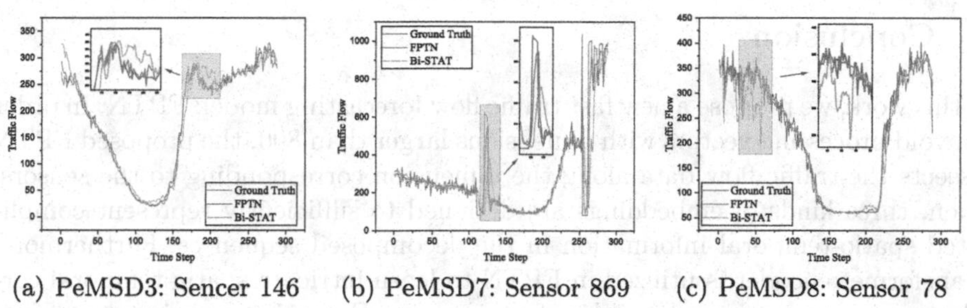

(a) PeMSD3: Sencer 146 (b) PeMSD7: Sensor 869 (c) PeMSD8: Sensor 78

Fig. 3. Visualizing forecasted traffic flow on PeMSD3, PeMSD7, and PeMSD8.

FPTN cannot achieve the best performance under the MAPE metric, but it is still comparable with state-of-the-art methods like FOGS and Bi-STAT. We found that is because FPTN is not sensitive when the target value of traffic flow is small (e.g., target value<5) which can result in a high value by calculating MAPE.

Visualization of Prediction Results. We've depicted both the actual and predicted curves produced by FPTN and Bi-STAT in Fig. 3. It's evident that FPTN can generate accurate predictive sequences, even in high-traffic areas like Sensor 78 in PeMSD8 as seen in Fig. 3(c). Though Bi-STAT performs reasonably well and often parallels our model's curve across numerous time steps, our model's predictions are significantly more precise in challenging scenarios. This is particularly evident in the boxed areas, where the time-points for Sensor 869 in PeMSD7 and Sensor 146 in PeMSD3 are highlighted.

Error for Each Horizon. We juxtapose our approach with two formidable contenders, GMAN and AGCRN, while adjusting the horizon between 1 and 12 as displayed in Fig. 4. It's discernible that our method consistently excels the other two techniques with a considerable margin, notably when the horizon exceeds 9. This substantiates FPTN's ability to formulate precise forecasts for both short-range flows (minor horizon) and long-range flows (major horizon).

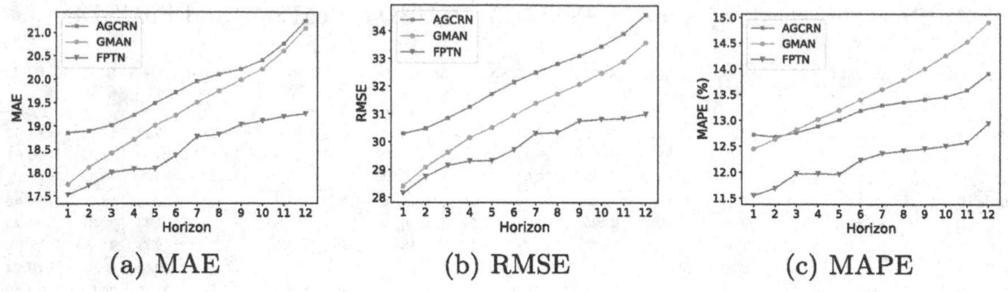

(a) MAE (b) RMSE (c) MAPE

Fig. 4. Performance comparison among different methods with varying horizons on the PeMSD4 dataset.

6 Conclusion

In this work, we propose a new fast traffic flow forecasting model: FPTN. In order to avoid processing vectors with dimensions larger than 800, the proposed FPTN dissects the traffic flow data along the dimension corresponding to the sensors. Then, three kinds of embeddings are designed to sufficiently represent complicated spatio-temporal information in the decomposed sequences. Furthermore, Transformer encoder is utilized in FPTN to learn intricate spatio-temporal correlations concurrently and speed up forecast time. Extensive experiments on four real-world datasets show that FPTN achieves favorable performance compared with other SOTA methods. In the meantime, FPTN only costs 23.27% inference time of other Transformer-base models. Moreover, FPTN holds potential applicability across various other tasks that require spatial-temporal prediction.

References

1. Bai, L., Yao, L., Kanhere, S.S., Yang, Z., Chu, J., Wang, X.: Passenger demand forecasting with multi-task convolutional recurrent neural networks. In: PAKDD (2019)
2. Bai, L., Yao, L., Li, C., Wang, X., Wang, C.: Adaptive graph convolutional recurrent network for traffic forecasting. In: NeurIPS (2020)
3. Cai, L., Janowicz, K., Mai, G., Yan, B., Zhu, R.: Traffic transformer: capturing the continuity and periodicity of time series for traffic forecasting. Trans. GIS **24**(3), 736–755 (2020). Jun
4. Chen, C., Liu, Y., Chen, L., Zhang, C.: Bidirectional spatial-temporal adaptive transformer for urban traffic flow forecasting. IEEE Trans. Neural Netw. Learn. Syst. (2022)
5. Choi, J., Choi, H., Hwang, J., Park, N.: Graph neural controlled differential equations for traffic forecasting. In: AAAI, pp. 6367–6374 (2022)
6. Fang, Y., Zhao, F., Qin, Y., Luo, H., Wang, C.: Learning all dynamics: traffic forecasting via locality-aware spatio-temporal joint transformer. IEEE Trans. Intell. Transport. Syst. **23**(12), 23433–23446 (2022)
7. Fu, H., Wang, Z., Yu, Y., Meng, X., Liu, G.: Traffic flow driven spatio-temporal graph convolutional network for ride-hailing demand forecasting. In: PAKDD (2021)

8. Hu, Y., Zhou, Y., Song, J., Xu, L., Zhou, X.: Citywide mobile traffic forecasting using spatial-temporal downsampling transformer neural networks. IEEE Trans. Netw. Serv. Manage. **20**(1), 152–165 (2023)
9. Li, G., et al.: A lightweight and accurate spatial-temporal transformer for traffic forecasting. IEEE Trans. Knowl. Data Eng., 1–14 (2022)
10. Li, M., Zhu, Z.: Spatial-temporal fusion graph neural networks for traffic flow forecasting. In: AAAI, pp. 4189–4196 (2021)
11. Li, Y., Yu, R., Shahabi, C., Liu, Y.: Diffusion convolutional recurrent neural network: data-driven traffic forecasting. In: ICLR (2018)
12. Li, Y., Ren, Q., Jin, H., Han, M.: LSTN: long short-term traffic flow forecasting with transformer networks. In: 2022 26th International Conference on Pattern Recognition (ICPR), pp. 4793–4800 (2022)
13. Lippi, M., Bertini, M., Frasconi, P.: Short-term traffic flow forecasting: an experimental comparison of time-series analysis and supervised learning. IEEE Trans. Intell. Transp. Syst. **14**(2), 871–882 (2013)
14. Liu, D., Wang, J., Shang, S., Han, P.: MSDR: multi-step dependency relation networks for spatial temporal forecasting. In: SIGKDD, pp. 1042–1050 (2022)
15. Liu, L., et al.: On the variance of the adaptive learning rate and beyond. In: ICLR (2020)
16. Rao, X., Wang, H., Zhang, L., Li, J., Shang, S., Han, P.: FOGS: first-order gradient supervision with learning-based graph for traffic flow forecasting. In: IJCAI, vol. 5, pp. 3926–3932 (2022)
17. Roy, A., Roy, K.K., Ali, A.A., Amin, M.A., Rahman, A.K.M.M.: SST-GNN: simplified spatio-temporal traffic forecasting model using graph neural network. In: PAKDD (2021)
18. Shen, Y., Li, L., Xie, Q., Li, X., Xu, G.: A two-tower spatial-temporal graph neural network for traffic speed prediction. In: PAKDD (2022)
19. SHI, X., Chen, Z., Wang, H., Yeung, D.Y., Wong, W.K., WOO, W.C.: Convolutional LSTM network: a machine learning approach for precipitation nowcasting. In: Advances in Neural Information Processing Systems, vol. 28 (2015)
20. Vaswani, A., et al.: Attention is all you need. In: NIPS, pp. 6000–6010 (2017)
21. Wu, Z., Pan, S., Long, G., Jiang, J., Zhang, C.: Graph WaveNet for deep spatial-temporal graph modeling. In: IJCAI, pp. 1907–1913 (2019)
22. Xu, M., et al.: Spatial-Temporal Transformer Networks for Traffic Flow Forecasting. arXiv preprint arXiv:2001.02908 (2021)
23. Zerveas, G., Jayaraman, S., Patel, D., Bhamidipaty, A., Eickhoff, C.: A transformer-based framework for multivariate time series representation learning. In: SIGKDD, pp. 2114–2124 (2021)
24. Zhang, J., Zheng, Y., Qi, D.: Deep spatio-temporal residual networks for citywide crowd flows prediction. In: AAAI, pp. 1655–1661 (2017)
25. Zheng, C., Fan, X., Wang, C., Qi, J.: GMAN: a graph multi-attention network for traffic prediction. In: AAAI, pp. 1234–1241 (2020)

GenTC: Generative Transformer via Contrastive Learning for Receipt Information Extraction

Xinrui Deng, Zheng Huang(✉), Kefan Ma, Kai Chen, Jie Guo, and Weidong Qiu

School of Electronic Information and Electrical Engineering, Shanghai Jiao Tong University, Shanghai, China
{kawhi1201rui,huang-zheng,entropy2333,kchen,guojie,qiuwd}@sjtu.edu.cn

Abstract. Information Extraction from visually rich documents has attracted increasing attention due to its various advanced applications in the real world. Most existing methods employ sequence labeling models to solve this problem. However, these approaches suffer from error propagation problems, especially when dealing with noisy OCR results. For this reason, this paper proposes GenTC, a **Gen**erative **T**ransformer enhanced by **C**ontrastive learning for receipt information extraction. GenTC extracts structural information in a generative manner. In addition, since the optimization objective is inconsistent with the task, we use an entity-order perturbation and optimize the model with contrastive learning to mitigate the incorrect bias. GenTC is able to tolerate annotation errors in OCR results, which is vital because correct annotation of numerous documents is laborious and expensive. Extensive experiments on three public benchmark datasets demonstrate that GenTC achieves competitive performance compared with previous state-of-the-art methods, and outperforms them by a large margin, especially in realistic scenarios.

Keywords: Document understanding · Key information extraction · Visually rich documents · Generative transformer

1 Introduction

In recent years, information extraction (IE) has attracted increasing attention. In the IE task, each given document may have structured information to be extracted. There have been numerous useful methods to solve this task like BiLSTM structure. However, most of these studies are based on plain text and cannot be applied to extract information from document images, such as scanned receipts or commercial invoices. Figure 1 shows an example of receipt information extraction. Understanding receipts is a very challenging task due to their complex layout, diverse formats, and poor quality of scanned images.

In general, mainstream methods solve this task in a two-stage manner: text reading and information extraction. Text reading implies capturing all the texts

L. Iliadis et al. (Eds.): ICANN 2023, LNCS 14259, pp. 394–406, 2023.
https://doi.org/10.1007/978-3-031-44223-0_32

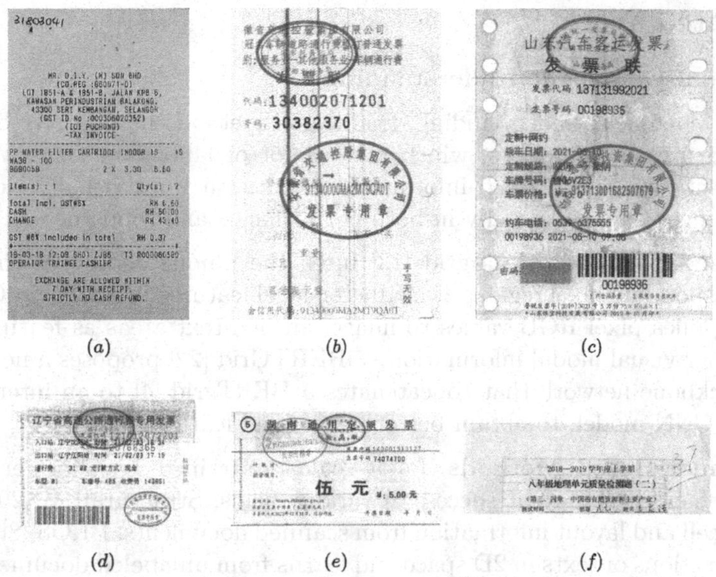

Fig. 1. Scanned image samples of receipts with complex layout and diverse formats. (a) and (f) are from SROIE and EPHOIE dataset, while $(b) \sim (d)$ are from SCID.

in a receipt image, which usually depends on a Optical Character Recognition (OCR) process, including text detection and recognition. And information extraction is responsible for mining key components from the captured texts.

Most existing methods [11,16,36,37] adopt sequence labeling models to extract information. However, these methods suffer from error propagation problems, especially in realistic scenarios where OCR results are noisier. To address the issues mentioned above, we introduce a generative Transformer for receipt information extraction. By transforming the target information into a token sequence, our model generates predictions auto-regressively. However, generative models tend to introduce incorrect bias. If previously generated entities are missing or noisy, it negatively affects the inference of subsequent entities. As a result, we introduce contrastive learning to mitigate these problems.

In summary, the contribution of this paper are as follows:

(1) We propose GenTC, which is a generative Transformer for receipt information extraction. GenTC extracts information by generating text auto-regressively and can mitigate error propagation problems from noisy OCR results compared with previous methods that rely on sequence labeling.
(2) To mitigate the incorrect bias, we propose an entity-order perturbation task and optimize the model with a contrastive loss, which is beneficial to help induce the model with better generalization performance.
(3) Extensive experiments on three benchmark datasets show that our proposed model achieves competitive performance compared with previous state-of-the-art baselines, to verify the effectiveness of our method.

2 Related Work

2.1 Visual Document Understanding

For visual document understanding, traditional methods mainly rely on handcrafted features or templates, which takes a lot of labor and time. With the development of deep learning, information extraction from visually rich documents has evolved substantially in both performance and robustness.

Grid-Based Methods. Chargrid [13] fuses the unique coding of characters with corresponding pixel regions as character-level features. VisualWordGrid [14] directly applies pixel RGB values to images in non-text areas as features, providing richer visual modal information. ViBERTGrid [22] proposes a new multimodal backbone network that concatenates a BERTgrid [4] to an intermediate layer of a CNN model, to obtain better text visual features.

Transformer-Based Methods. Large-scale pre-trained Transformer such as BERT [5] have shown great success in various fields. StructuralLM [20] jointly leverages cell and layout information from scanned documents. BROS [8] encodes relative positions of texts in 2D space and learns from unlabeled documents with an area-masking strategy. LayoutLM [34] proposes a document-level pre-training framework that integrates semantic and layout information. LayoutLMv2 [33] extends LayoutLM by introducing a multi-modal Transformer to fuse three modalities. including text, image, and layout. LayoutLMv3 [9] further improves cross-modal alignment through word-patch alignment pre-training.

End-To-End Methods. TRIE [37] proposes a unified end-to-end framework for text reading and information extraction, where the two tasks reinforce each other. Donut [15] proposes an OCR-free transformer for document understanding. Through pre-training on tremendous public and synthetic data, Donut achieves a strong generalization ability. GMN [2] proposes a multi-modal generation method without predefined label categories. Pix2Struct [17] proposes a pre-trained image-to-text model by learning to parse masked screenshots of web pages into simplified HTML.

2.2 Contrastive Learning

Contrastive learning [3,6,7,12,27,28] has evolved considerably in recent years. It aims to learn a better representation via contrasting positive and negative samples. To mitigate the exposure bias problem, contrastive learning is introduced into text generation [18], where negative examples are generated by adding small perturbations to the input sequence. SimCTG [29] introduces a novel decoding method that performs perform token-level contrastive learning to encourage diversity while maintaining coherence in the generated text. SeqCLR [1] proposes a contrastive framework for text recognition, which divides each feature map into different instances and computes the corresponding contrastive loss. CoNT [30] generates contrastive examples from its predictions through beam search algorithm and uses an N-pairs contrastive loss to address bottlenecks that prevent contrastive learning from being widely adopted in generation tasks.

3 Methodology

3.1 Overall Architecture

Figure 2 shows an overview of the framework of our proposed model. Given an input image, it is first fed into an OCR engine to perform text detection and recognition. Then we encode the image with an image Transformer and encode the OCR results with a layout-aware Transformer. The next part consists of two modules: a multi-modal fusion layer and an auto-regressive text decoder for extracting structural information.

Image Encoder. Given an origin receipt image X, we use an image Transformer to extract latent features. Different from previous methods that re-scale input images to a fixed resolution, we re-scale the input images while keeping the aspect ratio, which can be vital for understanding documents [17]. In this way, we extract the maximal number of patches that fit within the given sequence length. Concretely, we adopt Swin Transformer [23] as our image encoder due to its superior performance in document understanding [15].

$$F_{image} = \text{ImageEncoder}(X) \tag{1}$$

where $X \in \mathbb{R}^{H \times W \times C}$ represents the input image, and $F_{image} \in \mathbb{R}^{m \times d_i}$ denotes the feature map. m is the feature map size and d_i is the dimension of features.

Text Encoder. Intuitively, semantic and spatial information of text instances is significant for receipt understanding. In general, we acquire the OCR results by means of performing text detection and recognition, which contains the bounding boxes and texts for each document instance. To fully utilize the semantic

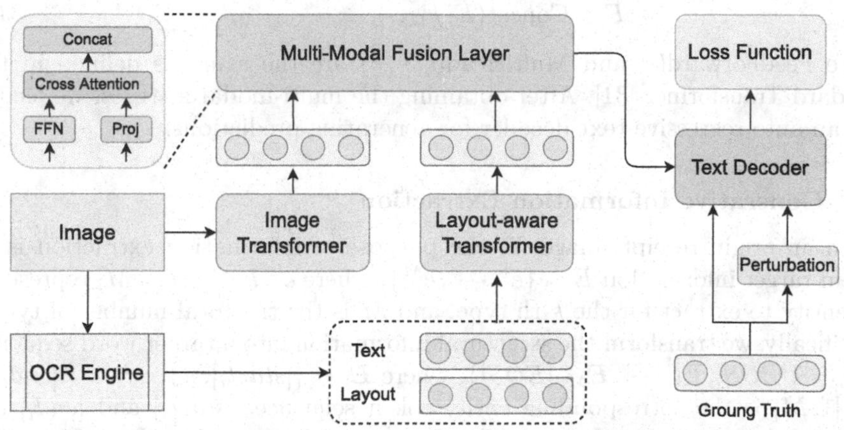

Fig. 2. Illustration of our proposed model. GenTC extracts multi-modal features and combines them with a fusion layer. Then an auto-regressive text decoder is employed to generate predictions, where we introduce the entity-order perturbation and optimize the model with a contrastive loss.

information and spatial coordinates, the text fragments are tokenized and the bounding boxes are normalized to the range of [0, 1000]. Then we encode them with a layout-aware Transformer following LayoutLM [34].

Formally, the text sequence is denoted as $T = \{[CLS], t_1, \cdots, t_l, [SEP]\}$, and the corresponding coordinates are $C_{x_0}, C_{x_1}, C_{y_0}$ and C_{y_1} separately. And we also introduce the width and height information denoted as C_w and C_h. Since character-level annotations are hard and expensive to acquire in realistic scenarios, we use the same layout information for each text instance. Then two embedding layers are applied to embed x-axis features and y-axis features, respectively. The calculation can be formulated as follows:

$$P_x = \text{PosEmbedding}_x(C_{x_0}, C_{x_1}, C_w) \tag{2}$$

$$P_y = \text{PosEmbedding}_y(C_{y_0}, C_{y_1}, C_h) \tag{3}$$

$$F_{text} = \text{TextEncoder}(T, P_x, P_y) \tag{4}$$

where P_x and P_y denotes the layout embedding, and $F_{text} \in \mathbb{R}^{n \times d_t}$ refers to the contextualized text feature. $\text{PosEmbedding}_x(\cdot)$ and $\text{PosEmbedding}_y(\cdot)$ are the layout embedding layers we used to embed the coordinates. d_t is the dimension of text features.

Multi-modal Fusion Layer. To integrate visual and textual information, a multi-modal fusion layer is employed. We apply a cross-attention layer to capture the correlation between text and image features.

$$\tilde{F}_{text} = \text{Projection}(F_{text}) \tag{5}$$

$$\tilde{F}_{image} = \text{FeedForward}(F_{image}) \tag{6}$$

$$\tilde{F} = \text{MultiHead}(\tilde{F}_{text}, \tilde{F}_{image}, \tilde{F}_{image}) \tag{7}$$

$$F = \text{Concat}(\tilde{F}, \tilde{F}_{text}) \tag{8}$$

where $\text{FeedForward}(\cdot)$ and $\text{MultiHead}(q, k, v)$ are the same as defined in the standard Transformer [31]. After obtaining the multi-modal features, we feed it into an auto-regressive text decoder for generating predictions.

3.2 Generative Information Extraction

Given an origin receipt image X, the purpose of information extraction is to obtain target information $E = \{e^1, \cdots, e^M\}$, where $e^k, k \in [1, t = M]$ represents the entity to extract for the k-th type, and M is the the total number of types. Specifically, we transform the structural information into a target word sequence as $Y = \{[BOS], E_1, \cdots, E_M, [EOS]\}$, where $E_i = \{[start_i], w_i^1, w_i^2, \cdots, [end_t]\}$, $i \in [1, M]$ is the corresponding entity token sequence. $[start_i]$ and $[end_i]$ are the special start and end token of i-th entity. We formulate the information extraction task in a generative way:

$$P(Y|X) = \prod_{t=1}^{N} P(y_t|X, Y_{<t}) \tag{9}$$

where y_0 is the special "start of sentence" token $[BOS]$ and N is the total length of target sequence. We use a BART-like [19] decoder to generate texts auto-regressively. Greedy search algorithm is used in the decoding process, where the most likely token is selected at each step.

During the training phase, it predicts the next word based on previous ground truth input. We minimize the negative log likelihood (NLL) loss as follows:

$$\mathcal{L}_{NLL} = -\sum_{t=1}^{N} \log p_\theta(y_t|X, Y_{<t}) \tag{10}$$

3.3 Entity-Order Perturbation

When the generative model is applied to information extraction, the optimization objective is inconsistent with the task [38]. Since we obtain entity sequence through a generative model with a pre-defined entity order, we tend to neglect the dependency between entities and introduce incorrect bias. In addition, if some entities are noisy or missing in a image, it will negatively affect the inference of subsequent entities. As a result, we introduce an entity-order perturbation and contrastive learning to mitigate the incorrect bias.

As shown in the Fig. 3, we construct an augmented entity sequence by sampling possible entity orders. Given an original target sequence, we randomly permute the order of the entities. For brevity, we randomly swap two entities in the sequence each time. The augmented sample is denoted as Y'.

Intuitively, contrastive learning seeks to learn a similarity function that drives the distance between the source sequence representation and its ground-truth target sequence representation closer. We use from-batch negative samples and minimize the InfoNCE loss [6,25] as follows:

$$\mathcal{L}_{CL} = -\log \frac{\exp(\cos(z_Y, z_{Y'})/\tau)}{\sum_{y \in \mathcal{B}} \exp(\cos(z_Y, z_y)/\tau)} \tag{11}$$

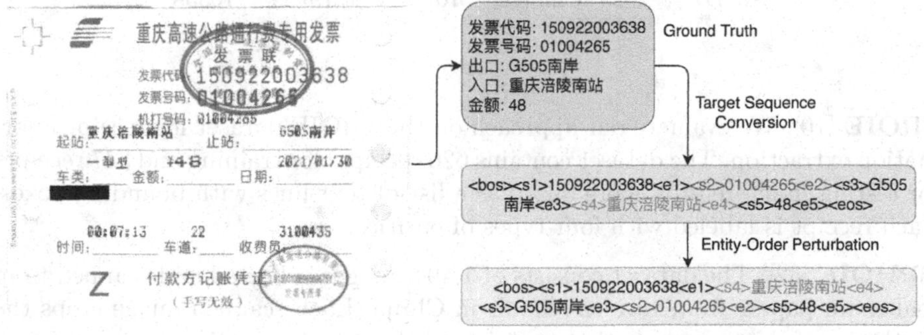

Fig. 3. Illustration of entity-order perturbation.

where $z_Y, z_{Y'}, z_y \in R^d$ denote the vector representation of ground truth x, perturbed ground truth x' and from-batch negative sample $y \in \mathcal{B}$, respectively. τ is the temperature and $\cos(\cdot, \cdot)$ refers to the cosine similarity function.

3.4 Training Objective

In the training phase, our proposed model GenTC can be trained in a generative manner, along with the weighted sum of the losses generated from two branches of information extraction and contrastive learning. The whole loss function can be formulated as follows:

$$\mathcal{L} = \mathcal{L}_{NLL} + \lambda \mathcal{L}_{CL} \tag{12}$$

where λ is the coefficient weight to control the trade-off between losses. Compared with methods based on sequence labelling, our model generates structural information and is capable of tolerating noisy OCR results. Through introducing contrastive entity-order perturbation, our model further mitigates the incorrect bias and achieves improved generalization ability.

4 Experiments

4.1 Datasets

In this paper, we applied our proposed model to three popular public benchmark datasets, including SROIE, EHPOIE, and SCID. Detailed dataset statistics are shown in Table 1. The introduction to the datasets is given below.

Table 1. Statistical analysis of datasets.

Dataset	Year	Language	#Entities	#Train	#Test
SROIE	2019	English	4	626	347
EPHOIE	2020	Chinese	10	1183	311
SCID	2022	Chinese	10	19999	10358

SROIE [10]. We evaluate our approach on the SROIE dataset for receipt information extraction. The dataset contains 626 receipts for training and 347 receipts for testing. Each receipt is organized as a list of text lines with bounding boxes. Each receipt is labeled with four types of entities.

EPHOIE [32]. The dataset consists of 1,494 images collected and scanned from real exam papers from various schools in China. Each scanned image crops the head area of the test paper that contains all the key information, where the text is composed of handwritten and printed Chinese characters

SCID[1]. This dataset is from CSIG 2022 Competition on Invoice Recognition and Analysis. It contains six types of invoices for key information extraction, including Taxi Invoice, Train Invoice, Passenger Invoice, Toll Invoice, Air Itinerary Invoice and Quota Invoice.

4.2 Implementation Details

Our experiments are performed on NVIDIA V100 GPU, implemented by the PyTorch framework. We use Swin Transformer as our vision encoder, LayoutXLM as our layout-aware text encoder, and BART as our text decoder. Specifically, we initialize our vision encoder and text decoder with pre-trained weights of multi-lingual `donut-base`[2] and random initialize the multi-modal fusion layer. Our text encoder is initialized with pre-trained weights of `layoutxlm-base`[3]. AdamW [24] optimizer is adopted in the training phase, with a scheduled learning rate of maximum 5e-5. The training batch size is 8. The weight decay is set to 1e-2, and the loss weight λ is set to 0.5. And the max length in the decoder is 128. As for other OCR-dependant baselines, we choose the open-source PaddleOCR [21] as our OCR engine due to its superior performance.

4.3 Comparisons with Previous Methods

Results on SROIE and EPHOIE. The experimental results on SROIE and EPHOIE benchmark datasets are elaborated in Table 2. Our proposed GenTC achieves competitive or superior performance compared with previous state-of-the-art methods. In detail, GenTC consistently outperforms all of the baselines in terms of precision, recall, and f1-score with a single exception of recall on EPHOIE where LayoutLMv2 is better. Compared with LayoutLMv2, the best among the listed baselines, GenTC can improve f1-score by 0.68% on the SROIE datasets, and 0.22% on the EPHOIE dataset. It demonstrates that our proposed method is capable of exploiting multi-modal features, and extracting information more accurately.

Results on SCID. The results of experiments on the SCID dataset are shown in Table 3. Under **Ground Truth** setting, all models are trained with accurate OCR annotations. Compared with BERT which only utilizes the textual modality, there is a significant boost observed on three metrics across all datasets. It validates the effectiveness of fusing multi-modal features, including vision, text, and layout. Experimental results show that our model achieves the best f1-score 91.80%, surpassing LayoutXLM by a margin of 0.47%.

Results Under End-To-End Setting. The robustness of our proposed model is more evident under the **End-to-End** setting where the OCR results are

[1] https://davar-lab.github.io/dataset/scid.html.
[2] https://github.com/clovaai/donut.
[3] https://github.com/microsoft/unilm.

Table 2. Experimental results on SROIE and EPHOIE datasets. The results of other baselines are cited from corresponding original papers. "-" means not available in the original paper. The best results are shown in bold. **P**, **R**, and **F1** represent Precision, Recall, and F1-score, respectively. "↑" indicates the improvement of our method compared with best results.

Model	SROIE			EPHOIE		
	P	R	F1	P	R	F1
PICK [36]	96.79	95.46	96.12	-	-	-
GraphIE [26]	-	-	94.46	-	-	90.26
TRIE [37]	-	-	96.18	-	-	93.21
BERT [5]	90.99	90.99	90.99	88.52*	86.04*	87.26*
BROS [8]	94.93	96.03	95.48	-	-	-
VIES [32]	-	-	96.12	-	-	95.23
LayoutLMv2 [35]	96.25	96.25	96.25	97.45*	**98.02***	97.73*
GenTC	**97.59**$^{\uparrow 0.80}$	**96.27**$^{\uparrow 0.02}$	**96.93**$^{\uparrow 0.68}$	**98.16**$^{\uparrow 0.71}$	97.74	**97.95**$^{\uparrow 0.22}$

Table 3. Experimental results on the SCID dataset. For other baselines, we use the implementation provided by the authors in the original paper to produce the results. And the best results are shown in bold.

Setting	Model	Precision	Recall	F1-score
Ground Truth	BERT	84.63*	68.19*	75.53*
	LayoutXLM	**95.68***	87.35*	91.33*
	GenTC	95.45	**88.43**$^{\uparrow 1.08}$	**91.80**$^{\uparrow 0.47}$
End-to-End	BERT	78.48*	62.29*	69.45*
	Donut	84.85*	81.22*	82.80*
	LayoutXLM	87.66*	79.34*	83.29*
	GenTC	**91.27**$^{\uparrow 3.61}$	**87.02**$^{\uparrow 5.80}$	**89.09**$^{\uparrow 5.80}$
Competition	Rank 1	88.90	87.37	87.88
	Rank 2	87.22	85.33	85.94
	Rank 3	86.61	84.84	85.46

noisy and less accurate. Compared with LayoutXLM, a sequence labeling-based method with error propagation problems, GenTC significantly outperforms it in terms of precision, recall, and f1-score. Specifically, GenTC improves the f1-score by a large margin (89.09% v.s. 83.29%), verifying the vulnerability of the sequence labeling approach to noisy OCR results, which our model can tolerate. Moreover, we compare GenTC with Donut, an end-to-end method that does not rely on OCR results. Since Donut generates predictions only from image pixels, it is hard to capture the fine-grained information such as layout connections between text instances, yielding a relatively lower performance.

In addition to the listed baselines, we also compare our method with the top three methods during CSIG 2022 competition which inevitably introduced delicate techniques like model ensemble. However, our proposed method achieves even better results (89.09 v.s. 87.88). Experimental results demonstrate that our generative Transformer is more practical in realistic scenarios and can mitigate the error propagation problems from the OCR process.

4.4 Ablation Study

To reveal the individual effects of entity-order perturbation (EOP), multi-modal fusion (MMF), and generative information extraction (GIE), we implement different variants of GenTC by removing them sequentially. The experimental results of ablation studies on EPHOIE and SCID are reported in Table 4.

Table 4. Ablation study results on EPHOIE and SCID datasets.

Model	EPHOIE (Ground Truth)			SCID (End-to-End)		
	P	R	F1	P	R	F1
GenTC	**98.16**	**97.74**	**97.95**	**91.27**	**87.02**	**89.09**
w/o EOP	97.75	97.46	97.70	90.77	86.71	88.69
w/o EOP & MMF	97.55	97.08	97.31	90.32	86.48	88.36
w/o GIE	97.45	97.03	97.24	86.78	80.39	83.46

Entity-Order Perturbation. As shown in the second line of Table 4, it can be observed that entity-order perturbation boosts performance. More concretely, the f1-score drops by 0.25% on EPHOIE dataset and 0.40% on SCID dataset, respectively. This is because, the generative model tends to introduce incorrect bias and neglects the correlation between entities to extract. Through introducing entity-order perturbation and contrastive learning, our proposed model can achieve better robustness and generalization ability.

Multi-modal Fusion. Our proposed GenTC utilizes multiple modalities and combines these features with a multi-modal fusion layer. Hence, we conduct experiments to validate its effectiveness by removing this fusion layer and concatenating features directly. The results show a 0.39% drop on EPHOIE dataset and a 0.33% drop on SCID dataset in terms of f1-score.

Generative Information Extraction. Since GenTC extracts information in a generative manner, we perform the ablation study by replacing text decoder with a sequence labeling layer. As shown in the last line of Table 4, replacing the text decoder hardly affects the performance on EPHOIE dataset under **Ground Truth** setting. However, a significant drop is observed on SCID dataset under **End-to-End** setting. Concretely, f1-score drops 4.9% (from 88.36 to 83.46), close to the results of LayoutXLM reported above. These results show that generative information extraction can tolerate noisy OCR results and mitigate the error propagation problems from OCR process in realistic scenarios.

5 Conclusion and Future Work

This paper proposes GenTC, a generative Transformer enhanced by contrastive learning for receipt information extraction. Our proposed aims to extract structural information in a generative manner and exploit different modalities. Moreover, we introduce an entity-order perturbation to alleviate the incorrect bias. Extensive experimental results on SROIE, EPHOIE and SCID benchmark datasets show that our proposed method achieves competitive or superior performance compared with previous state-of-the-art methods, and surpasses them, especially in realistic scenarios. Detailed ablation studies further validate the effectiveness of GenTC. Nevertheless, as an auto-regressive model, GenTC inevitably consumes comparatively more computing resources. Speeding up the training and inference without losing accuracy is the next important step for improvement.

Visual document understanding is a challenging task that requires knowledge of natural language processing and computer vision. There is still vast scope to explore in the future, including over-reliance on excellent OCR engines, complex layouts, and handling unknown entities in the wild. Therefore, it deserves more attention and further investigation. We hope that GenTC will inspire and facilitate follow-up works.

Acknowledgement.. This work was supported by the National Natural Science Foundation of China (Grant No. 92270201).

References

1. Aberdam, A., et al.: Sequence-to-sequence contrastive learning for text recognition. In: CVPR (2021)
2. Cao, H., et al.: GMN: generative multi-modal network for practical document information extraction. In: Proceedings of AACL (2022)
3. Chen, T., Kornblith, S., Norouzi, M., Hinton, G.E.: A simple framework for contrastive learning of visual representations. In: ICML (2020)
4. Denk, T.I., Reisswig, C.: BERTgrid: contextualized embedding for 2D document representation and understanding. CoRR (2019)
5. Devlin, J., Chang, M., Lee, K., Toutanova, K.: BERT: pre-training of deep bidirectional transformers for language understanding. In: Proceedings of AACL (2019)
6. Gao, T., Yao, X., Chen, D.: SimCSE: simple contrastive learning of sentence embeddings. In: EMNLP (1) (2021)
7. He, K., Fan, H., Wu, Y., Xie, S., Girshick, R.B.: Momentum contrast for unsupervised visual representation learning. In: CVPR (2020)
8. Hong, T., Kim, D., Ji, M., Hwang, W., Nam, D., Park, S.: BROS: a pre-trained language model focusing on text and layout for better key information extraction from documents. In: Proceedings of AAAI (2022)
9. Huang, Y., Lv, T., Cui, L., Lu, Y., Wei, F.: Layoutlmv3: pre-training for document AI with unified text and image masking. In: ACM Multimedia (2022)
10. Huang, Z., et al.: ICDAR2019 competition on scanned receipt OCR and information extraction. In: ICDAR (2019)

11. Jiang, Z., Huang, Z., Lian, Y., Guo, J., Qiu, W.: Integrating coordinates with context for information extraction in document images. In: ICDAR (2019)
12. Jiang, Z., Chen, T., Chen, T., Wang, Z.: Robust pre-training by adversarial contrastive learning. In: NeurIPS (2020)
13. Katti, A.R., et al.: CharGRID: towards understanding 2D documents. In: EMNLP (2018)
14. Kerroumi, M., Sayem, O., Shabou, A.: VisualWordGrid: information extraction from scanned documents using a multimodal approach. In: Barney Smith, E.H., Pal, U. (eds.) ICDAR 2021. LNCS, vol. 12917, pp. 389–402. Springer, Cham (2021). https://doi.org/10.1007/978-3-030-86159-9_28
15. Kim, G., et al.: OCR-free document understanding transformer. In: Avidan, S., Brostow, G., Cissé, M., Farinella, G.M., Hassner, T. (eds.) Computer Vision - ECCV 2022, ECCV 2022. Lecture Notes in Computer Science, vol. 13688, pp. 498–517. Springer, Cham (2022). https://doi.org/10.1007/978-3-031-19815-1_29
16. Lee, C., et al.: FormNet: structural encoding beyond sequential modeling in form document information extraction. In: ACL (1) (2022)
17. Lee, K., et al.: Pix2struct: screenshot parsing as pretraining for visual language understanding. CoRR (2022)
18. Lee, S., Lee, D.B., Hwang, S.J.: Contrastive learning with adversarial perturbations for conditional text generation. In: ICLR (2021)
19. Lewis, M., et al.: BART: denoising sequence-to-sequence pre-training for natural language generation, translation, and comprehension. In: ACL (2020)
20. Li, C., et al.: StructuralLM: structural pre-training for form understanding. In: ACL/IJCNLP (1) (2021)
21. Li, C., et al.: Pp-ocrv3: more attempts for the improvement of ultra lightweight OCR system. CoRR (2022)
22. Lin, W., et al.: ViBERTgrid: a jointly trained multi-modal 2D document representation for key information extraction from documents. In: Lladós, J., Lopresti, D., Uchida, S. (eds.) ICDAR 2021. LNCS, vol. 12821, pp. 548–563. Springer, Cham (2021). https://doi.org/10.1007/978-3-030-86549-8_35
23. Liu, Z., et al.: Swin transformer: hierarchical vision transformer using shifted windows. In: ICCV (2021)
24. Loshchilov, I., Hutter, F.: Decoupled weight decay regularization. In: ICLR (Poster) (2019)
25. van den Oord, A., Li, Y., Vinyals, O.: Representation learning with contrastive predictive coding. CoRR (2018)
26. Qian, Y., Santus, E., Jin, Z., Guo, J., Barzilay, R.: Graphie: a graph-based framework for information extraction. In: Proceedings of AACL (2019)
27. Schroff, F., Kalenichenko, D., Philbin, J.: FaceNet: a unified embedding for face recognition and clustering. In: CVPR (2015)
28. Sohn, K.: Improved deep metric learning with multi-class n-pair loss objective. In: NIPS (2016)
29. Su, Y., Lan, T., Wang, Y., Yogatama, D., Kong, L., Collier, N.: A contrastive framework for neural text generation. CoRR (2022)
30. Teng, Z., Chen, C., Zhang, Y., Zhang, Y.: Contrastive latent variable models for neural text generation. In: UAI (2022)
31. Vaswani, A., et al.: Attention is all you need. In: NIPS (2017)
32. Wang, J., et al.: Towards robust visual information extraction in real world: New dataset and novel solution. In: Proceedings of AAAI (2021)
33. Xu, Y., et al.: Layoutlmv2: multi-modal pre-training for visually-rich document understanding. In: ACL/IJCNLP (1) (2021)

34. Xu, Y., Li, M., Cui, L., Huang, S., Wei, F., Zhou, M.: LayoutLM: pre-training of text and layout for document image understanding. In: Proceedings of KDD (2020)
35. Xu, Y., et al.: LayoutxLM: multimodal pre-training for multilingual visually-rich document understanding. CoRR (2021)
36. Yu, W., Lu, N., Qi, X., Gong, P., Xiao, R.: PICK: processing key information extraction from documents using improved graph learning-convolutional networks. In: ICPR (2020)
37. Zhang, P., et al.: TRIE: end-to-end text reading and information extraction for document understanding. In: ACM Multimedia (2020)
38. Zhang, S., Shen, Y., Tan, Z., Wu, Y., Lu, W.: De-bias for generative extraction in unified NER task. In: ACL (1) (2022)

Hierarchical Classification for Symmetrized VI Trajectory Based on Lightweight Swin Transformer

Wuqing Yu, Linfeng Yang(✉), and Zixian He

School of Computer Electronics and Information, Guangxi Key Laboratory of Multimedia Communication and Network Technology, Guangxi University, Nanning 530004, China
{2113301058,2213394008}@st.gxu.edu.cn, ylf@gxu.edu.cn

Abstract. Non-intrusive Load Monitoring (NILM) is an important means to realize household energy management, and appliance identification is a significant branch of NILM. However, type II appliances, also called multi-state appliances, make it hard to correctly identify the type of appliance. In this paper, hierarchical classification based on swin transformer is proposed to improve the accuracy of appliance identification and reduce the adverse impacts of intra-class variety (IACV) mainly caused by type II electrical loads. By using k-means to pre-cluster target categories into more abstract subclasses, artificial classification operations in hierarchical classification are reduced. Meanwhile, VI trajectories with comprehensive and highly differentiated characteristics are generated, specifically, we skillfully symmetrize VI trajectories and map the higher order harmonic feature into the empty pixels in the background of the VI images for the first time, which improves the network's potential mining for features, and the symmetrical trajectory is more conducive to swin transformer's feature positioning and fine-grained learning through the shifted windowing configuration, and in order to effectively cope with the negative impacts of inter-class variety (IECV) and insufficient feature information in the existing load signatures, we adopt RGB color encoding to fuse multiple features. Compared with the existing methods, the experimental results indicate that our proposed method is more effective on the PLAID and Whited v1.1 datasets. The code is available at: https://github.com/linfengYang/HC_LST_NILM.

Keywords: Non-intrusive Load Monitoring (NILM) · Hierarchical classification · Appliance identification · k-means · Light swin transformer

1 Introduction

More and more countries in the world advocate the concept of sustainable development. A key element of sustainable development is energy storage and consumption. Appliance-level energy consumption, as a basic unit of electricity consumption, can be effectively managed to improve energy efficiency. Non-Intrusive Load Monitoring (NILM), as a monitoring method, was first proposed by Hart [1]. NILM is an attractive and available approach to identifying the operational states and electricity usage

L. Iliadis et al. (Eds.): ICANN 2023, LNCS 14259, pp. 407–420, 2023.
https://doi.org/10.1007/978-3-031-44223-0_33

of single appliance, given the overall energy signal of a household. The selection and recognition of load characteristics are always the key and difficult problems in NILM. Many studies have explored different strategies to deal with NILM using different load signatures like power, current, etc. The problem of appliance recognition is transformed into a classification issue if VI trajectories are used as load signatures.

Ham, H et al. use V-I trajectory as electrical features for the first time in 2007 [2], which maps the steady-state voltage and current waveforms to a 2D image, bringing a new way to represent electrical features. Inspired by their VI trajectory transformation, Du et al. [3] maps the VI trajectory to a grid, and assigns each grid a binary value, the value of the grid is set to 1 if there is a trajectory passing through the grid, and 0 otherwise. This significantly improves the recognition accuracy while reducing the computational cost, and many subsequent studies on VI trajectories are mostly based on their inspiration. De Baets et al. [4] transfers the VI trajectory into a weighted pixelated image such that the image has continuous values rather than binary values. In [5], the VI trajectory maps are color-coded in HSV space, and transfer learning is used to identify and classify them for the first time. However, their recognition effect for Type II appliances is unstable, which may be caused by the IACV. In [6], two classifiers, random forest (RF) and CNN, are used to classify VI trajectories. In their methods, random forest uses an outer closed contours curve (also called Elliptical Fourier Descriptors EFD) of the VI trajectories as the characterization of the corresponding appliance. The authors in [7] convert the current of one activation cycle into weighted recurrence graph, but the normalization of single feature leads to a large loss of information and the electrical characteristics are underutilized, which may result in a poor classification performance when the appliance category increases. Zhang et al. [8] first apply SVM to pre-cluster the target classes into several groups, then RF is used to further classify the appliances in these groups. The main problem is that the classification efficiency is not high when the number of appliances increases.

The authors in [9] introduces a branch convolutional neural network (B-CNN) to conduct hierarchical classification, it is the first time that the hierarchical classification implemented by a neural network has been proposed.

Inspired by the above-related works and their shortcomings, this paper proposes a hierarchical classification for symmetrized VI trajectory based on light swin transformer. First, we obtain the VI trajectories embedded with multiple features through RGB color encoding and background mapping. In addition, k-means is used to pre-cluster the VI trajectories into more abstract subclasses, and then a hierarchical classification model is built to perform the task of load recognition.

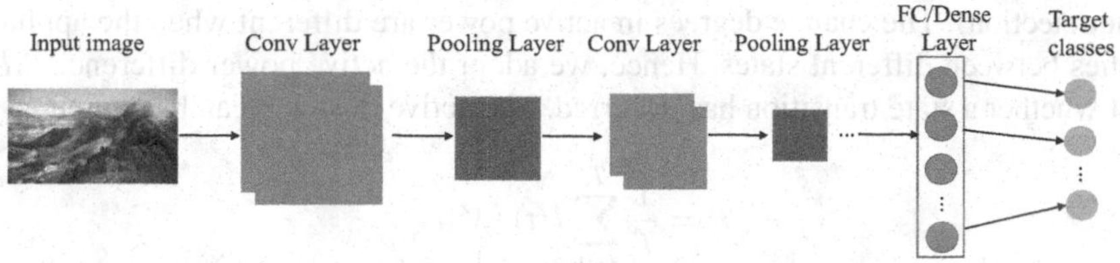

Fig. 1. Traditional convolutional neural network architecture for image classification (VGG Net-like architecture)

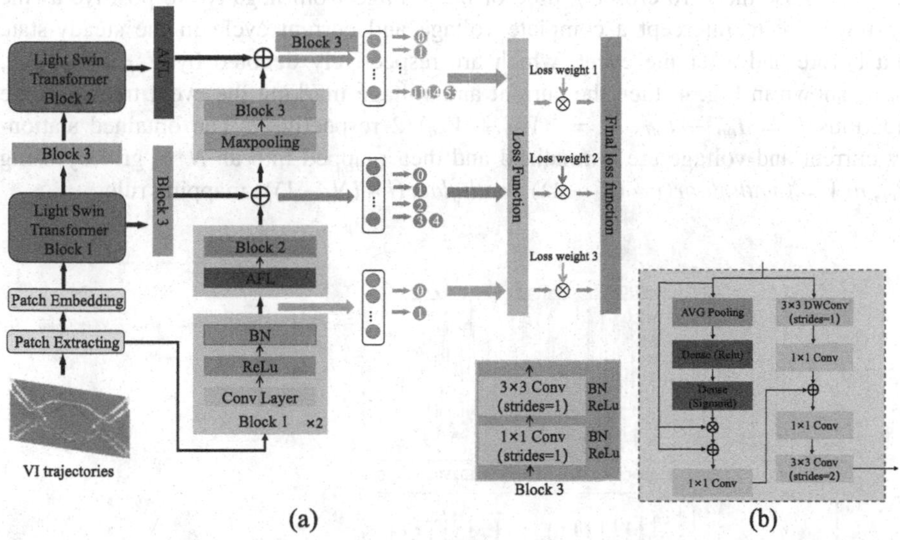

Fig. 2. (a) Illustration of our hierarchical classification structure for appliance identification. (b) AFL: Attention Fusion Layer.

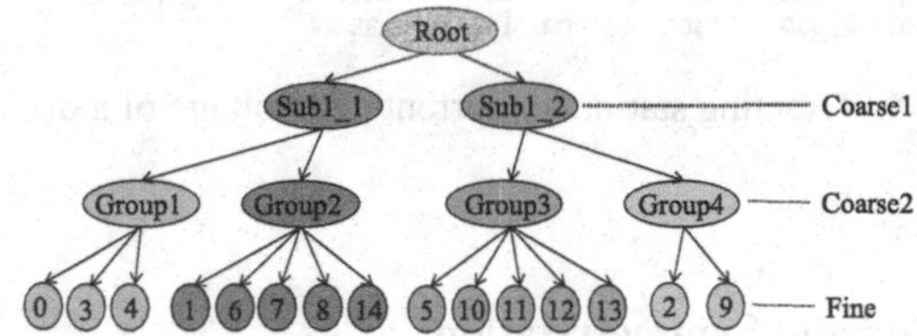

Fig. 3. A hierarchical label tree for PLAID 2018 Submetered dataset.

2 Method

2.1 VI Trajectory Acquisition

VI trajectories are used to mark the characteristics of appliance on-event, and they are generated from one steady-state voltage and current cycle in a mapping rule. A crucial problem before obtaining steady-state voltage and current is how to detect event transition (event detection). The change degrees in active power are different when the appliance switches between different states. Hence, we adopt the active power difference ΔP to detect whether a state transition has occurred. The active power P can be computed by:

$$P = \frac{1}{T}\sum_{t=1}^{T} I(t) \cdot V(t) \tag{1}$$

where T denotes the total number of data points in a cycle. *I(t)*, *V(t)* are the stationary current and voltage of a cycle, respectively.

We choose the zero crossing time of the voltage from negative to positive as the starting point to intercept a complete voltage and current cycle in the steady-state data before and after the event, which are respectively denoted by V_{off}, V_{on}, I_{off}, I_{on} as shown in Fig. 4, then the current and voltage marking the event transition are equations $I = I_{on} - I_{off}$, $V = (V_{on} + V_{on})/2$ respectively. The obtained stationary current and voltage are normalized and then mapped into an $N*N$ grid by using $\left(n_{v_i}, n_{i_j}\right) = (math.floor(v * (N-1)), math.floor(i * (N-1)))$ mapping rule.

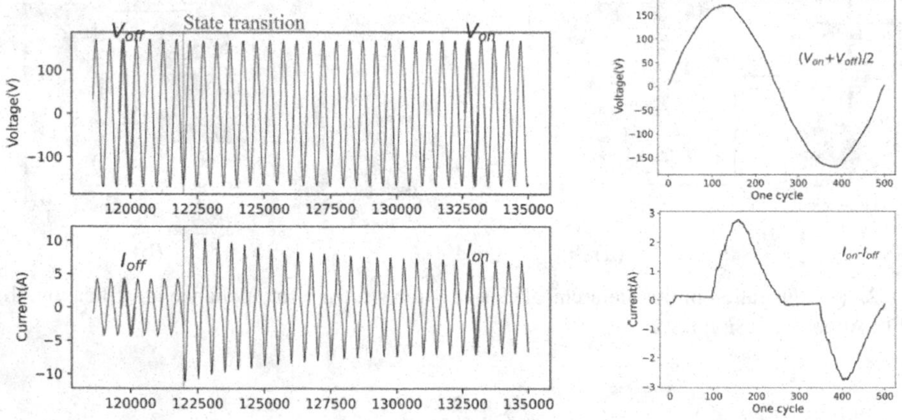

Fig. 4. Exacting stationary current and voltage of a cycle.

2.2 Feature Mapping and Symmetrization

For Type II appliances, they have multiple operational states, e.g. a washing machine has some states: washing, spinning, drying, standby, etc. Hence these multi-state appliances bring higher intra-class variety (IACV), and at the same time, some states of these appliances may also have similar VI trajectories with other appliances with similar running modes, (e.g., the warming mode of an air conditioner is similar to the working state of a hairdryer), which greatly increases the difficulty of appliance classification. Some similar VI trajectory samples are shown in the first row in Fig. 7. Therefore, in our paper, we encode nonactive current, active power, and phase difference of each grid into RGB three channels in VI trajectories (grid to grid). According to Fryze's power theory

[10], the current is divided into nonactive and active components, where the nonactive current is orthogonal to the voltage *V(t)*, so the nonactive current can be expressed as follows:

$$I(t) = I_a(t) + I_f(t) \tag{2}$$

$$I_a(t) = \frac{P}{V_{rms}^2} \cdot V(t) \tag{3}$$

$$I_f(t) = I(t) - \frac{\frac{1}{T}\sum_{t=1}^{T} V(t) \cdot I(t)}{V_{rms}^2} V(t) \tag{4}$$

where $I_a(t)$ and $I_f(t)$ are the active and nonactive components, respectively. V_{rms} denotes the effective value of the periodic voltage. Fryze's power theory can represent the non-active and active components as non-resistance and resistance information respectively, which can further help to enhance the variability of VI trajectories.

The phase difference can reflect the motion information of the trajectory, so we map the phase difference to the B channel, and the phase difference θ_j between adjacent points can be calculated by $\theta_j = \arctan\left((V_{j+1} - V_j)/(I_{j+1} - I_j)\right)$.

If an image has more features, the neural network can learn from these abundant features more sensibly. Hence, for the first time, we symmetrize the VI trajectory and introduce harmonic feature to the background to enhance the network's mining of potential features and provide a larger range of feature learning. Electrical appliances are mainly divided into linear loads (L) (can be inductive or resistive) and non-linear loads (NL). Higher-order harmonics provide information about the linearity of electrical appliances. Therefore, the introduction of harmonic features can make the VI trajectory carry more information, the sequence of coefficients $(c_j)_{j\in\mathbb{Z}}$ is written by:

$$c_j = \frac{1}{T}\int_{-\frac{T}{2}}^{\frac{T}{2}} y(t)e^{-2i\pi jFt}dt \tag{5}$$

where $F = \frac{1}{T}$ is defined as the frequency on $\mathbb{R}$ and $y(t)$ is the periodic function in the time period *T*. From the Fig. 5 we can see that: odd harmonics are more important than even harmonics, and harmonics higher than the fifth order do not contribute much to the feature discrimination. Therefore, after the periodic current is processed by the Fast Fourier Transform (FFT) method, we map the sum of harmonic coefficients at the first second order (1st-2nd) and at the first fifth order (1st-5th) to the R and B channels in the background empty pixels, respectively.

Nonactive current, active power, phase angle difference, and harmonics have large differences in numerical values. Since RGB color space can represent the darkest color with the maximum value 255, and the value 0 represents the lightest color, we propose a sigmoid-like function $\sigma(x) = 1/(1+e^{\frac{x-a}{-b}})$ to normalize the above four feature values to [0,1]. For nonactive current and phase angle difference, a and b are set to 0, 1, respectively, while for the normalization of active power, a is set to 100 and b is set to 200, and for harmonics, a and b are set to 4, 1. The normalization curves are shown in Fig. 6. One

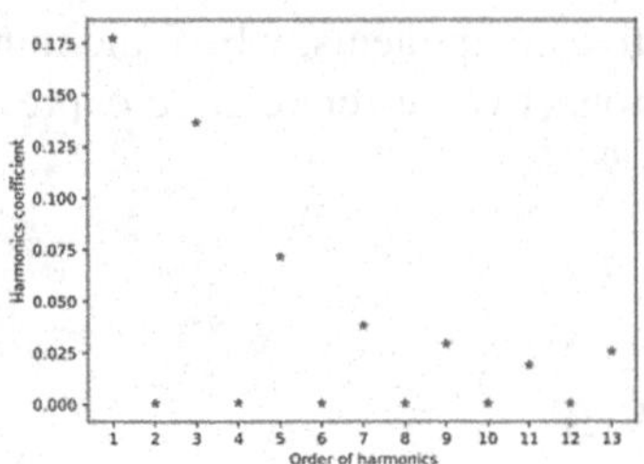

Fig. 5. The harmonics coefficient of current.

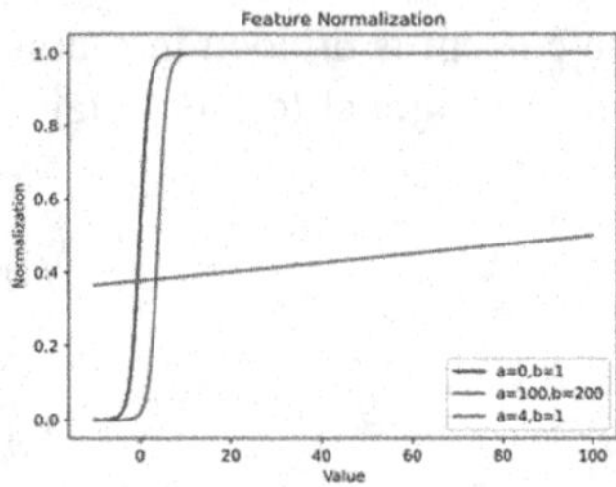

Fig. 6. Different feature normalization level.

benefit of normalizing the different features separately is that when faced with model migration to identify other countries or very different appliances, adjusting the degree of normalization can produce more diverse GRB VI images. Some RGB and background mapping samples are shown in Fig. 7.

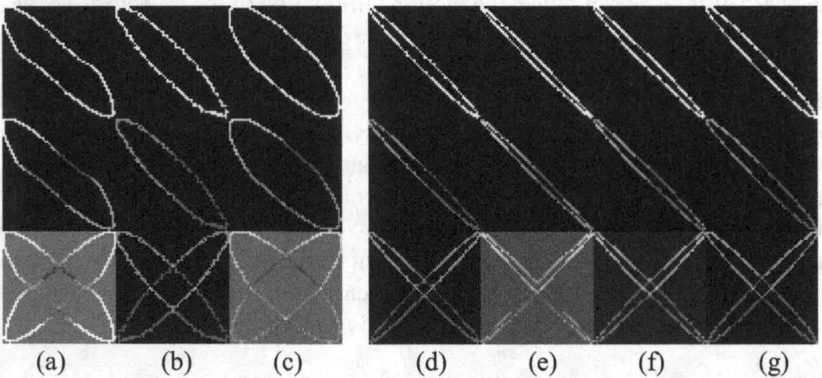

Fig. 7. Some samples of similar VI trajectories and the comparison with different preprocessing methods. (a) Air conditioner, (b) Fan, (c) Washing machine, (d) Incandescent Light Bulb, (e) Heater, (f) Hairdryer, (g) Air conditioner.

2.3 Hierarchical Classification

Traditional CNN-based classifiers, as shown in Fig. 1, output the predicted categories through the last layer of FC or Dense layer. They hypothesize that all categories are equally tough to discriminate. However, in the real world, there are some categories that are more difficult to distinguish, or there is an abstract hierarchical relationship between categories. Hierarchical classification can decompose a tricky classification task into multiple subtasks. It aims to learn inter-class classification levels by using multiple output layers with different class abstractions.

The overall classification framework we propose is shown in Fig. 2. We set up two abstract layers, and the label tree corresponding to the category division of the VI trajectory (obtained from PLAID2018S) is shown in Fig. 3. Fine labels are the real categories of appliances, which are the target classes to be predicted. The number of target classes is 15 and we use them as leaves for hierarchical classification. The 15 classes are initially divided into several more abstract classes Coarse2 based on their superficial features. We select a VI image (without harmonic mapping) from each type of appliance (one class one picking), the selected VI image is straightened into a one-dimensional vector along the channel direction, as shown in Fig. 8, and then the k-means algorithm is applied to cluster the flattened feature vector, and preliminarily determines how many leaf nodes are specifically subdivided by each node in Coarse2.

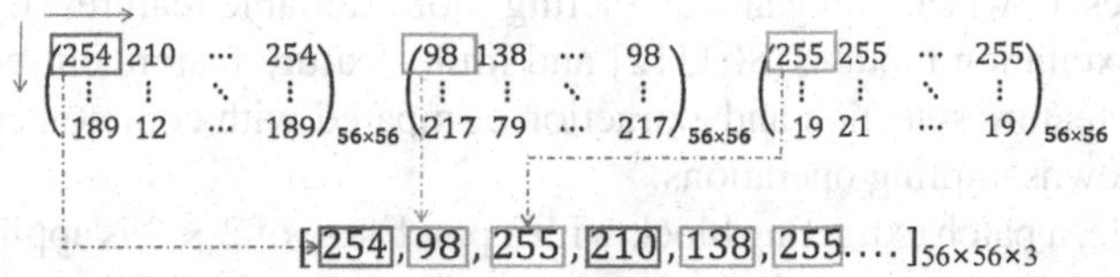

$$\begin{pmatrix} 254 & 210 & \cdots & 254 \\ \vdots & \vdots & \ddots & \vdots \\ 189 & 12 & \cdots & 189 \end{pmatrix}_{56\times56} \begin{pmatrix} 98 & 138 & \cdots & 98 \\ \vdots & \vdots & \ddots & \vdots \\ 217 & 79 & \cdots & 217 \end{pmatrix}_{56\times56} \begin{pmatrix} 255 & 255 & \cdots & 255 \\ \vdots & \vdots & \ddots & \vdots \\ 19 & 21 & \cdots & 19 \end{pmatrix}_{56\times56}$$

$$[254, 98, 255, 210, 138, 255 \ldots]_{56\times56\times3}$$

Fig. 8. Feature stretching of RGB three channels VI trajectory to realize pre-clustering.

Coarse 1, as the highest abstract level, is Coarse 2 layer's father node and connects to virtual root node. The setting of Coarse 1 will generate a more effective classifier when electrical appliances categories are large.

2.4 Swin Transformer

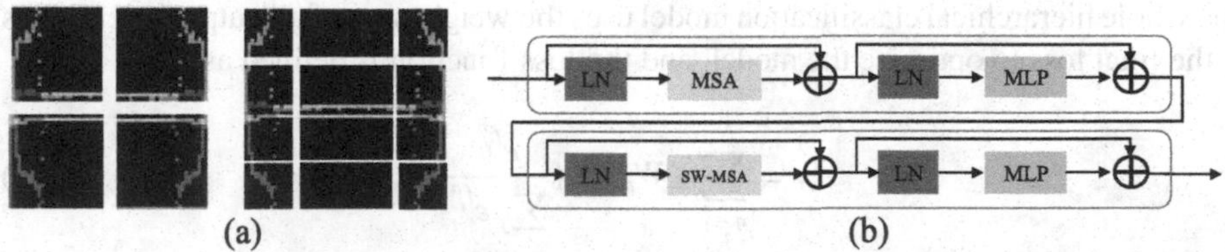

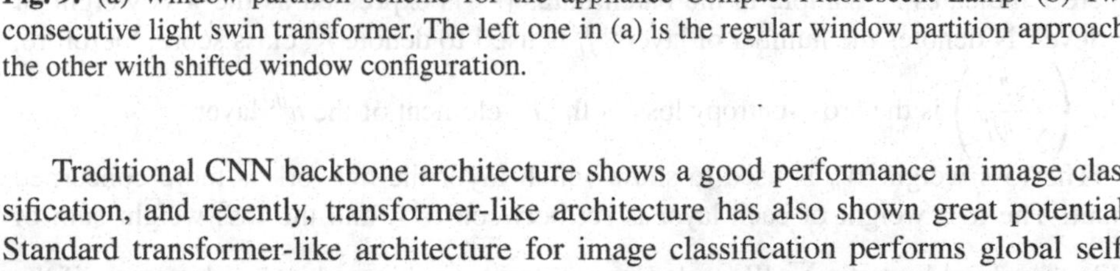

Fig. 9. (a) Window partition scheme for the appliance Compact Fluorescent Lamp. (b) Two consecutive light swin transformer. The left one in (a) is the regular window partition approach, the other with shifted window configuration.

Traditional CNN backbone architecture shows a good performance in image classification, and recently, transformer-like architecture has also shown great potential. Standard transformer-like architecture for image classification performs global self-attention with a fixed window scale, this may lead to high computational complexity [11]. Therefore, considering the accuracy speed trade-off, we optimize and migrate the swin transformer with shifted windowing scheme for appliance classification, generating a Lightweight Swin Transformer (LST) for NILM.

The distribution of features in VI trajectories affects the learning quality of the neural network. When LST performs self-attention computation on symmetrized VI trajectories, the rich features of each trajectory are divided into many patch tokes by the shifted window partitioning method. Due to the symmetry of VI trajectories, each local window is maximally likely to contain trajectory features that can be further extracted. Compared with asymmetric VI trajectories, the network can learn more meaningful features. The window partition comparison is visualized in Fig. 9(a). During our experiment, we find that swin transformer is sensitive to hyper-parameters when performing hierarchical classification. In order to alleviate this shortcoming and improve the performance of the transformer for recognizing VI trajectory, our proposed light swin transformer constitutes a parallel architecture with CNN blocks, together, they form the backbone of hierarchical classification (their contribution to classification performance is discussed in Sect. 3.3). In the parallel architecture, a Attention Fusion Layer (AFL) is designed to play two roles: downsampling and extracting more valuable features. By introducing Squeeze and Excitation module (SE) [12] and multi-feature fusion, our proposed AFL can strengthen feature selection and extraction compared with common convolution or max-pooling downsampling operations.

In our article, a patch extracting block with a patch size of 2×2 is applied to split the RGB VI trajectory into non-overlapping patches, the dimension of the resulting feature map is $2 \times 2 \times 3 = 12$. Then, a patch embedding layer projects the split patches to larger channel 64. Next, the lightweight swin transformer blocks are used to extract rich multi-scale features for these patch tokens. The latter block establishes the multi-head self-attention module with shifted windows (SW-MSA) rather than the regular windowing configuration, introducing cross-window interactions between adjacent non-overlapping windows.

2.5 Loss Function and Loss Weight

The whole hierarchical classification model uses the weight sum of all output layer losses as the final loss to optimize the model, and the loss function is defined as:

$$L_i = \sum_{n=1}^{N} -W_n \log\left(\frac{e^{f^n_{y_i}}}{\sum_j e^{f^n_j}}\right) \tag{6}$$

where i indicates i^{th} sample in the batch data, W_n is expressed as the loss weight of nth level, N denotes the number of layers. f_j is used to denote j^{th} class score, therefore, $-\log\left(\frac{e^{f^n_{y_i}}}{\sum_j e^{f^n_j}}\right)$ is the cross-entropy loss of the ith element of the nth layer.

The loss weight W_n is used to show which layer the network is more concerned about. The loss weight of each layer is set between 0–1, and the loss weight sum of all layers should satisfy $\sum_{n=1}^{N} W_n = 1$. In our three-layer hierarchical architecture, if the loss weight corresponding to each layer is [0, 0, 1], then the hierarchical classification is similar to a traditional single-branch training framework.

3 Experimental Implementation and Discussion

3.1 Dataset

In this paper, we use the publicly available datasets Whited v1.1 [13] and PLAID [14] for performance evaluation. Whited v1.1 includes 54 different appliances captured from around the world at 44.1 kHz sampling frequency, with a total of 1259 submetered measurements. For PLAID, there are multiple versions: PLAID 2018, PLAID 2017, and PLAID 2014. All PLAID datasets are obtained at 30 kHz sampling frequency. Additionally, PLAID 2018 includes aggregated and submetered records, denoted by PLAID 2018A and PLAID 2018S for easy description, respectively. First, we pre-classify the VI trajectory with RGB encoding but without background mapping, and the results of k-means pre-classification are shown in Table 1.

Table 1. The pre-clustering results.

Dataset	Coarse2	The index of appliances (Alphabetical sorting by appliances in the data set)
PLAID 2014 & 2017	0	(1), (7)
	1	(3), (10)
	2	(4), (8)
	3	(0), (2), (5), (6), (9)
Whited v1.1	0	(1), (6), (7), (12), (17), (19), (20), (22), (25), (40), (41), (46), (52)
	1	(3), (5), (15), (21), (27), (28), (31), (37), (39), (48)
	2	(0), (2), (8), (9), (11), (14), (16), (26), (38), (51)
	3	(29), (32), (33), (34), (35), (42), (45), (47), (49), (53)
	4	(4), (10), (13), (18), (23), (24), (30), (36), (43), (44), (50)

3.2 Implementation Details

All our experiments are conducted in a computer with GeForce RTX 2080Ti GPU and Stochastic Gradient Descent (SGD) is chosen as the optimizer for the model, the batch size is set to 16, and the number of training epochs is 75 or 90. The loss weight pair of the three outputs is initialized to [0.98, 0.01, 0.01], and then changed respectively with the number of iterations: [0.1, 0.8, 0.1] at epoch 8, [0.1, 0.2, 0.7] at epoch 18, [0, 0, 1] at epoch 28. The goal of this configuration for the network is to first learn the shallow features and then gradually shift its attention toward the Fine layers. The initial learning rate is set to 0.003, changes to 0.0018 after 40 epochs, and drops to 0.0006 after 55 epochs.

In order to compare with the current different methods, we use K-repeated K-fold cross-validation with the stratified strategy to evaluate the effectiveness of the model. The average value of K experiments is taken as the final classification result. For the K-fold cross-validation, the dataset is split into K subsets of equal size, uses K-1 folds for model training and the remaining 1 fold for evaluating model performance. Since the selection of K value does not have a completely consistent conclusion, in our comparison, K is set to 4, 5, and 10 consistent with the K values adopted in the comparison methods. We use the macro averaged F1 score to evaluate the performance of appliance classification, its definition can be expressed by:

$$F_{1-macro} = \frac{1}{M}\sum_{i=1}^{M} F_1^i \tag{7}$$

$$F_1 = \frac{2 \times P \times R}{P + R} \tag{8}$$

$$P = \frac{TP}{TP + FP} \tag{9}$$

$$R = \frac{TP}{TP + FN} \tag{10}$$

$$Accuracy = \frac{TP + TN}{TP + FN + FP + TN} \tag{11}$$

where *FN* is false negative and *FP*, *TP* denote false positive and true positive, respectively. *P* is Precision, measuring the performance of retrieving real appliances, and *R* is Recall, measuring the ability of discriminating real appliances. The F_1 can be considered as a weighted average of *R* and *P*, comprehensively reflecting the performance of a classifier.

3.3 Ablation Experiment

The contribution of preprocessing with or without color coding and symmetrization to the performance of appliance recognition is shown in Table 2. This result is obtained under the partition ratio of training set and test set 8:2 (also with stratified strategy), the results of repeated three times in the same condition are averaged as the final estimation. It can be seen from Table 2 that when the binary VI trajectory is not preprocessed, the F1-score is much lower due to the lack of features in the 2D image and the failure to distinguish similar trajectories. On the contrary, the classification performance is improved to a certain extent when any kind of preprocessing is applied to the VI trajectory. This demonstrates the effectiveness of our proposed preprocessing method and shows that each of our feature processing methods is not redundant. And the confusion matrix for including all preprocessing operations on the test set of PLAID 2017 is presented in Fig. 10.

The contributions of CNN and Lightweight Swin Transformer (LST) module to appliance recognition are shown in Table 3 (for PLAID 2017). During the experiment, we find that using only LST as the backbone to conduct hierarchical classification, its recognition performance remains way below the decent level at 93.91% (in the case

Table 2. The performance with or without preprocessing for the PLAID 2017

No	RGB encoding	Background mapping	Symmetrization	P	R	$F_{macro}(\%)$
1	×	×	×	90.08	90.24	90.04
2	√	×	×	92.40	92.75	92.59
3	√	√	×	94.44	94.27	94.35
4	√	×	√	94.59	94.61	94.57
5	√	√	√	**96.31**	**96.07**	**96.19**

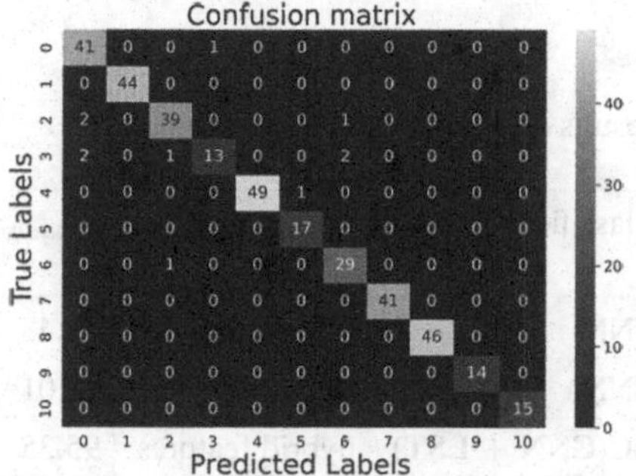

Fig. 10. The confusion matrix for the test set.

Fig. 11. RP representation.

of specially adjusted hyperparameters), while when we effectively fused the LST with convolutional blocks as well as the AFL block, it is able to perform the best recognition performance with a 2.34% average improvement of F_{macro} and to train only with 75 epochs or even less. Meanwhile, F_{macro} will decrease by about 0.5% if we replace AFL with two-layer convolution and max-pooling operations to achieve corresponding downsampling.

Table 3. The contribution of CNN and Light Swin Transformer to appliance identification.

No	CNN	LST	AFL	P (%)	R (%)	*Accuracy* (%)	F_{macro} (%)
1	√	×	×	94.66	94.24	94.11	94.40
2	√	×	√	94.78	94.89	94.56	94.83
3	×	√	×	94.21	93.74	92.84	93.91
4	×	√	√	94.63	94.35	93.13	94.47
5	√	√	×	95.97	95.80	97.02	95.87
6	√	√	√	**96.29**	**96.21**	**97.59**	**96.25**

3.4 Comparison and Discussion

Considering the dataset used, its partition (training mode), and data preprocessing, we choose [5–7, 15], and [8] methods for performance comparison. [15] classifies the transformed recurrence plot with their proposed a spacial pyramid pooling CNN architecture, their recurrence plot (RP) is similar to WRG in [7], using distance-similarity matrix to represent a temporal sequence. The RP representation is shown in Fig. 11. The comparison results are shown in the Table 4. Different datasets have different IECV (IACV), for dataset PLAID 2018S, it is widely known that it has higher IACV, however our proposed method has the best performance on this dataset. And, taking the results on PLAID 2018A for example, the F_1 index of our proposed method is 6.41% higher than [6], regardless of the training and validation pattern, our proposed method shows better classification performance.

Table 4. The comparison results on PLAID and Whited.

Dataset	Ref	K-repeated K-fold or 8:2	Classifier	Load features	$F_{macro}(\%)$
PLAID 2014	[5]	10K	CNN	VI in HSV	**95.4**
	[7]		CNN	WRG	93.01
	ours		HC(CNN + LST)	hybrid features	95.35
PLAID 2017	[15]	5K	CNN	RP	84.56
	ours		HC(CNN + LST)	hybrid features	**96.46**
PLAID 2018S	[7]	10K	CNN	WRG	95.63
	ours		HC(CNN + LST)	hybrid features	**97.20**
	[6]	4K	RF	EFD	80.4
	ours		HC(CNN + LST)	hybrid features	**96.69**
	[8]	8:2	SVM & RF	multi-features	93.75
	ours		HC(CNN + LST)	hybrid features	**95.87**
PLAID 2018A	[6]	4K	CNN	EFD	88
	ours		HC(CNN + LST)	hybrid features	**94.41**
Whited v1.1	[7]	10K	CNN	WRG	95.47
	ours		HC(CNN + LST)	hybrid features	**97.89**

4 Conclusion

This paper proposes a hierarchical classification architecture with multiple hierarchical outputs based on swin transformer for VI trajectories, which has higher classification performance compared to other methods that use traditional CNN architecture or other classifiers, and our classification method can avoid the trouble of manually clustering target classes into more abstract subclasses in the hierarchical classification. In addition, we propose a multi-feature dimensional VI trajectory preprocessing method, which makes the VI trajectory more distinguishable and can effectively mitigate the adverse impact of inter-class variety (IECV) in the type II appliances. Furthermore, lightweight swin transformer blocks with shifted window configuration can more efficiently compute self-attention for the symmetrized VI trajectories owing to the wider range of rich features captured by the local windows.

Acknowledgement. The work is partially supported by the Natural Science Foundation of Guangxi (2020GXNSFAA297173), and Innovation Project of Guangxi Graduate Education (YCSW2022050).

References

1. Hart, G.W.: Nonintrusive appliance load monitoring. Proc. IEEE. **80**(12), 1870–1891 (1992)
2. Ham, H., Fung, G., Lee, W.: A novel method to construct taxonomy electrical appliances based on load signaturesof. IEEE Trans. Consumer Electron. **53**(2), 653–660 (2007)
3. Du, L., He, D., Harley, R.G., Habetler, T.G.: Electric load classification by binary voltage-current trajectory mapping. IEEE Trans. Smart Grid. **7**(1), 358–365 (2016)
4. De Baets, L., Ruyssinck, J., Develder, C., Dhaene, T., Deschrijver, D.: Appliance classification using VI trajectories and convolutional neural networks. Energy Buildings **158**, 32–36 (2018)
5. Liu, Y., Wang, X., You, W.: Non-intrusive load monitoring by voltage-current trajectory enabled transfer learning. IEEE Trans. Smart Grid. **10**(5), 5609–5619 (2019)
6. De Baets, L., Dhaene, T., et al.: VI-Based Appliance Classification Using Aggregated Power Consumption Data. In: 2018 IEEE International Conference on Smart Computing (SMARTCOMP). pp. 179–186. IEEE, Taormina (2018)
7. Faustine, A., Pereira, L.: Improved appliance classification in non-intrusive load monitoring using weighted recurrence graph and convolutional neural networks. Energies **13**(13), 3374 (2020)
8. Zhang, Z., Shi, F., Liu, Y., Yan, H.: A Hierarchical classification method for Type II appliance recognition in NILM. In: 2022 5th International Conference on Renewable Energy and Power Engineering (REPE). pp. 121–126. IEEE, Beijing, China (2022)
9. Zhu, X., Bain, M.: B-CNN: branch convolutional neural network for hierarchical classification, http://arxiv.org/abs/1709.09890 (2017)
10. Teshome, D., Huang, T.D., Lian, K.-L.: A distinctive load feature extraction based on Fryze's time-domain power theory. IEEE Power Energy Technol. Syst. J. **3**, 1–1 (2016)
11. Liu, Z., Lin, Y., Cao, Y., et al.: Swin transformer: hierarchical vision transformer using shifted windows. In: Proceedings of the IEEE/CVF International Conference on Computer Vision. pp. 10012–10022 (2021)
12. Hu, J., Shen, L., Sun, G.: Squeeze-and-excitation networks. In: Proceedings of the IEEE Conference on Computer Vision and Pattern Recognition. pp. 7132–7141 (2018)
13. Kahl, M., Haq, A. U., et al.: Whited-a worldwide household and industry transient energy data set. In: 2016 3rd International Workshop on Non-Intrusive Load Monitoring, pp. 1–4. (2016)

14. Medico, R., De Baets, L., Gao, et al.: A voltage and current measurement dataset for plug load appliance identification in households. Sci. Data **7**(1), 49 (2020)
15. Wenninger, M., Bayerl, S.P., et al.: Recurrence Plot spacial pyramid pooling network for appliance identification in non-intrusive load monitoring. In: 2021 20th IEEE International Conference on Machine Learning and Applications (ICMLA), pp. 108–115. IEEE, Pasadena, CA, USA (2021)

Hierarchical Vision and Language Transformer for Efficient Visual Dialog

Qiangqiang He, Mujie Zhang, Jie Zhang, Shang Yang, and Chongjun Wang(✉)

State Key Laboratory for Novel Software Technology, Nanjing University, Nanjing, China
{qqh,mujiezhang,iip_zhangjie,yangshang}@smail.nju.edu.cn, chjwang@nju.edu.cn

Abstract. The visual dialog task requires a deep understanding of an image and a dialog history to answer multiple consecutive questions. Existing research focuses on enhancing cross-modal interaction and fusion but often overlooks the computational complexity and higher-level interaction between the two modalities. This paper proposes a hierarchical vision and language Transformer (HVLT) to address these issues. Specifically, HVLT employs a convolution-like design to learn the interaction and fusion of images and text at different levels. We employ a token merging module to aggregate four spatially adjacent image tokens and four temporally adjacent text tokens into one token and use the expanded $[CLS]$ token to fuse image and text information in a new dimension. This hierarchical architecture allows the model to focus on feature maps of different sizes and dialog history at word, phrase, and sentence levels and reduces the time overhead. We tailor two training objectives for HVLT: masked language regression (MLR) and next sentence prediction (NSP), which help the model understand images and language and learn their relationships. Experimental results on the VisDial v0.9 and v1.0 datasets demonstrate the competitive performance of HVLT. Finally, we visualize the attention to gain insights into how HVLT works in practice, shedding light on its interpretability.

Keywords: Visual Dialog · Hierarchical Transformer · Multi-Modal

1 Introduction

Visual dialog has gained significant attention from academia and industry as an emerging human-machine interaction method, propelled by the continuous advancement of artificial intelligence technology. It combines natural language processing and computer vision to enable machines to answer questions based on their comprehension of image content and dialog history. In contrast to visual question answering (VQA) [1–3], visual dialog goes beyond understanding the image and question at hand, requiring a profound understanding of the dialog history to generate relevant responses to the current question. This unique characteristic of visual dialog sets it apart and presents distinct challenges to developing effective solutions.

L. Iliadis et al. (Eds.): ICANN 2023, LNCS 14259, pp. 421–432, 2023.
https://doi.org/10.1007/978-3-031-44223-0_34

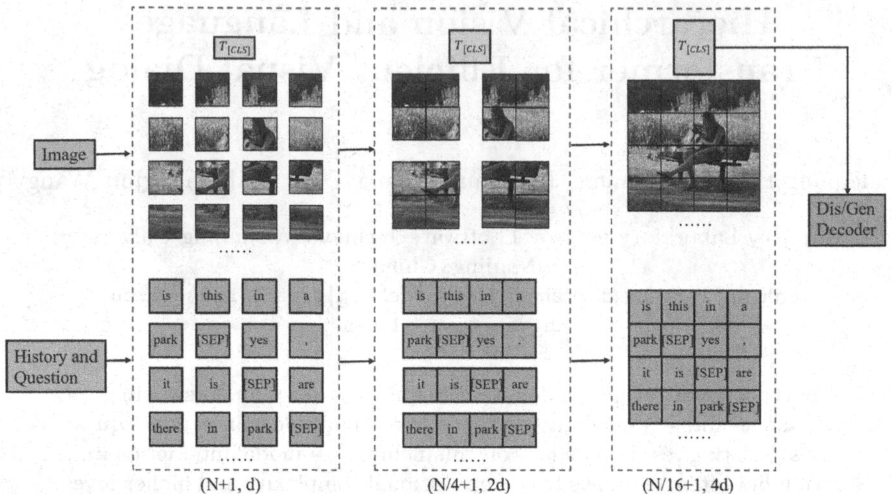

Fig. 1. The process of image and text tokens aggregation, where N denotes the number of image and text tokens and d denotes the initial dimension of tokens

In tackling the challenges of visual dialog, current approaches often employ specialized modules to process images and dialog history, followed by integrating the processed information using cross-modal attention mechanisms. For instance, DAN [5] and LTMI [6] utilize multi-head attention mechanisms to manage interactions between multiple modalities. Some methods leverage graph-based structures for learning cross-modal understanding. Furthermore, unified Transformer-based architectures, such as VD-BERT [7], VU-BERT [8], and ViLBERT [9], have also been utilized to facilitate cross-modal interactions and have demonstrated promising performance in addressing the challenges of visual dialog.

However, existing research lacks a hierarchical fusion of visual and textual information. The simple utilization of self-attention mechanisms to model the interaction between vision and text has limitations in advancing the Transformer architecture. Firstly, employing full attention mechanisms results in significant computational costs that increase quadratically with the number of input tokens. Secondly, relying solely on the $[CLS]$ token as the output of the Transformer encoder can lead to information loss, compromising the model's robustness and generalization ability. These limitations highlight the need for a more sophisticated approach that addresses these issues and promotes the development of more efficient and effective visual dialog models.

To address the aforementioned issues, this paper proposes a hierarchical vision and language Transformer (HVLT) that employs a convolution-like design to learn the interaction and fusion of image and text at different levels. As depicted in Fig. 1, we utilize linear projection layers and embedding layers with positional embeddings to obtain image and text tokens, respectively. Subsequently, we employ self-attention mechanisms to obtain a global representation based on the $[CLS]$ token and token merging module to aggregate four spatially adjacent image tokens and four temporally adjacent text tokens into one token. This hierarchical architecture allows the model to focus on feature maps of different sizes and dialog history at word, phrase, and sentence levels and reduces the time overhead. To train our framework, we tailor two objectives: masked language regression (MLR) and next sentence regression (NSP). The contributions of this paper can be summarized as follows:

- We propose the HVLT for efficient visual dialog to improve the expressiveness of the model while effectively reducing time overhead.
- We tailor MLR and NSP training objectives to train HVLT effectively.
- Experiments on the Visdial v0.9 and v1.0 datasets demonstrate the effectiveness of HVLT. We visualize the attention to gain insights into how HVLT works in practice.

2 Related Work

2.1 Visual Dialog

Visual dialog has been comprised of two main tasks, namely the VisDial task proposed by Das et al. [10], and the GuessWhat task [11], which is a goal-driven guessing game that requires models to guess the target image by answering yes/no questions. In this paper, our focus is on the VisDial task. Previous research has focused on developing various attention mechanisms to model the interaction between images and texts. For instance, Guo et al. [12] proposed DVAN, a two-layer attention model that captures both global and local visual information. Gan et al. [4] explored the interaction between images and dialogue history through multi-step reasoning. Additionally, some methods have utilized graph-based structures to learn cross-modal understanding. For instance, Li et al. [13] proposed the CARE framework to integrate environmental context and visual objects. Kang et al. [14] also proposed a sparse graph learning (SGL) method to represent visual dialog as a graph structure learning task.

2.2 Visual and Language Transformer

BERT [15] and ViT [16] have demonstrated remarkable performance in NLP and CV tasks, respectively, highlighting the powerful representation capabilities of Transformers. Many existing studies have attempted to incorporate Transformers into vision and language tasks and yield significant results. Vision and language Transformers can be broadly classified into two types: two-stream models and single-stream models. Two-stream models encode the image and text independently and then fuse the two modalities through mutual attention, such as ViLBERT [9], LXMBERT [17], and others. On the other hand, single-stream models simultaneously encode and fuse visual and textual information, such as

VisualBERT [18], VL-BERT [19], VD-BERT [7], VU-BERT [8], UTC [20], and others. However, existing research has not yet considered the fusion of visual and language information at different levels and the fully self-attention mechanism often results in expensive time and memory costs.

3 Method

Firstly, we formally describe visual dialog. Given an image, its caption, the previous $t-1$ rounds of dialogs, and the t-th question, the model needs to predict its answer. Typically, there are two types of decoders to give answers. The discriminative decoder ranks 100 candidate answers and is trained with cross-entropy loss, while the generative decoder generates answers and is trained with maximum log-likelihood loss. Figure 2 illustrates the architecture of our proposed approach.

3.1 Embedding

Vision Embedding. Different from object-level feature extraction methods, we use an image processing approach similar to ViT [16], which is faster than Faster-RCNN [21]. For an image $I \in \mathbb{R}^{H\times W\times C}$, we divide it into N_v patches of size $P\times P\times C$. Then, we flatten the patches and embed them into a latent space through $W_v \in \mathbb{R}^{P^2C\times d}$ to obtain patch embeddings $v \in \mathbb{R}^{N_v\times d}$.

Text Embedding. Given the previous $t-1$ rounds of dialog and t-th question and candiate answer represented by $D = \left\{C, Q_1, A_1, \ldots, Q_{t-1}, A_{t-1}, Q_t, \widehat{A}_t\right\}$ grounded in the image I, where C is the image caption. We use $[SEP]$ and $[END]$ as delimiters and the end marker for the dialog to obtain the processed dialog $H = \left\{C, [SEP], Q_1, [SEP], A_1, [SEP], \ldots, Q_t, [SEP], \widehat{A}_t, [END]\right\}$. We employ the WordPiece tokenizer [22] to split H into a word sequence. Then, a word embedding layer is adopted to get the text embedding $t \in \mathbb{R}^{N_t\times d}$.

Next, position and modal embeddings are added to patch embeddings v and text embeddings t respectively, and then concatenated with $[CLS]$ to obtain the input sequence $x^0 \in \mathbb{R}^{(N+1)\times d}$, where $N = N_v + N_t$. The formula is as follows:

$$x^0 = [t_{cls}; v + p_v + m_0; t + p_t + m_1] \tag{1}$$

Relative position embedding $p_v \in \mathbb{R}^{N_v\times d}$ and $p_t \in \mathbb{R}^{N_t\times d}$ are employed to model the position information. Similar to ViLT [23], we use modal embedding m_0 and $m_1 \in \mathbb{R}^{1\times d}$ to distinguish between image and text embeddings.

3.2 HVLT Architecture

Our HVLT consists of 8 Transformer blocks for image-text interaction and fusion and 3 token merging modules for enlarging receptive fields and reducing the number of tokens. The input sequence x^0 is first fed into two consecutive Transformer blocks for sufficient interaction between images and text and

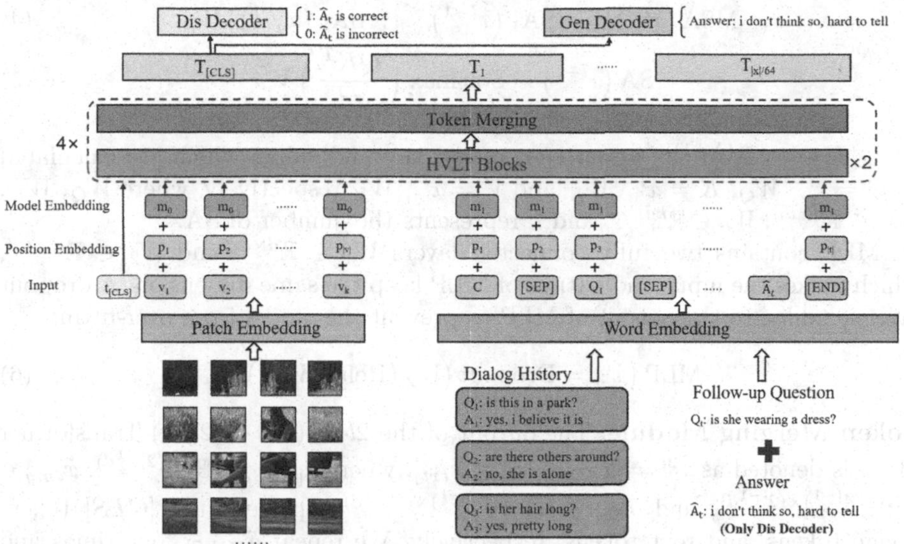

Fig. 2. The architecture of HVLT.

outputs $\tilde{x}^2$. Then, the token merging module aggregates four spatially adjacent image tokens and four temporally adjacent text tokens into one token and outputs $x^2 \in \mathbb{R}^{(N/4+1)\times 2d}$. We repeat this process four times to finally obtain $x^8 \in \mathbb{R}^{(N/64+1)\times 8d}$ (No aggregation after the 8th Transformer block). We take the first token of x^8, i.e., $T_{[CLS]}$, as the output of HVLT. In the discriminative decoder, $T_{[CLS]}$ is fed into a binary fully connected layer to judge whether $\widehat{A}_t$ is the correct answer. In the generative decoder, the input sequence x^0 does not include the candidate answer $\widehat{A}_t$. $T_{[CLS]}$ will be fed into the LSTM to generate the answer autoregressively.

Transformer Backbone. Following the setup of ViLT, each Transformer block comprises multi-head attention (MSA), multi-layer perceptron (MLP), skip connection and layer normalization (LN). Specifically, the output of the l-th Transformer block is as follows:

$$\widetilde{x}^l = \mathrm{LN}\left(\mathrm{MSA}\left(x^{l-1}\right) + x^{l-1}\right) \tag{2}$$

$$x^l = \mathrm{LN}\left(\mathrm{MLP}\left(\widetilde{x}^l\right) + \widetilde{x}^l\right) \tag{3}$$

The output of MSA is obtained by concatenating the outputs of multiple self-attention (SA) and utilizing the fully connected layer W_h to map them back to the original space. In the l-th Transformer block, the formulas of MSA and SA are as follows:

$$\mathrm{MSA}\left(x^{l-1}\right)=\left[\mathrm{SA}_1\left(x^{l-1}\right);\ldots;\mathrm{SA}_k\left(x^{l-1}\right)\right]W_h \quad (4)$$

$$\mathrm{SA}\left(x^{l-1}\right)=\mathrm{Softmax}\left(\frac{QK^T}{\sqrt{d_h}}\right)V \quad (5)$$

$Q, K, V \in \mathbb{R}^{(N+1)\times d_h}$ represent query, key and value, which are calculated as $Q = x^{l-1}W_Q$, $K = x^{l-1}W_K$ and $V = x^{l-1}W_V$ respectively, where W_Q, W_K, $W_V \in \mathbb{R}^{d\times d_h}$, $W_h \in \mathbb{R}^{kd_h\times d}$ and k represents the number of SA.

MLP contains two fully connected layers $W_1 \in \mathbb{R}^{d\times d_m}$ and $W_2 \in \mathbb{R}^{d_m\times d}$, which makes the input and output of MLP keep the same dimension. A dropout layer is added to the output of MLP to prevent the model from over-fitting.

$$\mathrm{MLP}\left(\widetilde{x}^l\right)=\mathrm{Dropout}\left(W_2\left(\mathrm{Relu}\left(W_1\widetilde{x}^l\right)\right)\right) \quad (6)$$

Token Merging Module. The output of the $2l$-th ($l \in \{1,2,3\}$) Transformer block is denoted as $\tilde{x}^{2l} = [\tilde{x}_{[CLS]}, \tilde{x}_{img}, \tilde{x}_{txt}]$, where $\tilde{x}_{[CLS]} \in \mathbb{R}^{1\times(2^{l-1}d)}$, $\tilde{x}_{img} \in \mathbb{R}^{(N_v/4^{l-1})\times(2^{l-1}d)}$, and $\tilde{x}_{txt} \in \mathbb{R}^{(N_t/4^{l-1})\times(2^{l-1}d)}$ represent the $[CLS]$ token, image tokens, and text tokens, respectively. We repeat $\tilde{x}_{[CLS]}$ four times and concatenate them to obtain $x_{[CLS]}$. We concatenate four spatially adjacent image tokens and four temporally adjacent text tokens to obtain $x_{img} \in \mathbb{R}^{(N_t/4^l)\times(2^{l+1}d)}$ and $x_{txt} \in \mathbb{R}^{(N_v/4^l)\times(2^{l+1}d)}$. Finally, we concatenate $x_{[CLS]}$, x_{img}, and x_{txt} and pass them through a fully connected layer $W_a \in \mathbb{R}^{(2^{l+1}d)\times(2^l d)}$ to obtain the aggregated output $x^{2l} \in \mathbb{R}^{(N/4^l+1)\times(2^l d)}$.

$$x^{2l}=\left[x_{[CLS]};x_{img};x_{txt}\right]W_a \quad (7)$$

3.3 Training Objectives

Masked Language Regression (MLR). Like MLM in BERT, we mask the tokens in the conversation with 15% probability and replace them with a special token $[MASK]$. HVLT aggregates $[MASK]$ and adjacent tokens into larger tokens, which prevents the model from predicting the content of $[MASK]$ tokens alone. Therefore, we propose MLR as the training objective. The model accepts visual features and unmasked words and outputs the $T_{[CLS]}$ into the LSTM decoder. The decoder outputs the complete conversation content in an autoregressive manner until the generation of the terminator $[END]$. This pre-training task is similar to the generative decoder and matches the model structure of HVLT well. The task drives the model to learn the dependencies of image and textual information as well as the dependencies of words in the sentence. Let the visual and textual embeddings be denoted as $v = v_1, ..., v_t$, $w = w_1, ..., w_n$. k is the index of the masked word and $w_{\backslash k} = \{w_1, \ldots, w_{k-1}, [MASK], w_{k+1}, \ldots, w_n\}$ denotes the masked sentence. MLR uses the maximizing the log-likelihood loss function with the following equation:

$$\mathcal{L}_{MLR}=-\mathbb{E}_{(v,w)\sim D}\sum_{i=1}^{n}\log p\left(w_t \mid w_{<t}, w_{\backslash k}, v\right) \quad (8)$$

Next Sentence Prediction (NSP). Let w and v denote the text embedding containing the candidate answer and the vision embedding. The NSP task aims to predict whether the given answer is correct based on the dialog history and the image.

$$\mathcal{L}_{NSP} = -\mathbb{E}_{(v,w)\sim D} \log P(y \mid B(v, w)) \quad (9)$$

where $B(\cdot)$ is a binary classifier to predict the probability based on the $T_{[CLS]}$ and $y \in \{0, 1\}$ indicates whether the candidate answer is correct.

4 Experiments

4.1 Experimental Settings

Dataset. We train HVLT on the large-scale visual dialog datasets, VisDial v0.9 and v1.0. VisDial v0.9 consists of 82,783 training images and 40,504 validation images, each paired with a caption and ten related questions. Each question has 100 candidate answers, among which only one is correct. The v1.0 is a reorganized version of v0.9, with the training, validation, and test sets containing 123,287, 2,064, and 8,000 images, respectively. Additionally, the v1.0 validation set provides dense annotations, which assigns relevance scores to the 100 candidate answers for calculating the NDCG metric.

Baseline. In our visual dialog task comparisons, we evaluate HVLT against various single and ensemble baselines, such as VD-BERT [7], VU-BERT [8], VisDial-BERT [24], LF [11], HRE [11], DVAN [12], DualVD [25], and CAG [26], which have demonstrated exceptional performance on the leaderboard or in previous publications.

Implementation Details. The shape of each image is resized to $224 \times 224 \times 3$ and divided into 256 patches of size 14×14. Text is padded with $[PAD]$ tokens until its length is 256. Image patches and text words are embedded into tokens of 512 dimensions. The input sequence is aggregated by HVLT into 9 tokens of dimension 4096. Where the first token corresponds to the $T_{[CLS]}$. HVLT consists of 8 Transformer blocks, each block containing 8 attention heads.

We conduct pre-training for 20 epochs using the MLR on the MSCOCO dataset [27], which comprises of 113k images and 567k captions. Specifically, we randomly mask 15% of the tokens in the captions and then use HVLT to generate the complete captions autoregressively by leveraging the images and unmasked tokens. For the MLR objective, we employ the Adam optimizer with a learning rate of 3e-5, while the NSP objective uses a lower learning rate of 5e-6 with the Adam optimizer. All experiments are conducted with a batch size of 64 on two Tesla V100 GPUs with 32G memory each. Our training and evaluation code is implemented using PyTorch 1.9.

We evaluate the performance of HVLT on the VisDial v0.9 and v1.0 datasets using four metrics: Recall@K, MRR, Mean, and NDCG. Recall@K measures the

Table 1. Performance of discriminative/generation models on VisDial v0.9 dataset. Higher is better for MRR and recall@k, while lower is better for Mean.

Model	MRR↑	R@1↑	R@5↑	R@10↑	Mean↓
LF	0.580/0.519	43.82/41.83	74.68/61.78	84.07/67.59	5.78/17.07
HRE	0.584/0.523	44.67/42.29	74.50/62.18	84.22/67.92	5.72/17.07
DVAN	0.667/0.559	53.62/46.58	82.85/**65.50**	90.72/71.25	**3.93**/14.79
FGA	0.652/0.413	51.43/27.42	82.08/56.33	89.56/71.32	4.35/**9.10**
VD-BERT	**0.700**/0.559	**55.79**/46.83	85.34/65.43	**92.68**/72.05	4.04/13.18
VU-BERT	0.633/0.540	48.71/44.50	81.03/62.60	89.10/71.70	4.19/12.49
HVLT	0.684/**0.561**	54.51/**46.84**	**85.35**/64.70	91.58/**72.82**	4.11/10.86

proportion of correct answers ranked in the top k positions. MRR measures the effectiveness of a model by taking the average of the reciprocal ranks of correct answers in a ranked list. Mean indicates the average ranking of correct answers. NDCG evaluates the quality of a ranked list by considering both the relevance and the position of the answers in the list, which is only employed in the v1.0.

4.2 Performance Evaluation

Performance on v0.9. We report the results of HVLT and several state-of-the-art baselines on v0.9 in both generative and discriminative settings in Table 1. HVLT outperforms other methods on most evaluation metrics, including MRR of 0.561 (Gen), R@1 of 46.84 (Gen), R@5 of 85.35 (Dis), and R@10 of 72.82 (Gen). These results on v0.9 indicate that our hierarchical architecture facilitates the fusion and interaction of visual and textual information, especially in the generative setting.

Performance on v1.0. Table 2 compares our results on the Visdial v1.0 validation set. HVLT demonstrates superior performance in all metrics except for R@1 and NDCG. Compared to other models, HVLT shows a 0.8% improvement in MRR, a 1.5% improvement in R5, a 1.6% improvement in R10, and a mean rank reduction of 0.3. These results suggest that our hierarchical architecture reduces computational time costs effectively and enhances the model's generalization ability.

The main improvement of HVLT over existing Transformer architecture models lies in its convolution-like structure, which enables the learning of interactions and fusion of image and text at different abstraction levels. The token merging module employs spatially adjacent aggregation for images and temporally adjacent aggregation for dialogues, enhancing the model's expressive power while reducing the number of tokens. However, we observed that HVLT's performance on NDCG is comparatively weaker than existing models, which could be attributed to HVLT's use of binary cross-entropy loss for training instead of

Table 2. Performance of discriminative models on VisDial v1.0 dataset. Higher is better for MRR, recall@k and NDCG, while lower is better for Mean.

Model	MRR↑	R@1↑	R@5↑	R@10↑	Mean↓	NDCG↑
NMN	0.5880	44.15	76.88	86.88	4.81	0.5810
GNN	0.6137	47.33	77.98	87.83	4.57	0.5282
DualVD	0.6323	49.25	80.23	89.70	4.11	0.5632
CAG	0.6349	**49.85**	80.63	90.15	4.11	0.5664
LF	0.5542	40.95	72.45	82.83	5.95	0.4531
FGA	0.6370	49.58	80.97	88.55	4.51	0.5210
VD-BERT	0.5117	38.90	62.82	77.98	6.69	**0.7454**
VisDial-BERT	0.5074	37.95	64.13	80.00	6.53	0.7447
VU-BERT	0.4909	33.60	67.20	81.60	6.12	0.7287
HVLT	**0.6451**	49.75	**82.48**	**91.75**	**3.82**	0.6209

ranking-based loss functions, limiting its ability to accurately understand the relevance of answers.

Analysis of parameters and MACs. We utilize the torchprofile library to calculate the MACs of various models. As shown in Table 3, the number of parameters in HVLT is notably higher than that of other Transformer-based models, mainly due to the exponential increase in token dimension caused by our aggregation operation. However, despite HVLT having seven times more parameters than the lightweight VU-BERT, its MACs are only half of VU-BERT's, which is primarily attributed to two reasons. Firstly, in the initial stage, HVLT and other models receive tokens of the same length as input, but HVLT has a lower input dimension. Secondly, during the later stages aggregation process, the tokens' dimension increases exponentially by the power of 2, but the quantity of tokens decreases exponentially by the power of 4. As a result, the computation time of attention mechanisms, which is quadratically correlated with the number of tokens, is significantly reduced.

4.3 Attention Visualization

To gain insights into the inner workings of HVLT, we examine the composition of attention by concatenating the correct candidate answers to the dialogue history

Table 3. The parameters and MACs of Transformer-based architecture.

Model	Visdial-BERT	VD-BERT	VU-BERT	HVLT
# Parameters	315.26M	174.51M	133.94M	951.70M
# MACs	45.93G	63.78G	48.32G	25.15G

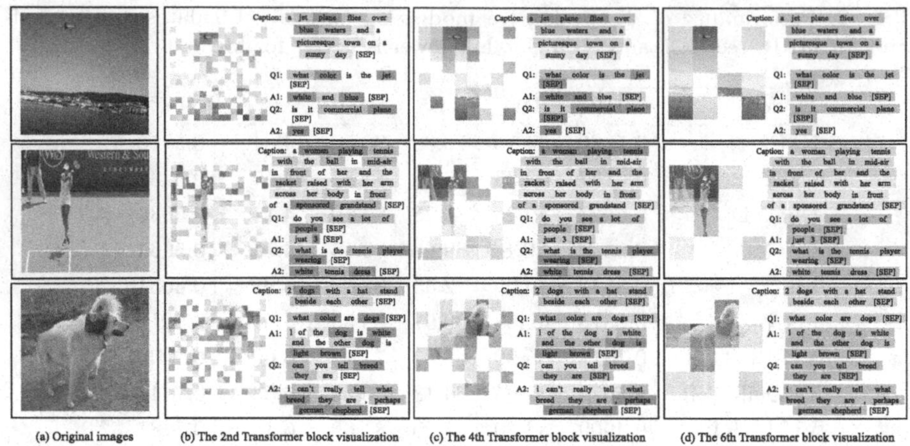

Fig. 3. Attention visualization of $[CLS]$ token. Best viewed zoomed in.

and visualizing the attention of the [CLS] tokens in the 2nd, 4th, and 6th layers of Transformer blocks, as shown in Fig. 3. In the visualization, each square box represents a patch, with the 2nd, 4th, and 6th Transformer blocks containing 256, 64, and 16 image patches respectively. The patches' opacity and the words' background color reflect their contributions to the discriminative visual dialogue task.

In our observation, we find that in the early stages of the model, the attention on image patches is more scattered, capturing both relevant and irrelevant information. However, as the patch size increases, the model's global perception ability strengthens, leading to more focused and accurate attention. For text tokens, the model initially focuses on capturing semantic information at the word level with varying granularity. In the middle stages, it better captures phrase-level semantic information; in later stages, it tends to focus on sentence-level semantic information. This hierarchical architecture allows the model to focus on feature maps of different sizes and dialog history at the word, phrase, and sentence levels.

5 Conclusion

In this work, we propose a hierarchical vision and language Transformer for effective visual dialog. HVLT employs a convolution-like design to learn the interaction and fusion of images and text at different levels. We follow the token merging module in every two Transformer blocks to aggregate four spatially adjacent image tokens and four temporally adjacent text tokens into one token and use the expanded $[CLS]$ token to fuse image and text information in a new dimension. This hierarchical architecture allows the model to focus on feature maps of different sizes and dialog history at word, phrase, and sentence levels and reduces the time overhead. We tailor masked language regression and next sentence prediction objectives for HVLT, which help the model understand images and language and learn their relationships. Experimental results on the VisDial v0.9 and v1.0 datasets show that HVLT maintains the SOTA performance while its MACs are much smaller than those of other Transformer architecture models. By visualizing the attention, we aim to gain a deeper understanding of the practical workings of HVLT and provide insights into its interpretability.

Acknowledgement. This paper is supported by the National Natural Science Foundation of China (Grant No. 62192783, U1811462), the Collaborative Innovation Center of Novel Software Technology and Industrialization at Nanjing University.

References

1. Antol, S., et al.: VQA: visual question answering. In: Proceedings of the IEEE International Conference on Computer Vision, pp. 2425–2433 (2015)
2. Kafle, K., Kanan, C.: Visual question answering: datasets, algorithms, and future challenges. Comput. Vis. Image Underst. **163**, 3–20 (2017)
3. Teney, D., Anderson, P., He, X., Van Den Hengel, A.: Tips and tricks for visual question answering: learnings from the 2017 challenge. In: Proceedings of the IEEE Conference on Computer Vision and Pattern Recognition, pp. 4223–4232 (2018)
4. Gan, Z., Cheng, Y., Kholy, A., Li, L., Liu, J., Gao, J.: Multi-step reasoning via recurrent dual attention for visual dialog. In: Proceedings of the 57th Annual Meeting of the Association for Computational Linguistics, pp. 6463–6474 (2019)
5. Kang, G. C., Lim, J., Zhang, B. T.: Dual attention networks for visual reference resolution in visual dialog. arXiv preprint arXiv:1902.09368 (2019)
6. Nguyen, V. Q., Suganuma, M., Okatani, T.: Efficient attention mechanism for visual dialog that can handle all the interactions between multiple inputs. In: Proceedings of Computer Vision-ECCV 2020: 16th European Conference, Part XXIV 16, pp. 223–240 (2020)
7. Wang, Y., Joty, S., Lyu, M., King, I., Xiong, C., Hoi, S. C.: VD-BERT: a unified vision and dialog transformer with BERT. In: Proceedings of the 2020 Conference on Empirical Methods in Natural Language Processing (EMNLP), pp. 3325–3338 (2020)
8. Ye, T., Si, S., Wang, J., Wang, R., Cheng, N., Xiao, J.: VU-BERT: a unified framework for visual dialog. In: ICASSP 2022–2022 IEEE International Conference on Acoustics, Speech and Signal Processing (ICASSP), pp. 6687–6691. IEEE (2022)
9. Lu, J., Batra, D., Parikh, D., Lee, S.: ViLBERT: pretraining task-agnostic visiolinguistic representations for vision-and-language tasks. In: Advances in Neural Information Processing Systems, vol. 32 (2019)
10. Das, A., et al.: Visual dialog. In: Proceedings of the IEEE Conference on Computer Vision and Pattern Recognition, pp. 326–335 (2017)
11. Chattopadhyay, P., et al.: Evaluating visual conversational agents via cooperative human-AI games. In: Proceedings of the AAAI Conference on Human Computation and Crowdsourcing **5**, pp. 2–10 (2017)
12. Guo, D., Wang, H., Wang, M.: Dual visual attention network for visual dialog. In: IJCAI, pp. 4989–4995 (2019)

13. Li, X., Gao, L., Zhao, L., Song, J.: Exploring contextual-aware representation and linguistic-diverse expression for visual dialog. In: Proceedings of the 29th ACM International Conference on Multimedia, pp. 4911–4919 (2021)
14. Kang, G.C., Park, J., Lee, H., Zhang, B.T., Kim, J.H.: Reasoning visual dialog with sparse graph learning and knowledge transfer. arXiv preprint arXiv:2004.06698 (2020)
15. Devlin, J., Chang, M.W., Lee, K., Toutanova, K.: BERT: pre-training of deep bidirectional transformers for language understanding. arXiv preprint arXiv:1810.04805 (2018)
16. Dosovitskiy, A., et al.: An image is worth 16×16 words: transformers for image recognition at scale. arXiv preprint arXiv:2010.11929 (2020)
17. Tan, H., Bansal, M.: LXMERT: learning cross-modality encoder representations from transformers. arXiv preprint arXiv:1908.07490 (2019)
18. Li, L.H., Yatskar, M., Yin, D., Hsieh, C.J., Chang, K.W.: VisualBert: a simple and performant baseline for vision and language. arXiv preprint arXiv:1908.03557 (2019)
19. Su, W., et al.: VL-BERT: pre-training of generic visual-linguistic representations. arXiv preprint arXiv:1908.08530 (2019)
20. Chen, C., et al.: UTC: a unified transformer with inter-task contrastive learning for visual dialog. In: Proceedings of the IEEE/CVF Conference on Computer Vision and Pattern Recognition, pp. 18103–18112 (2022)
21. Girshick, R.: Fast R-CNN. In: Proceedings of the IEEE International Conference on Computer Vision, pp. 1440–1448 (2015)
22. Wu, Y., et al.: Google's neural machine translation system: bridging the gap between human and machine translation. arXiv preprint arXiv:1609.08144 (2016)
23. Kim, W., Son, B., Kim, I.: ViLT: vision-and-language transformer without convolution or region supervision. In: International Conference on Machine Learning, pp. 5583–5594. PMLR (2021)
24. Murahari, V., Batra, D., Parikh, D., Das, A.: Large-scale pretraining for visual dialog: a simple state-of-the-art baseline. In: Proceedings of Computer Vision-ECCV 2020: 16th European Conference, pp. 336–352 (2020)
25. Jiang, X., et al.: DualVD: an adaptive dual encoding model for deep visual understanding in visual dialogue. Proc. AAAI Conf. Artif. Intell. **34**(07), 11125–11132 (2020)
26. Guo, D., Wang, H., Zhang, H., Zha, Z. J., Wang, M.: Iterative context-aware graph inference for visual dialog. In: Proceedings of the IEEE/CVF Conference on Computer Vision and Pattern Recognition, pp. 10055–10064 (2020)
27. Lin, T.Y., et al.: Microsoft COCO: common objects in context. In: Proceedings of Computer Vision-ECCV 2014: 13th European Conference, pp. 740–755 (2014)

ICDT: Maintaining Interaction Consistency for Deformable Transformer with Multi-scale Features in HOI Detection

Bingnan Guo, Sheng Liu(✉), Feng Zhang, Junhao Chen, and Ruixiang Chen

Zhejiang University of Technology, Hangzhou, China
{bingnan,edliu}@zjut.deu.cn

Abstract. Localization and interaction recognition are two main tasks in HOI (Human-Object Interaction) detection, which require high-level image and scene understanding. Existing HOI detection methods typically rely on single architecture to solve these tasks. However, such a strategy would frequently ignore the intrinsic links between two tasks. Meanwhile, the previous methods lack scale information, leading to a poor understanding of the visual scene. To overcome these drawbacks, we propose a method called ICDT(**I**nteraction **C**onsistency **D**eformable **T**ransformer). ICDT performs a pre-trained hierarchical backbone with a deformable transformer encoder to extract contextual multi-scale features for accurate feature representations. Moreover, ICDT utilizes a cascaded deformable decoder architecture with learnable anchors to consistently obtain interaction predictions in sophisticated surroundings. Experimental results show the effectiveness of our method on the HICO-DET and V-COCO benchmarks. The codes are available at https://github.com/bingnanG/ICDT.

Keywords: Human-Object Interaction · Transformer-Based · Interaction Consistency

1 Introduction

Human-Object Interaction (HOI) Detection is an important component of computer vision and interaction understanding, which focuses on the interaction between human and object. Compared with Object Detection, it pays more attention to action and scene understanding, which is of great significance for machines to understand human activities [2,4,6,7,15]. Specifically, HOI detection predicts a set of triplets <*human, interaction, object*> from an input image. The triplets include the localization representations of humans and objects

R. Chen—This work was supported by the National Key R & D Program of China(No.2018YFB1305200).

L. Iliadis et al. (Eds.): ICANN 2023, LNCS 14259, pp. 433–445, 2023.
https://doi.org/10.1007/978-3-031-44223-0_35

Fig. 1. Visualization HOI predictions. We compare the visualized HOI prediction results of our proposed and baseline method [3] under different scale sample inputs in complex, varying surroundings. The different scales of input samples consist mainly of (a) small object and small human. (b) large object and small human. (c) human and object of similar size and nearby distance. The complex surroundings in input samples mainly include occlusion, partial visible interactive subject and overlap. The visualized result shows ICDT exceeds the baseline in terms of localization and interaction recognition accuracy.

with the corresponding interaction classes. Intelligently and efficiently localizing human-object pairs and predicting corresponding interactions in complex, varying surroundings are always challenging for HOI detection tasks.

Convolutional HOI detection methods can be divided into two types: two-stage and one-stage HOI detectors. Most two-stage approaches utilize Faster R-CNN [20] as the backbone and use multi-branch architecture to build features representation, PD-Net [27] decodes visual polysemy of verbs and performs four feature streams to predict HOI triplets. But using multi-stream is rather challenging to find interactive human-object pairings in a large number of negative pairs using local region features. Instead, one-stage approaches utilize two-branch architecture to localize human-object pairs and recognition interactions. Some approaches [15,25] extract features from Hourglass-104 [18] and view the HOI detection as a point-of-interaction pairing problem. However, these methods utilize cropped and local region features to identify interactive human-object pairs [21], resulting in a performance loss. In addition, integrated features are inadequate and often polluted because of CNN training.

In recent years, there has been growing interest in Transformer [23]. Some HOI methods extract contextual features and global information with transformer-based architecture to address the HOI task. QPIC [21] and HOTR [12] first apply transformer on HOI. UPT [26] construct a unary-pairwise transformer to combine unary and pairwise representations in HOI. However, the single architecture methods always ignore the variation of spatial scale, which can make ambiguities in predictions in complex variable scenarios. So QAHOI [3] builds the deformable network to address the problem of the scale variability in the scene. Nevertheless, using the single transformer architecture to weigh up the task of locating human-object pairs against interaction recognition is challenging and hard to maintain consistency of interaction.

To solve the above problems, we propose ICDT, a multi-scale deformable transformer network that gradually transforms the visual features to the HOI knowledge. Instead of simply applying transformer architecture to predict HOI instances, we leverage a hierarchical backbone to extract multi-scale visual features and construct an innovative structure of introducing multi-scale features for cascaded deformable decoders to maintain consistency in interaction prediction. For details, we apply multi-scale features with deformable attention [29] and adopt the novel decoding structure for interaction consistency. Throughout the encoding-decoding process, the ICDT uses additional learnable anchors in the deformable attention process to introduce bounding box information to obtain HOI embeddings. Figure 1 shows that our proposed model accurately and consistently completes HOI predictions in various scenarios. The visualization results show that the ICDT provides more accurate interaction detection for complex and multi-scale scenarios than the baseline method in HOI detection. Furthermore, Experiments on two popular datasets show results outperforming previous works, demonstrating the effectiveness of proposed IDCT.

In summary, we make the following contributions:

- We propose ICDT to mine the intrinsic connection between localization and interaction recognition in HOI detection for better obtaining finer-grained feature representations.
- We present a novel architecture to accomplish effective and consistent interaction prediction in variable and complex scenarios. For details, we introduce a hierarchical backbone and a deformable encoder to extract multi-scale visual features. Moreover, we perform the cascaded deformable decoder architecture with learnable anchors as additional information, which frees the network from learning unnecessary embedding transformation and maintains interaction consistency.
- Experiments on HICO-DET and VCOCO datasets show promising results compared to previous methods and thus demonstrate the effectiveness of our method.

2 Related Work

2.1 Convolutional Approaches

In contrast to Object Detection, Human-Object Interaction (HOI) Detection tries to localize and identify the interaction of human-object pairs, it requires a deeper comprehension of the context. The existing conventional approaches in HOI can be grouped by two paradigms, i.e., two-stage and one-stage methods. Most two-stage methods [5,6,9,24,27] utilize Faster R-CNN [20] or Mask R-CNN [10] to locate target firstly. Then, the features extracted from backbone networks are cropped into the localized region. Generally, the cropped features are fed into multi-stream networks to generate the interaction results. Some of the two-stage methods [5,16,19,22] perform graph networks or incorporate human-pose information [9,14,27] to refine the features. However, the cropped features lead to unbalanced matching problems for interactive human-object pairings and results in performance degradation. So some one-stage approaches [11,15,25] utilize two-branch architecture to detect HOI triplets directly. Even though these methods seek to capture contextual information through integrated features, the features are inadequate and occasionally tainted due to insufficient contextual knowledge.

2.2 Transformer-Based Approaches

Recently, DETR [1] views object detection as a direct set prediction problem and successfully applied the transformer to object detection, so the transformer-based methods [3,4,12,21,30] use the self-attention mechanism to solve the problem of insufficient contextual knowledge during training. It has emerged as a new trend in the HOI detection task. However, it is difficult for these approaches to build a unified feature representation for two very distinct tasks: human-object detection and interaction classification. The interaction branch of above methods still suffers from multi learning tasks and cannot maintain the interaction consistency. The lack of granularity of feature representation in different tasks is still a pressing issue.

3 Methodology

In this section, we discuss each module and report the implementation details.

3.1 Multi-scale Feature Extractor

As shown in Fig. 2, we construct a hierarchical multi-scale feature extractor that consists of swin-transformer [17] and a deformable encoder to extract sequential visual multi-scale features V_m. Given an input image $x \in \mathbb{R}^{H \times W \times 3}$, we obtain hierarchical feature information, specifically described as three scale feature maps, $f_1 \in \mathbb{R}^{\frac{H}{8} \times \frac{W}{8} \times 2C_s}$, $f_2 \in \mathbb{R}^{\frac{H}{16} \times \frac{W}{16} \times 4C_s}$, $f_3 \in \mathbb{R}^{\frac{H}{32} \times \frac{W}{32} \times 8C_s}$. C_s is the dimension after the backbone network transformation. Following the Deformable DETR's implementation [29], an additional low resolution feature map $f_4 \in \mathbb{R}^{\frac{H}{64} \times \frac{W}{64} \times C_l}$, $C_l = 256$ is generated by 3×3 convolution. And after 1×1 convolution, the dimension C_s of feature maps is transferred to C_d. Then, we flatten and concatenate the feature maps into a sequence feature of length $=$ N_m with C_d dimensions. N_m is the number representing the sum of the pixels of the feature maps. The deformable transformer encoder takes the sequence feature with positional encoding [1] $P \in \mathbb{R}^{N_q \times C_d}$ to produce richer contextual information $V_m \in \mathbb{R}^{N_m \times C_d}$ in a multi-scale manner. The encoded features V_m are then provided for deformable decoders to decode HOI information.

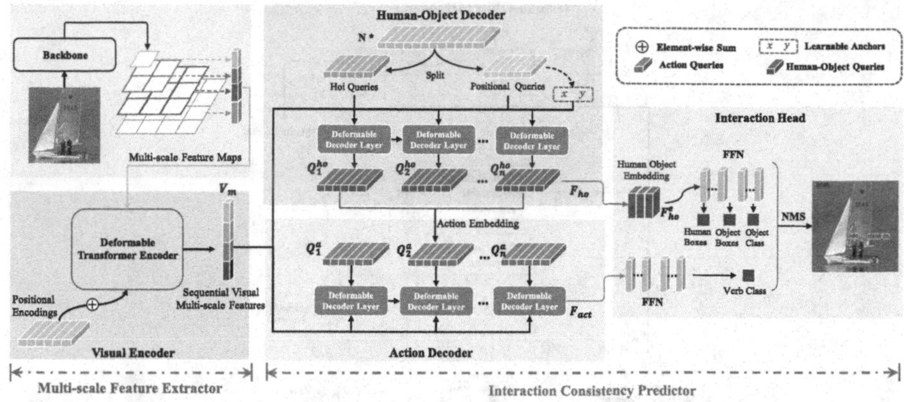

Fig. 2. Overview of ICDT. ICDT employs a hierarchical backbone network to extract multi-scale feature maps and a deformable encoder to encode the visual features for obtaining visual multi-scale sequence encoding features. The encoded features are passed to two cascaded deformable decoders in a shared manner. The two decoders complete the decoding of human-object and corresponding action interaction features based on different learnable queries. Finally, the human-object query is used to locate the human and object. The interaction predictions are obtained through the Interaction Head.

3.2 Interaction Consistency Predictor

For better decoding human-object and action features, we construct an Interaction Consistency Predictor that converts sequential visual features to interactive representations. Unlike the previous transformer-based methods, we perform two cascaded deformable decoders to generate efficient localization and interaction features, respectively. What's more, we combine learnable anchors into the human-object decoder for obtaining HOI embeddings with localization information.

Human-Object Decoder. The green part of the Fig. 2 shows the overall architecture of the human-object decoder. According to the Deformable DETR [29], we initialize the object queries $Q \in \mathbb{R}^{N_q \times C_d}$ and split it equally into two parts, i.e., hoi queries $Q_{hoi} \in \mathbb{R}^{\frac{N_q}{2} \times C_d}$ and positional queries $Q_{pos} \in \mathbb{R}^{\frac{N_q}{2} \times C_d}$. The learnable anchors $a \in \mathbb{R}^{N_q \times 2}$ are generated by a linear layer from Q_{pos}. As depicted in Fig. 3, we apply L deformable decoder layers for the human-object decoder and show the details of the first decoder layer. Each decoder layer is comprised of a multi-head attention and a multi-scale deformable attention. After formation of learnable anchors a, the human-object queries Q_{ho} are generated by concatenating those two queries:

$$Q_{ho} = [Q_{hoi}, Q_{pos}], \tag{1}$$

where $Q_{ho} \in \mathbb{R}^{N_q \times C_d}$. Next, the Q_{ho} are fed into a multi-head attention module. And then a multi-scale deformable attention operation is conducted between

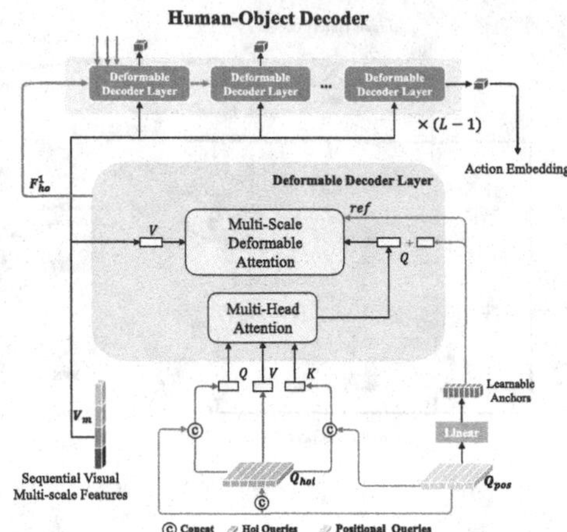

Fig. 3. Details of human-object decoder (the first layer). The human-object decoder is composed of multiple deformable decoder layers. Each deformable decoder layer performs the joint attention operation to decode the human and object features.

the queries and the sequential features V_m. Finally, we generate the decoded human-object features, it can be simply represented as:

$$F_{ho} = f_{ho}(Q_{ho}, V_m, P), \tag{2}$$

where f_{ho} denotes the joint attention operations of the entire decoding process in human-object decoder, and $F_{ho} \in \mathbb{R}^{bs \times N_q \times C_d}$ are the decoded human-object features. Instead of extracting the human interaction features directly from the visual feature sequence [3, 21], we use a separate deformable decoder to obtain the salient human-object features with location information. After that, the human-object features are transferred to the action decoder.

Action Decoder. To better combine human-object features to predict interaction information, a deformable action decoder is specially constructed to build action features individually in this network. The action decoder obtain the action features based on the visual features V_m and the action queries Q_a embedded by the updated human-object queries. Like the human-object decoder, the decoded action features of the action decoder can be simply represented as:

$$F_{act} = f_{act}(Q_a, V_m, P), \tag{3}$$

$F_{act} \in \mathbb{R}^{bs \times N_q \times C_d}$. During the process of feature generation, we convert multi-scale visual features into human-object and corresponding action features by employing the cascaded deformable decoders. In this way, interaction consistency can be further maintained. The interaction head network will output the predictions in the next step.

Interaction Head. The human-object features are embedded as F_{ho}^e after getting decoded human-object and action features. And then the interaction head

Table 1. Performance comparison with SOTA methods on HICO-DET. The 'A', 'S', 'P', 'L' represent the appearance feature, spatial feature, human pose information and the language feature, respectively. The best and the second best results are highlighted in **bold** and underline formats, respectively.

Method	Backbone	Feature	Default ↑ Full	Rare	Non-Rare	Known Object ↑ Full	Rare	Non-Rare
No-Frills [9]	R152	A+S+P	14.84	17.18	12.17	–	–	–
PMFNet [24]	R50-FPN	A+S	17.46	15.62	18.00	20.34	17.47	21.20
DRG [5]	R50-FPN	A+S	19.26	17.74	19.71	23.40	21.75	23.89
PPDM-Hourglass [15]	HG104	A	21.94	13.97	24.32	24.81	17.09	27.12
HOI-Trans [30]	R50	A	23.46	16.91	25.41	26.15	19.24	28.22
ConsNet [16]	R50-FPN	A+S+L	24.39	17.10	26.56	30.34	23.40	32.41
HOTR [12]	R50	A	25.10	17.34	27.42	–	–	–
GGNet [28]	HG104	A	29.17	22.13	30.84	33.50	26.67	34.89
QPIC-R50 [21]	R50	A	29.07	21.85	31.23	31.68	24.14	33.93
QPIC-R101 [21]	R101	A	29.90	23.92	31.69	32.38	26.06	34.27
UPT-R50 [26]	R50	A	31.66	25.94	33.36	35.05	29.27	36.77
UPT-R101 [26]	R101	A	32.31	**28.55**	33.44	35.65	**31.60**	36.86
QAHOI$_t$ [3]	Swin-Tiny	A	28.47	22.44	30.27	30.99	24.83	32.84
QAHOI$_b$ [3]	Swin-Base^{*+}	A	33.58	25.86	35.88	35.34	27.24	37.76
ICDT$_t$	Swin-Tiny	A	29.69	21.25	32.28	32.63	24.32	35.12
ICDT$_b$	Swin-Base^{*+}	A	**34.01**	27.60	**35.92**	**36.29**	29.88	**38.21**

in ICDT predicts the $\{h_{box}, o_{bbox}, o_{cls}, a_{cls}\}$ using FFN as follows:

$$h_{bbox} = \sigma(FFN_{hbox}(F^e_{ho})), \tag{4}$$

$$o_{bbox} = \sigma(FFN_{obox}(F^e_{ho})), \tag{5}$$

$$o_{cls} = FFN_{cls}(F^e_{ho}), \tag{6}$$

$$a_{cls} = FFN_{act}(F_{act}), \tag{7}$$

where $o_{cls} \in \mathbb{R}^{C_o}$ and $a_{cls} \in \mathbb{R}^{C_a}$ denote the object class and the action class respectively, C_o, C_a is the number of categories. The $h_{bbox}\{x, y, w, h\} \in \mathbb{R}$ and $o_{bbox}\{x, y, w, h\} \in \mathbb{R}$ are predicted with the center points and the normalized reference points.

4 Experiments

In this section, we conduct extensive experiments to show the efficacy of our proposed ICDT. First, we describe the datasets and evaluation metrics of our experiment settings in Sect. 4.1. Then we compare our ICDT with the previous state-of-the-art methods in Sect. 4.2. In addition, Fig. 4 visualizes the attention maps of two decoders. Finally, we do the ablation studies for different designs to check the effects of our proposed method in Sect. 4.4.

Table 2. The best performance comparison with SOTA methods on V-COCO.

Methods	Feature	AP_{role}^{S1} ↑	AP_{role}^{S2} ↑
iCAN [6]	A	45.3	52.4
TIN [14]	A+P	47.8	54.2
DRG [5]	A+S	51.0	–
VSGNet [22]	A+S	51.8	57.0
PMFNet [24]	A+S	52.0	–
IDN [13]	A	53.3	60.3
AS-Net [4]	A	53.9	–
GGNet [28]	A	54.7	–
QPIC [21]	A	58.8	61.0
UPT [26]	A	<u>59.0</u>	**64.5**
ICDT$_b$	A	**59.4**	<u>61.8</u>

4.1 Datasets and Evaluation Metrics

Datasets. We evaluate our model on two wildly-used datasets, i.e., HICO-DET [2], and V-COCO [8]. HICO-DET consists of 38,117 training and 9,658 test images and it provides over 150K annotated instances of human-object pairs, spanning the 600 HOI categories. V-COCO is a subset of MS-COCO that provides 5,400 images for training and 4,946 images for testing. It has 29 action categories and 80 object categories.

Evaluation Metrics. We evaluate our model by using the mean average precision (mAP) as the evaluation metric for both HICO-DET and V-COCO. For HICO-DET, we evaluate the performance in two different settings following [2] : *default* and *known-object* setting. In the former setting, each HOI category is evaluated on the full test set, while in the later setting, each HOI category is only evaluated on the images containing the target object category. Each setting includes the three different HOI category sets: all 600 HOI categories(*Full*), 138 HOI categories with less than 10 training instances(*Rare*), and 462 HOI categories(*Non-Rare*). For V-COCO, we evaluate performance in two scenarios: *scenario1* and *scenario2*, denoted as AP_{role}^{S1}, AP_{role}^{S2}, respectively.

4.2 Performance Comparison

We compare the performance of ICDT with previous methods on HICO-DET and V-COCO datasets, described in Table 1 and Table 2. On the two popular datasets, ICDT uses Swin Transformer [17](pre-trained on ImageNet) as the backbone network. On the V-COCO dataset, we compare the experimental results with the best performance of other methods. Our model uses the same backbone as the baseline on public datasets and performs better in all settings and scenarios. We achieve about 8.21% improvement in *default* setting on HICO-DET and 3.69% improvement on V-COCO comparing to baseline. These results demonstrate the ICDT's effectiveness and generalizability on both datasets.

4.3 Qualitative Analysis

We conduct a qualitative analysis of ICDT to observe how ICDT captures interactions in Fig. 4. The highlighted region represents the interest areas of the decoder. Intuitively, the human-object decoder captures the extremities of human and object. The action decoder focuses more on the interaction region. The attention maps of two decoders demonstrate the decoders indeed capture disentangled representations.

Fig. 4. Visualization of the HOI results and two type attention maps. In four sets of images, the first column represents the HOI results, the second and the third column represent the human-object and action decoder's attention maps, respectively.

4.4 Ablation Study

To examine the effectiveness of the components and the different design choices of our proposed IDCT, we conduct experiments on the V-COCO dataset with the Swin-Base*+ backbone.

Table 3. Ablation study on performance using different multi-scale feature maps.

Multi-scale feature maps	AP^{S1}_{role}	AP^{S2}_{role}
f_1, f_2, f_3, f_4	58.1	60.6
f_1, f_2, f_3	**59.4**	**61.8**
f_2, f_3	55.7	57.9
f_3	53.1	55.3

Multi-scale Feature Maps. Firstly, we analyze the effectiveness of multi-scale feature maps on the proposed method, shown in Table 3. Note that f_1, f_2, f_3 and f_4 are four scale feature maps defined in Sect. 3.1. We can observe that the additional generated feature map f_4 does not improve the performance. Comparing the second row with the fourth row, the two feature maps f_1, f_2 give a model accuracy improvement of 6.3 mAP (relatively 10.6%) on the AP^{S1}_{role} and 11.7% on the AP^{S2}_{role}. The multi-scale features benefit visual representations by introducing sufficient scale information. The significant performance improvement indicates the effectiveness of the multi-scale features.

Table 4. Ablation study on the effect of our proposed cascade decoder architecture. ✓ indicates that this part is used. MSf: Multi-scale features include f_1, f_2, f_3. CDA: The cascade decoder architecture.

MSf	CDA	AP^{S1}_{role}	AP^{S2}_{role}
✓		56.9	59.7
✓	✓	**59.4**	**61.8**

Effect of the Proposed Cascade Decoder Architecture. Secondly, to verify the effectiveness of proposed cascade decoder architecture on HOI detection, we design the ablation study in Table 4. Comparing the first row with the second row, we can observed that the mAP on V-COCO is improved by 4.4% and 3.5% in AP^{S1}_{role} and AP^{S2}_{role}, respectively. In contrast, the mAP falls when the cascade decoder architecture is removed. The improved performance proves the effectiveness of our proposed architecture. In summary, we combine the multi-scale feature extractor and the interaction consistency predictor to capture more fine-grained features and obtain more reasonable interaction information.

Table 5. Ablation study on the effect of decoder layer numbers on V-COCO test set. We maintain the same number of two decoder layers for matching consistency.

human-object decoder	action decoder	AP^{S1}_{role}	AP^{S2}_{role}
6	6	57.8	60.4
5	5	**59.4**	**61.8**
4	4	57.9	60.3
3	3	56.4	58.4

Effect of Decoder Layer's Number. Then, we analyze the layer's number of disentangled decoders in interaction consistency predictor, shown in Table 5. We set the same layer's number in human-object and action decoder for inter-matching. It can be found that the human-object decoder layer $L^{ho}_{de} = 3$ and the action decoder layer $L^{a}_{de} = 3$ get the worse performance. Too few decoding layers will result in insufficient feature representation for accomplishing highly accurate human-object interaction detection. The parameter combination of $L^{ho}_{de} = 5$ and

$L_{de}^{a} = 5$ gets the best performance. Thus, the improving feature representation requires the proper fine-grained separation of features.

5 Conclusions

In this paper, we propose a novel framework ICDT for Human-Object Interaction Detection. The proposed ICDT utilizes the hierarchical feature extractor to introduce multi-scale features for representing multi-level features in complex scenarios. In addition, applying the cascaded deformable decoders free the network from the incomplete feature representations and inconsistent interaction prediction. We empirically demonstrated that extracting finer-grained feature representations is an effective way to improve the performance of HOI detection. Experiments on two popular datasets verify the effectiveness and the superior performance of the proposed method.

References

1. Carion, N., Massa, F., Synnaeve, G., Usunier, N., Kirillov, A., Zagoruyko, S.: End-to-end object detection with transformers. In: Vedaldi, A., Bischof, H., Brox, T., Frahm, J.-M. (eds.) ECCV 2020. LNCS, vol. 12346, pp. 213–229. Springer, Cham (2020). https://doi.org/10.1007/978-3-030-58452-8_13
2. Chao, Y.W., Liu, Y., Liu, X., Zeng, H., Deng, J.: Learning to detect human-object interactions. In: 2018 IEEE Winter Conference on Applications of Computer Vision (WACV), pp. 381–389. IEEE (2018)
3. Chen, J., Yanai, K.: Qahoi: Query-based anchors for human-object interaction detection. arXiv preprint arXiv:2112.08647 (2021)
4. Chen, M., Liao, Y., Liu, S., Chen, Z., Wang, F., Qian, C.: Reformulating hoi detection as adaptive set prediction. In: Proceedings of the IEEE/CVF Conference on Computer Vision and Pattern Recognition, pp. 9004–9013 (2021)
5. Gao, C., Xu, J., Zou, Y., Huang, J.-B.: DRG: dual relation graph for human-object interaction detection. In: Vedaldi, A., Bischof, H., Brox, T., Frahm, J.-M. (eds.) ECCV 2020. LNCS, vol. 12357, pp. 696–712. Springer, Cham (2020). https://doi.org/10.1007/978-3-030-58610-2_41
6. Gao, C., Zou, Y., Huang, J.B.: iCAN: Instance-centric attention network for human-object interaction detection. arXiv preprint arXiv:1808.10437 (2018)
7. Gkioxari, G., Girshick, R., Dollár, P., He, K.: Detecting and recognizing human-object interactions. In: Proceedings of the IEEE Conference on Computer Vision and Pattern Recognition, pp. 8359–8367 (2018)
8. Gupta, S., Malik, J.: Visual semantic role labeling. arXiv preprint arXiv:1505.04474 (2015)
9. Gupta, T., Schwing, A., Hoiem, D.: No-frills human-object interaction detection: factorization, layout encodings, and training techniques. In: Proceedings of the IEEE/CVF International Conference on Computer Vision, pp. 9677–9685 (2019)
10. He, K., Gkioxari, G., Dollár, P., Girshick, R.: Mask R-CNN. In: Proceedings of the IEEE International Conference on Computer Vision, pp. 2961–2969 (2017)
11. Kim, B., Choi, T., Kang, J., Kim, H.J.: UnionDet: union-level detector towards real-time human-object interaction detection. In: Vedaldi, A., Bischof, H., Brox, T., Frahm, J.-M. (eds.) ECCV 2020. LNCS, vol. 12360, pp. 498–514. Springer, Cham (2020). https://doi.org/10.1007/978-3-030-58555-6_30

12. Kim, B., Lee, J., Kang, J., Kim, E.S., Kim, H.J.: HOTR: End-to-end human-object interaction detection with transformers. In: Proceedings of the IEEE/CVF Conference on Computer Vision and Pattern Recognition, pp. 74–83 (2021)
13. Li, Y.L., Liu, X., Wu, X., Li, Y., Lu, C.: Hoi analysis: integrating and decomposing human-object interaction. Adv. Neural. Inf. Process. Syst. **33**, 5011–5022 (2020)
14. Li, Y.L., et al.: Transferable interactiveness knowledge for human-object interaction detection. In: Proceedings of the IEEE/CVF Conference on Computer Vision and Pattern Recognition, pp. 3585–3594 (2019)
15. Liao, Y., Liu, S., Wang, F., Chen, Y., Qian, C., Feng, J.: PPDM: parallel point detection and matching for real-time human-object interaction detection. In: Proceedings of the IEEE/CVF Conference on Computer Vision and Pattern Recognition, pp. 482–490 (2020)
16. Liu, Y., Yuan, J., Chen, C.W.: ConsNet: learning consistency graph for zero-shot human-object interaction detection. In: Proceedings of the 28th ACM International Conference on Multimedia, pp. 4235–4243 (2020)
17. Liu, Z., et al.: Swin transformer: hierarchical vision transformer using shifted windows. In: Proceedings of the IEEE/CVF International Conference on Computer Vision, pp. 10012–10022 (2021)
18. Newell, A., Yang, K., Deng, J.: Stacked hourglass networks for human pose estimation. In: Leibe, B., Matas, J., Sebe, N., Welling, M. (eds.) ECCV 2016. LNCS, vol. 9912, pp. 483–499. Springer, Cham (2016). https://doi.org/10.1007/978-3-319-46484-8_29
19. Qi, S., Wang, W., Jia, B., Shen, J., Zhu, S.C.: Learning human-object interactions by graph parsing neural networks. In: Proceedings of the European Conference on Computer Vision (ECCV), pp. 401–417 (2018)
20. Ren, S., He, K., Girshick, R., Sun, J.: Faster R-CNN: towards real-time object detection with region proposal networks. In: Advances in Neural Information Processing Systems, vol. 28 (2015)
21. Tamura, M., Ohashi, H., Yoshinaga, T.: Qpic: query-based pairwise human-object interaction detection with image-wide contextual information. In: Proceedings of the IEEE/CVF Conference on Computer Vision and Pattern Recognition, pp. 10410–10419 (2021)
22. Ulutan, O., Iftekhar, A., Manjunath, B.S.: VSGNet: spatial attention network for detecting human object interactions using graph convolutions. In: Proceedings of the IEEE/CVF Conference on Computer Vision and Pattern Recognition, pp. 13617–13626 (2020)
23. Vaswani, A., et al.: Attention is all you need. In: Advances in Neural Information Processing Systems, vol. 30 (2017)
24. Wan, B., Zhou, D., Liu, Y., Li, R., He, X.: Pose-aware multi-level feature network for human object interaction detection. In: Proceedings of the IEEE/CVF International Conference on Computer Vision, pp. 9469–9478 (2019)
25. Wang, T., Yang, T., Danelljan, M., Khan, F.S., Zhang, X., Sun, J.: Learning human-object interaction detection using interaction points. In: Proceedings of the IEEE/CVF Conference on Computer Vision and Pattern Recognition, pp. 4116–4125 (2020)
26. Zhang, F.Z., Campbell, D., Gould, S.: Efficient two-stage detection of human-object interactions with a novel unary-pairwise transformer. In: Proceedings of the IEEE/CVF Conference on Computer Vision and Pattern Recognition, pp. 20104–20112 (2022)
27. Zhong, X., Ding, C., Qu, X., Tao, D.: Polysemy deciphering network for robust human-object interaction detection. Int. J. Comput. Vis. **129**(6), 1910–1929 (2021)

28. Zhong, X., Qu, X., Ding, C., Tao, D.: Glance and gaze: inferring action-aware points for one-stage human-object interaction detection. In: Proceedings of the IEEE/CVF Conference on Computer Vision and Pattern Recognition, pp. 13234–13243 (2021)
29. Zhu, X., Su, W., Lu, L., Li, B., Wang, X., Dai, J.: Deformable DETR: Deformable transformers for end-to-end object detection. arXiv preprint arXiv:2010.04159 (2020)
30. Zou, C., et al.: End-to-end human object interaction detection with hoi transformer. In: Proceedings of the IEEE/CVF Conference on Computer Vision and Pattern Recognition, pp. 11825–11834 (2021)

Imbalanced Conditional Conv-Transformer for Mathematical Expression Recognition

Shuaijian Ji[1], Zhaokun Zhou[1], Yuqing Wang[1], Baishan Duan[1], Zhenyu Weng[1], Liang Xu[2], and Yuesheng Zhu[1](✉)

[1] Communication and Information Security Lab, Shenzhen Graduate School, Peking University, Shenzhen, China
{210122809,zhouzhaokun,wyq,baishanduan}@stu.pku.edu.cn, {wzytumbler,zhuys}@pku.edu.cn

[2] Gamma Lab, OCFT, Shenzhen, China

Abstract. Mathematical Expression Recognition (MER), which aims to convert images into corresponding LaTeX markup, has been a long-standing research topic. Previous methods employ the paradigm of dense computing in both encoder and decoder would suffer from slow convergence, limited performance, and design complexity of extra backbone network before encoder. To alleviate the above limitation, we propose a fast-converging end-to-end ImBalanced Conditional Conv-Transformer (IBCCT) architecture that combines a light encoder and a heavy decoder. Besides, we extend the traditional encoder-decoder framework by further learning a lightweight network to generate for each image a conditional token to inject global position information. Extensive experiments show that our IBCCT-Base model can achieve better performance with faster convergence speed and the parameter is reduced by 33% compared with the SOTA method. In particular, our IBCCT-Large model has achieved 94.04% and 93.2% in the Match metric, which is 1.34% and 4.12% higher than the SOTA method.

Keywords: Mathematical expression recognition · Conditional token · Imbalanced architecture

1 Introduction

With the strong revival of deep learning, traditional Optical Character Recognition (OCR) has been significantly improved [9]. Despite the maturity of the research on OCR, recognizing mathematical expression images into structural markup representation rather than aligned characters is still challenging. Compared to traditional OCR, Mathematical Expression Recognition (MER) often requires the system to handle presentational aspects such as sub and super-script notation, special symbols, and nested fractions. Another unique property of MER is that their lengths may vary more drastically than other image-based sequence

L. Iliadis et al. (Eds.): ICANN 2023, LNCS 14259, pp. 446–458, 2023.
https://doi.org/10.1007/978-3-031-44223-0_36

$$f(x) = \frac{2\sqrt{2}cosx}{cos\frac{x}{2} - sin\frac{x}{2}}$$

$$f(x) = \frac{2\sqrt{2}cosx}{sin^{x} - sin^{x}}$$

$$\mathcal{E}\left(x\right) = \int \mathrm{d}^3 k \sqrt{\frac{2\omega}{(2\pi)^3}} \left\{ \begin{array}{c} c^3\left(e_3 + e_4\right)]\mathrm{e}^{-ikx} + \\ \left[c^{*2} e_1 + c^{*4}\left(e_3 + e_4\right)\right]\mathrm{e}^{ikx} \end{array} \right\}, \; \omega \equiv \sqrt{\vec{k}^2}$$

$$\mathcal{E}\left(x\right) = \int \mathrm{d}^3 k \sqrt{\frac{2\omega}{(2\pi)^3}} \left\{ \begin{array}{c} \left[c^1 e_1 + c^3\left(e_3 + e_4\right)\right]\mathrm{e}^{-ikx} + \\ \left[c^{*2} e_1 + c^{*4}\left(e_3 + e_4\right)\right]\mathrm{e}^{ikx} \end{array} \right\}, \; \omega \equiv \sqrt{\rightarrow k^2}$$

$$f_N' = \left\{ \pi^{-1/2} \sum_{n=0}^{N} \frac{(-1)^n}{n!} \left(\frac{\lambda}{4} x^4\right)^n e^{-x^2} \; for\,|x| < x_{c,N} 0 for\,|x| > x_{c,N} \right.$$

$$f_N' = \left\{ \pi^{-1/2} \sum_{n=0}^{N} \frac{(-1)^n}{(n)} \left(\frac{\lambda}{4} x^4\right)^n e^{-x^2} \; for\,|x| < x_{c,N} 0 for\,|x| > x_{c,N} \right.$$

Fig. 1. The predicted LaTeX sequence from EDSL and our methods. We also rendered the predicted LaTeX sequence into images for better visualization. Blue indicates the correct prediction of our IBCCT, red indicates that the wrong results predicted by EDSL. (Color figure online)

recognition tasks. Last but not least, MER is sensitive to the position of the nested characters, which means that the same character in different positions may represent several completely different semantics. Mathematics expression understanding has received much attention from both academia and industry due to its numerous applications such as arithmetical ex- ercise correction [7], student performance prediction [14], and automatic mark- ing [16].

Some attempts have been made to address this problem. For example, the algorithm in [3] first presents an encoder-decoder model with a scalable coarse-to-fine attention mechanism. [5] proposes the first Transformer-based method named EDSL, which achieved SOTA performance at that time. After that, DBN [13] introduces knowledge distillation and dual branch network based on the EDSL model while achieving slight performance improvement with unaffordable model parameters. Since then, the research on MER seems to have stagnated.

Though the EDSL-based model (EDSL and DBN) achieved SOTA performance, we argue that they exist critical problems: EDSL-based architecture generally consists of backbone network, encoder, and decoder three parts. The heavy backbone network (usually a VGG net) and encoder have large redundancy in extracting feature map for grayscale input images, which results in the paradigm difficult to converge in early stage and actually hurts the performance of the model. Besides, the performance is affected significantly by the length of math expression. EDSL employs the connected-component labeling algorithm to segment symbol blocks in an expression image during the preprocess aiming to obtain fine-grained features. This unsupervised manner destroys the integrity of the input images and harms the global position relationship. Though the paper additionally proposes the reconstruction module to recover the spatial dependencies of symbols in the encoder, it is still difficult for the EDSL-based model to correctly recognize the structural mathematical expression, especially when facing long sequences.

To address the problems mentioned above, we propose a simple end-to-end approach called ImBalanced Conditional Conv-Transformer (IBCCT), which has a light encoder and simplified architecture. The rationale behind the design of IBCCT is to improve the efficiency of parameters and convergence speed according to the characteristics of MER. A light encoder is enough to extract feature of the grayscale input image. Meanwhile, a heavy decoder is necessary because the core of MER is to model the layout relation. Thus, we choose depthwise separate convolution as the token mixer [11] in the encoder and remove the backbone network. Through our design, encoder parameter is only 1.6M accounting for less than 20% of the whole model. In the decoder, we use the Attention same as [12] to generate LaTeX sequence. The overall encoder-decoder architecture follows the design principle of MetaFormer [15], which is a general architecture abstracted from Transformers by not specifying the token mixer. To deal with the model robustness when facing long sequence, we further extend a lightweight neural network (Conditional Network) to enhance the global position information. The key idea is to make a token embedding conditioned on the global feature extracted from encoder to make the model have better ability to capture long sequence dependency.

Benefiting from the imbalanced design and simplified architecture, our IBCCT possesses faster convergence speed with fewer parameter. At the same time, the performance also has a comprehensive improvement with easy end-to-end training. Besides, the design of Conditional Network makes the model fully leverage the translation-invariance of CNN and the permutation-invariance of Transformer [2], which accounts for that the model can capture the long-distance dependency and dynamically adapt the receptive field according to the image content in the MER task.

To summarize, our key contributions are as follows.

- We design the imbalanced architecture IBCCT to reduce the model parameters and improve the convergence speed according to the characteristics of MER. IBCCT can acquire 42.0% in accuracy in ME-20K only in one epoch while the baseline model only acquires 9.9%.
- We additionally develop a light Condition Network to inject global position information to improve the ability of capturing long sequence dependency for IBCCT. Our model shows superior robustness when facing long mathematical sequence.
- Without bells and whistles, IBCCT-base model achieves the best overall performance with the model parameters reduced by 33%. Besides, IBCCT-L model has achieved 94.04% and 93.2% in the Match metric, which is 1.34% and 4.12% higher than the SOTA methods.

2 Related Work

The mainstream of MER methods can be divided into two categories: traditional multi-stage methods and recently popular end-to-end methods. Compared to multi-stage methods, end-to-end models are easier to train and the performances usually outperform a lot.

Traditional multi-stage MER involves two main components: symbol recognition and symbol-arrangement analysis [1,8]. Recent research on MER mainly inherited from the encoder-decoder architecture [3,5,14,17]. For example, WAP [17] uses a VGG network as the encoder and used RNN equipped with an attention mechanism to generate LaTeX sequence. [16] proposed a multi-scale attention mechanism to recognize symbols in different scales. [3] presents a neural encoder-decoder model with a scalable coarse-to-fine attention mechanism. EDSL uses the unsupervised manner to segment symbol block, and then send them to the pipeline of backbone network, encoder and decoder. DBN introduces knowledge distillation and dual branch network based on the EDSL. The recognition effect has been greatly improved by these two models.

In computer vision, ViT [4] opened the trend of Transformer. After that, MLP-like models [10], ConvMixer [11], and ConvNext [6] are proposed. In our view, these models conform to the design principles of MetaFormer, which argues that the competence of Transformer/MLP-like models primarily stems from the general architecture MetaFormer instead of the equipped specific token mixers [15]. Inspired by these models, IBCCT provides timely insight on how to design an efficient model that is suitable for MER.

3 Method

Below we first provide brief reviews on MER problem formalization. Then, we present the overview and technical details of our approach as well as the rationale behind the design.

3.1 MER Formalization

The Mathematical Expression Recognition (MER) problem is defined as converting a rendered source image to target presentational markup (LaTeX) that fully describes both its content and layout [1]. The source, x, consists of a grayscale and structural image. The target consists of a sequence of LaTeX expression $y =< y_1, y_2, \cdots, y_T >$ where T is the length of the sequence, and y_i is a token in the markup language.

We consider the model $f(x, \theta) = \hat{y}$, where θ are the parameters of f. In the view of vision, MER requires that rendering $\hat{y}$ with a LaTeX compiler equals math expression image x. In the view of language, we hope that y and $\hat{y}$ have the max semantic similarity and $\hat{y}$ can minimize the symbol redundancy (redundant brackets).

3.2 Model Overview

An overview of our approach is shown in Fig. 2. In this paper, we argue that heavy backbone and encoder result in more parameters and destroy the convergence speed (the experiments will be shown in the next section). According to this, we remove the backbone network in architecture meanwhile make the depth-wise

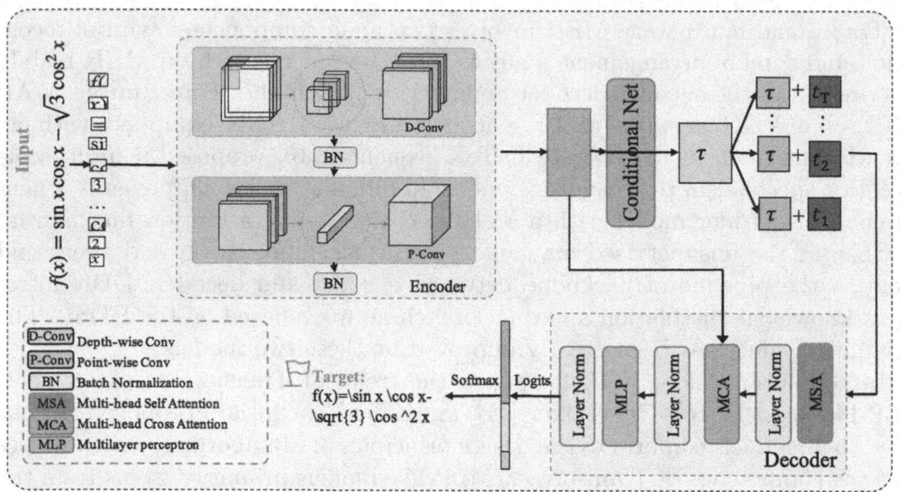

Fig. 2. The architecture of our Imbalanced Conditional Conv-Transformer (IBCCT) model.

Conv as the encoder's token mixer. Thanks to this design, IBCCT enjoys architectural simplicity without requiring dense attentional computation or explicit pyramid CNN networks in encoder. In the decoder, we keep the Attention the same as [12] to utilize its ability to capture long sequence dependency. Most importantly, we send the global feature map extracted from encoder to Conditional Network to condition it on the token embedding. The instance-conditional token embedding generalize better especially when facing long sequences because it shifts the focus away from delicate position encoding to feature map itself. Relevant experiment will be shown in Sect. 4.

3.3 Architecture Details

ConvMixer Encoder: It first splits an input grayscale image into non-overlapping patches with a patchify layer implemented using a 4×4, stride 4 convolutional layer. After the patchify layer, the feature dimension is $\frac{w}{4} \times \frac{h}{4} \times c$, where the w and h is the image size of width and height and c is the hidden dimension. We indicate the output of the patchify layer as z_0:

$$z_0 = \mathbf{BN}(\sigma\{\mathbf{Conv}(x, stride = 4, kernelsize = 4)\}) \tag{1}$$

The ConvMixer block consists of depthwise convolution followed by pointwise convolution. Each of the convolutions is followed by an activation and post-activation BatchNorm in the l_{th} layer:

$$z_l^{'} = \mathbf{BN}(\sigma\{\mathbf{DepthwiseConv}(z_{l-1})\}) + z_{l-1} \tag{2}$$

$$z_l = \mathbf{BN}(\sigma\{\mathbf{PointwiseConv}(z_l^{'})\}) \tag{3}$$

The same as [11],we chose depthwise convolution to mix spatial dimension and pointwise convolution to mix channel dimension. After 20 blocks with the same architecture, the feature dimension keeps unchanged. Finally, it will be flattened into the dimension $n \times c$ where n is $\frac{w}{4} \times \frac{h}{4}$ and we use V to indicate the flattened feature map.

Conditional Network: A straightforward way to implement Conditional Network is to build T neural networks to get T conditional tokens where T is the length of mathematical expression length. However, such a design would require $T\times$ the size of a neural network and T varies in different batch. To reduce the model parameters as far as possible, we adapt the parameter-efficient design that is more flexible. Specifically, we further learn a lightweight neural network, called Conditional Network (Con-Net), to generate for each input a conditional token (vector), which is then combined with the token embeddings. See Fig. 2. for a sketch of the architecture. Let $h_\theta(\cdot)$ denote the Con-Net parameterized by θ, each conditional token is now obtained by

$$\tau = h_\theta(V) \tag{4}$$

During training, we update the Con-Net's parameters θ by standard back-propagation. In our implementation, the Con-Net is built with a two-layer bottleneck structure (Linear-ReLU-Linear) similar to [18]. The input to the Con-Net is simply the output features produced by the light encoder.

Attention Decoder: It generates one token at each time according to the patch set and previous outputs. To facilitate minibatch processing, each mathematical expression sequence is encompassed with the $[SOS]$ and $[EOS]$ tokens and capped at the longest length of this minibatch. After that, the IDs are mapped to 256-dimension word embedding vectors. Let t denote the mathematical expression embedding and $t =< t_1, t_2, \cdots, t_T >$ where the $t_i \in \mathcal{R}^{256}$ is the token embedding. Then, each token presentation is now obtained by $y_i = t_i + \tau$ and $i \in 1, 2, \cdots, T$. The Attention block followed by [12] is then employed. The decoder is trained as a conditional language model to give the probability of the next token according to the image features V and history annotations. On top of the decoder, we define the following language model:

$$P(y_t|y_1, \cdots, y_{t-1}, V) = \mathbf{Softmax}(W_{out}o_{t-1}) \tag{5}$$

where y_t is the t_{th} target token in the output LaTeX sequence based on the previous output, o_{t-1} is the output of the transformer decoder in the $t-1_{th}$ step, $W_{out} \in \mathcal{R}^{|D| \times 256}$ are learned linear transformations and $|D|$ is the size of the vocabulary. The overall loss L is defined as the negative log-likelihood of the LaTeX token sequence:

$$L = \sum_{t=1}^{T} -logP(y_t|y_1, \cdots, y_{t-1}, V) \tag{6}$$

4 Experiment

As for the EDSL achieving relative better performance with acceptable number of parameters, we make EDSL as the direct rival to our approach. In fact, DBN achieves slightly better performance than EDSL but with heavy model parameters and does not provide available code, so we just list it as a reference. In this section, we will show the relevant information of the dataset and experiment results in detail.

4.1 Expreiments Setup

Datasets: We select two publicly available MER datasets used in EDSL, ME-20K, and ME-98K as our benchmark datasets. These two datasets constitute a comprehensive benchmark, which covers a diverse set of formulas collected from the online education system and research papers. ME-20K derives from public datasets Formula which collects math expression images and corresponding LaTeX representations from high school math exercises in Zhixue.com. It has 20686 images and corresponding LaTeX labels. ME-98K derives from the dataset IM2LATEX, which collects the printed formula and corresponding LaTeX representations from 60000 research papers. It contains 98676 images and labels. To make a fair comparison with EDSL, the datasets we use are completely consistent with it.

Metrics: We use Bleu-4, Rough-4, Match, and Match-WS as the four main metrics to comprehensively evaluate the model performance from the vision and language view. Bleu-4 and Rough-4 are to measure the precision and recall for predicted sequence and label sequence. These two metrics aim to evaluate the ability mainly from the language view. The metric Match is to check the matching accuracy of the rendered prediction image with a **LaTeX compiler** compared to the ground-truth image. Match-WS is a relatively easy metric that checks the matching accuracy after eliminating white space columns. These two metrics mainly evaluate the ability from the vision view.

Training Details: We adapt the split result of EDSL which randomly splits the dataset into the train, validation, and test sets according to the ratio of 8:1:1. The final result mainly refers to the result on the same test dataset. During training, we resize the input formula image to the size of 112×224. Training is done with Adam and an initial learning rate of 0.0003. For all datasets, the training batch size is set to 16 training on Tesla V100 GPU. As for the learning rate decay policy, we follow EDSL to halve the learning rate when the validation set accuracy decreases for three consecutive epochs and the training process will stop after ten epochs with the validation set accuracy not increasing.

4.2 Overall Performance Comparison

Quantitative results: With our simplified pipeline and Conditional Network, the model achieves better performance than EDSL with the model parame-

Table 1. Quantitative results on ME-20K and ME-98K.

DataSet	Methods	Bleu-4	Rough-4	Match	Match-WS	Param(M)
ME-20K	IM2Markup [3]	92.83	93.74	89.23	89.63	–
	DBN [13]	**94.73**	**95.60**	92.85	93.61	–
	EDSL [5]	94.23	95.10	92.70	93.45	14.6M
	IBCCT	94.49(+0.26)	95.29(+0.19)	**94.04**(+1.37)	**94.52**(+1.07)	**9.8M**(-33%)
	IBCCT-L	95.11	95.96	94.04	94.47	30.4M
ME-98K	IM2Markup [3]	91.47	92.45	84.96	85.16	–
	DBN [13]	92.90	93.34	89.71	90.01	–
	EDSL [5]	92.93	93.30	89.00	89.34	14.6M
	IBCCT	**93.49**(+0.56)	**93.80**(+0.50)	**91.30**(+2.30)	**91.45**(+2.11)	**9.9M**(-33%)
	IBCCT-L	93.53	93.95	93.2	93.46	30.5M

ters reduced by almost 33%, which fully proves the superiority of our proposed IBCCT model. The overview performance comparison is shown in Table 1. Specifically, IBCCT-base model outperforms EDSL by **1.04** percentages on average in two benchmark datasets with four metrics and our model parameter is less than 10M. DBN achieves better results in two metrics in ME-20K than our base model, but we infer its parameter is far greater than 14.6M because it inherits from EDSL and adds two heavy modules (DBN has no available code and does not indicate the model parameters in the paper). Thus, we additionally design the IBCCT-L model which has more heavy and larger input to compete against DBN. IBCCT-L demonstrated its strong ability when dealing with more complex dataset ME-98K and comprehensively outperforms DBN. Specifically, IBCCT-L model achieved 94.04% and 93.2% in the Match metric, which is much higher than the EDSL and DBN model.

Convergence Speed: We keep the same strategy to train EDSL and IBCCT and record their accuracy on ME-20K validation to investigate the convergence speed, as depicted in Fig. 3. IBCCT with assorted architecture significantly outperforms competitive EDSL with faster convergence speed. Thanks to our imbalanced design, IBCCT can acquire amazingly 42.0% accuracy in one epoch because the light encoder is easy to converge and the Conditional Network improves the balance of the model converge in the early stage. After six epochs, IBCCT achieves the accuracy of 79.8% while EDSL only achieves 79.4% after 12 epochs.

Robustness Analysis: The intuitive comparison between the two models is shown in Fig. 1. To better demonstrate the effect of expression length, we draw the model performance in two metrics (R4 curve is similar to B4 and Match-WS is similar to Match) with formulas length increasing. As illustrated in Fig. 4, IBCCT is superior EDSL and more robust when meeting extremely long expressions. As the length of expression increasing, the gap between the two models becomes larger. This sheds light on the benefit of end-to-end input and Conditional Network. In fact, when IBCCT converges insufficiently in the early stage, the Conditional token plays the role of position embedding in some way because the input feature of Conditional Network contains the global position information. We recommend checking out our supplementary materials for detailed comparison for rendered images with a LaTeX compiler. From the result, we can demonstrate that IBCCT has excellent advantages in processing long sequences.

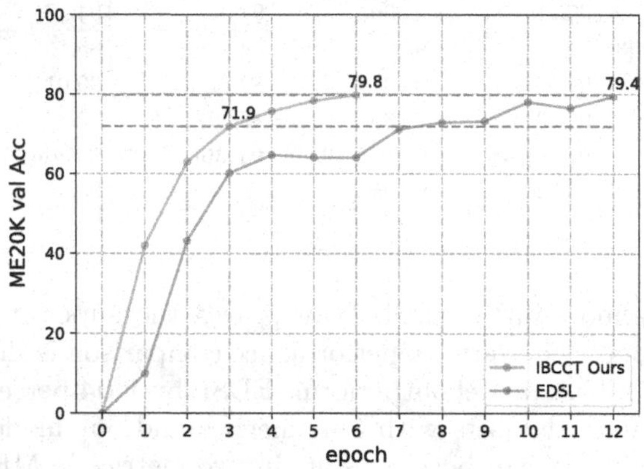

Fig. 3. Convergence curves of our IBCCT and EDSL on ME-20K validation.

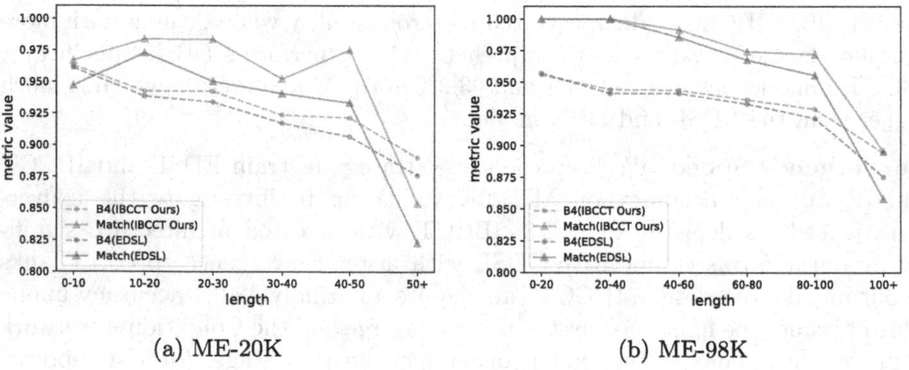

(a) ME-20K (b) ME-98K

Fig. 4. Model performance with different expression lengths on ME- 20K and ME-98K.

4.3 Data Augmentation

Data augmentation is critical to avoid overfitting in the training of deep neural networks. In this section, we will show the importance of suitable augmentation and compare the performance with baseline method in two situations: without data augmentation and with triple data augmentation. When without augmentation, we just train the model using the original dataset both for IBCCT and

EDSL. As for data augmentation, EDSL uses three segmentation thresholds as the augmentation. Considering the characteristics of MER, we focus on three kinds deformation-based augmentation: distort, stretch and perspective [7]. From the result shown in Table 2, we can conclude that augmentation strategies boost IBCCT's and EDSL's performance, which proves that data size is critical to the Attention-based model. However, whether with data augmentation or not, IBCCT can defeat EDSL, which proves the efficiency of IBCCT model itself.

Table 2. Performance with triple data augmentation.

DataSet	Methods	Aug	BLEU-4	ROUGH-4	Match	Match-ws
ME-20K	EDSL	✗	93.63	94.81	91.86	92.38
		✓	94.23	95.10	92.70	93.45
	IBCCT	✗	94.15	95.07	90.97	91.55
		✓	94.49	95.29	94.04	94.52
ME-98K	EDSL	✗	92.49	92.86	85.86	86.20
		✓	92.93	93.30	89.00	89.34
	IBCCT	✗	92.58	92.93	86.65	86.83
		✓	93.49	93.80	91.30	91.45

4.4 Hyper-parameters Analysis

Kernel Size: We mainly explore the influence of kernel size when resizing the input image into 112×224 and 160×320. For different input resolutions, there are different optimal kernel sizes. It may not pay off to spend huge resources to adjust such a hyper-parameter, but we hope that our experiments can provide general rules to guide the later research to select a suitable kernel size. The experiments in Fig. 5. are conducted in ME-20K by the IBCCT-base model without data augmentation. As illustrated, the kernel set to 5 can acquire the best performance when the input image size is 112×224 while the optimal choice is 9 when the input size is 160×320. It is reasonable because the kernel size is strongly correlated with the receptive field and a suitable kernel size can guarantee the stability of local correlation.

Not Keeping the Image Ratio: Considering the mathematical expression length may vary drastically, we try to keep image ratio during training. Concretely, we first delete the expression image blank space and then pad the deleted image the ratio to $1:2$. After that, we can resize the padded image into the specified shape 112×224. Another choice is to delete the blank space and directly resize the image into 112×224. The result is shown in Table 3. Interestingly, we find that keeping the image ratio instead destroys the model performance. We argue that this is because excessive padding makes the model difficult to correctly determine the boundary.

Table 3. IBCCT performance when keeping image ratio.

DataSet	keep ratio	B4	R4	Match	Match-WS
ME-20K	✗	94.15	95.07	90.97	91.55
	✓	93.77(−0.38)	94.58(−0.49)	90.63(−0.34)	91.66(+0.11)
ME-98K	✗	92.58	92.93	86.65	86.83
	✓	91.81(−0.77)	92.14(−0.79)	81.92(−4.73)	82.04(−4.79)

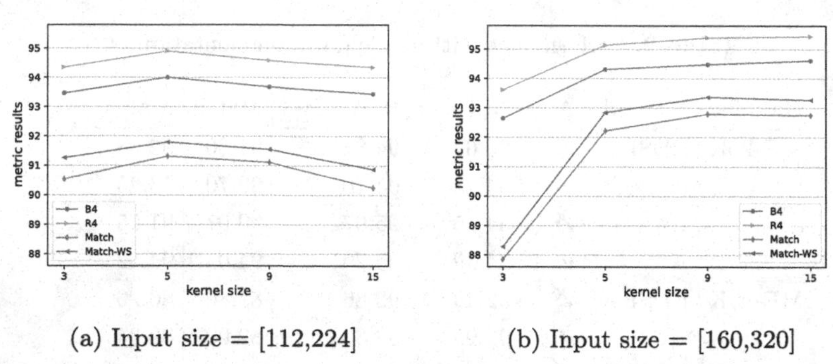

(a) Input size = [112,224]

(b) Input size = [160,320]

Fig. 5. Model performance of different kernel sizes for input size 112×224 and 160×320.

5 Conclusion

MER is a long-standing research topic, but current models still suffer from slow convergence, limited performance, and design complexity of extra backbone network before encoder. Our research provides timely insights on how to design a parameter-efficient model to solve the MER problem. Our IBCCT model comprehensively outperforms the SOTA methods with amazingly lightweight and simplified architecture. The results serve as strong evidence that IBCCT has the potential for other complex long-sequence recognition tasks.

The simplicity of IBCCT allows easy extension for future work and there remain many interesting questions to explore. IBCCT has relatively excellent robustness whether long sequences or complex deformation are encountered, which makes IBCCT have the potential to extend to the field of handwriting mathematical recognition and other structural markups. In the future, we will explore such structural image recognition problems and be devoted to providing a unified solution.

Acknowledgement. This work was supported in part by the National Innovation 2030 Major S&T Project of China under Grant 2020AAA0104203, and in part by the Nature Science Foundation of China under Grant 62006007.

References

1. Blostein, D., Grbavec, A.: Recognition of mathematical notation. In: Handbook of Character Recognition and Document Image Analysis, pp. 557–582. World Scientific (1997)
2. Chu, X., Tian, Z., Zhang, B., et al.: Conditional positional encodings for vision transformers. arXiv preprint arXiv:2102.10882 (2021)
3. Deng, Y., Kanervisto, A., Ling, J., et al.: Image-to-markup generation with coarse-to-fine attention. In: International Conference on Machine Learning, pp. 980–989. PMLR (2017)
4. Dosovitskiy, A., Beyer, L., Kolesnikov, A., et al.: An image is worth 16x16 words: Transformers for image recognition at scale. arXiv preprint arXiv:2010.11929 (2020)
5. Fu, Y., Liu, T., Gao, M., et al.: EDSL: An encoder-decoder architecture with symbol-level features for printed mathematical expression recognition. arXiv preprint arXiv:2007.02517 (2020)
6. Liu, Z., Mao, H., Wu, C.Y., et al.: A convnet for the 2020s. In: Proceedings of the IEEE/CVF Conference on Computer Vision and Pattern Recognition, pp. 11976–11986 (2022)
7. Luo, C., Zhu, Y., Jin, L., et al.: Learn to augment: joint data augmentation and network optimization for text recognition. In: Proceedings of the IEEE/CVF Conference on Computer Vision and Pattern Recognition, pp. 13746–13755 (2020)
8. Okamoto M, Imai H, T.K.: Performance evaluation of a robust method for mathematical expression recognition. In: Proceedings of Sixth International Conference on Document Analysis and Recognition, pp. 121–128. IEEE (2001)
9. Shi, B., Bai, X., Yao, C.: An end-to-end trainable neural network for image-based sequence recognition and its application to scene text recognition. IEEE Trans. Pattern Anal. Mach. Intell. **39**(11), 2298–2304 (2016)
10. Tolstikhin, I.O., et al.: MLP-mixer: An all-MLP architecture for vision. Adv. Neural. Inf. Process. Syst. **34**, 24261–24272 (2021)
11. Trockman, A., Kolter, J.Z.: Patches are all you need? arXiv preprint arXiv:2201.09792 (2022)
12. Vaswani, A., Shazeer, N., Parmar, N., et al.: Attention is all you need. In: Advances in Neural Information Processing Systems, vol. 30 (2017)
13. Wang, Y., Weng, Z., Zhou, Z., et al.: Dual branch network towards accurate printed mathematical expression recognition. In: Pimenidis, E., Angelov, P., Jayne, C., Papaleonidas, A., Aydin, M. (eds.) ICANN 2022. LNCS, vol. 13532, pp. 594–606. Springer, Cham (2022). https://doi.org/10.1007/978-3-031-15937-4_50
14. Wu, C., et al.: Stroke based posterior attention for online handwritten mathematical expression recognition. In: 2020 25th International Conference on Pattern Recognition (ICPR), pp. 2943–2949. IEEE (2021)
15. Yu, W., Luo, M., Zhou, P., et al.: Metaformer is actually what you need for vision. In: Proceedings of the IEEE/CVF Conference on Computer Vision and Pattern Recognition, pp. 10819–10829 (2022)
16. Zhang, J., Du, J., Dai, L.: A GRU-based encoder-decoder approach with attention for online handwritten mathematical expression recognition. In: ICDAR, vol. 1, pp. 902–907. IEEE (2017)

17. Zhang, J., Du, J., Zhang, S., et al.: Watch, attend and parse: an end-to-end neural network based approach to handwritten mathematical expression recognition. Pattern Recognit. **71**, 196–206 (2017)
18. Zhou, K., Yang, J., Loy, C.C., Liu, Z.: Conditional prompt learning for vision-language models. In: Proceedings of the IEEE/CVF Conference on Computer Vision and Pattern Recognition, pp. 16816–16825 (2022)

Knowledge Graph Transformer for Sequential Recommendation

Jinghua Zhu, Yanchang Cui, Zhuohao Zhang, and Heran Xi(✉)

School of Computer Science and Technology,
Heilongjiang University, Harbin 150080, China
xiheran@hlju.edu.cn

Abstract. The problem of sequential recommendation aims at predicting the most likely item that user will interact based on historical interaction sequence. However, the previous methods only consider the proximity correlations among items and neglect the internal correlations when exploiting auxiliary information, and thus are insufficient to obtain accurate item embedding. Inspired by the success of transformer in NLP, we propose a novel Knowledge Graph Transformer for Sequential Recommendation, KGT-SR for brevity. The main idea of KGT-SR is to extract the rich semantic information of items by utilizing knowledge graph and feed the fused position and item information into the transformer to well learn item representation. KGT-SR consists of embedding layer, knowledge extraction layer and prediction layer. Extensive experiments results on three real world recommendation scenarios show that KGT-SR not only outperforms state-of-the-art sequential recommendation methods but also alleviates the problem of data sparsity.

Keywords: Sequential recommendation · Knowledge graph · Graph neural collaborative filtering · Transformer

1 Introduction

With the rapid growth of information in Internet, recommendation systems have become important and necessary for alleviating the problem of information overload and selecting interested information in various Web applications. Users' preferences heavily depend on the context and thus sequential recommendation predicts the next item that users are likely to purchase by analyzing their history behaviors. Many sequential recommendation algorithms [9,14] have been proposed to better understand the sequential history of users. Among these algorithms, self-attention based models [5] have achieved excellent performance by learning the dependency relationships of sequence and capturing the users' current and recent preferences change. Recent research [13,15] have shown that auxiliary information is helpful to improve the recommend performance. Despite their excellent performance, most of the sequential recommendation models only focus on the sequence relationship among items in users' interaction records, and

L. Iliadis et al. (Eds.): ICANN 2023, LNCS 14259, pp. 459–471, 2023.
https://doi.org/10.1007/978-3-031-44223-0_37

ignore the rich semantic information which could enhance the representations of items. Furthermore, the existing sequential recommendation methods cannot deal with the noisy of sequences well.

As a rich source of auxiliary information, Knowledge Graph (KG) can enhance the representations of items because it contains a variety of related information about the items which can help recommendation systems to portray the items and their correlations. We regard KG as a heterogeneous network and use it as the main source of auxiliary information to extract rich semantic information about the items. Many previous studies [11] have proven that KG-based recommendation methods are superior to non-KG methods. Plenty of studies have shown that the dependency relationships between the items in user interaction records contain the users' current and recent preferences which is useful for accurate recommendations.

In this paper, we propose a Knowledge Graph Transformer for Sequential Recommendation (KGT-SR), which simultaneously integrates the rich semantic information of KG and the sequence information in the interaction sequence to improve the accuracy of recommendation and alleviate the problem of data sparsity in recommendation system. First, KGT-SR embeds a learnable position vector for each item in the input sequence and KG. Through learnable position embeddings, KGT-SR can flexibly handle the relative sequence order of the items in the interaction sequence. Then KGT-SR inputs the items in the sequence into knowledge extraction layer to aggregate the rich semantic information about the items and fuse the learnable position information of the items. Finally, KGT-SR uses a transformer to measure the relevance of the items in the interaction sequence from multiple perspectives. KGT-SR can reduce the influence of noise data by learning the dependencies in the interaction sequence and thus improve the accuracy and stability of the recommendation system.

The main contributions of this work are summarized as follows:

- We propose a novel knowledge graph assisted sequential recommendation model that extends the transformer by exploiting knowledge graph to capture the semantic and order information in the sequence.
- We propose to diversify the position embedding schemes that are used to encode the positions of the user-item interactions in a sequence. This is done by encoding the position of the items both in interaction sequence and knowledge graph.
- We conduct extensive experiments on real-world datasets to verify the effectiveness of our model and the experiments' results show that our model outperforms the state-of-art methods.

2 Methodology

In the real sequential recommendation scenario, given an interaction sequence between user u and items: $C^u = \left(C_1^u, C_2^u, \ldots, C_{|C^u|}^u\right)$, where $|C^u|$ represents the sequence length. The corresponding KG is defined as $\mathcal{G} = \{(h, r, t)\}$. During

KGT-SR training, the model relies on the previous interactions to predict the potential items that users are likely to interact. As shown in Fig. 1, we can simply understand that $\left(C_1^u, C_2^u, \ldots, C_{|C^u|-1}^u\right)$ will be used as the input of model and the model will output a transformed result sequence $\left(C_2^u, C_3^u, \ldots, C_{|C^u|}^u\right)$.

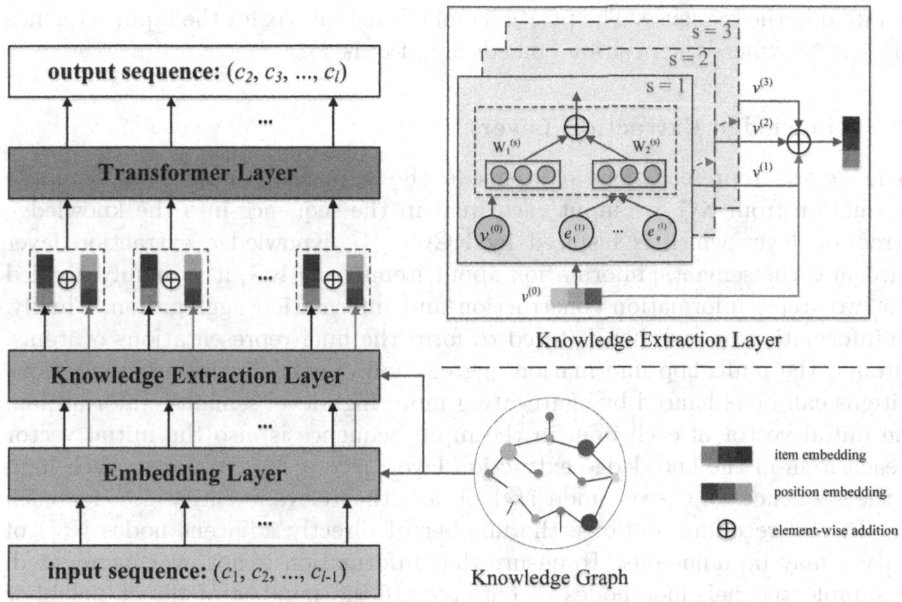

Fig. 1. The overall framework of KGT-SR model. The model consists of three layers: embedding layer, knowledge extraction layer and transformer layer.

2.1 Embedding Layer

First, we convert the user's interaction sequence $C^u = \left(C_1^u, C_2^u, \ldots, C_{|C^u|}^u\right)$ into a fixed-length input sequence $c = (c_1, c_2, \ldots, c_l)$, where l is the maximum sequence length that the model can handle. If the length of C^u is longer than l, we will intercept the last l interactions to form the input sequence c. Otherwise, we will use the padding items to pad on the left side of C^u until the length of C^u reaches l. In different recommendation scenarios, our model needs different sequence lengths to capture the corresponding features for recommendation. In the experiments, we analyze the impact of sequence length on our model in each recommendation scenario. We create a KG embedding matrix $K \in R^{|\omega| \times d}$, where d is the dimension of the embedding vector and ω represents the number of entities in KG. Then we retrieve the item embedding matrix $\mathrm{E} \in R^{|I| \times d}$ in the recommendation system from K, where $|I|$ denotes the number of items in recommendation system. Finally, we retrieve the embedding matrix $\mathrm{M} \in R^{l \times d}$

of the input sequence from E and $M_i = E_{c_i}$ means the item embedding in the input sequence. In this paper, we use the zero vector as the embedding vector to pad the sequence.

The ordinary transformer model [10] constructs a fixed position code for each element in the sequence. However, this setting is unreasonable for sequential recommendation because it will solidify the order of items in the interaction sequence. For the input sequence, we construct a learnable position vector for each item in the sequence. The position embedding matrix for the input sequence is $\mathrm{P} \in R^{l\times d}$, where the position embedding of c_i is P_i.

2.2 Knowledge Extraction Layer

To make the representations of items in the sequence contain rich semantic information from KG, we input each item in the sequence into the knowledge extraction layer which is inspired by KGCF [1]. Knowledge extraction layer aggregates the semantic information about items from KG, it is mainly divided into two steps: information construction and information aggregation. Finally, the information of each hop is fused to form the final representations of items. Through the multi-hop information aggregation operation, the representations of items can be enhanced by aggregating more high-level semantic information. The initial vector of each item in the input sequence is also the initial vector of each item in the knowledge extraction layer: $v^{(0)} = M_{c_i}$. We treat each item in the sequence as a seed node and obtain the relevant entity $e^{(s)}$ for each hop. In real recommendations, the number of directly adjacent nodes $\mathrm{N}(e)$ of entity e may be numerous. To ensure that information is not over aggregated, we sample the neighbor nodes of entity e. If the number of direct neighbor nodes of the entity e is less than q(i.e., $|\mathrm{N}(e)| < q$), we use random sampling with replacement, otherwise we use random sampling without replacement. We define the information of the s-th hop as follows:

$$\begin{cases} m^{(s)}_{v\leftarrow e_q^{(s)}} = \mathrm{w}_1^{(s)} e_q^{(s)} + \mathrm{w}_2^{(s)} \left(v^{(s-1)} \odot e_q^{(s)}\right) \\ m^{(s)}_{v^{(s-1)}\leftarrow v^{(s-1)}} = \mathrm{w}_1^{(s)} v^{(s-1)} \end{cases}, \tag{1}$$

where $m^{(s)}_{v\leftarrow e_q^{(s)}}$ represents the information construction of related entities, $e_q^{(s)}$ is the q-th related entity in the s-th hop, $\mathrm{w}_1^{(s)}$, $\mathrm{w}_2^{(s)} \in R^{d\times d}$ are the mapping matrices, $\mathrm{w}_1^{(s)}$ is the shared matrix, $\odot$ is the Hadamard product. In addition to constructing the information of neighbor-related entities, we also construct the loop information: $m^{(s)}_{v^{(s-1)}\leftarrow v^{(s-1)}}$. The self-loop information retains the original feature information of the previous hop to avoid excessive spread on KG and reduce noise. After completing the information construction, we define the information aggregation of the current hop as follows:

$$v^{(s)} = LeakyRelu\left(m^{(s-1)}_{v^{(s-1)}\leftarrow v^{(s-1)}} + \sum_{e\in e^{(s-1)}} \sum_{e_j\in N(e)} m^{(s)}_{v\leftarrow e_j}\right), \tag{2}$$

where $e^{(s-1)}$ denotes the $(s-1)$-th hop related set of entities, and $|\mathrm{N}(e)|$ denotes the neighbor sample set of entity e. Thus, we obtain the item representation vector of the s-th hop. After obtaining the item representation vector of each hop, we define the information fusion function as follows:

$$v = v^{(0)} + v^{(1)} + \cdots + v^{(s)}. \tag{3}$$

After fusing the item representation of each hop, we can get the input matrix M^{kg} composed of the final representation vector of each item in the sequence. We will update the final representation vector of each item in the sequence to the KG embedding matrix and item embedding matrix. In the next section, we will complete the fusion of information between item embedding and learnable position embedding.

After the items in the input sequence have been passed through the knowledge extraction layer, we obtain the updated KG embedding matrix, item embedding matrix and input sequence embedding matrix. In this part, we will use wise-element addition to achieve the fusion of item information and learnable position information. We define the fusion operation as follows:

$$\widehat{M} = \begin{bmatrix} M_1^{kg} + \mathrm{P}_1 \\ \cdots \\ M_{c_l}^{kg} + \mathrm{P}_{c_l} \end{bmatrix}, \tag{4}$$

where M_i^{kg} is the updated item embedding, P_i is the learnable position vector.

2.3 Transformer Layer

Self-Attention Layer. The scaled dot product attention [10] can be defined as follows:

$$\text{Attention}\left(\mathrm{Q}, \mathrm{K}, \mathrm{V}\right) = \text{softmax}\left(\frac{QK^T}{\sqrt{d}}\right)V, \tag{5}$$

where $\mathrm{Q}, \mathrm{K}, \mathrm{V}$ represent the query, key and value respectively, $\sqrt{d}$ is a scale factor. Intuitively, each row in V represents the embedding vector of a item. In our model, we define the attention function as follows:

$$\text{SATT}(\hat{M}) = \text{Attention}\left(\hat{M}W^Q, \hat{M}W^K, \hat{M}W^V\right), \tag{6}$$

where W^{Q}, W^{K}, $W^{\mathrm{V}} \in R^{d \times d}$ and $\hat{M}$ is the input sequence embedding matrix. In the self-attention layer, it considers all the items in the sequence to calculate a weighted sum. However, in a real sequential recommendation, the model should actively predict the $(t+1)$-th potential item to be interacted by considering the previous t sequence items. Therefore, to avoid information leakage in sequential recommendation (i.e., use future interaction behavior to predict the current potential interaction), we mask all the similarity calculations of Q_i and $K_j (j > i)$.

To measure the correlation weights between the items in the sequence from multiple perspectives, we generalize the single-head attention to the multi-head attention. Following [12], We define multi-head attention as follows:

$$\mathrm{C} = \mathrm{MH}(\widehat{M}) = \mathrm{concat}\left(\mathrm{head}_1, \mathrm{head}_2, \ldots, \mathrm{head}_h\right) W^{(3)}, \tag{7}$$

where $\mathrm{head}_i = \mathrm{Attention}\left(\widehat{M}W_i^Q, \widehat{M}W_i^K, \widehat{M}W_i^V\right)$. After obtaining the output of the multi-head attention, we concatenate the output of each head and finally restore as the shape of the original embedding matrix through linear projection.

Point-Wise Feed-Forward Network. To increase the nonlinearity of the model and the interaction between embedding vector dimensions, we use a point-level two-layer Feed-Forward Network (shared parameters) for all item vectors c_i. We define the Feed-Forward Network function as follows:

$$F_i = FFN\left(C_i\right) = \mathrm{ReLu}\left(C_i W^{(4)} + b^{(1)}\right) W^{(5)} + b^{(2)}, \tag{8}$$

where $W^{(4)}$, $W^{(5)} \in R^{d \times d}$ are the weight matrices and $b^{(1)}$, $b^{(2)} \in R^d$ are the bias vectors. It is worth noting that in order to avoid information leakage in sequential recommendation, we mask the interaction between c_i and c_j $(j > i)$.

To avoid overfitting the model and enable the model to learn abundant features between layers, we define the following functions to regularize the input and pass low-level features to the output layer:

$$\hat{C} = \mathrm{LayerNorm}\ (C + \mathrm{Dropout}(MH(C))), \tag{9}$$

$$\mathrm{F} = LayerNorm\left(\hat{C} + \mathrm{Dropout}\left(\mathrm{LeakyRelu}\left(\hat{C}W^{(4)} + b^{(1)}\right) W^{(5)} + b^{(2)}\right)\right). \tag{10}$$

Stacking Self-attention Layer. For different recommendation scenarios, the model may need to learn more complicated item association information, so we stack multiple self-attention layers to extract more complicated association information between items in the sequence. We define the b-th $(b > 1)$ layer as follows:

$$C^{(b)} = SATT\left(F^{(b-1)}\right), \tag{11}$$

$$F_i^{(b)} = FFN\left(C_i^{(b)}\right), \quad \forall i \in \{1, 2, \ldots, l\}. \tag{12}$$

2.4 Prediction and Loss Function

After the information of each item in the sequence relative to its previous items is adaptively extracted through the b self attention layers, we predict the item that the user will interact with next time based on $F_t^{(b)}$. We use an prediction layer to compute the score of item i, the formula is as follows:

$$y_{i,t} = F_t^{(b)} M_i^T, \tag{13}$$

where $y_{i,t}$ is the score of next interaction between user and item i based on the given previous t interactions, $\mathrm{M} \in R^{|I| \times d}$ is the item embedding matrix. By sorting the scores of candidate items, we can generate a list of recommended items.

In order to obtain the sequence $\mathrm{c} = \{c_1, c_2, \ldots, c_l\}$ with a fixed-length l, we truncate or pad the user's interaction sequence. We define the t-th interaction in the sequence as follows:

$$p_t = \begin{cases} < pad >, & \text{if } c_t \text{ is a padding commdity} \\ c_{t+1}, & 1 \leq t \leq l \\ c^u_{|c^u|}, & t = l \end{cases}, \tag{14}$$

where $< pad >$ represents the item padding in the sequence. Our model takes the sequence c as input and outputs the corresponding sequence. In our model, we apply cross-entropy to construct the loss function as follows:

$$\mathcal{L} = -\sum_{C^u \in C} \sum_{t \in [1,2,\ldots,l]} \left[\log\left(\sigma\left(y_{p_t,t}\right)\right) + \sum_{j \in C^u} \log\left(1 - \sigma\left(y_{j,t}\right)\right) \right]. \tag{15}$$

It is worth noting that when $p_t =< pad >$, we ignore this item.

3 Experiment

3.1 Datasets and Evaluation Metrics

We use three public datasets (MovieLens[1], Last.FM[2] and Book[3]) to evaluate the effectiveness of our model. These sparse datasets are often used in recommendation systems, as shown in Table 1. In experiments, we mainly use Hit-ratio@k [6] and NDCG@k [4] as evaluation metrics.

Table 1. Datasets Statistics.

Dataset	users	items	interactions	entities	relations	KG triples
Movie	6036	2445	753772	182011	12	160519
music	1872	3846	42346	9366	60	15518
book	17860	14967	139746	77903	25	151500

[1] https://grouplens.org/datasets/movielens/.
[2] https://grouplens.org/datasets/hetrec-2011/.
[3] http://www.informatik.uni-freiburg.de/cziegler/BX/.

3.2 Experiment Setup

For each dataset, we discard the users whose historical interaction sequence length is less than 5 and divide the historical interaction sequence C^u of each user into three parts: (1) the most recent interaction $C^u_{|C^u|}$ as the test interaction, (2) the second recent interaction $C^u_{|C^u|-1}$ which is close to the current interaction as the validation interaction, (3) the remaining part of the input sequence as the training sequence of the model. It is worth noting that when we are testing, the input sequence includes training interaction and validation interaction. In order to ensure the fairness of comparative experiments, we keep the same validation and test sets for comparative experiments and each comparative experiment uses its original paper settings or default parameters in the code. KGT-SR's hyper-parameter settings are shown in Table 2, where l denotes the maximum sequence length that the model can process, d denotes the dimension of embedding vector, b denotes the number of self-attention blocks, h is the number of heads in multi-head attention, q is the number of neighbor samples, and s is the hop of aggregated information.

Table 2. Hyper-parameter settings.

Dataset	l	d	b	h	q	s
Movie	60	96	3	2	6	2
music	100	64	3	1	4	3
book	80	64	2	2	4	3

3.3 Baselines

The comparision benchmarks of this paper is as follows:

- **NCF** [2]. NCF uses neural network architecture instead of dot product, it solves the dot product in matrix factorization which is not enough to capture the complex structural interaction information.
- **LRML** [8]. LRML is a recommendation method based on metric learning, which aims to learn the correlations between users and items.
- **Caser** [7]. Caser applies both hierarchical and vertical convolutional networks to model the historical interactions of users.
- **AttRec** [17]. AttRec uses self-attention mechanism to model the dependencies and importance of users' short-term behavior patterns.
- **GRU4Rec+** [3]. GRU4Rec+ uses an improved loss function and sampling strategy to improve GRU4Rec's recommendation accuracy.
- **TCN** [16]. TCN makes improvements and refinements in the CNN part and adds a residual mechanism to the deep CNN.
- **SASRec** [5]. SASRec uses the transformer to process user's historical interaction sequence to predict the user's next interaction behavior.

3.4 Analysis of Results

The experimental results of all models are shown in Table 3 and Fig. 2, where Table 3 shows the performance comparison on NDCG@k evaluation metric of all models, and Fig. 2 shows the performance comparison on hit@k evaluation metric of all models. By comparing and analyzing the experimental results of each model, we can draw the following conclusions:

Table 3. Performance comparison in terms of NDCG@k on all datasets.

Model	Movie			music			book		
	@1	@5	@10	@1	@5	@10	@1	@5	@10
NCF	0.281	0.431	0.507	0.124	0.144	0.171	0.081	0.092	0.120
LRML	0.228	0.400	0.525	0.094	0.124	0.144	0.075	0.089	0.109
Caser	0.219	0.383	0.427	0.084	0.123	0.141	0.076	0.100	0.108
AttRec	0.209	0.371	0.407	0.099	0.112	0.135	0.080	0.098	0.115
GRU4Rec+	0.106	0.122	0.153	0.082	0.102	0.130	0.068	0.095	0.105
TCN	0.333	0.500	0.540	0.240	0.332	0.363	0.138	0.291	0.320
SASRec	0.322	0.492	0.540	0.220	0.346	0.385	0.190	0.302	0.331
KGT-SR	**0.335**	**0.512**	**0.557**	**0.242**	**0.365**	**0.400**	**0.200**	**0.316**	**0.500**

- In general, we can find that all models perform better on the movie dataset than on the music and book datasets. In addition, we can also find that the performance of all models on the book dataset is the worst. Because compared with the music and book dataset, the movie dataset is denser and more conducive to model learning.
- Compare the performance of the models on the three datasets, we can find that the performance of the sequential recommendation models are mostly better than the global recommendation models because sequential models can learn personalized interaction information in user interaction sequences. However, in the case of relatively sparse data, some sequential models cannot learn the sequence of items well, which results in poor performance. Especially simple sequential models such as GRU4Rec+ are easily affected by data sparsity and noise data. Some can see that GRU4Rec+'s performance is not very good from the experimental results.
- We can see that the performance of TCN is better than the Caser model on all three datasets. Compared with Caser, TCN improves and refines the CNN part and adds the residual mechanism to the deep CNN. TCN proposes a high-level representation that can be extracted from short and long-range item dependency, which improves the performance of the model.
- For the experimental results of all sequential recommendation models, we can find that KGT-SR outperforms all comparison models on three datasets. At

the same time, the performance of KGT-SR is better than all global recommendation models. Because KGT-SR not only considers the sequence information in the users' interaction records but also takes into account the rich semantic information of the items, KGT-SR can more accurately mine the correlations between the items, which enhances the expression ability of the model and improves the recommendation accuracy.

3.5 Parameter Sensitivity

The KGT-SR is mainly affected by six hyper-parameters. l, d and b are the first type of hyper-parameters, where l is the maximum sequence length that the model can handle, d is the dimension of embedding vector, b denotes the number of self-attention blocks, h denotes the number of multi-head attention heads. From Tables 4, 5, 6 and 7, we can see that for movie, music and book dataset, when $l = 60, 100, 80$, $d = 96, 64, 64$, $b = 3, 3, 2$, $h = 2, 1, 2$, KGT-SR achieves optimal performance. In different recommendation scenarios, the users' historical information has different effects on the users' current interaction behavior. The dimension of embedding vector also affects the information amount of model fusion. The second type of hyper-parameters are q and s, where q represents the number of neighbor samples and s represents the order of the fusion information. These two parameters determine how much semantic information about the item is fused from the KG. From Tables 8 and 9, we can see that for the movie, music and book datasets, when $q = 6, 4, 4$, $s = 2, 3, 3$, KGT-SR achieves the best performance.

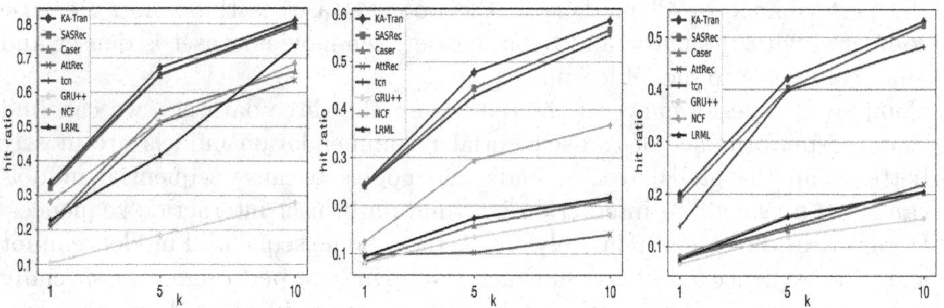

Fig. 2. The result of hit@k on movie, music and book.

Table 4. The hit@10 results of KGT-SR with different input sequence lengths.

l	20	40	60	80	100
Movie	0.630	0.753	0.768	0.726	0.700
music	0.468	0.487	0.488	0.495	0.533
book	0.477	0.506	0.517	0.529	0.516

Table 5. The hit@10 results of KGT-SR with different embedding dimensions.

d	32	48	64	80	96	112
Movie	0.700	0.720	0.740	0.746	0.810	0.691
music	0.496	0.524	0.548	0.533	0.530	0.526
book	0.524	0.525	0.529	0.521	0.518	0.514

Table 6. The hit@10 results of KGT-SR with different self-attention blocks.

b	1	2	3	4
Movie	0.705	0.767	0.7829	0.734
music	0.446	0.551	0.554	0.527
book	0.465	0.529	0.509	0.502

Table 7. The hit@10 results of KGT-SR with different heads of multi-head attention.

h	1	2	4	6	8
Movie	0.780	0.783	0.726	0.721	0.715
music	0.540	0.506	0.487	0.482	0.474
book	0.500	0.511	0.506	0.510	0.490

Table 8. The hit@10 results of KGT-SR with different sizes of neighbor sample.

q	2	4	6	8	10
Movie	0.783	0.789	0.795	0.778	0.773
music	0.574	0.577	0.573	0.568	0.567
book	0.524	0.530	0.510	0.506	0.500

Table 9. The hit@10 results of KGT-SR with different hops of aggregation information.

s	2	3	4	5
Movie	0.811	0.778	0.786	0.777
music	0.576	0.586	0.573	0.547
book	0.526	0.530	0.513	0.503

4 Conclusion

In this paper, we propose a new knowledge graph auxiliary sequence recommendation model, referred to as KGT-SR. KGT-SR makes good use of the auxiliary information of items in the knowledge graph, feeds back the fused position and item information to the converter, and integrates the sequential information in the interactive sequence to extend the converter. We implemented a variety of location embedding schemes by encoding location information in interactive sequences and knowledge graphs. To validate the above work, we conducted extensive experiments on three real-world datasets. The experimental results showed that KGT-SR outperformed state-of-the-art sequential recommendation baselines in terms of accuracy, alleviated the problem of data sparsity, and also improved the interpretability of recommender systems by leveraging the link relationships between items in the knowledge and user interaction history.

Acknowledgement. This work was supported by the Natural Science Foundation of Heilongjiang Province of China[grant numbers LH2022F045].

References

1. Cai, M., Zhu, J.: Knowledge-aware graph collaborative filtering for recommender systems. In: 2019 15th International Conference on Mobile Ad-Hoc and Sensor Networks (MSN), pp. 7–12. IEEE (2019)
2. He, X., Liao, L., Zhang, H., Nie, L., Hu, X., Chua, T.S.: Neural collaborative filtering. In: Proceedings of the 26th International Conference on World Wide Web, pp. 173–182 (2017)
3. Hidasi, B., Karatzoglou, A.: Recurrent neural networks with top-k gains for session-based recommendations. In: Proceedings of the 27th ACM International Conference on Information and Knowledge Management, pp. 843–852 (2018)
4. Järvelin, K., Kekäläinen, J.: IR evaluation methods for retrieving highly relevant documents. In: ACM SIGIR Forum, vol. 51, pp. 243–250. ACM New York, NY, USA (2017)
5. Kang, W.C., McAuley, J.: Self-attentive sequential recommendation. In: 2018 IEEE International Conference on Data Mining (ICDM), pp. 197–206. IEEE (2018). https://arxiv.org/pdf/1808.09781
6. Karypis, G.: Evaluation of item-based top-n recommendation algorithms. In: Proceedings of the Tenth International Conference on Information and Knowledge Management, pp. 247–254 (2001)
7. Tang, J., Wang, K.: Personalized top-n sequential recommendation via convolutional sequence embedding. In: Proceedings of the Eleventh ACM International Conference on Web Search and Data Mining, pp. 565–573 (2018)
8. Tay, Y., Anh Tuan, L., Hui, S.C.: Latent relational metric learning via memory-based attention for collaborative ranking. In: Proceedings of the 2018 World Wide Web Conference, pp. 729–739 (2018)
9. Tian, Y., Chang, J., Niu, Y., Song, Y., Li, C.: When multi-level meets multi-interest: a multi-grained neural model for sequential recommendation. In: Annual International ACM SIGIR Conference on Research and Development in Information Retrieval, pp. 1632–1641 (2022)
10. Vaswani, A., et al.: Attention is all you need. arXiv preprint arXiv:1706.03762 (2017)
11. Wang, H., et al.: Ripplenet: propagating user preferences on the knowledge graph for recommender systems. In: Proceedings of the 27th ACM International Conference on Information and Knowledge Management, pp. 417–426 (2018)

12. Wang, S., Hu, L., Wang, Y., Cao, L., Sheng, Q.Z., Orgun, M.: Sequential recommender systems: challenges, progress and prospects. arXiv preprint arXiv:2001.04830 (2019)
13. Wang, Z., Guangyan, L., Tan, H., Chen, Q., Liu, X.: CKAN: collaborative knowledge-aware attentive network for recommender systems, pp. 219–228 (2020)
14. Xie, Y., Zhou, P., Kim, S.: Decoupled side information fusion for sequential recommendation, pp. 1611–1621 (2022)
15. Yang, Y., Huang, C., Xia, L., Li, C.: Knowledge graph contrastive learning for recommendation, pp. 1434–1443 (2022)
16. Yuan, F., Karatzoglou, A., Arapakis, I., Jose, J.M., He, X.: A simple convolutional generative network for next item recommendation. In: Proceedings of the Twelfth ACM International Conference on Web Search and Data Mining, pp. 582–590 (2019)
17. Zhang, S., Tay, Y., Yao, L., Sun, A.: Next item recommendation with self-attention. In: arXiv preprint arXiv:1808.06414 (2018)

LorenTzE: Temporal Knowledge Graph Embedding Based on Lorentz Transformation

Ningyuan Li[1], Haihong E[1(✉)], Li Shi[2], Xueyuan Lin[1], Meina Song[1], and Yuhan Li[3]

[1] School of Computer Science, Beijing University of Posts and Telecommunications, Beijing 100876, China
ehaihong@bupt.edu.cn

[2] National Computer Network Emergency Response Technical Team/Coordination Center of China, Beijing 100029, China

[3] School of Artificial Intelligence, Beijing University of Posts and Telecommunications, Beijing 100876, China

Abstract. Inferring missing facts in knowledge graphs(KGs) has been proved to be a significant task due to the incompleteness problem. Temporal knowledge graphs(TKGs) in which each fact is incorporated with a timestamp to model the dynamic properties of facts, suffer from the incompleteness either. Thus temporal knowledge graph completion(TKGC) is introduced to infer missing dynamic facts. However, most of the existing TKGC models are proposed based on existing static KG embedding models and then try to learn embeddings for timestamps and incorporate them into the score functions, which, in several cases, impairs models' expressivity and interpretabilities. In this paper, we provide a novel physical view for TKGC and propose LorenTzE, an embedding based model inspired by Lorentz transformation [1] in which each embedding is endowed with physical meanings. We also prove that LorenTzE is capable of modeling various relation patterns under temporal settings. Experimental results on three main TKGC benchmarks demonstrate the effectiveness and superiorities to several static and temporal models of our proposed method.

Keywords: Temporal Knowledge Graph · Lorentz Transformation · Temporal Knowledge Graph Completion

1 Introduction

Knowledge Graphs(KGs) store various facts in the form of (h, r, t) in which r is a real-world relation while h and t represent head entity and tail entity entailed in r. KGs are prevalent as well as crucial in many downstream applications such as recommender systems [2], information retrieval [3] and question answering [4]. However, in practice, most KGs are incomplete which generates the motivation

L. Iliadis et al. (Eds.): ICANN 2023, LNCS 14259, pp. 472–484, 2023.
https://doi.org/10.1007/978-3-031-44223-0_38

of developing knowledge graph completion(KGC) models to infer missing facts in KGs. Among existing KGC approaches, knowledge graph embedding turns out to be an effective method, in which entities and relations are embedded into low dimensional space and during the training process, those embedding representations are gradually adjusted for evaluating scores of potential missing facts afterwards.

Traditional KGs can be viewed as a static snapshot of real-world facts, which ignores the constraints between time and plausibility of facts. In other words, triplets in traditional KGs may not be true perpetually. Thus temporal knowledge graphs(TKGs) are introduced to model dynamic properties of facts, in which each fact is associated with a timestamp τ. Consequently, each fact in TKGs is represented as a quadruple (h, r, t, τ) indicating that (h, r, t) holds at timestamp τ. There are several well-known TKGs like: Integrated Crisis Early Warning System(ICEWS) and Global Database of Events, Language, and Tone (GDELT).

However, inevitably, TKGs suffer from the incompleteness problem either, which generates the extension from KGC to temporal knowledge graph completion(TKGC) in order to inferr missing facts in TKGs. Most of the existing approaches tend to extend static KGC models to TKGs just through embedding timestamps into the low dimensional space and proposing new score functions to take temporal information into consideration during inference. Although, to a certain extent, this idea turns out to be effective, physical meanings of time in these models are significantly neglected, which intensifies the lack of interpretabilities of embedding based models. Besides, for some TKGC models which are designed in the way mentioned above, their capablilities of modeling different relation patterns are impaired. We will detail to this in the third section.

In this paper, we consider TKGC from a novel physical point of view in which entities, relations and timestamps have their corresponding physical meanings. Entities are considered as various points in four dimensional spacetime whose coordinates are observed from its entity-specific coordinate system, while relations describe relative motions between any two coordinate systems. Under this settings, inspired by the Lorentz transformation formula, we propose LorenTzE, an embedding based model without any static KGC model prototypes. In physics, the Lorentz transformations are linear transformations from a coordinate frame in spacetime to another frame that moves at a constant velocity relative to the former. In LorenTzE, observed three-dimensional coordinates of entities as well as relative motions defined by relations are embedded into vector space. Besides, apart from a three dimensional spatial coordinate, each entity possesses a time dimension value which is dependent on an entity specific vector and a timestamp specific matrix. Then, through Lorentz transformation, the head entity's coordinates will be transformed to another coordinates in the tail entity specific coordinate system with another time dimension value due to the relative motion defined by a relation. Afterwards we define and utilize the scoring function $f_r(\mathbf{h}, \mathbf{t})$ in the tail entity specific coordinates system to compute the confidence of (h, r, t, τ) being true. Additionally, we also prove that LorenTzE is fully expressive and is capable of modeling various properties of relations including antisymmetry, inversion and composition.

Our contributions are as follows:

- We model the TKGC task in a novel background and propose LorenTzE, which to our best knowledge is the first model that solves TKGC task from a physical view and provides better interpretabilities than common embedding based TKGC models.
- We prove that LorenTzE is capable of modeling various relation patterns including inversion, anti-symmetry and composition, under temporal settings.
- Experimental results show that LorenTzE achieves better performances than several classic KGC and TKGC models on three standard TKG datasets.

2 Related Work

2.1 Static Knowledge Graph Embedding

Numerous efforts have been devoted into static KG embedding learnings, which can be approximately divided into two categories: translation-based models and bilinear models. TransE [5] is one of the most representative translation-based models, which regards relation r as a translation in the embedding space operating on head entity h and resulting a vector close to tail entity t, i.e. $\mathbf{h}+\mathbf{r} \approx \mathbf{t}$. Subsequently, there emerge several improvements based on TransE such as TransH [6] and TransR [7] which project entity embeddings into relation specific hyperplane and relation specific space before processing translation r from h to t. RotatE [8] embeds entities and relations into complex space and views relations as rotation operations from h to t in complex space. RESCAL [9], Dismult [10] and ComplEx [11] are representative bilinear models which intend to score missing facts by matching latent semantics of entities and relations. In RESCAL, each relation is embedded as a full rank matrix which is used together with two entity embedding vectors to compute a bilinear product score. Due to the proneness to overfitting of RESCAL, Dismult constrains the relation matrices in RESCAL to be diagonal. ComplEx extends Dismult to complex space, in which entities have conjugated embeddings when they serve as different elements (heads or tails) in multiple facts.

2.2 Temporal Knowledge Graph Embedding

Temporal knowledge graphs are introduced to model the dynamic properties of real-world facts, which, however, suffers from incompleteness as KGs do. Hence, more efforts are being devoted into TKGC tasks. TTransE [12] is the first TKGC model which extend TransE to TKGs by naturally embedding timestamps into low dimensional space and adding time embeddings into the translation functions i.e. $\mathbf{h}+\mathbf{r}+\tau=\mathbf{t}$. HyTE [13] can be viewed as an extension of TransH, in which entity embeddings and relations embeddings are projected onto a timestamp specific hyperplane before calculating the distance between $\mathbf{h}+\mathbf{r}$ and $\mathbf{t}$. TA-TransE and TA-Dismult [14] create time-aware representations by introducing recurrent neural networks and utilizing relations and characters in timestamps as inputs.

Then replace relation embeddings in TransE and Dismult with the obtained time-aware representations. Diachronic embeddings [15] are proposed to model temporal information at any timestamps through combining entity embeddings with timestamp embeddings which results different hidden entity embeddings at different time. ConT [16] is a TKGC model based on Tucker decomposition, which learns a timestamp specific core tensor for Tucker decomposition at each timestamp in order to capture temporal properties under TKG settings. TeRo [17] embeds time into complex vector space and the time embeddings operate rotations on entity embeddings before a score is calculated by the score function of TransE. BoxTE [18] extends BoxE [19] to TKGC task by introducing time bumps to generate time embeddings, which are incorporated in the final entity embeddings to provide relation specific dynamic information. However, for most of the extended TKGC models above, the introduction of time impairs the interpretability or intuitions of the models.

3 Proposed Method

3.1 Notations and Task Definition

Notations. In this paper, lower case letters denote scalars, lower case letters in bold denote vectors, while upper case letters represent matrices. Specially, $\mathcal{E}$, $\mathcal{R}$ and $\mathcal{T}$ represent all the entities, relation and timestamps respectively. While $|\mathcal{E}|$ and $|\mathcal{R}|$ denote the number of entities and relations. For vectors $\mathbf{v}_1, \mathbf{v}_2 \in \mathbb{R}^d$, $\mathbf{v}_1 * \mathbf{v}_2$ denotes the element-wise product of $\mathbf{v}_1$ and $\mathbf{v}_2$, $\langle \mathbf{v}_1, \mathbf{v}_2 \rangle = \mathbf{v}_1^T \mathbf{v}_2$ represents the inner product of $\mathbf{v}_1$ and $\mathbf{v}_2$. As for $[\mathbf{v}_1; \mathbf{v}_2]$, it denotes the concatenation of $\mathbf{v}_1$ and $\mathbf{v}_2$.

Temporal Knowledge Graph Completion. TKG can be considered as a sequence of graphs i.e. $\mathcal{G} = \{G_1 ... G_n\}$ in which $G_i = \{(h, r, t, \tau_i)\}$ where $h, t \in \mathcal{E}$, $r \in \mathcal{R}$ and $\tau_i \in \mathcal{T}$. The TKGC task aims to generate ranks of candidate entities given queries $(h, r, ?, \tau_i)$ or $(?, r, t, \tau_i)$ where $(h, r, t) \notin G_i$ but (h, r, t, τ_i) is actually true however missed in the TKG.

3.2 Lorentz Transformation

Lorentz transformations are linear transformations from a coordinate frame in spacetime to another frame that moves at a constant velocity relative to the former. In other words, an object o whose spacetime coordinates (x,y,z,t) observed in coordinate frame A, can have a totally different coordinates even a different time when o is observed from B if B moves at a constant but high velocity relative to A. For simplicity, in the common form of Lorentz transformation, the relative velocity is confined to the x axis direction, which can be written as below:

$$\begin{cases} t' = \gamma\left(t - \frac{vx}{c^2}\right) \\ x' = \gamma\left(x - vt\right) \\ y' = y \\ z' = z \end{cases}$$

where c is the light speed and $\gamma = (1 - \frac{v^2}{c^2})^{-\frac{1}{2}}$ is called Lorentz factor. From the calculation of γ, we can discover a latent constraint which is that the relative velocity v has to be smaller than light speed c to ensure the square root making sense.

However, in general cases, the relative motions between any two coordinate frames can be in arbitrary directions. The main idea of the derivation of general form of Lorentz Transformation can be described as: first compute the angles between the relative velocity and x, y, z axis and then rotating the coordinate frame so that the x axis is aligned with the relative velocity. Finally leverage formulae in the simple form above to obtain the general version. And the formulae are:

$$\begin{bmatrix} t' \\ x' \\ y' \\ z' \end{bmatrix} = \begin{bmatrix} \gamma & \frac{-\gamma v_x}{c} & \frac{-\gamma v_y}{c} & \frac{-\gamma v_z}{c} \\ \frac{-\gamma v_x}{c} & 1 + (\gamma - 1)\frac{v_x^2}{v^2} & (\gamma - 1)\frac{v_x v_y}{v^2} & (\gamma - 1)\frac{v_x v_z}{v^2} \\ \frac{-\gamma v_y}{c} & (\gamma - 1)\frac{v_y v_x}{v^2} & 1 + (\gamma - 1)\frac{v_y^2}{v^2} & (\gamma - 1)\frac{v_y v_z}{v^2} \\ \frac{-\gamma v_z}{c} & (\gamma - 1)\frac{v_z v_x}{v^2} & (\gamma - 1)\frac{v_z v_y}{v^2} & 1 + (\gamma - 1)\frac{v_z^2}{v^2} \end{bmatrix} \begin{bmatrix} t \\ x \\ y \\ z \end{bmatrix}$$

where γ is the Lorentz factor and v_x, v_y, v_z denotes projections of the relative velocity on x, y, z axis (Fig. 1).

3.3 LorenTzE

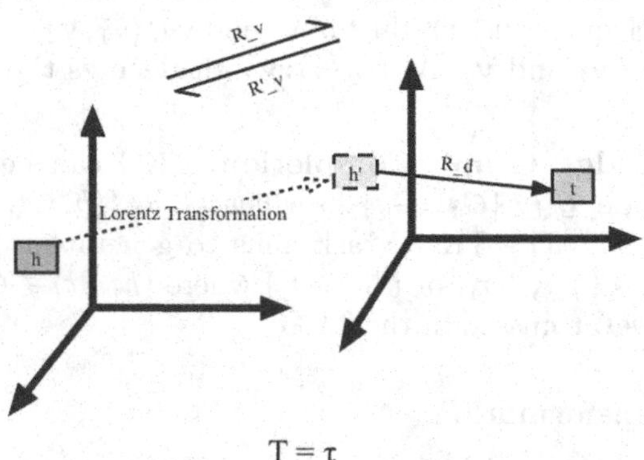

Fig. 1. Translation process of LorenTzE

Relation Specific Lorentz Transformation. In LorenTzE, each $r \in \mathcal{R}$ defines a Lorentz transformation from the coordinates frame of the head to the coordinates frame of the tail, which is denoted by three vectors $\mathbf{r_x}, \mathbf{r_y}, \mathbf{r_z} \in \mathbb{R}^d$ and describe the projections of relative velocity on x, y, z axis. However, considering the constraint that relative velocities have to be smaller than light speed, in LorenTzE, we set $c = 1.0$ and use $sigmoid(\mathbf{r_v})$ to denote $\frac{v}{c}$ where $\mathbf{r_v} = \sqrt{\mathbf{r_x}^2 + \mathbf{r_y}^2 + \mathbf{r_z}^2}$ is the original relative velocity. Besides, when processing Lorentz Transformation, a time dimension vector $\mathbf{h}_\tau \in \mathbb{R}^d$ is needed which will be introduced in the following sections.

Entity and Relation Embedding. In LorenTzE, each entity $h \in \mathcal{E}$ is represented by three vectors $\mathbf{h_x}, \mathbf{h_y}, \mathbf{h_z} \in \mathbb{R}^d$ which together denote its three dimension spatial coordinates observed from its **entity specific coordinates frame.** These three vectors are completely independent on each other. While, each $r \in \mathcal{R}$, apart from the Lorentz transformation defined by r, is also represented by three vectors $\mathbf{d_{rx}}, \mathbf{d_{ry}}, \mathbf{d_{rz}} \in \mathbb{R}^d$, which are utilized to do the translation in the coordinates frame of the tail entity.

Time Embedding. Intuitively, for $(h, r, t, \tau_i) \in G_i$, the time dimension vector of h should just be the embedding of τ_i, however, we should notice that this τ_i is observed from our point of view instead of from the coordinates frames specific to h or t. We call the timestamps in all quadruples absolute time. Since we cannot define or obtain the relative velocity between each entity specific coordinate frame and the frame where we observe the absolute timestamps, we build a mechanism transforming absolute time to time observed from any entity specific coordinate frame. For each entity $e \in \mathcal{E}$, we define a time core vector $\mathbf{e_{core}} \in \mathbb{R}^m$ and for each $\tau \in \mathcal{T}$, we define a transform matrix $\mathbf{M}_\tau \in \mathbb{R}^{d \times m}$. Then the final time embedding vector e_τ of e at timestamp τ is computed as follows:

$$\mathbf{e}_\tau = \mathbf{M}_\tau \mathbf{e_{core}}$$

Inspired by BoxTE, the main idea of the transform above is that we use matrix $\mathbf{M}_\tau$ which contains m d-dimensional vectors to capture the temporal information at τ from our absolute vision. While $\mathbf{e_{core}}$ represents the information of relative motion between the e specific coordinate frame and our absolute coordinate frame, which mathematically calculates the linear combination of the m d-dimensional vectors in $\mathbf{M}_\tau$ to give the temporal vector of $\mathbf{e}_\tau$ with respect to its own coordinate frame.

Training and Inference. The loss function of LorenTzE consists of two parts: the spatial loss $\mathcal{L}_s$ and the temporal loss $\mathcal{L}_t$. For a quadruple (h, r, s, τ), we first obtain the time embedding $\mathbf{e}_\tau$ of h with the mechanism we propose above and then through utilizing the general form of Lorentz transformation, we compute the coordinates vectors $(\mathbf{h'_x}, \mathbf{h'_y}, \mathbf{h'_z}, \mathbf{h_\tau}')$ of h in t specific coordinates system:

$$(\mathbf{h'_x}, \mathbf{h'_y}, \mathbf{h'_z}, \mathbf{h_\tau}') = Lorentz_r(\mathbf{h_x}, \mathbf{h_y}, \mathbf{h_z}, \mathbf{e}_\tau)$$

where $Lorentz_r$ represents Lorentz transformation with respect to relative velocity defined by r and $\mathbf{h'_x}, \mathbf{h'_y}, \mathbf{h'_z}, \mathbf{h'_\tau}$ are results of Lorentz transformation. Then we calculate the spatial score and temporal score in the t specific coordinates system:

$$\begin{aligned} score_s(h, r, t, \tau) =& \langle \mathbf{h'_x} + \mathbf{d_{rx}}, \mathbf{t_x} \rangle + \langle \mathbf{h'_y} + \mathbf{d_{ry}}, \mathbf{t_y} \rangle + \langle \mathbf{h'_z} + \mathbf{d_{rz}}, \mathbf{t_z} \rangle \\ score_t(h, r, t, \tau) =& \langle \mathbf{h'_\tau}, \mathbf{t_\tau} \rangle \end{aligned}$$

And the spatial and temporal loss function can be defined as:

$$\begin{aligned} \mathcal{L}_s &= -\log \sigma(score_s(h, r, t, \tau)) \\ \mathcal{L}_t &= -\log \sigma(score_t(h, r, t, \tau)) \end{aligned}$$

The final loss $\mathcal{L}$ is calculated as:

$$\mathcal{L} = \alpha\mathcal{L}_s + (1-\alpha)\mathcal{L}_t$$

where α controls the contributions of spatial loss and temporal loss.

During training process, we leverage negative sampling to effectively optimize LorenTzE. We propose the following loss function incorporating negative loss:

$$\mathcal{L}_{train} = -\mathcal{L}(h,r,t,\tau) - \frac{1}{n}\sum_{i=1}^{n}\mathcal{L}(h'_i,r_i,t'_i,\tau)$$

where n is the number of negative quadruples and (h'_i,r,t'_i,τ) is the $i-th$ negative quadruple.

3.4 Properties

Table 1. Properties of multiple KGC and TKGC models

Model	Temporal	Inverse	Anti-symmetry	Composition
TransE	✗	✓	✓	✓
RotatE	✗	✓	✓	✓
HyTE	✓	✗	✓	✗
TTransE	✓	✗	✓	✗
TA-TransE	✓	✗	✓	✗
DE-TransE	✓	✗	✓	✗
TeRo	✓	✗	✓	✗
BoxTE	✓	✓	✓	✗
LorenTzE	✓	✓	✓	✓

In this section, first we give the definition of various relation patterns and then discuss the issue that for some TKGC models extended from static KGC models, the incorporation of time embeddings impairs their abilities to model relations patterns. And finally, we prove that LorenTzE is able to model various relation patterns including anti-symmetry, inversion and transition.

Definition 1. For relation r, and $\forall h,\ t,\ \tau$, if $r(h,t,\tau)$ then,

$$\neg r(t,h,\tau)$$

we call r is antisymmetric.

Definition 2. For relation r, and $\forall h,\ t,\ \tau$, if $r(h,t,\tau))$ then,

$$\exists r',\ r'(t,h,\tau)$$

we call r is invertible.

Definition 3. For relation r_1, r_2, and $\forall h,\ t,\ q,\ \tau$, if $r_1(h,t,\tau) \wedge r_2(t,q,\tau)$ then,

$$\exists r_3,\ r_3(h,q,\tau)$$

we call r is transitive(composition property).

It is noted that many static-model-based TKGC models have difficulties in modeling different relation patterns under temporal settings. For example, many TransE based TKGC models lost the capabilities to model inverse and composition properties. The detailed information is listed in Table 1.

Now we demonstrate that LorenTzE can model relation patterns including: inversion, anti-symmetry and composition.

Lemma 1. LorenTzE can model inverse relations.

Proof. Since Lorentz transformation is inverse, let

$$\begin{aligned} \mathbf{d_{rx}}, \mathbf{d_{ry}}, \mathbf{d_{rx}} &= \mathbf{0} \\ \mathbf{r_x} &= -\mathbf{r'_x} \\ \mathbf{r_y} &= -\mathbf{r'_y} \\ \mathbf{r_z} &= -\mathbf{r'_z} \end{aligned}$$

then for $\forall h, t$, if $r(h,t,\tau)$ holds, we have $r'(t,h,\tau)$

Lemma 2. LorenTzE can model anti-symmetric relations.

Proof. Let $\mathbf{d_{rx}}, \mathbf{d_{ry}}, \mathbf{d_{rx}} = \mathbf{0}$ and $\mathbf{r_x}, \mathbf{r_y}, \mathbf{r_z} \neq \mathbf{0}$, then for $\forall h, t$, if $r(h,t,\tau)$ holds, we have $\neg r(t,h,\tau)$.

Lemma 3. LorenTzE can model transitive relations.

Proof. Since Lorentz transformation is also transitive, let

$$\begin{aligned} \mathbf{d_{rx}}, \mathbf{d_{ry}}, \mathbf{d_{rx}} &= \mathbf{0} \\ \mathbf{r_{3x}} &= \mathbf{r_{1x}} + \mathbf{r_{2x}} \\ \mathbf{r_{3y}} &= \mathbf{r_{1y}} + \mathbf{r_{2y}} \\ \mathbf{r_{3z}} &= \mathbf{r_{1z}} + \mathbf{r_{2z}} \end{aligned}$$

then for $\forall h, t, q$, if $r_1(h,t,\tau) \wedge r_2(t,q,\tau)$ holds, we have $r'_3(h,q,\tau)$.

Intuitively, the above proofs can be understood from a physical view. First, we consider $\mathbf{d_{rx}}, \mathbf{d_{ry}}, \mathbf{d_{rx}}$ as bias to make the model more expressive. As we set $\mathbf{d_{rx}}, \mathbf{d_{ry}}, \mathbf{d_{rx}}$ to $\mathbf{0}$, a Lorentz transformation is all we do in the translation process. For the proof of inversion, we just find the inverse transformation of the Lorentz transformation defined by relations. It is obvious that anti-symmetry holds for Lorentz transformation. Because the relative speed has a value and a direction which is surely not "symmetric". As for the proof of composition, we find the relative motion between coordinates frames of h and q, which can be computed by adding the two relative speeds together.

4 Experiments

4.1 Experimental Setup

Table 2. Statistics of ICEWS14, ICEWS05-15 and ICEWS18

	N_{train}	N_{valid}	N_{test}	$\mathcal{E}$	$\mathcal{R}$	$\mathcal{T}$
ICEWS14	72,826	8,941	8,963	7,128	230	365
ICEWS0515	386,962	46,275	46,092	10,488	251	4017
GDELT	2,735,685	341,961	341,961	500	20	366

Datasets. We evaluate LorenTzE on three datasets: GDELT [20], ICEWS14 and ICEWS05-15 [14]. GDELT is a subset of Global Database of Events, Language, and Tone, which stores facts of human societal behaviours with timestamps starting from April 1, 2015 to March 31, 2016. ICEWS14 and ICEWS05-15 are subsets of Integrated Crisis Early Warning System (Boschee et al., 2015), which store political events taking place in 2014 and from 2005 to 2015 respectively. Comparatively, GDELT is a dense dataset containing over 2.7 million facts with 500 entities and 20 different relations included. The detailed statistics of the three datasets are shown in Table 2.

Metric. The metrics we use to evaluate our model are: mean reciprocal rank (MRR) and Hits@1/3/10. For N testing queries, the MRR is computed as $MRR = \frac{1}{N}\sum_i \frac{1}{rank_i}$ and Hits@K is calculated as $Hits@K = \frac{1}{N}\sum_i \mathbf{I}(rank_i < K)$, where $\mathbf{I}$ is the indicator function.

Implementation Details. We implement LorenTzE in PyTorch. For all datasets, we train the model for 3000 epochs and set the learning rate = 0.0001, batch size = 1024 for ICEWS14 and GDELT, while 512 for ICEWS05-15. Besides, the embedding dimension is tuned from $\{100, 200, 300\}$, α is tuned from $\{0.25, 0.5, 0.75, 0.9\}$, dropout value is tuned from $\{0.2, 0.4, 0.5, 0.7\}$ and the negative sampling size is tuned from $\{4, 8, 16, 32\}$. We search the optimal hyperparameters according to the metrics on validation sets. For GDELT and ICEWS14, we set the embedding dimension to be 300, α to be 0.75 and negative sampling size to be 16. While the embedding dimension is restricted to 200 and $\alpha = 0.75$, negative size = 8 on ICEWS05-15. As for time embedding dimension, we set it to be 2 for ICEWS14 and 5 for ICEWS05-15 and GDELT.

Baseline Methods. In this paper, we select both static and temporal translation based models as baselines. For the static models, we use TransE and RotatE. While under temporal settings, we select HyTE, TTransE, TA-TransE and DE-TransE. All the results are taken from [15] and [17] (Fig. 2).

Table 3. Results of LorenTzE on ICEWS14, ICEWS05-15 and GDELT.

	ICEWS14				ICEWS05-15				GDELT			
Model	MRR	Hits@1	Hits@3	Hits@10	MRR	Hits@1	Hits@3	Hits@10	MRR	Hits@1	Hits@3	Hits@10
TransE	0.280	9.4	–	63.7	0.294	9.0	–	66.3	0.113	0.0	15.8	31.2
RotatE	**0.418**	**29.1**	**47.8**	69.0	0.304	16.4	35.5	59.5	–	–	–	–
HyTE	0.297	10.8	41.6	65.5	0.316	11.6	44.5	68.1	0.118	0.0	16.5	32.6
TTransE	0.255	7.4	–	60.1	0.271	8.4	–	61.6	0.115	0.0	16.0	31.8
TA-TransE	0.275	9.5	–	62.5	0.299	9.6	–	66.8	–	–	–	–
DE-TransE	0.326	12.4	46.7	68.6	0.314	10.8	45.3	68.5	0.126	0.0	18.1	**35.1**
LorenTzE	0.320	10.2	47.0	**70.4**	**0.354**	**16.8**	**47.1**	**70.8**	**0.176**	**9.4**	**18.6**	34.1

4.2 Results

Table 3 reports results of LorenTzE on three widely used datasets. We can observe that LorenTzE outperforms all the classical translation based KGC as well as TKGC models that we select on ICEWS05-15 and GDELT. Specifically, LorenTzE leads 4% and 5% MRR points on ICEWS05-15 and GDELT respectively. It also surpasses the second best results up to %5.2 and %9.4 Hits@1 points on ICEWS05-15 and GDELT. While, on ICEWS14, LorenTzE is not the best, but still gives competitive results on MRR and Hits@10 comparing to RotatE which is the best baseline that we select on ICEWS14.

4.3 Ablation Study

In this section, we discuss the effects of hyperparameters choices on ICEWS14. To be specific, we study 1) the embedding dimension; 2) α, the ratio between temporal loss and spatial loss; 3) m, the dimension of time embedding.

From the top left figure we can see that the choices of α slightly impact the performance. $\alpha = 0.9$ gives best Hits@3,10 and worst Hits@1 and $\alpha = 0.75$ makes a better trade-off. Besides, given the results of $\alpha = 0.2, 0.5$, we argue that both spatial and temporal information contribute to inference missing facts. However, spatial information is more important for relatively more general inference performance, since as Hits@1 fluctuates, Hits@3,10 are constantly improved as the ratio of spatial loss gets higher. Intuitively, spatial information consists of three "dimension" (x,y,z) and predicting more precisely on these three dimension would benefit more for finding the correct answer compared to predicting on the time dimension. From the right figure, we observe that the lowest time dimension $m = 2$ gives the best performance. And Hits@1, 3 drops more drastically than Hits@10 as m goes high. Since the number of time stamps in ICEWS14 is relatively small, we can reasonably think that $m = 2$ is enough for capturing temporal information and larger dimension might cause relatively lower distinctions. From the bottom figure, we can see how embedding dimension affects the performance of LorenTzE. Hits@3, 10 get improved as embedding dimension gets higher, while Hits@1 decreases at the same time.

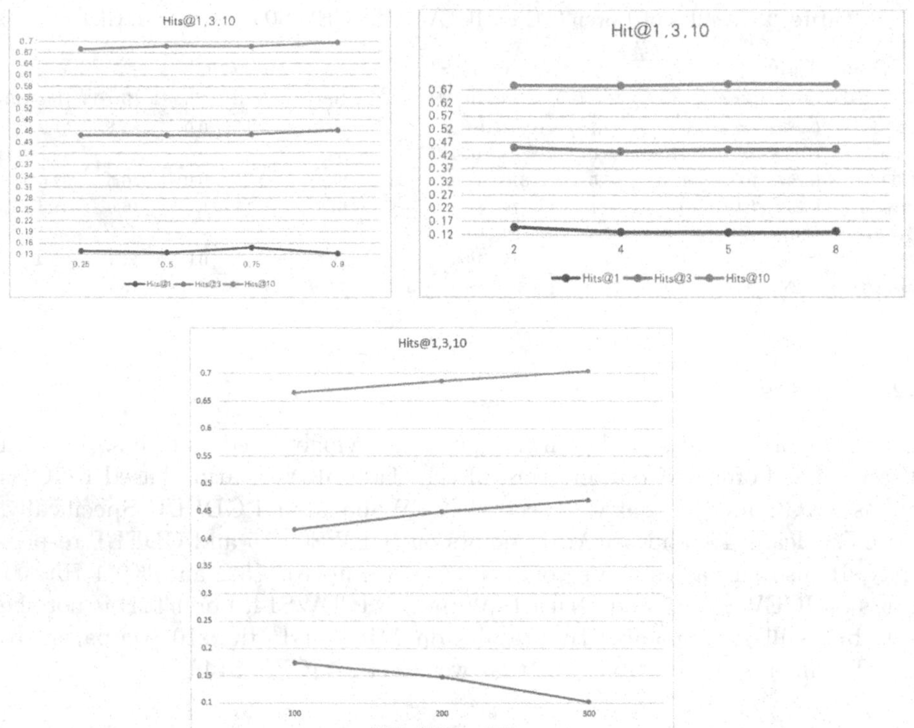

Fig. 2. Influence of alpha(top left),time dimension(top right), dimension(bottom) on Hits@1,3,10(blue, orange and grey lines). The results of various α are evaluated with fixed embedding dimension = 200 and $m = 2$; results of different m are evaluated with fixed embedding dimension = 200 and $\alpha = 0.75$; results of various embedding dimension are evaluated with fixed $\alpha = 0.75$ and $m = 2$. (Color figure online)

5 Conclusion

In this paper, we provide a novel as well as reasonable point of view to model the temporal knowledge graph completion task and propose LorenTzE which is able to model various relation patterns under the temporal settings. LorenTzE is designed upon the Lorentz transformation in physics, which endows embeddings in LorenTzE with physical meanings and makes LorenTzE more interpretable. Experimental results show that our model achieves competitive performances on three TKG datasets. Our future works involve exploring more effective mechanism to generate time embeddings and try to extend LorenTzE to TKG extrapolation tasks.

Acknowledgement. This work is supported by the National Science Foundation of China (Grant No. 62176026) and Beijing Natural Science Foundation (M22009).

References

1. Lorentz, H.A., Lorentz, H.: Electromagnetic phenomena in a system moving with any velocity smaller than that of light. In: Collected Papers, pp. 172–197. Springer, Dordrecht (1937). https://doi.org/10.1007/978-94-015-3445-1_5
2. Hildebrandt, M., et al.: A recommender system for complex real-world applications with nonlinear dependencies and knowledge graph context. In: Hitzler, P., et al. (eds.) ESWC 2019. LNCS, vol. 11503, pp. 179–193. Springer, Cham (2019). https://doi.org/10.1007/978-3-030-21348-0_12
3. Liu, Z., Xiong, C., Sun, M., Liu, Z.: Entity-duet neural ranking: Understanding the role of knowledge graph semantics in neural information retrieval. arXiv preprint arXiv:1805.07591 (2018)
4. Hao, Y., et al.: An end-to-end model for question answering over knowledge base with cross-attention combining global knowledge. In: Proceedings of the 55th Annual Meeting of the Association for Computational Linguistics (Volume 1: Long Papers), pp. 221–231 (2017)
5. Bordes, A., Usunier, N., Garcia-Duran, A., Weston, J., Yakhnenko, O.: Translating embeddings for modeling multi-relational data. In: Advances in Neural Information Processing Systems, vol. 26 (2013)
6. Wang, Z., Zhang, J., Feng, J., Chen, Z.: Knowledge graph embedding by translating on hyperplanes. In: Proceedings of the AAAI Conference on Artificial Intelligence, vol. 28 (2014)
7. Lin, Y., Liu, Z., Sun, M., Liu, Y., Zhu, X.: Learning entity and relation embeddings for knowledge graph completion. In: Proceedings of the AAAI Conference on Artificial Intelligence, vol. 29 (2015)
8. Sun, Z., Deng, Z.H., Nie, J.Y., Tang, J.: Rotate: Knowledge graph embedding by relational rotation in complex space. arXiv preprint arXiv:1902.10197 (2019)
9. Nickel, M., Tresp, V., Kriegel, H.P., et al.: A three-way model for collective learning on multi-relational data. In: Icml, vol. 11, pp. 3104482–3104584 (2011)
10. Yang, B., Yih, W.t., He, X., Gao, J., Deng, L.: Embedding entities and relations for learning and inference in knowledge bases. arXiv preprint arXiv:1412.6575 (2014)
11. Trouillon, T., Welbl, J., Riedel, S., Gaussier, É., Bouchard, G.: Complex embeddings for simple link prediction. In: International Conference on Machine Learning, pp. 2071–2080. PMLR (2016)
12. Leblay, J., Chekol, M.W.: Deriving validity time in knowledge graph. In: Companion Proceedings of the the Web Conference 2018, pp. 1771–1776 (2018)
13. Dasgupta, S.S., Ray, S.N., Talukdar, P.P.: HyTE: hyperplane-based temporally aware knowledge graph embedding. In: EMNLP, pp. 2001–2011 (2018)
14. García-Durán, A., Dumančić, S., Niepert, M.: Learning sequence encoders for temporal knowledge graph completion. arXiv preprint arXiv:1809.03202 (2018)
15. Goel, R., Kazemi, S.M., Brubaker, M., Poupart, P.: Diachronic embedding for temporal knowledge graph completion. In: Proceedings of the AAAI Conference on Artificial Intelligence, vol. 34, pp. 3988–3995 (2020)
16. Ma, Y., Tresp, V., Daxberger, E.A.: Embedding models for episodic knowledge graphs. J. Web Semant. **59**, 100490 (2019)
17. Xu, C., Nayyeri, M., Alkhoury, F., Yazdi, H.S., Lehmann, J.: Tero: A time-aware knowledge graph embedding via temporal rotation. arXiv preprint arXiv:2010.01029 (2020)
18. Messner, J., Abboud, R., Ceylan, I.I.: Temporal knowledge graph completion using box embeddings. In: Proceedings of the AAAI Conference on Artificial Intelligence, vol. 36, pp. 7779–7787 (2022)

19. Abboud, R., Ceylan, I., Lukasiewicz, T., Salvatori, T.: Boxe: a box embedding model for knowledge base completion. Adv. Neural. Inf. Process. Syst. **33**, 9649–9661 (2020)
20. Leetaru, K., Schrodt, P.A.: GDELT: global data on events, location, and tone, 1979–2012. In: ISA Annual Convention, vol. 2, pp. 1–49. Citeseer (2013)

MFT: Multi-scale Fusion Transformer for Infrared and Visible Image Fusion

Chen-Ming Zhang[1], Chengbo Yuan[1], Yong Luo[1], and Xin Zhou[2(✉)]

[1] School of Computer Science and Hubei Key Laboratory of Multimedia and Network Communication Engineering, Wuhan University, Wuhan, China
{mingming,michael.yuan.cb,luoyong}@whu.edu.cn

[2] Jiangxi Science and Technology Normal University, Nanchang, China
zhouxin@jxstnu.edu.cn

Abstract. This paper studies the problem of fusing the infrared and visible images to improve the quality of target image. Traditional image fusion algorithms usually utilize convolutional neural network (CNN) for feature extraction and fusion, and thus can only exploit local information. Some recent approaches combines CNN and Transformer to capture long-range dependencies, but the global contextual information in the images still cannot be full exploited. To improve the ability of capturing global information, we propose a novel multi-scale fusion transformer (MFT) to fuse the infrared and visible images. In the encoder of our MFT, a multi-head pooling attention module is utilized to extract both local features and long-range dependencies for the input image. Then a novel dual-branch fusion module is designed to simultaneously exploit the global contextual and infrared-visible complementary information in the fusion process. Experimental results show that the proposed method can effectively improve the subjective visual experience of the infrared-visible fused image, and outperforms many recent and competitive counterparts in terms of most objective evaluation criteria.

Keywords: Image fusion · Infrared-visible · Transformer · Multi-scale

1 Introduction

In the real world, it is often difficult to capture high-quality scene images from a single sensor due to the physical limitations of imaging sensors. The combination of infrared and visible sensors makes image processing and analysis more flexible and comprehensive, and helps to improve the understanding and processing of complex scenes. Recently, infrared and visible image fusion technology has been widely used in diverse fields, such as surveillance [1], intelligent driving [2], military [3], target tracking [4] and medical imaging [5].

Traditional image fusion algorithms have achieved certain success, but there are still some challenges to be addressed, such as the fusion efficiency and quality, and the robustness to changes in lighting and temperature. To address these

L. Iliadis et al. (Eds.): ICANN 2023, LNCS 14259, pp. 485–496, 2023.
https://doi.org/10.1007/978-3-031-44223-0_39

issues, many image fusion algorithms based on deep learning have been proposed in recent years, and significantly advanced image fusion. Existing image fusion algorithms usually extract features using convolutional neural network (CNN) [19–22]. Hence, only the local features can be obtained and the global conextual information may be ignored [23]. Some recent approaches introduce Transformer [15] to capture the long-range dependencies, such as by adding a Transformer branch in the fusion [23], but the global information still cannot be fully exploited.

To remedy this drawback, we propose a novel multi-scale fusion transformer (MFT) for infrared and visible image fusion. In particular, an encoder incorporated with a multi-head pooling attention module is utilized to extract both local and global features at different scales. Then in the fusion process, we integrate the axial attention [17] and multi-head pooling attention to exploit the complementary between the infrared and visible modalities and minimize the information loss.

Our main contributions can be summarized as follows:

- We propose a novel multi-scale auto-encoder network for infrared and image fusion, where multi-head pooling attention is introduced to extract the global contextual information at different scales.
- We design a novel dual-branch module to simultaneously exploit the global contexts and complementary information of the infrared and visible modalities during the fusion process.

We conduct extensive experiments by utilizing the popular MS-COCO [24] and KAIST [25] datasets for training, and TNO [26] dataset for test. The results demonstrates that our method outperforms many existing counterparts in most cases both subjectively and objectively.

2 Related Work

2.1 Image Fusion

Traditional image fusion methods mainly include methods based on sparse representation (SR) [6], multiscale transformation [7], and low-rank representation (LRR) [8]. Although these methods have achieved competitive performance, they have some drawbacks: 1) High-performance fusion heavily relies on manual features [9], and it is difficult to find a universal feature extraction method for different fusion tasks; 2) For methods based on SR and LRR, dictionary learning is very time-consuming, and the runtime of fusion algorithms highly depends on the dictionary learning operator [10]; 3) The generalization ability is poor, and different fusion strategies are often needed for different source image datasets.

In recent years, to address the aforementioned problems, many new image fusion algorithms based on deep learning have been proposed. These algorithms have shown great potential and often achieve better fusion results than traditional methods. For example, Li et al. [11] proposed an image fusion framework that utilizes a pre-trained network, which is the first that uses multi-layer deep features to handle infrared and visible light image fusion tasks. Li and Wu [13] proposed a novel fusion framework based on dense blocks and auto-encoder structures. Ma et al. [14] used generative adversarial networks (GAN) for infrared and visible image fusion tasks.

Due to the powerful nonlinear fitting ability of multi-layer neural networks, deep learning has made good progress in low-level visual tasks in recent years, and more and more convolutional neural network (CNN)-based network models have been applied to the field of image fusion. Among them, the auto-encoder network structure has achieved remarkable achievements in the field of image fusion due to its powerful feature extraction and reconstruction capabilities.

However, due to the inherent defects of CNNS, existing deep learning-based methods often focus on learning spatial local features between source images, without considering the long-term dependencies that exist in source images. Therefore, we introduce global information in the process of feature extraction and fusion to further improve the fusion quality.

2.2 Transformer

The Transformer was initially to improve the efficiency of machine translation in the field of natural language processing. Due to its simple and flexible network structure and powerful self-attention mechanism, it can extract and process multiple input features, and has been widely applied in various fields beyond natural language processing, such as visual recognition [29–31].

For one-dimensional sequence-formatted image data, the essence of the self-attention mechanism is to calculate the association information between each point in the feature sequence and all other points in the feature sequence. Therefore, each feature itself can use the self-attention mechanism to explore the interdependence between internal information. Transformer can reconstruct input features to some extent and generate high-quality feature representations, which makes it possible to extract image features using Transformers [15]. Meanwhile, the self-attention mechanism can be applied across multiple modalities to mine the data relationships between different modality feature values and complete information interactions between different modalities, thus Transformer also performs well in the field of feature fusion [16].

Therefore, in this work, we use two Transformer-based networks (Axial Transformer [17] and MultiScale Vision Transformer [18]) to model the self-attention mechanism, allowing our proposed model to encode long-term dependencies in images and obtain better fused images.

3 The Proposed Framework

The network architecture of our end-to-end image fusion method based on auto-encoder is shown in Fig. 1. It mainly consists of three components: encoder (left), fusion network (middle), and decoder (right). Here, I_{ir} and I_{vi} represent the

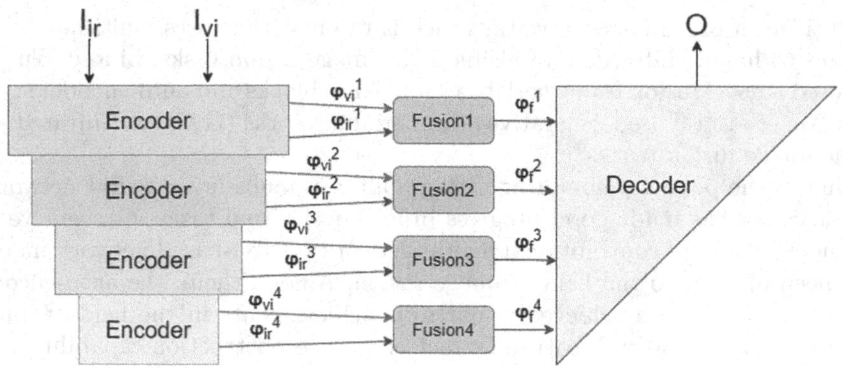

Fig. 1. Network Architecture of our multi-scale fusion Transformer.

input source images (infrared and visible images, respectively), O is the output fused image. "Fusion m" refers to the deep feature fusion at the m-th scale, where φ_{vi}^m and φ_{ir}^m represent the visible and infrared image features extracted by the encoder, and φ_f^m is the feature obtained by the fusion network. In this framework, the features of infrared and visible images are extracted and fused at four different scales (i.e., $m \in 1, 2, 3, 4$), and then a decoder is utilized to reconstruct the multi-scale fused features to obtain the fused image.

Inspired by DenseFuse [13], we employ a two-stage training strategy: first train the multi-scale auto-encoder using the visible images, and then train the fusion part using the infrared-visible image pairs. More details are depicted as follows.

3.1 The Multi-scale Auto-encoder

At this stage, only the visible images are utilized. Our goal is to first obtain an auto-encoder network, where the encoder can extract multi-scale depth features of the input image and the decoder can reconstruct the input image from these features. The network architecture is shown in Fig. 2, where I and O represents the input and output image, respectively. The encoder network consists of a 1×1 convolution layer ("Conv"), four convolutional blocks ("ECB", Encoder ConvBlock), each containing two 3×3 convolution layers, and a multi-scale vision transformer (MViT) block, where a multi-head pooling attention module is incorporated to exploit the global contextual information [23]. The encoder is utilized to extract both local and global features at different scales, and then the obtained multi-scale deep features are fed into the decoder network with a nested connection architecture [27] to reconstruct the input image.

In this paper, we simplify the nested connection to enable it to efficiently reconstruct the fused image. In Fig. 2, $\varphi_{vi}^m (m \in 1, 2, 3, 4)$ represents the multi-scale features obtained by the encoder, "DCB" (Decoder ConvBlock) denotes the convolutional module in the decoder, which consists of two convolutional layers. Nested connections are utilized in the decoder network to process the

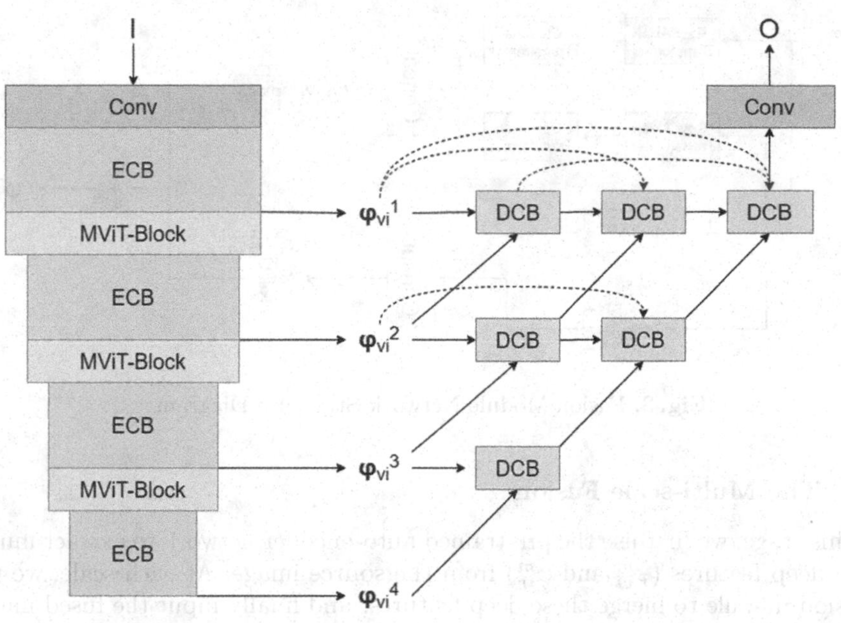

Fig. 2. Multi-scale auto-encoder network structure.

multi-scale depth features extracted by the encoder. In each row of the decoder, convolutional blocks are connected by short-distance residual connections similar to the dense block architecture. Due to the short cross-layer connections, the decoder can fully utilize the multi-scale depth features to reconstruct the input image.

Our auto-encoder network is trained according to the following loss:

$$L_{auto} = L_{pixel} + \lambda\, L_{ssim}, \tag{1}$$

where the pixel loss L_{pixel} and structural similarity (SSIM) loss L_{ssim} are used to measure the difference between the input and output images, λ is a balance hyper-parameter. The pixel loss is given by:

$$L_{pixel} = \|Output - Input\|_F^2. \tag{2}$$

Here, $\|\cdot\|_F^2$ signifies the L_2-norm. The loss constrains the reconstructed image to be as similar as possible to the input image at the pixel level.

The structural similarity loss L_{ssim} is given by:

$$L_{ssim} = 1 - SSIM(Output, Input), \tag{3}$$

which enforces the structures between the input and output image to be similar.

The goal of this stage is to obtain an auto-encoder network with good feature extraction and reconstruction capabilities. After training the auto-encoder network, the parameters are fixed during the training process of the fusion module.

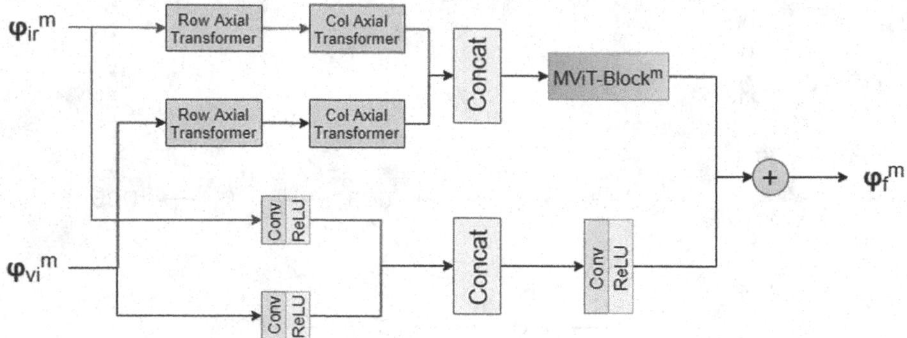

Fig. 3. Fusion Module Network Structure Diagram

3.2 The Multi-scale Fusion

At this stage, we first use the pre-trained auto-encoder network to extract multi-scale deep features (φ_{vi}^m and φ_{ir}^m) from the source image. At each scale, we use a fusion module to merge these deep features, and finally input the fused multi-scale features (φ_f^m) into the decoder network.

As shown in Fig. 3, our fully learnable feature fusion module consists of two branches: a CNN branch and a Transformer branch. The features φ_{vi}^m and φ_{ir}^m are fed into both the CNN branch and Transformer branch. In the CNN branch, we use multiple convolutional layers to obtain local information, where the first convolutional layer is used to further processing the features extracted by the encoder, and the second convolutional layer is adopted to resize the output feature dimension of this branch. In the Transformer branch, we utilize self-attention mechanism to model long-range dependencies for acquiring global information. The axial Transformer [17] based on axial attention mechanism is employed for further processing of the extracted features by the encoder. Meanwhile, the multi-scale vision transformer block based on multi-head attention mechanism is used to resize the feature dimension. Finally, the image features obtained from the two branches are averaged to obtain the final fusion feature φ_f^m. We apply this fusion strategy to the multi-scale features extracted by the encoder and input the fusion result into the decoder network to obtain the final fused image.

The fusion module is trained according to the following loss:

$$L_{fuse} = \alpha L_{detail} + L_{feature}, \tag{4}$$

where L_{detail} and $L_{feature}$ represents the background detail preservation loss and salient object feature enhancement loss, respectively, and α is a balancing hyper-parameter.

In the infrared and visible image fusion, most of the background detail information comes from the visible image, so loss term

$$L_{detail} = 1 - SSIM(O, I_{vi}) \tag{5}$$

will mainly performed on the visible image, aiming to preserve the detail information and structural features in the visible image, as well as constrain the background detail information during reconstruction.

Since the infrared image contains more salient object features than the visible image, the loss term

$$L_{feature} = \sum_{m=1}^{M} w_1(m)||\varphi_f^m - (w_{vi}\varphi_{vi}^m + w_{ir}\varphi_{ir}^m)||_F^2 \tag{6}$$

constrains the deep features in the fusion module to maintain the salient structure. Here, M is the number of multi-scale depth features (i.e., 4), w_1, w_{vi}, and w_{ir} are all balancing coefficients. Among them, w_1 is used to balance the different scales, and w_{vi} and w_{ir} are trade-off hyper-parameters for the visible and infrared image features. Since this loss term mainly performs on the infrared image (the thermal source in the infrared image will have a larger pixel value, which can better reconstruct the salient objects), w_{ir} is usually larger than w_{vi}.

4 Experiments

In this section, we first describe the experimental settings. Then, we perform ablation studies to verify effectiveness of several major modules of our method. Finally, we subjectively and objectively compare the proposed method with several competitive counterparts in terms of diverse evaluation criteria (En, MI, SCD and MS-SSIMM).

4.1 Experimental Settings

In this training phase, we use the MS-COCO dataset [24] to train our auto-encoder network (without fusion), where 80, 000 images are selected for training, and these images are converted into grayscale images of size 256 × 256. The balanced parameter λ is set to be 10, and the batch size and epoch are set to be 4 and 2, respectively, with a learning rate of 1×10^{-4}. After training, the network parameters are stored.

After the first stage of training the auto-encoder module, the parameters of the encoder and decoder are fixed. During the training of the fusion module, we choose the KAIST dataset [25], and convert the images to grayscale and resize them to be 256 × 256. The batch size and epoch were set to be 4 and 2, respectively, and the learning rate was set to be 110^{-4}. The balancing parameter $\alpha = 30$, $w_{ir} = 1.5$, $w_{vi} = 1.0$, $w_1 = \{1, 10, 100, 1000\}$.

In the test phase, we use two datasets: the first set consists of 21 pairs of infrared and visible images collected from the TNO dataset [26], and the second set consists of 40 pairs of infrared and visible light images collected from the VOT2020-RGBT dataset [28].

Table 1. Objective ablation study for the encoder.

	En	MI	SCD	MS-SSIM
Traditional auto-encoder	6.9080	13.8160	1.7898	**0.9419**
Ours	**7.0160**	**14.0320**	**1.7987**	0.9401

Table 2. Objective comparison for different fusion strategies.

Fusion Strategy	En	MI	SCD	MS-SSIM
Add	6.7456	13.4911	**1.8126**	**0.9476**
Avg	6.7452	13.4904	**1.8126**	**0.9476**
Max	6.8681	13.7361	1.5455	0.8913
SPA	6.9529	13.9057	1.5281	0.8859
RFN	6.9421	13.8842	1.7654	0.9338
Transformer branch	6.8031	13.7716	1.6018	0.8816
CNN branch	6.9536	13.9011	1.7603	0.9271
Ours	**7.0160**	**14.0320**	1.7987	0.9401

4.2 Ablation Study of the Encoder

In this section, we discuss the impact of the Multiscale Vision Transformer block on the feature extraction of the encoder. We train the fusion network using a traditional auto-encoder (replacing Multiscale Vision Transformer with Max-Pooling) with the same training strategy and loss function. The fused results examples and objective evaluation values for four quality metrics are shown in Table 1.

Compared with using a traditional auto-encoder in the fusion network, our proposed network can obtain three best objective metric values. This indicates that the multi-head pooled attention module plays a crucial role in enhancing the feature extraction ability of the encoder network. Through the multi-scale vision transformer block, the encoder can extract deep features with multi-scale global information, which is beneficial for utilizing global information in the subsequent fusion process, leading to more natural and clearer fusion images.

4.3 Ablation Study of Fusion Strategy

This section analyzes the importance of the fusion module designed in our fusion network. We compared three traditional fusion strategies ("Add", "Avg", and "Max"), one traditional attention-based fusion strategy ("SPA"), and one deep learning-based fusion strategy ("RFN") through comparative experiments. Meanwhile, to verify the effectiveness of the dual-branch fusion strategy, we also show the experiment results of using only the CNN branch and only the self-attention branch.

We conducted comparative experiments on a 21-pairs test set and evaluated them based on the above four quality metrics, as shown in Table 2. Our fusion network achieved the best comprehensive results overall, indicating that our proposed fusion module outperforms other similar image fusion methods.

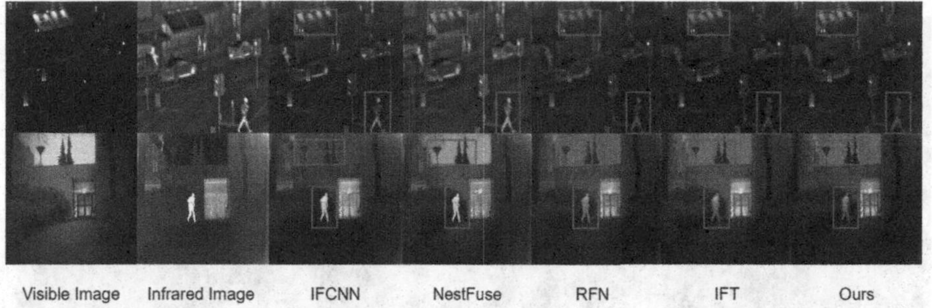

Fig. 4. Examples of subjective comparison of fused results on the 21-pairs test set.

Table 3. An objective comparison with other approaches on the 21-pairs test set.

Methods	En	MI	SCD	MS-SSIM
Densefuse	6.6715	13.3431	1.8350	0.9289
IFCNN	6.5954	13.1909	1.7137	0.9052
NestFuse	6.9197	13.8394	1.7335	0.8624
FusionGan	6.3628	12.7257	1.4568	0.7318
U2Fusion	6.7570	13.5141	1.7983	0.9253
RFN	6.8413	13.6826	**1.8367**	0.9145
IFT	6.9862	13.9725	1.7818	0.8606
Ours	**7.0160**	**14.0320**	1.7987	**0.9401**

4.4 Comparison with Other Approaches

This section mainly compares the fusion performance of our proposed fusion model with existing algorithms. We selected several representative fusion methods for comparison, including DenseFuse [12], IFCNN [19], NestFuse [20], FusionGan [14], U2Fusion [21], RFN-Nest [22], and IFT [23]. To compare the subjective visual effects of the fusion results, we selected several open-source models from the above methods (the network parameters were set according to the optimal values in the original paper) and used two pairs of visible and infrared images for comparison. The fusion images obtained by the existing fusion approaches and our method are shown in Fig. 4. It can be seen that our proposed method achieved the best subjective fusion result in preserving image background details (such as billboard text and trees in the blue box), while maintaining a better balance between visible light background information and infrared features. We still use the above four quality metrics to objectively evaluate the fusion performance, comparing the performance of the above fusion models and our proposed fusion framework on the 21-pairs dataset. The results are shown in Table 3, where the best value is marked in bold.

Fig. 5. Examples of subjective comparison of fused results on the 40-pairs test set.

Table 4. An objective comparison with other approaches on the 40-pairs test set.

Methods	En	MI	SCD	MS-SSIM
Densefuse	6.7763	13.5526	1.7486	0.9294
NestFuse	6.9934	13.9869	1.6754	0.8861
U2Fusion	6.9497	13.8993	1.7478	0.9314
RFN	6.9295	13.8590	**1.7611**	0.9089
Ours	**7.1149**	**14.1239**	1.7537	**0.9533**

From Table 3, it can be seen that compared with other approaches, our method achieve three best values (En, MI, MS-SSIM) and one third-best value (SCD). Compared with other existing fusion models, our fusion network achieved good fusion performance, generating clearer content and having more visual information fidelity.

The results on the 40-pairs test set are shown in Fig. 5. It can be seen that our proposed method achieve a more natural-looking fusion result while ensuring good expression of salient information (such as the red box) and obtaining clearer background details (such as the blue box). The results in terms of the objective evaluation criteria are reported in Table 4, where the best value is marked in bold. From the results, we observe that compared with other approaches, our proposed fusion method achieve three best values (En, MI, and MS-SSIM) and one second-best value (SCD), and thus the best overall performance.

5 Conclusion

In this paper, we propose a multi-scale method for infrared and visible image fusion. We combine multi-scale vision transformer with convolutional neural network (CNN) to improve traditional encoder networks. Besides, we design a learnable dual-branch fusion strategy, where the Transformer branch with axial attention and multi-head pooling attention is used to capture global information and better exploit the complementary information. Experimental results on two public test sets show that our proposed model achieves better results in both subjective visual experience and objective evaluation criteria compared with existing infrared-visible image fusion counterparts.

Acknowledgement. This work is supported by the National Natural Science Foundation of China (No. 62262026 and 62276195), the project of Jiangxi Education Department (No. GJJ211111), and the Fundamental Research Funds for the Central Universities (No. 2042023kf1033).

References

1. Paramanandham, N., Rajendiran, K.: Infrared and visible image fusion using discrete cosine transform and swarm intelligence for surveillance applications. Infrared Phys. Technol. **88**, 13–22 (2018)
2. Gao, H., Cheng, B., Wang, J., et al.: Object classification using CNN-based fusion of vision and LIDAR in autonomous vehicle environment. IEEE Trans. Industr. Inf. **14**(9), 4224–4231 (2018)
3. Ma, J., Ma, Y., Li, C.: Infrared and visible image fusion methods and applications: a survey. Inf. Fusion **45**, 153–178 (2019)
4. Kristan, M., Matas, J., Leonardis, A., et al.: The seventh visual object tracking VOT2019 challenge results. In: Proceedings of the IEEE/CVF International Conference on Computer Vision Workshops (2019)
5. Lopez-Molina, C., Montero, J., Bustince, H., et al.: Self-adapting weighted operators for multiscale gradient fusion. Inf. Fusion **44**, 136–146 (2018)
6. Wright, J., Yang, A.Y., Ganesh, A., et al.: Robust face recognition via sparse representation. IEEE Trans. Pattern Anal. Mach. Intell. **31**(2), 210–227 (2008)
7. He, K., Zhou, D., Zhang, X., et al.: Infrared and visible image fusion based on target extraction in the nonsubsampled contourlet transform domain. J. Appl. Remote Sens. **11**(1), 015011–015011 (2017)
8. Liu, G., Lin, Z., Yan, S., et al.: Robust recovery of subspace structures by low-rank representation. IEEE Trans. Pattern Anal. Mach. Intell. **35**(1), 171–184 (2012)
9. Liu, C.H., Qi, Y., Ding, W.R.: Infrared and visible image fusion method based on saliency detection in sparse domain. Infrared Phys. Technol. **83**, 94–102 (2017)
10. Zhang, Q., Fu, Y., Li, H., et al.: Dictionary learning method for joint sparse representation-based image fusion. Opt. Eng. **52**(5), 057006–057006 (2013)
11. Li, H., Wu, X.J., Kittler, J.: Infrared and visible image fusion using a deep learning framework. In: 2018 24th International Conference on Pattern Recognition (ICPR), pp. 2705–2710. IEEE (2018)
12. Simonyan, K., Zisserman, A.: Very deep convolutional networks for large-scale image recognition. arXiv preprint arXiv:1409.1556 (2014)

13. Li, H., Wu, X.J.: DenseFuse: a fusion approach to infrared and visible images. IEEE Trans. Image Process. **28**(5), 2614–2623 (2018)
14. Ma, J., Yu, W., Liang, P., et al.: FusionGAN: a generative adversarial network for infrared and visible image fusion. Inf. Fusion **48**, 11–26 (2019)
15. Hu, R., Singh, A.: Transformer is all you need: Multimodal multitask learning with a unified transformer. arXiv preprint arXiv:2102.10772 (2021)
16. Chen, C.F.R., Fan, Q., Panda, R.: CrossViT: cross-attention multi-scale vision transformer for image classification. In: Proceedings of the IEEE/CVF International Conference on Computer Vision, pp. 357–366 (2021)
17. Ho, J., Kalchbrenner, N., Weissenborn, D., et al.: Axial attention in multidimensional transformers. arXiv preprint arXiv:1912.12180 (2019)
18. Fan, H., Xiong, B., Mangalam, K., et al.: Multiscale vision transformers. In: Proceedings of the IEEE/CVF International Conference on Computer Vision, pp. 6824–6835 (2021)
19. Zhang, Y., Liu, Y., Sun, P., et al.: IFCNN: a general image fusion framework based on convolutional neural network. Inf. Fusion **54**, 99–118 (2020)
20. Li, H., Wu, X.J., Durrani, T.: NestFuse: an infrared and visible image fusion architecture based on nest connection and spatial/channel attention models. IEEE Trans. Instrum. Meas. **69**(12), 9645–9656 (2020)
21. Xu, H., Ma, J., Jiang, J., et al.: U2Fusion: a unified unsupervised image fusion network. IEEE Trans. Pattern Anal. Mach. Intell. **44**(1), 502–518 (2020)
22. Li, H., Wu, X.J., Kittler, J.: RFN-Nest: an end-to-end residual fusion network for infrared and visible images. Inf. Fusion **73**, 72–86 (2021)
23. Vs, V., Valanarasu, J.M.J., Oza, P., et al.: Image fusion transformer. In: 2022 IEEE International Conference on Image Processing (ICIP), pp. 3566–3570. IEEE (2022)
24. Lin, T.-Y., et al.: Microsoft COCO: common objects in context. In: Fleet, D., Pajdla, T., Schiele, B., Tuytelaars, T. (eds.) ECCV 2014. LNCS, vol. 8693, pp. 740–755. Springer, Cham (2014). https://doi.org/10.1007/978-3-319-10602-1_48
25. Hwang, S., Park, J., Kim, N., et al.: Multispectral pedestrian detection: benchmark dataset and baseline. In: Proceedings of the IEEE Conference on Computer Vision and Pattern Recognition, pp. 1037–1045 (2015)
26. Toet, A.: The TNO multiband image data collection. Data Brief **15**, 249–251 (2017)
27. Zhou, Z., Rahman Siddiquee, M.M., Tajbakhsh, N., Liang, J.: UNet++: a nested U-Net architecture for medical image segmentation. In: Stoyanov, D., et al. (eds.) DLMIA/ML-CDS -2018. LNCS, vol. 11045, pp. 3–11. Springer, Cham (2018). https://doi.org/10.1007/978-3-030-00889-5_1
28. Kristan, M., et al.: The eighth visual object tracking VOT2020 challenge results. In: Bartoli, A., Fusiello, A. (eds.) ECCV 2020. LNCS, vol. 12539, pp. 547–601. Springer, Cham (2020). https://doi.org/10.1007/978-3-030-68238-5_39
29. Zhang, Q., Xu, Y., Zhang, J., et al.: VSA: learning varied-size window attention in vision transformers. In: Avidan, S., Brostow, G., Cissé, M., Farinella, G.M., Hassner, T. (eds.) ECCV 2022. LNCS, vol. 13685, pp. 466–483. Springer, Cham (2022). https://doi.org/10.1007/978-3-031-19806-9_27
30. Xu, Y., Zhang, Q., Zhang, J., et al.: Vitae: vision transformer advanced by exploring intrinsic inductive bias. Adv. Neural. Inf. Process. Syst. **34**, 28522–28535 (2021)
31. Zhang, Q., Xu, Y., Zhang, J., et al.: ViTAEv2: vision transformer advanced by exploring inductive bias for image recognition and beyond. Int. J. Comput. Vision 1–22 (2023)

NeuralODE-Based Latent Trajectories into AutoEncoder Architecture for Surrogate Modelling of Parametrized High-Dimensional Dynamical Systems

Michele Lazzara[1,2(✉)], Max Chevalier[2], Corentin Lapeyre[3], and Olivier Teste[2]

[1] Airbus Operations, 31300 Toulouse, France
michele.lazzara@airbus.com
[2] Université de Toulouse - IRIT UMR5505, 31400 Toulouse, France
[3] CERFACS, 31100 Toulouse, France

Abstract. Data-driven modelling has recently gained interest in the scientific computing community with the purpose of emulating complex large scale systems. Surrogate modelling based on autoencoders (AEs) is widely employed across several engineering fields to model the time-history response of nonlinear high-dimensional dynamical systems from a set of design parameters. In this direction, this paper introduces an efficient deep learning scheme consisting of a two-steps autoencoding framework in conjunction with Neural Ordinary Differential Equations (NODEs), a novel approach for modelling time-continuous dynamics. The proposition aims at alleviating the drawbacks of similar methodologies employed for the same task, namely Parametrized NODE (PNODE) and the two-steps AE-based surrogate models, to provide a more powerful predictive tool. The effectiveness of the conceived methodology has been assessed by considering the task of emulating the spatiotemporal dynamics described by the 1D viscous Burgers' equation. The outcomes of our empirical analysis demonstrate that our approach outperforms the alternative state-of-the-art models in terms of predictive capability.

Keywords: Surrogate modelling · Deep Learning · NODE · Dynamical Systems

1 Introduction

High-fidelity numerical simulations of spatiotemporal dynamics play a critical role in understanding physical processes, e.g. turbulence and fluid-structure interaction in aerodynamic and thermal design activities [7,19,23,28].

Non-intrusive, i.e. purely data-driven, reduced-order modeling (ROM) have been studied and proposed as effective approaches for reducing the computational burden associated to these high-fidelity simulations for high-dimensional dynamical systems. [8,11,13,22,27,28]. Prominent among these approaches is

L. Iliadis et al. (Eds.): ICANN 2023, LNCS 14259, pp. 497–508, 2023.
https://doi.org/10.1007/978-3-031-44223-0_40

the use of Neural ODEs (NODEs) [3], a family of deep learning models that parametrizes the time-continuous dynamics of hidden states in the form of a system of ordinary differential equations. However, in the original form, NODEs are not designed for dealing with external static or time-varying inputs [4]. Indeed, as pointed out in [2,6,16], NODEs optimize a set of trainable parameters defining only one dynamics for the whole training dataset, meaning that a single dynamics is accounted for distinctive model inputs. This results in limited expressiveness of the model when it is intended to learn, and predict, multiple trajectories depending on various input instances. An extension to NODEs that enables the learning of multiple trajectories with a single set of network weights, called PNODE [16], has been proposed for modelling parameter-dependent time-dependent solutions. However, this approach makes the deep learning model tend to overfit because of the weak variability of the learned hidden multiple trajectories.

In a similar manner, low generalization capability related to weak variability is encountered in the two-steps autoencoder-based surrogate modelling, where an autoencoder (AE) and a fully-connected neural network (FCNN) regressor are subsequently trained for the prediction of a multivariate time-series from a set of parameters [15,22,35]: the low spectrum of latent values provided to the decoder triggers the propagation of the input-to-latent mapping function error, resulting in poor predictive capabilities of the model.

In this paper we deploy a deep learning architecture, named "SuMo-LatentNODE" and involving a combination of an AE-based network and a FCNN-based regressor, for (surrogate) modelling of parametrized dynamical systems, i.e. for predicting parameter-dependent multivariate time-series. In the proposed framework, a NODE block is integrated into an AE-based architecture, where the ODE integration occurs in the lower-dimensional space for generating the temporal evolution of the hidden state. Inspired by the beneficial relationship between variability and generalization capability [25,31], the main intuition behind this proposition is to expose the decoding network to more variable and wavering data, leading indeed to a more robust predictive model. Furthermore, by enhancing the robustness of the model in this way, a desired level of accuracy is achieved by using less training data.

2 Related Work

2.1 Data-Driven Reduced-Order-Modeling

To alleviate the computational burden of high-fidelity simulations, many research activities focused on data-driven strategies to provide a reduced-order model (ROM) to learn the original dynamics in a lower-dimensional space. Typically, the equation free evolution of dynamics into the reduced space is modelled through recurrent convolutional autoencoder [10,12,17,21] or by learning the temporal evolution of Proper Orthogonal Decomposition (POD) modal coefficients [24,34]. In this framework, also Neural ODE has been widely exploited for learning non-linear spatio-temporal dynamics [5,23,29] delivering a very competitive tool over long short-term memory networks (LSTMs), as demonstrated in [18]. NODES hold many advantages over the conventional neural networks: the use of adaptive numerical integration reduces the auto-regressive error propagation; it bypasses the look-back windowed sequences strategy for RNN/LSTMs; and it is memory efficient because there is no need to store any intermediate quantities of the forward pass while backpropagating. In the domain of ROMs, surrogate modelling of parametrized dynamical systems relying on the use of autoencoders have recently gained interest in the scientific community. This approach consists on learning a direct mapping function from input-space to the latent space, where the low-dimensional representations are formerly computed by applying autoencoders [8,15,22,28,35] or variational autoencoders [9,20,30,33] on the high-dimensional solutions. For a new input parameter, the prediction is given by decoding the latent representation delivered by the learned mapping function. In particular, when used for dealing with time-dependent prediction, such AE-based models generate a (multivariate) sequence from the latent vector generally using "Unpooling" or "Repeat Vector" strategies. This leads to an important shortcoming: these (quasi)-static sequences limit the classes of functions and variability of values that can be treated, triggering overfitting phenomena.

2.2 NODE for Time-Series and Parametrized NODE

Neural ODE [3] is a continuous-depth deep neural network model that can be interpreted as the continuous counterpart of the discrete traditional models such as recurrent and residual neural network. The framework of NODE envisions the parametrization of the derivative of time-continuous representation of a hidden state $\mathbf{z}(t)$ using an ordinary differential equation (ODE) specified by a neural network f_Θ:

$$\frac{d\mathbf{z}(t)}{dt} = f_\Theta(\mathbf{z}(t), t; \Theta) \tag{1}$$

From an initial condition $\mathbf{z}_{t_0}$, a hidden state at any time index t_* can be defined by solving the ODE initial value problem (Eq. 1) via a numerical black-box differential equation solver:

$$\mathbf{z}_{t_1}, \mathbf{z}_{t_2}, \ldots, \mathbf{z}_{t_*} = ODESolver(f_\Theta, \mathbf{z}_{t_0}, t_1, t_2, \ldots, t_*) \tag{2}$$

PNODE proposition [16] extends NODEs and allows the learning of multiple trajectories that depend on the input parameters with a single set of network weights by expressing the hidden dynamics as:

$$\frac{d\mathbf{z}(t;\mu)}{dt} = f_\Theta(\mathbf{z}(t;\mu), t; \mu, \Theta) \tag{3}$$

with a parametrized initial condition $\mathbf{z}_{t_0}(\mu)$, where μ denotes problem specific input parameters. In practice, f_Θ is a velocity function that takes $\mathbf{z}$ and μ as input and produces $\frac{d\mathbf{z}}{dt}$ as output. In a situation where the influence of the parameters on the parametrized initial condition is low, e.g. $dim(\mathbf{z}_0) >> dim(\mu)$

or $||\mathbf{z}_0|| >> ||\mu||$, and where the initial state $\mathbf{z}_0$ is the same across all data samples, one can suppose that the multiple trajectories depending on different input parameter instances actually share the same waveform and present weak variability, limiting the spectrum of learnable dynamics.

3 Proposed Methodology

The proposed approach has been conceived to provide a performing tool in the context of surrogate modelling for parameter-dependent dynamical systems.

Problem Statement. Let f denote a matrix-valued function on the space Ω, a subset of the space $\mathbb{R}^{N_x}$ ($N_x \in \mathbb{N}$). For a data-driven estimation of f, a set of n observations $\mathcal{S}_n := \{(\mathbf{x}_i, \mathbf{Y}_i = f(\mathbf{x}_i)), i \in [1; n]\}$ is exploited, where $\mathbf{x}_i = (x_1^i, ..., x_{N_x}^i)^T$ represents the input parameter vector and $\mathbf{Y}_i = (\mathbf{y}_1^i, ..., \mathbf{y}_{N_y}^i)^T$ is the corresponding solution of the high-fidelity model, where $\mathbf{y}_k^i$ is a time-ordered sequence. Exploiting the dataset $\mathcal{S}_n$, a parametrized function $\hat{f}$ can be learned with the objective to approximate $f : \mathbb{R}^{N_x} \to \mathbb{R}^{N_y \times N_T}$.

To achieve this goal, we leverage the Neural ODE approach within a two-steps autoencoder-based architecture, allowing for learning multiple trajectories depending on different input parameter instances.

Training Phase. The *offline* phase or (training phase) consists of two successive steps as illustrated in Fig. 1. Firstly the autoencoding-fashioned deep learning model is trained over the n solutions $\mathbf{Y}_i$ to reconstruct the multivariate time series given in input and obtain their reduced representations $\mathbf{z}_i \in \mathbb{R}^{N_z}$: the LSTM encoding function annotated e_ϕ, the NODE network f_δ and the decoding network d_θ are jointly trained to minimize the reconstruction function $L(\mathbf{Y}_i, \hat{\mathbf{Y}}_i)$. The forward pass is reported in Algorithm 1. Then, a FCNN is trained to learn the function $g_\psi : \mathbb{R}^{N_x} \to \mathbb{R}^{N_z}$ which relates the input parameter space to the low-dimensional representation of the physical space. The supervised learning is performed by using the pair samples $\mathcal{U}_n := \{(\mathbf{x}_i, \mathbf{z}_i), i \in [1; n]\}$, where the set of $\mathbf{z}_i$ is extracted from the previous step.

Algorithm 1 Forward propagation into the autoencoder-based architecture

1. The LSTM recognition net e_ϕ consumes the multivariate time-series $\mathbf{Y_i}$ sequentially backwards in time and outputs a reduced representation $\mathbf{z}_i = e_\phi(\mathbf{Y_i})$;
2. The encoded representation, equivalent to the reduced initial state $\mathbf{z}_i \equiv \mathbf{z}_{t_0}$, is used as initial condition to solve a system of ODEs as defined by the NODE framework:

$$\mathbf{z}_{t_1}, \mathbf{z}_{t_2}, \ldots, \mathbf{z}_{t_{N_T}} = ODESolver(f_\delta, \mathbf{z}_{t_0}, t_1, t_2, \ldots, t_{N_T}) \tag{4}$$

3. The generated sequence in the reduced space is processed by the decoder to provide the high-dimensional approximated solution $\hat{\mathbf{Y}}_i = d_\theta(\mathbf{z}_{t_1}, \mathbf{z}_{t_2}, \ldots, \mathbf{z}_{t_{N_T}})$.

Prediction Phase. For a new set of parameters $\mathbf{x}^*$, the trained FCNN is employed to obtain the reduced representation of the corresponding solution $\mathbf{z}^*$, used as initial condition to solve the reduced ODEs system and generate the temporal evolution of the low dimensional state.

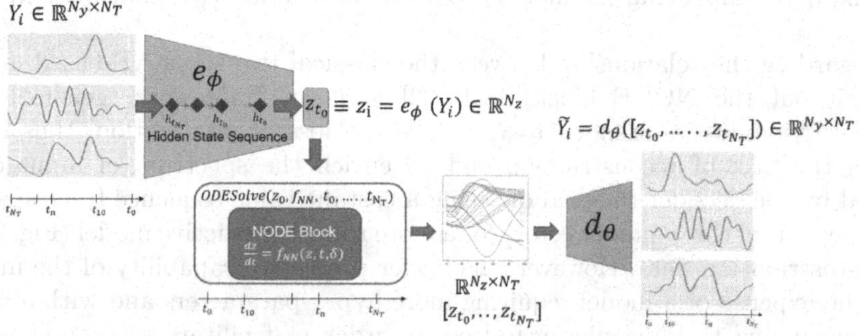

(a) **Step 1:. Encoder, NODE function and Decoder are trained together to reconstruct the input, delivering meaningful low-dimensional representation of the input data.**

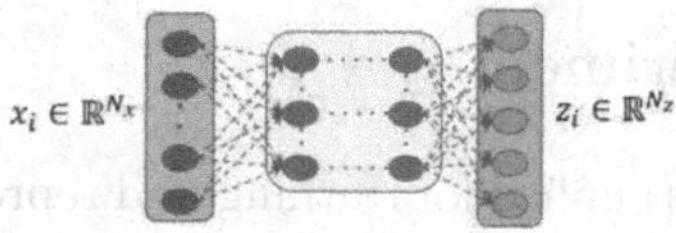

(b) **Step 2: Training FCNN for $x \rightarrow z_i$ mapping. The FCNN is trained by using the low dimensional representation of the original solution from AE.**

Fig. 1. The training phase of the autoencoder-based surrogate modeling approach.

The pre-trained decoder maps the reduced hidden sequence back to the original space, delivering the surrogate model solution:

$$\hat{\mathbf{Y}}^* = d_\theta(ODESolver(f_\delta, g_\psi(\mathbf{x}^*), t_1, t_2, \ldots, t_{N_T})) \tag{5}$$

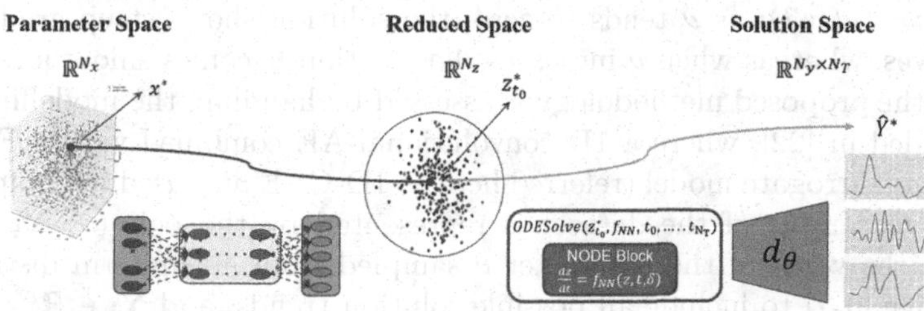

Fig. 2. In the prediction phase, FCNN, NODE block and the decoder are assembled to form the final surrogate model.

Compared to the PNODE, where $\mathbf{z}_{t_0}(\mu) = [e_\phi(\mathbf{Y}_{t_0}), \mu]$, in our SuMo-LatentNODE the initial condition for the ODESolver is explicitly function of the entire time-history response $\mathbf{Y}_i$, i.e. of possible inter and intra-temporal correlations depending on a particular parameter instance, retaining pertinent information about the dynamics of the high-dimensional state space vector. This is supposed to increase the variability of the initial hidden states for the entire training data, improving the model capability in dealing with multiple trajectories.

Regarding the relationship between the classical two-steps AE-based model (i.e. without the NODE block) [8,15,22] and our framework, generating a reduced dynamics is intended to *i)* reduce the loss of information, thus facilitating the task of reconstruction and *ii)* enrich the spectrum of input data treated by the decoder (instead of seeing a costant value sequence from upsampling/repeating the context vector) for a more robust predictive model (Fig. 2) to out-of-distribution data. However, the better predictive capability of the model is at the expense of a model requiring more hyper-parameters and with a more time-consuming training phase. Indeed, in order to facilitate a comprehensive exploration of the hyper-parameter space for building the proposed AE-NODE model, efforts need to be directed at accelerating the training times.

4 Numerical Experiments

The proposed framework is applied for learning and reproducing the behaviour of large-scale parametrized dynamical systems. The PNODE and the two steps AE-based surrogate model are considered and will serve as baselines in our numerical experiments to provide comparison with the proposed approach. The effectiveness is assessed by analysing the outcomes of the experiments performed on the viscous 1D Burgers equation [1], a convection-diffusion equation widely used in the scientific deep learning (SciDL) community [8,18,22], whose physics is governed by the following partial differential equation:

$$\frac{\partial u}{\partial t} + u\frac{\partial u}{\partial x} = \nu \frac{\partial^2 u}{\partial x^2} \tag{6}$$

where ν is the diffusion parameter that regulates the trend of the velocity field solution $u = u(x, t)$: as ν tends to zero, the solution shows steep gradients as time evolves, whereas when ν increases the solution becomes smoother.

Here, the proposed methodology is assessed by handling the modelling problem provided in [22], where a 1D convolutional-AE combined with a FCNN is proposed as surrogate model (referred here as 1D-CAE and used as competitor).

The *i-th* sample of the dataset is represented by the pair $(x_i, \mathbf{Y_i})$, where $x_i \in \mathbb{R}$ is the value of the parameter ν sampled from an uniform distribution in the range $[0, 1]$ to include all possible solution trends, and $\mathbf{Y_i} \in \mathbb{R}^{N_y \equiv N_s \times N_T}$ is the associated velocity matrix solution, gathered discretizing Eq. 6 with a finite difference scheme leading to $N_s = 200$ and $N_T = 100$ spatial and time points, respectively. The initial conditions were taken as $u(x, 0) = -sin(\pi x)$ with

$x \in [-1, 1]$ and the boundary conditions $u(\pm 1, t) = 0$ with $t \in [0, 5]$ and maintained constant for all the samples of the dataset. For training, we set the loss function as the mean squared error and optimize the network weights using Adam [14] with minibatches of 8 samples, 3000 training epochs and learning rate equal to 0.001 with step-decay. These hyperparameters have been set by a grid search strategy. Train-validation split (0.9–0.1) has been randomly performed, ensuring that the statistical distributions are consistent within each other such that the model can efficiently learn and emulate the spectrum of velocity field trends. For the performance evaluation metric, we measure the error of approximated solutions with respect to the reference solutions, using an averaged normalized error defined as:

$$\epsilon_{avg} = \frac{1}{N} \sum_{i=1}^{N} \frac{\|\mathbf{Y^i} - \mathbf{\hat{Y}^i}\|}{\|\mathbf{Y^i}\|} \tag{7}$$

Besides the 1D-CAE, a PNODE framework has been build as further competitor on the basis of the architecture used in [16]. The network architecture consists of two FCNNs for the encoder and the neural network approximating the hidden dynamics, and by a decoder formed by 1D convolutional layers. For PNODE and our implementation we took advantage of the software package used in [3,26]. The architecture of our proposed approach is described in Table 1.

Table 1. Deep learning model configuration. The convolutional layers have kernel filter length $k = 5$ and strides $s = 1$. Best ϵ_{avg} error is achieved with $N_z = 8$.

Component	e_ϕ	f_δ	d_θ	FCNN
Layers	Input(N_T, N_y)	Input(N_z)	Input(N_T, N_z)	Input(N_x)
	LSTM(N_T,96)	ELU(128)	Conv1D(64; ReLU)	ReLU(256)
	LSTM(N_T,64)	ELU(128)	Conv1D(128; ReLU)	ReLU(256)
	LSTM(1,N_z)	ELU(128)	Conv1D(N_y; Linear)	ReLU(256)
		Linear(N_z)		Linear(N_z)

Two studies have been conducted to assess the accuracy of the proposed model and to investigate the influence of the training dataset size. Initially, a dataset of $n = 200$ pairs (x_i, $\mathbf{Y}_\mathrm{i}$) has been considered for a comparative analysis to get the most performing surrogate model. The results of the numerical experiments are illustrated in Fig. 3. Our proposed approach outperforms both PNODE and 1D-CAE in terms of predictive capability considering the metric defined in Eq. 7. The interesting outcome to highlight is that PNODE approach is less competitive than the other two frameworks. Although these two latter need for two subsequent neural network models (AE and FCNN mapping), consequently triggering error propagation, their decoding frames actually benefit from processing the time series in the first step training. Furthermore, all the models increase their performance by increasing the number of tunable weights (as expected) and with a larger dimension of the latent space.

However, an optimal dimension has to be selected in a two-steps AE-based framework, seeking for a trade-off between the autoenconding reconstruction and the increasing complexity in learning the mapping function. For example, the proposed model with $N_z = 24$, having around 400000 parameters, has an autoencoding error lower than the same model with $N_z = 8$ as theoretically expected, but a worse prediction performance regarding the overall surrogate model: this is often related to the propagation of the mapping error through the reconstruction, probably emphasized by an overfitting tendency of the autoencoder which leads to an unsmoothed distribution of latent points.

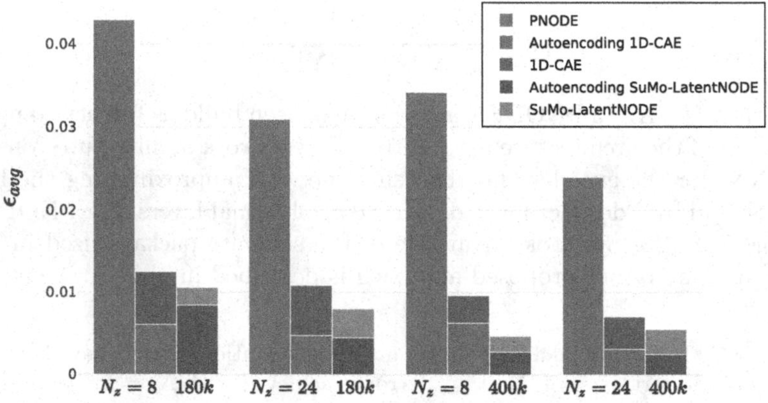

Fig. 3. Comparative analysis for the three frameworks in terms of ϵ_{avg} (lower is better). For each framework two N_z values and two amount of trainable weights have been considered.

In Fig. 4 we illustrate the generated sequence of the reduced hidden state $\mathbf{z}_{t_1}, \mathbf{z}_{t_2}, \ldots, \mathbf{z}_{t_{N_T}}$ of dimension $N_z = 2$, from the PNODE (Fig. 4a) and the proposed SuMo-LatentNODE (Fig. 4b) for the validation parameter instances. The initial hidden state condition plays a key role in learning multiple trajectories. Processing the entire temporal solution (our approach) instead of concatenating the initial encoded state with the relative parameter value (PNODE), allows the NODE model to learn and generate distinctive trajectories: the variability of the "latent" trajectories enriches the data processed by the decoder, consequently leading to better generalization capacity.

The second analysis aimed at investigating the influence of the size of the training dataset on the performance of the surrogate models. Three training datasets have been selected, respectively with $n_1 = 200$, $n_2 = 600$ and $n_3 = 1000$ pairs, each sharing the same distribution of the sampled parameters. A dataset with $n = 2010$ samples has been kept aside from the learning process and used for testing purpose. The three trainings shared the same autoenconding architectures (models with 400000 weights and $N_z = 8$) and optimization hyperparameters.

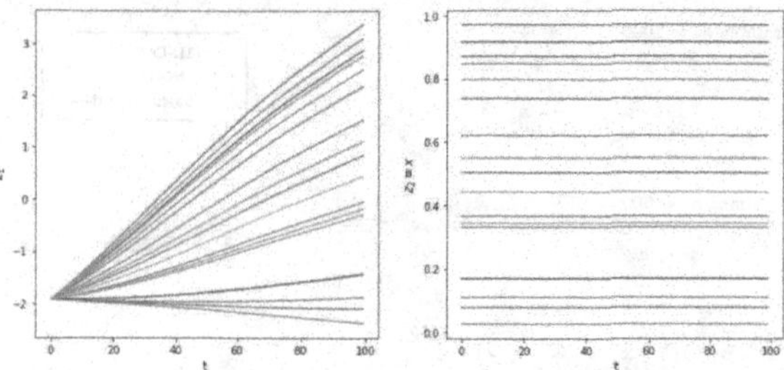

(a) Temporal evolution of the reduced hidden states for PNODE. The variable z_2 coincides with the input parameter value.

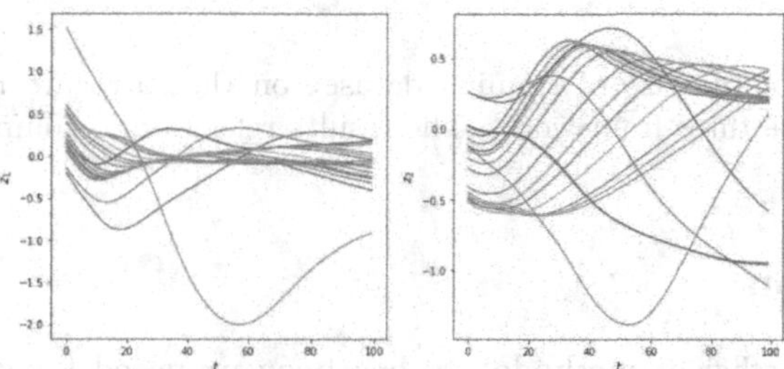

(b) Temporal evolution of the reduced hidden states in the proposed framework, being $\mathbf{z}_{t_0} = e_\phi(\mathbf{Y})$.

Fig. 4. Expressivity of the multiple reduced state trajectories of the generated from the NODE block in our approach vs PNODE. Each color corresponds to a validation parameter instance.

Only the $\mathbf{x} \rightarrow \mathbf{z}$ mapping networks have been modified: to avoid underfitting issues of the initial 5-layers 32-neurons FCNN, the number of neurons in each layer doubled as the size of the dataset increased. Indeed, augmenting the complexity of the FCNNs has reduced the error propagation through the decoder caused by an improper mapping. The results illustrated in Fig. 5 show once again the better prediction capability of the proposed surrogate model with respect to the two competitors considered for this study. A noteworthy outcome is that only the PNODE has a considerable improvement passing from n_1 to n_3, while for the others two autoencoding frameworks the gain is less important. Particularly, the investigation highlights another key element: if on the one hand the performances of the three models are quite similar when exploiting a bigger training dataset, on the other the proposed approach is much more powerful when exploiting a smaller dataset. This characteristic is very significant because it would possible building a surrogate model by exploiting a limited number of samples, i.e. reducing the computational burden of running a substantial number of high-fidelity simulations.

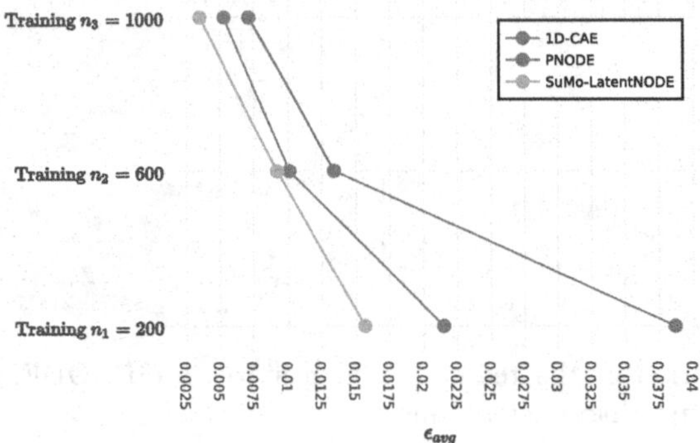

Fig. 5. Influence of the size of training dataset on the surrogate model predictive performance for the three frameworks. The results refer to ϵ_{avg} computed on the test set.

5 Conclusion

In this work, an efficient methodology has been proposed for data-driven surrogate modelling of parametrized high-dimensional dynamical systems. The framework consists of integrating a Neural ODE block within an autoencoding architecture trained to reconstruct the spatiotemporal response defined by a parameter-dependent dynamical system. The strategy has been proposed to overcome the main drawbacks of existing approaches. By comparison with state-of-the art models for the equivalent problem, namely the two-steps 1D-CAE and the PNODE, the results demonstrated that the proposed model more accurately predicts the parametrized time-history response regarding the spatio-temporal solution of the 1D Burger's equation.

The outcomes are encouraging for further investigations on more complex and/or different problems regarding the modelling of multivariate time-series, whose temporal evolution is regulated by a set of design parameters. Besides the studies related to how physics-informed strategy could be combined with NODE [32] for non-academic benchmark problems, another area of future investigation regards the influence of various hyperparameters the NODEs depend on to improve their understanding for time-series modelling.

Acknowledgement. This work has been supported by Airbus Operations SAS and the French National Agency for Technological Research (ANRT) within the CIFRE framework (grant N° 2019/1815).

References

1. Burgers, J.: A mathematical model illustrating the theory of turbulence. Adv. Appl. Mech. **1**, 171–199 (1948)
2. Chalvidal, M., Ricci, M., VanRullen, R., Serre, T.: Neural optimal control for representation learning. arXiv abs/2006.09545 (2020)

3. Chen, R.T.Q., Rubanova, Y., Bettencourt, J., Duvenaud, D.K.: Neural ordinary differential equations. In: Advances in Neural Information Processing Systems, vol. 31. Curran Associates, Inc. (2018)
4. Chen, X., et al.: Forecasting the outcome of spintronic experiments with neural ordinary differential equations. Nat. Commun. **13**(1), 1016 (2022)
5. Dikeman, H.E., Zhang, H., Yang, S.: Stiffness-reduced neural ode models for data-driven reduced-order modeling of combustion chemical kinetics. In: AIAA SCITECH 2022 Forum, p. 0226 (2022)
6. Dupont, E., Doucet, A., Teh, Y.W.: Augmented neural odes. In: Advances in Neural Information Processing Systems, vol. 32 (2019)
7. Dupuis, R., Jouhaud, J.C., Sagaut, P.: Surrogate modeling of aerodynamic simulations for multiple operating conditions using machine learning. AIAA J. **56**(9), 3622–3635 (2018)
8. Fresca, S., Dede', L., Manzoni, A.: A comprehensive deep learning-based approach to reduced order modeling of nonlinear time-dependent parametrized PDEs. J. Sci. Comput. **87**, 1–36 (2021)
9. Gergs, T., Borislavov, B., Trieschmann, J.: Efficient plasma-surface interaction surrogate model for sputtering processes based on autoencoder neural networks. J. Vac. Sci. Technol. B **40**(1), 012802 (2022)
10. Gonzalez, F.J., Balajewicz, M.: Deep convolutional recurrent autoencoders for learning low-dimensional feature dynamics of fluid systems. arXiv preprint arXiv:1808.01346 (2018)
11. Guo, M., Hesthaven, J.S.: Reduced order modeling for nonlinear structural analysis using gaussian process regression. Comput. Methods Appl. Mech. Eng. **341**, 807–826 (2018)
12. Hasegawa, K., Fukami, K., Murata, T., Fukagata, K.: Machine-learning-based reduced-order modeling for unsteady flows around bluff bodies of various shapes. Theoret. Comput. Fluid Dyn. **34**, 367–383 (2020)
13. Hesthaven, J., Ubbiali, S.: Non-intrusive reduced order modeling of nonlinear problems using neural networks. J. Comput. Phys. **363**, 55–78 (2018)
14. Kingma, D.P., Ba, J.: Adam: a method for stochastic optimization. In: 3rd International Conference on Learning Representations, ICLR 2015, San Diego, CA, USA, 7–9 May 2015, Conference Track Proceedings (2015)
15. Lazzara, M., Chevalier, M., Colombo, M., Garcia, J.G., Lapeyre, C., Teste, O.: Surrogate modelling for an aircraft dynamic landing loads simulation using an LSTM autoencoder-based dimensionality reduction approach. Aerosp. Sci. Technol. **126**, 107629 (2022)
16. Lee, K., Parish, E.J.: Parameterized neural ordinary differential equations: applications to computational physics problems. Proc. Roy. Soc. A Math. Phys. Eng. Sci. **477**(2253), 20210162 (2021)
17. Maulik, R., Lusch, B., Balaprakash, P.: Reduced-order modeling of advection-dominated systems with recurrent neural networks and convolutional autoencoders. Phys. Fluids **33**(3), 037106 (2021)
18. Maulik, R., Mohan, A., Lusch, B., Madireddy, S., Balaprakash, P., Livescu, D.: Time-series learning of latent-space dynamics for reduced-order model closure. Physica D **405**, 132368 (2020)
19. Milan, P.J., Torelli, R., Lusch, B., Magnotti, G.: Data-driven model reduction of multiphase flow in a single-hole automotive injector. At. Sprays **30**(6) (2020)
20. Na, J., Jeon, K., Lee, W.B.: Toxic gas release modeling for real-time analysis using variational autoencoder with convolutional neural networks. Chem. Eng. Sci. **181**, 68–78 (2018)

21. Nakamura, T., Fukami, K., Hasegawa, K., Nabae, Y., Fukagata, K.: Convolutional neural network and long short-term memory based reduced order surrogate for minimal turbulent channel flow. Phys. Fluids **33**(2), 025116 (2021)
22. Nikolopoulos, S., Kalogeris, I., Papadopoulos, V.: Non-intrusive surrogate modeling for parametrized time-dependent partial differential equations using convolutional autoencoders. Eng. Appl. Artif. Intell. **109**, 104652 (2022)
23. Portwood, G.D., et al.: Turbulence forecasting via neural ODE. arXiv preprint arXiv:1911.05180 (2019)
24. Rahman, S.M., Pawar, S., San, O., Rasheed, A., Iliescu, T.: Nonintrusive reduced order modeling framework for quasigeostrophic turbulence. Phys. Rev. E **100**, 053306 (2019)
25. Raviv, L., Lupyan, G., Green, S.C.: How variability shapes learning and generalization. Trends Cogn. Sci. **26**(6), 462–483 (2022)
26. Rubanova, Y., Chen, R.T., Duvenaud, D.K.: Latent ordinary differential equations for irregularly-sampled time series. In: Advances in Neural Information Processing Systems, vol. 32 (2019)
27. Salvador, M., Dede, L., Manzoni, A.: Non intrusive reduced order modeling of parametrized PDEs by kernel pod and neural networks. Comput. Math. Appl. **104**, 1–13 (2021)
28. Sekar, V., Jiang, Q., Shu, C., Khoo, B.C.: Fast flow field prediction over airfoils using deep learning approach. Phys. Fluids **31**(5), 057103 (2019)
29. Shankar, V., et al.: Learning non-linear spatio-temporal dynamics with convolutional neural odes. In: Third Workshop on Machine Learning and the Physical Sciences (NeurIPS 2020) (2020)
30. Sharif, S.A., Hammad, A., Eshraghi, P.: Generation of whole building renovation scenarios using variational autoencoders. Energy Build. **230**, 110520 (2021)
31. Tenenbaum, J.B., Griffiths, T.L.: Generalization, similarity, and bayesian inference. Behav. Brain Sci. **24**(4), 629640 (2001)
32. Thangamuthu, A., Kumar, G., Bishnoi, S., Bhattoo, R., Krishnan, N.M.A., Ranu, S.: Unravelling the performance of physics-informed graph neural networks for dynamical systems. In: Thirty-sixth Conference on Neural Information Processing Systems Datasets and Benchmarks Track (2022)
33. Wang, J., He, C., Li, R., Chen, H., Zhai, C., Zhang, M.: Flow field prediction of supercritical airfoils via variational autoencoder based deep learning framework. Phys. Fluids **33**(8), 086108 (2021)
34. Wang, Z., Xiao, D., Fang, F., Govindan, R., Pain, C.C., Guo, Y.: Model identification of reduced order fluid dynamics systems using deep learning. Int. J. Numer. Meth. Fluids **86**(4), 255–268 (2018)
35. Xu, J., Duraisamy, K.: Multi-level convolutional autoencoder networks for parametric prediction of spatio-temporal dynamics. Comput. Methods Appl. Mech. Eng. **372**, 113379 (2020)

RRecT: Chinese Text Recognition with Radical-Enhanced Recognition Transformer

Xinrui Deng, Zheng Huang[(✉)], Kefan Ma, Kai Chen, Jie Guo, and Weidong Qiu

School of Electronic Information and Electrical Engineering, Shanghai Jiao Tong University, Shanghai, China
{kawhi1201rui,huang-zheng,entropy2333,kchen,guojie,qiuwd}@sjtu.edu.cn

Abstract. Text recognition has attracted continuous attention in recent years and reaches increasingly high performance on English datasets. Nevertheless, little attention is emphatically paid to Chinese Text Recognition (CTR), leading to a barely satisfying accuracy on Chinese datasets. Due to the complex glyph structure and large size of character set, CTR is more challenging and requires a powerful capacity of feature extraction. In this paper, we propose a novel network for CTR named **R**adical-enhanced **Rec**ognition **T**ransformer (RRecT). It firstly introduces a customized Recognition Transformer (RecT) to extract multi-grained features, then exploits radical decomposition as an auxiliary supervision signal and enhances character representation with radical information by Radical Prediction Module (RPM) and Radical-Character Fusion Module (RCFM). Thus, final feature contains both character-level and fused radical-level information. The experimental results show that RRecT outperforms the state-of-the-art methods by a margin of 1.4% on Scene dataset, 1.8% on Document dataset and reaches a competitive performance on Web and Handwritten dataset. Moreover, RRecT requires much less computation cost and is a lightweight and effective model.

Keywords: Chinese text recognition · OCR · radical prior

1 Introduction

Text recognition task aims to recognize text in images, which has increasingly attracted attention in recent years and acted as an important role in several downstream visual applications (e.g., vehicle license plate recognition [35], autonomous driving [38], real-time translation etc.). Since texts in scene images may be shaped irregularly, arbitrarily and designed with diverse font types, Scene Text Recognition (STR) has been a spotlight in this filed. In recent years, with the rapid advance in deep learning, extensive novel and effective methods have been proposed for scene text recognition [1,11,12,19,26,32]. However,

L. Iliadis et al. (Eds.): ICANN 2023, LNCS 14259, pp. 509–521, 2023.
https://doi.org/10.1007/978-3-031-44223-0_41

these methods mainly focus on and are evaluated on Indo-European language datasets, especially on English. In contrast, few efforts have been emphatically devoted to East Asian languages deriving from ancient Chinese (e.g., modern Chinese, Japanese and Korean), one of the most widely spoken languages with more than 20% of population using them. Unlike Indo-European languages, East Asian languages, especially Chinese, have entirely different and complex glyph structures, hence existing methods suffer from a bottleneck on them.

Figure 1 lists the character accuracy of top methods on ICDAR 2019 Robust Reading Challenge on Arbitrary-Shaped Text leaderboard [6]. An obvious performance gap is observed between Chinese and English datasets. The character accuracy reaches over 70% on English datasets, while drops by approximately 10+% on Chinese datasets. We attribute the gap to the huge character set, complex character structures, and series of similar characters in Chinese Text Recognition (CTR). In other words, algorithms designed and evaluated on English datasets are incapable of performing well on Chinese datasets.

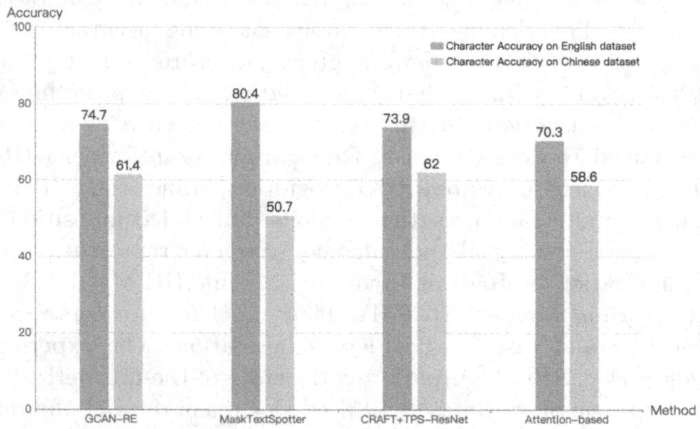

Fig. 1. The character accuracy of top methods on ICDAR 2019 Robust Reading Challenge on Arbitrary-Shaped Text leaderboard. There is a clear gap observed between English and Chinese datasets among four methods.

Due to the complex glyph structure and large size of character set, CTR algorithms require superb capacity of extracting multi-grained features. Inspired by language education of Chinese characters, researchers [4,34,42] have fused various component prior. However, most of these methods are designed for single-character recognition with matching strategy, thus unable to work on text line.

In this paper, we propose a CTR method named Radical-enhanced Recognition Transformer (RRecT), which introduces a Radical Prediction Module (RPM) and a Radical-Character Fusion Module (RCFM) based on a Recognition Transformer (RecT) backbone. An input image is first fed into RecT backbone to extract multi-grained feature, which is sequentially fed into radical and character feature compression modules respectively. Radical feature is directly applied for radical sequence prediction in RPM, while character feature is fused with the former in RCFM. To exploit the radical prior and prevent from learning the certain character-to-radicals mapping relationship, we utilize a parallel CTC-based [14] decoder, leading to a faster inference speed meanwhile. Therefore, radical and character ground truth could optimize our model synergistically. Moreover, we conduct a series of experiments to validate the effectiveness of our method. The experimental results demonstrate that RRecT achieves a competitive or better performance compared with the state-of-the-art methods on Scene, Web, Document, and Handwritten datasets [5]. In addition, since our architecture consists of only a customized RecT with an additional cross-attention operator and several linear layers, there is a significant advantage in training or inference speed.

To summarize, the contributions of this paper are three-fold:

1) We propose a CTR method named RRecT that exploits radical prior as an auxiliary supervision signal to promote recognition performance.
2) We introduce a Radical Predication Module and a Radical-Character Fusion Module based on customized Recognition Transformer, which improve the capacity of recognizing Chinese structures and characters.
3) The RRecT outperforms the state-of-the-art methods by a margin of 1.4% on the Scene and 1.8% on the Document dataset, while RRecT requires much less computation cost with parameters of 7.27M and inference speed of 5.2 ms.

2 Related Work

2.1 Scene Text Recognition

STR has been a focus of research for a long time, which could be divided into classical machine learning methods and deep learning methods.

Classical Machine Learning Methods. Traditional text recognition methods [2,24,25] utilize standard image features (such as HOG [8] and SIFT [23]) and handcrafted features with machine learning classifiers such as SVM [31]. Be confined to the expense and quality of feature extraction, traditional methods suffer from low speed and accuracy, especially on irregular texts.

Deep Learning Methods. With the explosive development of deep learning, researchers have adopted deep neural networks on STR. Early CNN-based methods [16,27,33] require location annotation of each character, suffering from complex and irrelevant backgrounds. Jaderberg [17] proposed to extract word-level representation and classify from 90k words. Considering that the text is organized as a character sequence, CRNN [26] utilized a CTC-based decoder and introduced LSTM to deal with the neglects of long distance dependencies. Seq2seq-based methods first produce a semantic visual representation, then transcribes it in auto-regressive manner. Currently, Du [11] demonstrated that a single visual model could also achieve a competitive performance in STR task.

2.2 Chinese Text Recognition

Experiments on Chinese datasets have shown [5] that these above advanced methods initially designed for English performs unsatisfactorily, and what makes it so difficult has been concluded by us as follow aspects:

Huge Character Set. According to Chinese national standard **GB18030-2005**[1], there are 70,244 Chinese characters. The size is much larger than English, leading to two intractable task [9], large-scale classification and few-shot learning.

Characters with Similar Forms. Similar patterns may mislead recognition. Taking English for example, *l*, *I* and *1* often confuse STR models. In pictograph Chinese, huge character set leads to more challenges, e.g., 戊, 戌, 戍, 戎 are slightly different on only one stroke but almost indistinguishable.

Further-Subdivided Characters. Characters may be mis-decomposed or mis-merged, e.g., *m* are recognized as *rn* and *vv* as *w* in English. Since Chinese radicals themselves could be legitimate characters, recognizer tends to misidentify Chinese more offen, e.g., 的 is recognized as 白勺 and 彳亍 as 行 ambiguously.

To address above problems, a series of work have attempted to incorporate component prior. Zhang [40] proposed RAN, utilizing RNN with attention to decode radical sequence and introducing a radical-to-character matcher. Wang [34] proposed DenseRAN, also following the paradigm of radical sequence prediction and character mapping. Chen [4] decomposed Chinese character into 5 categories of strokes and also utilized a matcher. Zu [42] utilized the number of radicals, the number of strokes and the total length of strokes to produce augmented character profiles, and then select the closest candidate through joint matching.

Although the above methods have achieved an excellent performance, most of them are CCR methods rather than CTR methods, which is designed for **single-character** datasets and constrained by **radical-to-sequence matching**. In this paper, we exploit the radical prior. Specifically, we utilize no radical-to-character matcher but still introduce radical prediction to supervise training. As a result, our model could capture radical information and produce radical-fused features for character recognition. To our knowledge, Our usage of radical prior is novel, effective and different from [4,34,40,42].

3 Method

3.1 Overall Architecture

An overview of the RRecT architecture is illustrated in Fig. 2. Given an input RGB image of size $H \times W \times 3$, it is firstly fed into an overlapping patch embedding block and transformed into $\frac{H}{4} \times \frac{W}{4}$ patches of dimension d_0 like ViT [10]. Each patch is regarded as a token with certain information. Then, three RecT blocks are carried out to reduce the size into $1 \times \frac{W}{4} \times d_3$. Through the adaptive

[1] https://zh.wikipedia.org/wiki/GB_18030.

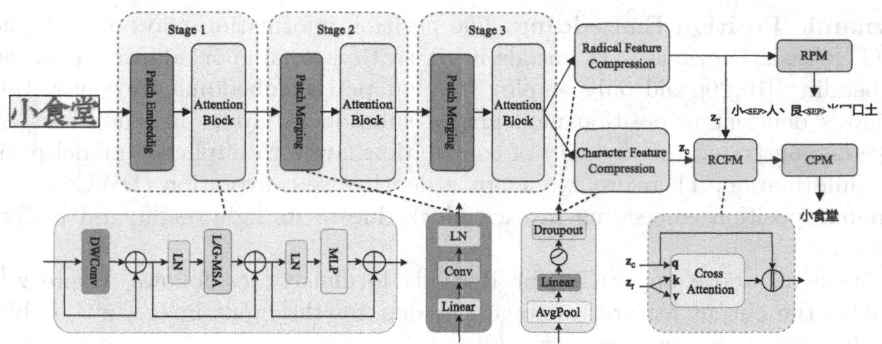

Fig. 2. Illustration of the RRecT. The three-stage RecT extracts multi-grained feature, the RPM supervises training by radical ground truth and the RCFM enhances character representation with radical feature. Each block is further illustrated at the bottom.

perception of self-attention mechanism in RecT blocks, both local patterns and global dependencies at multiple scales are captured. To exploit the multi-grained features, a Radical Prediction Module (RPM) is introduced to supervise training explicitly. Specifically, the feature map is transformed into radical feature and character feature, while the former is fed into a CTC-based parallel classifier to predict radical sequence. Furthermore, a Radical-Character Fusion Module (RCFM) is conducted to integrate the previous character feature with radical structure knowledge and produce radical-enhanced character feature. Finally, we utilize another CTC-based classifier to generate output character sequence.

3.2 Recognition Transformer Backbone

The standard ViT architecture utilizes global self-attention, which conducts attention computation between each patch and all other patches. To address the low efficiency of quadratic complexity and make it suitable for CTR task, we narrow the receptive field of self-attention, modify the reducing direction of patch merging and introduce dynamic position embedding in our RecT.

Local/Global Hybrid Attention Operation. Since shallow layers are expected to capture fine-grained patterns, we restrict attention within a local window in first several layers, denoted by L-MSA in this paper (G-MSA for vanilla version). Concretely, supposing that the window size K is set to $k_h \times k_w$, the attention receptive field is a $k_h \times k_w$ rectangle centered at each patch. Meanwhile, the computational complexity is reduced from quadratic to linear.

Width-Kept Patch Merging. Unlike image classification task requiring a holistic feature, CTR task prefers sequential features and thus the width of feature map is supposed to be long enough for recognition. We employ convolution layers with stride 1 in the width dimension and 2 in the height dimension so that the width is kept as a constant while the height is halved.

Dynamic Position Embedding. The position information plays a vital clue in CTR task. Previous ViTs encode it via static learnable or adaptive position embedding [10,20] and only employ it upon patch embedding. However, this usage is deficient in position modeling of subsequent layers. Recent works [7] have demonstrated the capacity of convolution layers to implicitly model position information. Therefore, we adopt a depth-wise convolution (DWConv) as dynamic position embedding in each block due to its lightweight and performance.

With all above approach, our RecT is formulated as follows, where $\mathbf{z}^{(l)}$ denotes the output features of stage l, $\mathbf{x}$ denotes the input image, $\hat{\mathbf{z}}^{(l-1)}$, $\mathbf{h}^{(l)}$ and $\hat{\mathbf{h}}^{(l)}$ denote intermediate embeddings.

$$\hat{\mathbf{z}}^{(0)} = \text{PatchEmbedding}\ (\mathbf{x}), \tag{1}$$

$$\hat{\mathbf{z}}^{(l-1)} = \text{PatchMerging}\ (\mathbf{z}^{(l-1)}), \tag{2}$$

$$\mathbf{h}^{(l)} = \hat{\mathbf{z}}^{(l-1)} + \text{DWConv}\ (\hat{\mathbf{z}}^{(l-1)}), \tag{3}$$

$$\hat{\mathbf{h}}^{(l)} = \text{L/G-MSA}\ (\text{LN}\ (\ \mathbf{h}^{(l)})) + \mathbf{h}^{(l)}, \tag{4}$$

$$\mathbf{z}^{(l)} = \text{MLP}\ (\text{LN}\ (\hat{\mathbf{h}}^{(l)})) + \hat{\mathbf{h}}^{(l)}. \tag{5}$$

3.3 Radical Prediction Module

Our method introduces a Radical Prediction Module (RPM) explicitly. Instead of using radical prediction for matching, we just regard it as an auxiliary task. We follow GB18030-2005 to decompose Chinese characters into radical sequences. As shown in Fig. 3, there are 12 basic glyph structures and thus each character could be decomposed into a radical tree. Nevertheless, predicting a tree structure implies additional model design and time cost, hence we adopt its inorder traversal as ground truth. We remove glyph structure symbols since recognizing structure requires more global information but we expect RPM to focus on radical patterns themselves. Furthermore, the ⟨SEP⟩ token is utilized to separate the radical sequence of different characters.

With the final feature map $\mathbf{z}^{(3)} \in \mathbb{R}^{1\times\frac{W}{4}\times d_3}$ extracted from RecT, we conduct a feature compression to produce radical feature, which is computed as:

$$\hat{\mathbf{z}}_r = \text{Linear}\ (\text{AvgPooling}\ (\mathbf{z}^{(3)})), \tag{6}$$

$$\mathbf{z}_r = \text{Dropout}\ (\text{Activation}\ (\hat{\mathbf{z}}_r)). \tag{7}$$

Firstly, an average pooling operator is employed to sample the size to $1 \times m$, where m denotes the maximum length of radical sequence. Then the pooled feature is further transformed by a linear layer, an activation and a dropout. Through above operations, we get information-rich radical feature.

To exploit radical prior implicitly, we utilize a linear layer as N_r-class classifier for recognition, where N_r is the number of radicals and special symbols. Here for the consideration that a Seq2Seq-based serial methods might tend to learn a character-to-radicals mapping relationship, we choose a parallel CTC-based [14] decoder. After classification, radical features is transcribed to radical

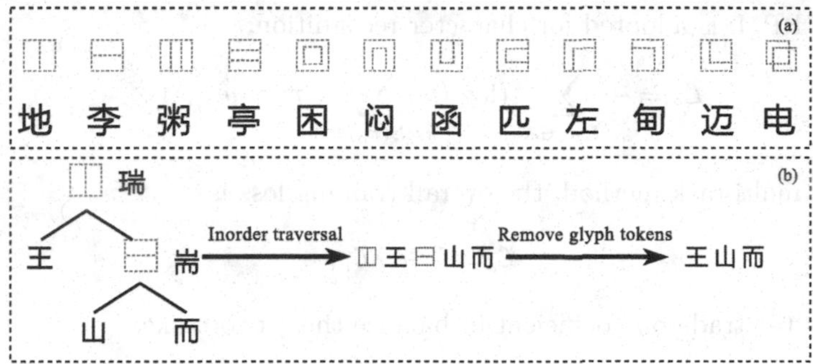

Fig. 3. (a) Twelve glyph structures of Chinese character. (b) An example of ground truth generation from tree glyph decomposition.

sequence with repetition, where non-text and non-Chinese characters are transcribed to blank and a special symbol. In the training stage, we employ CTC-Loss to supervise radical recognition and optimize parameters synergistically. Denoting the training dataset by $\mathcal{X} = \{I_i, r_i, c_i\}$, in which I_i is the training image, r_i is radical sequence label and c_i is character sequence label, the radical loss function is:

$$\mathcal{L}_r = -\sum_{I_i, r_i \in \mathcal{X}} (\log (\sum_{\pi_r : \mathcal{B}_r(\pi) = r_i} p(\pi_r | y_{(r)i}))). \tag{8}$$

In this equation, $\mathcal{B}_r$ is a mapping function from π_c onto r_i by removing repeated radicals and blank symbols, while $y_{(r)i}$ is the sequence produced by classifier. In the testing stage, the sequence is condensed to final deduplicated result.

3.4 Radical-Character Fusion Module

With radical prior introduced in RPM, we refocus on CTR task and attempt to utilize it in character recognition module. We propose a Radical-Character Fusion Module (RCFM) to integrate radical components inspired by the learning process of Chinese characters. Compared with RPM, RCFM exploit radical prior in a more explicit manner. Before RCFM, the semi-processed character feature is produced by another feature compression. Then a cross-attention mechanism is employed to capture and fuse corresponding radical information of characters:

$$\hat{\mathbf{z}}_c = \text{Linear}\ (\text{AvgPooling}\ (\mathbf{z}^{(3)})), \tag{9}$$

$$\mathbf{z}_c = \text{Dropout}\ (\text{Activation}\ (\hat{\mathbf{z}}_c)), \tag{10}$$

$$\mathbf{z}'_c = [\text{Attention}\ (\mathbf{z}_c, \mathbf{z}_r, \mathbf{z}_r) \parallel \mathbf{z}_c]. \tag{11}$$

where Attention is a standard attention operator with q, k and v as input. In the consideration of reducing information loss, we concatenate the semi-processed feature and radical-fused feature. Finally, Character Prediction Module (CPM), similar to RPM, is adopted for character recognition.

$$\mathcal{L}_c = -\sum_{I_i, c_i \in \mathcal{X}} (\log (\sum_{\pi_c : \mathcal{B}(\pi_c) = c_i} p(\pi_c | y_{(c)i}))). \tag{12}$$

Thus as a multi-task method, the overall training loss is:

$$\mathcal{L} = \mathcal{L}_c + \lambda \mathcal{L}_r. \tag{13}$$

where λ is the trade-off coefficient to balance these two tasks.

4 Experiments

4.1 Datasets

Extensive experiments are conducted on four public standard Chinese benchmarks collected by [5], including Scene, Web, Document and Handwritten dataset. Here not only scene text but also other types of datasets are chosen to demonstrate the capacity of our architecture on various kinds of data.

Scene dataset collects 636,455 scene text images from five benchmarks, RCTW [29], ReCTS [41], LSVT [30], ArT [6] and CTW [37]. The images are randomly split at a ratio of 8:1:1 into three parts. There are 509,164 samples for training, 63,645 samples for validation and 63,646 samples for testing.

Web dataset contains 140,589 images *on the Taobao Website* from the training set of MTWI [15]. 112,471 images are used in the training stage, while 14,059 images in the validation stage and the rest 14,059 images in the testing stage.

Document dataset is generated by Text Render with corpus from *wiki, films, amazon and baike.* This dataset comprises of 400,000 images for training, 50,000 images for validation and 50,000 images for testing.

Handwritten dataset is cropped from SCUT_HCCDoc [39], which captures unconstrained Chinese handwritten images. These 93,254 images are divided into 74,603 for training, 18,651 for validation and 23,389 for testing.

4.2 Implementation Details

For all datasets, the image is resized to 32×320 before being fed into RRecT. The maximum length is 80 for radical and 40 for character. The embedding size is set to 64, 128, 256 for three RecT stages respectively and 96 for radical and character feature. Empirically, we set the trade-off coefficient λ to 0.5 in loss function. We train RRecT models for 150 epochs on each dataset, containing the first 2 warm-up [13] epochs. We use AdamW [22] optimizer with β_1 of 0.9, β_2 of 0.99, weight decay of 0.05 and cosine learning rate scheduler [21]. We implement the RRecT with PaddlePaddle and conduct experiments on two NVIDIA GeForce GTX 1080 Ti GPU 11GB with the batch size of 128.

$$\text{CACC} = \frac{1}{N}\sum_{i=1}^{N}\mathbb{I}(y_i = \hat{y}_i) \tag{14}$$

$$\text{NED} = 1 - \frac{1}{N}\sum_{i=1}^{N}\frac{\text{EditDistance}(y_i, \hat{y}_i)}{\max(\text{len}(\text{y}_\text{i}), \text{len}(\hat{\text{y}}_\text{i}))} \tag{15}$$

For evaluation, we choose two measures, Character Accuracy (CACC) and Normalized Edit Distance (NED) as metrics.

4.3 Comparison with Existing Methods

We compare RRecT with previous well-known models, including CRNN [26], ASTER [28], SAR [19], SRN [36], TransOCR [3], SVTR [11], DenseRAN [34] and ACPM [42]. CRNN adopts LSTM to encode sequential feature from CNN backbone. ASTER is a rectification-based method that introduces a Spatial Transformer Network (STN) [18] to address the irregularity of text. SAR focuses on curved texts and utilizes a 2D attention for decoding. SRN designs a parallel visual attention architecture for correction. SVTR utilizes a single visual model and show superiority in STR. The DenseRAN and ACPM are single-character CCR methods. DenseRAN predicts radical sequence and exploits radical-to-character matching. ACPM produces several augmented character profiles and then select the closest candidate through joint matching.

For general methods, we cite the results in [5] and follow the pipeline of original paper to test the speed. For DenseRAN and ACPM, we first cut the image in width to get potential single-character images, then feed them into the model sequentially. Since the characters are predicted in one-by-one manner, the NED is not calculated for DenseRAN and ACPM.

The experimental results are elaborated in Table 1 and the RRecT yields a competitive or higher performance compared with existing state-of-the-art methods across all datasets. In detail, RRecT reachs the best CACC on the Scene and Document, while the second best on the Web. Compared with the TransOCR, the best performing among the listed general, there is a 1.4% CACC increase observed on the Scene and 1.8% on the Document, demonstrating the benifit of RRecT to exploit radical prior and further promote recognition. Compared with the ACPM, the best Chinese-specific method, the RRecT outperforms by a wide margin in the Scene, web and Document, which also demonstrates the wonderful performance on various scenarios.

Although the CACC is slightly lower than TransOCR on the Web and Handwritten, our RRecT requires far fewer computing power and reaches a significantly higher performance than all other methods. Compared with DenseRAN and ACPM, the RRecT performs slightly worse on the Handwritten, we hold the view that the radical-to-character matcher in these methods is more applicable on scrawl and irregular samples. In addition, these two methods are originally proposed for offline handwritten CCR. Even so, our RRecT achieves a superior CACC than all methods except heavyweight TransOCR, proving the effectiveness and efficiency of our method.

Table 1. Experimental Results on four Chinese benchmarks against existing methods, using CACC and NED as metrics. The first 6 rows are general methods while the rest 2 rows are single-character CCR methods. The best results are shown **in bold**.

Method	Scene		Web		Document		Handwritten		Params(M)/Speed(ms)
	CACC	NED	CACC	NED	CACC	NED	CACC	NED	
CRNN	53.4	0.734	54.5	0.736	97.5	0.994	46.4	0.840	8.3/6.3
ASTER	54.5	0.695	52.3	0.689	93.1	0.989	39.9	0.720	27.2/-
SAR	62.5	0.785	53.3	0.725	93.8	0.987	31.4	0.655	27.8/120
SRN	60.1	0.778	52.3	0.706	96.7	0.995	18.0	0.512	64.3/25.4
TransOCR	63.3	0.802	**62.3**	0.787	96.9	0.994	53.4	0.849	83.9/132
SVTR	61.7	0.786	55.7	0.737	96.9	0.997	44.1	0.834	**6.1/4.5**
DenseRAN	54.9	-	46.3	-	97.4	-	54.3	-	67.2/423
ACPM	58.2	-	49.7	-	97.9	-	**60.1**	-	80.9/745
RRecT	**64.7**	**0.804**	62.1	**0.788**	**98.7**	**0.998**	52.9	**0.856**	7.27/5.2

Moreover, experimental results show an improvement of NED on all benchmarks, thus verify that RRecT could capture enriched radical information to reduce wrong recognition and redundant prediction. Also, parameter and the inference speed per image are depicted in Table 1. Compared with similar magnitude of model, encouragingly, our RRecT shows a noticeable lead in both CACC and NED with a wonderful inference speed across all datasets, which further indicates the advantage of RRecT.

4.4 Ablation Study

To specify the independent contribution of each design and better understand RRecT, we conduct ablation studies by removing DPE, RPM and RCFM sequentially. All experiments are carried out on the Scene and Web datasets.

Dynamic Position Embedding. As shown in Table 2, a slight drop is observed after eliminating DPE from RRecT. Our ultimate RRecT model achieves a higher performance by 0.6%/0.004 and 0.3%/0.006 on CACC/NED, demonstrating that DPE is a suitable position embedding strategy on CTR.

Radical Prediction Module. Since we introduce radical prior knowledge through RPM, it is quite necessary to investigate whether this design leads to improvement. By blocking the supervision from radical sequence ground truth, as seen in Line 4 of Table 2, the CACC and NED drops considerably by 2.4% (from 64.7% to 62.3%) and 0.014 (from 0.804 to 0.790) on the Scene dataset, 2.7% (from 62.1% to 59.4%) and 0.020 (from 0.788 to 0.768) on the Web dataset. Therefore, observing such a clear margin, we could draw a conclusion that our multi-task joint training strategy with hybrid loss could capture more comprehensive information and enhance the feature representation.

Radical-Character Fusion Module. In our RRecT, RCFM introduces radical information explicitly into character feature, hence we conduct a experiment to validate its effectiveness. Specifically, we remove RCFM along with RPM and the experimental results show a 1%/0.006 drop on the Scene dataset and a 1.1%/0.008 drop on the Web dataset from the variant model *without DPE*. This significant decrease illustrates the necessity of RCFM.

Table 2. Ablation studies with respect to the DPE, RPM and RCFM of our method. Superscript "↓" indicates the performance drop compared with ultimate RRecT.

Model	Scene		Web	
	CACC	NED	CACC	NED
RRecT	64.7	0.804	62.1	0.788
w/o DPE	$64.1^{\downarrow 0.6}$	$0.800^{\downarrow 0.004}$	$61.8^{\downarrow 0.3}$	$0.782^{\downarrow 0.006}$
w/o DPE & RCFM	$63.1^{\downarrow 1.6}$	$0.794^{\downarrow 0.010}$	$60.7^{\downarrow 1.4}$	$0.774^{\downarrow 0.014}$
w/o RPM	$62.3^{\downarrow 2.4}$	$0.790^{\downarrow 0.014}$	$59.4^{\downarrow 2.7}$	$0.768^{\downarrow 0.020}$

5 Conclusion

This paper proposes a novel network named RRecT for Chinese text recognition. We design an excellent architecture for CTR and exploit radical prior knowledge of Chinese in a multi-task manner to train a more general and robust visual encoder. The RRecT first extracts multi-grained features with our proposed customized RecT backbone. Then, it utilizes radical decomposition as an auxiliary supervision signal and enhances character representation by radical feature through cross-attention mechanism. Extensive experimental results and detailed ablation analysis on four benchmark datasets show that our method is superior compared with existing state-of-the-art methods. With much fewer parameters, RRecT is also more effective, economical and environment-friendly.

There is still vast scope to explore in CTR field. Firstly, we tend to further customize RecT backbone to better and faster extract adaptive recognition features. Secondly, from our point of view, exploiting more fine-grained information like stroke decomposition may further promote the performance. However, the sequence of stroke decomposition will be far longer than that of radical decomposition and requires an effective pre-processing strategy. Hence, we hope that our RRecT could inspire and foster follow-up works.

Acknowledgement. This work was supported by the National Natural Science Foundation of China (Grant No. 92270201).

References

1. Borisyuk, F., Gordo, A., Sivakumar, V.: Rosetta: large scale system for text detection and recognition in images. In: Proceedings of KDD (2018)
2. de Campos, T.E., Babu, B.R., Varma, M.: Character recognition in natural images. In: VISAPP (2) (2009)
3. Chen, J., Li, B., Xue, X.: Scene text telescope: text-focused scene image super-resolution. In: CVPR (2021)
4. Chen, J., Li, B., Xue, X.: Zero-shot Chinese character recognition with stroke-level decomposition. In: Proceedings of IJCAI (2021)
5. Chen, J., et al.: Benchmarking Chinese text recognition: datasets, baselines, and an empirical study. CoRR (2021)
6. Chng, C.K., et al.: ICDAR2019 robust reading challenge on arbitrary-shaped text - RRC-art. In: ICDAR (2019)
7. Chu, X., Zhang, B., Tian, Z., Wei, X., Xia, H.: Do we really need explicit position encodings for vision transformers? CoRR (2021)
8. Dalal, N., Triggs, B.: Histograms of oriented gradients for human detection. In: CVPR (1) (2005)
9. Deng, J., Berg, A.C., Li, K., Fei-Fei, L.: What does classifying more than 10,000 image categories tell us? In: Daniilidis, K., Maragos, P., Paragios, N. (eds.) ECCV 2010. LNCS, vol. 6315, pp. 71–84. Springer, Heidelberg (2010). https://doi.org/10.1007/978-3-642-15555-0_6
10. Dosovitskiy, A., et al.: An image is worth 16x16 words: transformers for image recognition at scale. In: ICLR (2021)
11. Du, Y., et al.: SVTR: scene text recognition with a single visual model. In: Proceedings of IJCAI (2022)
12. Fang, S., Xie, H., Wang, Y., Mao, Z., Zhang, Y.: Read like humans: autonomous, bidirectional and iterative language modeling for scene text recognition. In: CVPR (2021)
13. Goyal, P., et al.: Accurate, large minibatch SGD: training imagenet in 1 hour. CoRR (2017)
14. Graves, A., Fernández, S., Gomez, F.J., Schmidhuber, J.: Connectionist temporal classification: labelling unsegmented sequence data with recurrent neural networks. In: ICML (2006)
15. He, M., et al.: ICPR2018 contest on robust reading for multi-type web images. In: ICPR (2018)
16. Jaderberg, M., Simonyan, K., Vedaldi, A., Zisserman, A.: Synthetic data and artificial neural networks for natural scene text recognition. CoRR (2014)
17. Jaderberg, M., Simonyan, K., Vedaldi, A., Zisserman, A.: Reading text in the wild with convolutional neural networks. Int. J. Comput. Vis. **116**, 1–20 (2016)
18. Jaderberg, M., Simonyan, K., Zisserman, A., Kavukcuoglu, K.: Spatial transformer networks. In: NIPS (2015)
19. Li, H., Wang, P., Shen, C., Zhang, G.: Show, attend and read: a simple and strong baseline for irregular text recognition. In: Proceedings of AAAI (2019)
20. Liu, Z., et al.: Swin transformer: hierarchical vision transformer using shifted windows. In: ICCV (2021)
21. Loshchilov, I., Hutter, F.: SGDR: stochastic gradient descent with warm restarts. In: ICLR (Poster) (2017)
22. Loshchilov, I., Hutter, F.: Decoupled weight decay regularization. In: ICLR (Poster) (2019)

23. Lowe, D.G.: Distinctive image features from scale-invariant keypoints. Int. J. Comput. Vis. **60**, 91–110 (2004)
24. Pan, Y., Hou, X., Liu, C.: Text localization in natural scene images based on conditional random field. In: ICDAR (2009)
25. Sawaki, M., Murase, H., Hagita, N.: Automatic acquisition of context-based image templates for degraded character recognition in scene images. In: ICPR (2000)
26. Shi, B., Bai, X., Yao, C.: An end-to-end trainable neural network for image-based sequence recognition and its application to scene text recognition. IEEE Trans. Pattern Anal. Mach. Intell. **39**(11), 2298–2304 (2017)
27. Shi, B., Wang, X., Lyu, P., Yao, C., Bai, X.: Robust scene text recognition with automatic rectification. In: CVPR (2016)
28. Shi, B., Yang, M., Wang, X., Lyu, P., Yao, C., Bai, X.: ASTER: an attentional scene text recognizer with flexible rectification. IEEE Trans. Pattern Anal. Mach. Intell. **41**(9), 2035–2048 (2019)
29. Shi, B., et al.: ICDAR2017 competition on reading Chinese text in the wild (RCTW-17). In: ICDAR (2017)
30. Sun, Y., et al.: ICDAR 2019 competition on large-scale street view text with partial labeling - RRC-LSVT. In: ICDAR (2019)
31. Suykens, J.A.K., Vandewalle, J.: Least squares support vector machine classifiers. Neural Process. Lett. **9**, 293–300 (1999)
32. Tang, X., Lai, Y., Liu, Y., Fu, Y., Fang, R.: Visual-semantic transformer for scene text recognition. CoRR (2021)
33. Wang, T., Wu, D.J., Coates, A., Ng, A.Y.: End-to-end text recognition with convolutional neural networks. In: ICPR (2012)
34. Wang, W., Zhang, J., Du, J., Wang, Z., Zhu, Y.: Denseran for offline handwritten Chinese character recognition. In: ICFHR (2018)
35. Yang, Y., Li, D., Duan, Z.: Chinese vehicle license plate recognition using kernel-based extreme learning machine with deep convolutional features. IET Intell. Transp. Syst. **12**(3), 213–219 (2018)
36. Yu, D., et al.: Towards accurate scene text recognition with semantic reasoning networks. In: CVPR (2020)
37. Yuan, T., Zhu, Z., Xu, K., Li, C., Mu, T., Hu, S.: A large Chinese text dataset in the wild. J. Comput. Sci. Technol. **34**, 509–521 (2019)
38. Zhang, C., Ding, W., Peng, G., Fu, F., Wang, W.: Street view text recognition with deep learning for urban scene understanding in intelligent transportation systems. IEEE Trans. Intell. Transp. Syst. **22**(7), 4727–4743 (2021)
39. Zhang, H., Liang, L., Jin, L.: SCUT-HCCDoc: a new benchmark dataset of handwritten Chinese text in unconstrained camera-captured documents. Pattern Recognit. **108**, 107559 (2020)
40. Zhang, J., Du, J., Dai, L.: Radical analysis network for learning hierarchies of Chinese characters. Pattern Recognit. **103**, 107305 (2020)
41. Zhang, R., et al.: ICDAR 2019 robust reading challenge on reading Chinese text on signboard. In: ICDAR (2019)
42. Zu, X., Yu, H., Li, B., Xue, X.: Chinese character recognition with augmented character profile matching. In: ACM Multimedia (2022)

S^2R: Exploring a Double-Win Transformer-Based Framework for Ideal and Blind Super-Resolution

Minghao She, Wendong Mao(✉), Huihong Shi, and Zhongfeng Wang(✉)

School of Electronic Science and Engineering, Nanjing University, Nanjing, People's Republic of China
{mhshe,wdmao,shihh}@smail.nju.edu.cn, zfwang@nju.edu.cn

Abstract. Nowadays, deep learning based methods have demonstrated impressive performance on ideal super-resolution (SR) datasets, but most of these methods incur dramatically performance drops when directly applied in real-world SR reconstruction tasks with unpredictable blur kernels. To tackle this issue, blind SR methods are proposed to improve the visual results on random blur kernels, which causes unsatisfactory reconstruction effects on ideal low-resolution images similarly. In this paper, we propose a double-win framework for ideal and blind SR task, named S^2R, including a light-weight transformer-based SR model (S^2R transformer) and a novel coarse-to-fine training strategy, which can achieve excellent visual results on both ideal and random fuzzy conditions. On algorithm level, S^2R transformer smartly combines some efficient and light-weight blocks to enhance the representation ability of extracted features with relatively low number of parameters. For training strategy, a coarse-level learning process is firstly performed to improve the generalization of the network with the help of a large-scale external dataset, and then, a fast fine-tune process is developed to transfer the pre-trained model to real-world SR tasks by mining the internal features of the image. Experimental results show that the proposed S^2R outperforms other single-image SR models in ideal SR condition with only 578K parameters. Meanwhile, it can achieve better visual results than regular blind SR models in blind fuzzy conditions with only 10 gradient updates, which improve convergence speed by 300 times, significantly accelerating the transfer-learning process in real-world situations. Codes will be found in https://github.com/berumotto-vermouth/S2R.

Keywords: Super-Resolution · Image Processing · Blind Super-Resolution · Transformer

This work was supported in part by National Key R&D Program of China under Grant 2022YFB4400604.

L. Iliadis et al. (Eds.): ICANN 2023, LNCS 14259, pp. 522–537, 2023.
https://doi.org/10.1007/978-3-031-44223-0_42

1 Introduction

Super-Resolution (SR) is proposed to increase the resolution of low-quality images and enhance their clarity. As a fundamental low-level vision task, single image super-resolution (SISR), which aims to recover plausible high-resolution (HR) images from their counterpart low-resolution (LR) images, has attracted increasing attention. With the remarkable success of convolutional neural networks (CNNs), various deep learning based methods with different network architectures and training strategies have been proposed for SISR and achieved prominent visual results. Most of them are optimized upon a large number of external training dataset, which uses the fixed bicubic operation to downsample HR images for obtaining LR images and constructing paired training datasets. For imitating low-resolution images in ideal conditions, in regular tasks, the LR images are generated by down-sampling in the noise-free bicubic condition. In this way, several previous deep learning based methods [8,20,23,30,41] show excellent performance in ideal conditions.

In real-world situations, noise and blur are inevitable and influenced by actual equipment, such as camera lens condition, shooting conditions, which is sometimes different from the ideal one. And these blur kernels affected by real-world conditions are unpredictable in most cases. Thus, to imitate the actual degradation blur condition of real-world images, most blind SR methods [2,12,35] assume that the LR input image is obtained by down-sampling the counterpart HR image by an unpredictable blur kernel. As revealed in [9], learning-based methods will suffer severe performance drops when the blur kernels in the test phase and the training phase are inconsistent. This kind of kernel mismatch will introduce undesired artifacts to output images. Thus, the problem with unpredictable blur kernels, also known as blind SR, has limited the application of some deep learning based SR methods in real-world situations. To solve this limitation, several novel methods have been proposed. For instance, some blind SR methods [2,12,35] are model-based, which introduce prior knowledge to the deep learning area and usually involve complicated optimization procedures. These methods do not calculate the SR kernel directly, but assume that SR networks are robust and transferable to variations in the downsampling kernels. [29] exploited the recurrence of small image patches across scales of a single image to estimate the unknown SR kernel directly from the LR input image. However, it fails when the SR scale is larger than 2, and the runtime is very long. ZSSR [32] does not adopt the regular training process on the external datasets and trains from scratch for each test image, so that specific models pay more attention to information in the picture. Nevertheless, the runtime is greatly increased, limiting its application in the real scene. The current challenge is that in the above SR models, no one can show ideal performance simultaneously on both SISR and blind SR tasks. Thus, it's urgent to propose an SR method to solve this challenge.

In this paper, we propose a novel framework S^2R. In it, inspired by the great success of transformer in computer vision tasks, a light-weight transformer-based model is proposed to achieve excellent performance in the ideal LR condition, and a novel coarse-to-fine training strategy is performed to boost the scalability for guaranteeing the real-world applications and achieving fast convergence by extremely few gradient updates. The detailed contributions are shown as follow:

- To achieve excellent performance in ideal and blind SR conditions, we propose a new framework S^2R, containing a light-weight transformer-based model where the excellent visual results can be achieved in ideal conditions, and a novel coarse-to-fine training strategy where the proposed model can be extended to the real-world applications.
- For the network architecture, we propose a light-weight transformer-based model for super resolution, which enhances the representational power by combining several light-weight efficient blocks, achieving good performance in ideal SISR tasks.
- To boost the scalability of the proposed model in real-world situations, we further propose a new coarse-to-fine training strategy, which is to pre-train the proposed model on a large-scale external dataset, and then, perform transfer-learning on a new internal real-world dataset to take advantage of external and internal learning, realizing better performance and fast-adaption for real-world applications.
- The experiment result shows the superiority of the proposed framework. For SISR tasks, compared to sort-of-the-art (SOTA) transformer-based models, our methods can achieve comparable performance with minimum number of parameters. And for blind SR tasks, our methods can achieve better performance and clearer outputs than other blind SR models. Moreover, the proposed framework reduces the number of backpropagation gradient updates by 300 times.

2 Related Work

2.1 Single Image Super Resolution

SISR is based on the image degradation model as

$$I_{LR} = (I_{HR} * k_s) \downarrow_s, \tag{1}$$

where I_{HR}, I_{LR}, k_s, s denote HR, LR image, SR kernel, and scaling factor, respectively. Recently, CNN-based methods [8,18,20,30,33] have demonstrated impressive performance in SR tasks. SRGAN [21] first introduced residual blocks into SR networks. EDSR [24] also used a deep residual network for training SR model but removed the unnecessary batch normalization layer in the residual block. Zhang *et al.* [42] achieved better performance than EDSR by introducing the channel attention to residual block to form a very deep network. Haris *et al.* [11] proposed deep back-projection networks to exploit iterative up and down sampling layers, providing an error feedback mechanism for projection errors at each stage. SRMD [40] proposed a stretching strategy to integrate kernel and noise information to cope with multi-degradation kernels in an SR network. The breakthrough of transformer networks in natural language processing (NLP) inspires researchers to use self-attention (SA) in vision tasks. Thus, the transformer-based SR models come into being. SwinIR [23] adapted the Swin Transformer [25] to image restoration, which combines the advantage of both CNNs and transformers. ELAN [41] based on SwinIR [23], removed redundant designs such as masking strategy and relative position encoding to make the network more slim. Reducing the number of parameters of transformer-based methods and alleviating performance drops is a feasible direction. Based on this, we introduce some light-weight blocks to reduce parameters further, and boost the representational power, achieving good visual results.

2.2 Blind Super-Resolution

Compared to SISR, blind SR assumes that the degradation blur kernels are unpredictable. In real-world applications, the SR kernel of images is influenced by the sensor optics. In recent years, some blind SR methods [12,35] introduce prior knowledge into the deep learning area. However, these methods are to make their models more robust to variations, rather than explicitly calculating the SR kernel. In contrast, [29] estimates the kernel based on the recurrence of small image patches (5×5, 7×7) across scales of a single image but fails for SR scale factors larger than 2. KernelGAN [3] based on Interal-GAN [31] estimates the SR kernel that best preserves the distribution of patches across scales of the LR image. ZSSR [32] trains a small full convolution network for each image from scratch to learn image-specific internal structure, rather than adapting the training process to big data. However, it drastically increases the runtime for thousands of backpropagation gradient updates at test time. In contrast, the proposed methods can significantly reduce the runtime with the help of our pre-train model on a large-scale external dataset.

3 The Proposed S^{2}R Framework

In this section, we introduce a double-win framework for ideal and blind SR (S^{2}R), which consists of a light-weight transformer-based model (S^{2}R transformer) and a novel coarse-to-fine training strategy, as shown in Fig. 1. With the proposed training strategy, the proposed model can achieve significant performance with a few backpropagation gradient updates and great scalability for the real-world applications. The learning process of the framework is mainly divided to two stages, coarse-level learning on the general dataset and fast fine-tune on real-world images. The first stage is to pre-train the proposed model on a large scale external dataset to guarantee its great visual results on ideal LR conditions and fast-adaption when the proposed model is extended to the real-world situations. The second stage is to boost the scalability of our model, to extend the real-world applications.

3.1 Network Architecture

As shown in Fig. 1(a), the proposed S^{2}R transformer contains three modules, a shallow feature extraction module (SF), a deep feature extraction module (DF)

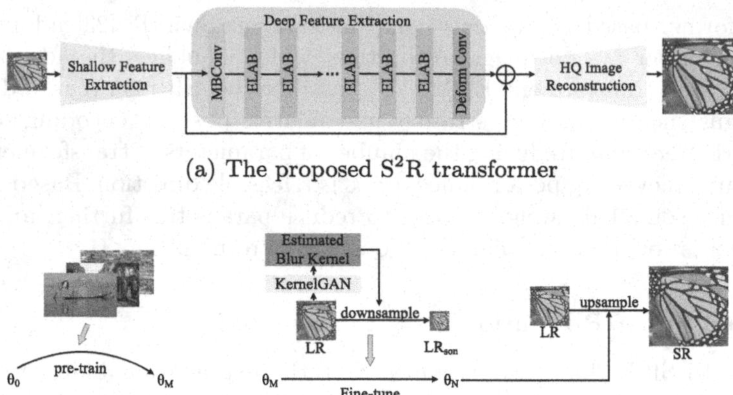

(a) The proposed S^2R transformer

(b) The proposed coarse-to-fine training strategy

Fig. 1. Illustration of the proposed S^2R framework. (a) The architecture of the proposed model, S^2R transformer. (b) The overall pipeline of the proposed coarse-to-fine training strategy.

and a high-quality image reconstruction module (RC). Specifically, given a low-resolution (LR) input $I_{LR} \in \mathbb{R}^{3\times\mathbb{H}\times\mathbb{W}}$, where H and W are the height and width of the LR image, respectively, we first use the shallow feature extraction module denoted by $H_{SF}(\cdot)$, which only consists of a single 3×3 convolution, to extract local feature $I_{local} \in \mathbb{R}^{\mathbb{C}\times\mathbb{H}\times\mathbb{W}}$, the deep feature extraction module consists of a mobile bottleneck convolution (**MBConv**), denoted by H_{mbconv}, N cascaded efficient long-range attention blocks (**ELAB**), denoted by H_{ELAB}, a deformable convolution [6] (**Deform Conv**), denoted by H_{deform} and a 3×3 convolution:

$$I_{local} = H_{SF}(I_{LR}), \tag{2}$$

where C is the feature channel number.

I_{local} then goes to the deep feature extraction module, denoted by $H_{DF}(\cdot)$. That is:

$$I_{deep} = H_{DF}(I_{local}), \tag{3}$$

where $I_{deep} \in \mathbb{R}^{\mathbb{C}\times\mathbb{H}\times\mathbb{W}}$ denotes the output of the deep feature extraction module. More specifically, intermediate features I_{mbconv}, I_{deform}, $I_1, I_2, \ldots, I_N$, and the output deep feature I_{deep} are extracted block by block as

$$\begin{aligned} I_{mbconv} &= H_{mbconv}(I_{local}) \\ I_i &= H_{ELAB_i}(I_{i-1}), \qquad i = 1, 2, \ldots, N \\ I_{deform} &= H_{deform}(I_N) \\ I_{deep} &= H_{CONV}(I_{deform}), \end{aligned} \tag{4}$$

where $H_{ELAB_i}(\cdot)$ denotes the i-th ELAB and H_{CONV} is the last convolutional layer. Finally, taking I_{deep} and I_{local} as inputs, the HR image I_{HQ} is reconstructed as:

$$I_{RHQ} = H_{RC}(I_{deep} + I_{local}), \quad (5)$$

where H_{RC} is the reconstruction module. Here we choose a sub-pixel convolution layer [30] to upsample the feature. The proposed model can be optimized with the commonly used loss functions for SR, such as L_2 [7] and L_1 [20,24,43]. For simplicity, we choose L_1 as our loss function by minimizing the L_1 pixel loss.

ELAB. Despite the great success of transformer on computer vision tasks, it greatly suffers from explosive parameters and high computational complexity. Thus, inspired by [41], we introduce ELAB to achieve a good performance in the case of a relatively low number of parameters. In ELAB, the regular multi-layer perception is replaced with two shift-conv [36] with a simple ReLU activation. It can help enlarge the receptive field of the proposed model preliminarily, while sharing the same arithmetic complexity as two cascaded 1×1 convolutions. Moreover, to significantly reduce parameters, the accelerated attention mechanism (ASA) is utilized. In the self-attention calculation procedure, three independent 1×1 convolutions, denoted by θ, ϕ, ψ, are employed to map the input feature X into three different feature maps. In ELAB, θ is set the same as ϕ, which can save 1×1 convolution in each self-attention. For compensating for performance drops caused by the reduced number of parameters, instead of the regular self-attention, the group-wise multi-scale self-attention (GMSA) is used. The computational complexity of the regular window-based self-attention [25] is determined by the window size M. Thus, in GMSA, the input feature map is divided into three groups, and then set a flexible window size for each group. In this way, the relative position bias in regular transformer-based SISR models, which makes models fragile to the resolution change [38], can be removed. Based on this, the proposed model can also extract information with different scales and be more flexible to the input, which makes it feasible to extend the proposed model to real-world applications. Finally, batch normalization (BN) [16] is utilized to replace layer normalization (LN), accelerating the calculation by avoiding fragmenting the calculation into many element-wise inefficient operations.

MBConv. For further performance improvement, inspired by the intuition that the bottleneck actually contains all the necessary information, MBConv is introduced to enhance the representational power. It is based on depthwise separable convolution [5], which inherently has fewer parameters than the full convolution. Thus, it will not bring lots of parameters. Furthermore, a squeeze-and-excitation optimization [13] is added to enlarge the receptive field further. For its inverted design, it is more memory efficient which will further decrease running time and parameter count for bottleneck convolution. Therefore, this light-weight block can help the proposed model get a larger receptive field and better performance. Recent studies [10,37] suggest that using convolutions in early stages benefits the performance of Vision Transformers. Thus, we follow this design to put MBConv in early stages.

Deform Conv. To extract irregular structural features, a Deform Conv is added. It is based on the idea of augmenting the spatial sampling in the modules with additional offsets and learning the offsets from the target tasks, without introducing additional supervision. Thus, it is lightweight on its own, without sacrificing computing resources to trade off the performance. Furthermore, as the receptive field is further enlarged, it can facilitate generalization to new tasks possessing unpredictable geometric transformations, improving the performance in SISR tasks, and supporting subsequently migrating the proposed model into the real-world applications.

3.2 The Proposed Coarse-to-Fine Training Strategy

To guarantee impressive performance in ideal SR conditions while extending the proposed model to applications in the real world, we propose a coarse-to-fine training strategy. Figure 1(b) shows the pipeline of the proposed fast training strategy. It consists of two stages, coarse-level learning on the general dataset and fast fine-tune on real-world images.

Coarse-Level Learning on the General Dataset. Considering that most blind SR methods directly train on the input test dataset, without fully exploiting the large-scale external dataset. Thus, as shown on the left side of the dotted line in Fig. 1(b), we firstly pre-train S^2R transformer on the external dataset (noise-free "bicubic" dataset). This procedure can guarantee the good performance on SISR tasks, even if the proposed model is migrated to the real-world applications.

Fast Fine-Tune on Real-World Images. Avoiding deviating from the goal of calculating the blur kernel to deal with blind SR tasks, rather than just make the proposed model robust to variations in the degradation LR kernel, it's necessary to estimate the SR kernel that best preserves the distribution of patches across scales of the LR image, which can compensate for the performance drop caused by the blur kernel mismatch. Recent studies [3,29,44] have exploited the kernel estimation well, we estimate the blur kernel by the method in [3], where its *Generator* is trained to generate a downscaled image of the LR test image, such that its *Discriminator* cannot distinguish between the patch distribution of the downscaled image and the origin.

The diversity of the LR-HR relations within a single image is significantly small, related to noise and blur kernel. Thus, as shown on the right side of the dotted line in Fig. 1(b), given an LR real-world test image I_{LR}, we use the estimated blur kernel K to generate the lower resolution image I_{LRson}, and synthesize them as a data pair LR-LR_{son}. Then, we use the pre-trained model generated in *Coarse-Level Learning on the General Dataset* to generate the corresponding high-resolution version I_{SR} of the I_{LRson}, and optimize to learn the residual between I_{SR} and I_{LR}. With the help of training with the external dataset and the proposed light-weight transformer-based model, the runtime can be drastically reduced. Thus, only 10 iterations are needed. Furthermore, a learning-rate update policy is performed, where we start with a learning rate of β_0, and then, change to β_1 when the iteration is not larger than 4, and keep β_2 until the end. Finally, the method in [24], where 8 different outputs for several rotations and flips of the test image I are generated and combined, is utilized to improve the performance on images in real-world situations. Moreover, their mean is replaced with the median of these 8 outputs. We further combine it with the back-projection of [17], so that each of the 8 output images goes through multiple iterations of the back-projection and the final correction of the median image can also be done through the back projection.

Compared to conventional blind SR methods, such as ZSSR [32], and conventional SISR methods, such as SwinIR [23], the advantages of the proposed framework are twofold:

- In terms of network architecture, compared to ZSSR, whose backbone is a fully convolutional network, our model is based on transformer blocks which have more powerful learning and representation, thus achieving better performance than ZSSR.
- In terms of training strategy, ZSSR trains from scratch on the small dataset for implementing the SR task, while we pre-train the proposed model on the external dataset, and then, transfer-learning is performed on the proposed model to extend our model to a new SR task. It makes our model fast-adaption on downstream tasks and real-world applications and further boosts the performance of the proposed model.

4 Experiments and Results

4.1 Training Details

For the pre-trained stage, we employ the DIV2K dataset [34] with 800 training images to train our model, which consists of 10 ELABs with 60 channels, an MBConv, and a Deformable Conv. The model is trained using the ADAM [19] optimizer with the learning rate $\beta = 2 \times 10^{-4}$. Following ELAN [41], our multi-scale window sizes are set: 4×4, 8×8 and 16×16. The model training is conducted by Pytorch on NVIDIA 2080Ti GPUs. For the transfer-learning stage, our model is fine-tuned for 10 iterations, using the ADAM [19] optimizer with the learning rate $\beta_0 = 2 \times 10^{-2}$, and then, change to $\beta_1 = 1 \times 10^{-2}$ when the iteration is not larger than 4, and keep $\beta_2 = 5 \times 10^{-3}$ until the end.

4.2 Evaluations on Ideal Super-Resolution Dataset

We evaluate our model with several popular SISR models, including CNN-based models CARN [1], IMDN [15], LAPAR-A [22], LatticeNet [26], and transformer-based models SwinIR-light [23] and ELAN-light [41] on popular benchmarks:

Set5 [4], Set14 [39], BSD100 [27], Urban100 [14] and Manga109 [28], for performance comparison. Peak Signal-to-Noise Ratio (PSNR) and Structural SIMilarity (SSIM) are used as evaluation metrics, which are calculated on the Y channel after converting RGB to YCbCr format.

Quantitative Comparison. The quantitative indexes of different methods are reported in Table 1. The transformer-based methods outperform many CNN-based methods, by exploiting the self-similarity of images. However, among them, SwinIR-light [23] suffers from its high number of parameters, which will place a heavy burden on the deployment, limiting its applications in real-world situations. Compared to it, ELAN-light [41] improves the performance and accelerates the inference for real-world applications. Among all light-weight CNN-based SR models, parameters of the proposed model are a little more than LAPAR-A [22], while the PSNR/SSIM of the proposed model outperforms all of them greatly. Among all light-weight transformer-based SR models, our model has the lowest number of parameters 578K. Compared to the SOTA model ELAN [41], the PSNR/SSIM of the proposed model is comparable to it with almost identical visuals as shown in Fig. 2(e) and Fig. 2(f). It's worth mentioning that our model outperforms ELAN significantly on real-world tasks, detailed can be seen in Sect. 4.3.

Table 1. Performance comparison of different light-weight SR models in ideal SR conditions. #Params indicates the total number of network parameters. The efficiency proxies (#Params) is measured under the setting of upscaling SR images to 1280 × 720 resolution. Best and second-best PSNR/SSIM indexes are marked in red and blue colors, respectively.

Scale	Model	#Params (K)	Set5 [4] PSNR/SSIM	Set14 [39] PSNR/SSIM	BSD100 [27] PSNR/SSIM	Urban100 [14] PSNR/SSIM	Manga109 [28] PSNR/SSIM
×2	CARN [1]	1592	37.76/0.9590	33.52/0.9166	32.09/0.8978	31.92/0.9256	38.36/0.9765
×2	IMDN [15]	694	38.00/0.9605	33.63/0.9177	32.19/0.8996	32.17/0.9283	38.88/0.9774
×2	LAPAR-A [22]	548	38.01/0.9605	33.62/0.9183	32.19/0.8999	32.10/0.9283	38.67/0.9772
×2	LatticeNet [26]	756	38.06/0.9607	33.70/0.9187	32.20/0.8999	32.25/0.9288	-/-
×2	SwinIR-light [23]	878	38.14/0.9611	33.86/0.9206	32.31/0.9012	32.76/0.9340	39.12/0.9783
×2	ELAN-light [41]	582	38.17/0.9611	33.94/0.9207	32.30/0.9012	32.76/0.9340	39.11/0.9782
×2	S^2R transformer (Ours)	578	38.15/0.9611	33.88/0.9206	32.30/0.9013	32.61/0.9333	39.01/0.9780

Qualitative Comparison. We then qualitatively compare the SR quality of different light-weight models. For a more prominent comparison, we compare the ×4 SR results on the example image instead of ×2 SR, as shown in Fig. 2. From Fig. 2(a), Fig. 2(b) and Fig. 2(c) and 2(d), we can see that SwinIR-light [23] and all the CNN-based models result in blurry and distorted edges in ideal SR conditions. However, compared to Fig. 2(g), Fig. 2(e) and Fig. 2(f) show that the transformer-based models can restore more accurate and clear structures and have the potential to recover clear and sharp edges in ideal SR conditions, demonstrating the effectiveness of introducing self-attention. It's worth mentioning that the visuals of the proposed model are almost comparable to ELAN-light [41], while parameters of the proposed model are fewest among the light-weight transformer-based SR models.

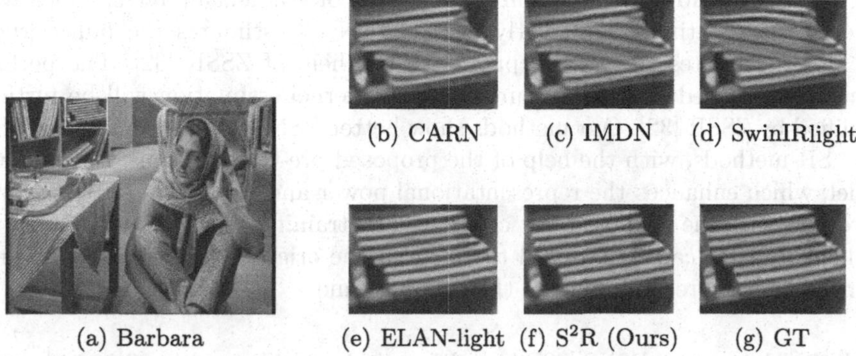

Fig. 2. Qualitative comparison of state-of-the-art light-weight SR models for ×4 upscaling in ideal super-resolution conditions, where the enlarged local patch of output image is shown in the right. (b) The result of CARN [1]. (c) The result of IMDN [15]. (d) The result of SwinIR-light [23]. (e) The results of ELAN-light [41]. (f) The result of ours. (g) Ground truth.

4.3 Evaluations on Real-World Images with Unpredictable Blur Kernels

For imitating the real-world images, we randomly generate various blur kernels to characterize different fuzzy conditions of real-world images caused by various unpredictable factors, and then, we evaluate the proposed framework on these blur kernel conditions. We assume four scenarios: severe aliasing, isotropic Gaussian, anisotropic Gaussian, and isotropic Gaussian, followed by *bicubic subsampling*. PSNR and SSIM are used as evaluation metrics, which are calculated on the Y channel after converting RGB to YCbCr format.

- $g^d_{0.2}$: isotropic Gaussian blur kernel with width $\lambda = 0.2$ followed by *direct* subsampling.
- $g^d_{2.0}$: isotropic Gaussian blur kernel with width $\lambda = 2.0$ followed by *direct* subsampling.
- g^d_{ani}: anisotropic Gaussian with widths $\lambda_1 = 4.0$ and $\lambda_2 = 1.0$ with $\Theta = -0.5$ from

$$\sum = \begin{bmatrix} cos(\Theta) & -sin(\Theta) \\ sin(\Theta) & cos(\Theta) \end{bmatrix} \begin{bmatrix} \lambda_1 & 0 \\ 0 & \lambda_2 \end{bmatrix} \begin{bmatrix} cos(\Theta) & sin(\Theta) \\ -sin(\Theta) & cos(\Theta) \end{bmatrix} \tag{6}$$

followed by *direct* subsampling.

- $g^b_{1.3}$: isotropic Gaussian blur kernel with width $\lambda = 1.3$ followed by *bicubic* subsampling.

Quantitative Comparison. The results on various kernels are shown in Table 2. ZSSR [32] is a classical blind SR model, when it comes to the LR input images, it trains from scratch for each LR input image to recover the counterpart HR image. However, it requires thousands of gradient updates, which will increase the run time significantly. KernelGAN [3] estimates the blur kernel, and then, generates the HR outputs with the help of ZSSR [32]. The performance drop caused by the inaccuracy of blur kernel estimation will be further amplified by ZSSR [32]. Our methods show better PSNR/SSIM than the regular blind SR methods, with the help of the proposed pre-trained transformer-based model, which enhances the representational power and accelerate the inference. Moreover, with the proposed fast coarse-to-fine training strategy, the number of gradient updates can be reduced to 10, from the origin 3000 in ZSSR [32] and KernelGAN [3], greatly reducing the running time.

Table 2. The average PSNR/SSIM results on various kernels with ×2 in real-world conditions. Best and second-best PSNR/SSIM indexes are marked in red and blue colors, respectively.

Scale	Kernel	Dataset	ZSSR [32]	KernelGAN [3]	ELAN [41]	SwinIR [23]	S^2R (Ours)
×2	$g^d_{0.2}$	Set5	28.45/0.8592	21.11/0.5903	28.51/0.8694	28.46/0.8686	28.47/0.8684
×2	$g^d_{2.0}$	Set5	29.16/0.8602	26.17/0.8074	29.17/0.8612	29.17/0.8613	30.06/0.8890
×2	g^d_{ani}	Set5	28.41/0.8374	25.74/0.7802	28.44/0.8392	28.43/0.8390	28.93/0.8583
×2	$g^b_{1.3}$	Set5	31.59/0.8991	29.17/0.8811	31.54/0.9000	31.58/0.9005	33.37/0.9239

Furthermore, from Table 3, we find that transformer-based models also show relatively good performance in real-world tasks, further proving the importance of introducing self-attention to extract features. At the $g^d_{0.2}$ condition, the blur kernel width is relatively small, resulting in a relatively incorrect blur kernel estimation, subsequently, amplified by the proposed coarse-to-fine training strategy, leading to a result that is a little bit worse than ELAN [41]. Besides, the proposed framework shows better PSNR/SSIM than others.

Table 3. The average PSNR/SSIM results on "bicubic" downsampling scenario with ×2 on benchmarks. Those with better PSNR/SSIM will be bolded.

scale	Dataset	ZSSR [32]	S^2R (Ours)
×2	Set5 [4]	36.93/0.9554	**38.15/0.9611**
×2	BSD100 [27]	31.43/0.8901	**32.30/0.9013**
×2	Urban100 [14]	29.34/0.8941	**32.61/0.9333**

Qualitative Comparison. We then qualitatively compare the SR quality of different blind SR methods in real-world conditions with the kernel $g^b_{1.3}$. As shown in Fig. 3, the visual results outperform other methods. Our method can better mine the internal features of the image, obtaining sharper edges and higher contrast results. Compared with Fig. 3(a), Fig. 3(b), Fig. 3(c) and Fig. 3(d), the results of ours are far clearer than them, and closest to GT.

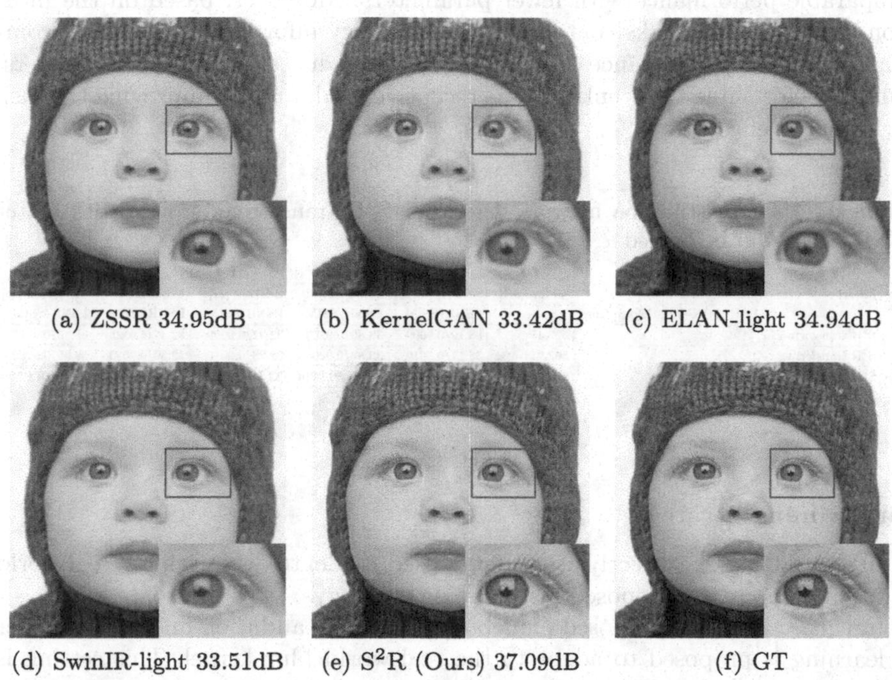

(a) ZSSR 34.95dB (b) KernelGAN 33.42dB (c) ELAN-light 34.94dB

(d) SwinIR-light 33.51dB (e) S²R (Ours) 37.09dB (f) GT

Fig. 3. Qualitative comparison of state-of-the-art blind SR methods for ×2 upscaling in real-world SR conditions with the kernel $g^b_{1.3}$, where the enlarged local patch of output image is placed in the lower right corner of the image. (a) The result of ZSSR [32]. (b) The result of KernelGAN [3]. (c) The results of ELAN-light [41]. (d) The result of SwinIR-light [23]. (e) The result of ours. (f) Ground truth.

4.4 Ablation Study

In order to further verify the necessity of the modules in our network and our proposed training recipe, we conduct ablation experiments on the corresponding dataset.

For Network Architecture

- This setting only contains ELAB in the deep feature module, so it can be used to observe the effect of ELAB.

- This setting contains ELAB and MBConv in the deep feature module, so it can be used to observe the effect of MBConv.
- This setting is full model, containing ELAB, MBConv and Deform Conv, so it can be used to verify the effect of Deformable Conv.

The results are shown in Table 4. Benefit from the efficient design of ELAB, compared with conventional SR models, such as SwinIR [23], our model achieves comparable performance with fewer parameters. Moreover, based on the intuition that the bottlenecks contain all the necessary information, MBConv compensates for the performance drop caused by the reduced number of parameters. Finally, Deformable Conv enlarges the receptive field, further improving the task performance effectively.

Table 4. Ablation study on network design for S^2R transformer. Those with better PSNR/SSIM will be bolded.

Scale	Model	Different components			#Params(K)	Set5 [4]	Set14 [39]	BSD100 [27]	Urban100 [14]	Manga109 [28]
		ELAB	MBConv	Deform Conv		PSNR/SSIM	PSNR/SSIM	PSNR/SSIM	PSNR/SSIM	PSNR/SSIM
×2	S^2R transformer	✓			523.45	38.12/0.9609	33.80/0.9203	32.27/0.9009	32.45/0.9325	38.85/0.9777
×2	S^2R transformer	✓	✓		562.94	38.14/0.9610	33.83/0.9205	32.28/0.9010	32.50/0.9330	38.95/0.9780
×2	S^2R transformer	✓	✓	✓	578	**38.15/0.9611**	**33.88/0.9206**	**32.30/0.9013**	**32.61/0.9333**	**39.01/0.9780**

For Training Strategy

- In this setting, we directly use the proposed model to deal with the real-world tasks without the proposed fast training strategy.
- In this setting, the proposed model is pre-trained, and then fine-level transfer learning is proposed to adapt to the real-world blur kernel. This setting is used to verify the effect of the proposed coarse-to-fine training strategy.

The key point of our training recipe is to fine-tune on several other blur kernels after pre-training our model. Our purpose is to broaden the scalability of our model and reduce the runtime simultaneously. With the help of self-similarity, transformer-based models benefit the performance on blind SR tasks. Moreover, the per-trained model avoids up to 3000 backpropagation gradient updates, reducing the runtime significantly (Table 5).

Table 5. Ablation study on training strategy for S^2R transformer. Those with better PSNR/SSIM will be bolded.

Scale	Model	Training Strategy	Set5($g^d_{0.2}$)	Set5($g^d_{2.0}$)	Set5(g^d_{ani})	Set5($g^b_{1.3}$)
			PSNR/SSIM	PSNR/SSIM	PSNR/SSIM	PSNR/SSIM
×2	S^2R transformer		28.36/0.8664	29.17/0.8614	28.43/0.8391	31.58/0.9007
×2	S^2R transformer	✓	**28.47/0.8684**	**30.06/0.8890**	**28.93/0.8583**	**33.37/0.9239**

5 Conclusion

In this paper, we proposed a novel framework S^{2}R, which consists of a light-weight transformer-based model and a novel coarse-to-fine training strategy, achieving excellent performance and good visual results in both SISR and blind SR tasks. On one hand, some light-weight blocks are utilized in the proposed model to reduce the number of parameters further while maintaining a great performance. On the other hand, the proposed training strategy broadens the scalability of the proposed model in real-world situations. From our extensive experiments, regardless of whether in real-world applications or in ideal conditions, the proposed model outperforms previous methods in terms of visual results with the lowest number of parameters 578K. Moreover, the proposed framework accelerates the transfer-learning process in real-world situations by extremely reducing the number of backpropagation gradient updates, Compared to ZSSR [32], the reduction is as high as 300 times.

References

1. Ahn, N., Kang, B., Sohn, K.A.: Fast, accurate, and lightweight super-resolution with cascading residual network. In: Proceedings of the European Conference on Computer Vision (ECCV), pp. 252–268 (2018)
2. Begin, I., Ferrie, F.: Blind super-resolution using a learning-based approach. In: Proceedings of the 17th International Conference on Pattern Recognition, ICPR 2004, vol. 2, pp. 85–89. IEEE (2004)
3. Bell-Kligler, S., Shocher, A., Irani, M.: Blind super-resolution kernel estimation using an internal-GAN. In: Advances in Neural Information Processing Systems, vol. 32 (2019)
4. Bevilacqua, M., Roumy, A., Guillemot, C., Alberi-Morel, M.L.: Low-complexity single-image super-resolution based on nonnegative neighbor embedding (2012)
5. Chollet, F.: Xception: deep learning with depthwise separable convolutions. In: Proceedings of the IEEE Conference on Computer Vision and Pattern Recognition, pp. 1251–1258 (2017)
6. Dai, J., et al.: Deformable convolutional networks. In: Proceedings of the IEEE International Conference on Computer Vision, pp. 764–773 (2017)
7. Dong, C., Loy, C.C., He, K., Tang, X.: Image super-resolution using deep convolutional networks. IEEE Trans. Pattern Anal. Mach. Intell. **38**(2), 295–307 (2015)
8. Dong, C., Loy, C.C., Tang, X.: Accelerating the super-resolution convolutional neural network. In: Leibe, B., Matas, J., Sebe, N., Welling, M. (eds.) ECCV 2016. LNCS, vol. 9906, pp. 391–407. Springer, Cham (2016). https://doi.org/10.1007/978-3-319-46475-6_25
9. Efrat, N., Glasner, D., Apartsin, A., Nadler, B., Levin, A.: Accurate blur models vs. image priors in single image super-resolution. In: Proceedings of the IEEE International Conference on Computer Vision, pp. 2832–2839 (2013)
10. Graham, B., et al.: LeViT: a vision transformer in convnet's clothing for faster inference. In: Proceedings of the IEEE/CVF International Conference on Computer Vision, pp. 12259–12269 (2021)
11. Haris, M., Shakhnarovich, G., Ukita, N.: Deep back-projection networks for super-resolution. In: Proceedings of the IEEE Conference on Computer Vision and Pattern Recognition, pp. 1664–1673 (2018)

12. He, H., Siu, W.C.: Single image super-resolution using gaussian process regression. In: CVPR 2011, pp. 449–456. IEEE (2011)
13. Hu, J., Shen, L., Sun, G.: Squeeze-and-excitation networks. In: Proceedings of the IEEE Conference on Computer Vision and Pattern Recognition, pp. 7132–7141 (2018)
14. Huang, J.B., Singh, A., Ahuja, N.: Single image super-resolution from transformed self-exemplars. In: Proceedings of the IEEE Conference on Computer Vision and Pattern Recognition, pp. 5197–5206 (2015)
15. Hui, Z., Gao, X., Yang, Y., Wang, X.: Lightweight image super-resolution with information multi-distillation network. In: Proceedings of the 27th ACM International Conference on Multimedia, pp. 2024–2032 (2019)
16. Ioffe, S., Szegedy, C.: Batch normalization: accelerating deep network training by reducing internal covariate shift. In: International Conference on Machine Learning, pp. 448–456. PMLR (2015)
17. Irani, M., Peleg, S.: Improving resolution by image registration. CVGIP Graph. Models Image Process. **53**(3), 231–239 (1991)
18. Kim, J., Lee, J.K., Lee, K.M.: Deeply-recursive convolutional network for image super-resolution. In: Proceedings of the IEEE Conference on Computer Vision and Pattern Recognition, pp. 1637–1645 (2016)
19. Kingma, D.P., Ba, J.: Adam: a method for stochastic optimization. arXiv preprint arXiv:1412.6980 (2014)
20. Lai, W.S., Huang, J.B., Ahuja, N., Yang, M.H.: Deep laplacian pyramid networks for fast and accurate super-resolution. In: Proceedings of the IEEE Conference on Computer Vision and Pattern Recognition, pp. 624–632 (2017)
21. Ledig, C., et al.: Photo-realistic single image super-resolution using a generative adversarial network. In: Proceedings of the IEEE Conference on Computer Vision and Pattern Recognition, pp. 4681–4690 (2017)
22. Li, W., Zhou, K., Qi, L., Jiang, N., Lu, J., Jia, J.: LAPAR: linearly-assembled pixel-adaptive regression network for single image super-resolution and beyond. Adv. Neural. Inf. Process. Syst. **33**, 20343–20355 (2020)
23. Liang, J., Cao, J., Sun, G., Zhang, K., Van Gool, L., Timofte, R.: Swinir: image restoration using swin transformer. In: Proceedings of the IEEE/CVF International Conference on Computer Vision, pp. 1833–1844 (2021)
24. Lim, B., Son, S., Kim, H., Nah, S., Mu Lee, K.: Enhanced deep residual networks for single image super-resolution. In: Proceedings of the IEEE Conference on Computer Vision and Pattern Recognition Workshops, pp. 136–144 (2017)
25. Liu, Z., et al.: Swin transformer: hierarchical vision transformer using shifted windows. In: Proceedings of the IEEE/CVF International Conference on Computer Vision, pp. 10012–10022 (2021)
26. Luo, X., Xie, Y., Zhang, Y., Qu, Y., Li, C., Fu, Y.: LatticeNet: towards lightweight image super-resolution with lattice block. In: Vedaldi, A., Bischof, H., Brox, T., Frahm, J.-M. (eds.) ECCV 2020. LNCS, vol. 12367, pp. 272–289. Springer, Cham (2020). https://doi.org/10.1007/978-3-030-58542-6_17
27. Martin, D., Fowlkes, C., Tal, D., Malik, J.: A database of human segmented natural images and its application to evaluating segmentation algorithms and measuring ecological statistics. In: Proceedings Eighth IEEE International Conference on Computer Vision, ICCV 2001, vol. 2, pp. 416–423. IEEE (2001)
28. Matsui, Y., et al.: Sketch-based manga retrieval using manga109 dataset. Multimedia Tools Appl. **76**, 21811–21838 (2017)
29. Michaeli, T., Irani, M.: Nonparametric blind super-resolution. In: Proceedings of the IEEE International Conference on Computer Vision, pp. 945–952 (2013)

30. Shi, W., et al.: Real-time single image and video super-resolution using an efficient sub-pixel convolutional neural network. In: Proceedings of the IEEE Conference on Computer Vision and Pattern Recognition, pp. 1874–1883 (2016)
31. Shocher, A., Bagon, S., Isola, P., Irani, M.: InGAN: Capturing and retargeting the "DNA" of a natural image. In: Proceedings of the IEEE/CVF International Conference on Computer Vision, pp. 4492–4501 (2019)
32. Shocher, A., Cohen, N., Irani, M.: "Zero-shot" super-resolution using deep internal learning. In: Proceedings of the IEEE Conference on Computer Vision and Pattern Recognition, pp. 3118–3126 (2018)
33. Tai, Y., Yang, J., Liu, X.: Image super-resolution via deep recursive residual network. In: Proceedings of the IEEE Conference on Computer Vision and Pattern Recognition, pp. 3147–3155 (2017)
34. Timofte, R., Agustsson, E., Van Gool, L., Yang, M.H., Zhang, L.: NTIRE 2017 challenge on single image super-resolution: methods and results. In: Proceedings of the IEEE Conference on Computer Vision and Pattern Recognition Workshops, pp. 114–125 (2017)
35. Wang, Q., Tang, X., Shum, H.: Patch based blind image super resolution. In: Tenth IEEE International Conference on Computer Vision (ICCV 2005), vol. 1, pp. 709–716. IEEE (2005)
36. Wu, B., et al.: Shift: a zero flop, zero parameter alternative to spatial convolutions. In: Proceedings of the IEEE Conference on Computer Vision and Pattern Recognition, pp. 9127–9135 (2018)
37. Xiao, T., Singh, M., Mintun, E., Darrell, T., Dollár, P., Girshick, R.: Early convolutions help transformers see better. Adv. Neural. Inf. Process. Syst. **34**, 30392–30400 (2021)
38. Xie, E., Wang, W., Yu, Z., Anandkumar, A., Alvarez, J.M., Luo, P.: SegFormer: simple and efficient design for semantic segmentation with transformers. Adv. Neural. Inf. Process. Syst. **34**, 12077–12090 (2021)
39. Zeyde, R., Elad, M., Protter, M.: On single image scale-up using sparse-representations. In: Boissonnat, J.-D., et al. (eds.) Curves and Surfaces 2010. LNCS, vol. 6920, pp. 711–730. Springer, Heidelberg (2012). https://doi.org/10.1007/978-3-642-27413-8_47
40. Zhang, K., Zuo, W., Zhang, L.: Learning a single convolutional super-resolution network for multiple degradations. In: Proceedings of the IEEE Conference on Computer Vision and Pattern Recognition, pp. 3262–3271 (2018)
41. Zhang, X., Zeng, H., Guo, S., Zhang, L.: Efficient long-range attention network for image super-resolution. In: Avidan, S., Brostow, G., Cissé, M., Farinella, G.M., Hassner, T. (eds.) ECCV 2022. LNCS, vol. 13677, pp. 649–667. Springer, Cham (2022). https://doi.org/10.1007/978-3-031-19790-1_39
42. Zhang, Y., Li, K., Li, K., Wang, L., Zhong, B., Fu, Y.: Image super-resolution using very deep residual channel attention networks. In: Proceedings of the European Conference on Computer Vision (ECCV), pp. 286–301 (2018)
43. Zhang, Y., Tian, Y., Kong, Y., Zhong, B., Fu, Y.: Residual dense network for image super-resolution. In: Proceedings of the IEEE Conference on Computer Vision and Pattern Recognition, pp. 2472–2481 (2018)
44. Zontak, M., Irani, M.: Internal statistics of a single natural image. In: CVPR 2011, pp. 977–984. IEEE (2011)

Self-adapted Positional Encoding in the Transformer Encoder for Named Entity Recognition

Kehan Huangliang[1,2], Xinyang Li[1,2], Teng Yin[1,2], Bo Peng[1,2], and Haixian Zhang[1,2](✉)

[1] Machine Intelligence Laboratory, College of Computer Science, Sichuan University, Chengdu, China
{huangliangkehan,xinyang,tengyin}@stu.scu.edu.cn, zhanghaixian@scu.edu.cn

[2] Grid Planning and Research Center of Guangdong Power Grid Corporation, Guangzhou, China
pengbo@gd.csg.cn

Abstract. The task of named entity recognition (NER) is fundamental to natural language processing (NLP), as it forms the basis for various downstream applications such as question answering, text summarization, and machine translation. With the development of Transformer architecture, it has gained popularity in NLP due to its ability to model parallel distant contextual dependencies. Although positional encoding is crucial in transformer-based NER models for capturing the sequential feature of natural language and improving their accuracy in NER, most approach, which uses a fixed mathematical formula to assign a unique vector to each position, is a hard-coded encoding To address this issue, a self-adapted positional encoding module called self-adapter is proposed in a Transformer model. The proposed self-adapter incorporates two information fusers aimed at enhancing the embedding representational ability of the model. The first information fuser integrates information across different positions, enhancing the embedding representational ability for different ranges. The second information fuser integrates diverse dimensional information for one position, resulting in improved embedding representation. Besides, We modify the calculation of the attention score to enhance the utilization of the self-adapter. A mathematical analysis based on Fourier series is presented to demonstrate the effectiveness of the proposed method. This approach allows for dynamic positional encoding adjustment, facilitating adaptation to varying contextual inputs and more flexibility to capture word relationships. To evaluate the model, four NER datasets, including one English and three Chinese datasets, are used. The results show that the self-adapter substantially improves the Transformer's performance in the NER task.

Keywords: Transformer · Positional Encoding · Adapter · NER

L. Iliadis et al. (Eds.): ICANN 2023, LNCS 14259, pp. 538–549, 2023.
https://doi.org/10.1007/978-3-031-44223-0_43

1 Introduction

NER involves identifying specific entities, categorized according to semantic types such as person, location, or organization, from the text. NER is a crucial component in several NLP applications, such as relation extraction, question answering, text summarization, and machine translation.

The neural network model used for NER generally consists of three components: Distributed representations [1–5], Context encoder [6–8], and Tag decoder [7,9]. Since its introduction by Vaswani et al. in 2017, the vanilla Transformer [10] has demonstrated remarkable performance across a variety of NLP tasks. The Transformer architecture has served as a foundation for the development of various pre-training models such as BERT [11], GPT [12], T5 [13], XLNet [14] and others, which have greatly advanced NLP. As the positional relationships between words are critical in NER, the encoding of positional information requires adaptation. Several efforts have been undertaken to enhance the Transformer model's compatibility with NER. Examples of such variants include TENER [15], which employs directional relative positional encoding, reduces parameter count, and improves attention distribution, and FLAT [16], designed for Chinese NER, which converts lattice structures into spans and introduces a specific positional encoding. Recently, [17] proposed a hybrid Transformer that employs fused additional feature embeddings, such as char embedding, bigram embedding, lattice embedding, and BERT embedding, as distributed representations to enhance the representational capability of the model. And a relative positional encoding, which enhances the positional awareness of the vanilla Transformer, is also used in the hybrid Transformer. These studies have explored improved positional encoding methods to make the Transformer more compatible with NER. Therefore, one observation is that positional encoding remains an important issue in making the Transformer more compatible with NER. Although there exist several methods for self-adapted positional encodings for other tasks, such as RNN-Transformer [18] for machine translation and learnable fourier features [19] for computer vision, limited research has been conducted on self-adapted positional encoding for NER task.

This paper proposes a novel approach for self-adapted positional encoding, which markedly improves the performance of the Transformer Encoder in NER. And we also provide mathematical reasoning to support the efficacy of the proposed approach. To improve the utilization of the self-adapter, we made adjustments to the calculation of the attention score. Furthermore, the self-adapter is easily transferable to various Transformer models.

Our contributions can be summarized as follows:

1) We propose the self-adapter, a data-driven module that integrates positional information into the transformer, enhancing the performance of the self-attention mechanism for NER.
2) To better exploit the self-adapter and leverage the Fourier series form within the attention scores, we utilize a single learnable parameter in the computation of attention scores. And we provide mathematical evidence to support the effectiveness of our proposed method.

3) The experimental evaluation is performed on four distinct NER datasets. The experimental results demonstrate that our method substantially enhances the Transformer's performance in the NER task.

2 Related Work

2.1 Positional Encoding in Vanilla Transformer

Incorporating positional information into self-attention is critical because self-attention does not have the ability to intrinsically recognize positional information. To address this, Vaswani et al. [10] introduce position encoding, which is generated from sine and cosine functions with various frequencies, to enable self-attention to capture positional information. The position encoding for the pth token is formulated as follows:

$$PE_{(p,2i)} = \sin(pos/10000^{2i/d}) \tag{1}$$

$$PE_{(p,2i+1)} = \cos(pos/10000^{2i/d}) \tag{2}$$

where p is the position, d is the dimension, and $i \in [0, d/2]$. Positional encoding is added to the input embedding, endowing self-attention with the ability to model tokens between different distances.

2.2 Relative Positional Encoding

The utilization of relative positional encodings within the embedding space has been suggested as a promising approach for improving the efficacy of Transformer-based architectures. In the Transformer model, the input embedding with positional encoding is mapped into query, key and value by three groups of linear layers. The general form of relative positional encoding can be described by the following formula [20]:

$$[Q_x, K_x, V_x]^T = E_x \odot [W_q, W_k, W_v]^T + [0, R_{i-j}, R_{i-j}]^T \tag{3}$$

Q_x, K_x and V_x are the inputs of multi-head attention, E_x generated from the input embedding module is embedded input. R_{i-j} is the relative position encoding. W_q, W_k and W_v are the weight value matrices of the three groups of linear layers. With the study of Transformer, [21] proposed an improved relative positional encoding and applied it to self-attention:

$$\begin{aligned} A^{rel}_{i,j} &= \underbrace{E^T_{x_i} W^T_q W_{k,E} E_{x_j}}_{(a)} + \underbrace{E^T_{x_i} W^T_q W_{k,R} R_{i-j}}_{(b)} \\ &+ \underbrace{u^T W_{k,E} E_{x_j}}_{(c)} + \underbrace{v^T W_{k,R} R_{i-j}}_{(d)} \end{aligned} \tag{4}$$

Each item has its own significance: term (a) signifies content-based addressing, term (b) represents content-dependent positional bias, term (c) governs global content bias, and term (d) encodes global positional bias.

3 Proposed Method

Our proposed self-adapter enhances the performance of the self-attention mechanism, as shown in Fig. 1. The model comprises three primary components: an embedding module, a Self-adapted Transformer, and a CRF. The subsequent sections will provide detailed descriptions of the three components.

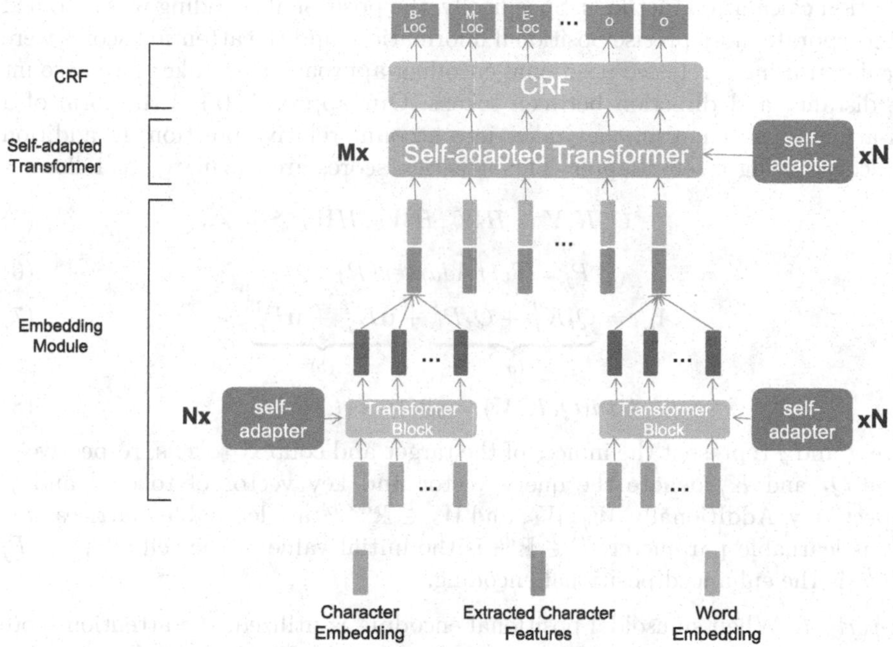

Fig. 1. The model structure for English NER.

3.1 Embedding Module

Word-level representation [22–24] is one of the dominant approaches for distributed representations. However, a challenge with word-level representation is the handling of out-of-vocabulary (OOV) words. To overcome this issue, character-level representation has been proposed, utilizing two common architectures for extraction: CNN-based [4,25,26] and RNN-based [27,28] models.

In the embedding module, for English NER, we use a Transformer block to extract character features. We further enhance this approach by adding a self-adapter to the Transformer block. By combining the pre-trained word embeddings and character embeddings, we obtain the representation for each word in the Embedding Module. The character and bigram embeddings provided by [29] are utilized for Chinese NER.

3.2 Self-adapted Transformer

The Transformer model has demonstrated impressive performance across a variety of NLP tasks, but it has been observed that its performance in NER is suboptimal [15,30]. The vanilla Transformer has limitations in NER, including ineffective capture of contextual information on both sides of a token and a tendency to break distance awareness in the attention mechanism. To overcome these limitations, [15] proposed improvements to the positional encoding and attention calculation methods. Specifically, the positional encoding was modified to incorporate more precise positional information, and the attention scores were calculated using a relative positional encoding approach that takes into account the distance and direction between tokens. Our approach takes the form of a self-attention mechanism that takes into account relative position, in addition to incorporating a self-adapter. The attention scores are calculated as follows:

$$Q, K, V = HW_q, HW_k, HW_v \tag{5}$$

$$P_j = SelfAdapter(P) \tag{6}$$

$$A_{t,j} = \underbrace{Q_t K_j^T + Q_t P_j^T}_{(a)} + \underbrace{\mathbf{u} K_j^T + \mathbf{u} P_j^T}_{(b)} \tag{7}$$

$$Attn(Q, K, V) = softmax(A)V \tag{8}$$

Here, t and j represent the indices of the target and context tokens, respectively, while Q_t and K_j denote the query vector and key vector of token t and j, respectively. Additionally, W_q, W_k, and $W_v \in \mathbb{R}^{d \times d_k}$ are learnable matrices. $u \in R^{d_k}$ is learnable parameter, $P \in \mathbb{R}^{d_k}$ is the initial value of the self-adapter. $P_j \in \mathbb{R}^{d_k}$ is the enhanced positional encoding.

Property 1. When sinusoidal positional encoding is utilized, the attention score in the form of Eq. 7 implicitly adopts the form of the Fourier series.

Proof. Eq. 7 can be expressed as:

$$A_{t,j} = \underbrace{Q_t (K_j + P_j)^T}_{(a)} + \underbrace{\mathbf{u}(K_j + P_j)^T}_{(b)} \tag{9}$$

And the P_j is the j-th position vector

$$P_j = \begin{bmatrix} \sin(p_1) \\ \cos(p_2) \\ \vdots \\ \sin(p_{d-1}) \\ \cos(p_d) \end{bmatrix} \tag{10}$$

Let S be the sum of K_j and position embeddings P_j. Then, each element in S

$$s_i(j) = k_i + p_i(j) = \begin{cases} k_i + \sin(p_i), & \text{if } i \text{ is odd} \\ k_i + \cos(p_i), & \text{if } i \text{ is even} \end{cases} \tag{11}$$

After multiplying with Q_t, S is transformed as $A = Q_t S$ with each element

$$a_i(t) = \sum_{i=1}^{D} q_{t,i} k_i + \sum_{i=1}^{D/2} \left(q_{t,2i-1} \sin\left(p_{2i-1}\right) + q_{t,2i} \cos\left(p_{2i}\right) \right) \tag{12}$$

The RHS of Eq. 12 is a Fourier series form [31] in physics and signal processing. It is commonly accepted that an infinite number of terms and appropriate frequencies in the Fourier series can accurately represent continuous functions within a given interval. However, since using an infinite number of terms is impractical, it is advantageous to allocate a limited number of frequencies in a data-driven manner for more generalized approximations. Additionally, we have taken account of fusing the information about various positions. Based on these reasons, we designed the self-adapter.

3.3 Self-adapter

The length of the sequence is denoted as l, while m represents the dimension of the embedding at each position. The initial values matrix $P \in \mathbb{R}^{l \times m}$ is a real-valued matrix. The matrix is processed into the self-adapter as follows:

$$P_{final} = Sinusoidal(\underbrace{f(f(...f(P)))}_{N}) \tag{13}$$

where f represents a self-adapter block. N is the number of stacked self-adapters. The self-adapter showed in Fig. 2(a).

The self-adapter block is composed of two information fusers. Figure 2(b) shows the information fuser. The following equations describe its details.

$$U = \sigma\left(W_3 \sigma\left(W_2 \sigma\left(W_1 I\right)\right)\right) \tag{14}$$

$$O = I + \text{LayerNorm}(\sigma\left(W_5 \sigma\left(W_4 U\right)\right)) \tag{15}$$

The input and output of the information fuser, denoted by I and O respectively, are obtained using the following equations. σ is a nonlinearity activation function Tanh. The first information fuser facilitates the exchange of different position information, while the second exchanges information about different embeddings within the same position. And we employ a skip-connection in the information fuser. The input and output dimensions of the information fuser remain consistent. Finally, the position encoding matrix is obtained by processing each column with alternating sine and cosine functions. In summary, the overall calculation process of the self-adapter is shown in Algorithm 1.

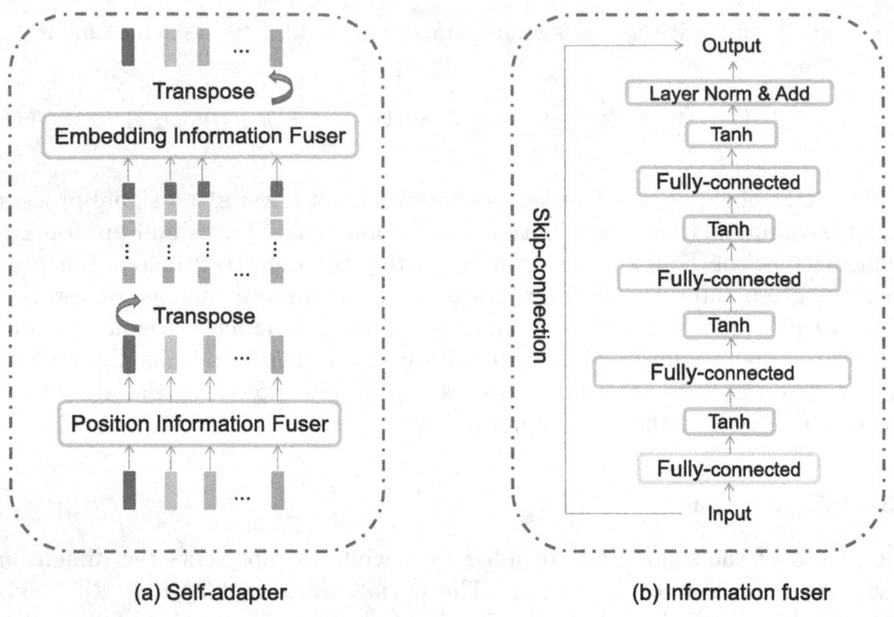

Fig. 2. The structure of the self-adapter and information fuser.

Algorithm 1. Generating self-adapted positional encoding.

Input: $P = \{P1, P2..., Pn\}$: the initialized matrix. n is the n-th position. $Pn = [\dots\left(\frac{n-m}{10000^{2i/d_k}}\right)\left(\frac{n-m}{10000^{2i/d_k}}\right)\dots]$;

Output: Enhanced positional encodings, EP;

N is the depth of the self-adapter.

for $l = 1; l \leq N; l \leftarrow l + 1$ **do**

  Fusing information from different positions, based on Eq. 14, 15;

  $EP \leftarrow$ TRANSPOSE(EP);

  Fusing information from different dimensions of embedding, based on Eq. 14, 15;

  $EP \leftarrow$ TRANSPOSE(EP);

end for

$EP \leftarrow$ SINUSOIDAL(EP);

return EP;

3.4 CRF

Conditional Random Field (CRF) is a probabilistic model used to describe the conditional probability distribution of output random variables given input random variables. Given an input sequence x and its corresponding golden label sequence y, the set of all valid label sequences for x is denoted as $Y(x)$.

$$P(y \mid x) = \frac{\sum_{t=1}^{T} e^{f(y_{t-1}, y_t, x)}}{\sum_{y'}^{Y(x)} \sum_{t=1}^{T} e^{f\left(y'_{t-1}, y'_t, x\right)}} \tag{16}$$

where $f(y_{t-1}, y_t, x)$ computes the transition score from y_{t-1} to y_t and the score for y_t.

4 Experiment

4.1 Datasets

Our approach is evaluated on four NER datasets: CoNLL2003 [32] for English, and Weibo [33], Resume [29], and MSRA [34] for Chinese. CoNLL2003 is an English NER dataset with four named entity types. Weibo NER is a Chinese dataset based on social media text from Sina Weibo, consisting of four entity types. Resume NER is built from summary data of senior executives' resumes on Sina Finance and contains eight entity types. MSRA is a news domain NER dataset annotated by Microsoft Research Asia, with three entity types.

4.2 Experimental Settings

For CoNLL2003, a self-adapter with a depth and width of 4 and 1, respectively, was utilized. And we employed a depth of 3 and a width of 2 for Weibo, whereas for Resume, we augmented the depth to 3 and the width to 4. For MSRA, we used a depth of 3 and a width of 1. We utilized SGD optimization with a batch size of 16 and momentum of 0.9 to train the model.

4.3 Results on English NER Datasets

We conducted experiments on CoNLL2003 and compared multiple methods, with the results presented in Table 1. Our method outperforms the other approaches shown in Table 1, as indicated by the experimental results. Our method utilizes an adjusted computational method for attention scores that leverages the hidden Fourier series in the attention scores. Additionally, our method accounts for spatial information in multiple dimensions, which enhances the Transformer's adaptability for NER. By virtue of the enhancements mentioned above, our approach achieves superior performance.

4.4 Results on Chinese NER Datasets

We conducted experiments on three Chinese NER datasets (Weibo, Resume, and MSRA) and compared our results with other methods, which are presented in Table 2. The results indicate that our method is inferior to FLAT on MSRA, but outperforms the other methods on all remaining datasets. Notably, our method effectively improved the results on Weibo. We attribute this improvement to the effectiveness of data-driven approaches in selecting more suitable frequencies for the self-attention mechanism, particularly on smaller datasets like Weibo, where such approaches are advantageous.

Table 1. F1 scores on English Dataset.

Models	CoNLL2003
BiLSTM-CRF [35]	88.83
CNN-BiLSTM-CRF [36]	90.91
BiLSTM-BiLSTM-CRF [28]	90.94
CNN-BiLSTM-CRF [4]	91.21
BiLSTM-BiLSTM-CRF [37]	91.11
CN^3 [38]	91.10
Transformer	89.57
TENER	91.32
Ours	**91.58**

Table 2. F1 scores on Chinese Dataset.

Models	Weibo	Resume	MSRA
BiLSTM [29]	56.75	94.41	91.87
Transformer	47.42	94.13	88.35
TENER	57.18	94.85	92.26
FLAT	60.11	94.48	93.42
Ours	**60.21**	**95.32**	**92.71**

4.5 Impact of the Depth of Self-adapter

This experiment aims to evaluate the impact of self-adapter depth on performance. We set the width of the self-adapter to 1. Table 3 summarizes the performance comparison of self-adapters with depths of 1, 2, 3 and 4 on four different datasets. The results indicate that a self-adapter with a relatively deeper depth can yield better results. However, a self-adapter with excessive depth may cause performance to degrade. We consider that stacking too many self-adapters can negatively impact its performance on certain datasets by affecting parameter updates and potentially weakening the positional information. Considering that the self-adapter is data-driven, the distribution of the dataset is also an important factor. Therefore, we consider it important to carefully balance the depth of self-adapters in order to achieve optimal results.

Table 3. F1 scores of different depths on English and Chinese Datasets.

N	CoNLL2003	Weibo	Resume	MSRA
1	91.48	59.78	95.01	92.57
2	91.37	58.79	94.84	92.67
3	91.49	59.53	95.05	92.71
4	91.58	59.79	94.81	92.30

4.6 Impact of the Width of Self-adapter

To investigate how the width of the self-adapter affects the performance of the model, we conducted a comparison across various widths. To enhance clarity, we

Table 4. The index corresponding to different widths. E is the embedding dim, L is the length of the sentence. The format "(a, b)" represents the input dimension and output dimension of a fully connected layer.

Index	1	2	3	4	5
W	(E, 300)	(E, 500)	(E, 800)	(E, 1100)	(E, 1500)
	(300, 500)	(500, 800)	(800, 1200)	(1100, 2000)	(1500, 2500)
	(500, 400)	(800, 600)	(1200, 900)	(2000, 1400)	(2500, 1800)
	(400, E)	(600, E)	(900, E)	(1400, E)	(1800, E)
	(L, 1800)	(L, 2000)	(L, 2200)	(L, 2600)	(L, 3000)
	(1800, 2800)	(2000, 3000)	(2200, 3200)	(2600, 3500)	(3000, 4000)
	(2800, 2000)	(3000, 2200)	(3200, 2300)	(3500, 2400)	(4000, 2500)
	(2000, L)	(2200, L)	(2300, L)	(2400, L)	(2500, L)

indexed the various widths, as demonstrated in Table 4. We set the depth of the self-adapter to 1.

Table 5 displays that the model's performance exhibits a positive correlation with the increment in the width of self-adapter until it reaches a specific threshold, beyond which a slight degradation in performance is evident. To attain optimal performance, it is suggested to avoid exceeding the ideal width of the self-adapter.

Table 5. F1 scores of different widths on English and Chinese Datasets.

W	CoNLL2003	Weibo	Resume	MSRA
1	91.30	59.78	94.07	92.57
2	91.10	59.87	94.78	92.50
3	91.41	59.21	94.94	92.15
4	91.22	59.09	94.69	92.37
5	91.15	58.55	94.39	92.16

5 Conclusion

We propose the self-adapter that leverages the underlying Fourier series in the attention score and enhances information exchange among different positions and dimensions within the same position. And the calculation of attention scores is modified to better utilize the self-adapter. Our method substantially enhances the effectiveness of Transformer architecture in the NER task and can be effortlessly incorporated into models based on Transformer. To demonstrate the effectiveness of the proposed method, we conducted a mathematical analysis based on Fourier series. Experimental results on four NER datasets show that the self-adapter substantially enhances the Transformer's performance in the NER task.

References

1. Chiu, J.P.C., Nichols, E.: Named entity recognition with bidirectional LSTM-CNNs. In: Proceedings of the Transactions of the Association for Computational Linguistics, pp. 357–370 (2016)
2. Yang, J., Liang, S., Zhang, Y.: Design challenges and misconceptions in neural sequence labeling. In: COLING, pp. 3879–3889 (2018)
3. Yao, L., Liu, H., Liu, Y., Li, X., Anwar, M.W.: Biomedical named entity recognition based on deep neutral network. Int. J. Hybrid Inf. Technol. **8**(8), 279–288 (2015)
4. Ma, X., Hovy, E.: End-to-end sequence labeling via bidirectional LSTM-CNNS-CRF. In: ACL (2016)
5. Lin, B.Y., Xu, F.F., Luo, Z., Zhu, K.: Multi-channel bilstm-crf model for emerging named entity recognition in social media. In: Proceedings of the 3rd Workshop on Noisy User-generated Text, pp. 160–165 (2017)
6. Collobert, R., Weston, J., Bottou, L., Karlen, M., Kavukcuoglu, K., Kuksa, P.: Natural language processing (almost) from scratch. J. Mach. Learn. Res., 2493–2537 (2011)
7. Strubell, E., Verga, P., Belanger, D., McCallum, A.: Fast and accurate entity recognition with iterated dilated convolutions. In: ACL (2017)
8. Žukov-Gregorič, A., Bachrach, Y., Coope, S.: Named entity recognition with parallel recurrent neural networks. In: ACL (2018)
9. Zhai, F., Potdar, S., Xiang, B., Zhou, B.: Neural models for sequence chunking. In: Proceedings of the AAAI Conference on Artificial Intelligence, vol. 31, no. 1, pp. 3365–3371 (2017)
10. Vaswani, A., et al.: Attention is all you need. In: NIPS, pp. 5998–6008 (2017)
11. Devlin, J., Chang, M.W., Lee, K., Toutanova, K.: BERT: pre-training of deep bidirectional transformers for language understanding. In: NAACL-HLT, pp. 4171–4186 (2019)
12. Radford, A., Narasimhan, K., Salimans, T., Sutskever, I.: Improving language understanding by generative pre-training. Technical Report, OpenAI (2018)
13. Raffel, C., et al.: Exploring the limits of transfer learning with a unified text-to-text transformer. J. Mach. Learn. Res. **21**(1), 5485–5551 (2020)
14. Yang, Z., Dai, Z., Yang, Y., Carbonell, J., Salakhutdinov, R.R., Le, Q.V.: XLNet: generalized autoregressive pretraining for language understanding. In: Advances in Neural Information Processing Systems, vol. 32 (2019)
15. Yan, H., Deng, B., Li, X., Qiu, X.: TENER: adapting transformer encoder for named entity recognition. arXiv preprint: arXiv:1911.04474 (2019)
16. Li, X., Yan, H., Qiu, X., Huang, X.: FLAT: Chinese NER using flat-lattice transformer. In: ACL, pp. 6836–6842 (2020)
17. Jin, Z., He, X., Wu, X., Zhao, X.: A hybrid transformer approach for Chinese NER with features augmentation. Expert Syst. Appl. **209**, 118385 (2022)
18. Neishi, M., Yoshinaga, N.: On the relation between position information and sentence length in neural machine translation. In: Proceedings of the 23rd Conference on Computational Natural Language Learning (CoNLL), pp. 328–338 (2019)

19. Li, Y., Si, S., Li, G., Hsieh, C.J., Bengio, S.: Learnable fourier features for multi-dimensional spatial positional encoding. In: Advances in Neural Information Processing Systems, vol. 34, pp. 15816–15829 (2021)
20. Wang, B., et al.: On position embeddings in BERT. In: ICLR (2021)
21. Dai, Z., Yang, Z., Yang, Y., Carbonell, J., Le, Q.V., Salakhutdinov, R.: Transformer-XL: attentive language models beyond a fixed-length context. In: ACL, pp. 2978–2988 (2019)
22. Mikolov, T., Chen, K., Corrado, G., Dean, J.: Efficient estimation of word representations in vector space. arXiv preprint: arXiv:1301.3781 (2013)
23. Nguyen, T.H., Sil, A., Dinu, G., Florian, R.: Toward mention detection robustness with recurrent neural networks. arXiv preprint: arXiv:1602.07749 (2016)
24. Zheng, S., Wang, F., Bao, H., Hao, Y., Zhou, P., Xu, B.: Joint extraction of entities and relations based on a novel tagging scheme. In: ACL (2017)
25. Li, P.H., Dong, R.P., Wang, Y.S., Chou, J.C., Ma, W.Y.: Leveraging linguistic structures for named entity recognition with bidirectional recursive neural networks. In: Proceedings of the 2017 Conference on Empirical Methods in Natural Language Processing, pp. 2664–2669 (2017)
26. Peters, M.E., et al.: Deep contextualized word representations. In: NAACL-HLT, pp. 2227–2237 (2018)
27. Kuru, O., Can, O.A., Yuret, D.: CharNER: character-level named entity recognition. In: Proceedings of COLING 2016, the 26th International Conference on Computational Linguistics: Technical Papers, pp. 911–921 (2016)
28. Lample, G., Ballesteros, M., Subramanian, S., Kawakami, K., Dyer, C.: Neural architectures for named entity recognition. In: NAACL, pp. 260–270 (2016)
29. Zhang, Y., Yang, J.: Chinese NER using lattice LSTM. In: ACL, pp. 1554–1564 (2018)
30. Guo, Q., Qiu, X., Liu, P., Shao, Y., Xue, X., Zhang, Z.: Star-transformer. In: NAACL, pp. 1315–1325 (2019)
31. Arfken, G.B., Weber, H.J.: Mathematical methods for physicists (1999)
32. Sang, E.F., De Meulder, F.: Introduction to the CoNLL-2003 shared task: language-independent named entity recognition. In: NAACL, pp. 142–147 (2003)
33. Peng, N., Dredze, M.: Named entity recognition for Chinese social media with jointly trained embeddings. In: EMNLP, pp. 548–554 (2015)
34. Levow, G.A.: The third international Chinese language processing bakeoff: word segmentation and named entity recognition. In: Proceedings of the Fifth Workshop on Chinese Language Processing, SIGHAN@COLING/ACL 2006, Sydney, Australia, pp. 108–117 (2006)
35. Huang, Z., Xu, W., Yu, K.: Bidirectional LSTM-CRF models for sequence tagging. arXiv preprint: arXiv:1508.01991 (2015)
36. Chiu, J.P., Nichols, E.: Named entity recognition with bidirectional LSTM-CNNs. In: TACL, vol. 4, pp. 357–370 (2016)
37. Akhundov, A., Trautmann, D., Groh, G.: Sequence labeling: a practical approach. arXiv preprint: arXiv:1808.03926 (2018)
38. Liu, P., Chang, S., Huang, X., Tang, J., Cheung, J.C.K.: Contextualized non-local neural networks for sequence learning. In: AAAI, vol. 33, no. 01, pp. 6762–6769 (2019)

SHGAE: Social Hypergraph AutoEncoder for Friendship Inference

Yujie Li[1(✉)], Yan Chen[1], Tianliang Qi[1], Feng Tian[1], Yaqiang Wu[2], and Qianying Wang[2]

[1] College of Computer Science and Technology, Xi'an Jiaotong University, Xi'an, Shaanxi, China
3121351010@stu.xjtu.edu.cn
[2] Lenovo Research, Beijing, China
wuyqe@lenovo.com

Abstract. Location-Based Social Networks (LBSNs) present a significant challenge for inferring social relationships from both social networks and user mobility. While traditional rule-based walk graph representation learning methods predict friendship based on user proximity, they fail to distinguish contributions of different mobile semantics (temporal, spatial, and activity semantics). On the other hand, graph-based autoencoder models have shown promising results, but they are not suitable for heterogeneous information in LBSNs, and they perform poorly when users lack initial features. In this paper, we propose the Social Hypergraph Autoencoder (SHGAE) model, a novel autoencoder designed specifically for social hypergraphs formed by LBSNs data, which combines the strengths of these two methods. We initialize nodes vectors via hypergraph-jump-walk embedding strategy to capture features of the hypergraph, then use a well-designed autoencoder with heterogeneous message passing and attention mechanisms to model different semantic node influences. Extensive experiments demonstrate that our model outperforms state-of-the-art methods on the social relationship inference task. Moreover, in the ablation study, we find that our two proposed modules contribute differently to datasets with different sparsity, which can provide valuable insights for future research.

Keywords: Graph autoencoder · Graph Neural Networks · Graph attention networks · Location based social network · Link prediction

1 Introduction

With the development of online social networks, friendship inference has gradually become a research hotspot. Location-based social networks(LBSNs) such as Foursquare [1], Facebook, Gowalla, and Brightkite have emerged and gained millions of users who share their real-time presence in the form of check-ins. A check-in includes a timestamp, a semantic category (e.g., shopping or having supper), and a point of interest (POIs) (e.g., school or a cinema), as shown in

L. Iliadis et al. (Eds.): ICANN 2023, LNCS 14259, pp. 550–562, 2023.
https://doi.org/10.1007/978-3-031-44223-0_44

Fig. 1. Studying the mobility of users is crucial for friendship inference in LBSNs [2] since people tend to engage in activities with friends. Users with similar trajectories are more likely to have common interests and more encounters, making them more likely to become friends.

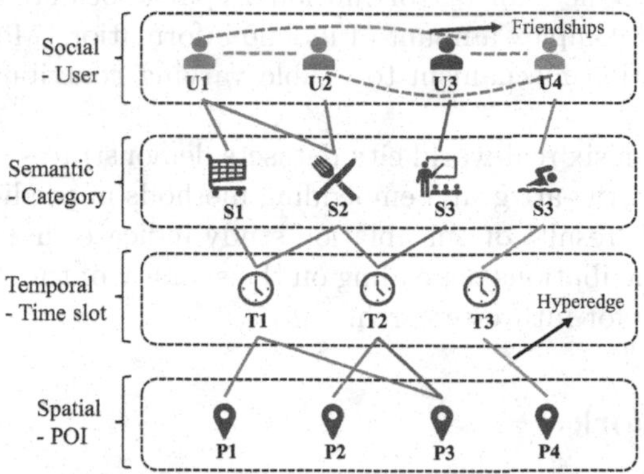

Fig. 1. LBSN with Friendship edges and Check-ins Hyperedges.

Early works on social inference primarily relied on manual feature engineering [3,4]. However, this type of method exhibits poor generalization and requires significant time and effort. In order to automatically represent graph data and overcome the limitations of manual methods, several rule-based walk representation learning methods have been proposed [5–7]. However, these methods treat the timestamp, semantic category, point of interest, and users equally, although different semantics may have distinct impacts on social inference. For instance, co-occurrences of users in certain locations or at specific times may have different effects on social inference. Moreover, some users may be more influential in promoting friendships than others. Recently, graph representation learning methods based on Graph Convolutional Neural Networks (GNNs) have received significant attention. Many studies have combined autoencoder ideas with GNNs to construct latent graph representations [8–10]. However, current graph autoencoder techniques are only suitable for graph datasets with explicit node features (such as Cora [11], a citation network whose explicit node features can be generated from the words in this paper).

To solve the above problems, we propose social hypergraph autoencoder **(SHGAE)**, a novel social hypergraph representation framework, which combines the advantages of rule-based walk graph representation learning and graph autoencoder. Our contributions can be summarised as follows:

- We design a novel social hypergraph walk: social hypergraph Jump walk (SHJ-walk), which learns the features of users and mobile nodes by jumping walk with weights between social and different mobile layers. SHJ-walk can fully and efficiently capture complex social and mobile features (timestamp, semantic

category, and POIs) in the social hypergraph, which provides a suitable initial representation for graph autoencoders.
- We introduce Heterogeneous Message Passing Graph Attention Networks (HMP-GAT) to adapt the graph convolutional neural network to social hypergraphs. Specifically, we propose a modification to the direction of message passing to address the challenge of dilution of sparse social relationships caused by the large and complex amount of mobile information. Moreover, we incorporate an attention mechanism to enable varying contributions of different semantic nodes.
- Our evaluation on six real-world city datasets demonstrates that SHGAE outperforms state-of-the-art graph embedding methods in predicting friendships. Furthermore, the results of our ablation study indicate that the two modules have varying contributions depending on the sparsity of the dataset, providing valuable insights for future research.

2 Related Work

Rule-Based Walk Graph Representation. The series of approaches utilize a rule-based walk strategy to obtain node sequences and maximize the probability of co-occurring words in a window to represent nodes. Bruna et al. [6] first proposed deepwalk on social graph, Aditya Grover et al. [5] made improvements on deepwalk and proposed node2vec, which controls the transition probability of the walk through the two parameters p and q. Dingqi Yang et al. [12] proposed LBSN2vec, which is a specially designed walk strategy for social hypergraph.

Graph Neural Networks. In recent years, with the rapid development of graph neural networks, a series of approaches have been proposed. Max Welling et al. [10] applies the idea of convolutional neural network(CNN) to graph proposed GCN. Will Hamilton et al. [9] proposed an inductive approach graphSAGE through sample and aggregate neighbor nodes generates representations. Petar Velikovi et al. [13] introduces attention mechanism and proposes GAT, which has stronger performance and is suitable for directed graphs. However the GNN methods are not suitable for LBSNs without node explicit features.

Social Inference in LBSNs. Walk2friends [14] tried social inference with user mobility alone. Wu Yongji et al. [15] proposed Heter-GCN for social heterogeneous graph, but lacks considering check-in information with various semantics. Zhao WayneXin et al. [16] considers the timing relationship of check-in locations and multi-Grained sequential contexts. Dingqi Yang et al. [12] proposed LBSN2vec, which fuses social features with multi-semantic check-in features. But in LBSN2vec, various check-in semantic information contribute the same in social inference.

3 Problem Definition

As shown in Fig. 1, a friendship is represented by an edge (a blue dotted line) that links two user nodes, while a check-in is represented by a hyperedge (a thick colored line) that links four nodes.

Table 1. Summary of notation

Notations	Descriptions
$G = (V, E)$	Hypergraph of LBSN
V_i	Set of nodes in hypergraph of type $i(u, s, t, p)$
α	Probability of jumping to hyperedge
E_i	Set of edges in hypergraph of type $i(f, h)$
v_i	Nodes of type $i(u, s, t, p)$
e_i	edges of type $i(f, h)$
N^n, N^e	The number of nodes, edges in hypergraph
$Z_I \in \mathbb{R}^{N \times F}$	Initial embedding vectors of nodes
$Z_G \in \mathbb{R}^{N \times F}$	Encoded vectors of nodes
$A', A \in \mathbb{R}^{N \times N}$	The (reconstructed) adjacency matrix of graph

Each user is represented by a single node denoted as u. Semantic categories, or activity types, such as shopping or having supper, are represented by nodes denoted as s. Temporal time slots, obtained by dividing continuous time into fixed intervals, are represented by nodes denoted as t. Spatial points of interest (POIs), such as schools or cinemas, are represented by nodes denoted as p. The LBSN, a hypergraph, can be represented as $G = (V, E)$, which is an undirected graph. Other symbol definitions are shown in the Table 1. The main downstream tasks can be defined as follow:

Social Relationship Inference in LBSN: Given a hypergraph $G = (V, E)$ and pairs of nodes $v_u^i, v_u^j \in V, (v_u^i, v_u^j) \notin E$, inference the friendship link (v_u^i, v_u^j) whether will be formed in the future.

4 Model Architecture

4.1 Overview of Model

The architecture of our proposed model, Social Hypergraph AutoEncoder (SHGAE), is depicted in Fig. 2. The autoencoder framework comprises three main components: Social Hypergraph Jump Walk(SHJ-walk), Heterogeneous Message Passing Graph Attention Network (HMP-GAT), and Decoder.

To obtain the initial node representations $Z_I \in \mathbb{R}^{N \times F}$ of the user and mobility nodes, we utilize skip-gram [17] to process the sequences generated from the

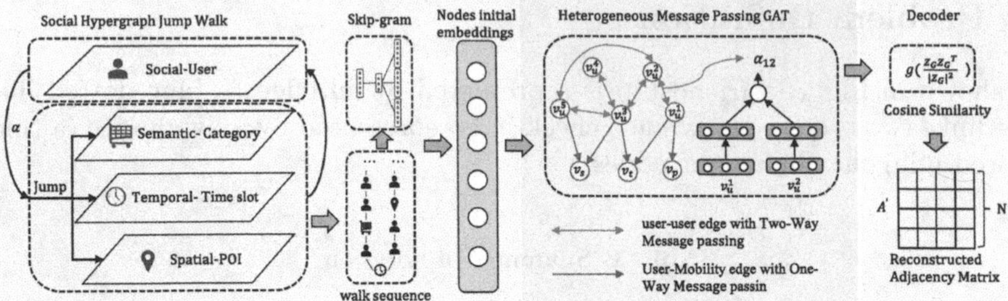

Fig. 2. The overview of SHGAE which consists of three parts: social hypergraph jump walk, heterogeneous message passing graph attention network, and decoder.

SHJ-walk. HMP-GAT is a Graph Neural Network with our improved messaging pattern and heterogeneous graph structure. The initial representations Z_I are fed to the HMP-GAT to further extract features of nodes $Z_G \in \mathbb{R}^{N \times F}$. The Decoder component implements the generative model to reconstruct a new adjacency matrix $A^{'} \in \mathbb{R}^{N \times N}$, which can be utilized to predict social links.

4.2 Social Hypergraph Jump Walk

Walk Strategy: SHJ-walk is designed to perform a classic random walk at the social layer, with the probability of jumping to a hyperedge being α. After landing on a hyperedge, SHJ-walk jumps to one of the layers (activity category, timestamp, or POI) with a weight assigned to each mobility layer. After sampling a node from the hyperedge based on its frequency of occurrence, SHJ-walk returns to the social layer. As illustrated in Fig. 3, a sequence of SHJ-walk contains not only user nodes but also check-in nodes, making it a comprehensive representation of social and multi-semantic information.

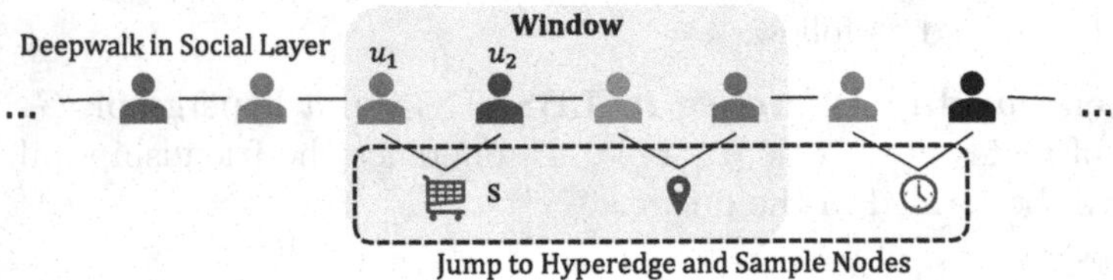

Fig. 3. An example sequence of SHJ-walk.

Our proposed approach aims to include users who have co-occurrences in check-ins but do not have direct social links, in the same sequence for representation learning (u_1 and u_2 are in the same sequence due to s). Additionally, the weight jump strategy is designed such that if check-in nodes have more co-occurrences with users, they are more likely to be jumped to, which aligns with the idea of social prediction: more co-occurrences imply a higher likelihood of friendship.

W_i is the weight of jumping to layer i(s,t,p) of check-ins. $w_i(j)$ is the weight of sampling node v_j after jumping to layer i. W_i and $w_i(j)$ can be calculated in the Eq. 1:

$$W_i = num(V_i) \quad w_i(j) = \frac{count(v_j)}{num(V_i)} \quad i \in s,t,p \tag{1}$$

The pseudo-code for SHJ-walk is given in Algorithm 1.

Algorithm 1 Social hypergraph jump walk (SHJ-walk)

Input: Hypergraph of LBSNvec $G = (V, E)$, Four types of node sets (V_u, V_s, V_t, V_p), Start node u, Length l, Jump to Hyperedge Probability α, weight of jumping to layer i: W_i, weight of sampling v_i in layer i: $w_i(j)$.
Output: A sequence of SHJ-walk.

```
for int i=1 to N do
    curr = walk[-1]
    if curr ∈ V_u then
        if random() < α then
            choice_stp = WeightedChoice(W_t, W_s, W_p)
            V^m_curr = GetMobilityNeighbors(curr, choice_stp, G)
            s = WeightedSampling(V^m_curr, weight(V^m_curr))
        else
            V^u_curr = GetUserNeighbors(curr, G)
            s = RandomSampling(V^u_curr)
        end if
    else
        V^u_curr = GetUserNeighbors(curr, G)
        s = RandomSampling(V^u_curr)
    end if
    Append s to walk
end for
return walk
```

Learning by Skip-Gram Model: The embedding model adopts the classsic skip-gram [17], we extend it to graph by optimizing the following objective function 2, which maximizes the log-probability co-occurrences of nodes in window $N_s(u)$ and a node u :

$$\Theta = \sum_{u \in V} \sum_{n_i \in N_s(u)} \left(f(n_i) \cdot f(u) - log \sum_{v \in V} f(v) \cdot f(u) \right) \tag{2}$$

Due to calculating $log \sum_{v \in V} f(v) \cdot f(u)$ requires summation over all nodes in G, it is expensive to compute for large networks, we adopt the negative sampling [18].

4.3 Heterogeneous Message Passing GAT

Heterogeneous Message Passing: In order to adapt the graph autoencoder to hypergraphs of LBSN, we introduce a novel approach called Heterogeneous Message Passing graph attention networks (HMP-GAT), which is built upon the concept of GAT. As illustrated in the second part of Fig. 2, messages are exchanged bidirectionally on the user-user edges, while on the user-mobility edge, messages flow from the user to the mobility node. This can be mathematically expressed as:

$$\vec{h}_i' = \sigma(\frac{1}{K}\sum_{k=1}^{K}\sum_{j\in N_i}\alpha_{ij}^k W^k \vec{h}_j') \quad N_i \in V_u \tag{3}$$

where σ is a nonlinearity function, K is the number of heads of attention, α_{ij}^k is attention coefficients [13], W^k is linear transformation's weight matrix, All nodes only receive information from the user node V_u.

The two-way passing of messages on the social edge is to ensure the extraction of all social features, and the one-way passing of messages on the check-in edge is due to that the number of check-in edges in heterogeneous graph is much larger than that of user social edges, and receiving check-in node messages would dilute the social features of user nodes, leading to poor representation.

Learning: The HMP-GAT is a model with two-layer GAT witch can deep encode the graph structure:

$$Z_G = HMP - GAT(X, A) \tag{4}$$

The decoder reconstruct the graph adjacency matrix A' by the encoded vector Z_G and minimize the reconstruction loss $\mathcal{L}$:

$$\mathcal{L} = difference(A, A') \tag{5}$$

However, due to the extreme sparsity of the heterogeneous graph, penalizing all unlinked nodes in the reconstruction error is computationally expensive. To address this issue, we employed negative sampling. Moreover, penalizing all unlinked users is not appropriate since future social links may emerge between them. The edges involved in training include: user-user links, user-check links, sampling negative user-user links and sampling negative user-check links:

$$\begin{aligned}\mathcal{L} = &\sum_{u\in V_u}\sum_{u'\in V_u} log(a_{uu'}^1) + \sum_{u\in V_u}\sum_{c\in V_{stp}} log(a_{uc}^1)\\ &- \sum_{u\in V_u}\sum_{u'\in V_u} log(a_{uu'}^0) - \sum_{u\in V_u}\sum_{c\in V_{stp}} log(a_{uc}^0)\end{aligned} \tag{6}$$

where $a_{uu'}^1$, a_{uc}^1 $a_{uu'}^0$, and a_{uc}^0 are reconstructed value of links, and negative links, respectively, which can be calculate by:

$$a_{ij} = sigmoid(z_i z_j^T) \tag{7}$$

4.4 Decoder Model

After training, we obtain the embedding Z_G of each node through our model. We use the commonly used cosine similarity to reconstruct the adjacency matrix A':

$$A' = \frac{Z_G Z_G^T}{|Z_G|^2} \tag{8}$$

5 Experiments

5.1 Experimental Setup

Datasets: We use six real-world datasets from Foursquare social network. These datasets are collected from Foursquare dataset containing a set of check-ins over about two years (from Apr.2021 to Jan.2014) by Yang, Dingqi et al. [12], which has two snapshots of the corresponding user social network before (in Mar. 2012) and after (in May 2014) the check-in data collection period. Table 2 shows the details of the datasets.

Table 2. Statistics of the datasets

Dateset	NYC	TKY	IST	JK	KL	SP
#User	4,024	7,232	10,367	6,395	6,432	3,954
#POI	3,628	10,856	12,693	8,826	10,817	6,286
#Check-ins	105,961	699,324	908,162	378,559	526,405	249,839
#Friendships(Before)	8,723	37,480	21,354	11,207	16,161	9,655
#Friendships(After)	10,545	51,704	36,007	16,950	31,178	14,402

We use three metrics to measure the characteristics of the dataset, D^s and D^m measures the sparsity of sociality and mobility of social graph. $D^{s\&m}$ measures the ratio of mobile and social sparsity of the social graph:

$$D^s = norm(\frac{|E_f|}{|V_u|^2}) \quad D^m = norm(\frac{|E_h|}{|V_u|}) \quad D^{s\&m} = norm(\frac{D^m}{D^s}) \tag{9}$$

where, E_f is the number of friend edges, E_h is the number of check-ins, $|V_u|$ is the number of users, $norm$ is the normalization function.

Metrics: We use three common metrics: precision, recall, F1-score for the top-K prediction. Due to the number of candidate pairs of nodes is too large, we randomly selecting 50 users who have no friendship link as candidates for every user.

Baselines: We compared our method with the following state-of-the-art baselines: DeepWalk [6], Node2vec [5], Walk2Friends [14], DHNE [19], LBSN2vec [12], LINE [20]. The hypergraphs can not directly to most of baseline methods, we use three settings to make these methods applicable to LBSN:

- (S): Only consider user nodes and user-user edges in this case. This setting applies to Deepwalk, Node2vec, LINE.
- (M): Only consider user nodes, check-in nodes, hyperedges in this case. This setting applies to Walk2friends, DHNE.
- (S&M): Consider all nodes and edges in this case. This setting applies to Deepwalk, Node2vec, LINE, LBSN2Vec and our model.

Training Configuration: For SHJ-walk module 4.2, we set walk length to $l = 80$, the number of walks per node to $r = 10$, and the context window size for the SkipGram model to $k = 10$, the dimension of nodes' embedding to $d = 64$, the probability of jumping to hyperedge $\alpha = 0.2$. For HMP-GAT module 4.3, we used two layers of GAT, the dimensions of hidden layer is 64. We set attention head to $h = 5$, learning rate to $l = 0.001$, use the validation set for early stopping during training to prevent overfitting.

To prevent accidental errors, each experiment was repeated 10 times and averaged. The code of our experiment is publicly available at https://github.com/LYJAntelope/mySHGAE

5.2 Results of Social Relationship Inference

The experimental results of social relationship inference are shown as Fig. 4. For ease of observation, we discard the poorly performing methods in some settings.

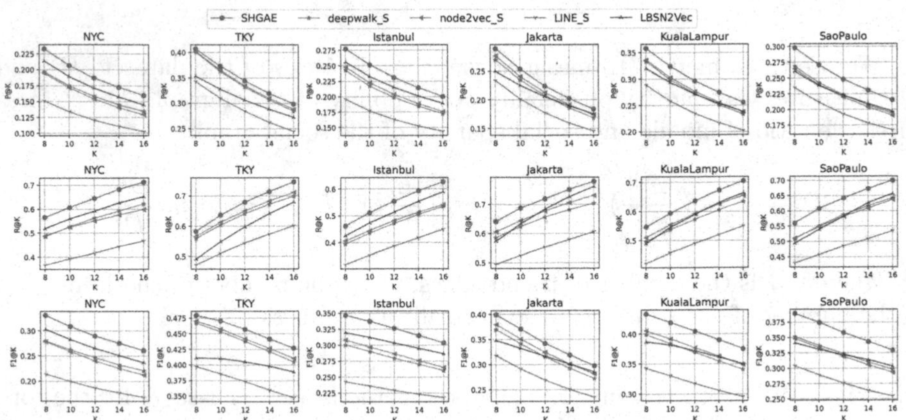

Fig. 4. The results of social relationship inference compared with baselines.

Our evaluation results demonstrate that our proposed SHGAE model outperforms all baseline methods across all metrics and datasets. LBSN2vec, as a hypergraph embedding method, performs well compared with other baselines because it captures the social and mobile information of the large social hypergraph. Compared with LBSN2vec, our method extracts all the features of the social hypergraph while making various semantics nodes exert different influences, thereby extracting more social features. It is worth noting that we removed all M and S&M settings results from the display because they were all too poor, which shows that traditional methods tend to extract the check-in information and ignore the social features of users when faced with the huge check-in data of LBSN.

5.3 Ablation Study

To further study the impact of each module in our framework, we conducted the following ablation experiments:

- SHGAE-A1: Feed random initial vector into HMP-GAT to verify the effectiveness of SHJ-walk.
- SHGAE-A2: Remove the check-in edges to verify the effectiveness of heterogeneous structure of HMP-GAT.
- SHGAE-A3: Let the messages are passed in both directions on all edges to verify the effectiveness of heterogeneous message passing.
- SHGAE-A4: Remove HMP-GAT module.

Table 3. The Experimental Results of Ablation study

Methods	NYC		TKY		Istanbul		Jakarta		KualaLampur		SaoPaulo	
	P@K	R@K	P@K	R@K	P@K	R@K	P@K	R@K	P@K	R@K	P@K	R@K
SHGAE-A1	0.147	0.414	0.241	0.379	0.158	0.309	0.169	0.430	0.211	0.356	0.206	0.416
SHGAE-A2	0.198	0.584	0.366	0.619	0.237	0.471	0.246	0.652	0.312	0.562	0.261	0.577
SHGAE-A3	0.168	0.488	0.220	0.347	0.195	0.412	0.212	0.563	0.239	0.438	0.196	0.430
SHGAE-A4	0.187	0.553	0.366	0.621	0.249	0.511	0.248	0.676	0.318	0.571	0.259	0.587
SHGAE	**0.207**	**0.607**	**0.373**	**0.636**	**0.257**	**0.523**	**0.254**	**0.688**	**0.324**	**0.594**	**0.271**	**0.608**

Table 3 shows the experimental results (repeat ten times, top-10) of each ablation study. The results demonstrate that SHGAE outperforms all other models on all datasets.

It is worth noting that different modules perform differently. Figure 5 shows the sparsity comparison of datasets (D^s, D^m, $D^{s\&m}$, explained in 5.1). Setting the threshold $D^{s\&m} = 0.15$, we can divide the datasets into two sets: $\{NYC, SP, TKY\}$, $\{IST, JK, KL\}$. Combining with Fig. 5 and Table 3 for analysis, we can draw the following conclusions:

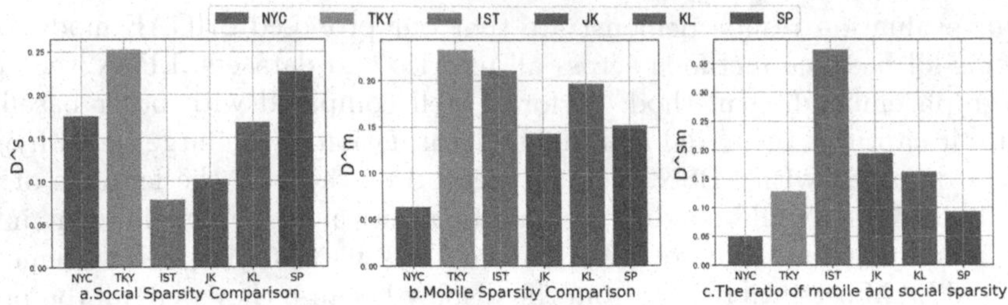

Fig. 5. The sparsity comparison of datasets.

- On LBSNs with relatively sparse friendships and dense check-ins such as IST, JK and KL, the performance of SHGAE-4 is closer to SHGAE, which shows that the random walk based module performance better, and SHJ-walk contribute more in social feature extraction on such LBSNs;
- On LBSNs with relatively dense social and sparse check-ins such as NYC, SP and TKY the performance of SHGAE-2 is closer to SHGAE, which shows that the graph convolutional neural network performs better, and HMP-GAT contribute more in social feature extraction on such LBSNs;

6 Conclusion

In this paper, we proposed a novel autoencoder for social hypergraphs, named SHGAE, which combines the strengths of rule-based walk graph representation learning and graph autoencoder. Experimental results show that SHGAE consistently outperforms the state-of-the-art graph embedding methods on the friendship prediction task. Our ablation study verifies the effectiveness of each module, and we discovered that the two proposed modules contribute differently to datasets with varying sparsity. These findings can serve as guidelines for future research in this area.

In the future, we plan to further extend SHGAE by considering the complex mixed probability distribution of social hypergraph data to get a more comprehensive representation of datasets with different sparse distributions.

Acknowledgement. This work was supported by National Key Research and Development Program of China (2020AAA0108800), National Natural Science Foundation of China (62137002, 61721002, 61937001, 61877048, 62177038, 62277042). Innovation Research Team of Ministry of Education (IRT_17R86), Project of China Knowledge Centre for Engineering Science and Technology. MoE-CMCC "Artificial Intelligence" Project (MCM20190701), Project of Chinese academy of engineering "The Online and Offline Mixed Educational ServiceSystem for'The Belt and Road' Training in MOOC China". "LENOVO-XJTU" Intelligent Industry Joint Laboratory Project.

References

1. Noulas, A., Scellato, S., Mascolo, C., Pontil, M.: An empirical study of geographic user activity patterns in foursquare. In: Proceedings of the International AAAI Conference on Web and Social Media, vol. 5, no. 1, pp. 570–573 (2011)
2. Eagle, N., Pentland, A., Lazer, D.: Inferring friendship network structure by using mobile phone data. Proc. Nat. Acad. Sci. **106**(36), 15274–15278 (2009)
3. Cheng, R., Pang, J., Zhang, Y.: Inferring friendship from check-in data of location-based social networks. In: Proceedings of the 2015 IEEE/ACM International Conference on Advances in Social Networks Analysis and Mining 2015, pp. 1284–1291 (2015)
4. Scellato, S., Noulas, A., Mascolo, C.: Exploiting place features in link prediction on location-based social networks. In: Proceedings of the 17th ACM SIGKDD International Conference on Knowledge Discovery and Data Mining, pp. 1046–1054 (2011)
5. Grover, A., Leskovec, J.: node2vec: scalable feature learning for networks. In: Proceedings of the 22nd ACM SIGKDD International Conference on Knowledge Discovery and Data Mining, pp. 855–864 (2016)
6. Perozzi, B., Al-Rfou, R., Skiena, S.: DeepWalk: online learning of social representations. In: Proceedings of the 20th ACM SIGKDD International Conference on Knowledge Discovery and Data Mining, pp. 701–710 (2014)
7. Yang, D., Qu, B., Yang, J., Cudré-Mauroux, P.: Lbsn2vec++: heterogeneous hypergraph embedding for location-based social networks. IEEE Trans. Knowl. Data Eng. **34**(4), 1843–1855 (2020)
8. Guo, Z., Wang, F., Yao, K., Liang, J., Wang, Z.: Multi-scale variational graph autoencoder for link prediction. In: Proceedings of the Fifteenth ACM International Conference on Web Search and Data Mining, pp. 334–342 (2022)
9. Hamilton, W., Ying, Z., Leskovec, J.: Inductive representation learning on large graphs. In: Advances in Neural Information Processing Systems, vol. 30 (2017)
10. Kipf, T.N., Welling, M.: Semi-supervised classification with graph convolutional networks (2016)
11. Sen, P., Namata, G., Bilgic, M., Getoor, L., Galligher, B., Eliassi-Rad, T.: Collective classification in network data. AI Mag. **29**(3), 93–93 (2008)
12. Yang, D., Qu, B., Yang, J., Cudre-Mauroux, P.: Revisiting user mobility and social relationships in LBSNs: a hypergraph embedding approach. In: The World Wide Web Conference, pp. 2147–2157 (2019)
13. Veličković, P., Cucurull, G., Casanova, A., Romero, A., Lio, P., Bengio, Y.: Graph attention networks. arXiv preprint: arXiv:1710.10903 (2017)
14. Backes, M., Humbert, M., Pang, J., Zhang, Y.: walk2friends: inferring social links from mobility profiles. In: Proceedings of the 2017 ACM SIGSAC Conference on Computer and Communications Security, pp. 1943–1957 (2017)
15. Wu, Y., Lian, D., Jin, S., Chen, E.: Graph convolutional networks on user mobility heterogeneous graphs for social relationship inference. In: IJCAI, pp. 3898–3904 (2019)
16. Zhao, W.X., Fan, F., Wen, J.-R., Chang, E.Y.: Joint representation learning for location-based social networks with multi-grained sequential contexts. ACM Trans. Knowl. Discov. Data (TKDD) **12**(2), 1–21 (2018)
17. Mikolov, T., Chen, K., Corrado, G., Dean, J.: Efficient estimation of word representations in vector space. arXiv preprint: arXiv:1301.3781 (2013)

18. Mikolov, T., Sutskever, I., Chen, K., Corrado, G.S., Dean, J.: Distributed representations of words and phrases and their compositionality. In: Advances in Neural Information Processing Systems, vol. 26 (2013)
19. Tu, K., Cui, P., Wang, X., Wang, F., Zhu, W.: Structural deep embedding for hyper-networks. In: Proceedings of the AAAI Conference on Artificial Intelligence, vol. 32, no. 1 (2018)
20. Tang, J., Qu, M., Wang, M., Zhang, M., Yan, J., Mei, Q.: Line: large-scale information network embedding. In: Proceedings of the 24th International Conference on World Wide Web, pp. 1067–1077 (2015)

Temporal Deformable Transformer for Action Localization

Haoying Wang, Ping Wei(✉), Meiqin Liu, and Nanning Zheng

Institute of Artificial Intelligence and Robotics, Xi'an Jiaotong University, Xi'an, China
pingwei@xjtu.edu.cn

Abstract. Temporal action localization (TAL) is a challenging task that has received significant attention in video understanding. Recently, Transformer-based models have demonstrated their effectiveness in capturing contextual information and achieved outstanding performance on various TAL benchmarks. However, these methods still face challenges in computational efficiency and contextual modeling rigidity. In this paper, we propose a method to address those problems in Transformer-based models. Our model introduces a temporal deformable Transformer module and the corresponding time normalization, enabling flexible aggregation of temporal context information in videos, leading to enhanced video representations. To demonstrate the effectiveness of the proposed method, we construct a Transformer-based anchor-free model with a simple prediction head, which yields superior performance on widely used benchmarks. Specifically, it achieves an average mAP of 67.4% on THUMOS14 and an average mAP of 36.8% on ActivityNet-v1.3.

Keywords: Temporal Action Localization · Transformer · Deformable Attention · Video Understanding

1 Introduction

One of the most formidable endeavors in video understanding is the temporal action localization (TAL) task. Recently, this task has garnered considerable attention due to its potential applicability across various scenarios, including smart surveillance, autonomous driving, and human-robot interaction. TAL aims to regress the boundaries (i.e., start and end time of actions) of each action instance in untrimmed videos and give their corresponding action categories in the meantime.

Early classical TAL methods [15,16] used a bottom-up approach to generate a large number of action proposals, refine proposal reliability, and classify proposals using an additional classifier. Other methods [7,10,22,29], which rely on pre-defined anchors, focus on adjusting these anchors. However, these methods have inherent limitations, including generating redundant action proposals that increase computational costs and dependence on hyperparameters, such

L. Iliadis et al. (Eds.): ICANN 2023, LNCS 14259, pp. 563–575, 2023.
https://doi.org/10.1007/978-3-031-44223-0_45

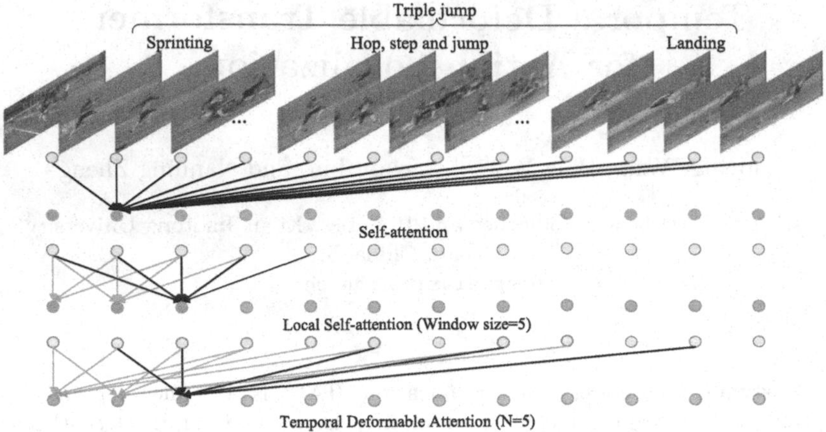

Fig. 1. Temporal deformable attention, self-attention and local self-attention.

as the anchor quantity and size. To address these issues, anchor-free methods [14,19,32,33] have emerged, generating only one proposal per temporal location represented as a pair of values indicating the distance between the start and end moments to the current location. Anchor-free methods are efficient and easy to train for the reduced computation and integrated boundary regression and classification in a single model. However, they require more robust video representations as they generate limited action proposals.

This paper aims to improve the performance of TAL by mining the video features enriched with temporal context through a flexible method. We propose a temporal deformable attention mechanism and develop a Transformer-based anchor-free model for TAL, drawing inspiration from the success of Transformers [25] in object detection [5,35] and TAL [19,33]. Our method takes in video representations and dynamically attends to temporal locations of interest along the time axis, guided by a sub-network, and performs feature aggregation.

The proposed temporal deformable Transformer module is a dynamic approach for incorporating temporal contextual information in videos, which can be applied at different stages of the model. The module gives the attention score of every moment in the video. It is more flexible when facing complex actions. The proposed module changes the way that the commonly used self-attention [25] and local self-attention [33] assign the importance to different parts of the input video. Figure 1 is an illustration comparing our proposed temporal deformable attention with the commonly used self-attention and local self-attention.

Our model integrates the temporal deformable Transformer module to extract an enhanced feature pyramid from the input video. Then it utilizes a lightweight convolutional prediction head on the pyramid for classification and regression. We perform extensive experiments on THUMOS14 [11] and ActivityNet-v1.3 [4] datasets. Our model achieves an average mAP of 67.4% on THUMOS14, which outperforms other comparison methods. On ActivityNet-v1.3, our results are also competitive and surpass other anchor-free models.

2 Related Work

Transformer [25] has brought remarkable improvements in various NLP and vision tasks [13,20]. ViT [9] proposed the first Transformer-based model for image classification that achieved state-of-the-art performance. MSIT [23] proposed a specially designed top-down interaction Transformer structure for temporal action proposal generation. DETR [5] proposed a new paradigm for object detection by leveraging the attention mechanism in Transformer. Deformable DETR [35] proposed a deformable attention module for object detection. This module focuses on selecting a few sampling points as a preliminary filter to identify significant key elements among all the feature map pixels. Deformable DETR provides significant inspiration for our work.

Earlier approaches [7,16] employed feature fusion techniques to account for temporal context in TAL. Besides, several methods have been proposed to create robust representations through temporal context modeling, including frame context [10,30,33] and boundary feature context [2,14]. Recently, there has been a growing interest in leveraging Transformer-based approaches [19,33] to model temporal context information in TAL, with attention mechanisms playing a pivotal role. Attention mechanisms are used to weigh the importance of different video clips based on their relevance to the action being localized, allowing the model to focus on the most salient temporal context information. These methods typically utilize either self-attention or local self-attention. Our proposed method tries to overcome the limitations of traditional attention mechanisms in temporal context modeling.

3 Method

Given an untrimmed input video $\boldsymbol{I}$, the aim of temporal action localization is to predict a label set $\boldsymbol{Y} = \{\boldsymbol{y}_i\}_{i=1}^{n}$, where $\boldsymbol{y}_i$ is the label of the ith action instance and n is the number of the instances in video $\boldsymbol{I}$. Each label $\boldsymbol{y}_i$ can be depicted as a tuple $(t_i^{start}, t_i^{end}, c_i)$, where c_i denotes the action category, and (t_i^{start}, t_i^{end}) indicate the start and the end time respectively. It should be noted that n may vary in different videos.

3.1 Model Overview

We construct a purely anchor-free architecture using multi-head temporal deformable attention shown in Fig. 2. The overall framework of our model is similar to the work [33]. In this model, we employ the proposed temporal deformable Transformer module as depicted in Fig. 3, which will be further described in the subsequent section. To be specific, we employ the I3D model [6] to extract features from the input video $\boldsymbol{I}$ and use a 1D convolution layer and a LayerNorm layer to embed the features. In this way, the video is represented as the clip feature $\boldsymbol{f} \in \mathbb{R}^{T \times C}$, where T is the number of video clips and C is the feature dimension of each video clip. Then, three temporal deformable Transformer modules are used for extracting temporal context information.

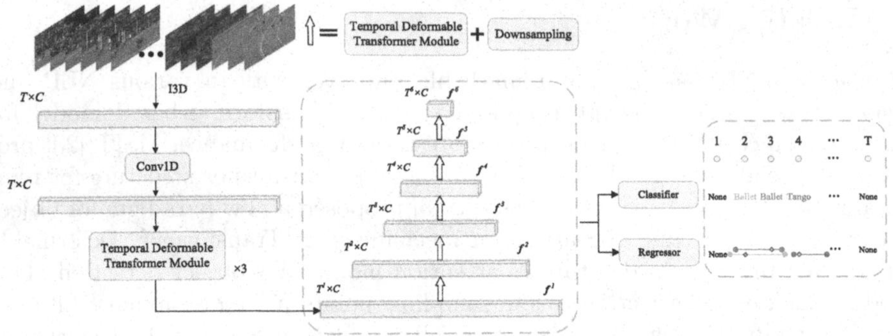

Fig. 2. The overall architecture of our model.

Several studies have demonstrated the significance of multi-scale features in object detection [17] and TAL [14,33]. We utilize additional five temporal deformable Transformer modules with 2x down-sampling module to generate multi-scale features. This process is summarized as follows:

$$\bar{\boldsymbol{f}}^l = TDTM(\boldsymbol{f}^{l-1}), \quad \boldsymbol{f}^l = \downarrow (\bar{\boldsymbol{f}}^l), \quad l = 2, 3, \ldots, 6, \tag{1}$$

where $TDTM()$ denotes the temporal deformable Transformer module. $\boldsymbol{f}^l \in \mathbb{R}^{T^l \times C}$ is the feature input to the l-th temporal deformable Transformer module. $\downarrow ()$ indicates the 2x down-sampling. $\boldsymbol{f}^1$ is the output from the previous module. Then we get a 6-layer feature pyramid $\boldsymbol{F} = [\boldsymbol{f}^1, \boldsymbol{f}^2, \ldots, \boldsymbol{f}^6]$, each layer of which is input to the prediction head to output the action candidates.

Our prediction head is a lightweight 1D convolutional network composed of a classifier and a regressor. The classifier is implemented using 3-layer 1D convolution with kernel size=3 and a sigmoid function is used to predict the probability of action categories. It classifies each temporal location across all 6 levels on the pyramid $\boldsymbol{F}$. The structure of the regressor is comparable to the classifier, except for a ReLU activation added for the distance prediction.

In inference, given the current temporal location as specified by the classifier within the duration of an action, the regressor predicts the distances to the action boundaries $(\Delta t^{start}, \Delta t^{end})$. Then these candidates are post-processed by Soft-NMS [3] to eliminate the redundant instances, resulting in the final predictions.

In our model, we use the same label assignment strategy as the work [14,33]. Concretely, we assign each temporal location t on the l-th level $\boldsymbol{f}^l$ as a positive sample to the i-th ground truth when $t_i^{start} < t < t_i^{start}$ is satisfied. We also use the center sampling method to modify the strategy and a predefined output regression range is established for each pyramid level [33].

3.2 Temporal Deformable Transformer Module

The temporal deformable Transformer module, as shown in Fig. 3, is proposed as a means of effectively modeling contextual information among clip features, guided by the context-dependent moments associated with each temporal location in the feature embeddings. The approach takes inspiration from deformable DETR [35], wherein the attention module focuses on a fixed number of spatial sampling points in the feature maps for each query. While our proposed module takes an approach by attending to N context-dependent moments surrounding each temporal location. These relevant moments are generated by a sub-network, whose inputs are the queries.

With the learnable parameters $\boldsymbol{W}_q \in \mathbb{R}^{C\times C}$, $\boldsymbol{W}_k \in \mathbb{R}^{C\times C}$ and $\boldsymbol{W}_v \in \mathbb{R}^{C\times C}$, the clip feature $\boldsymbol{f} \in \mathbb{R}^{T\times C}$ is projected into $\boldsymbol{Q}$, $\boldsymbol{K}$ and $\boldsymbol{V}$, referred to as query, key and value, respectively:

$$\boldsymbol{Q} = \boldsymbol{f}\boldsymbol{W}_q, \quad \boldsymbol{K} = \boldsymbol{f}\boldsymbol{W}_k, \quad \boldsymbol{V} = \boldsymbol{f}\boldsymbol{W}_v. \tag{2}$$

According to the clips feature $\boldsymbol{f} \in \mathbb{R}^{T\times C}$, we use a series of uniform time points $\boldsymbol{t} = \{0, 1, 2, \ldots, T-1\} \in \mathbb{R}^T$ index the grid moments, which indicate the clip feature of each moment. Then we normalize them to the range [0,1] according to T. Next, we input the query $\boldsymbol{Q}$ into a neural network $\Psi(\cdot)$ that produces N context-dependent offsets for each moment:

$$\boldsymbol{\Delta t} = TimeNorm(\Psi(\boldsymbol{Q})). \tag{3}$$

Specifically, $\Psi(\cdot)$ contains a 1D convolution and a linear projection with ReLu activation and $\boldsymbol{\Delta t} \in \mathbb{R}^{T\times N}$. We then use a time normalization method $TimeNorm$ to normalize $\boldsymbol{\Delta t}$ and stabilize the training process. We will provide the definition of $TimeNorm$ later.

Then we define a sampling function $\Phi(\cdot,\cdot)$, utilizing bilinear interpolation, that samples $\boldsymbol{V}$ according to the $\boldsymbol{t} + \boldsymbol{\Delta t}$ to obtain $\widetilde{\boldsymbol{V}} = \left\{\widetilde{V}_1, \widetilde{V}_2, \ldots, \widetilde{V}_T\right\} \in \mathbb{R}^{N\times C\times T}$, i.e.,

$$\widetilde{\boldsymbol{V}} = \Phi(\boldsymbol{V}, \boldsymbol{t} + \boldsymbol{\Delta t}). \tag{4}$$

It should be noted that $\boldsymbol{t}$ is broadcast to match the shape of $\boldsymbol{\Delta t}$.

We use a network $\Psi'(\cdot)$, which is similar to $\Psi(\cdot)$, to generate the attention weights $\boldsymbol{W} \in \mathbb{R}^{N\times T}$:

$$\boldsymbol{W} = \Psi'(\boldsymbol{K}) \tag{5}$$

wherein $\boldsymbol{W}$ can be rewritten as $\boldsymbol{W} = \{W_1; W_2; \ldots; W_T\}$. Then the temporal deformable attention (TDA) feature can be calculated by:

$$TDA = \left\{\widetilde{V}_1^T W_1; \widetilde{V}_2^T W_2; \ldots; \widetilde{V}_T^T W_T\right\}. \tag{6}$$

Based on the proposed module, following Transformer [25] and Deformable DETR [35], we extend the deformable attention mechanism to the multi-head deformable attention. It is implemented by dividing the input through channels into multiple parallel heads, each with its own set of context-dependent moments and learned attention weights. Then, by aggregating the outputs from all the attention heads, the model can capture a more comprehensive representation of the input, enhancing its ability to handle complex context information. It can

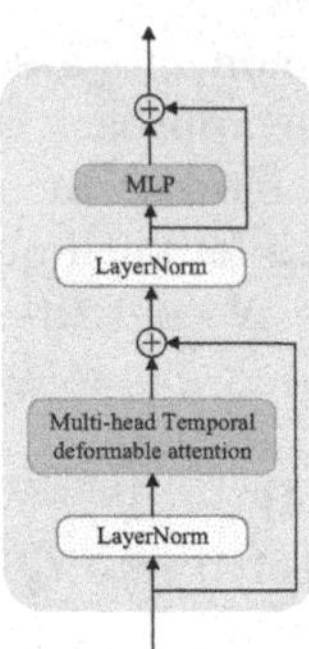

Fig. 3. Temporal deformable Transformer module.

substitute self-attention in the Transformer and be used at various model stages, with consistent input and output dimensions.

TimeNorm. We present an additional normalization step following the network $\Psi(\cdot)$ in order to induce moderate context-dependent offsets for each moment, thereby facilitating easier model training. The *TimeNorm* standardizes the offsets using the mean and standard deviation across every moment. It is formulated as:

$$\bar{\Delta t^i} = \frac{s}{\sigma}(\Delta t^i - \mu) + b \tag{7}$$

where s and b are learnable parameters scaling the normalized offsets. Δt^i is the offset of moment i. μ and σ are calculated as:

$$\begin{aligned} \mu &= \frac{1}{MN}\sum_{m=1}^{M}\sum_{n=1}^{N}\Delta t^i_{mn} \\ \sigma &= \sqrt{\frac{1}{MN}\sum_{m=1}^{M}\sum_{n=1}^{N}(\Delta t^i_{mn} - \mu)^2} \end{aligned} \tag{8}$$

where M denotes the number of attention heads. We demonstrate through ablation experiments that incorporating TimeNorm improves the performance of the model.

4 Experiments

4.1 Datasets and Setup

We test the proposed method on two datasets. THUMOS14 [11] contains 413 videos with 20 categories of actions labeled for TAL. Following the previous studies [14,33], we train our model on the validation videos and report the results on the test videos. ActivityNet-v1.3 [4] is composed of 19,994 untrimmed videos with 200 categories of actions labeled for TAL. Following the previous studies

[14,33], we use the training set to train our model and report the results on the validation set.

We conduct sampling of both RGB and optical flow frames at a rate of 10 frames per second for the THUMOS14 and 15 frames per second for the ActivityNet-v1.3. We use the two-stream I3D [6] model pre-trained on Kinetics to extract features of clips. Moreover, we also use the pre-training method from the work [14,33] with the R(2+1)D model [24] extracting features of clips, to make a fair comparison with other methods and show that our method can improve the performance with different features. Additionally, we merged the external classification results from the work [28] following other studies [2,14,30,33]. We present mean average precision (mAP) at different temporal-intersection-over-union (tIoU) thresholds. Specifically, the tIoU thresholds are [0.3 : 0.1 : 0.7] for THUMOS14 and [0.5 : 0.05 : 0.95] for ActivityNet-v1.3.

Our model is trained for 30 epochs using Adam [12] with a warm-up of 5 epochs. We set the initial learning rate to 10^{-4} and a cosine learning rate schedule is used. We set the batch size to 2 and weight decay to 0.04. We train our model with the basic loss function $\mathcal{L} = \ell_{cls} + \lambda\ell_{reg}$ where λ is a learnable parameter and its initial value is set to 1.0. ℓ_{cls} is the focal loss [18] for classification, and ℓ_{reg} is the DIoU loss [34] for regression. The parameters of Soft-NMS follow the work [33] and the final predictions are obtained by averaging the results of RGB and optical flow frames.

4.2 Results

As shown in Table 1 and 2, we present a comprehensive comparison of our model with other methods, specifying in the table the feature extraction methods they employed, namely I3D [6], TSN [26] and R(2+1)D [24].

Table 1 shows the results on THUMOS14. Our method reaches an average mAP of 67.4%, with an mAP of 78.8% at tIou=0.4 and an mAP of 71.5% at tIOU=0.5, outperforming all other advanced methods on all thresholds. It should be noted that A^{2}NET [32], TadTR [19], AFSD [14] and ActionFormer [33] are anchor-free methods. However, most of them utilize complex supplementary modules. Our model adopts a straightforward design and predicts results with a single shot, without including any refinement modules, thereby demonstrating the superiority of our module for anchor-free methods.

Table 2 shows the results on ActivityNet-v1.3. Our method achieves an average mAP of 36.8% using the pre-training method from TSP [1], with an mAP of 54.8% at tIou=0.5 and an mAP of 38.0% at tIOU=0.75. Especially, our method outperforms the state-of-the-art method with I3D features, whether they are actionness-based, anchor-based, or anchor-free. Despite not achieving the top performance on this difficult dataset, where the methods TCANet [21] and RCL [27] that surpass our method are not anchor-free, our method achieves competitive results using a relatively simple approach.

Table 1. Comparison with other methods on THUMOS14. We report mAP (%) at different tIoU thresholds and the average mAP (%) in [0.3 : 0.1 : 0.7].

Method	Feature	0.3	0.4	0.5	0.6	0.7	Avg.
BMN [15]	TSN	56.0	47.4	38.8	29.7	20.5	38.5
G-TAD [30]	TSN	54.5	47.6	40.3	30.8	23.4	39.3
BC-GNN [2]	TSN	57.1	49.1	40.4	31.2	23.1	40.2
TCANet [21]	TSN	60.6	53.2	44.6	36.8	26.7	44.3
RCL [27]	TSN	70.1	62.3	52.9	42.7	30.7	57.1
DCAN [8]	TSN	68.2	62.7	54.1	43.9	32.6	52.3
A^2NET [32]	I3D	58.6	54.1	45.5	32.5	17.2	41.6
TadTR [19]	I3D	62.4	57.4	49.2	37.8	26.3	46.6
ContextLoc [36]	I3D	68.3	63.8	54.3	41.8	26.2	50.9
AFSD [14]	I3D	67.3	62.4	55.5	43.7	31.1	52.0
BCNet [31]	I3D	71.5	67.0	60.0	48.9	33.0	56.1
ActionFormer [33]	I3D	82.1	77.8	71.0	59.4	43.9	66.8
Ours	I3D	**82.4**	**78.8**	**71.5**	**59.8**	**44.3**	**67.4**

Table 2. Comparison with other methods on ActivityNet-v1.3. We report mAP (%) at different tIoU thresholds and average mAP (%) in [0.5 : 0.05 : 0.95].

Type	Method	Feature	0.5	0.75	0.95	Avg.
Others	BMN [15]	TSN	50.1	34.8	8.3	33.9
	G-TAD [30]	TSN	50.4	34.6	9.0	34.1
	BC-GNN [2]	TSN	50.6	34.8	**9.4**	34.3
	DCAN [8]	TSN	51.8	36.0	9.5	35.4
	TCANet [21]	TSN	52.3	36.7	6.9	35.5
	RCL [27]	TSN	54.2	36.2	9.2	36.0
	ContextLoc [36]	I3D	**56.0**	35.2	3.6	34.2
	RCL [27]+TSP [1]	R(2+1)D	55.2	**39.0**	8.3	**37.7**
Anchor-free	A^2Net [32]	I3D	43.6	28.7	3.7	27.8
	TadTR [19]	I3D	49.1	32.6	8.5	32.3
	AFSD [14]	I3D	52.4	35.3	6.5	34.4
	ActionFormer [33]	I3D	53.5	36.2	8.2	35.6
	ActionFormer [33]+TSP [1]	R(2+1)D	54.7	37.8	**8.4**	36.6
	Ours	I3D	54.1	36.9	8.2	36.0
	Ours+TSP [1]	R(2+1)D	**54.8**	**38.0**	**8.4**	**36.8**

4.3 Ablation Study

We conduct ablation experiments using I3D features on THUMOS14.

Impact of the Number of Context-Dependent Moments. The number of context-dependent moments, denoted by N, plays a critical role in determining

Table 3. Ablation studies on THUMOS14. We report mAP (%) at $tIoU$ =0.3, 0.5, 0.7 and average mAP (%) in [0.3 : 0.1 : 0.7] by varying N.

N points	0.3	0.5	0.7	Avg.
2	81.9	70.5	44.0	66.5
4	82.2	71.5	44.0	66.9
6	**82.4**	**71.6**	43.9	67.0
8	**82.4**	71.5	**44.3**	**67.4**
10	82.3	**71.6**	44.1	67.1
12	82.6	71.4	44.2	67.2
18	82.0	70.8	43.0	66.5
24	81.3	69.7	42.5	65.6

Table 4. Ablation studies on the temporal deformable module. We report mAP (%) at tIoU=0.5 and average mAP (%) in [0.3 : 0.1 : 0.7].

Model	Stage 1			Stage 2			mAP	
	$S.$	$L.$	$D.$	$S.$	$L.$	$D.$	@0.5	Avg.
Baselines	✓			✓			68.6	65.3
			✓	✓			70.5	66.5
	✓					✓	69.7	65.8
		✓			✓		71.3	66.6
Ours			✓			✓	71.3	67.1
Ours+TimeNorm			✓			✓	**71.5**	**67.4**

the quantity and extent of temporal context information. Our experiments, detailed in Table 3, evaluate the impact of N on the performance of our model on THUMOS14. We test values of N varying $N \in [2, 4, 6, 8, 10, 12, 18, 24]$ and observe that our method stably improves performance across a broad range of N. The optimal results are achieved with $N = 8$, which is used in our experiments. Besides, the experimental results present the observation that larger values of N do not always result in better performance, which may contradict our initial expectations. The possible reason is that the network designed to generate Δt may not be optimal and that the choice of context-dependent moments may have caused features to become obscured, thereby diminishing the model's performance. These issues will be addressed as our next research objective.

Transformer-Based Network. We build a Transformer-based model as a baseline using vanilla self-attention [25]. Concretely, we replace all the temporal deformable Transformer modules with the standard Transformer modules. The feature embedding network, classifier, regression, and training strategy are the same as our model. It achieves an average mAP of 65.3% on THUMOS14, as shown in the first row of Table 4.

Impact of the Temporal Deformable Module. To evaluate the effectiveness of our proposed method, we replace the standard Transformer modules in the baseline model with the proposed temporal deformable Transformer module. The process is divided into two phases: Stage 1 is the context information mining stage and Stage 2 is the pyramid construction stage. We also implement an ActionFormer-like model that uses local self-attention in the Transformer module. The experimental results are presented in Table 4, where $S.$ denotes the self-attention Transformer module, $L.$ stands for the local self-attention Transformer module, and $D.$ is the temporal deformable Transformer module. This result shows that our proposed module is useful for every stage of the model.

Table 5. Comparison of parameters and MACs.

Method	Params	MACs
Self-attention	29.53M	45.56G
Local self-attention	29.20M	45.06G
Ours	27.39M	43.40 G

Comparison of Parameters and MACs. As shown in Table 5, we calculate the number of parameters and multiply-accumulate operations (MACs) for the models (excluding the backbone) that employ self-attention, local self-attention, and our proposed method on the same settings. By combining the previous experimental results, it is apparent that our method achieves higher performance with fewer parameters and lower computational demands.

5 Conclusion

In this paper, we present a new temporal deformable attention mechanism that tackles the issues of inefficiency and inflexibility in temporal context modeling. Our method enhances the adaptability in aggregating temporal context information from videos, resulting in stronger video representations. Our experiments on THUMOS14 and ActivityNet-v1.3 show the remarkable performance of our method for the anchor-free model. However, it is important to note that the temporal deformable attention mechanism is currently limited to temporal relationships and does not take into account other factors such as spatial and semantic information. Thus, our future work will focus on incorporating additional contextual information into the model to further improve its performance.

Acknowledgement. This research was supported by the grants National Key Research and Development Program (No. 2020YFB1406900), National Natural Science Foundation of China (No. 62088102), Youth Innovation Team of Shaanxi Universities, and Fundamental Research Funds for the Central Universities.

References

1. Alwassel, H., Giancola, S., Ghanem, B.: TSP: temporally-sensitive pretraining of video encoders for localization tasks. In: International Conference on Computer Vision, pp. 3173–3183 (2021)
2. Bai, Y., Wang, Y., Tong, Y., Yang, Y., Liu, Q., Liu, J.: Boundary content graph neural network for temporal action proposal generation. In: Vedaldi, A., Bischof, H., Brox, T., Frahm, J.-M. (eds.) ECCV 2020. LNCS, vol. 12373, pp. 121–137. Springer, Cham (2020). https://doi.org/10.1007/978-3-030-58604-1_8
3. Bodla, N., Singh, B., Chellappa, R., Davis, L.S.: Soft-NMS-improving object detection with one line of code. In: International Conference on Computer Vision, pp. 5561–5569 (2017)
4. Caba Heilbron, F., Escorcia, V., Ghanem, B., Carlos Niebles, J.: ActivityNet: a large-scale video benchmark for human activity understanding. In: IEEE Conference on Computer Vision and Pattern Recognition, pp. 961–970 (2015)
5. Carion, N., Massa, F., Synnaeve, G., Usunier, N., Kirillov, A., Zagoruyko, S.: End-to-end object detection with transformers. In: Vedaldi, A., Bischof, H., Brox, T., Frahm, J.-M. (eds.) ECCV 2020. LNCS, vol. 12346, pp. 213–229. Springer, Cham (2020). https://doi.org/10.1007/978-3-030-58452-8_13
6. Carreira, J., Zisserman, A.: Quo Vadis, action recognition? A new model and the kinetics dataset. In: IEEE Conference on Computer Vision and Pattern Recognition, pp. 6299–6308 (2017)
7. Chao, Y.W., Vijayanarasimhan, S., Seybold, B., Ross, D.A., Deng, J., Sukthankar, R.: Rethinking the faster R-CNN architecture for temporal action localization. In: IEEE Conference on Computer Vision and Pattern Recognition (2018)
8. Chen, G., Zheng, Y.D., Wang, L., Lu, T.: DCAN: improving temporal action detection via dual context aggregation. In: AAAI Conference on Artificial Intelligence, vol. 36, pp. 248–257 (2022)
9. Dosovitskiy, A., et al.: An image is worth 16x16 words: transformers for image recognition at scale. arXiv preprint: arXiv:2010.11929 (2020)
10. Gao, J., et al.: Accurate temporal action proposal generation with relation-aware pyramid network. In: AAAI Conference on Artificial Intelligence, vol. 34, pp. 10810–10817 (2020)
11. Idrees, H., et al.: The Thumos challenge on action recognition for videos "in the wild". Comput. Vis. Image Underst. **155**, 1–23 (2017)
12. Kinga, D., et al.: A method for stochastic optimization. In: International Conference on Learning Representations, vol. 5, p. 6 (2015)
13. Li, H., Wei, P., Li, J., Ma, Z., Shang, J., Zheng, N.: Asymmetric relation consistency reasoning for video relation grounding. In: Avidan, S., Brostow, G., Cisse, M., Farinella, G.M., Hassner, T. (eds.) ECCV 2022. Lecture Notes in Computer Science, vol. 13695, pp. 125–141. Springer, Cham (2022). https://doi.org/10.1007/978-3-031-19833-5_8
14. Lin, C., et al.: Learning salient boundary feature for anchor-free temporal action localization. In: IEEE Conference on Computer Vision and Pattern Recognition (2021)
15. Lin, T., Liu, X., Li, X., Ding, E., Wen, S.: BMN: boundary-matching network for temporal action proposal generation. In: International Conference on Computer Vision, pp. 3889–3898 (2019)

16. Lin, T., Zhao, X., Su, H., Wang, C., Yang, M.: BSN: boundary sensitive network for temporal action proposal generation. In: Ferrari, V., Hebert, M., Sminchisescu, C., Weiss, Y. (eds.) ECCV 2018. LNCS, vol. 11208, pp. 3–21. Springer, Cham (2018). https://doi.org/10.1007/978-3-030-01225-0_1
17. Lin, T.Y., Dollár, P., Girshick, R., He, K., Hariharan, B., Belongie, S.: Feature pyramid networks for object detection. In: IEEE Conference on Computer Vision and Pattern Recognition, pp. 2117–2125 (2017)
18. Lin, T.Y., Goyal, P., Girshick, R., He, K., Dollár, P.: Focal loss for dense object detection. In: International Conference on Computer Vision, pp. 2980–2988 (2017)
19. Liu, X., et al.: End-to-end temporal action detection with transformer. IEEE Trans. Image Process. **31**, 5427–5441 (2022)
20. Ma, Z., Wei, P., Li, H., Zheng, N.: HOIG: end-to-end human-object interactions grounding with transformers. In: IEEE International Conference on Multimedia and Expo (ICME), pp. 1–6 (2022)
21. Qing, Z., et al.: Temporal context aggregation network for temporal action proposal refinement. In: IEEE Conference on Computer Vision and Pattern Recognition, pp. 485–494 (2021)
22. Ren, S., He, K., Girshick, R., Sun, J.: Faster R-CNN: towards real-time object detection with region proposal networks. In: Advances in Neural Information Processing Systems, vol. 28 (2015)
23. Shang, J., Wei, P., Li, H., Zheng, N.: Multi-scale interaction transformer for temporal action proposal generation. Image Vis. Comput. **129**, 104589 (2023)
24. Tran, D., et al.: A closer look at spatiotemporal convolutions for action recognition. In: IEEE Conference on Computer Vision and Pattern Recognition, pp. 6450–6459 (2018)
25. Vaswani, A., et al.: Attention is all you need. In: Advances in Neural Information Processing Systems, vol. 30 (2017)
26. Wang, L., et al.: Temporal segment networks: towards good practices for deep action recognition. In: Leibe, B., Matas, J., Sebe, N., Welling, M. (eds.) ECCV 2016. LNCS, vol. 9912, pp. 20–36. Springer, Cham (2016). https://doi.org/10.1007/978-3-319-46484-8_2
27. Wang, Q., Zhang, Y., Zheng, Y., Pan, P.: RCL: recurrent continuous localization for temporal action detection. In: IEEE Conference on Computer Vision and Pattern Recognition, pp. 13566–13575 (2022)
28. Xiong, Y., et al.: Cuhk & ethz & siat submission to activitynet challenge 2016. arXiv preprint: arXiv:1608.00797 (2016)
29. Xu, H., Das, A., Saenko, K.: R-c3d: region convolutional 3d network for temporal activity detection. In: International Conference on Computer Vision, pp. 5783–5792 (2017)
30. Xu, M., Zhao, C., Rojas, D.S., Thabet, A., Ghanem, B.: G-TAD: sub-graph localization for temporal action detection. In: IEEE Conference on Computer Vision and Pattern Recognition, pp. 10156–10165 (2020)
31. Yang, H., et al.: Temporal action proposal generation with background constraint. In: AAAI Conference on Artificial Intelligence, vol. 36, pp. 3054–3062 (2022)
32. Yang, L., Peng, H., Zhang, D., Fu, J., Han, J.: Revisiting anchor mechanisms for temporal action localization. IEEE Trans. Image Process. **29**, 8535–8548 (2020)
33. Zhang, C.L., Wu, J., Li, Y.: ActionFormer: localizing moments of actions with transformers. In: Avidan, S., Brostow, G., Cisse, M., Farinella, G.M., Hassner, T. (eds.) ECCV 2022. Lecture Notes in Computer Science, vol. 13664, pp. 492–510. Springer, Cham (2022). https://doi.org/10.1007/978-3-031-19772-7_29

34. Zheng, Z., Wang, P., Liu, W., Li, J., Ye, R., Ren, D.: Distance-IoU loss: faster and better learning for bounding box regression. In: AAAI Conference on Artificial Intelligence, vol. 34, pp. 12993–13000 (2020)
35. Zhu, X., Su, W., Lu, L., Li, B., Wang, X., Dai, J.: Deformable DETR: deformable transformers for end-to-end object detection. arXiv:2010.04159 (2020)
36. Zhu, Z., Tang, W., Wang, L., Zheng, N., Hua, G.: Enriching local and global contexts for temporal action localization. In: International Conference on Computer Vision, pp. 13516–13525 (2021)

Trans-Cycle: Unpaired Image-to-Image Translation Network by Transformer

Kai Tian, Mengze Pan, Zongqing Lu, and Qingmin Liao(✉)

Tsinghua University, Hai Dian, Beijing, China
liaoqm@tsinghua.eu.cn

Abstract. Transformer recently has made remarkable progress in various computer vision tasks. In this paper, we design a novel transformer-based framework for image-to-image translation under the condition of limited computing resources. We conducted a comparative analysis between the model introduced in this paper and mainstream methodologies prevalent in the field, employing various publicly available datasets. The evaluation encompassed the assessment of numerical metrics and the examination of visualization outcomes. Compared with the recent unpaired translation network, our model has a more powerful deformation ability and a more refined distinction between image sub-regions. It has better performance on multiple datasets and much development potential.

Keywords: Transformer · Image-to-Image Translation

1 Introduction

Image-to-image translation is a crucial and intricate task within the realm of image generation, which involves intricate cross-domain conversions across various image categories. Such conversions can encompass the depiction of seasonal transitions within specific scenes, the representation of landscapes with diverse artistic styles, or the modification of objects with unique similarities. Conventional image translation tasks necessitate paired datasets, which may not adequately capture the complexities of real-world scenarios, thereby limiting the generality and applicability of the models. Therefore, we contend that unpaired image translation techniques have significant potential for simulating data, generating virtual imagery, and facilitating high-degree-of-freedom style transfers. Accordingly, this paper focuses on unpaired image translation and presents an innovative model structure designed for this task.

CycleGAN [25] is a pioneering paradigm in unpaired image translation that leverages dual adversarial generative networks to facilitate domain conversion. This approach utilizes cycle consistency loss to ensure the coherence and consistency of image translation, while incorporating adversarial loss and identity loss

K. Tian and M. Pan—Supported by Tsinghua University. Contribute equally to this paper.

L. Iliadis et al. (Eds.): ICANN 2023, LNCS 14259, pp. 576–587, 2023.
https://doi.org/10.1007/978-3-031-44223-0_46

to govern the realism of the generated images. Despite the numerous improvements to the CycleGAN-based framework, most of these advancements focus on training pipelines or losses. By contrast, this paper emphasizes the model structure of generators and discriminators. We contend that the intrinsic limitations of convolutional neural networks (CNNs) constitute a significant obstacle hindering the progress of unpaired translation models, particularly in handling complex scenes and intricate image relationships.

In recent years, the Transformer [20] architecture has exhibited remarkable performance across a range of computer vision tasks. For example, Segformer [23] has achieved state-of-the-art outcomes in semantic segmentation, while DETR [2] and Deformable DETR [26] have surpassed conventional CNN models in object detection. Nevertheless, the complexity and convergence issues pose significant challenges for the effective application of Transformers in image generation, particularly in the context of generative adversarial tasks. Moreover, research on Transformers in cross-domain translation remains limited. Prior work has either used attention exclusively as an auxiliary module or utilized Transformers solely as a low-resolution translation module, with the primary structure largely governed by CNNs.

Building on the foundation of CycleGAN, this paper integrates the Transformer framework into the network structure, leveraging the inherent global feature modeling capabilities of the Transformer architecture to enhance accuracy and translation performance. In contrast to previous work that used a full CNN structure or used only the Transformer or attention module as a high-level semantic translator, we use Transformer as the main architecture from top to bottom hoping to obtain stronger detail discrimination and better semantic transformation ability. A novel generator, based on the Transformer architecture, is meticulously designed, in conjunction with a discriminator that combines global domain information and local feature texture information. The model seamlessly blends the global self-attention advantages of Transformers with the local feature extraction capacities of CNNs, ultimately yielding superior results compared to competing methods. This fusion approach fosters more robust cross-domain transformations, with the potential to propel the field forward and contribute to a wide range of real-world applications.

2 Related Works

2.1 Unpaired Image-to-Image Translation

Various approaches have been proposed to address the challenge of unpaired image-to-image translation. CoGAN [14] adopts a weight-sharing strategy to learn feature representations across different domains, while Liu at el. [13] employs auto-encoders and generative networks to improve translation performance. Park at el. [18] uses contrastive learning to utilize mutual information. CycleGAN is the first unpaired translation model that achieves comparable performance to paired image-to-image translation models. This approach utilizes two sets of generative adversarial networks to train images from different domains, employing consistency loss to ensure the cross-domain transformation is reversible. As a result, CycleGAN can train unpaired samples and has broad applications.

Subsequent works such as StarGAN [3] and MUNIT [8] extend CycleGAN to more diverse transformation tasks across multiple domains. DRIT enables multi-domain mapping by disentangling representations, while UGATIT [10] introduces an attention mechanism and ADAIN [7] for auxiliary functions in CycleGAN.

2.2 Transformers in Generative Models

Transformers have achieved outstanding performance in natural language processing, and ViT introduced this architecture to computer vision. Various improvements and variants have been proposed to adapt the transformer to computer vision tasks. Compared with traditional convolutional neural network models, transformers perform better on many tasks. However, the training process of transformer models consumes more computing resources and requires more demanding conditions.

Although many models have been improved based on the transformer model and applied to downstream tasks such as classification, detection, and semantic segmentation, few generative adversarial networks are based on the transformer model. The two main works are TransGAN [9] and ViTGAN [12]. ViTGAN utilizes an adaptive norm layer to constrain the generator according to the initial noise w and employs implicit neural mapping to improve the high-frequency information of the generated results while saving computation. The discriminator part improves the self-attention calculation formula to make it more suitable for Leibniz continuity.

Despite recent advancements, the use of transformers in GANs remains challenging due to the instability of the GAN network and the difficulty in the convergence of the transformer.

2.3 Efficient Transformers

Numerous methods have been proposed to mitigate the computational complexity of transformers. These methods can be broadly categorized into two types. The first type pertains to reducing the number or size of tokens. For instance, Swin Transformer [15] employs local attention to confine the attention operation within a small patch at the cost of accuracy. Additionally, CSWin [5] proposed cross-shaped window attention, and TWINS [4] applied group attention to transformers to avoid global computation costs. PVT [22] utilizes spatial reduction to decrease the dimension of the correlation matrix, whereas NesT [24] aggregates block attention-based transformers from bottom to top.

The second type of methods employs alternative operations to vanilla attention to achieve linear computation complexity. For example, Reformer [11] uses locality-sensitive hashing to decrease the computational complexity of self-attention. Linformer [21], on the other hand, maps the attention matrix to a low-dimensional space using projection layers. In contrast, SOFT [16] uses a specialized kernel function rather than SoftMax and introduces a novel correlation calculation method. This approach compresses the correlation matrix, transforms it into a low-rank matrix, and subsequently decomposes it for linear computation.

The current image-to-image translation model based on convolutional neural networks (CNNs) generally encounters various challenges. For instance, the model faces difficulties in accurately distinguishing between foreground and background, modeling complex scenes, and preventing schema collapse. In response to these issues, we propose an image translation network that utilizes the transformer model, which aims to overcome the limitations of previous models through the superior abilities of transformers.

3 Transcycle

3.1 Dumbbell Transformer Genorator

In this study, we propose a novel transformer generator architecture that incorporates a texture augmentation branch. The core of this generator is a dumbbell-shaped transformer structure, which is composed of three distinct stages: a spatially optimized pyramid transformer structure for downsampling, a pixel-wise transformer in the middle, and an inverted pyramid transformer structure for upsampling. Our proposed generator is designed to effectively capture texture details while maintaining the global context of the input image. The structure of generator is show in Fig. 1.

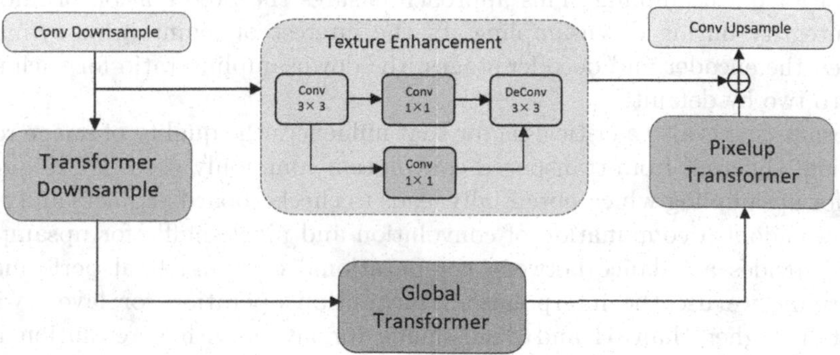

Fig. 1. The Generator Structure

In the first and third part of our model, Patch-wise Vision Transformer is adopted with spatially optimized attention. When comes to high resolution, vanilla attention will bring huge computational consumption and unnecessary global interaction. The solution we give is to optimize the self-attention module from both inside and outside separately.

For the inside part, spatial pooling method is adopted in the generation of keys and values in attention. We simply adopt depth-wise convolution for the dynamic pooling of input features, the spatial optizmized attention can be written as following:

$$Attention = Softmax(\frac{Q * Pool(K)^T}{\sqrt{d_{head}}})Pool(V) \quad (1)$$

For the outside part, window attention is adopted for high resolution stages, and we use a window size of 8*8 and calculate the global attention only for all pixels in the current window by default. Assuming that the current input resolution is (H, W, d), the computation cost of vanilla transformer is $(HW)^2 * d$, while our window transformer's cost is only $64 * HW * d$. When combined with spatial optimization strategy, the cost is even reduced to $64 * HW * d/r$, where r is the ratio of spatial compression. With the help of these efficient transformers, our model even require less computation/memory cost than typical CNN generators.

The transformer in the middle layer employs a 4-block global attention module similar to the Vision Transformer(ViT). We do not apply spatial optimization here to get better high-level semantic transformation.

Downsample and Upsample Methods. In the present study, downsampling play crucial roles in feature extraction. Similar to Convolutional Neural Network (CNN) models, we utilize progressive downsampling methods in our proposed generator. Specifically, for the output of each downsampling transformer layer, we adopt a lossless patch embedding module. The module first resizes the features to a (H, W, C) dimension and then integrate image information onto the channel for downsampling. This approach ensures the preservation of information integrity during downsampling. In the interest of maintaining symmetry between the encoder and decoder stages, the downsampling ratio for each stage is set to two by default.

Upsampling is also a critical factor that influences the quality of image reconstruction. Different from transposed convolution commonly used in CNN generators for upsampling which potentially leads to checkerboard artifacts and ripple noise, we adopt a combination of convolution and pixel shuffle for upsampling, which provides a balance between computational cost and final performance. Specifically, we use the interpolation convolution operation for layers with a resolution higher than 64 and pixel-shuffle for layers with a resolution lower than 64.

Texture Augmentation Branch. During our experiment, we observed that although the generator we designed performed well in terms of image semantics, it suffered from a shortcoming that drew our attention. Specifically, the texture details of the image were lost to some extent, and certain local regions of the image appeared to be too monotonous. We attribute this phenomenon to the transformer structure utilized in the up-and-down sampling process. In the higher spatial resolution stage, the current visual transformers cannot operate at the pixel attention level due to computational constraints, and our model was no exception. The windowed self-attention mechanism employed in our model resulted in the loss of some small-scale textures.

To address this issue, we introduced a texture enhancement branch into our model. The branch is connected to the stage of the first downsampling core and the last upsampling stage, and it comprises two small branches. The first branch applies a downsampling convolution operation to extract local textures, which are then subjected to further conversion through a 1*1 convolution kernel, and eventually reconstructed at the original resolution via deconvolution. The second branch is relatively simple, involving only a 1*1 convolution operation to transform the non-textured image background. The two branches are subsequently merged.

We note that our texture enhancement branch incorporates multiple convolutional transformations rather than simple skip connections. This design aims to better match the image cross-domain translation task, as skip connections may impose unreasonable constraints on the model, particularly in cases where the source and target domains exhibit significant differences.

3.2 Discriminator-PatchViT

Few methods in the image translation field have improved the discriminator, but we believe that the design of the discriminator is also an important aspect. Among the existing works, PatchGAN is a common discriminator model which predict the classification score of multiple regions. In this paper, we use the Transformer architecture as the main body of the discriminator and construct a concise and efficient discriminator that considers both domain-wide and block-level features, not only utilizing the long-range dependencies of the Transformer but also enabling better collaboration between the generator and the discriminator, resulting in better convergence consistency. The structure of discriminator is shown in Fig. 2. The discriminator consists of two parts: a feature discriminator module that is merged from top to bottom and a domain vector discriminator module, as shown in the figure. First, the input image is decomposed into 16*16 tokens using OverlapEmbedding, then channel-expanded to 128 after patch embedding and joined with the category token. After multi-stage, multi-layer Transformer blocks perform self-attention calculations, with spectral normalization ensuring training stability, the class token and feature queries are finally processed through an MLP network to obtain classification outputs. The classification result of the class token is used as the domain discrimination score, while the classification output of the feature sequence is used as the block feature discrimination score. The final output of the discriminator is shown below:

$$y = \lambda * y_{domain} + (1 - \lambda) * y_{query} \quad (2)$$

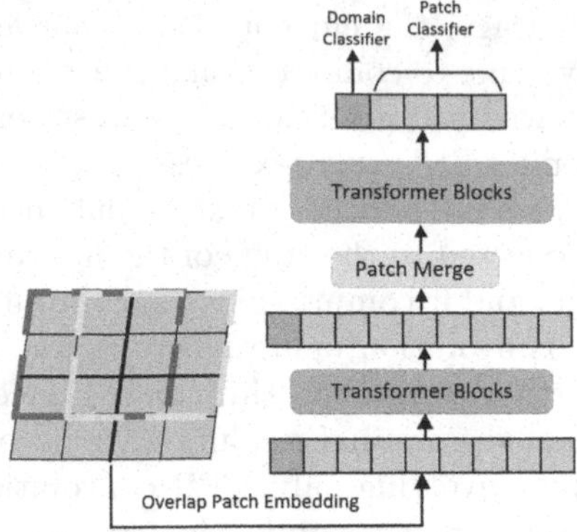

Fig. 2. The Discriminator Structure

We use losses in LSGAN [17] as our default adversarial loss.

4 Experiments

4.1 Experiments Setup

Datasets. The same methodology that will be subjected to comparison in subsequent analyses was also employed in our experimentation on two distinct datasets, namely, the selfie-to-anime dataset and the male-to-female dataset.

Selfie-to-anime: The training set of the dataset in question comprises a total of 3400 facial photographs and 3400 anime avatars. Similarly, the test set includes 100 images for each category. Notably, all images in the dataset are of uniform size, specifically 256 pixels by 256 pixels.

Male-to-female: The male-to-female dataset comprises facial images that were cropped from the CelebA dataset. The dataset contains a total of 68,261 and 16,173 images of males in the training and test sets, respectively. Similarly, it also includes 94,509 and 23,656 images of females in the training and test sets, respectively. It is noteworthy that all images in the dataset are of uniform size, specifically 218 pixels by 178 pixels.

Glass: The dataset used in this study of Glass dataset is a subset of the CelebA dataset, which was cropped from CelebA. However, it should be noted that the glass dataset is not inherently balanced, which may lead to biased results in certain analyses. In order to ensure fairness and accuracy in our comparisons, we have employed the same dataset processing methodology as that used in the UVCGAN, as described in the present article.

4.2 Evaluation Metrics

FID Scores. [6] The FID score is a widely recognized metric for evaluating the results generated by the GAN network. FID takes advantage of Inception

V3 [19] and measures the distance between the generated results and the two distributions of the real image. For the image translation task, we compare the FID scores of our model and the CycleGAN model on different datasets and under different domain transformations to compare the generation quality of our model quantitatively.

KID Scores. [1] The Kernel Inception Distance (KID) metric serves as a significant metric in evaluating the convergence of Generative Adversarial Networks (GANs). Distinct from the Frechet Inception Distance (FID), KID does not necessitate the assumption of normal distribution and exhibits an impartial estimation of network convergence.

Train Details. The training method of the network is generally consistent with CycleGAN. The difference is that we design different initial learning rates for different batch sizes and the embedding dimension of the discriminator part of the transformer. In most cases, when the batch size is 1, we usually use an embedding dimension of 128 and an initial learning rate of 0.0001.

4.3 Ablation Study

In this study, we conducted an empirical investigation to evaluate the feasibility of a selection of proposed techniques, namely, dumbbell generators, texture branches, and discriminators that are more closely aligned with the generators. Our evaluation was performed using the selfie2anime dataset, and we employed the fid score as our metric of choice. Specifically, we utilized the cycleGAN model as the baseline in this compatibility experiment, and all the aforementioned methods were trained until convergence was achieved.

Table 1. Results of Ablation experiment on selfie-to-anime dataset(from selfie to anime). CycleGAN is chosen as our baseline. DT denotes the Dumbbell Transformer without Texure Augment Branch, TAB denotes the Texure Augment Branch, and DP denotes Discriminator-PatchViT.

Method	DT	TAB	DP	FID	KID
CycleGAN				92.1	0.0272
Ours	✓			86.0	0.0253
Ours	✓	✓		83.2	0.0177
Ours	✓	✓	✓	78.4	0.0154

4.4 Quantitative Results

In this study, a comparative analysis was conducted to evaluate the performance of our proposed model against other mainstream models of similar nature. To achieve this, we conducted performance assessment of the models in both forward and backward directions, using two distinct datasets. The findings of these experiments are presented in a series of tables below.

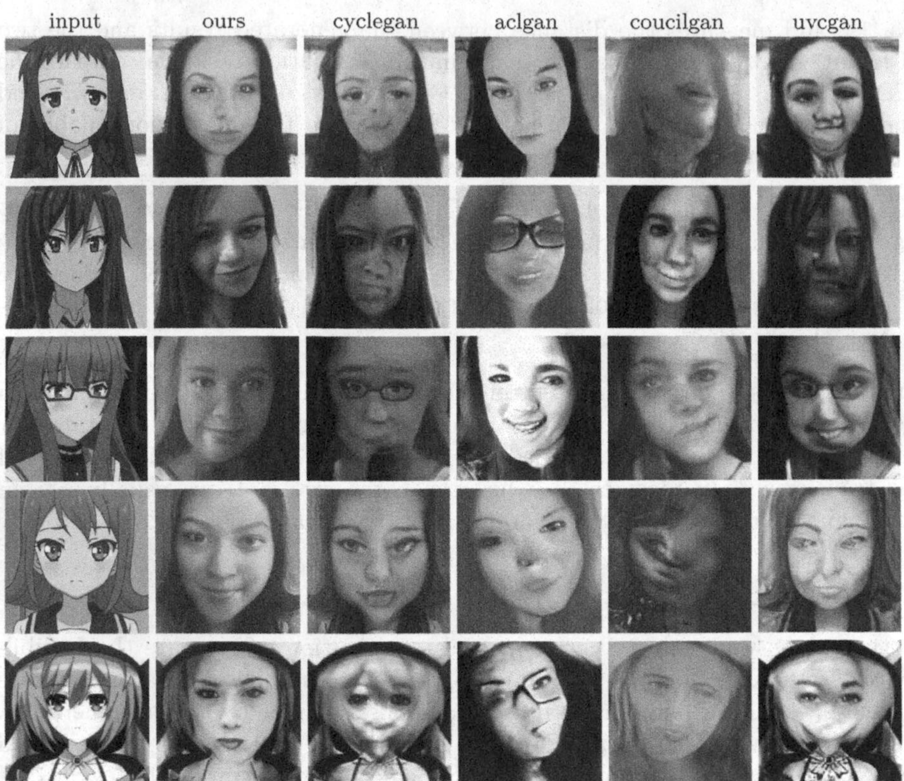

Fig. 3. Comparsion results of Trans-Cycle and other methods on Anime2selfie task.

Table 2. Results on selfie-to-anime dataset

Method	Selfie-	to-Anime	Anime-	to-Selfie
Score	FID	KID	FID	KID
CycleGAN	92.1	0.0272	127.5	0.0252
ACL-GAN	99.3	0.0322	128.6	0.0349
U-GAT-IT	95.8	0.0274	108.8	0.0148
Council-GAN	91.9	0.0274	126.0	0.0257
UVCGAN	79.0	0.0135	122.8	0.0233
Ours	78.4	0.0154	118.3	0.0178

Upon scrutinizing the comparative outcomes depicted in Fig. 3, it becomes evident that our model possesses a significant advantage in the domain of anime-to-selfie translation. Notably, our model exhibits a heightened comprehension of the distinct elements constituting the source image, thereby resulting in a diminished occurrence of incongruities evident in the generated output.

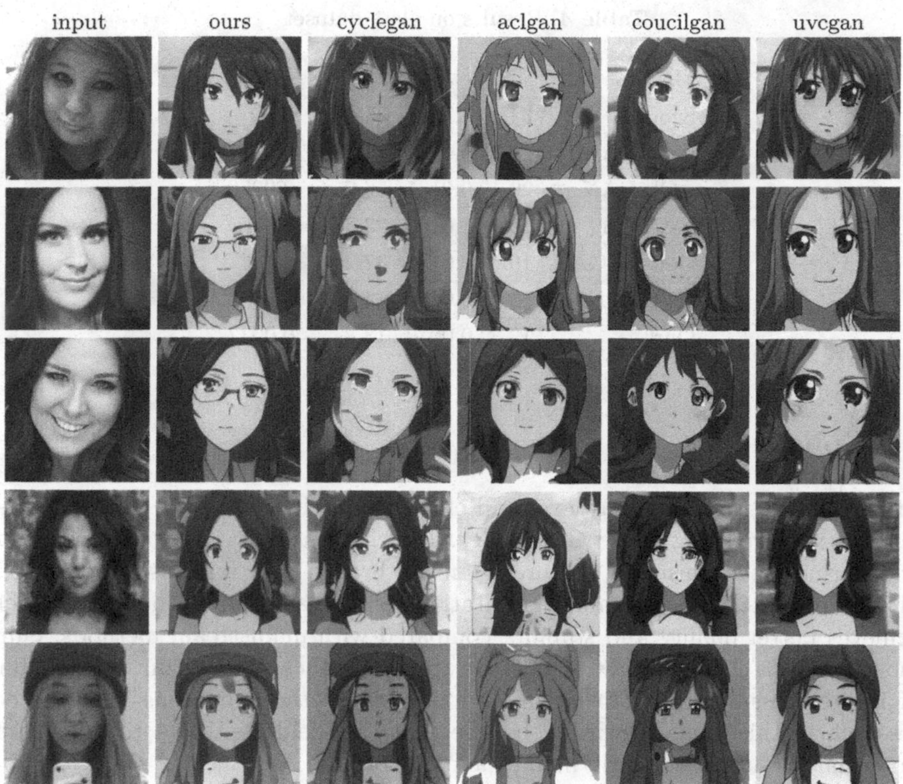

Fig. 4. Comparsion results of Trans-Cycle and other methods on Selfie2anime task.

Table 3. Results on male-to-female dataset

Method	Male-	to-Female	Female-	to-Male
Score	FID	KID	FID	KID
CycleGAN	15.2	0.0129	22.2	0.0174
ACL-GAN	9.4	0.0058	19.1	0.0138
U-GAT-IT	24.1	0.0220	15.4	0.0094
Council-GAN	10.4	0.0074	24.1	0.0179
UVCGAN	9.6	0.0068	13.9	0.0091
Ours	8.6	0.0057	13.7	0.0103

The findings presented in Fig. 4 elucidate the notable advantages inherent in our proposed approach when it comes to effectively managing the coordination of individual image blocks. Moreover, it is apparent that our methodology showcases superior performance in faithfully preserving intricate texture details within the generated images. This assertion is exemplified by the intricate depiction of hair textures observed in the generated results, thereby reinforcing the efficacy of our approach.

Table 4. Results on glass dataset

Method	add	glass	remove	glass
Score	FID	KID	FID	KID
CycleGAN	19.8	0.0136	24.2	0.0187
ACL-GAN	20.1	0.0135	16.7	0.0070
U-GAT-IT	19.0	0.0108	23.3	0.0169
Council-GAN	19.5	0.0133	37.2	0.0367
UVCGAN	13.6	0.0060	14.4	0.0068
Ours	13.3	0.0073	13.8	0.0037

5 Conclusions

In this paper, we propose a noval and efficient unpaired image-to-image translation structure using pure transformers. To achieve this, we integrates efficient transformer mechanism, a texture augment branch and a transformer-based discriminator. Qualitative and quantitative results have shown that our model achieves better quality and stability compared with mainstream methods. Our model extends the investigation of transformers' applicability within the domain of image cross-domain translation, contributing to the expanding frontiers of research in this area. We firmly believe that this field continues to hold vast potential for future scholarly inquiry and exploration.

References

1. Bińkowski, M., Sutherland, D.J., Arbel, M., Gretton, A.: Demystifying mmd gans. arXiv preprint arXiv:1801.01401 (2018)
2. Carion, N., Massa, F., Synnaeve, G., Usunier, N., Kirillov, A., Zagoruyko, S.: End-to-end object detection with transformers. In: Vedaldi, A., Bischof, H., Brox, T., Frahm, J.-M. (eds.) ECCV 2020. LNCS, vol. 12346, pp. 213–229. Springer, Cham (2020). https://doi.org/10.1007/978-3-030-58452-8_13
3. Choi, Y., Choi, M., Kim, M., Ha, J.W., Kim, S., Choo, J.: Stargan: Unified generative adversarial networks for multi-domain image-to-image translation. In: Proceedings of the IEEE Conference On Computer Vision and Pattern Recognition, pp. 8789–8797 (2018)
4. Chu, X., et al.: Twins: revisiting the design of spatial attention in vision transformers. Adv. Neural Inform. Process. Syst. **34** 9355–9366 (2021)
5. Dong, X., et al.: Cswin transformer: A general vision transformer backbone with cross-shaped windows. arXiv preprint arXiv:2107.00652 (2021)
6. Heusel, M., Ramsauer, H., Unterthiner, T., Nessler, B., Hochreiter, S.: Gans trained by a two time-scale update rule converge to a local nash equilibrium. Adv. Neural Inform. Process. Syst. **30** (2017)
7. Huang, X., Belongie, S.: Arbitrary style transfer in real-time with adaptive instance normalization. In: Proceedings of the IEEE International Conference on Computer Vision, pp. 1501–1510 (2017)

8. Huang, X., Liu, M.Y., Belongie, S., Kautz, J.: Multimodal unsupervised image-to-image translation. In: Proceedings of the European Conference on Computer Vision (ECCV), pp. 172–189 (2018)
9. Jiang, Y., Chang, S., Wang, Z.: Transgan: two pure transformers can make one strong gan, and that can scale up. Adv. Neural Inform. Process. Syst. **34**, 14745–14758 (2021)
10. Kim, J., Kim, M., Kang, H., Lee, K.: U-gat-it: Unsupervised generative attentional networks with adaptive layer-instance normalization for image-to-image translation. arXiv preprint arXiv:1907.10830 (2019)
11. Kitaev, N., Kaiser, Ł., Levskaya, A.: Reformer: The efficient transformer. arXiv preprint arXiv:2001.04451 (2020)
12. Lee, K., Chang, H., Jiang, L., Zhang, H., Tu, Z., Liu, C.: Vitgan: Training gans with vision transformers. arXiv preprint arXiv:2107.04589 (2021)
13. Liu, M.Y., Breuel, T., Kautz, J.: Unsupervised image-to-image translation networks. Adv. Neural Inform. Process. Syst. **30** (2017)
14. Liu, M.Y., Tuzel, O.: Coupled generative adversarial networks. Adv. Neural Inform. Process. Syst. **29** (2016)
15. Liu, Z., et al.: Swin transformer: Hierarchical vision transformer using shifted windows. In: Proceedings of the IEEE/CVF International Conference on Computer Vision, pp. 10012–10022 (2021)
16. Lu, J., et al.: Soft: Softmax-free transformer with linear complexity. Adv. Neural Inform. Process. Syst. **34**, 21297–21309 (2021)
17. Mao, X., Li, Q., Xie, H., Lau, R.Y., Wang, Z., Paul Smolley, S.: Least squares generative adversarial networks. In: Proceedings of the IEEE International Conference on Computer Vision, pp. 2794–2802 (2017)
18. Park, T., Efros, A.A., Zhang, R., Zhu, J.-Y.: Contrastive learning for unpaired image-to-image translation. In: Vedaldi, A., Bischof, H., Brox, T., Frahm, J.-M. (eds.) ECCV 2020. LNCS, vol. 12354, pp. 319–345. Springer, Cham (2020). https://doi.org/10.1007/978-3-030-58545-7_19
19. Szegedy, C., Vanhoucke, V., Ioffe, S., Shlens, J., Wojna, Z.: Rethinking the inception architecture for computer vision. In: Proceedings of the IEEE Conference On Computer Vision and Pattern Recognition, pp. 2818–2826 (2016)
20. Vaswani, A., et al.: Attention is all you need. Adv. Neural Inform. Process. Syst. **30** (2017)
21. Wang, S., Li, B.Z., Khabsa, M., Fang, H., Ma, H.: Linformer: self-attention with linear complexity. arXiv preprint arXiv:2006.04768 (2020)
22. Wang, W., et al.: Pyramid vision transformer: a versatile backbone for dense prediction without convolutions. In: Proceedings of the IEEE/CVF International Conference on Computer Vision, pp. 568–578 (2021)
23. Xie, E., Wang, W., Yu, Z., Anandkumar, A., Alvarez, J.M., Luo, P.: Segformer: Simple and efficient design for semantic segmentation with transformers. Adv. Neural Inform. Process. Syst. **34**, 12077–12090 (2021)
24. Zhang, Z., Zhang, H., Zhao, L., Chen, T., Pfister, T.: Aggregating nested transformers. arXiv preprint arXiv:2105.12723 (2021)
25. Zhu, J.Y., Park, T., Isola, P., Efros, A.A.: Unpaired image-to-image translation using cycle-consistent adversarial networks. In: Proceedings of the IEEE International Conference on Computer Vision, pp. 2223–2232 (2017)
26. Zhu, X., Su, W., Lu, L., Li, B., Wang, X., Dai, J.: Deformable detr: Deformable transformers for end-to-end object detection. arXiv preprint arXiv:2010.04159 (2020)

Author Index

L. Iliadis et al. (Eds.): ICANN 2023, LNCS 14259, pp. 589–591, 2023.
https://doi.org/10.1007/978-3-031-44223-0

Printed in the United States
by Baker & Taylor Publisher Services